EDUCATIONAL PSYCHOLOGY
Theory and Practice

ADDISON-WESLEY PUBLISHING COMPANY

Reading, Massachusetts • Menlo Park, California

London • Amsterdam • Don Mills, Ontario • Sydney

GARY A. DAVIS

University of Wisconsin

EDUCATIONAL PSYCHOLOGY

Theory and Practice

TO DOT AND R. C. NELSON, EMILY AND MERLE BOE

Sponsoring Editor: Linda Fisher
Production Editor: Herb Merritt

Text Designer: Melinda Grosser
Illustrator: Textbook Art Associates
Cover Designer: Ann Scrimgeour Rose
Cover Illustration: *New England Country School,* by Winslow Homer.
Courtesy of the Addison Gallery, Phillips Academy, Andover, Mass.
Classroom photograph by Ted Kawalerski, The Image Bank.
Art Coordinator: Robert Gallison

Production Manager: Karen Guardino
Production Coordinator: Peter Petraitis

The photographs for Figures 6.5 and 15.4 are by the author.
The photograph for Figure 15.2 is by the Psychological Corporation.
The photograph on page 548 is from Argus Communications.
All other photographs in this book are by Elizabeth Crews.
The text of this book was composed in Trump by Monotype Composition Company.

Library of Congress Cataloging in Publication Data

Davis, Gary A., 1938–
   Educational psychology.

   Includes bibliographical references and indexes.
   1. Educational psychology. I. Title. [DNLM:
1. Psychology, Educational. LB 1051 D261e]
LB1051.D314 1983   370.15   82-8750
ISBN 0-201-10253-6   AACR2

PREFACE

A successful teacher in today's schools is informed on academic and professional issues; understands students' motives, personalities, abilities, learning and thinking styles, and social and antisocial behaviors; is effective in transmitting knowledge and skills; is respected and accepted by both colleagues and students; and, not least of all, feels good about doing an important job in a competent, informed fashion. This book can help you become a more successful teacher. For example, it will help you understand how children learn and think, and how these patterns of learning and thinking change over the childhood and adolescent years. It will help you understand the many forms of motivation which control both student learning and student disruptiveness. It will help you become acquainted with issues and innovations—for example, mainstreaming, intelligence testing, microcomputers, humanistic education, the education of the gifted and talented, and, interestingly, characteristics and techniques of successful teachers.

Never before has education made greater demands on the professional knowledge and training of teachers than today. For example, the main-streaming law (Public Law 94-142) has made it necessary for teachers at all levels to understand exceptional students. Sections in several chapters of this book focus on the problems and tactics needed to cope with and to teach students who are learning disabled, emotionally disturbed, mildly retarded, or environmentally disadvantaged. Also, most states and many individual school districts and schools have initiated programs for culti-vating one of our greatest natural resources—our gifted, talented, and creative students. One chapter will acquaint you with the topic of crea-tivity—creative people, the creative process, and the teaching of creative thinking in the schools. Another chapter will familiarize you with the field of education of the gifted, and with a step-by-step approach to the identi-fication of and programming for gifted and talented students.

In the area of technology, a minor revolution called "microcomputers" has hit the schools. The "micro's" can teach content, they can teach problem-solving and thinking techniques via simulations and games, they can make both teachers and students "computer literate"—and they can be purchased for less than the price of an electric typewriter. One section will familiarize you with the uses and vocabulary of the microcomputer movement.

Educational Psychology: Theory and Practice is intended to be an eclectic approach to learning, teaching, and managing a classroom. (e-klek'-tic. 1: Selecting what appears to be best in various doctrines, methods or styles; 2: Composed of elements drawn from various sources.) There are a great many fine theories, principles, insights, and techniques emanating from many different perspectives—from traditional psychology of learning, from more current information-processing theory, from developmental psychology, from the cognitive view of learning and teaching of D. P. Ausubel, from principles and theories of motivation and classroom man-agement, from the humanistic perspective, from contemporary theories of instruction, from research on individual differences, and from many other points of view. It is your author's point of view that a teacher, as a professional educator, should be acquainted with many academic viewpoints on a problem, and armed with a variety of specific tactics for teaching and managing students.

This text tries to achieve a balance between the academic and the applied. As an educated person, you should be familiar with the main thrusts of psychology and educational psychology—for example, with theories of learning, development, motivation, social learning, principles and theories of classroom management, instructional models, and main dimensions of personality and cognitive styles. However, you also need to know how these ideas will help you understand students, and how these theories and principles will help you make good decisions in the professional problems you will face daily. Of course, some academic theory and knowledge will be more practical than others. For example, our section on genetics and prenatal development is mainly for your education; however, chapters on instructional models and theories, behavior modification, planning programs for the gifted, managing disruptiveness, and other matters present you with some time-tested strategies for effectively helping and teaching students. Sometimes the applications are in context; sometimes they are emphasized in boxed inserts; they certainly appear in the sections titled *To Improve Your Teaching*; and they often appear in the *Topics for Thought and Discussion* and the *Projects* sections which appear at the end of each chapter.

As a final suggestion, read this book constructively and creatively; think about what the information and strategies mean for teaching and how they can help you become a better, more professional teacher. They can.

Madison, Wisconsin
November 1982

G.A.D.

CONTENTS

THE TEACHER IN THE CLASSROOM   25   2

DEVELOPMENT   57   PART II

PHYSICAL, PERSONALITY, AND MORAL DEVELOPMENT   59   3

COGNITIVE DEVELOPMENT AND LANGUAGE DEVELOPMENT   89   4

PSYCHOLOGY OF LEARNING   121   PART III

LEARNING: THEORY AND PRINCIPLES   123   5

BEHAVIOR MODIFICATION, PROGRAMMED INSTRUCTION, AND MICROCOMPUTERS IN EDUCATION   155   6

INFORMATION PROCESSING, 7
MEMORY, AND TRANSFER   189

A COGNITIVE STRUCTURE VIEW OF LEARNING AND 8
TEACHING: AUSUBEL   217

INDIVIDUAL DIFFERENCES   *397*   PART VI

THE NATURE OF INDIVIDUAL DIFFERENCES   *399*   14

INTELLIGENCE   *433*   15

EDUCATIONAL PSYCHOLOGY

PART I

Educational Psychology
and Teaching

1

The teacher as problem-solver and decision-maker /
Subtle influences upon learning and teaching / The field
of educational psychology / Research methods in
educational psychology / Problems and challenges in
education / To improve your teaching / Summary /
Topics for thought and discussion / Projects /
Recommended reading

3

THE TEACHER AS PROBLEM-SOLVER AND DECISION-MAKER

Teachers at all levels solve problems and make important decisions virtually every day. As a teacher you will have students who are unable to learn, refuse to learn, have no friends, have low self-esteem, are mildly retarded, are profoundly gifted, or are aggressive, disruptive, dishonest, or perhaps even abusive. Intuition and good judgment are helpful in coping with such matters, but any teacher will be a more effective problem solver and decision maker when armed to the pedagogical teeth with an assortment of relevant educational theories and strategies. Engineers study engineering and administrators study administration in order to make informed decisions and solve professional problems. The effective professional teacher also must be acquainted with theories, principles, and strategies which will enable him or her to understand and cope with problems of teaching, learning, and managing a classroom. The purpose of this book is to help you better understand students and their problems, and to suggest tested methods of dealing with both.

Examples of Problem Areas

To review just a handful of topic areas that will require professional decision making and problem solving, as a teacher you will face challenges related to:

- Teacher-student interactions, including classroom atmospheres, expectations, and effects of teacher personality.
- Different developmental levels in cognitive functioning, personality, and moral thinking.
- Subtleties in learning, memory, and transfer—together known as information processing.
- The role of affective and humanistic learning—values, self-esteem, attitudes—in your cognitive-oriented curriculum.
- Understanding and even controlling student motivation, especially with disadvantaged students.
- Managing a classroom to minimize disruption and maximize effort and satisfaction.
- Setting and using instructional objectives, and teaching for "higher-level" objectives such as the abilities to analyze, synthesize, and evaluate.
- Selecting instructional models consistent with classroom goals.
- Accommodating individual differences in intelligence, learning styles, motivation, and personality.
- Fostering creative development.
- Deciding what to do with those one or two gifted children who are bored to tears with work they understood three years ago.

INSET 1.1

**WHAT IS A TEACHER? A
PRINCIPAL? A SCHOOL
BOARD?**

The teacher is the head of the class who picks on everyone.   *G. J., Age 10*

A teacher knows a lot of children's tricks, I found.   *G. F., Age 11*

A teacher is a educated person who is to help other people. She does not go to school for her own good.   *J. B., Age 12*

A principal tells the teachers what they can do and where they can go.   *M. L., Age 11*

He [the principal] is the one who calls everyone to the office and talks in a deep voice.   *M. D., Age 10*

A school board is a board that the principal uses to spank his customers.   *D. B., Age 8*

A school board is something we wright on and erase it, too.   *D. L., Age 9*

- Understanding and recognizing learning disabilities.
- Effectively teaching handicapped mainstreamed students.
- Understanding the needs of economically disadvantaged and minority students.
- Writing tests which fairly test what you want them to test.

A great many thoughtful researchers and scholars have devoted their professional lives to unraveling specific student and classroom problems. Many of these people are called educational psychologists, and many of their best ideas are summarized in these pages. With a thoughtful and constructive approach to reading these chapters, you should become a more effective problem solver and decision maker, and a better-informed, more professional teacher. And you might even become a better person.

SUBTLE INFLUENCES ON LEARNING AND TEACHING

Many psychological influences on student attitudes, conduct and achievement, and on teacher attitudes and behavior, are sufficiently subtle that teachers frequently are quite unaware of the dynamics at work. An experienced teacher can easily cause problems for himself or herself for 20 years or longer without understanding *why*, and therefore without a hint as to how to improve the situation.

Personality, Management Practices, Climate, and Expectations

For example, both the teacher's personality and his or her classroom management practices will influence student attitudes, motivation, misbehavior, and achievement. These are reasonably important topics for the beginning teacher who wishes to realize some degree of career success. Intimately related to the effects of teacher personality and classroom management practices are the topics of classroom climate (atmosphere) and teacher expectations. These also have a direct, although subtle influence on student attitudes and achievement. The effects of teacher expectations upon student achievement (and even IQ scores!) are so subtle that even the experts cannot agree on the dynamics at work. Chapter 2 will take a closer look at the effects of classroom climate and teacher expectations. The effects of teacher personality and classroom management strategies are explored in several sections, particularly in Chapters 2, 9, 10, 13, and 14.

Subtle Forms of Student Motivation

Another subtlety lies in the topic of motivation itself. Motivation experts can easily argue that *all* forms of human behavior are motivated. They also argue with one another about which kinds of motivation are at work in the classroom. Chapter 9 will acquaint you with at least eight broad views of motivation, including motives based in instincts, curiosity, rewards and punishments, needs for achievement, needs for competency, needs to make correct cause-and-effect "attributions," and needs to remove unpleasant "cognitive dissonance" due to conflicting ideas. Your intuition and insight may be keen, but this chapter will sensitize you to student motives you never dreamed of. Motivation, we add with emphasis, is *every* teacher's number one concern—it wins hands down in every survey of teachers' classroom problems.

Developmental Changes

It is possible that you are taking a child or adolescent development course separate from this educational psychology course. The subtleties of developmental changes in language, thought, personality, self-perception, moral values, and other matters—including that magnificent metamorphosis known as puberty—deserve at least one entire college course. Despite the present space limitations, Chapters 3 and 4 will present some of the more significant concepts in physical development, personality and moral development, and development of children's thinking and learning (cognitive development). As an example of a common problem, many teachers often expect a level of understanding and abstract thinking considerably *above* a child's current stage of cognitive development. Conversely, a teacher may expect, and get, performance which is *below* a child's level of cognitive development. The continuing challenge is to fit the curriculum to children and adolescents who are developing at different rates.

Especially subtle are the growing child's conceptions of moral values, such as honesty, fairness, loyalty, and obedience, and ever-increasing ability to understand another person's attitude or point of view. In its earliest months and years, for example, a child can perceive the external world only in relation to himself or herself—the **egocentric thinking** stage. Also, in the early years "right" and "wrong" are understood only in terms of outcomes—either rewards or punishments.

Subtleties in Classroom Rewards and Punishments

Now, everyone knows about rewards and punishments and that students like one but not the other. At the same time, however, many of today's teachers inadvertently administer severe punishments and then are surprised to find that students show little enthusiasm for classroom activities and assignments. Some examples of subtle (?) punishments are yelling at a sensitive adolescent, demanding that an excruciatingly difficult speech be given *again* (usually next week, so the child has plenty of time to suffer), habitual grouchiness, or being unreasonable and unfair in grading practices. Your author's children experience these and other punishments quite regularly; they never appreciate it.

Students work harder when they like the class; and if they like the teacher, they also will like the class (Kounin, 1970; see Chapter 10).

As with punishments, rewards also function in subtle ways. Rewards strengthen desirable behavior and attitudes, but they can also strengthen undesirable behaviors, and a teacher must try to be aware of the latter situations as well. For example, teacher attention may reward disruptiveness; tripping off to the pencil sharpener may serve as an escape from frustrating seatwork; even getting expelled leads to a two-week vacation. We will see more regarding the subtleties and dynamics of rewards and punishments in Chapters 5 and 6, with applications to motivation, classroom management, and the teaching of handicapped children in Chapters 9, 10, 18 and 19.

Test Construction and Interpretation

Your author has been designing college-level tests for about 15 years. In the process of gathering information for Chapter 19, he discovered that he had been making some very basic mistakes for a very long time. When should you use multiple-choice questions? When should you use true-false or matching items? When should essay (long or short) questions be used? Exactly how do you write good multiple-choice, true-false, matching, or fill-in-the-blanks questions? And how does one evaluate the "goodness" of different types of test questions? And then there is the very critical distinction between norm-referenced and criterion-referenced tests. You truly must know the difference between norm-referenced and criterion-referenced tests, or your tests will not serve their purposes as well as they should. Besides, you do wish to appear professionally literate. Anyone can make up a test (your author has been doing it for years), but to do it sensibly and effectively requires attention to subtleties of test construction. See Chapter 19.

The Hidden Curriculum: Psychological Subtlety at its Finest

One feature of school learning is so subtle that educational psychologists have named it the "hidden curriculum" or sometimes the "hidden agenda." Chapter 2 will uncover the hidden curriculum in more detail, but for now it refers to all of those usually unwritten and unspoken rules and policies and teacher quirks and expectations which the student must master in order to succeed in school.

THE FIELD OF EDUCATIONAL PSYCHOLOGY

The field of educational psychology originally was an offspring of its more senior parent, psychology. Earlier in this century it seemed logical that teachers should be exposed to principles of human behavior, and so most teachers' colleges and education departments required at least one psychology course. It soon became apparent that some psychological topics were more relevant to teacher training than others. Among the more relevant topics were principles of learning, memory, transfer, cognitive development, intelligence, motivation, and some aspects of social psychology, most notably leadership styles. Among the less relevant topics were the anatomy of the ear, eyeball, and brain; demonstrations of conditioning cockroaches and worms; discussions of communist brainwashing; optical illusions which fool everyone; teaching brain-damaged rats to run a maze; and exploring the world of the catatonic schizophrenic. Educational psychology courses were created in order to emphasize those aspects of psychology most relevant to problems of teaching. Actually, not much of their content was.

Originally, and even up until about two decades ago, educational psychology was fairly defined as "principles of psychology applied to education." In these recent decades however, educational psychology has assumed an identity of its own and no longer accepts the obsolete psychology-applied-to-education label. The following are just some of the topics unique to educational psychology:

- Theories and models of classroom learning and instruction.
- Dynamics of teacher-student interaction.
- Principles of affective learning and personality development specifically in classroom settings.

- Principles of classroom motivation and management.
- Strategies for fostering creative development and for accommodating gifted learners.
- Strategies for writing and using instructional objectives in teaching and testing.
- Coordinating teaching methods with individual differences in ability, personality, or thinking style.

While educational psychology has its roots in traditional psychology, it currently is a unique field in its own right. A summary diagram of the major components of educational psychology appears in Figure 1.1. Of course, it resembles the table of contents of this book. You might also note that the diagram describes or relates to a good share of your own future professional activities and obligations.

Figure 1.1 Everything anyone would ever want to know about educational psychology.

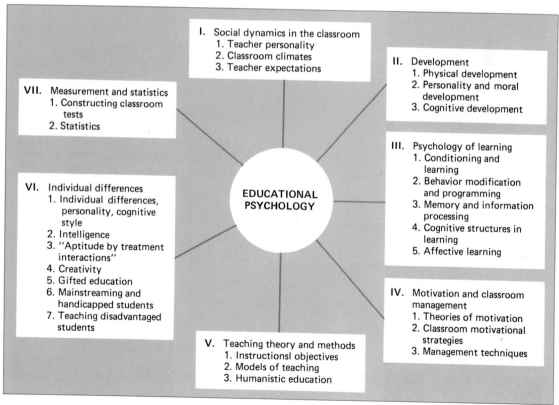

RESEARCH METHODS IN EDUCATIONAL PSYCHOLOGY

Many problems and questions in education require a research approach. For example, consider such basic questions as:

- How can curriculum be best organized to foster memory and transfer (application)?
  What is the course of cognitive and personality development and exactly what are the implications for learning and teaching?
- Are there important sex differences in learning (e.g., math) or personality (e.g., aggressiveness)?
- Do such well-known learning-readiness programs as Head Start and Sesame Street produce a significant effect?
- Is an innovative school organization (e.g., combining grades and teaching with teams) superior to traditional self-contained classrooms? If so, in what ways?
- What happens when students teach one another (peer tutoring)?
- What programs for creative development or for teaching gifted and talented students are worth the time and money?
- What are the effects of "mainstreaming" handicapped students into the regular classroom, as required by federal law?

A scientific, research-based approach seems to be the most objective way to answer these and other important questions. Accordingly, many educational psychologists are active researchers, and many conventional journals and convention programs bulge with new research evidence, new viewpoints, and new theories—all aimed at improving the education of children and youth.

There are four main types of research: observational, correlational, experimental, and product-development.

Observational Research

With observational or "naturalistic" research, information is obtained by observing students and classrooms as they function naturally. Some educators, psychologists, and sociologists have devised systematic behavior recording (rating) scales to help them record instances of, for example, asking questions, seeking help, being aggressive, working furiously, wandering, interrupting the teacher, and so on. Clinical case studies of individual students include descriptive reports based on naturalistic observation.

Correlational Research

With correlational research, the educational psychologist may wish to learn whether there is a relationship between two (or more) characteristics or behaviors; for example, self-confidence and achievement. The researcher might give a self-confidence test to a large group of high school students, probably 50 to 500 or so. The scores on the self-confidence test would be statistically correlated with, say, grades in American history, algebra, biology or physical education. The size of the correlation coefficient would indicate the strength of the relationship on a scale from 0 to 1.0. Correlation coefficients also can be negative, on a scale from 0 to −1.0, indicating that an increase in one factor (say stupidity) is related to a decrease in another factor (say grades in mathematics).

Correlations, including their meaning and formulas, will be further described in Chapters 14 and 19. For now, we should note one additional principle of correlational research: A correlation coefficient indicates degree or strength of a relationship, but it does not demonstrate causation. For example, a positive correlation between self-confidence and grades does not permit one to conclude that high self-confidence "causes" high grades. Actually, (a) the reverse may be true or (b) a third factor such as high intelligence could be "causing" both high confidence and high grades.

Experimental Research

It is experimental research which permits one to identify cause-effect relationships. In its simplest form, an experimental group receives a particular training or treatment experience while a control group does not.

Any later differences in the measured learning or behavior should be due to (or caused by) the treatment difference.

For example, let's say that researcher Norman Nervous developed a training program which he thought would strengthen students' feelings of self-confidence, and perhaps even lead to better school performance. At the beginning of the school year, Norman randomly assigned students to either the experimental group, which received the confidence training, or the control group, which watched Road Runner cartoons. After the training experience, if the experimental group scored significantly higher than the control group on tests of self-confidence, Norman Nervous probably would conclude that the training caused the students to have more self-confidence. Our experimenter would have had more confidence in his own conclusions if he (a) administered the confidence test to the experimental and control groups *before* the training began, in order to ensure that the groups were not different in self-confidence *before* any training (pretesting), and (b) tested the students again a month or so after the training to determine if the training effect lasted for a while (delayed post-testing).

Furthermore, if at the end of the year grades were higher for the students in the experimental group than for those in the control group, Norman probably would conclude that the self-confidence training experience also led to (or caused) the higher achievement.

Experimental research includes a specialized vocabulary. The factors which the experimenter manipulates are the *independent variables*. The present reseach design included one independent variable: self-confidence training (experimental group) vs. cartoon watching (control group). In this example the experimenter also could have used a *pretest* to ensure *group comparability*. The scores which measure the performance, ability, or trait (e.g., test scores, number of correct answers, ratings on a rating scale, minutes to complete a task, observed frequencies of occurrence of an event, number of problems completed) are the *dependent variables* (or dependent measures). The present example mentioned three dependent measures: the *immediate post-test* scores on the self-confidence test, the *delayed post-test* self-confidence scores, and the students' average grades at the end of the year. These concepts are appropriate terms to use when discussing experimental research.

Product-Development Research

A fourth type of research involves development of instructional products—either curriculum materials or teaching methods—which must be experimentally evaluated (field-tested) and usually modified. Product-development research usually is similar to experimental research in that an experimental group is taught a particular set of concepts or skills using the new materials or methods, while a control group is taught the same content via a more

"standard" teaching procedure. The product developer-researcher is interested (a) in whether the new materials or methods produce higher achievement and perhaps better attitudes compared with existing methods, and (b) in receiving ideas for improving the innovation.

For example, let's say that educational researcher Nellie Numero has devised a new strategy for teaching sixth-grade math, and so she writes a workbook based upon her brainchild. The puzzle-laden book is designed to raise math scores and improve attitudes toward math as a school subject. Ms. Numero might persuade teachers in 20 (experimental) schools to use her workbook for one semester. Teachers in another 20 (control) schools, similar in such characteristics as average ability, socioeconomic level, and racial and ethnic composition, would proceed in their usual way. At the end of the trial semester reseacher Numero would evaluate students' math achievement, students' attitudes toward mathematics, and teachers' reactions to the clarity, difficulty, organization, writing, illustrations, etc. of the workbook. Students' comments and reactions also are solicited. The data would tell Nellie Numero whether or not her new method was superior to standard methods in teaching math skills and fostering positive attitudes, and also how her workbook could be improved. Product-development research sometimes requires years of developing, testing, refining, retesting, re-refining, and on and on.

PROBLEMS AND CHALLENGES IN EDUCATION

To end our first chapter, it seems proper to review a few of the current challenges, problems, and criticisms of education. While some of these matters are beyond the control of the individual teacher, many are not.

Problems and Criticisms
When students do not learn or when they drop out before graduation, it is difficult to point the accusing finger in exactly the right direction. Is it the fault of the teachers? The school program? Peer pressure? Cultural influences? Is "society" at fault? Perhaps it's some combination of all these. Idealists would say that schools should teach students to value learning and educational achievement as the best route to personal development and economic success in the world. Perhaps eventually such humanistic values can be transmitted strongly enough to offset peer and cultural influences and the short-sighted attractions of a high-paying job in the local chicken pluckery. As it is, however, many young Americans are not mastering basic skills and an astounding number drop out before graduation. The various sets of statistics which summarize our "educational failures" are partly inconsistent with one another, but sobering nonetheless. According to a 1969 Digest of Educational Statistics:

- One student in four has a significant reading deficiency.
- Over three million people in America are illiterate.
- Half of our unemployed youth are "functionally illiterate"; their reading, writing, and arithmetic skills are too poor to be useful in common occupations.

These figures underestimate those reported in a 1979 news release describing a two-year Ford Foundation study. That study concluded that ". . . as many as 64 million Americans are illiterate" and that ". . . 23 million adults—about 15 percent of the population—are too illiterate to function competently in our society. There are nine states . . . in which more than half of the residents never finished high school."

According to a report in *TIME* magazine (September 24, 1979), the nonprofit National Assessment of Educational Progress organization concluded that math skills have declined notably in the five preceding years.

"A fourth of the nation's 17-year-old students cannot multiply 671 by 402 and get the right answer. . . . About 60 percent of the teenagers knew that the area of a rectangle equals its length times its width, and that the sides of a square are equal. But less than half of them could reckon the area of a square when the length of only one side was labeled." Only 29 percent of poor 17-year-olds could solve this problem: "The floor of a rectangular room has an area of 96 square feet. Its width is 8 feet. How long is the room?"

In a 1979 speech former U.S. Commissioner of Education Ernest L. Boyer reported:

- A full 25 percent of our high school students drop out before graduation. In some city schools the rate is 40–50 percent. These figures were accurately described as a "national disgrace."
- About 11 percent (2.4 million) of our secondary school students have something stolen from them *each month.* About 1.3 percent (282,800) are physically attacked (each month). (And so are teachers; see Chapter 2.)
- About 20 percent of all senior high schools report five or more crimes per month.
- Each year about 600 million dollars is spent on repairing vandalism damage.
- High schools are impossibly overcrowded.

- Student counseling is pathetic. New York City has one counselor per 942 students; Detroit has one for every 627; Baltimore has one per 856. Other cities have similar understaffed counseling services.

Challenges of the 1980s

At present virtually all high schools offer some student choices so that vocationally oriented students can load up with machine shop, welding, auto mechanics, bookkeeping, shorthand, typing, and other job-related subjects. More academically oriented students can register for advanced math, chemistry, composition, speech, debate, and so on. Nonetheless, a major urgency in today's secondary schools is to accommodate *individual differences* in needs, goals, and talents so that schooling will be seen as a road to success and fulfillment, not as Prisoner's Island. Ernest Boyer's plan for restructuring the schools (see Inset 1.2) would go a long way toward accommodating different needs and abilities. The concept of "magnet" high schools (Inset 1.2), which offer specialized training to bused-in students, currently is meeting the needs of many young people—but only in a handful of large school systems. Unless the high school curriculum is seen as valuable and relevant, much hostility and resentment will remain.

Apart from restructuring the entire system, many educational psychologists are examining the effects of very specific personal differences in relation to effective learning and teaching styles. Chapters 14 and 15 will look at individual differences in motivation, cognitive thinking styles, personality, and intelligence, and will explore teaching methods which try to accommodate these differences.

A voucher system currently is attracting national attention. With this program, families are given vouchers which may be used to pay for either public, private, or parochial schooling. The idea is to force public schools—in a good old-fashioned American free-enterprise fashion—to compete with traditionally more effective private schools. Opponents of the voucher system, namely public school administrators, are nurturing ulcers over the prospect of losing large chunks of their funds. And with good reason. A recent widely publicized speech by James S. Coleman, who achieved fame with his "Coleman Report" on racial segregation (Coleman, 1966, 1975a, 1975b), concluded that private schools do indeed produce higher levels of achievement than public schools (Coleman, 1981). Of course, the issue is complex and clouded by the obvious selection factor: Children from academically and economically impoverished backgrounds typically do not attend expensive private schools (Cronbach, 1981).

Mainstreaming will continue to be implemented. Chapter 18 will describe some fine points of Public Law 94-142, the mainstreaming law. Chapter 18 also will look at the problems of learning-disabled, retarded,

INSET 1.2

NEW SCHOOL STRUCTURE FOR THE 1980s?

In a September, 1979, newspaper interview, former U.S. Commissioner of Education Ernest L. Boyer outlined his plan for overhauling America's school system. Said Boyer, "I think it's time to reshape the structure to meet the greater diversity of students." His proposed plan for the 1980s includes a three-step sequence: In a *basic school* youngsters will learn fundamental language and other basic skills. In a *middle school* junior-high age students will focus on "general knowledge," which will involve a mix of contemporary issues and traditional disciplines. Finally, in a *transition school* students specialize and develop talents in such areas as the arts, science, business, or trade skills.

Many large school systems, including Boston, Cincinnati, Milwaukee, and St. Louis, are experimenting with "magnet" schools, a concept which fits Boyer's transition-school notion. Magnet schools offer specialized training in (for example) math, science, and the performing arts. Students are bused in from all corners of the city to attend the particular high school which suits their educational and occupational interests.

It is true that student hostility is partly a result of the often large gap between the goals of the institution and the needs and goals of individual students. Whether or not Boyer's model becomes a reality, some changes are in order. The magnet-school idea seems to be a good beginning.

and emotionally disturbed children, and will describe some strategies for teaching these children. More and more handicapped children are being mainstreamed into regular classes, and teachers are learning to cope. Many, not well.

There also is rapidly growing attention to that other large category of exceptional students, the *gifted, talented, and creative.* Many states are passing laws earmarking funds for the development of G/T programs at all levels. Universities are beginning to offer special courses in teaching creative and gifted children, and some are offering new M.S. degree programs specializing in the care and feeding of gifted kids. This trend will continue to grow; we cannot afford to continue to ignore those bored but talented students who will be tomorrow's leaders and innovators (Chapters 16 and 17).

Accountability and Competency-Based Education

You may recall a widely publicized 1977 news story. The parents of one Long Island, New York, high school graduate sued their local school district for five million dollars because their 18-year-old could barely read and write, and could not add or subtract at all. As a reaction to the apparently easy school standards and lower achievement levels of the late 1960s and the 1970s, evidenced by substantially lower scores on the Scholastic Aptitude Test (SAT) and the American College Test (ACT), parents and educators alike have been united in a back-to-basics (with few frills) movement.

Part of this no-nonsense effort has been labeled **educational accountability**, or sometimes **competency-based education**. The similar labels mean that teachers, students, or both will be held accountable for the students' mastery of minimum "competencies" (outcomes or objectives). According to Mitchell and Spady (1978), the competency effort is based on (a) the belief that the schools have failed to fulfill their major purposes, (b) an endorsement of explicit expectations for better student outcomes, and (c) the conviction that schools lack a good base for program design and operation. For many parents and educators, specifying competencies (objectives) and holding students and/or teachers accountable for mastering those competencies provides the educational base needed for improving student achievement. For example, states such as California, Florida, Oregon, New Jersey, New York, and Virginia require students to pass a minimum competency test in order to graduate from high school.

In 1973, the Greenville County, Virginia, system carried the accountability concept one step further—students could not enter the *next higher grade* unless they passed a standardized year-end test. To prove the school system was not bluffing, in the first year of the program 1300 of the county's 3700 students were retained—a stunning 35 percent! Two reasonable fears were that (a) students would drop out *en masse* and (b) black children would suffer because of cultural biases in the standardized tests. In fact, the true long-term outcomes were (a) a *reduction* in drop-out rates, (b) tremendously higher achievement scores, and (c) much better self-images among the students, most of whom were black.

Unfortunately, and in complete accord with the Jello Theory (when you jiggle here, something over there also wiggles), competency-based programs and competency testing have caused problems. In many states students in inferior segregated schools were much more likely to flunk the competency tests, which makes the tests discriminatory and therefore unconstitutional. Accordingly, in July of 1979 one federal judge ruled that the Florida School System cannot make its "functional illiteracy test" a requirement for a high school diploma until all remnants of school segregation are gone. Another more common problem is that many teachers, threatened by the tests, focus their best efforts on ensuring that students can meet the objectives and pass the tests. Interesting enrichment activities, field trips, creativity exercises, educational movies, and rich discussions of current events unfortunately are shelved in favor of meeting the basic competencies.

TO IMPROVE
YOUR TEACHING

First and foremost, take this book and this class seriously. The concepts, ideas, theories, and methods in these pages have evolved from the efforts of a great many dedicated psychologists and educators over many decades. Read constructively, which means you should think about how the ideas and principles can help you understand students and their problems, and how the strategies can help you become a more effective teacher. Consider keeping this text as an on-the-job reference. If it helps you solve *one* problem, it will be worth more than the bookstore will give you for it.

Be sure to become sensitive to the psychological subtleties described in this chapter. Your cheery (or grouchy) personality *will* affect student attitudes, motivations, and achievement. Your classroom management practices (see Chapter 10) and expectations (Chapter 2) also will have a surprisingly strong impact on attitudes and achievement. Be aware of the large variety of sources of motivation (Chapter 9); it is every teacher's number-one problem.

Keep in mind also subtleties in developmental changes, in the some-times-unexpected effects of rewards and punishments, and especially in the "hidden curriculum" itself. Students must master the hidden curriculum; staff also should think about the unwritten procedures students must follow in order to succeed (Chapter 2).

You especially must acquaint yourself with the nitty-gritty of major educational movements. Take a course in special education to better enable you to work with mainstreamed students. Also take a course in the education of the gifted and talented (or read a few good books, if no course is available; some are recommended at the end of Chapter 17). It is not difficult to become a minor expert in "G/T education."

Your school may or may not wish to formalize an accountability system in which (a) students do not graduate or get promoted, or (b) you get fired if students do not achieve. However, you should be conscious of the "competencies" which you want your students to acquire. Chapter 11 takes a longer look at the virtues of using instructional objectives to plan teaching and testing. Objectives and competencies are about the same thing.

SUMMARY

The teacher is a problem solver and decision maker. Intuition and experience are nice, but a good base of knowledge will enable a teacher to make effective, informed decisions.

A partial list of areas in which problems must be solved and decisions made would include: Teacher-student interactions, developmental phenomena, dynamics of learning and memory, affective learning and humanistic concerns, motivation, classroom management, using objectives, using instructional models, allowing for individual differences, fostering creative growth, programming for the gifted, coping with mainstreaming, teaching handicapped students, teaching disadvantaged students, and evaluating learning. This book and this course will help you solve problems and make decisions in these and other areas.

There are many subtle psychological dynamics at work in the classroom. Some examples are: (a) the effects of teacher personality, management practices, classroom climate, and teacher expectations; (b) the many subtle forms of student motivation; (c) subtleties in developmental trends in thinking, self-perceptions and morality; (d) subtleties in dynamics of reward and punishment; (e) subtleties in developing a good classroom test; and (f) the innately subtle "hidden curriculum" itself.

Educational psychology grew out of traditional psychology, but now has an identity of its own. It claims areas of research and theory not found in traditional psychology, namely, classroom learning and instruction, affective and humanistic learning in the classroom, classroom motivation and management, programming for gifted, talented, and creative students, instructional objectives, and coordinating teaching strategies with individual differences.

There are four main types of research methods in educational psychology: observational research, correlational research, experimental research, and product development.

Problems and criticisms of education include: high drop-out rates (25 percent!); poor achievement which sometimes borders on illiteracy; theft and vandalism; physical attacks on students and teachers; overcrowding; and pathetic counseling services.

Continuing challenges for the teacher of the 1980s include efforts to accommodate individual differences, perhaps via "magnet" high schools or other forms of specialized "transition" high schools. Also, in some states a voucher system may force public schools to compete with private schools for funds.

The mainstreaming of handicapped children into regular classrooms makes it necessary for teachers to learn to cope with and teach handicapped students. At the other end of the scale, programs for gifted learners also are rapidly growing.

One solution to poor achievement is the accountability, or competency-based, approach. With this educational design, students or teachers are held accountable for student achievement. Operationally, some states have required students to pass standardized minimum competency tests in order to graduate from high school.

TOPICS FOR THOUGHT AND DISCUSSION

1. What do you think are the most common problems and decisions a teacher must deal with? What would be some of the most difficult problems and decisions? Why are they difficult?
2. Think about (or discuss) some distinctly "good" or "bad" classroom climates in your own elementary or secondary school. What caused the climate? What were the effects?
3. What sort of motives or motivations improve school achievement? What motives prevent high achievement? Can these motives be altered?
4. This chapter listed high drop-out rates, poor achievement and illiteracy, theft, vandalism, physical attacks, poor counseling, and overcrowding as major problems. Did we miss anything? Are these real problems where you expect to teach? Why or why not?
5. Which might be the most effective way to improve student achievement: (a) holding students accountable; (b) holding teachers accountable; or (c) holding both accountable? How might you hold students or teachers accountable? Be clever.

PROJECTS

1. Visit with two or three teachers. Ask them about their most common problems and most difficult problems. Do the teachers agree? Do they handle the problems well?
2. Observe a classroom in action for a few hours. See if you can detect effects of (a) teacher personality, (b) teacher management practices, (c) teacher expectations, or (d) effects of reward or punishment.

RECOMMENDED READING

Featherstone, J. *Schools where children learn.* New York: Liveright Publishing, 1971.

Holt, J. *How children fail.* New York: Pitman, 1964.

Mitchell, D. E., and W. G. Spady. Organizational contexts for implementing outcome based education. *Educational Researchers* **7**(7), 1978, 9–17.

Pediwell, A. The saber-tooth curriculum. New York: McGraw-Hill, 1939. Partially reprinted in G. A. Davis and T. F. Warren (eds.), *Psychology of education: New Looks.* Lexington, Mass.: Heath, 1974. Pp. 5–13.

Peterson, P. L., and H. J. Walberg (eds.). *Research on teaching: Concepts, findings and implications.* Berkeley, Calif.: McCutcheon, 1979.

The Teacher in the Classroom

2

The teaching business / Teacher style and personality /
The hidden curriculum / Sex differences / Classroom
climate / Classroom typologies / Teacher expectations
and self-fulfilling prophecies / To improve your teaching
/ Summary / Topics for thought and discussion /
Projects / Recommended reading

THE TEACHING BUSINESS

The perfect occupation has yet to be discovered. This section will summarize some of the obligations and expectations related to teaching, then will look at some of the good parts and bad parts.

**Role
Expectations:
Your Job**

In many elementary schools you will have the same 25 to 30 students all day. You will be expected to plan all lessons for all subjects all week— English, math, science, social studies, health, physical education, and perhaps even art and music. If your elementary school is departmentalized or uses teaching teams, there will be fewer preparations for you to do, but more students for you to monitor; and with team teaching, you will have even more planning.

In junior high or high school you might have three sections of one subject or grade and two sections of another. You probably will not have the stamina to personally stand in front of the class lecturing, demonstrating, leading discussions, and quizzing the troops for five hours every day. You will need to schedule seat work, reading or group projects not only for the students' benefit, but for your own. You also will need to schedule written reports and exams in such a way that you do not find yourself with 125 to 150 10-page reports on "carbon," "communism," or "Robert Burns" which must be graded by tomorrow.

You will be expected to keep attendance records and records of books, basketballs, media and equipment, lunch money, lockers, and parent permissions for field trips, to say nothing of academic records and grades. Skip basketballs and lunch money if you teach high school. Other requirements and nonteaching duties can include holding parent conferences, monitoring lunch rooms and study halls, preparing reports, doing committee work, taking in-service courses, chaperoning school dances and ski trips, perhaps enforcing dress codes, and others.

There are outside pressures and problems to deal with also. Your school district may require you to cover a certain content outline and to use particular textbooks. Generally, the larger the system the more detailed will be the district guidelines for materials and subjects. If you decide, in your proper youthful idealism, to include training in creative thinking, critical thinking, values clarification, moral thinking, or other humanistic, person-oriented topics (Chapters 3, 13, 16 and 17), you have a choice of asking permission from your principal and/or your school district or else bootlegging the material into your class when the prescribed material has been lightly covered. Don't forget, tenure will normally be awarded after a three-year trial period. Will your "extras" be seen as dedicated, creative contributions or irresponsible violations of time-tested policies and regulations? School districts and individual principals differ tremendously in their interest in nonbasic, personal development training.

In addition to district requirements, your elected school board also will exert pressure for more of this and less of that; often, more basic skills and fewer frills. You may be required to use books and subject outlines reviewed and approved by members of the school board. Your fellow teachers also will have input on your teaching. Teachers at higher and lower grades will want to be certain that the curriculum is continuous and consistent. Teachers of other sections of the same class will need to coordinate subject matter, tests, and other requirements. It will not do for one teacher to assign less work, but award higher grades, than another teacher of supposedly the same course.

The Good Parts and the Bad Parts

The good part is that you are doing an important job: training America's young people in basic skills, knowledge of science and their culture, artistic skills, and skills of thinking and creating. The bad part is that your important job sometimes will be repetitious, dull, frustrating, and perhaps even unappreciated by rebellious students and parents. You are the villain when the public searches for answers to "Why can't Johnny read?"

The good part is that you will be a person of authority, a trained professional who is a respected member of the community. You will also have a secure job, once you acquire tenure. The bad part is that you will not earn a lot of money, unless your spouse or other person with whom you share expenses also has a respectable income.

The good part is that you will develop some warm and close relationships with many fine young people and many intelligent and energetic colleagues. The bad part is that (a) some students will have problems—for example, poverty or nasty parents—which you can do nothing about, (b) some teenage students, in school only because of the law, will detest you and your school, and (c) some colleagues may be unpleasant and difficult to work with—year after year after year.

The good part is that you will have plenty of swell vacation time—spring break, Christmas, and all summer. The bad part is that correcting papers and examinations can take you until three A.M. or even shoot a whole weekend. And there are plays, parties, dances, PTA meetings, Saturday field trips, basketball games, etc., which require teacher supervision or chaperoning, all part of the job.

In the elementary school, the good part is that (a) most children are eager to learn, (b) you can easily see their progress, and (c) many of them will adore you. The bad part is that (a) progress will sometimes be slow, (b) attention will be difficult to sustain, (c) some students will continuously

INSET 2.1

**TEACHER "BURNOUT"
DRAWS ATTENTION
FROM EDUCATORS***

DETROIT (AP)—Emmitt Williams almost quit teaching this spring after 23 years of doing the best job he could at a profession he loves. Why continue, he wondered, after your house is ransacked and set afire by a student you've struggled to help.

"I was thinking 'What's the use,' " he recalled during an interview at the National Education Association's convention which ends tonight. "You break your butt trying to help kids . . ." His voice trailed off.

Williams, a junior high school teacher from Downey, Calif., is a victim of what educators call—ironically in his case—teacher "burnout."

Frustrated by discipline problems, fearful of violence in their classrooms and hallways, and besieged by critics who denounce them because Johnny can't read, teachers are buckling under to the stress.

They suffer high blood pressure, insomnia, and sometimes emotional collapse. Many simply "burn out" and give up.

Williams isn't sure why 14-year-old Don, deemed a problem case by school officials who placed him in Williams' class, and two buddies broke into his home last December, smashed his furniture, and finally torched the house. The teacher said he had been working with Don and thought the youngster was making progress.

He's been told the boy was angry because Williams stopped letting the student mow his lawn in return for some spending money—an action Williams says he took when Don stopped doing the job right.

seek your attention, and (d) you will be talking all day at the level of your first or second graders. Before long, you may be asking your doctor, "Guess what we have today! That's right, more pain in our ankle! Raise your hand if you know where my ankle is. Very good!"

In junior and senior high school, the good part is that students are capable of comprehending complex, abstract concepts, which sometimes will lead to keen excitement about learning, discovering, and producing quality projects and reports. The bad part is that (a) some resentful students expect to fail, (b) some will try to cheat, (c) some will argue about grades, (d) many will ignore rules and laws about attendance, drinking and smoking, and (e) it may be difficult to maintain your own enthusiasm through three or four repetitions of the same material or same movie in a single day.

But in spite of despair at how difficult it's become to teach, and unlike many of his colleagues across the country, Williams decided against leaving the profession—"Sure, you get hurt by kids, but there's always that one you can help," he says.

But the situation is not without hope and many teachers are searching for ways to cure teacher "battle fatigue."

One education association conducts workshops on how to handle stress, another began a public relations campaign to let the community know about the problems leading to teacher burnout. A program being developed at Eastern Michigan University features a "teacher stress hotline" and confidential sessions with psychiatrists.

During contract negotiations last fall in Tacoma, Wash., teachers bargained in a provision that set up a committee to study stress—a goal set after a survey revealed that 75 percent of the teachers there had been subjected to verbal abuse and 25 percent had been assaulted.

The Tacoma committee found that involuntary transfers caused teachers the most stress, followed by notification of unsatisfactory performance, assaults on school colleagues, and managing disruptive children.

Involuntary transfers, in fact, were the major problem in Tacoma last fall, when teachers staged a 29-day strike, said association president Diana Landahl.

"People who had been teaching high school German were teaching fourth grade," related Landahl. "I had teachers in tears in my office saying, 'What do I do? I don't know how to handle junior high school kids.'

"One man was so unable to cope," she continued, "that now he's on long-term disability because of being emotionally upset."

* From an Associated Press article published in 1979. Reprinted with permission of the Associated Press.

TEACHER STYLE AND PERSONALITY

It is not difficult for an educational psychologist to study characteristics of "good" and "bad" teachers. The researcher gathers data on students' achievement, students' perceptions of their teachers, and attitudes toward particular classes and compares this information against the teachers' self-perceptions, training, intellectual ability, teaching style, and personality. Students fill out questionnaires, teachers fill out questionnaires, records are probed for facts and figures about students and teachers, and teacher behaviors are observed and recorded as they conduct class. Generally, the results show that good teaching and good teachers can be identified.

Of course, the issue is not simple. One good teacher may be quite different from other good teachers. Also, certain teachers may get good results only with certain types of students. Many powerful factors rooted in the students' experiences and abilities will influence educational outcomes, and the teacher is just one of those factors (Centra and Potter, 1980)

Stephans (1967) even proposed—incredibly enough—that the teacher has *no effect whatsoever* on student achievement. Rather, he argued, students learn because of their own abilities and motivational forces based in their personal histories, homes, and communities. MacDonald (1976) also concluded that socioeconomic level and student aptitudes are very strong determiners of achievement. However, he did concede that teaching style and personality also have a noteworthy effect. We certainly need not accept Stephans' extreme viewpoint, particularly since a half-century of instructional research has uncovered many recurring commonalities in the styles and traits which characterize "good" teachers—teachers who are effective, respected, and usually well-liked. (For reviews, see Centra and Potter, 1980; Rosenshine and Furst, 1971.)

Characteristics of Good Teachers

Good teachers tend to be knowledgeable in their subject areas. Strong academic preparation has been consistently related to effective teaching ability. It is not only the weighty knowledge itself which counts, but the good academic habits which led to the higher college grades and superior knowledgeability: These people work harder, prepare more thoroughly, are better organized, and even read more than less knowledgeable, less effective teachers.

One little research project involving 2043 teachers (Ryans, 1959) showed that effective teachers tended to have wider interests, were generally better informed, and indicated a greater interest in music and the arts. It is noteworthy that these traits also are characteristic of creative persons (see Chapter 16).

Several educators have emphasized that good teachers are task oriented, businesslike, and responsible (Centra and Potter, 1980). They have goals and objectives for their students, and they expect the objectives to be met. They are organized, monitor their classes closely, and have established routines for everyday procedural matters. Learning activities thus are well structured (Soar, 1973), and the teachers maintain control and use good classroom management procedures (Evertson and Brophy, 1973; see Chapter 10).

Good teachers are described as imaginative, stimulating, open to new strategies, materials, and activities, progressive in attitude, and especially enthusiastic (Centra and Potter, 1980; Rosenshine, 1971; Shavelson and Stern, 1981). Indeed, teacher enthusiasm may be the single most critical teacher characteristic. From kindergarten through graduate school, students

do respond well to a genuinely interested, enthusiastic instructor (although some days you will have to work at it).

As we will see in Chapter 13 on humanistic education, good teachers also know and care about their students. "Humanness" includes being reasonable, fair, empathetic, easy to relate to, open, humorous, understanding, and trusting. The humanistic teacher also is willing to admit having feelings and imperfections and sometimes making mistakes.

In one early survey of 3725 high school students (Hart, 1934), the best-liked teachers were described as "interested in and understands students" and as "human, friendly, companionable, and one of us." The least-liked teachers were too cross, crabby, grouchy, never smiling, nagging, sarcastic, snooty, aloof, superior in attitude, overbearing, "losing their tempers," "flying off the handle," and "does not know you out of class."

In their continuing investigations of behaviors of effective teachers, Evertson, Anderson, Anderson and Brophy (1980; see also Anderson, Evertson, and Brophy, 1979; Evertson and Brophy, 1973) recently recorded the classroom behaviors of 68 English and mathematics teachers in urban junior

---

INSET 2.2

SELF-RATING SCOREBOARD

This section summarizes some of the traits and behaviors which often characterize teachers who are effective and well-liked. Take the inventory; the scoring key is at the bottom.

	Yes	No
1. Are you knowledgeable in your subject matter?	___	___
2. Do you have good work habits?	___	___
3. Do you have wide interests?	___	___
4. Are you interested in art, music?	___	___
5. Can you be task-oriented and businesslike?	___	___
6. Are you responsible? Organized?	___	___
7. Will you use goals and objectives?	___	___
8. Are you flexible and imaginative?	___	___
9. Are you generally energetic and enthusiastic?	___	___
10. Do you like and care about students?	___	___
11. Can you be fair and reasonable?	___	___
12. Empathetic and understanding?	___	___
13. Do you have a good sense of humor?	___	___
14. Can you admit feelings? Mistakes?	___	___
15. Are you crabby, grouchy, nagging, sarcastic?	___	___
16. Do you lose your temper easily?	___	___
17. How about snooty, are you snooty?	___	___
18. Do you perceive and evaluate students positively?	___	___
19. Do you have good self-esteem?	___	___
20. Would you be strongly in favor of stimulating on-task effort (academic engagement)?	___	___
21. Are you active, enthusiastic?	___	___
22. Will you solicit and use student ideas?	___	___

Scoring Key: One point for "yes" to items 1–14, 18–22; one point for "no" to items 15, 16 and 17. **Interpretation:** If you said "yes" to items 15, 16 and 17, you might consider another line of work, away from people. If you said "yes" to all other questions, you're probably too good to be true.

high schools. These teaching styles and activities were compared with student achievement test scores and attitudes toward the teachers. As a first finding, these two outcome measures generally were positively related—students who achieved at higher levels also rated their teachers more favorably. Other findings seem to reconfirm many of the above earlier conclusions. The most effective teachers:

- Were active and enthusiastic.
- Were nurturant and affectionate.
- Were well-organized, strongly academically oriented, and academically effective.
- Encouraged and accepted student ideas.
- Managed their classes efficiently, "nipping trouble in the bud."
- Were confident and competent.
- Did *not* try to catch nonvolunteers off-guard—asking them questions they could not answer.
- In mathematics, gave more lecture-demonstrations and less seatwork.

In Chapter 12 we will make a closer examination of what appears to be the single most critical determinant of student achievement. It is not a personality trait as such, nor is it a factor in teachers' training or background. It is an approach to teaching. Rosenshine (1979) coined the terms **direct instruction** and **academic engaged time** to describe the key points of this approach. It seems that the more time students spend actively engaged in academic tasks, the more they learn. That is, the more time teachers spend directly instructing and the more time students spend in on-task activities, the more content they cover and the higher are their achievement scores. (This discovery would not be so profound if it were not for 50 years of searching for teacher characteristics and teacher behaviors which produce high achievement.) On the affective side, these no-nonsense, high academic engagement classes also tend to be warm and pleasant—the teacher cares about the welfare and progress of each student—and the high achievement leads to good feelings of self-esteem and accomplishment.

THE HIDDEN CURRICULUM

When you think about it, there are two curricula which must be dealt with by successful students in any classroom from K through college. First, there is the official content-related curriculum: the concepts, principles, and skills outlined by the school district and found in textbooks. The other curriculum is a hidden one, the unwritten routines and policies along with the teacher's expectations and feelings which must be accommodated by

the student who wishes to succeed with a minimum of pain and conflict. A few obvious examples are neatness, pleasantness, docility, good manners, and an appearance of exerting effort. Some of the teachers' hidden expectations actually may contradict what they teach students. For example, teachers may laud independence, creativity, and standing up for one's rights, yet the message is sent via facial expressions, glares, and innuendos that students are expected to conform and to follow the rules, preferably without questioning them.

In addition, successful students learn to accept interruption of an engaging activity, forfeiting their own interests whenever asked. And all students learn to wait—for the bus, for the doors to be unlocked, for teacher attention, for books and materials, for recess, for lunch, for slower students to finish, and for dismissal.

One study of student perceptions of high school showed that many students view school learning strictly as a teacher-managed activity. They rarely even thought of independent study or intellectual discussions with other students (Sprinthall and Mosher, 1969). Another survey of nearly 7000 high school students found that two-thirds of them did see themselves as powerless victims of a high-handed, autocratic school system (DeCecco, 1972). It is conceivable that bureaucratic behavior patterns (part of the hidden curriculum) are not consistent with creative independence, entrepreneurship, or even self-initiated intellectual development. Fortunately, many energetic students are able to sustain their natural enthusiasm and individuality while accommodating the demands of the hidden curriculum.

Sexism in the Schools

Despite a growing awareness of women's rights, there remain several forms of sexism in elementary and secondary schools. An easy example is the school staff itself—the secretaries are all women; the custodians are almost always men in elementary schools, although the occasional large high school may have a cleaning woman or two; elementary school teachers are mostly women; teachers at all levels are subservient to principals, 80 percent of whom are male.

Publishers are more and more aware of sexism in textbooks (believe me!), yet reading materials still are likely to portray women as bed makers, baby feeders and cookie bakers. In professional careers they may be shown typing men's letters or as nurses assisting male doctors. The roles women have played in American history form an increasingly popular high school topic, but we have yet to hear about our Founding Mothers.

SEX DIFFERENCES

Actually, there are sex differences in cognitive, social, and physical characteristics (Lips and Colwill, 1978). For example, in elementary and secondary school, boys cause more trouble than girls and so the majority of reprimands and punishments are aimed at boys (Brophy and Good, 1970). Boys also are much more likely to become classroom disrupters and even juvenile offenders.

Boys not only cause more trouble, they also are worse students, particularly in elementary and junior high school. In the elementary school two-thirds of all grade repeaters are boys. Indeed, more boys "fail" course-work than girls—in every grade and in every subject except math and science, in which boys seem to surpass girls (Fennema, 1982; Kahl, 1982). Boys are more likely to drop out of school than girls, since boys tend to dislike school more than girls. On the average, boys score between 6 and 18 months below girls on standardized achievement tests. Maccoby and Jacklin (1974) studied elementary school abilities and achievement of boys vs. girls, concluding that girls are generally superior in verbal fluency, reading, and spelling. Boys were superior in mathematical reasoning and in tasks involving spatial relationships. Girls get higher grades.

One suggested reason for the higher grades of girls is simply that their mothers overprotected them in childhood, leading to attitudes of dependence, conformity, and a desire to please (Lois W. Hoffman, 1972; Moss, 1967). Boys, according to Hoffman, are encouraged to be independent and not seekers of approval, and therefore tend to work hard only in subjects which interest them. At the time of her research, Hoffman concluded that despite their lower school grades, boys tend to achieve at higher levels in many activities later in life.

One recent line of research focused specifically on the repeated finding that girls score higher than boys in reading, but lower than boys in math (Aiken, 1973; Backman, 1972; National Assessment of Educational Progress, 1975), a difference which seems to widen over the years (Hilton and Berglund, 1974). Leinhardt, Seewald, and Engel (1979) observed 49 second-grade teachers as they taught math and reading. Their conclusions: The teachers made more "instructional contacts" and spent more time teaching reading to girls; conversely, there were more contacts and more time was invested in teaching math to boys. While average reading ability was equal in September, by June the girls could read better than the boys.

There also seem to be sex differences in interpreting school failure. Dweck and Bush (1976) found boys tend to attribute school failures to lack of effort—perhaps due to a history of criticism for "not trying," or for being unnecessarily careless, messy, thoughtless, or absent minded. Girls, on the other hand, tend to attribute failure to lack of ability (Dweck and Repucci, 1973; Nichols, 1979). This difference is important. If one attributes failure to lack of *effort*, the situation is not hopeless and one may be inclined to work harder and achieve more on later tasks (Bar-Tal, Raviv, Raviv, and Bar-Tal, 1982; Dweck, 1975; Weiner, 1972, 1980). However, if failure is attributed to lack of *ability*, the problem is considerably more serious, and the person is less likely to work harder to improve. Boys often perform better than girls in high school and on SAT tests. It also appears that high school males desire and expect to attain higher levels of educational achievement in college than do females (Marini and Greenberger, 1978).

CLASSROOM CLIMATE

The topic of classroom climate or psychological atmosphere is closely related to the topic of teacher style and personality discussed above and to the topics of motivation and classroom management presented in Chapters 9 and 10. Certainly, different teacher personalities, teaching styles, and management practices will create very different classroom atmospheres; compare any college or high school class in which you felt safe and productive with another in which you were anxious and threatened. Classroom atmosphere influences student achievement, satisfaction with the class, and feelings toward the teacher. For example, one recent study of the social environments of 19 high school classes showed that absenteeism, one form of silent rebellion, was highest in classes rated as competitive, high in teacher control, and low in personal supportiveness (Moos and Moos, 1978). Also, as we will see later and in Chapter 10, teachers who early in the year use clear classroom rules to help establish their authority are able to be businesslike yet warm and supportive; and students in such an atmosphere usually have higher morale and greater satisfaction, and they earn higher grades (Kaye, Trickett, and Quinlan, 1977).

For now, we will summarize three studies which identify important classroom climate factors, all based on teacher personality and classroom leadership and interaction patterns, and then turn to two analyses of classroom "types." You probably will look for yourself in these descriptions.

The Lewin, Lippitt and White Study

One of the most profound—and certainly one of the best known—studies of the effects of leadership style on the attitudes and behaviors of children was the research by Lewin and his colleagues, Lippitt and White (1958). The subjects were 11-year old boys invited to participate in some after-school "clubs." The researchers attempted to create three politically-loaded leadership styles, authoritarian (autocratic), democratic, and laissez-faire. The groups of boys were exposed to all three of the leadership styles (or "climates"). However, different groups experienced the three climates in different orders, so that the effects of changing from one leadership style to another could be evaluated.

In accord with instructions, the authoritarian leader gave plenty of orders and nonconstructive criticisms. He also awarded praise and approval for correct, conforming behavior. Interestingly enough, under the dictator two patterns of behavior emerged: Some groups became apathetic and submissive while others became aggressive, discontented, and critical. Not too surprisingly, work productivity was higher in the conforming, submissive groups than in the aggressive groups. Either way however, most boys in the authoritarian climate became very dependent on the leader for direction. When the leader left the room—a deliberate maneuver—work activity almost stopped cold, picking up again the instant he returned. Morale was low.

The democratic leader gave suggestions and stimulated self-guidance. He was generally jovial, confident, and matter-of-fact. This climate led to friendly, work-oriented conversations and a higher rate of after-hours, out-of-club conversations. Clearly, morale was the highest. However, work productivity was lower than in the leader-present authoritarian situation. When the democratic leader left the room, work continued without interruption.

As per his instructions, the laissez-faire leader mainly provided information about procedures and activities—but only when asked. Students in this situation scored very high in "asking for information." Would you be surprised to hear that work productivity was rock-bottom lowest in the laissez-faire groups? Interestingly, when the leader left the room, work productivity *increased*. It seems that the frustrating lack of structure encouraged leaders to emerge from the group to direct activities and get something done.

The effects of changes in leadership styles led to observations and conclusions which have influenced educators for several decades. It seems that a transition from a no-nonsense authoritarian climate to a more democratic one improved attitudes and satisfaction. Vice versa, a switch from a laissez-faire or friendly democractic style to a tougher authoritarian approach led to poor productivity, frustration, restlessness, and, to be redundant, low morale.

Now, some experienced teachers give this advice to newcomers: Get tough and clamp down early in the year, then ease up later. As we will see in Chapter 10, however, classroom management experts Good and Brophy (1978) point out that a too-tough beginning will establish you as "the enemy," complete with student feelings of hostility, mistrust, and alienation. A better approach is to try to establish respectability, likeability, and trustworthiness by communicating to students that (a) you enjoy teaching and interacting with students, (b) you look forward to knowing each student better, (c) you are always willing to help students with any sort of problem, (d) you expect to teach the subject matter, and (e) certain behaviors are expected, others are forbidden. A set of clear classroom rules and other management tactics will help emphasize these points and reduce management problems—the restlessness, frustration, and low productivity described by Lippitt and White (1958).

We might note also that Summerhill and other unstructured free schools popular in the late 1960s and early 1970s produced behaviors resembling those of Lewin's laissez-faire climate. Overall academic accomplishment in these schools usually was low, but many students did develop initiative and responsibility, mainly to relieve boredom and get something done.

As a final pair of observations on this classic, influential study of leadership styles: (a) The researchers used artificially extreme forms of the three climates—few teachers are likely to be as authoritarian or as laissez-faire as the trained leaders of Lewin, Lippitt, and White. (b) The point is made, however, that leadership style does have an effect on morale, productivity, and patterns of social interactions.

Three Personality and Leadership Patterns: Heil and Washburne

Heil and Washburne (1962) summarized three teacher "styles" which seem to combine the topics of personality and leadership. Briefly, the Style A teacher was described as sentimental, with a strong personal identification with students. This teaching style tends to be impulsive and variable, sometimes unplanned and slipshod except in topics in which the teacher is highly interested. Student achievement also tends to be inconsistent and variable. Insecure and low ability students do not learn well with this personality-leadership style, and their emotional security tends to stay low.

The Style B teacher, a white-hatted hero, tends to be warm and understanding and is willing to listen to and accept student ideas and feelings. Her or his approach to teaching is described as responsible, businesslike, orderly and work-oriented, yet at the same time stimulating,

flexible and imaginative. The Style B teacher praises and encourages, administers rewards fairly, and carefully explains reasons for constructive criticisms of students' work. Student achievement is high and consistent. She or he appears to possess most of the characteristics of effective teachers described above and follows most of the principles for good classroom management (Chapter 10) and effective "direct instruction" (Chapter 12).

Style C teachers are about the opposite of the sentimental Style A teacher, although student outcomes are similar. The Style C teacher tends to be excessively fearful, aloof, and anxious about how others feel toward him or her. In the classroom this teacher may be dominating, critical, unreasonable, and demanding. The catchy terms "dull" and "routine" seem to describe the classroom environment. Most likely due to fear motivation, achievement probably will be high, although independent-thinking "rebellious" students may fight back and, consequently, not do well.

The three Heil and Washburne teacher styles—sentimental/impulsive, warm/businesslike, and anxious/demanding—clearly are oversimplifications of complex behaviors. In a very general way however, the three styles characterize some common personality and leadership traits of a great many teachers.

Direct and Indirect Teaching: Flanders

Classroom climates are determined virtually entirely by the nature of the interactions between teachers and students. Flanders (1970; Amidon and Flanders, 1967) devised a 10-category interaction analysis system for objectively recording these interactions. As shown in Table 2.1, the scale includes seven categories of **teacher talk**, broken down into four categories of **indirect influence** and three categories of **direct influence,** and three categories of **student talk.** Flanders considers direct and indirect teaching to be two major teaching (or interaction) styles.

Teachers who score high on **indirect teaching** frequently ask open-ended questions—soliciting ideas and opinions—and then build on the response, incorporating the ideas into the lesson. They also tend to offer more praise and encouragement and they accept and clarify student feelings (e.g., "Of course you're disappointed about the cancellation," "You're very upset, aren't you?"). In contrast, **direct teachers** talk—almost in monologues—for about 85 percent of the class period.

In comparing student achievement under the two teaching styles, Flanders found higher achievement with indirect teaching in math, social studies, and English. As you might guess, student attitudes toward the teacher, toward learning activities, and toward school in general were also more positive with indirect teaching. There is one depressing note: On the average, these teachers were observed to "accept and clarify student feelings" only about five times per 1000 codable interactions.

Table 2.1 Categories for Flanders interaction analysis.

Teacher talk

Indirect Influences

1. *Accepts feelings.* Accepts and clarifies the tone of feeling of the students in an unthreatening manner. Feelings may be positive or negative. Predicting or recalling feelings are included.
2. *Praises or encourages.* Praises or encourages student action or behavior. Jokes that release tension, but not at the expense of another individual, nodding head and saying "um hm?" or "go on" are included.
3. *Accepts or uses ideas of students.* Clarifies, builds, or develops ideas suggested by a student. As teacher brings more of his own ideas into play, shift to #5.
4. *Asks questions.* Asks a question about content or procedure with the intent that the student answer.

Direct Influence

5. *Lecturing.* Gives facts or opinion about content or procedure; expresses his own ideas, asking rhetorical questions.
6. *Giving directions.* Directs, commands, or gives orders that students are expected to comply with.
7. *Criticizing or justifying authority.* Statements intended to change student behavior from unacceptable to acceptable pattern; bawling someone out; stating why the teacher is doing what he is doing; extreme self-reference.

Student talk

8. *Student talk—response.* Talk by students in response to teacher. Teacher initiates the contact or solicits student statement.
9. *Student talk—initiation.* Talk initiated by students. If "calling on" student is only to indicate who may talk next, observer must decide whether student wanted to talk.

10. *Silence or confusion.* Pauses, short periods of silence, and periods of confusion in which communication cannot be understood by the observer.

From N. A. Flanders, *Analyzing Teacher Behavior* (Reading, Mass.: Addison-Wesley, 1970), p. 34. Reprinted by permission.

Flanders' criticism of **direct teaching** would appear to contradict the beneficial effects of **direct instruction** outlined by Rosenshine (1979; see above and Chapter 12). However, Rosenshine's direct instruction includes sincere concern for student achievement and success plus a close monitoring of individual and group work—not simply lecturing to students for almost the entire class period. In fact, Evertson, Anderson, Anderson, and Brophy (1980) found that the most successful (effective, well-liked) junior high school math teachers were both receptive to student ideas (Flanders' indirect teaching) and high in task orientation (Rosenshine's direct instruction).

CLASSROOM TYPOLOGIES

We already have reviewed three classifications of important teacher leadership, personality, and teaching styles, each with just two or three main categories. Two more analyses of classroom types identify additional informative social climate factors, producing taxonomies with nine and six categories, respectively.

Moos Typology

Moos (1978; see also Moos, 1974; Price, 1974) statistically analyzed 200 junior and senior high school classrooms according to scores on a *Classroom Environment Scale*, which measures such characteristics as student-teacher relationships, student-student relationships, student involvement, degree of order and organization, rule clarity, amount of teacher control, teacher support, task orientation, competition, and openness to innovation. The results suggested nine "types" of high school classrooms.

1. *Control oriented.* The classes were high in teacher control, with little emphasis on personal relationships or even task orientation.
2. *Innovation oriented.* These classes were strong on trying new activities and materials, and were above average in interpersonal relationships. However, they scored low on task orientation, goal clarity, and teacher control.
3. *Affiliation oriented—structured.* These classes were highest in student-student interaction and participation. They also were high in organization and clarity of rules and procedures.
4. *Affiliation oriented—unstructured.* These also were high in student-student interaction, but lacked organization, rule clarity, and teacher control.
5. *Task oriented—structured.* These classes were high in task orientation, teacher support, rule clarity, and teacher control. There was little interaction among students and little innovation.
6. *Task oriented—unstructured.* While also task oriented, these classes tended to be low in teacher support, teacher control, and rule clarity. As in Type 5, there was little interaction and little innovation.

7. *Competition oriented—structured.* These competitive classes were high in organization, clarity, teacher control, and student involvement.
8. *Competition oriented—unstructured.* Also competitive, these classes were rated as *low* in organization, clarity, teacher control, and student involvement.
9. *Competition oriented—supportive.* This third competitive atmosphere emphasized working together, for example, with homework. Organization and clarity were high, as in Type 7, but teacher control was low.

Students were most satisfied with: Type 3, structured affiliation-oriented classes; Types 9 and 7, supportive and structured competition-oriented classes; and Type 2, innovation-oriented classes.

Students least liked: Type 1, control-oriented classes; Type 5, structured task-oriented classes.

Teachers were most satisfied with: Type 9, supportive competition-oriented classes; Type 6, unstructured task-oriented classes.

Teachers were least satisfied with: Type 8, unstructured competition-oriented classes; Type 5, structured task-oriented classes; Type 1, control-oriented classes.

Reasonably enough, neither teachers nor students were wildly enthusiastic about classes which overstress teacher control and discipline and minimize personal relations and student interaction (Types 1 and 5). Both students and teachers seemed to enjoy a competitive yet supportive, working-together class with clear organization but low teacher control (Type 9).

Holland's Typology

Holland (1973; see also Hearn and Moos, 1978) proposed a six-part typology of classrooms based on the frequent observation that, for example, biology and physics classes seem to resemble each other more than do French and theatre classes, which also resemble each other. The typology is summarized in Table 2.2. According to Holland, the main reason for the differences among the six types is in the students who take the classes. Thus it is assumed that art students are likely to be creative, impulsive, independent, etc. (refer to Table 2.2 and Chapter 16), and chemistry students are supposed to be more analytic, intellectual, and so on. These personality and vocational factors "... create characteristic interpersonal environments" (Holland, 1973, p. 9).

In contrast with all of the above studies, which emphasize the influence of the teacher and his or her personality and teaching style, Holland's typology points out that student personality and interests, combined with the subject matter of the class, contribute greatly to the nature of the classroom's climate.

TEACHER EXPECTATIONS AND SELF-FULFILLING PROPHECIES

You see, really and truly, ... the difference between a lady and a flower girl is not how she behaves, but how she's treated. I shall always be a flower girl to Professor Higgins, because he ... treats me as a flower girl, ... but I know I can be a lady to you, because you always treat me as a lady, and always will. [Pygmalion, George Bernard Shaw.]

As you begin your teaching career you will find it impossible to avoid forming impressions of student capabilities. Logically, these impressions of capability will influence your expectations of each student. You expect rapid, high quality learning and thinking from the alert, highly verbal, high-SES student whose record shows an IQ score of 135. Conversely, you do not expect much from disadvantaged Eliza Doolittle, whose records show low grades, slow work, and numerous comments about poor spelling and comprehension.

Table 2.2 Holland's typology of high school classrooms

Classroom type	Relevant classroom subjects	Characteristic personality and environmental type
Realistic	Auto repair, carpentry, electronics, general shop, machine shop, power mechanics	Asocial, conforming, frank, genuine, materialistic, persistent, practical, stable, thrifty, uninsightful
Investigative	Algebra, biology, chemistry, geometry, mathematics, physics, physical science, science	Analytical, curious, independent, intellectual, introspective, introverted, passive, unassuming, unpopular
Artistic	Art, band, composition, drama, English, French, German, Italian, literature, music, Spanish, theatre	Complicated, disorderly, emotional, imaginative, impractical, impulsive, independent, intuitive, nonconforming, original.
Social	Civics, economics, government, history, political systems, social studies, sociology	Friendly, helpful, idealistic, insightful, persuasive, responsible, sociable, tactful, understanding.
Enterprising	Independent creative work	Acquisitive, ambitious, dependent, domineering, energetic, impulsive, optimistic, self-confident, sociable
Conventional	Bookkeeping, clerical office practice, retailing, shorthand, stenography, typing	Conforming, defensive, efficient, inflexible, inhibited, obedient, orderly, persistent, practical, prudish

From Hearn, J. C., and R. H. Moos. Subject matter and classroom climate: A test of Holland's environmental propositions. *American Educational Research Journal* **15**, 1978, 113, Table 1. Reprinted by permission.

While these expectations are reasonably normal—and often reasonably accurate—the bad part is that teacher expectations may have a direct effect, good or bad, on student achievement. The expectations may become self-fulfilling prophecies (Braun, 1976; Brophy, 1982; Cooper, 1979; Rist, 1970; Rosenthal and Jacobson, 1968).

Dynamics of Expectations

The actual dynamics of self-fulfilling prophecies in the classroom are not particularly simple. For example, the teacher who expects high accomplishment may give assignments consistent with this expectation. These students are thus tacitly required to put forth more effort. The quality of their work is therefore higher and they generally learn more and earn higher grades.

Even without giving more demanding work to "capable" students, the teacher's high expectations can be communicated to the students by what the teacher says and how he or she says it, by facial expressions and perhaps by other physical gestures (Chaiken, Sigler, and Derlega, 1974; Page, 1971; Rosenthal and Jacobson, 1968). These direct and indirect messages not only convey to the student that he or she must work hard; they also improve the student's self-image: "Gee whiz, Mr. Euclid thinks I'm good at math! I bet if I work hard I can get straight A's on the tests!" Students who sense that their teacher thinks highly of their ability feel increased confidence in that ability, expect more from themselves, and have higher self-esteem.

In addition to communicating his or her expectations to the students, the teacher with great expectations also simply may improve his or her teaching strategies. For example, if English teacher Bill Shakespeare is honestly convinced that he has an extraordinarily talented drama class, he probably will invest more effort in selecting materials, exercises, and productions that will elicit the best from his superior thespians.

It also can be enlightening to turn things around: Do teacher expectations determine student achievement—or does student achievement determine teacher expectations? Most likely both. We also can ask: How do student expectations affect the teacher? (Feldman and Prohaska, 1979)

In one interesting study which complicates the dynamics of expectancies even more, Gagné, Hoy, Hauck, and Moore (1979) deliberately conveyed either high or low expectations to high-achieving fourth-grade students ("I think you will do very well on this lesson," or "I believe this lesson will be difficult for you"). After the lesson, students received either positive or negative feedback ("You did an excellent job on that lesson," or "You did very poorly on that lesson"). They found that students who received inconsistent combinations—high expectancy followed by negative feedback or low expectancy followed by positive feedback—tended to become uncertain about their chances for success and therefore "psychologically aroused." This state of arousal led to improved attention, more effort, and better performance. This experiment was duplicated with low-achieving high school students in a reading program (Means, Moore, Gagné, and Hauck, 1979). Those students who received inconsistent combinations of expectancy and feedback got higher comprehension scores—due to improved attention and performance—than those who received consonant expectancy and feedback information.

Weiner (1974, 1980) explains expectancy effects in terms of attributions. That is, students can attribute their performance to *luck*, to *effort*, to *ability*, or to *task difficulty*. As we noted earlier, in relation to sex differences in learning, if the teacher conveys to the student that his or her performance is attributable to lack of ability, the student may conclude that there is little he or she can do about the situation and continue to perform poorly.

However, if a teacher indicates that a poor performance is due to lack of effort, to an unusually difficult learning task, or perhaps to bad luck, the student may retain his or her feelings of having adequate ability and will be willing to work harder to achieve better grades.

The Oak School Experiment: Rosenthal and Jacobson

It was a book by psychologists Robert Rosenthal and Lenore Jacobson (1968), *Pygmalion in the Classroom: Teacher Expectations and Pupils' Intellectual Development*, which launched a stormy I-knew-it-all-the-time reaction in American intellectual circles. For example:

> *Can the child's performance in school be considered the result as much of what his teachers' attitudes are toward him as of his native intelligence or his attitude as a pupil?* . . . Pygmalion in the Classroom *is full of charts and graphs and statistics and percentages and carefully weighed statements, but there are conclusions that have great significance for this nation.* . . . *Among the children of the first and second grades, those tagged "bloomers" made astonishing gains.* . . . *TOIA's putative prophecy was fulfilled so conclusively that even hard-line social scientists were startled.* [Coles, *The New Yorker*, April 9, 1969]

> *Here may lie the explanation of the effects of socio-economic status on schooling. Teachers of a higher socio-economic status expect pupils of a lower socio-economic status to fail.* [Hutchins, *San Francisco Chronicle*, August 11, 1968]

> *In one study conducted by Robert Rosenthal of Harvard University, the test results given to teachers were rigged, but the children performed just as teachers had been led to expect based on the IQ scores.* [McCurdy, *Los Angeles Times*, January 31, 1969]

Other comments appeared in the *Saturday Review* (October 19, 1968), and a special issue of *The Urban Review* (September 1968) was devoted solely to the topic of expectancy and contained a selection from *Pygmalion*. Rosenthal was even invited to discuss his research on NBC's "Today" show, thus reaching millions of viewers with the expectancy-achievement relationship.

Of most significance, the demonstration of the effects of teacher expectations led to a rapid and widespread reappraisal of IQ testing and ability grouping—both of which obviously create clear expectations in the minds of teachers. In many school districts, both IQ testing and ability grouping have been dropped entirely as a result of the Rosenthal and Jacobson study.

The research itself took place in the west coast "Oak School." At the beginning of the year all children in the school were given the "Harvard Test of Inflected Acquisition." The test was described to teachers as a valid predictor of "academic blooming." Actually, it was an intelligence test, comprised of verbal (picture-vocabulary) and abstract reasoning subtests, which combined to produce a total IQ score.

In each of the 18 classes, three each of grades 1 through 6, teachers were given the names of "academic spurters," children who ". . . during the academic year ahead, would show unusual intellectual gains" (Rosenthal and Jacobson, 1968). The names, of course, were selected at random. The only difference between the "bloomers" and the other 80 percent of the class was in the minds and expectations of the teachers.

The "Harvard Test of Inflected Acquisition" was administered four months later and again at the end of the school year, ostensibly as ". . . further efforts to predict intellectual growth."

The famous "Pygmalion effect" results appear in Table 2.3. All classes showed an average gain in test scores from the fall to the spring testing, probably due to general growth and to having taken the test twice before. The important figures are for the first and second graders. The "expectancy advantage" column shows that the first-grade experimental children (bloomers) gained 15.4 more IQ points than did the control students (everybody else). For the second grade, the expectancy advantage was 9.5 points. Reports Rosenthal and Jacobson (1968, p. 261), "In 15 of the 17 classrooms in which the abstract reasoning subtest . . . was administered, the experimental group children gained more than did the control group children. . . . In the first

Table 2.3 Mean gain in IQ in one year by experimental and control children in each grade

Grade	Control		Experimental		Expectancy advantage	
	N	Gain	N	Gain	IQ points	One-tail p
1	48	+12.0	7	+27.4	15.4	.002
2	47	+ 7.0	12	+16.5	9.5	.02
3	40	+ 5.0	14	+ 5.0	0.0	
4	49	+ 2.2	12	+ 5.6	3.4	
5	26	+17.5	9	+17.4	−0.1	
6	45	+10.7	11	+10.0	−0.7	
Total	255	+ 8.42	65	+12.22	3.80	.02

From R. Rosenthal and L. Jacobson. *Pygmalion in the classroom.* Copyright © 1968 by Holt, Rinehart and Winston, Inc. Reprinted by permission of Holt, Rinehart and Winston, CBS College Publishing.

and second grades combined, 19 percent of the control group children gained 20 or more IQ points. Two-and-a-half times that many, or 47 percent, of the experimental group children gained 20 or more IQ points."

The teachers' expectations apparently led to growth not only in the cognitive areas, but in the nearby affective area as well. At the end of the year Rosenthal and Jacobson asked all teachers to describe the classroom behavior of their students. Interestingly, the experimental "bloomers" were described as more curious, more interesting, more happy, better adjusted, more affectionate, lower in needs for social approval, and as having a better chance for success.

Criticisms of the Rosenthal and Jacobson Research

The highly publicized Rosenthal and Jacobson study touched off that national reaction because their data seemed to confirm what many people suspected anyway. Particularly in regard to schools in low SES and disadvantaged areas, the expectancy effect seemed to be a logical and scientifically proven reason for poor student performance. However, many very severe cricitism may have been aimed at the Rosenthal and Jacobson research. The main attacks have come from the verbal machine guns of Jung (1971) and Elashoff and Snow (1971). For example:

> The RJ [Rosenthal and Jacobson] report is misleading. The text and tables are inconsistent, conclusions are overdramatized, and variables are given prejudicial labels. The three concluding chapters represent only superficial, and frequently inaccurate, attempts to deal with the study's flaws. Descriptions of design, basic data, and analyses are incomplete . . . charts and graphs are frequently drawn in a misleading way . . . statistical discussions are frequently oversimplified or completely incorrect. . . . After the study the teachers could not remember the names on the original list of 'bloomers,' and reported having scarcely glanced at the list.   [Elashoff and Snow, 1974, pp. 268–271]

At present, the Rosenthal and Jacobson research can be classified somewhere between "questionable" and "discredited." Several hundred post-Pygmalion studies—reviewed by Cooper (1979), Braun (1976), Brophy (1982), Dweck (1975), Rosenthal (1976), and West and Anderson (1976)— have produced both positive and negative results. Apparently the expectancy effect is not easily and predictably produced by educational researchers. However, it sometimes is demonstrated experimentally (see Inset 2.3) and most likely occurs when some teachers inadvertently inform some students that they have low ability and are not expected to succeed.

INSET 2.3

**GEMS FROM RECENT
RESEARCH ON
EXPECTATIONS**

The 1970s produced a minor flood of research on expectations and reviews of research on expectations. A few thoughtful conclusions are:

1. "... the existence of expectation effects seems well-established. It is equally clear, however, that expectation effects do not occur invariantly" (Cooper, 1979).
2. Over 300 studies were examined by Rosenthal (1976); of these, 37 percent reported statistically significant results confirming an expectancy influence on behavior.
3. "The impact of expectations has been measured on outcomes as varied as swimming ability, job performance, and absenteeism" (Cooper, 1979).

TO IMPROVE YOUR TEACHING

Think about the job requirements, obligations, and role expectations associated with a teaching career. Be sure that the satisfactions, challenges, and rewards more than offset the potential disappointments and frustrations. Your mental health may depend on it.

Be sure you understand the position of your principal, your school district, and the elected school board regarding their objectives and expectations, especially if you are interested in nontraditional personal development activities such as creativity, critical thinking, or the development of values and morals. Your job may depend on it.

Think about the personality traits and teacher styles which often characterize "good" teachers. Is this you? Can you cultivate patterns of self-confidence, friendliness, concern for students, imaginativeness, and enthusiasm, together with a responsible businesslike approach to setting and meeting teaching goals? If so, you should be great.

The topics of teacher personality and classroom climate are inseparable. As you review your own personality styles, relate these to their effects on

4. "The literature does suggest . . . that naturally formed, relatively accurate expectations can serve to *sustain* the pre-existing achievement variations among students" (Cooper, 1979).
5. West and Anderson (1976) and Cooper (1979) concluded that research evidence supports the notion that student achievement causes expectations *and* that expectations cause achievement.
6. Chaikin, Sigler, and Derlega (1974) and Page (1971) concluded that teachers create a "warmer socioemotional atmosphere" for students they think are bright. When teachers thought they were dealing with bright students, they smiled and nodded more, they physically leaned toward them, and they looked them in the eyes.
7. Brophy and Good (1974) found that teachers praise high-expectation students more, while low-expectation students are criticized more.
8. Higher overall grades are expected of middle-class students than of lower-class students (Cooper, Baron, and Lowe, 1975).

classroom atmosphere. Can you create a pleasant, achievement-oriented climate? Different students—especially those from disparate socio-economic levels—will complicate (perhaps prevent) the creation of an ideal classroom atmosphere.

Try to be aware of a hidden curriculum. Many of your feelings, policies, and expectations could be made explicit, so that each student does not have to deduce for herself or himself how to get along with you and succeed in your class. Clear classroom rules (Chapter 10) might provide some guides. Try to be especially aware of any contradictions between your stated and your "real" (hidden) expectations of students.

Prepare yourself to cope with the boys' problems of disruptiveness, aggressiveness, and more frequent academic problems. That's not being sexist; that's the way it is.

Be aware of your expectations and their effects on your teaching and on the students' self-concepts and motivation. Don't routinely accept poorly done assignments from Clem Kadiddlehopper because the school file shows an IQ of 75. With encouragement, even Clem can improve his work, his skills, and his education. You owe it to Clem.

SUMMARY

Teaching in the elementary school requires the planning of all lessons for all subjects all week. Teaching in the junior high or high school requires scheduling to keep physical and mental demands within reasonable limits. At any level, there will be much record keeping and many nonteaching duties.

There will be outside pressures, such as district and school board requirements, which may complicate such humanistic objectives as developing creativity or clarifying values. You also must coordinate your teaching with higher and lower grades and other sections at the same grade.

Some positive, rewarding facets of teaching are that: (a) You will have the knowledge that you are training our youth, an important job; (b) you will be an authoritative, respected, professional member of the community; (c) you will develop warm relations with students and colleagues; (d) you will have lots of vacation time; (e) elementary children are eager to learn and will adore you; (f) high school students think abstractly and produce exciting, high-quality work.

Some drawbacks to teaching are that: (a) Your job sometimes will be repetitious, frustrating, and unappreciated by students; (b) you will not earn a high salary; (c) you may become upset because you cannot help some troubled students; (d) some students may actively dislike you, and some of your colleagues may be unpleasant; (e) you will have to give up much of your personal time to keep up with the requirements of your job; (f) in the elementary school, inattentiveness and slow progress will be problems; (g) in high school, poor student attitudes and rule violations may take some of the fun out of teaching.

Teacher styles and personalities are studied by means of classroom observation, inventories, and school records. Some characteristics are used repeatedly to describe "good" (effective, repected, well-liked) teachers: good academic preparation, good work habits, friendly and humanistic feelings for students, imaginativeness, enthusiasm, and especially a responsible and businesslike approach to teaching. Ineffective teachers have been described as overbearing, self-centered, superior in attitude, and prone to anger.

One recent conclusion is that with more "academic engaged time" by students and more "direct instruction" by teachers, student achievement is higher.

The hidden curriculum refers to the teacher's unwritten rules, policies, expectations, and feelings which must be accommodated by a successful student. Some examples are neatness, docility, conformity, pleasantness, and a willingness to wait.

Sexism remains, particularly in the form of models: Custodians and most principals are men, secretaries and most elementary teachers are women.

However, there are consistent sex differences in the school: Boys are the trouble-makers and the grade repeaters. Academically, elementary boys tend to be superior to girls only in mathematical reasoning, science, and tasks involving spatial relations. One viewpoint is that conformity has been encouraged in girls, independence in boys.

One line of research concluded that boys attribute failure to lack of effort, but girls attribute failure to lack of ability. Boys are therefore more likely to work harder for improvement and to have higher college and career aspirations.

The classic boys' club research of Lippitt, Lewin, and White has been taken as evidence that a democratic climate leads to high morale and self-directed productivity; authoritarianism produces low morale, apathy, and dependence; and laissez-faire leadership leads to low productivity. Changing from authoritarianism to democracy improved attitudes and satisfaction, while going the opposite way produced the opposite effect. However, a "get tough early" approach may do more harm than good.

Heil and Washburne described three common teacher personality/leadership styles: Style A—sentimental, impulsive, and slipshod; Style B—friendly, responsible, and businesslike; Style C—anxious, critical, demanding, and dull.

Flanders' classroom interaction analysis system records different forms of teacher talk and student talk. Indirect teachers solicit and use ideas, give praise and encouragement, and accept and clarify student feelings. Direct teachers talk for about 85 percent of the class period. Achievement and satisfaction are higher with indirect teachers. (Do not confuse Flanders' *direct teaching* with Rosenshine's *direct instruction*.)

Moos' (1978) classroom typology included nine categories. Neither teachers nor students liked classes in which control and discipline were overstressed. Both liked competitive yet supportive classes with clear organization but low teacher control.

The Holland (1973) typology, which studied how different student personalities are attracted to different subject matters, included six types of classes: (1) realistic—e.g., auto repair; (2) investigative—e.g., biology; (3) artistic; (4) social—e.g., government; (5) enterprising—e.g., independent creative work; and (6) conventional—e.g., typing.

Teachers form expectations which can influence student achievement in many ways. For example, if a teacher has high expectations of a student, he or she may give the student more demanding work, the student's self-image may be improved, and/or the teacher may do a better teaching job.

Students who attribute poor performance to lack of effort (or bad luck, or the difficulty of the task) may work harder; those who attribute failure to lack of ability may give up.

The famous Rosenthal and Jacobson Oak School experiment appeared to prove that high expectations of teachers can cause IQ scores of students to increase. While this research has been severely criticized, other studies have sometimes (not always) shown that teacher expectancies do have an effect on student achievement. Publicity given the Rosenthal and Jacobson research resulted in policy changes related to IQ testing and ability grouping.

TOPICS FOR THOUGHT AND DISCUSSION

1. Is teaching a good career? Think about or discuss the good parts and the bad parts.
2. What personality traits will help a teacher succeed? What traits will interfere with running a productive classroom? Think about or discuss traits of good teachers you have had. Ditto for the traits of poor teachers.
3. Are some teachers unsuited for teaching? Why? What are the effects of their "poor" teaching style or poor characteristics on the students? On themselves?
4. How does classroom climate relate to Question 2? What influences classroom climate? What is an ideal classroom atmosphere? What is an ideal leadership pattern?
5. Try to think of examples of a hidden curriculum. What have you had to learn about instructors' hidden expectations in order to succeed in college?
6. Can anything be done about sex differences which interfere with success in school, namely, boys' aggressiveness and learning problems?
7. How have *your* teachers' expectations influenced your own self-concept and achievement?

PROJECTS

1. Meet with teachers, individually or as a group, who have 2 years, 10 years, or 20 years of teaching experience. Ask them what makes a teacher successful. Categorize the answers into (a) teacher personality, (b) teaching style or behavior, and perhaps (c) "tricks that work."
2. Identify two or more college instructors who have totally different personalities and teaching styles. Analyze (itemize) the differences and judge whether each item contributes to or detracts from student achievement and/or satisfaction.
3. As you observe classes in action, perhaps during your student teaching, see whether the climate seems to fit the Moos types, the Holland types, and/or the Lewin *et al.* authoritarian, democratic, or laissez-faire types. Are the teachers Type A, B, or C (Heil and Washburne)? Do they use "direct" or "indirect" influence (Flanders)?

RECOMMENDED READING

Brophy, J., and T. Good. *Teacher-student relationships: Causes and consequences.* New York: Holt, 1974.

Cooper, H. M. Pygmalion grows up. *Review of Educational Research* **49,** 1979, 389–410.

Centra, J. A., and D. A. Potter. School and teacher effects: An interrelational model. *Review of Educational Research* **50,** 1980, 273–291.

Dusck, J. Do teachers bias children's learning? *Review of Educational Research* **45,** 1975, 661–684.

Evertson, C. E., C. W. Anderson, L. M. Anderson, and J. E. Brophy. Relationships between classroom behaviors and student outcomes in junior high mathematics and English classes. *American Educational Research Journal* **17,** 1980, 43–60.

Rosenthal, R. *On the social psychology of the self-fulfilling prophecy.* New York: MSS Modular Publications, 1974.

DEVELOPMENT

PART II

Physical, Personality, and Moral Development

3

About human development / Genetics and behavioral
genetics / Physical development / Personality
development / Theories of personality / Kohlberg's
stages of moral development / To improve your teaching /
Summary / Topics for thought and discussion /
Projects / Recommended reading

ABOUT HUMAN DEVELOPMENT

Some growth-related changes are obvious, such as changes in size and the dramatic changes associated with puberty. Other changes are more subtle, such as changes in personality, in ability to think abstractly, or in understanding right and wrong. The developmental psychologist takes a close look at a great many facets of human growth and development, beginning with conception and progressing through infancy, childhood, adolescence, young adulthood, and even to middle and old age. The psychologist traces the course of physical development, cognitive development (including intelligence, language, thinking, and reasoning), and personality and emotional development. He or she studies such specifics as the workings of genetics and heredity, transitions in self-concept, social behavior, sex-role behavior, moral thinking, political attitudes, motivation, anxiety and emotional growth, perceptual ability, creativity, and even the effects of television on aggression and skill development (Yussen and Santrock, 1982).

Often, the developmental theorist will identify age-related stages of development. While the process of growth virtually always is smooth and continuous, the growing child nonetheless passes through a sequence of major recognizable stages in his or her physical and mental growth. Some interesting features about most analyses of developmental stages are that: (a) A new stage can involve a major reorganization in thinking or personality. (b) The stages will overlap, with different children entering the next higher state at different ages. (c) The identification of a child's stage of, say, emotional or moral development, tells us a lot about other characteristics we may expect that are associated with that stage. (d) Growth in an area may "plateau" short of the highest stage, usually due to some developmental "failure" or frustration, producing an adult with a pattern of reasoning, morality, or emotional development characteristic of a less mature chronological age.

This chapter will summarize briefly the workings of genetics and the influence of heredity on physical and mental development, then sketch the course of physical development from conception through adolescence. We will then turn to personality development and some prominent theories of personality, and then to the stages in moral thinking identified by Lawrence Kohlberg. Chapter 4 will review insightful stages of cognitive development originated by Swiss psychologist Jean Piaget, summarize Jerome Bruner's model of cognitive development, and, finally, discuss language development.

GENETICS AND BEHAVIORAL GENETICS

To a greater or lesser degree, physical and intellectual characteristics—and even some personality and behavioral characteristics—are inborn. Physical traits such as sex, eye and hair color, and height are almost entirely determined by genetic heritage. Mental and behavioral characteristics—including intelligence, personality, and even mental illness—are determined both by heredity and by environment (learning). We will look first at some of the basics of heredity and genetics, then briefly review evidence for a genetic influence on intelligence and retardation, schizophrenia, and personality and temperament.

Chromosomes and Genes

Our genetic blueprint for physical and some psychological characteristics is contained in chromosomes, small rodlike structures which are transmitted from parent to child. At conception, the 23 chromosomes of a sperm cell combine with the 23 chromosomes of the ovum, producing a fertilized cell containing 46 chromosomes in 23 pairs (Figure 3.1). Pair number 23, the sex chromosomes, determines one's sex. Female sex chromosomes are all X chromosomes; male sex chromosomes can be X or Y. If the male X chromosome combines with the female X chromosome, the resulting XX pair develops into a female offspring. If the male Y combines with the female X, the XY pair becomes a male.

Growth is a process of cell division. During cell division each of the 46 chromosomes duplicates itself, resulting in two cells which contain exactly the same genetic information. Occasionally, the division of a single fertilized egg cell will produce two individuals, each with identical genetic

Figure 3.1
Representation of the 23 pairs of chromosomes.

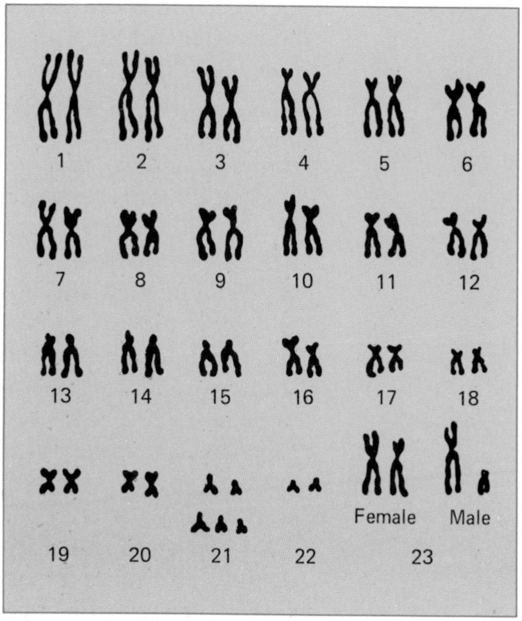

make-up. The result, of course, is identical twins, two siblings of the same sex who look alike and, as we will see below, sometimes even think alike and act alike. Fraternal twins, developing from two egg cells fertilized by two sperm cells, have similar but not identical genetic structures. They will not resemble each other any more than other pairs of siblings. However, if they happen to be of the same sex and strongly resemble each other, it is virtually impossible to know for certain whether they are fraternal or identical.

Each chromosome contains thousands of genes, complex molecules which carry the coded genetic information. Each molecule, known now as DNA (deoxyribonucleic acid) takes the form of a spiraling ladder—the famous *double helix* shape described by scientists Watson and Crick (Watson, 1968). The process of "growth" takes place when the double helix "unzips" down the middle of the ladder steps and each half then selects the necessary chemicals to build two complete and identical DNA molecules. Quite miraculous, when you think about it.

The sum total of a person's unique genetic inheritance is referred to as his or her **genotype.** The observed and measurable physical, mental, and behavioral characteristics are referred to as a person's **phenotype.** We turn now to relationships between genotypes and phenotypes.

Intelligence and Retardation

The topic of intelligence is sufficiently important to merit a chapter of its own (Chapter 15). Evidence for the heritability of intelligence also is explained in more detail in that chapter. Briefly, however, an early study comparing the IQ's of 428 father-child pairs and 538 mother-child pairs concluded that, in general, children's IQ scores resembled their parents' IQ scores (Conrad and Jones, 1940). It is quite possible, however, that bright parents provide more intellectually stimulating environments and opportunities, and so the Conrad and Jones data is quite ambiguous. Better evidence comes from studies comparing parents' intelligence with the IQ's of adopted children, or else comparing IQ's of identical twins, fraternal twins, siblings reared together, or siblings reared apart. For example, one study found that the IQ's of adopted children resembled the IQ's of their biological parents more closely than the IQ's of the foster parents, a clear argument for the heritability of intelligence (Leahy, 1935). Also, several studies of identical twins separated at birth have shown the twins to have extremely similar IQ scores.

At least some forms of mental retardation can be inherited, most notably *phenylketonuria*, or PKU. From their parents, some children inherit an enzyme deficiency that prevents an essential amino acid, phenylalanine, from being processed by the liver. The result is mental deterioration due to the build up of phenylalanine, which blocks the normal action of the nervous system. PKU is a *recessive* trait, which means it will appear only if both parents possess PKU genes. Fortunately, tests for PKU are now routinely performed, and when detected it can be easily treated with a diet which keeps phenylalanine at a low level.

The most common form of retardation is *Down's syndrome*, or mongoloidism. Children with Down's syndrome have smaller brains, a skull flattened in the back and front, a round face with almond-shaped eyes, an extra fold of skin over the eyelids, a thick tongue which may protrude, and retarded motor development. Also, they are often of shorter than normal stature. Mongoloid children—whose parents may be very intelligent people—have 47 chromosomes instead of the usual 46. The source of the extra chromosome is a mystery, but it may be due to the health of the female egg cell. Women over 40, who may produce less healthy ova, are statistically more likely to have mongoloid children; the age of the male is not a factor.

Schizophrenia

Schizophrenia ". . . includes a group of disorders manifested by characteristic disturbances of thinking, mood, and behavior. Disturbances in thinking are marked by alterations of concept formation that may lead to misinterpretations of reality and sometimes to delusions and hallucinations" (American Psychiatric Association, 1968, p. 33). The closer two persons are related, the more likely it is that if one is schizophrenic the other will be also. Thus a child with a schizophrenic parent is more likely to develop schizophrenia than is a child whose nearest schizophrenic kin is, say, a grandparent. Also, if one identical twin is schizophrenic, the chances are greater that the other also will develop schizophrenia, compared with fraternal twins or regular siblings. While less than one percent of the U.S. population becomes schizophrenic, about 16 percent of the children of schizophrenics become schizophrenic (Kallman, 1953).

Personality and Behavior

While personality undoubtedly is shaped by environmental circumstances and learning, there is strong evidence that some personality, temperament, and everyday patterns of behavior also are partly inherited. Shortly after birth, some babies are more energetic and active than others; some adore cuddling while others fuss and fret; some remain blissfully calm while others become startled and upset with very slight changes in their environment; and some actively explore their environment for long periods of time, while others seem not at all curious (Bridger, 1965; Schaffer and Emerson, 1964). These differences must be inborn.

Willerman (1973) found that identical twins were much more similar than fraternal twins in such activities as eating, watching television, playing, studying, and even sleeping. Scarr (1966, 1969, 1981) also found that identical twins resembled each other in physical activity, nervousness, anxiousness, patience, and degree of introversion and extroversion.

There seems little doubt that, like physical traits, intelligence, retardation, and schizophrenia, one's personality and even some behavioral patterns are at least partially determined by genetic roots.

PHYSICAL DEVELOPMENT

Many lengthy tomes have been written about the course of human physical development (e.g., Lodge, 1968; Tanner, 1970). Present space will permit just a cursory overview of four major human growth periods, the prenatal period, infancy, childhood, and adolescence.

Prenatal Development

Germinal period (first two weeks). Within a day after conception the process of cell division begins. The fertilized ovum divides into two cells, these two become four, then eight, and so on. As explained above, each new cell contains the same 23 pairs of chromosomes as the original cell. After about a week or 10 days, when approximately 60 or 70 cells have been formed, the tiny lump attaches itself to the wall of the uterus. The outer part of the mass will become the placenta; the inner part will become the fetus.

Embryonic period (two to eight weeks). At 30 days the growing mass still is smaller than an average pea but has the beginnings of a few rudimentary organs. Hands and feet begin to develop, and by 45 days the embryo begins to look human. Height: one inch. Weight: $\frac{1}{2}$ ounce. It has a head which is half the size of the total body, plus a trunk, arms, legs, and, if you look closely enough, even eyes, ears, toes, and fingers. It also has a primitive heart and heartbeat, circulatory activity, and even liver, kidney, glandular, and nervous-system activity.

The embryonic period also includes the development of the life-support system. The blood stream of the mother will remain separate from the blood stream of the embryo. However, in the area where the placenta attaches to the uterine wall, semipermeable membranes allow oxygen, vitamins, sugar, and protein from the mother to pass through to the embryo. Blood cells are too large to penetrate the membranes. The umbilical cord transports waste materials to the semipermeable membranes of the placental barrier, through which they enter the mother's system.

It is during the embryonic period that the baby-to-be is most susceptible to damage by nutritional deficits, disease, drugs, pollution, and even the emotional state of the mother. For example, malnutrition in the mother may cause a protein deficiency, sometimes leading to abnormal brain development and mental retardation (Naeye, Blanc, and Paul, 1973; Zeskind and Ramey, 1978). It also is suspected that emotional upset in mothers during the embryonic period creates hormonal imbalances which can cause physical abnormalities such as cleft palate. If the mother contracts German measles during the first three months of pregnancy, damage to the highly vulnerable nervous system can result in blindness, deafness, or brain damage and retardation. Diabetes in the mother can cause breathing and circulatory problems in the infant which may lead to death shortly after birth.

In the 1960s, hundreds of mothers took the tranquilizer thalidomide during the early months of pregnancy. This drug inhibited the growth of extremities in the fetus; thalidomide babies may be missing hands, arms, legs, or ears. While some mental impairment may occur, the majority of the thalidomide victims have IQ's in the normal range (McFie and Robertson, 1973). Babies born of heroin addicts are themselves addicts at the time of birth and will show withdrawal symptoms if they do not receive the drug. Very recent research also suggests that even moderate alcohol consumption during early pregnancy can cause a variety of learning and developmental disorders, including retardation, jitteriness, reduced height and weight, and malformed skeleton and organ systems (Hanson, 1979; Rosman, 1978). Even smoking and air pollution can cause lower birth weights (Davis, Gray, Ellwood, and Abernathy, 1976; Howes and Krakow, 1977; Spiker, 1975). There also is strong recent evidence that the formaldehyde in foam-type home insulation and in the plywood paneling used in mobile homes may cause physical or mental deficiencies in the newborn (Sauter, 1981).

Fetal period (eight weeks to birth). By the end of the third month the fetus has grown to a sturdy three inches in height and weighs in at one ounce. The most noticeable growth is in muscle development. The fetus can open and close its mouth, thrash its arms and legs about, and move its head. It also has a discernible nose, chin, and eyelids. The genitals are sufficiently developed that he or she can be identified as he or she.

By four months the fetus is six inches long and weighs four ounces. The mother can now feel the stronger arm and leg movements. The fetus may acquire its first habit: thumb sucking.

During the fifth month hair, skin, fingernails, and toenails appear. By the end of the sixth month our 14-inch, two-pound fetus shows a grasping reflex and can open its eyelids to show completely formed eyes.

At seven months the brain is developing rapidly. Almost all functions are in operation and the infant usually can survive a premature birth, although susceptibility to infection is high. An incubator usually would be needed to provide the necessary environment. During the eighth and ninth months growth is rapid, the fetus is very active and organ functions increase rapidly. At the end of nine months mother experiences a lot of pain and may even holler a bit, but somehow the experience of childbirth makes her very happy.

The Infant   The infancy period extends from birth to 18–24 months, about when the toddler begins saying a few words. The newborn infant's eyes are squinty, its skin is red and wrinkled, its head is big and maybe misshapen, and it may be screaming as loudly as it can. Friends and relatives observe, "Oh what a beautiful baby. Look at those big eyes and that gorgeous hair!"

The neonate has just a few obvious reflex responses: It will suck and swallow and it will cry when hungry or uncomfortable. However, a closer look by infant researchers has produced a longer list of infant reflexes which are summarized in Table 3.1. In addition to these, the infant also comes equipped with some eye-movement capabilities. It will blink in response to a bright light or loud noise, fixate on a small light, and will even visually follow a slowly moving object, at least briefly.

It is through the infant's sensory organs and its reflexes that it begins to develop its perceptual-motor, learning, cognitive, and eventual language

Table 3.1 Reflex behaviors in infants (from Freedman, 1978)

Reflex	Behavior
Moro reflex (startle)	Sudden stimulus such as loud noise causes full extension of legs, arms, and fingers, with back arched and head thrown back. Disappears in third or fourth month.
Rooting reflex (searching and sucking)	Stroking cheek causes turn in direction of stroke; mouth opens and sucks. Obviously enables infant to find nipple and nurse.
Babinski reflex	Stroking sole of foot causes toes to fan and foot arch up. At about six months replaced by adult reflex with foot arching downward and toes curling.
Darwinian reflex (grasping)	When palm is stroked, infant makes a fist and grasps whatever is in the palm. The grip is remarkably strong, perhaps a holdover from a time when newborns had to hold onto their parent's fur or body.
Swimming reflex	Put into water face down, baby will make swimming movements.
Walking reflex	If held under arms with bare feet touching the floor or other surface, infant makes movements similar to walking. The reflex disappears at about eight weeks. This and the swimming reflex are very early preparations for behavior that appears much later; yet both the swimming and walking reflex disappear before the more advanced behavior develops.

From Freedman, J.L. *Introductory Psychology.* © 1978 Addison-Wesley, Reading, MA, p. 311. Reprinted with permission.

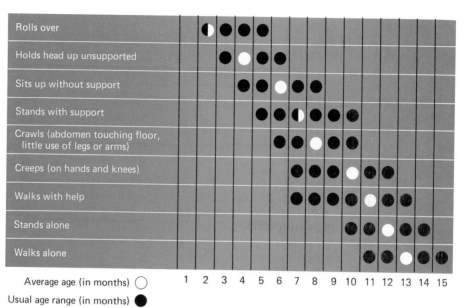

From Freedman, J. L. *Introductory Psychology.* © 1978, Addison-Wesley, Reading, MA, p. 312. Reprinted with permission.

Figure 3.2 This diagram shows the average age in months (white circles) and the range in age (black circles) at which early motor behaviors appear. The behaviors usually appear in the same sequence for each infant.

capabilities. The order in which various cognitive and motor skills appear is reasonably invariant—all normal babies develop these skills in the same order. However, the exact age at which the skills appear will vary; some infants walk and talk early, some late, with most in-between. For example, Figure 3.2 shows the average age at which early motor behaviors appear and the amount of variation among infants; but remember, the order in which these responses appear will be the same for each baby.

Accelerating Infant Motor Development

Some parents who are anxious for a precocious, rapidly developing child have tried to teach their youngsters to stand, walk, climb stairs, or use scissors at a too-early age. Researchers also have tried to speed up infant development with special exercises (Hilgard, 1932; Zelazo, Zelazo and Kolb, 1972). The results have been consistent: It is possible to slightly speed up or delay development of a particular infant motor skill; however, the effect is small and it soon disappears. That is, children who have not had special training soon catch up with those who have; or if a skill has been delayed, the delayed child soon catches up with the others. Two examples of nondelayed motor growth are, first, Hopi Indian babies, many of whom spend their early weeks bound tightly to a carrying board. They crawl, stand up and walk on about the same schedule as Hopi children who had not been bound to the board (Dennis, 1940). Second, Russian infants who had been tightly swaddled tended to walk a little later than unswaddled children, but soon caught up with them in ability.

Periods of Childhood

The end of infancy primarily is marked by the child's ability to talk in short phrases. The end of infancy also is marked by the onset of what parents have informally labeled the "terrible twos." Most, but not necessarily all, of these youngsters are curious about anything within reach, and they frequently dump it (the flower pot, the sugar bowl), break it (the camera, the last piece of great-grandmother's china), or try to eat it (puppy's nose, the can of Drain-O), and will scream loudly in public places if they do not

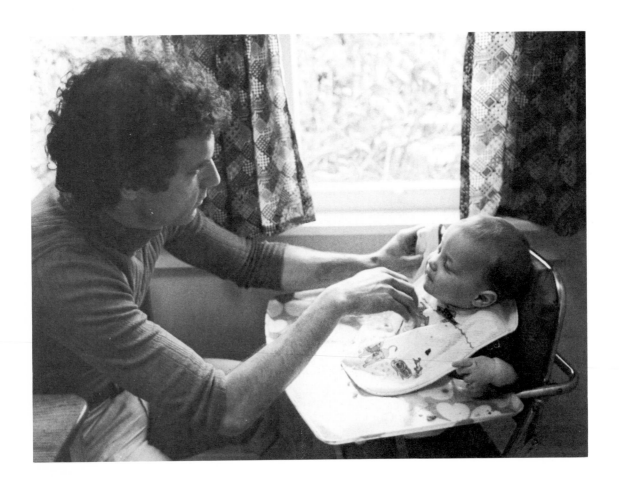

get precisely what they want. The youngsters cannot be reasoned with, although persuasion in the form of distracting bribes is known to be effective.

Early childhood, which includes the terrible twos, extends from the end of infancy to five or six years of age. In this period, the child's main accomplishments are learning to care for himself or herself (dressing, washing, toiletry) and developing such school-readiness skills as using pencils and crayons, identifying letters and numbers, and following instructions (Yussen and Santrock, 1982). **Middle childhood** includes the years from about age six to age eleven, the elementary school years. Basic academic skills are mastered and there is simplified exposure to such cultural matters as government, business, art, music, history, and some topical social problems.

Adolescence

Adolescence begins at puberty, that time at which we magically and dramatically change from a child to an adult. This event usually occurs in the very early teens, but can happen anytime from the ages of 10 to 17 for girls and 12 to 18 for boys. Sometimes even earlier or later. Both sexes undergo rapid physical growth; they can grow four or five inches and 15 or 20 pounds heavier in one year. The shape of the body itself changes. Males become taller and apparently thin, later to fill out with broader shoulders and greater muscularity, while females show the even more obvious growth of breasts and hips. With males, beards begin to grow and the voice deepens. With both sexes pubic hair appears and reproductive organs develop rapidly. Males produce sperm and females begin menstruating.

On the average, girls reach puberty about two years ahead of boys, which means that between the ages of 11 and 15 girls will be more developed *and* taller than boys, on the average. Also, in the same age groups there will be a lot of variation, with many underdeveloped girls and small boys and many shapely young women and tall awkward males with funny voices. Many books have been written about the physical and mental changes in adolescence (for example, see Adelson, 1979, *Handbook of Adolescent Psychology,* only $39.95; also Muus, 1975; Santrock, 1981), describing such matters as biological and hormonal changes, the growth of sexuality, the development of identity, moral thinking, personality, values, reasoning, learning ability, political thinking, friendship patterns, delinquent behavior, giftedness, and many others. We have space for only a few common sources of embarrassment and uncertainty: Boys, for example, may be self-conscious about their awkwardness or skinniness—they have grown in height too fast for their coordination or their weight to keep pace. Early maturing girls may be self-conscious about their shapely figures, their menstruation, or because they are attracting boys' attention. They may not be ready to cope with their sexual and physical maturity. Late-developing boys and girls may be self-conscious about their childlike physiques and may envy the attention the more developed males and females receive from members of the opposite sex. Adolescence is not a period of storm and stress for everyone, but it is a difficult time for many.

PERSONALITY DEVELOPMENT

What Is Personality?

Personality refers to enduring personal qualities, one's typical way of reacting to particular situations and to other people. For example, some people seem consistently extroverted, the "life of the party," while others are shy, low in self-confidence, and introverted; some may be cheerful and agreeable, while others are quarrelsome and quick to anger; some are ambitious and conscientious, others are lazy and slovenly; some are emotionally stable, others insecure and neurotic; and so on. There actually are over 18,000 words in the English language to describe characteristics of people (Mischel, 1981).

We also can distinguish between the way we *act* (our "social face"), the way we *see ourselves* (our "personal face"), and the way we *really are* (our "real face"). Our **social face** may quickly change, depending on whom we wish to impress. For example, in a new college classroom a person may put on an unconcerned "cool" mask to impress classmates, but try to appear knowledgeable and intelligent to impress the instructor. Most of us are concerned about our public image, and we sometimes put on an appropriate social face to present ourselves well.

Our **personal face** shows the person we think we are, how we perceive ourselves. Our judgments may be reasonably accurate, we may grossly exaggerate our talents and charm, or we may judge ourselves far too harshly. Our **real face,** of course, is our true self, the reality which could be seen if we were able to strip away all pretense, pride, and self-deception.

As we grow and change, all three of our "faces" also change—how we want others to see us, how we see ourselves, and how we really are.

THEORIES OF PERSONALITY

Trait Theory

Traditional trait theory, or dispositional theory, assumes that each of us possesses a set of relatively stable and consistent personality traits or dispositions. These traits exert a general and pervasive influence on our behavior, causing us to react in consistent ways in many different circum-

stances. Psychological researchers who follow this approach continually
search for important personality traits which seem to have a broad impact
on one's behavior. In the words of trait-researcher Goldberg (1973), the
quest is for "... the most important individual differences in mankind."
For example, Eysenck (1961) developed his *Eysenck Personality Inventory,*
a test of introversion-extroversion and neuroticism, two seemingly important traits which should strongly influence a person's behavior in a variety
of circumstances (more about extroversion in Chapter 14). Anxiety also is
a trait with wide impact on behavior (Spielberger, 1966). As you might
guess, anxiety is related to introversion and neuroticism. Cattell (1965)
identified a long list of traits, including integrity vs. dishonesty, disciplined
thoughtfulness vs. foolishness, ego strength vs. neuroticism, and dominance
vs. submission. Norman (1963) identified five personality traits which he
felt were the most basic, underlying dimensions of personality: extroversion,
agreeableness, conscientiousness, emotional stability, and "culture" (art-
istically sensitive, intellectual, refined). Wiggins' (1980) more recent list of
four dimensions of personality is quite similar to that developed by Norman:

ambitious-lazy, extroverted-introverted, agreeable-quarrelsome, and unassuming-arrogant.

The problem with the trait approach to personality is that people frequently do not behave in a predictably consistent way when reacting to different people, to different situations, or even at a different time. In fact, it has been argued that only severely disturbed and less mature individuals respond "indiscriminately"—that is, in a repeated and predictable way regardless of the circumstances (Mischel, 1973, 1981; Moos, 1968).

Social Behavior Theory: The Person-Situation Approach

Mischel (1973, 1979, 1980, 1981) and other social-behavior theorists have argued that both the characteristics of the *person* and the circumstances of the *situation* must be known before a person's behavior can be predicted. Any given individual is not necessarily consistent in behavior and reactions from situation to situation. Rather, for example, teacher Frank N. Friendly may be friendly in the morning, with his principal, with cheerleaders and football players, in a bar, and with the policeman giving him a ticket, but he might be aloof or even hostile at lunchtime, with secretaries, with below-average students, or when frustrated because he cannot find his comb or his checkbook. For other teachers, with different idiosyncratic organizations of traits and behaviors, the patterns of cheerfulness, aloofness, aggressiveness, extraversion, etc., will be totally different.

A given situation may exert a major influnce on a person's reactive behavior (e.g., funerals have a sobering and depressing effect on everyone), or a relatively minor influence (joggers in the road upset just a few drivers). Also, the person-situation theory tells us that the impact of a situation will depend on the person in the situation (Mischel, 1981). Thus a creativity training session or other educational experience may benefit some students, but not others. Consistency vs. variability in behavior—that is, a trait approach vs. a person-situation approach—continues to be a major source of debate in personality psychology (e.g., see Bowers, 1973; Mischel, 1973, 1980, 1981).

Psychoanalytic Theory: Freud

As a brilliant psychoanalyst who worked directly with neurotic and psychotic patients, Sigmund Freud had a great deal to say about the causes and dynamics of personality development, although many of his ideas are not widely accepted today. Briefly, Freud divided mental life into three components, the **id, ego,** and **superego.** The id is made of instinctive drives, most notably sexual and aggressive ones, which continually demand satisfaction. The superego is the voice of the social conscience—which directs the person to behave himself. According to Freud, the superego acts to inhibit, postpone, or prevent the basic urges of the id by using mechanisms of guilt and shame. Between these two battling forces we find the ego, a sort of referee. Most often, the ego redirects the urges of the id into outlets acceptable to the superego.

The ability of the ego to deal with the drives of the id and the forces of the superego is said to be a measure of a person's mental health. If either side, id or superego, becomes dominant, the result will be personality maladjustment or neurosis.

Freud's Stages in Personality Development

As the child grows, not only are the id, superego, and ego developing, but beginning at birth the personality of the child is said to pass through five distinguishable stages: **oral, anal, phallic, latent,** and **genital.**

The oral stage (0 to 1½ years). During this stage, pleasure is focused on the mouth area, with satisfaction derived from sucking, biting, chewing, and, as we parents know, spitting. According to Freud, future feelings of trust and dependence and traits of gullibility or sarcastic argumentativeness are formed during this stage.

The anal stage (1½ to 3 years). So named because it is the time of bowel training, this is also the period when independence and control, along with possible traits of orderliness, stinginess, cruelty, and destructiveness supposedly develop.

The phallic stage (3 to 7 years). This is a particularly stressful stage. Boys and girls become acutely aware of their sexual equipment and of the difference between the two basic models, thus beginning a sexual-identity component of personality. It is during the phallic stage that *Oedipus* and *Electra* complexes begin, problems which will require up to a decade to resolve. During the oedipal phase, according to Freud, a boy develops a vague sexual attraction to his mother. Father is seen as a competitor for mother's affection, a competitor who will castrate the boy if he oversteps his bounds. Castration anxiety and the love-hate conflict with father are said to be resolved by the boy identifying with the father, incorporating dad's behaviors and attitudes into his own personality. Social values of aggression and opposition to incest are said to result from identifying with the father.

The Electra complex is roughly the reverse of the oedipal problem. The 3- to 6-year old girl, Freud believed, develops a passion for her father and feels threatened by her competitor mother. While she cannot very well suffer castration anxiety, Freud did give her a moderately serious case of penis envy, jealousy over the male organ. (Women's liberation leaders consider this concept untrue and laughable.) Due in part to penis envy, girls never quite identify completely with mother, and so the ambivalent love-hate attitude is retained, not resolved as with boys.

Table 3.2 A summary of Freud's stages of personality development

Stage	Age	Activity	Outcome
Oral	0 to 1½	Sucking, biting, chewing	Feelings of trust and dependence
Anal	1½ to 3	Control of elimination	Independence and control
Phallic	3 to 6–7	Awareness of anatomy, Oedipus and Electra complexes	Identity, especially sexual
Latency	6–7 to 12–13	Exploration, mastery of skills	Copes with society
Genital	12–13 to 19	Interest in opposite sex	Stable and personal sexual identity

According to Freud, these first three stages, from age 0 to 6 or 7 years, are the most crucial for personality development. If the instinctual needs are met without undue trauma, the person is on the road to sound psychological health. If they are not, severe personality problems could arise; for example, alcoholism, miserliness, frigidity, or impotence.

The latency stage (6 or 7 to 12 or 13 years). Freud's latency stage is the long period of middle childhood. During this period the problems of the Oedipus and Electra complexes are repressed, and children channel their energies into safe outlets, exploring their world and learning skills for mastering their environment and coping with society.

The genital stage (12 or 13 to 18 or 19 years). Finally, Freud's genital stage includes, with puberty, a new interest in the opposite sex and in sexual matters. Over these years the adolescent forms a stable personal and sexual identity—a reasonably clear concept of who he or she is. A summary of Freud's five stages appears in Table 3.2.

Defense Mechanisms

Freud's **defense mechanisms** of the ego are considerably less controversial than his five stages of personality development and his Oedipus and Electra complexes. They also may have more relevance for understanding students' behavior in the sometimes stressful classroom. Defense mechanisms are psychological devices, usually unconscious, for reducing tension and restoring psychological equilibrium. Tension, as we know it every day, stems from anxieties and frustrations due to disappointments, failures, unmet needs, deadlines, disagreements, threats to the self-concept, and so on. In the classroom the teacher will see countless instances of defense mechanisms used by students to justify a poor test score or repeated tardiness, or else to vent aggression in a safer direction. Teachers also will use defense mechanisms to protect their valuable egos against feelings of failure or inadequacy.

One defense mechanism is **repression,** in which the anxiety-producing thought is pushed from the conscious to the unconscious. Thus some students simply will "forget" an important but worrisome test, assignmnent, or other responsibility. A related mechanism is **denial,** a favorite of young children who are not yet concerned about logical thinking or reality. As the name suggests, the child simply denies that an event occurred—"I didn't spill my paints!" "I wasn't late, the bus left without me!" With **projection,** an unacceptable thought is shifted or "projected" to someone else. We may find that a characteristic that causes us concern in others is really something we worry about in ourselves—"Nancy's makin' too much noise!" "Joey stole an eraser!" "Mr. Brown is putting on a little weight!" or "They both smoke and drink too much!"

A **reaction formation** is a defense which, amazingly, transforms a troublesome feeling or thought into its opposite. A politician who accepts bribes and kickbacks may yell loud and long about law, order, and respect for the police. A student who dislikes the teacher may reduce his or her anxiety about such feelings by frequently volunteering to help.

INSET 3.1

**ANNA FREUD'S
ADOLESCENT DEFENSE
MECHANISMS**

Anna Freud (1958), Sigmund Freud's daughter, described some defense mechanisms adolescents are likely to use. The reversal of affect is the peculiar switching of an expected emotion. The teenager who should be angry might become very calm and pleasant; the one needing closeness may appear unusually aloof. With withdrawal, the adolescent psychologically "hides out," becoming physically or mentally distant from friends or adults. Asceticism may be used to combat unacceptable feelings of pleasure by rejecting usual comforts, such as food and a soft bed. The uncompromising defense is the adoption of a rigid, inflexible ideology in an attempt to avoid the complexities of difficult "grey area" decisions. Teenagers also use regression to cope with conflicts and frustrations. This is simply an attempt to avoid growing up, to deny the obvious bodily changes.

Displacement, a reaction to anger or frustration, is usually shown by aggression toward an object or person that is a safer target than the original cause of the feeling. Children punished by teachers might punch a smaller child, or else return at night to redesign a few windows. Vandalism is probably an excellent example of displaced hostility and aggression. The similar mechanism of **sublimation** is the redirection of unacceptable needs into socially acceptable outlets. For example, the energy of the aggressive or disruptive student could be rechanneled into playing football, being a hall monitor, or some other acceptable outlet. As we will see in Chapter 16, Freud claimed that creativity is the sublimation of sexual urges into socially acceptable behavior.

The ever-popular **rationalization** is probably the most common and effective defense mechanism. Everyone makes excuses for, or "rationalizes," poor behavior in order to remove potentially upsetting conflicts. You might hear, for example, "The test was unfair," "But I had to play my clarinet at the basketball game," "The math teacher doesn't like me," "These students just will not learn," or "But officer, the sun was in my eyes."

Another favorite for protecting one's ego in school is **compensation**— high achievement or success in one area which psychologically offsets or "compensates for" below-par performance in another area. If we cannot get A's, we play football well; if we are too small for football we become fine skiers, artists, flute players, church leaders, hot-rod builders, etc. We all do this in order to maintain a healthy view of ourselves as worthwhile and valuable members of the species.

Finally, **identification** is a more subtle means of achieving feelings of self-worth by accepting the values and attitudes of a powerful, respected, or admired person—for example, a teacher, rock star, or movie star. You will see more than one student wearing a John Lennon or BeeGees T-shirt and showing values matching those of their idol.

Erikson's Eight Stages of Personality Development

As a bright young painter of children's portraits, Erik Erikson was invited to a villa in Austria to do a portrait of one of Sigmund Freud's children. After a series of informal discussions, Freud invited Erikson to join the Psychoanalytic Institute of Vienna and study child analysis. Erikson did join, and eventually became an internationally recognized theorist in the development of personality across the life span. In 1950, for example, a conference report on his basic theoretical framework was accepted in its entirety by the White House Conference on Children.

Since Erikson studied with Freud, it is not surprising to find considerable similarity in their thinking. Indeed, Erikson's (1963) eight developmental stages may be considered a modification of Freud's five stages, plus extensions to cover the rest of the life span. An important distinction is

that Erikson's stages are "psychosocial," based on problems in human relationships, while Freud's stages are psychosexual. Also, Erikson emphasizes conscious and rational thinking processes, contrasting with Freud's heavy reliance on unconscious conflicts and forces. Erikson further assumes that the personality is positive, productive, and constructive, which contrasts with the basic struggle-with-evil views of Freud (e.g., id vs. superego; the Oedipus and Electra complexes).

In each of Erikson's eight developmental stages, the individual is assumed to deal with a social-based emotional conflict which is dominant during that period. The conflict—always between a healthy, positive outcome and a pessimistic, unhealthy one—is said to determine the later shape of personality and mental health. Indeed, to Erikson, each of the eight developmental stages is no less than a "potential crisis" in personality development.

Stage 1, Oral-sensory—Basic trust vs. mistrust (0 to $1\frac{1}{2}$ years). Erikson's first stage corresponds to Freud's oral stage. According to Erikson, the quality of mother's care, warmth, and affection will foster lifetime attitudes of confidence and trust, or of feelings of mistrust and uncertainty.

Stage 2, Muscular-anal—Autonomy vs. shame and doubt (1½ to 3 years). This stage resembles Freud's anal stage. On the positive side, the child is now walking, running, talking, eating with silverware, and getting housebroken, and generally is not so dependent on mother. Reasonably, the child develops feelings of autonomy, independence, and self-direction. It is during this period of independence and exploration that the child both "gets into everything" and develops strong **competency** motivation, a strong need to master the environment (Chapter 9). On the negative side, demands are made upon the child for proper bladder and bowel activity and proper speech. Also, parents may be too overprotecting and interfering, thereby frustrating the attempts at exploration and autonomy and producing feelings of shame at the child's misbehavior and doubt about his or her competence. The conflict between autonomy and shame and doubt will determine one's later sense of control over oneself and one's environment, according to Erikson.

Stage 3, Locomotor-genital—Initiative vs. guilt (3 to 6 years). This corresponds to Freud's genital stage, during which children form their sexual identity and learn who and what they are. Little boys begin modeling adult male behavior and little girls copy mother's behavior. According to Erikson, this identification with the same-sexed parent includes an Oedipus/Electra attraction to the opposite-sexed parent—or to the kindergarten or first-grade teacher. Such romantic attachments may surface when the little girl expresses a wish for mommy to vanish so she can care for father, or when a kindergarten boy becomes broken-hearted when his kindergarten teacher gets married.

During these early years, children's feelings of initiative—of being the initiator of action—develop as they discover ways to express their maleness and femaleness. At the same time, children are especially vulnerable to feelings of guilt if they are punished for asserting themselves. For example, if the broken-hearted boy whose teacher jilted him for a grownup is ridiculed for his sadness, he will experience deep guilt over the matter. The conflict between initiative and guilt will influence children's later traits of goal-directedness and purpose. Supporting male and female identities in these years should help emotional growth and thus aid in the preparation for the next stage.

Stage 4, Latency—Industry vs. inferiority (juvenile period, 6 to 12 years). The years between 6 and 12 are especially critical in the development of personal competence and mastery. Children are enthusiastically learning to read and write and add and subtract. They explore new avenues of experience never before available—the Sunday funnies, writing notes and letters to friends and grandmother, and calculating the cost of new sneakers or a portable radio. And think of the activities, games, and sports mastered (sort of) during these years: swimming, baseball, roller skating, skiing, cooking, board games, card games, collecting stamps or money, and many more.

At the same time, it's during these years that the developing child is becoming more and more involved with friends and school-mates and with the general peer culture. Quite reasonably, the child begins to evaluate his or her capabilities in comparison with peers. Unfavorable comparisons will create attitudes and self-concepts of inferiority, while favorable comparisons will create feelings of mastery or industry. It is thus very, very important for children to master many skills during this period, not only for the valuable capabilities themselves but for the healthy development of feelings of industry and self-worth.

Stage 5, Puberty and adolescence—Identity vs. role confusion (12 to 18 years). This adolescent stage is the most critical of Erikson's stages, since it centers on the development of a stable, lifelong personality and identity (Erikson, 1968). The individual must decide who and what he or she is. A major portion of this identity involves planning a career, a social role which will be highly visible to the person, to his or her friends and family, and to the rest of society. Can the person confidently see himself or herself as a professional business person? A secretary? A cab driver? Will the adolescent girl plan to stay home and bake cookies for a swell husband, two children, and a St. Bernard? How the young see themselves, and how they see others seeing them, is the crux of the struggle between identity and role confusion.

Western society does not make identity a particularly easy task for our youth. At home and in school, the virtues of honesty, responsibility, clean living, happy marriage, and concern for others are presented as universal truths. Meanwhile, on the evening news, teenagers learn of politicians who take kickbacks and put girl friends on the payroll, bankers who embezzle, husbands who beat their wives, movie stars who pass out cocaine at cocktail parties, and millionaires who fritter away fortunes on pet cats while across town other people are starving. Forming a positive identity and a constructive approach to the adult world may not be easy, as evidenced by high rates of adolescent crime, murder, and suicide.

Stage 6, Young adulthood—Intimacy vs. isolation. The first five stages in Erikson's theory parallel those of Freud and cover the usual school years. You, the young adult reader, will be more interested in applying Stage 6 to yourself. The years of early adulthood are significant as a time for developing an intimate relationship with a member of the opposite sex. Marriage and children happen, often in that order. Friendships with neighbors and fellow workers also develop. If the friendships and the love relationship become unpleasant, or in Erik's words, ". . . competitive and combative," a lifestyle of isolation can result.

Stage 7, Adulthood—Generativity vs. stagnation (middle age). "Generativity" is helping the next generation to develop healthy personalities and to lead productive lives. "Stagnation" (or "self-absorption"), according to Erikson, is the unhealthy outcome of failing to guide the growth of ones own children, adopted kids, or perhaps children of friends and relatives.

Stage 8, Maturity—Ego integrity vs. despair (old age). Virtually every older, perhaps retired, person reminisces about the past and reviews his or her life. According to Erikson, if the person has achieved a positive outcome for each of the previous seven crisis stages, these looks into the past will show a satisfying, well-spent life. This satisfaction is ego integrity. On the other hand, if some of the earlier crises (stages) produced a negative outcome—for example, role confusion in Stage 5 (adolescence), personal isolation in Stage 6 (young adulthood), or stagnation in Stage 7 (middle age)—the life review in Stage 8 may produce disappointment (despair) over the perceived worth of his or her life. The frustration is augmented by the realization that time is now too short to try out alternative, more productive routes to integrity.

(Don't let the negative possibilities of these stages scare you. Certainly, positive outcomes at each stage are highly desirable, but many people who have not made all positive adjustments have found self-understanding and self-acceptance even in late Stage 7 or Stage 8. One *can* be happy.)

Erikson's ideas have had a substantial impact on many segments of our culture. Indeed, Erikson's phrase "identity crisis" has become part of our common language. Erikson especially has made us more conscious of the significance of forming an identity—a synthesis of how we come to see ourselves and how we expect others to see us. Identity formation in adolescence includes creating a sense of direction, purpose, perspective, and unity that integrates childhood experience with the expectations and hopes of adulthood. Erikson's stages are summarized in Table 3.3.

KOHLBERG'S STAGES OF MORAL DEVELOPMENT

Moral development might be loosely defined as understanding what's right and why. At three-year intervals, Lawrence Kohlberg (1974, 1976) presented moral dilemmas to the same group of 75 boys (from ages 10–16 until they were 22–28). The issues dealt with, for example, mercy killing and obedience to authority. He also studied moral development in Great Britain, Canada, Taiwan, Turkey, and Mexico. The outcome was a rather profound age-related theory of stages in moral development.

Table 3.3 Summary of Erikson's eight stages of man

Age	Stage	Psychosocial crisis	Optimal outcome
0 to 1½	Oral-sensory	Trust vs. mistrust	Basic trust and optimism
1½–3	Muscular-anal	Autonomy vs. shame, doubt	Sense of control over oneself and the environment
3–6	Locomotor-genital	Initiative vs. guilt	Goal-directedness and purpose
6–12	Latency	Industry vs. inferiority	Competence
12–18	Puberty and adolescence	Identity vs. role confusion	Reintegration of past with present and future goals; fidelity
Young adulthood	Young adulthood	Intimacy vs. isolation	Commitment, sharing, closeness and love
Middle age	Adulthood	Generativity vs. stagnation	Production and concern with the world and future generations
Old age	Maturity	Ego Integrity vs. despair	Perspective; satisfaction with one's past life; wisdom

According to Kohlberg, his stages are true invariant stages, which means that:

- They occur one at a time.
- They always occur in the same order.
- Movement is always forward, never backward.
- A person may be in only one stage at a time.
- Every person proceeds through the stages in the same order.
- Steps are never skipped.
- Growth may stop at any stage and at any age.

As an introduction, Kohlberg's stages of moral development are divided into three levels, each containing two discrete stages. Both stages of the **preconventional** level are oriented toward the physical consequences of an action, regardless of any humanistic meaning or value the action may have. Thus, being obedient and well-behaved is good because it avoids punishment or obtains rewards. Children at this age (4–10 years) can be cruel and dishonest when there are gaps in the power structure.

The **conventional** level also includes conformity, but now good and bad are defined by the expectations and rules of the person's family, group, or nation. Good behavior is that which pleases and is approved by others, or else is dictated by authority or law. A lot of unthinking people never get beyond this level.

The **postconventional** level includes universal and personal moral principles that are valid apart from authority. For example, the concept expressed by the golden rule—"Do unto others as you would have them do unto you"—appears in most major religions and philosophies. It is best to think at this level.

Let's take a closer look at each of the six stages.

Preconventional Level

Stage 1. The person's orientation is toward rewards and punishments. There is complete deference to physical power. Why obey rules? To avoid punishment.

Stage 2. Right action is that which satisfies one's own needs and sometimes the needs of others who will reciprocate. For example, concepts of "fairness" and "equal sharing" are based on very practical considerations, not on loyalty, justice, or gratitude. Why obey rules? To obtain rewards or have favors returned.

Conventional Level

Stage 3. "Good behavior" and "being nice" are good because they please others. In this "good boy/good girl" stage there is much conformity to stereotypes. The idea of *intention* (e.g., "he means well") appears for the first time. Why obey rules? To avoid disapproval or dislike.

Stage 4. This stage includes an orientation toward rules and authority and maintenance (not revision) of the social system. "Good behavior" includes doing one's duty and respecting authority and the law for their own sake. Respect is earned through such dutiful conformity. Why obey rules? To avoid censure from legitimate authority and to avoid the resultant guilt.

Postconventional Level

Stage 5. Here, right action is defined by general rights and standards which have been examined and agreed on by the larger society—for example, as stated in the *Constitution of the United States.* Independent personal values and opinions suggest the possibility of rationally changing these rights, standards, rules, laws, etc., instead of freezing them, as in Stage 4. Kohlberg

considers this stage to represent the "official morality" of American government. Why obey rules? To maintain community welfare and gain the respect of others.

Stage 6. Finally, for the Chosen Few, the highest stage of moral development is an orientation toward decisions of personal conscience and self-chosen ethics, based on consistent universal principles and rights, such as justice, equality of human rights, respect for individual differences, dignity, and the Golden Rule.

At higher stages of development the same moral concept becomes more differentiated and more integrated with the larger value system. Also, Kohlberg discovered that children and adolescents comprehend all stages up to their own—and understand only one additional stage. Significantly, "... *they prefer this next stage*" (Kohlberg, 1974; italics his). A child tends to move to the next higher stage when he or she is confronted by the appealing views of a peer who is in this next higher stage.

Teaching for Moral Development

Kohlberg makes a number of suggestions related to teaching for moral development. For example, a teacher might expose children to concepts one step higher than their current stage and encourage them to think at the more mature stage. Also, children can be given opportunities to think about moral problems by (a) role-playing someone who has been cheated, treated rudely, abused by a principal, or who must put to sleep their suffering dog, or by (b) practicing making decisions in moral issues, decisions requiring a higher level of moral thinking (see Rest, 1976). Kohlberg himself has produced filmstrips portraying moral dilemmas which children discuss and attempt to resolve.

In high school, Kohlberg's six stages themselves might be good curriculum content for stimulating an understanding of moral development. Discussions might center on well-known persons or groups who seem "stuck" at some more primitive level (e.g., "law 'n order" thinkers or unthinking followers of charismatic religious leaders). Are some adults thinking at the lowest stages—stealing is fine if you do not get caught? Is the average school system more concerned with Stage 4 (law and order) instead of Stage 5 (agreed-on but modifiable rights)?

TO IMPROVE YOUR TEACHING

If you are a pregnant person, eat well and avoid the measles, drugs, alcohol, smoking, air pollution, and jangled nerves. You also might instruct your women students to do the same.

Acquaint yourself thoroughly with the typical personality and adjustment problems of the age group you expect to teach. Some students will need understanding and empathy. Also, you should be able to determine whether some personality traits are interfering with adjustment and schoolwork—for example, extroversion, anxiety, quarrelsomeness, or laziness. Perhaps you can help students to understand and correct some of these problems. Erikson's stages suggest focal periods for strengthening important traits—for example, fostering initiative and goal-directedness (3–6 years), industry and feelings of competence (6–12 years), and a healthy identity (12–18 years).

Since the latent years, ages 6 to 12, are so critical for the development of all kinds of skills, be sure that all your students have a chance to develop important skills—for example, those related to using lab, art and sports equipment, musical instruments, and so on—in addition to "regular" academic and social skills.

The adolescent years are especially critical to the development of personality and a stable identity. Chapter 13 on affective and humanistic education suggests ways in which students may be helped to view themselves as valuable persons of adequate ability, high honesty and integrity, and initiative.

Students at any level might be accelerated in the growth of moral thinking. Try to determine the stage of moral development of most students in your class. Discuss various problems, issues, and dilemmas, and try to stimulate a higher level of moral thinking. You may wish to obtain Kolhberg's filmstrips.

In secondary school, try to raise students' understanding of the thinking in Kohlberg's Levels 5 and 6. If they understand and appreciate postconventional morality, there is a good chance they will adopt such a thinking style. Discuss with your fellow teachers the possibility of an "Ethics and Moral Philosophy" course. The world has enough rigid thinkers, stagnated at Levels 3 and 4.

Be aware that all of us use defense mechanisms to preserve our feelings of value and self-esteem. Many "flimsy excuses" you hear will unconsciously serve to protect the ego of the poorly performing student. Anna Freud's description of adolescent defense mechanisms points out even more subtle efforts to cope with frustrations and conflicts.

SUMMARY

The developmental psychologist traces human growth from conception through old age, looking at many aspects of physical, cognitive, and personality development. The psychologist often identifies developmental stages, including characteristics typically associated with a given stage.

The blueprint for physical and some mental characteristics is passed from parent to child in 46 chromosomes, 23 from each parent. Each chromosome contains thousands of genes, the double-helix shaped DNA molecules. A person's genotype is his genetic make-up; his phenotype is his observed and measured traits and behaviors.

IQ's of children are similar to those of their parents, evidence for a large heritability factor. Schizophrenia is more likely if a parent or sibling is schizophrenic, and retardation—Down's syndrome and especially PKU—seems to be inherited. Many personality traits and behavioral patterns seem to be partly determined by genetics, as evidenced by similarities between twins and differences between newborn babies.

Stages of prenatal development include (a) the germinal period, (b) the embryonic period, and (c) the fetal period. The baby-to-be is very susceptible to damage during the first three months.

The infant is born with a number of reflexes and with functioning sensory organs. Efforts to accelerate or delay early motor development have a small effect which soon disappears.

Periods of childhood are (a) infancy, 0 to 18–24 months (walking and talking), (b) early childhood, 18–24 months to 5–6 years (self-care), and (c) middle childhood, 5–6 years to about age 11 (basic academic skills, simple cultural concepts).

Puberty occurs from ages 10 to 17 for girls and 12 to 18 for boys. There is rapid physical and sexual growth, and often some self-consciousness and embarrassment.

Personality refers to personal qualities and ways of reacting to persons and situations. We all have a personal face (how we see ourselves), a social face (how we act), and a true face (our real selves).

The trait theory of personality emphasizes the search for stable, basic personality traits, such as extraversion, anxiety, agreeableness, and emotional stability. The person-situation (social behavior theory) approach emphasizes that characteristics of both the person and the situation are necessary to determine a person's reactions and behavior.

According to Freud's analysis of personality development, a person's mental health and personality depend on the ability of the ego to deal with the drives of the id (especially sex and aggression) and the forces of the superego (social conscience). Freud also divided personality development into five psychosexual stages of growth, each critical for the development of certain personality traits: oral (trust, dependence), anal (independence), phallic (identity, especially sexual), latency (mastery, coping), and genital (identity).

Freud's "defense mechanisms of the ego" are repression, denial, projection, reaction formation, displacement, sublimation, rationalization, compensation, and identification. Some adolescent mechanisms suggested by daughter Anna Freud were reversal of affect (flip-flopping an emotion), withdrawal (hiding), asceticism (rejecting comforts), uncompromising (adopting rigid attitudes), and regression (avoiding growing up).

Erick Erikson outlined eight psychosocial stages of development which extend across the entire life span. Each of Erikson's stages is seen as a "potential crisis" in which a conflict is resolved in either a healthy or unhealthy manner. The stages were:

1. Oral sensory (0 to $1\frac{1}{2}$ years), trust vs. mistrust.
2. Muscular-anal ($1\frac{1}{2}$ to 3 years), autonomy vs. shame and doubt.
3. Locomotor-genital (3 to 6 years), initiative vs. guilt.
4. Latency (6 to 12 years), industry vs. inferiority.
5. Puberty and adolescence (12 to 18 years), identity vs. role confusion.
6. Young adulthood, initimacy vs. isolation.
7. Adulthood, generativity vs. stagnation.
8. Maturity, ego integrity vs. dispair.

Kohlberg's six stages of moral development are true invariant, sequential stages, with no skipping and no regression. There are three main levels with two substages within each. At the preconventional level the main considerations are rewards and punishments, not humanistic values. At the conventional level there is strong conformity to expectations and rules. The highly desirable postconventional level includes universal, humanistic moral principles, the awareness that rules can be changed, and at Stage 6, self-chosen ethics. The attainment of each new stage includes an understanding of all earlier stages, but only one additional stage.

TOPICS FOR THOUGHT AND DISCUSSION

1. Which of your own personality characteristics do you think were strongly determined by heredity? Which by environment (home, school, peers)? Rate yourself on a scale of 1 to 10 on the traits mentioned in the Personality Theory section of this chapter.
2. What would (or could) you do if a child in your class were unusually jittery, unable to pay attention, and underweight, and you and your school psychologist thought it might be due to the formaldehyde in the child's mobile home?
3. When is a "social face" phony, and when is it proper?
4. How would you handle students who overuse defense mechanisms to justify poor performance? Or is there a problem here?
5. What is your own level of moral thinking? Do you know people who never quite made it to Kohlberg's postconventional level?

PROJECTS

1. If a paper is required for this or another education or psychology course, review recent literature on *behavior genetics*. Is the average doctor, lawyer, beggarman, or thief born or made?
2. Take a survey of teachers to find if any deliberately try to teach moral thinking and values. How do they do it? Are they successful?
3. Design a junior high or high school course in "Ethics and Moral Philosophy." Find references for books and AV materials. Look into values clarification (Chapter 13).

RECOMMENDED READING

Erickson, E. H. *Identity: Youth and crisis.* New York: Norton, 1968.
Freud, S. *An outline of psychoanalysis.* New York: Norton, 1949.
Lickona, T. (ed.). *Moral development and behavior.* New York: Holt, Rinehart & Winston, 1976.
Mischel, W. *Introduction to personality,* third edition. New York: Holt, Rinehart & Winston, 1981.
Muus, R. E. *Theories of Adolescence,* third edition. New York: Random House, 1975.
Santrock, J. W. *Adolescence: An introduction.* Dubuque, Iowa: W. C. Brown, 1981.
Scarr, S. *Race, social class, and individual differences in IQ: New studies of old issues.* Hillsdale, N.J.: Erlbaum, 1981.

Cognitive Development and Language Development

4

STAGES IN DEVELOPMENT

We mentioned at the beginning of Chapter 3 that developmental psychologists often describe growth and development in terms of identifiable stages. We looked briefly at stages in prenatal development; the stages of early childhood, middle childhood, and adolescence; Freud's five psychosexual stages and Erikson's eight psychosocial stages in personality development; and Kohlberg's six stages in the development of moral thinking. We also noted that the identification of a particular developmental stage alerts us to expect other sorts of thinking and behavior which usually accompany that stage. In this chapter we will survey that most famous set of developmental stages, the four stages of cognitive development identified by Swiss psychologist Jean Piaget. We also will see that a child's ability to take another person's point of view—his "perspective-taking stage"—is closely related to his Piagetian stage of cognitive development. We also will examine Bruner's three-stage analysis of cognitive development, and then turn briefly to language and language development.

ABOUT JEAN PIAGET

When you hear the phrase *cognitive development* you should think of Jean Piaget, just as *Santa* elicits *Claus*. Piaget was born in Switzerland in 1896 and died there in 1980. He was a precocious genius; at 10 years of age he published a paper on an albino sparrow which he found hopping around a public garden. From sparrows he turned to shellfish, and before he was 21 had published no less than 20 papers on mollusks. Before he graduated from secondary school he had been offered the curatorship of mollusks at the University of Geneva. With a doctorate in biology from Geneva, Piaget turned to developmental psychology. His discoveries and interpretations in children's thinking are appropriately colored with a biological evolutionary perspective: How does the changing cognitive organization help the growing child adapt to its environment? Both heredity and the environment interact to shape processes of thought. And it was the processes (the "how"), not the content (the "what"), which interested Piaget.

Now psychology has been measuring intelligence for 80 years, and IQ tests have confirmed beyond doubt that with age children develop better vocabularies, acquire bigger and more differentiated stores of information, reason better, and understand spatial relationships better. Piaget, however, used observation and some creative experimentation, often with his own now-famous children, Jacqueline, Laurent, and Lucienne, to nail down patterns and stages of specific conceptual and inferential processes. His fantastic productivity resulted in over 20 full-length books plus thousands of pages describing over 180 major studies, none of which are easy reading even if you understand French.

No brief statement such as this chapter can do Piaget justice. As a preliminary overview, Piaget's research and theories help us understand invariant stages in children's thinking processes. As we saw in Chapter 3, *invariant* means that everyone proceeds through all stages in the same order, nobody skips a stage, and normally nobody returns to an earlier stage. One process must develop before another can follow. Naturally, there are individual differences in *when* a given child enters a stage, and in *how long* he or she remains there. Also, the transition between stages is smooth, not abrupt. Critically, the stages differ in quality, not quantity; that is, the child entering a new stage does not think "faster," but in a different, more sophisticated way. Piaget's stages include insights into how moral thought develops, how imagination develops, how empathy and role-taking evolve, how perceptual abilities grow, how experience is incorporated into a nonegocentric world view, how scientific and logical thought develops, how language and symbol systems grow, and how abilities to generalize, discriminate, and categorize change with succeeding stages.

Sensorimotor Stage (0–2 Years)

For the first month of life, the cognitive activity of the newborn is largely reflexive, based upon immediate sensory experience. The infant sucks anything that touches its face, including teddy bears, rattles, little fists and daddy's nose, from which it also reflexively grabs daddy's glasses. The child soon undergoes a transition from a body-centered (self-centered) to an object-centered world. Through vision, hearing, touch, taste, etc., objects change from mere sensory impressions into real objects—with multiple properties and relationships to other objects. The child's activity is very practical during this period, and virtually always in direct response to immediate experience. The child is developing the very important ability to coordinate physical movements—grasping, looking, biting, etc.—with perceptions of appropriate stimuli.

Life is exciting during the sensorimotor stage, since virtually every experience is something new. The infant will watch a mobile dangling over its crib for hours. The seven- or eight-month-old will stand up by clinging to the bed rail and its saucer eyes will take in everything in sight. The 18- to 24-month-old, of course, gets into everything—sugar bowls get dumped, magazine racks and ash trays are overturned, and colorful books are examined, dismembered, and frequently eaten. The "terrible twos," which we noted in Chapter 3, are so called because the child wants what it wants when it wants it, and no amount of reasoning or explaining does a bit of good. Parents who embarrass easily tend to avoid restaurants, airplanes, movie theatres and church unless the two-year old is parked with grandparents.

By the end of the sensorimotor period, the child has learned to discriminate objects and people, and has learned a primitive symbol system (language). He or she also has learned the notion of **object permanence:** When mommy or a toy disappears, they are not gone forever. This ability reflects the child's capacity to form and hold mental images. The capacity for mental representation, as demonstrated in the child's attainment of object permanence, is the "crowning achievement" of the sensorimotor period. Mental representation is considered the primary prerequisite for language development (Bowerman, 1978; see also Corrigan, 1978, 1979).

Repeated experience with objects leads to the formation of mental **schemata,** memories of the appearance and meanings of particular objects and classes of objects. For example, after a child repeatedly sees, touches, tastes, and bounces a number of toy balls, it forms a schema for balls and remembers exactly what to do when it receives a new one.

It's important to note that a lack of experience, especially visual, will result in a lack of development of cognitive schemata. According to Piaget, a visually rich environment is the best way to develop a young child's intelligence; a deprived sensory environment can retard cognitive growth very substantially. In the classic research by Spitz (1945) it was discovered that institutionalized infants whose sensory environment was severely restricted suffered extensive intellectual, emotional, and social deficits.

Preoperational Stage (2–7 Years)

The preoperational stage is subdivided into two parts, the **preoperational phase** (age 2–4 years) and the **intuitive phase** (age 4–7 years). Some consider the latter to be a transitional period before the next stage (concrete operations), since some behaviors give the appearance of concrete operational thinking. The *entire* preoperational period is characterized by increasing symbolic activities, including language, imagery, and use of memory. The child responds to more than just the here-and-now experience of the sensorimotor stage.

The first phase—yes, it's the preoperational phase of the preoperational stage—is characterized largely by (a) a rapid increase in vocabulary and language ability, (b) egocentrism, the inability to take another person's point of view, and (c) the ability to classify, but only according to a single criterion. Egocentrism, a very salient trait, is characteristic of the entire preoperational stage.

As for language ability, the average two-year-old has a vocabulary of about 200 words and uses just one- and two-word sentences. The four-year-old owns about 2000 words and uses eight- to ten-word sentences which are grammatically correct. However, the concepts formed may be incorrect and amusing. The church hymn, "Gladly the cross I'd bear" becomes "Gladly, the cross-eyed bear," and another hymn, "Up up in the sky, where the little birds fly," usually is "A pup in the sky . . ." The child also experiments with language, making up new words and expressions such as "poopoo head" and other moderately colorful bathroom phrases.

THE FAMILY CIRCUS® **By Bil Keane**

Copyright 1981
The Register and Tribune
Syndicate. Inc

"Diddle, diddle, dumpling, mice and John. . . ."

Another symbolic ability appears in what Piaget called *deferred imitation*, a sort of delayed copying. The three- or four-year-old will remember mother's cake-mixing behavior and can imitate it a few hours later.

Egocentrism is reflected in the child's concept of time, which includes only "now," "before now," and "not yet." Space concepts also are me-based; to the child taken for an evening walk, it seems that the moon follows the child. The inability to see things from another's perspective might show up in spontaneous winners such as "Hey daddy, look at this man's big red nose!" Every teacher in the lower elementary grades raises her left hand when asking the class facing her to "Show me your right hand." Nobody catches it, except visiting adults. Also, having to ask the child to be quiet while you are on the phone, or to stop jumping on you while you are talking to someone else, similarly reflects his or her inability to understand how others think or feel (Glucksberg, Krauss, and Higgins, 1975; Shantz, 1976). Perspective taking will be further described later in this chapter.

In the classroom, such egocentrism does not help a child learn to follow rules. The preschool child may have difficulty understanding and accepting rules that protect the rights of others because he or she has never been able to think about the rights of others.

Classifying according to just one salient criterion means that the child may not recognize an object or person out of context. For example, the local butcher may not be recognized without a blood-stained apron and white pants. At the age of two years and seven months, Jacqueline Piaget did not even recognize baby sister Lucienne in a new bathing suit.

The **intuitive phase** (age 4–7 years) of this preoperational stage includes a process of **decentering,** a gradual understanding of a spatial world and a time scale which are independent of the child itself. The moon no longer follows the child, and clocks and calendars have new, nondecorative significance. The idea of *number* also appears. The child counts and is not so willing to trade two big pennies for one little dime.

Language is becoming ever more complex, although conversation tends to be "at" others rather than "with" them. This is an egocentric form of conversation in which each kid jabbers independently of others—just talking, rarely listening.

One of Piaget's most famous discoveries is that the preoperational child is unable to **conserve** mass, weight, number, and volume (Beilin, 1971; Brainerd, 1974). The nonconservation-of-mass demonstration goes about like this: A four-year-old child will agree that two equal-sized balls of clay are, in fact, equal. When one ball is rolled into a shape resembling a snake (or frankfurter) before the childs' very eyes, he or she illogically says the longer object contains more clay. At age five, about half of the children understand that the amount of clay does not change when the clay is rolled out. The conservation-of-weight demonstration is similar, but requires about another year of growth to understand. A five-year-old child will see that two balls of clay will balance a scale, indicating equal weight. Nonetheless, when one ball is rolled into a snake, the snake is judged heavier than the remaining ball. By age six, the child probably will understand that weight does not change with changes in shape. The child's inability to conserve volume was demonstrated quite easily by Piaget, and has been by hundreds of psychologists since. Water is poured from a short, fat glass container into a tall, thin glass container. The preoperational child will now say there is more water. By age seven, he or she probably is more accurate. Failure to conserve number is demonstrated in the child's belief that when a stack of pennies is scattered about, there suddenly are more pennies. If only it worked that way.

The preoperational child makes judgments based on perceptual appearance—the clay snake looks bigger and heavier, and there appears to be more water in the tall thin container. However, when the child begins to think of quantity in *units,* he or she naturally realizes that units do not change with changes in appearance.

With **animism,** another interesting preoperational phenomena, children believe that stones, clouds, and trees are living and conscious, and have motives and intentions (Looft and Bartz, 1974). After some amount of questioning children of different ages, Piaget concluded that children from

four to six years old attribute life to anything showing activity or usefulness: The sun is alive because it gives light. Later (age 6–7), life is attributed only to things that move: A rock is alive because it rolls, a table is not alive because it does not move. Finally, at age 8–10, spontaneous movement is required for something to be alive: A fly and a stream are alive because they move without help, a bicycle is not alive because we have to make it go. At age 11, kids have the adult concept of life, which includes only plants and animals.

Phenomenalistic causality refers to the preoperational child's tendency to infer causation when two events occur in sequence. That is, the first one is taken to cause the second one. If dad opens the door for mom to walk in, opening the door may be seen as causing mom to appear on the porch.

Nominal realism is the preoperational tendency for children not to understand that names are arbitrary designations of objects. They think the name is part of, or a property of, the object itself—the name of the sun is in the sun, and has always been there. (Hmmm, how *did* astronomers learn the planets' names!)

The increased symbolizing ability of the preoperational stage also includes having nightmares and developing strong phobias; for example, fear of dogs or of certain people. The fears usually do not seem to be based on experience, that is, they are not conditioned fears (Chapter 5).

Very generally, the improved symbolization abilities of the preoperational stage have tremendous adaptive characteristics. The child can use his or her language and experiences to deal with present problems. He or she also is capable of anticipation—having a foreknowledge of impending events. The child's reality includes the past, the future, and settings which are spatially removed. In Piaget's biological frame of reference, such abilities certainly would have survival value for the species.

Concrete-Operational Stage (7–11 Years)

In the stage of concrete operations, the logical flaws of the preoperational stage disappear. Also, the child shows a new capacity for reasoning—figuring out what to do before doing it. Thought precedes action. The child might, for example, work on a puzzle "in his or her head" rather than on a jam-it-together, trial-and-error basis. But always the thinking is about (or with) representations of concrete objects, not with abstract ideas and symbols.

Logical thinking (with concrete objects) is especially characteristic of this period. For one thing, children now conserve. They understand units of measurement and you can't fool them by pouring water from a fat glass into a skinny one—it's still the same amount of water. They also are able to conserve mass, weight, and number. The child can imagine the operation and accurately predict the results, despite attempts by the developmental psychologist to fool him or her. Quantification of thought, or the understanding of units and measurement, is one of the most salient characteristics of the concrete-operational child.

While the egocentrism of the preoperational child made rule-learning and rule-following difficult, the concrete-operational child has no such difficulty. He or she masters social rules (such as when to say "please" and "excuse me") along with other rules of conduct in specific social settings (breakfast, the classroom, visiting grandmother, etc.). He or she learns what to do when the firebell rings, how to behave in the library, and how to play bingo, baseball, and Monopoly. Importantly, to the concrete-operational child these rules are seen as fixed and unchangeable—engraved in stone somewhere and not subject to modification.

As a related tendency, since representations are tied to concrete objects and events, the concrete-operational child often fails to distinguish between his or her representations (or hypotheses) and reality. For example, if a child thinks "Freddy is mean" or "peas are yuk," then these are facts, not just possibilities which could be disconfirmed.

The concrete-operational child understands classifications, subclassifications and multiple classifications. A rose is a flower and a flower is a plant. A rose also is a red thing, something that smells good, and something that makes a nice surprise for mom. Collections—for which concrete-operational children are notorious—reflect the ability to perceive that an object is the same as other members of its class, yet unique in its position within that class.

We might mention also the **literal mindedness** of concrete-operational children. Literal mindedness refers to the often humorous tendency to interpret words directly, not as figures of speech. If you ask a 10-year old if you can "fix" him or her a hamburger, you're likely to get a grin and a question: "How'd it get broken?"

The child also thinks logically, and is able to handle such relationships as, "All dogs bark, Fido is a dog, therefore Fido barks." In addition, the child easily orders objects (e.g., sticks) according to size, without making painstakingly careful pairwise comparisons. He or she realizes that a stick is both longer than one neighbor and shorter than another, and that a new stick can be readily fitted into the series. Piaget called this **seriation.** A study by White, Yussen, and Docherty (1976) showed that particular exercises in a Montesorri nursery school enabled a number of these preoperational thinkers to perform seriation tasks which normally require concrete operational thought. The children could not solve conservation problems, however—the snake still weighed more than the clay ball it was created from. The authors concluded that the Montessori exercises probably enabled some children to perform some concrete-operational tasks. However, such training did not really accelerate movement from preoperational to concrete-operational thinking as some have argued (Kohlberg, 1968; Miezitis, 1972).

Another characteristic of the concrete stage is **reversibility** of thinking. Children can mentally add ducks and chickens to produce total fowl; then subtract chickens from fowl to produce ducks. They also can mentally pour water back and forth from fat to skinny jars and "see" the consequences.

As a final educational note, the ability of the concrete operational children (age 7 to 11) to solve problems mentally is limited to thinking with *things*. They must have concrete representations to manipulate. The kids do not, and cannot, think like adults, that is, with highly abstract symbols, concepts, and reasoning.

Formal Operations (Begins about age 11–14 Years)

With the stage of formal operations, which coincides with puberty and adolescence, the individual can think abstractly and logically and achieve a reality which is much like that of an adult. The adolescent can conceive of the possible, as well as the concrete here and now. He or she may create hypothetical events, imaginary possibilities, and abstract propositions, and then proceed to reason with them (Yussen and Santrock, 1982).

Teenagers also are capable of thinking about thinking, a phenomenon sometimes called **metathinking** or **metacognition** (Flavell and Wellman, 1979; Yussen and Levy, 1975). The adolescents' working vocabulary will include such thought-related abstractions as "belief," "intelligence," "reasonable," "values," and maybe "hypocrisy."

The adolescents' ability to think about thinking also includes the ability to think about other people's thinking. This leads to the common adolescent self-consciousness, which includes the exaggerated feeling that others are thinking *about them*. Teenagers are extremely concerned with their appearance, and fads and conformity are rampant. Developmental psychologist David Elkind (1970) considers these feelings to be a form of **adolescent egocentrism,** which includes what Elkinds calls the **personal fable,** a strong belief in one's personal uniqueness ("No one in the world can possibly understand how I feel"). The adolescent also creates an **imaginary audience—** perhaps feeling, for example, that everyone in the city is waiting each morning to see how the adolescent dresses and to hear what he or she thinks. Adolescent egocentrism also may include both excessive self-criticism ("Everyone will laugh at me") and excessive self-admiration ("I've got the coolest socks in the whole school").

The over-concern with what others think can lead to severe depression and even suicide for the teenager with a physical handicap or some other (often exaggerated) stigma, such as unfashionable clothes, weight problems, pimples, scars, etc. Of course the clothes, weight, pimples, etc., do play a role in the adolescent's unhappiness, but formal operational thinking can balloon these matters into serious personality difficulties.

Adolescent idealism is common. The young person can conceive of "perfect parents," "ideal teachers," "ideal schools," and a "perfect adulthood." A common adolescent stress is the disappointment and disillusionment which occurs when the ideal is compared with the actual. It makes very good TV drama material ("Oh mother, how could you!! I'll never be able to face my friends again! [sob]"). Elkind (1976, p. 101) noted that young people leave adolescence and become truly adult not when they give up their idealism, but when they realize that they can and must work toward their own ideal goals. A good thought.

The stage of formal operations expands the adolescent's ability to deal with higher mathematics and complex conceptions of space and time. The adolescent understands the meaning of "one mile" and "one month," though neither is very concrete. A younger child without such a time sense might ask if Aunt Minny was a pilgrim or if grandma ever saw a dinosaur.

Metaphorical thinking also becomes possible. The adolescent can see that one statement can have both a literal and a metaphorical meaning ("Look before you leap," "All that glitters is not gold," etc.). Also, stories with a moral—for example, *Androcles and the Lion*—will now make more profound sense.

Piaget's insightful stages of cognitive development are summarized in Table 4.1.

Table 4.1 Piaget's stages of cognitive development

Age	Stage	Description
0–2	Sensorimotor	Child organizes and coordinates perceptions with physical movements. The stage begins with reflexive actions, ends with primitive language. Significant accomplishment: object permanence (use of images).
2–7	Preoperational	
	Preoperational phase	Vocabulary growth; classification according to one characteristic.
	Intuitive phase	Understanding a world independent of self (decentering); concept of number.
	All of preoperational phase	Egocentrism; failure to conserve; Animistic thinking; Phenomenalistic causality; nominal realism.
7–11	Concrete operations	Thought precedes action; thinks with or about things; conservation; learns rules; multiple classifications; logical relations; seriation; reversibility.
Begins 11–14	Formal operations	Abstract, adultlike thought; adolescent idealism; metathinking; accurate concepts of time and space; metaphorical thinking; self-consciousness; conformity.

Beyond Formal Thought

Piaget's writings have stimulated tons of research. One moderately obvious question was: Is there a stage of cognitive development beyond formal operations? Reviews by Hooper and Sheehan (1977) and Colby and Kohlberg (1975) produced three relevant conclusions. First, fully developed operational thought seems to occur a bit later than Piaget's 11–14 age range. In some problems requiring formal operational thinking, adults 19–21 years old usually outperformed adolescents aged 12–15. Second, thought processes do not change much from young adulthood (age 19–21) through middle adulthood (age 30–50), although skills and experiences naturally grow. Third, formal operational thinking seems to decline during older adulthood, from about 65 years onward.

The Process of Change and Adaptation

We have already noted the biological, adaptive bias of Piaget. Each cognitive change of the growing human enables it to cope better and more independently with its big, bright world. Adaptation is change in cognitive organization. The dynamics run about like this: When a child encounters a new problem, conflict, or experience, his or her equilibrium is disturbed. Since nobody likes this disturbance, there is motivation to remove it and restore balance. Piaget's **equilibration** is the restoration of equilibrium by mental work which solves the problem. In other words, a person whose current thinking is inadequate to resolve a particular conflict will need to better organize his or her thoughts to resolve the issue. The new, improved, better-balanced organization is a higher stage of cognitive development. For example, to a child in the late-preoperational stage, a stack of pennies appears to increase in number when it is scattered. Reasonably, the child may wonder where the extra cents came from. But when his or her number ability tells the child that the number of pennies is the same, whether stacked or scattered, the issue is resolved and she or he makes a big step toward concrete operational thinking.

Two principal mechanisms of adaptation are **assimilation** and **accommodation.** With assimilation, a new idea or phenomenon is fitted into the existing cognitive organization by changing the new idea to fit. For example, a zebra, as a new concept, may be interpreted as a "wild, striped horse in Africa." The troublesome new phenomenon now fits nicely into current schemata related to horses, stripes, and Africa. "Zebra" is understood and equilibrium is restored.

Accommodation is the altering of the cognitive system to fit the new concept. For example, while learning about zebras, the child's schema for "horse" will be broadened to include (accommodate) the new information.

It should be apparent that assimilation and accommodation occur simultaneously. The learner alters the new information to fit existing structures (assimilation), and at the same time the current schemata are altered by the new information (accommodation). Through assimilation and accommodation, schemata become more structured and elaborated, and become related to other schemata. For example, with cognitive growth, *zebra* becomes a more sophisticated idea than before and is related to other systems of ideas, such as African geography and ecology, evolution, zoos, and so on.

The concepts of assimilation and accommodation also apply to the development and integration of **motor** and **attentional** schemata. Piaget describes how an infant will accommodate (fit its own action to the environment) a nipple by shaping its mouth to fit. The infant also assimilates (fits the environment to the action) by sucking on every object that brushes his or her mouth. When the infant begins to look at what he or she sucks, Piaget calls this a coordination of the "sucking schema" with the "looking schema," a cognitive reorganization which certainly is adaptive.

The reader should note that Ausubel's idea of *progressive differentiation of a concept in cognitive structure* (Chapter 8) is about the same as the Piagetian notion of developing, elaborating and coordinating cognitive schemata. As we will see, Ausubel emphasizes the ease of learning and understanding which takes place through relating new information to what the learner knows.

Development of Role-Taking

One very critical component of development is the child's role-taking ability, the ability to take another person's perspective. We have already noted that the preoperational (age 2 to 6 or 7) child thinks egocentrically, and cannot "decenter" and recognize that his or her own thoughts, feelings, and perceptions may be different from those of others. Further, the preoperational child is unaware of the limitations of his or her own viewpoint (Flavell, 1963; also Feffer, 1970).

INSET 4.1

A FUNNY THING HAPPENED ON THE WAY TO THE FRONT DOOR: A TEST OF SOCIAL ROLE TAKING

Chandler (1973) devised a series of short episodes, each illustrated by a cartoon, to measure the ability of children to take another person's perspective. Your author's favorite is:

> JOE WAS PRACTICING HITTING A BASEBALL. HE GAVE IT A HARD HIT BUT IT FLEW INTO AND BROKE THE WINDOW OF A CAR PARKED ACROSS THE STREET. HE RAN HOME VERY FRIGHTENED. HE LOOKED OUT HIS WINDOW TO SEE IF ANYBODY FOLLOWED HIM HOME. HIS FATHER SAW HIM LOOKING OUT THE WINDOW. THERE WAS A KNOCK AT THE DOOR AND JOE STOOD IN FRONT OF THE DOOR TO STOP ANYONE FROM ANSWERING IT. HE WAS SO FRIGHTENED, HE RAN AWAY CRYING.
>
> I AM JOE's FATHER. I WAS AT HOME ONE DAY WHEN . . . . (Child completes the story).

From Chandler, M. Egocentrism and antisocial behavior: The assessment and training of social perspective-taking skills. *Developmental Psychology* **9**, 1973, 1–6. Reprinted by permission.

Table 4.2 Selman's perspective-taking stages

Cognitive stage	Perspective-taking stage
Preoperational	Stage 0 (egocentric) Unaware of alternative viewpoints
Transitional preconcrete	Stage 1 (subjective) Differentiates own and others' views
Concrete	Stage 2 (self-reflective) Understands that other person can view child as a subject
Transitional concrete/early formal	Stage 3 (mutual) Can take another's point of view; understands that other person can take his or her point of view
Basic formal	Stage 4 (social and conventional system) Interpersonal awareness; can compare perspectives

Selman (1976, 1978; Selman and Byrne, 1974) developed a five-stage model of social role taking which ties social role-taking ability to the Piagetian stages of cognitive development (see Table 4.2). At the preoperational Stage 0, the egocentric child is unaware of alternative viewpoints. At Selman's Stage 1, at a transition between preoperational and concrete-operational thinking, the child at least differentiates between his or her own viewpoint and that of others. At Selman's Stage 2, corresponding to Piaget's concrete stage, the child not only understands that others have a different view, but further understands that the other person also can view the child as a subject. The Stage 2 child thus understands role taking as a mechanism. He or she also can anticipate the reactions of others. At Selman's Stage 3, in which the child is in a transition between Piaget's

INSET 4.2

SPATIAL PERSPECTIVE TAKING: THE THREE-SIDED MOUNTAIN

Piaget and his colleague Barbel Inhelder (1956) studied egocentric perspective taking with the three-sided mountain task. They asked the child to describe the mountain as seen by a doll which was sitting in a position different from the child. While some early concrete-operational children (age 7 to 11) sometimes could report a perspective different than their own, Piaget and Inhelder found that children did not consistently and accurately describe the doll's point of view until age 9 or 10.

concrete and early formal stages, the child is capable of taking the view of another person. Further, the child understands that the other person can take the child's point of view. Finally, at Selman's Stage 4, the formal operational thinker is fully capable of all possible third-person perspectives. The individual thus is capable of deep interpersonal awareness and can compare different perspectives on a problem.

Recursive thinking—I know that you know that I know—is a formal operational (Selman's Stage 4) capability. If you like, you may call this phenomenon *reciprocal coordination of perspectives,* although you may lose friends with that kind of talk.

PIAGET AND CLASSROOM LEARNING

The major and hopefully obvious upshot of Piaget's theory of cognitive development is that teaching must be coordinated with the child's stage of development.

In the typical preschool, the preoperational child will find blocks, toys, magnetic letters and numbers, xylophones and drums, paints and clay, dress-up clothes, pets, pots and pans, dinnerware, and so on. The emphasis clearly is on exploration and discovery; the child takes an active role in learning, while the teacher selects and organizes some activities.

In preschools which deliberately follow a Piagetian curriculum (Kamii, 1972), children acquire a general knowledge of physical objects—that is, schemas are enriched—by exploring how things work, feel, taste, and smell. They learn logico-mathematical skills in the form of classification and seriation problems; they acquire some representational symbols (e.g., letters, numbers, music notes); social rules; and self-control (Cowan, 1978). The teacher should not attempt to be a transmitter of complex knowledge, but focus on the assimilative aspects of learning—helping each child understand new objects and concepts by relating them to existing schemata.

At the concrete operational level, Piagetian teaching encourages the combining of content areas in order to develop a unity in cognitive organization—an interrelatedness among mental schemata. Cowan (1978) suggested teaching by the project method. Many kinds of projects may be arranged which combine various areas of knowledge and skill. Map making, for example, teaches concepts in social studies, politics, geography, and topology, as well as the skills of art, mathematics, and measuring, including the conservation of distance and space. If students work in groups, the learning will include social skills, language development, and probably a reduction in egocentrism. The teacher should "... keep an eye out for opportunities to teach the content of two or more subject areas simultaneously" (Cowan, 1978, p. 239).

In both secondary school and college, teachers and texts focus more on the curriculum and less on the developmental characteristics of students, which probably explains why there is virtually no information about teaching according to Piagetian principles at these levels. One principle which has emerged, however, is that many junior high school, high school, and even college students do not function at a formal operational level, and so effective teaching for these students must be at the concrete operational level. The teacher of students in the 12- to 15-year-old range especially must be aware that while some students will be thinking at a formal operational level, others still will be in concrete operational thinking. Those who do think at the formal level tend to get higher grades (Sayre and Ball, 1975).

Generally, Piagetian theory makes several clear recommendations for teaching. First, as we noted at the outset of this section, teaching must be coordinated with the cognitive developmental stage of the learners. Requiring young children to memorize abstract concepts and formulas by rote does not help them to develop logical thinking abilities, abilities which Piaget felt are much more important for the elementary school child than mastering facts. Second, as we have seen above, preoperational (and concrete-operational) children should be permitted to manipulate, touch, and explore—activities which lead to the discovery, understanding, and integration of meaningful knowledge. Concepts learned in this way create a good foundation for the later formal operational stage, in which the adolescent can deal more strictly with language and symbols.

Third, Piagetian theory supports a spiral curriculum. With increasing stages of development children return every few years to a more differentiated and integrated version of the same content material. Finally, and importantly, questions, problems, challenges, and incongruities should be posed at all levels. These cause disequilibration, leading to reasoning, accommodation, assimilation, and higher levels of cognitive development.

BRUNER'S THEORY OF COGNITIVE DEVELOPMENT

In 1967, psychologist Jerome Bruner criticized Piaget's description of cognitive stages, arguing that Piaget's theory describes only changes in the nature of children's knowledge, and does not constitute an adequate description of the processes of cognitive growth. Piaget undoubtedly would not have agreed. Bruner's alternative approach includes three stages which differ in the processes children use to form mental representations of their world: enactive, iconic, and symbolic modes of thinking.

Enactive, Iconic, and Symbolic Modes of Thought

The first form of representation, available for infants, is through action. This is the **enactive** mode. The child's motor behavior leads to motoric representations—what the child *does* is what he or she thinks. Such experiences as touching, tasting, moving, and grasping lead to enactive representations. In Bruner's words: "In earliest childhood, events and objects are defined in terms of the actions taken toward them. . . . .An object is what one does to it" (Bruner, 1967, p. 12).

The second, more advanced form of representation is the **iconic** mode, which includes visual imagery and other sensory representations. This tremendously important ability enables the child to reproduce things that no longer are present. Images also are "...great summarizers of action" (Bruner, 1967, p. 13), in the sense that one picture is worth a thousand descriptive words. The availability of mental images, along with the natural tendency for perceptual organization and completeness, permits the two- or three-year-old child to make predictions, to extrapolate, and to otherwise fill in missing information (Yussen and Santrock, 1982). According to Bruner, the three-year-old child is virtually a slave to sensory distractions—whatever is bright, colorful, noisy, or smelly will capture his or her undivided attention, at least for the moment.

Finally, with language comes representation in the **symbolic** mode, which begins around age five or six. Gradually, words come to be used to represent objects which are not present. The child now can deal with reality in far more flexible ways than with nonthinking action (enactive mode) or even perceptual understanding (iconic mode). Vast amounts of information are stored in and retrieved from our language and symbol systems. Bruner noted that symbolic thinking has "high compactibility." A large and profound statement can be condensed into a few symbols: $E = MC^2$, or "Look before you leap." Language is used to reason and solve problems, and eventually to make hypothetical, metaphorical, and conditional (if-then) propositions.

Bruner sees the child progressing successively from enactive to iconic to symbolic modes of representation and thought. The simpler modes are not scrapped, however. We continue to grow in all three modes. Adults continue to develop motor (enactive) representations for swimming, hitting a nail, petting a snake or playing the violin; we obviously acquire and use new iconic representations (that is, we form images or *icons*); and we all use growing symbol systems for communication, problem solving, and as vehicles for thinking about things.

Bruner and Education

It would seem that Bruner's model supplements—not contradicts or improves on—Piaget's enlightening analyses of stages of cognitive growth. Bruner's three modes of enactive, iconic, and symbolic thinking further support the use of manipulation and discovery with young children. Concrete objects and phenomena are consistent with the child's strong capability for sensorimotor learning and for his or her ability to form and retain images. Concepts and principles acquired in this fashion form a strong foundation for later, more verbal and symbolic forms of teaching and learning.

As a final thought-stimulating note, Bruner's single most famous statement is that "... any subject can be taught effectively in some intellectually honest form to any child at any stage of development." Unfortunately, some curriculum planners have incorrectly interpreted this statement to mean that it is just fine to try to teach, for example, abstract science, math, and social studies concepts in the elementary grades. The statement was intended to suggest that many complex concepts can be sufficiently simplified—structured for the appropriate cognitive developmental level—so that normal children can comprehend them at a level consistent with their stage of cognitive development. If one wishes to accept Bruner's challenge and incorporate sophisticated material into an elementary curriculum, one would need to attend very carefully to the age-related capabilities outlined by Bruner and Piaget.

LANGUAGE DEVELOPMENT

In the work of Piaget and Bruner we already have seen many insights into the process of language development. Piaget, for example, emphasized the growth of vocabulary and language ability (symbolization) during the preoperational stage (age 2–7), permitting the child to escape the here-and-now thinking of the sensorimotor stage (age 0–2). Throughout the concrete operational stage (age 7–11) the child uses words and other symbols to think, reason, and solve problems. These capabilities take a more abstract, often theoretical or philosophical form in the stage of formal operations (beginning at age 11–14). Bruner's symbolic mode of representation, of course, is based entirely on the use of language and other symbols to store information and solve problems, and eventually to think in terms of hypothetical, metaphorical, etc., propositions.

Cognitive Prerequisites for Language

We should note at the outset that language development and cognitive development are closely tied together. Psychologists studying the relationship between cognitive ability and language ability—a topic sometimes labeled "cognitive prerequisites for language"—have concluded that a child's speech will reflect only what he or she is capable of dealing with cognitively (Dale, 1973). The child will not use words or phrases whose meanings are beyond his or her stage of cognitive development. We will see below that early speech reflects important objects, events, and actions in the child's environment (e.g., "mama," "milk," "allgone truck"), quite appropriate for early preoperational thought and language. As the cognitive ability becomes more complex and sophisticated, language development becomes complex and sophisticated in a perfectly parallel fashion. Some psychologists have argued that cognitive development and language development are basically the same academic topic (Flavell, 1977).

The Conditioning-and-Learning View of Language Development

An older, traditional view of language learning is based on principles of conditioning and learning explained in Chapter 5. Briefly, one basic idea is that word meanings are acquired through a process of association. For example, in childhood the word *pencil* is paired with the object pencil ("Johnny, this is a pencil. Can you say 'pencil'?") until an association is formed between the word and the object. Affective meanings are acquired in a similar associative fashion: The *flag, patriotism,* and *motherhood* are learned to be good; *rotten fruit, mean dogs,* and *prejudice* are bad; *Mickey Mouse* is funny; a *sunset* is beautiful; and so on.

Another basic notion is that sentences are viewed as verbal chains. Each word (link in the chain) is considered to be both a stimulus and a response. That is, due to past word-word associations, each word in the sentence serves as a stimulus which elicits the next word as a response; this word then becomes a stimulus which elicits the next response word, and so on. Throughout language learning children are assumed to be rewarded (reinforced) for correct verbalizations—correct naming of objects, correct pronunciations, correct grammar—and punished for incorrect verbalizations. Modeling and imitation also are assumed to play an important role, with children learning language by mimicking words and phrases of adults.

There have been two main criticisms of the conditioning and learning (or behavioristic) approach to language. First, the theory does not adequately explain how a young child—or an adult, for that matter—is easily able to create a totally new, grammatically correct sentence, a sentence the child has never heard before nor ever been reinforced for producing. An explanation based on learning linguistic rules, discussed below, is much more convincing. Second, the notions of modeling, reinforcement, and punishment as mechanisms for language learning are considered inadequate and misleading, if not dead wrong. Harvard psycholinguists Roger Brown, Courtney Cazden, and Ursala Bellugi (1966) found that parents tended to correct (reinforce) the truthfulness of children's speech much more often than the grammatical correctness. For example, "doggie run" would likely elicit a correction of "No, that's a sheep" or "Yes, that's a nice doggie," with no comment on the incorrect plural verb (*run* instead of *runs*). As we will soon see, grammatical rules, enabling the child to produce correct sentences, seem to be acquired on the basis of widespread language experience, along with the innate capability for learning language.

Rule Learning and Transformational Grammar

It is true that some principles of conditioning and learning do apply to some aspects of language learning. However, the newer, more sophisticated and more widely accepted approach is based on (1) a built-in capability and motivation for language learning, (b) the conceptualization of language as a system of rules, and (c) the belief that language learning is a matter of learning those rules. We will look briefly at some linguistic rules.

Phonemes are the basic sounds used in a language. English employs about 36 phonemes, mainly consonant and verb sounds. Phonological rules allow us to use such sounds as *ad, kl, ini* and *br*, but not *dn, pq, fp* or *bc*. As children we learn rules for combining phonemes into basic units of meaning, **morphemes.** Some morphemes are complete words (*dog, plane, cap, run*); others may be prefixes (*pre-, re-, bi-*), suffixes (*-tion, -ly, -est*), or verb tense markers (*-ing, -ed, -s*). Morphological rules allow us to properly combine morphemes into words. Note that some morpheme combinations exist (*dogs, rerun, biplane, caption*), while others are not allowed (*bidog, planetion, runest*).

At the level of **syntax** we find rules for combining words into phrases and sentences. It is these syntactical linguistic rules which are learned by children, and which allow even a three-year-old child to create brand new, yet grammatically perfect sentences. Of course, the syntactical rules of children are not the same as the more sophisticated rules used by adults. Evidence that children do use systematic morphological and syntactical rules (and which confirms that these rules are not particularly accurate) can be found in the often amusing grammatical mistakes children make. For example, children learn that *-ed* marks a past tense, and so we frequently hear "We goed to the airport," plus *maked, bitted, builded*, and so on. Also, children learn that combining *her* with *self* produces *herself*, and so the rule is generalized to combine *his* with *self* to produce *hisself*. Almost every child makes this particular mistake. Adding *-s* or *-es* produces the plural, and so this rule leads to *mouses, mooses, gooses* and *fishes*.

In 1957 Noam Chomsky revolutionized thinking about language learning with his description of **generative grammar,** which includes the learning of **transformational rules.** Briefly, Chomsky defined **deep structure** roughly as the meaning or intent you wish to convey. Deep structures are the same worldwide (i.e., they are **linguistic universals**) in the sense that, for example, a person can be thirsty and want a drink of water regardless of the native language. The **surface structure** consists of the exact words spoken or heard. A person is said to use transformational rules to literally transform the deep structures (intended meanings) into a grammatically correct sentence, or surface structure. Space will not pemit an extended examination of Chomsky's famous transformational rules, but consider these simple examples based on Chomsky (1965):

1. An intended message in deep structure (S) may be transformed into a noun phrase (NP) and a verb phrase (VP).
2. A noun phrase may be transformed into a noun (N; *Joe, car, street, apple,* etc.), plus an optional article (A; *a, an, the,* etc.), and an optional adjective (Adj; *big, red, ripe,* etc.).
3. A verb phrase may be transformed into a verb (V; *runs, works, squashes,* etc.), plus an optional adverb (Adv; *quickly, quietly,* etc.), and an optional noun phrase (NP).

These rules alone—and there are many, many more dealing with verb tenses, subject verb agreement, negatives, interrogatives, etc.—would enable a young child or adult to produce the grammatically correct sentences "Joe works" or "The big car quickly squashed the ripe apple." In the diagram note how the rules are applied. Parentheses indicate optional transformations.

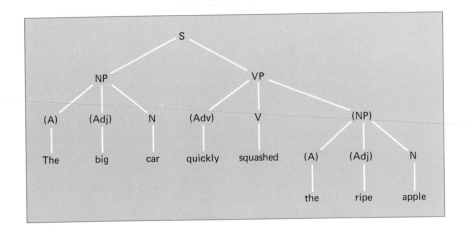

It is rules like the three just listed which are acquired as one main process of language development. It is the inborn capability and motivation for language which enables children to learn linguistic rules. McNeill (1970) described the language-learning child as possessing an imaginary internal machine, a *Language Acquisition Device* (LAD). The LAD (a) receives language input, (b) analyzes it, aided by an existing knowledge of language and a built-in capability for linguistic analysis, and (c) derives further ideas, hypotheses, and rules about the nature of language (see also Chomsky, 1965; Lenneberg, 1967).

As a related concept, we should distinguish between **linguistic competence** and **linguistic performance.** Linguistic competence is the child's language ability, his or her knowledge of linguistic rules. Linguistic performance is the language the child actually produces, his or her use of the linguistic rules. Normally, linguistic competence is more advanced than actual linguistic performance, which means that most children can understand words and phrases which they cannot yet use in spoken language. One clear implication is that language performance is not a good measure of overall linguistic ability.

Early Speech

At birth, the infant can only *cry.* Parents often can distinguish between hunger cries, fear cries, and pain cries (Wolff, 1966). For the next few months we also hear *cooing*—one-syllable sounds usually including a long *u* (*moo, roo, woo, doo,* etc.), but sometimes other vowel sounds as well. *Babbling*—strings of fairly complex but utterly unintelligible syllables—begins at about six or seven months.

Around one year of age, give or take a couple of months, the infant utters its first clear, single words: *Mama, dada, ball* (or "baw"), *doggie* (or "goggie"), *milk, juice, byebye, allgone* and *no* are common. The child now uses considerably fewer phonemes than in the babbling stage. By about 15 months the child has roughly a 50-word vocabulary, consisting of familiar action verbs (e.g., *go, walk, hit, drink*) and nouns (e.g., *milk, cookie, mama, shoe, TV*). These words represent actions, events, and objects in the child's environment that have demanded the child's attention (Dale, 1973). Indeed, it seems that in this one-word stage the child is busily learning words for things that have been enactively experienced, emotionally felt, or which capture the child's attention. Emotional content may be expressed, for example, by a loud and emphatic "Milk!" or "No!," signaling strong feelings of urgency, while softer pronunciations convey a message of contentment.

Interestingly, in the one-word stage the child becomes extremely adept at picking single words which convey a great deal of information. For example, "Byebye" may mean "I would like to go somewhere," "Hurt" means "I am injured," and "ball" usually means "get me that ball." The term **holophrase** was coined to refer to the child's single word which actually serves as an entire phrase or sentence.

Brown's Stages of Language Development

Psycholinguist Roger Brown (1973) studied the speech of young children and identified five stages of language development. Each stage is based on the average number of words per sentence, from a sample of 50 to 100 sentences for each child. The *mean length of utterance* (MLU) in each stage is:

Stage	MLU
1	2.0
2	2.0 to 2.5
3	2.5 to 3.0
4	3.0 to 3.5
5	3.5 to 4.0

Now it would be trivial to simply tape record a bunch of children's utterances, hire a graduate student to tediously compute the average sentence length for each child, and then ceremoniously assign each child to the "correct" stage. As with other analyses of developmental stages, there are other interesting language phenomena which are related to the five MLU stages. For example, Brown's MLU is a much better index of language development than is the child's chronological age. Children may differ six to nine months in age, yet be in the same stage of language development, that is, they use similar patterns of speech with similar rule systems.

Turning to characteristics of children in each stage, in Stage 1 (MLU = 2 words) the sentence length actually varies, with the child producing one-word, two-word, three-word and a few four-word sentences. Sentences like "Car broke," "Daddy gone," and "Mama want ball" sound like the clipped speech used in a telegram or classified ad, leading Brown to dub these phrases **telegraphic speech.** McNeill (1970) noted that children in the two-word stage of language development use a relatively small number of **pivot** words—such as *more, big, go, sit, see, my, hit,* and *there*—in combination with a larger number of **open** words, usually nouns, such as *milk, cookie, juice, mommy, daddy, ball,* and others. The child thus will say "more cookie," "more juice," "more milk," "see cookie," "see mommy," "see ball," "daddy go," "cookie go," and so on.

Note that such two-word sentences already reflect fairly sophisticated semantic concepts and linguistic rules. For example the child demonstrates mastery of the semantic relations of *identification* ("see truck"), *repetition* ("more cookie"), *nonexistence* ("allgone ball"), plus the correct pairing of *agents with actions* ("daddy spank"), *actions with objects* ("hit ice cream"), *actions with locations* ("sit floor"), and others (see Slobin, 1972).

In Stage 2 (MLU = 2.0 to 2.5), the sentence length ranges from one to four or five words. Now the child begins to use proper *inflections*—proper word endings that express grammatical relations. Especially, the child pluralizes nouns (*trucks* instead of *truck*) and begins to use a past tense of verbs. Such past tenses as *goed, hitted* or *eated* stem from an *overregulation* of linguistic rules; there is no allowance for exceptions. The child also begins to use prepositions (*in, on, by,* etc.) and articles (*a, the,* etc.) in appropriate places.

In Stages 3, 4, and 5 (MLU's of 2.5 to 3.0, 3.0 to 3.5, and 3.5 to 4.0, respectively), the length of sentences obviously increases. Also, the child masters important new linguistic rules, for example, *negative* forms ("The ball is not here"), *interrogative* forms ("Where is daddy?"), *imperative* ("Give me the candy!"), *relative clauses* ("The man who was here went home"), and *compound phrases* ("Mommy went to the store and bought me some ice cream"). The use of each of these requires the mastery of complex linguistic rules, rules for transforming deep structures into appropriate surface structures.

Beyond Stage 5, linguistic competence and performance continues to improve. The child uses longer sentences and may combine many of the above forms in one sentence (e.g., "Did daddy come home and not bring my bike?"). There are fewer childish rules (*hitted, goed, mouses, gooses*) and fewer ungrammatical constructions. Children become able to speak more precisely as their linguistic rules become more adultlike. They also learn to better comprehend the meaning of complex sentences, that is, to extract the deep structure from the surface structure. Sometimes, extremely fine discriminations are required as in, for example, "The dog is eager to see" vs. "The dog is easy to see."

Critical Period: The Child as Linguistic Genius

We end our discussion of language development with a comment on the profoundly remarkable language-learning talent of children. From about age 2 to around age 6 or 7 every child becomes a "linguistic genius" (Chukovsky, 1968). The child is in a *critical period* for language development, possessing a unique linguistic ability that—perhaps due to a changing brain structure (Lenneberg, 1967)—he or she will never possess again. The child rapidly learns vocabulary, pronunciations, semantic relations, and morphological and syntactical rules. In a bilingual environment the child will easily become fluent in both languages, much to the envy of adults who struggle for years to master pidgin Spanish or German.

As for speaking itself, a fine-muscle activity, the child demonstrates a phenomenally precise control of the breathing apparatus, diaphragm, vocal cords, mouth, and tongue. Such precision is not evident anywhere else in the behavior of the stumbling, spilling child who is unable to button buttons, zip zippers, or slide shoes on the correct feet. The talent is uniquely verbal.

TO IMPROVE
YOUR TEACHING

As we noted in Chapter 3, you must become thoroughly acquainted with the developmental characteristics of the children or adolescents you intend to teach. This knowledge will help you recognize situations in which students are developmentally unable to understand a principle or a viewpoint and may simply memorize the material on a rote basis. Many principles learned in this fashion are meaningless and soon forgotten (Chapter 8).

A good grasp of Piaget's stages of cognitive development also will help you recognize individual differences in developmental stages. The description of a child as "slow," "immature," or "retarded" should take on new meaning to you. The process of developmental growth includes not only improved intelligence, but qualitatively different thinking capabilities. There also are corresponding changes in moral thinking (Chapter 3) and in the related ability to take another person's perspective. Perhaps there would be less adolescent crime and violence if delinquent teenagers were able to comprehend their actions from the point of view of the victim.

Most importantly, Piaget's stages have direct implications for teaching, managing learning, and preparing curriculum materials. The early preoperational child, for example, learns best by directly interacting with materials and directly resolving conflicts and problems. This child does not gain much from formal instruction, cannot readily memorize mathematical facts, and even will have difficulty following instructions (Elkind, 1976). The concrete operational years of the elementary school are a time for skill building. Vocabulary, reading, writing, and math are quite within the associative capabilities of the concrete-operational thinker. However, many complex "if . . . then" or "either . . . or" constructions must wait. The concrete thinker can memorize such statements, but will not achieve a full connotative grasp until the formal operational stage (Elkind, 1976). Always try to tie new concepts—especially confusing, abstract verbal ones—to the student's existing knowledge. And remember that language development is closely tied to cognitive development; the child cannot sensibly verbalize what he or she cannot deal with mentally.

As noted in this chapter, combining content and skill areas, when possible, encourages the interrelatedness of knowledge schemata, a point which Piaget emphasized strongly.

Adolescence, of course, includes not only the high-level reasoning and perspective-taking of the formal operational stage, but many problems of self-consciousness and feelings of low self-worth. The teacher of junior high and high school students should look very carefully into the dynamics of adolescent development. You will not be able to figure it all out on the job.

The fact that children form and use grammatical rules should help you understand the frequent "I gotted a bunny," "He did it hisself," "Eddy runned to the gym," and "Look at my foots." If you teach language arts, you will be helping students consciously learn grammatical rules, and you will be emphasizing those critical exceptions which make correct adult English.

SUMMARY

Jean Piaget was a precocious youth, an authority on mollusks before finishing secondary school. His famous set of invariant stages describes developmental change in (among other things) logical, mathematical, and abstract thinking, in imagination, language, discrimination and classification abilities, and in egocentric thinking, role-taking, and moral thinking.

In the sensorimotor stage (0–2 years) a baby's activities initially are largely reflexive. He or she soon coordinates perceptions with motor movements. Object permanence develops. Experience with objects leads to the formation of mental and motor schemata. A deprived environment retards cognitive growth.

The preoperational stage (2–7 years) often is subdivided into the preoperational (2–4 years) and intuitive (4–7 years) phases. The earlier phase sees a huge spurt in language development, egocentrism, the ability to classify according to one criterion, and deferred imitation.

During the intuitive phase, egocentrism decreases and the idea of number appears. One famous characteristic is the child's inability to conserve mass, weight, volume, or number. Another trait is animistic thinking. Phenomenalistic causality, in which a first event causes a second event, and nominal realism, thinking that a name is part of the object, also appear at this time. The improved language ability of the older preoperational child allows him or her to use experience to solve problems and to anticipate events. The child's reality includes the past, present, and future.

In the stage of concrete operations (7–11 years), thinking is about or with representations of concrete objects, not abstract ideas or symbols. Amusing logical flaws (e.g., failure to conserve) disappear. The child understands units of measurement, along with lots of social rules. The ability to see "sameness" and "differentness" in the same object leads to the common phenomenon of collecting things. The child understands subclassifications and multiple classifications.

Logical relationships are understood at this stage—for example, as demonstrated in seriation ability. Rules, however, are seen as fixed and unchangeable. The concrete-operational child also tends to interpret statements literally. Further, his or her ideas or hypotheses about something are often taken as facts, not possibilities. Finally, another characteristic of the concrete-operational child is reversibility of thinking, the ability to reverse actions.

In the final stage of formal operations, beginning about 11–14 years, the individual can think abstractly and logically, achieving a reality much like an adult. Metathinking, or thinking about thinking, is now possible. Adolescent idealism, including concepts of "perfect parents" or a "perfect society," is common. The ability to deal with higher mathematics and metaphorical thinking also is possible. Further, a time sense unfolds.

One often troublesome formal operations ability is the capacity to think about what other people are thinking, leading to a form of adolescent egocentrism, which includes a "personal fable" (belief in uniqueness), an "imaginary audience" (belief that everyone is concerned about the adolescent), strong self-consciousness, conformity, and sometimes depression and even suicide.

Some recent authors have suggested that there may be a more fully developed stage of formal operational thinking which occurs later than Piaget's stage of formal operations.

To Piaget, the biologically adaptive process of cognitive change involves equilibration. When a problem is encountered, one's equilibrium is disturbed. The resolution of the problem (equilibration) restores equilibrium and results in a new, improved cognitive organization—a higher stage of development. Assimilation is a mechanism of adaptation in which a new concept is fitted into the existing cognitive organization; accommodation is the alteration of that cognitive organization to accommodate the new idea or experience.

The ability to take another person's perspective is closely related to the child's Piagetian stage of development. Selman described five stages in role-taking ability, from the preoperational *egocentric* stage, in which the child is unaware that others have different viewpoints (Stage 0), to the formal operational *social and conventional system*, in which the child shows deep interpersonal awareness and can even think about and compare different perspectives (Stage 4).

The clear educational implication of Piaget's brilliant analysis of stages of cognitive development is that teaching must be coordinated with the child's developmental level. For example, preoperational children need to explore and discover to gain practical knowledge and intelligence. At the concrete-operational level Piagetian teaching recommends the combining of content areas in order to foster the interrelatedness of schemata. Also, a spiral curriculum should aid in the development of differentiated and integrated mental schemata. Problems, questions, and challenges will create disequilibration, leading students to reason, accommodate, and assimilate—and achieve higher levels of cognitive development.

Jerome Bruner's three stages in cognitive development are three ways of forming mental representations of the world. With the enactive mode, motor behavior leads to motoric representations—what the infant does is what he or she thinks. The iconic mode (age 2–3 years) includes mental imagery and other sensory representations, which allow the child to reproduce things which are not present and to extrapolate and make predictions. With language comes representation in the symbolic mode, permitting the accumulation of vast amounts of information and the capacity for flexible manipulation.

Bruner's model also endorses the need for manipulation and self-discovery in early years, building a strong base for later verbal and symbolic forms of teaching and learning. Bruner's famous claim that ". . . any subject can be taught effectively in some intellectually honest form to any child at any stage of development" would seem to demand close attention to the capabilities present at the stages of development identified by Piaget and Bruner.

Language development is closely tied to a child's level of cognitive development; a child will not say what he or she cannot think.

The behavioristic approach to language includes the formation of mental associations, reinforcement, punishment, modeling, and viewing sentences as stimulus-response word chains. The theory does not adequately explain the production of novel sentences.

The current view emphasizes language learning as the learning of rules, phonological rules, morphological rules, syntactical rules, and Chomsky's transformational rules. Transformational rules transform deep structures (meanings) into surface structures (sentences). A hypothetical "language acquisition device" receives and analyzes input and derives further linguistic rules. Linguistic performance lags behind linguistic competence (language ability).

Early speech progresses from crying to cooing to babbling to the one-word stage. A holophrase is a one-word utterance containing the meaning of a phrase or sentence.

Brown's five MLU stages include telegraphic speech and the use of pivot and open words in his Stage 1 (MLU = 2.0 words). Stage 2 includes the use of inflections and proper word endings. Stages 3, 4, and 5 see the development of rules for negatives, interrogatives, use of relative clauses, and so on.

From age 2 to 6 or 7 the child is an incredible linguistic genius.

TOPICS FOR THOUGHT AND DISCUSSION

1. Think about your own adolescent years. Were you self-conscious? Were you too much of a conformist? Did you have an "imaginary audience"?
2. Now that you can understand the perspectives of others, how do you think some of the "outcasts" in your elementary school felt? As a teacher, do you think that "empathy training" can help elementary students understand the feelings of ignored students (who may be shy, disabled, unattractive, not too bright, etc.). See Chapter 13.

3. Is teaching always aimed at raising students' levels of cognitive development? Is cognitive development in the Piagetian "stage" sense affected? Why or why not?

4. Do colleges fail to integrate knowledge areas, creating knowledge "schemas" which should be, but are not, related to one another? Can you think of some solutions?

PROJECTS

1. Visit an elementary school. Try some of the Piagetian tasks (conservation, seriation, classification) with students at two or three grade levels. Is Piaget right? Are there exceptions?

2. Do the same with role-taking problems. See if students can take another's perspective in viewing a physical object or a social event. You may wish to use one or more of Chandler's (1973) cartoons.

3. Examine one or two elementary school textbooks to see if the required thinking skills are appropriate to the age level (see Elkind, 1973, or other Piaget-based education texts).

4. Plan a lesson (or unit) in which at least a half-dozen knowledge areas are combined.

5. Survey books applying Piaget's thinking to teaching. Itemize a list of principles for Piagetian teaching at the grade level you expect to teach.

6. If you visit an elementary school, ask teachers which grammatical mistakes are the most common, that is, which incorrect childish rules are the most difficult to correct. Do they have good solutions?

RECOMMENDED READING

Brown, R. *A first language: The early stages.* Cambridge, Mass.: Harvard University Press, 1973.

Bruner, J. S. *Toward a theory of instruction.* Cambridge, Mass.: Harvard University Press, 1967.

Cowan, P. A. *Piaget with feeling.* New York: Holt, Rinehart & Winston, 1978.

Dale, P. S. *Language development,* second edition. New York: Holt, Rinehart & Winston, 1973.

Elkind, D. *Child development and education: A Piagetian perspective.* New York: Oxford University Press, 1976.

Flavell, J. H. *Cognitive development.* Englewood Cliffs, N.J.: Prentice-Hall, 1977.

Kamii, C. An application of Piaget's theory to the conceptualization of a preschool curriculum. In R. F. Parker (ed.). *The preschool: Exploring early childhood programs.* Boston: Allyn & Bacon, 1972.

Looft, W. R., and W. H. Bartz. Animism revived. In G. A. Davis and T. F. Warren (eds.), *Psychology of education.* Lexington, Mass.: Heath, 1974, pp. 155–169.

McNeill, D. The development of language. In P. H. Mussen (ed.), *Carmichael's manual of child psychology,* third edition, vol. 1. New York: Wiley, 1970.

Yussen, S. R., and J. W. Santrock. *Child development,* second edition. Dubuque, Iowa: W. C. Brown, 1982.

PSYCHOLOGY OF LEARNING

PART III

Learning: Theory and Principles

5

Why study basic principles of learning? / Two kinds of conditioning / Classical conditioning / Instrumental conditioning / Social learning theory / Behaviorism and cognitive psychology / To improve your teaching / Summary / Topics for thought and discussion / Projects / Recommended reading

WHY STUDY BASIC PRINCIPLES OF LEARNING?

Research psychologists interested in the dynamics of learning and memory accept the proposition that the large majority of our cognitive, affective, and motor behavior is *learned*. Therefore, they have sought to understand human behavior by studying how that behavior was acquired. For a hundred years psychologists have studied basic principles of learning, conditioning, and memory as a key to understanding human behavior.

Chances are excellent that you already have some acquaintance with popular learning concepts. For example, you probably know that the Russian physiologist Ivan Pavlov conditioned dogs to salivate to the sound of a bell by pairing the bell with the dog's dinner, thus giving birth to the concept of classical or Pavlovian conditioning. You also probably know that B. F. Skinner taught hungry rats to press a bar for a food pellet, leading eventually to a popular knowledge of the effects of rewards and punishments in controlling behavior. Principles and processes derived from studies rooted in the classical conditioning of Pavlov and the "operant conditioning" procedures of Skinner and others have contributed greatly to our understanding of human learning, thinking, remembering, and behaving.

The teacher who becomes acquainted with these principles and processes of learning will better understand student learning and behavior, will be better equipped to control and manage students in the classroom, and may even become a more effective transmitter of knowledge and skills. The principles and dynamics of learning are at work every day in every classroom.

Learning Theory and Instructional Theory

Learning theory is primarily *descriptive*. Research and theory in the psychology of learning have tried to describe conditions, processes, and dynamics which influence learning and which control behavior. Instructional theory, however, is *prescriptive*. It attempts to prescribe what the educator can or should do to optimize learning and reach educational goals. As with many clear-cut distinctions, there is overlap between learning theory and instructional theory. For example, some instructional theory prescriptions, such as behavior modification, token reinforcement strategies, and programmed learning (Chapter 6) come to us directly from descriptive learning theory. Also, Ausubel's instructional theory (Chapter 8) includes a description of the process of learning. As we will see in Chapter 12, however, most instructional theories and models are not rooted in traditional learning theory.

TWO KINDS OF CONDITIONING

After some 100 years of conditioning dogs, cats, rats, monkeys, and sometimes people, most experimental psychologists have reached the conclusion that there are two basic, identifiably different, and irreducibly simple types of learning: **Pavlovian (or classical) conditioning** and **instrumental conditioning.** An argument can easily be made that your most complex thoughts and actions are merely combinations of these two simple forms of learning (e.g., see Staats, 1968). Most of this chapter is devoted to explaining how a conditioning-oriented psychologist thinks. That is, we will try to explain how seemingly complex behavior may be "reduced" to comprehendible principles of conditioning and learning—relationships among stimuli, responses, and reinforcements.

CLASSICAL CONDITIONING

Pavlov (1927) repeatedly rang a bell at the same instant he fed his dog. After a number of such stimulus-stimulus (bell-food) pairings, the not-so-dumb animal came to expect food when it heard the bell. The dog quite naturally began salivating to the sound of the bell, even when it was not followed by food. To the dog, the bell became a signal that food was about to be served. Therefore, the name **signal learning** sometimes is used interchangeably with classical conditioning.

The important circumstance for classical conditioning was the *contiguity* of the bell stimulus with the food stimulus. They occurred together, and so they became mentally associated. Thus we have two more equivalent terms, **contiguity learning** and **stimulus-stimulus** (S-S) learning, along with signal learning, Pavlovian conditioning, and classical conditioning. B. F. Skinner coined yet a sixth name for classical conditioning, **respondent conditioning,** because the dog "responded to" the bell stimulus controlled by Pavlov. Most psychologists prefer **classical conditioning,** with the understanding that the other five terms are virtually synonymous.

The dog food (actually meat powder) elicited the salivation response without any training, and so the food was called the **unconditioned stimulus** (UCS). The salivation is the **unconditioned response** (UCR; see Figure 5.1). The bell elicited no particular response (other than a "What-is-it?" reaction)

Figure 5.1
Diagram of classical conditioning.

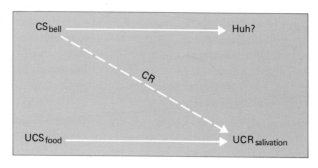

until after the conditioning, and so the bell was called a **conditioned stimulus** (CS).* The learned salivation response to the bell alone is the famous **conditioned response** (CR) or **conditioned reflex.** The latter term is used to emphasize the automatic "reflex" nature of some conditioned responses, such as salivation, fear responses, and even some word associations. (For example, *up* automatically elicits _____.)

Conditioning in Advertising

Do you remember ever hearing a commercial like this? "Can't sleep? Try Soporific! Can't sleep? Try Soporific! Can't sleep? Try Soporific!" and so on. Someone may have asked a conditioning-oriented psychologist how to get people to buy Soporific for sleeplessness, and of course the psychologist's answer would be to condition people to associate Soporific with their inability to sleep. You can do this simply by exposing the "learner" to the two stimuli in contiguity: "Can't sleep? Try Soporific!" Actually, all advertising tries to "condition" the public to mentally associate its products with, for example, dashing macho masculinity (trucks, cigarettes, aftershave lotion), romance (toothpaste and mouthwash), pleasure and excitement (beer and more cigarettes), success and prestige (big cars), saving money (little cars), beauty (soap and make-up), or good health (breakfast cereals, vitamins).

Repetition

A number of learning principles evolved from Pavlov's research. He noted that the strength of the conditioned reflex—measured by the number of drops of saliva—increased with the number of stimulus-stimulus pairings. This was the first scientific demonstration that *repetition* systematically strengthens learning.

Extinction

If the bell were repeatedly presented without the food, the conditioned salivation to the bell would diminish and eventually stop. We would say that the response was extinguished; the process itself is called **extinction.**

Extinction is not the same as forgetting. Ivan's dog might have remembered that the bell *used to be* followed by lunch. However, after hearing the disappointing bell all day without receiving the meat powder, the dog learned to ignore the bell and suppress the useless salivation. Extinction might include some actual forgetting, eventually, but not necessarily.

In the eighth-grade classroom of Mrs. Patience Timeclock, the 3:15 dismissal bell used to signal students to jump up and dash out the door, a

---

* Some writers prefer to call the bell a "conditional stimulus," probably because, strictly speaking, the bell is not a "conditioned stimulus" until after the training is completed.

virtual conditioned reflex. Then she began asking students to wait until she dismissed them and then to walk quietly. For a few days, the bell stimulated many false starts and dashes, then everyone learned to comply. The jumping and dashing were not forgotten, but they were extinguished.

Overlearning

Back in Pavlov's lab, the greater the degree of original learning (that is, the more times the food stimulus was paired with the bell stimulus) the longer it would take to extinguish the well-learned conditioned response. Thus hatched the principle of **overlearning** as a means of slowing the rate of extinction. Overlearning also reduces forgetting, as every piano player or dog trainer well knows.

Spontaneous Recovery

Let's assume it is one day after Pavlov's dog's conditioned salivation response was extinguished. Our cooperative dog again is strapped into the experimental apparatus. What happens when Pavlov rings the bell? Right, more salivation. After a rest period, an extinguished response normally will **spontaneously recover.** Of course, with no additional contiguous presentations of the meat stimulus (UCS) with the bell stimulus (CS), the conditioned reflex (CR) will quickly extinguish again. And again, and again, and again, until no spontaneous recovery occurs.

Back in Mrs. Timeclock's classroom, Arnold Absent had been gone for two weeks. On his first day back the 3:15 bell sent him flying out the door and halfway to his locker while Mrs. Timeclock was trying to think of the word "Wait!" His jumping and dashing had spontaneously recovered.

Generalization and Discrimination

In some of his experiments with the dogs, Pavlov used tuning forks to present either a high tone or a low tone in a random sequence. Meat powder would follow only, say, each high tone. At first, the dog innocently salivated to both tones. We would say the dog **generalized,** which means that the response given to one stimulus also is given to a similar stimulus. Such **stimulus generalization** is not unreasonable. Eventually, the dog forms a **discrimination,** salivating to the high tone, but not to the low tone. Both generalization and discrimination are necessary adaptive phenomena.

Examples of generalization and discrimination are countless. Whenever students apply a math or chemistry skill to a new problem—correctly or incorrectly—they are generalizing. Students generalize whenever they identify new objects as members of a class; for example, if rats, mice, and rabbits are rodents, then guinea pigs and hamsters probably are too.

Discriminations are difficult whenever stimuli are very similar, but must be associated with different ideas or responses. For example, most

young children have to look more than twice to discriminate *p* from *q* and *b* from *d*. Which is the correct spelling, *knowledgable* or *knowledgeable*? How old were you before you could correctly discriminate Theodore Roosevelt and Franklin D. Roosevelt?

Classical Conditioning in Language and Thought

The basic idea of classical conditioning may be stated simply as: Things which occur together tend to become associated. Therefore, with just a little imagination we may see many word meanings and word associations as instances of simple classical conditioning. For example, as we saw in Chapter 4, word meanings may be acquired through the pairing of the object, say a pencil, with the word *pencil;* or a picture of a lion with the word *lion.* Affective meanings also become associated with particular words—for example, by pairing the word *candy* with a sweet taste, *hot* with a bad burn, or *Mickey Mouse* with cartoons and humor. Word-word associations also are learned. For example, the word *salt* elicits the word *pepper, up* elicits *down, haunted* elicits *ghosts,* and so on, because these word pairs have been experienced in contiguity and therefore became associated.

Associations among words are much more complex than simple word-word relations. We have **divergent associations** in which, for example, the word *salt* elicits not just *pepper*, but *table, shaker, white, mines, sea,* and so on. Associations also can be **convergent,** as when several stimulus words elicit the same response. For example, *lion, tiger, leopard, panther,* and *Tabby* and *Morris* all elicit the word ＿＿＿(see Figure 5.2).

Actually, each word in our language elicits other words and meanings, and each of these is associated with still more words, ideas, and meanings. Many classic-minded psychologists use the label "associative network" to describe the fantastic web of mental associations among words, connotative meanings, affective meanings, concepts, and images.

Note that we are discussing not only word associations, but real human *thinking.* If you "think about," say, New York City, you recall words, ideas, and events associated with New York City (Times Square, Broadway, Wall Street, United Nations, Central Park, and so on). Since the time of Aristotle, philosophers speculating on the workings of the mind had observed that "things which occur together" tend to become mentally associated. Aristotle called this his **law of contiguity.** In the 16th century, Thomas Hobbes wrote "From St. Andrew the mind runneth to St. Peter, and from St. Peter to

Figure 5.2
Examples of divergent and convergent associations. "S" refers to the stimulus word(s), and "R" to the response word(s).

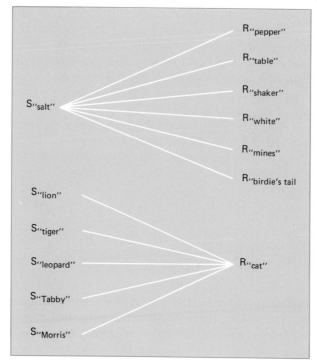

stone," which shows that an apparently disjointed and spontaneous chain of ideas actually follows the lawful law of contiguity. In Hobbes' experience, *St. Andrew* often contiguously occurred with *St. Peter*, and *St. Peter* with *stone*.

Pavlov himself argued that the mental association of the philosophers was one and the same as his conditioned reflex (Pavlov, 1976). Furthermore, the development of such mental associations follows the same principles of contiguity, repetition, overlearning, generalization, discrimination, and extinction, as does the development of a conditioned salivation response.

The associationist view of thinking has persisted in psychology for a very long time. "Associationism" is not a complete picture of human mental life, but the concept is alive and well and often informative.

Behavior Therapy and Desensitization Therapy   Many clinical psychologists and some psychiatrists have used a classical conditioning model in treating phobias and other behaviors considered undesirable or maladaptive (Eysenck, 1960; Masserman, 1943; Wolpe, 1969). The following newspaper column describes one commercial conditioning device, originally invented by psychologist O. H. Mowrer in 1938:

> *Dear Abby,*
>
> *I read your article about the thirty-one year old married man who still wets the bed, and I sure felt sorry for him because I'm 15 now, and I used to do the same thing until two years ago. Then my parents sent for something they saw advertised in a Sears catalog. It's like a rubber bed sheet with a buzzer connected to it. I'd sleep on that, and the minute it started to get wet, the buzzer would go off, and I'd wake up and go to the bathroom.*
>
> *At first I had to change the bed sheets, but after a while, the buzzer seemed to wake me up in time to stay dry all night.*
>
> *I hope you print this, but please don't print my name, or everybody in Worthington, Minn., will tease me. Just sign it "How Dry I Am."*
>
> *Dear Dry:*
>
> *Trust me! You're nice to want to share your solution with others.*
>
> (Copyrighted by Abigail Van Buren. Reprinted by permission.)

In conditioning terms, the buzzer is an unconditioned stimulus which easily elicits a waking-up response (unconditioned response). If the child's stretched bladder, an internal and very urgent stimulus, is paired with the buzzer sufficiently often, then the full bladder (or "urgency") will become a conditioned stimulus eliciting a conditioned wake-up response. At least this is the hope of frazzled mothers who would rather sleep than change soggy bed sheets at 4:00 A.M.

The conditioning-based treatment of drug addiction and alcoholism also has followed a simple conditioning formula. With addicts, a needle-in-the-arm stimulus has been paired with a strong shock, hoping to condition an aversion to needles and drugs. With alcoholism, the drug antabuse causes the patient to become nauseated if he drinks alcohol. The strategy obviously is intended to decrease the joy and increase the pain associated with even light drinking.

Psychologists and psychiatrists extinguish phobias by following a slightly modified classical conditioning model which Joseph Wolpe (1969) dubbed **desensitization training.** A formal desensitization procedure begins with the preparation of a **hierarchy of fears,** a list of disturbing stimuli ranked from least to most frightening. For example, with snake phobia the hierarchy might include thinking about a small garter snake, seeing a picture of a snake, viewing a small caged snake, viewing a larger caged snake, handling small snakes, to perhaps even wrapping a boa constrictor around one's neck. The desensitization therapist would ask the patient to sit quietly and relax. The patient would remain relaxed and reassured as the therapist leads him or her through the hierarchy of fears, beginning with the least frightening. Eventually, the patient can remain calm and relaxed while confronting the most frightening aspect of the phobia. A great many individuals have been cured of phobias through desensitization procedures.

Classical Conditioning in the Classroom	We have already emphasized that learning principles, including classical conditioning, tend to be descriptive; they describe human learning and behavior, but tend not to prescribe how to improve classroom learning. Indeed, the instructor faced with teaching American history to 25 lively seventh graders will find that the practical use of Pavlovian conditioning definitely is limited. Teaching involves much more than just the contiguous presentation of ideas and objects which are supposed to become associated with each other. However, such concepts as contiguity, repetition, over-learning, generalization, discrimination, extinction, and spontaneous recovery run through all forms of human learning, including classroom learning.

Classical conditioning research tells us that affective responses such as fear, anger, and likes and dislikes can be acquired very rapidly. However, the removal (extinction) of such emotional responses usually is a slower, more gradual process. This means that a teacher who is unpleasant may have a very difficult time extinguishing students' bad reactions to him or her. Also, negative reactions associated with frustrating assignments can last for years.

As a review, let's consider a few possible occurrences of classical conditioning in the typical, everyday urban school. Ten-year-old student Claude Klutske chipped a tooth and cut his lip while hurriedly slurping from the drinking fountain. He remembers the incident every time he passes that fountain. Fortunately, he generalized to other fountains and now slurps very cautiously.

Sally Square-root used to receive rotten grades in junior high algebra, which upset her. She doesn't take math classes anymore.

Monty Miniwork used to study multiplication tables until he could barely recite them correctly just once. No overlearning for him. His multiplication tables were quickly forgotten, but fortunately he now carries a pocket calculator.

First-grader Alphie learned that the word *rough* was to be associated with the sound "ruff." He did not yet discriminate among "-ough" words, reading *though, through,* thorough, trough, and thought as "thuff," "thruff," "thoruff," "truff," and "thufft." His teacher needed to pay special attention to situations involving difficult discriminations.

High school teacher Pauline Pedant gave an essay exam on the American Revolution. On many of her students' papers, the left margin contained a list of associations to the stimulus question, which were then developed into proper written prose.

Sophie Sponge overheard her teachers say that all Slobbovians are grubby, lazy, smell of garlic, and have funny ears. She never liked Slobbovians after that, although she never met one.

Teacher Carl Careful wants students to respond quickly and appropriately to safety signals. He required his students to practice responding to fire bells and tornado warnings. He also showed them how splintered banisters, frayed electrical wiring, excavations, railroad signals, and traffic lights should "signal" cautious behavior.

On Monday, teacher Dorothy Doright corrected a mistake made by geography ace Matthew Mapreader: The capitol of California is Sacramento, not San Francisco. On Tuesday's test, San Francisco spontaneously recovered as the capitol of California. "I guess we needed more repetition, overlearning, and discrimination," concluded Doright.

INSTRUMENTAL CONDITIONING

Instrumental conditioning is the second basic type of learning. The essence of instrumental conditioning is that reward strengthens behavior, while punishment weakens it. Not mysterious at all. Other names for instrumental conditioning are **operant conditioning** and **stimulus-response (S-R) learning.**

You do not need to be a psychologist or Sherlock Holmes to understand how rewards and punishment control behavior. Parents, teachers, police, and porpoise trainers have been dishing out spankings, threats, hugs, grades, praise, parking tickets, kisses, lashes, money and dead fish for a long time in order to teach the appropriate responses to the appropriate stimuli, whether it's hanging up coats, paying attention, feeding the meter, or jumping through a hoop. The idea has obvious credibility and appeal.

As an historical note, Edward L. Thorndike (1911), who was a protege of philosopher William James and one of the earliest American learning theorists, summarized the actions of rewards and punishments in his famous **Law of Effect:** Responses leading to satisfying effects (i.e., to rewards or "satisfiers") will be strengthened; responses leading to annoying effects (punishment or "annoyers") will be weakened.

B. F. Skinner, easily the most influential living psychologist, coined the name "operant conditioning."* The prototype operant conditioning situation includes a hungry white rat and a Skinner box, a small cage in which a food pellet drops into a cup each time a lever is pressed. Having just arrived from the rat plant, Mr. rat initially knows nothing about pressing

---

* As noted earlier in this chapter, Skinner used *respondent conditioning* to label Pavlovian conditioning, implicitly accepting the wisdom of distinguishing between the two elementary forms of learning.

levers for pellets. Psychologist Skinner sits quietly near his box with a finger on the remote control button for dispensing pellets. He rewards the rat for getting closer and closer to the lever. Before long, Skinner rewards the rat only for sniffing, biting, nosing, scratching, or placing his little paw on the lever. The rat soon will accidentally press the lever with enough force to release a pellet. After a little more preliminary bumbling, the rat will learn to press the lever with confidence and dash to the food cup for his reward. Skinner used the word **shaping** to describe this successive-approximations method of rewarding only behaviors which come closer and closer to the desired final behavior.

Beyond Freedom and Dignity: B. F. Skinner

Skinner built a very comprehensive theory of behavior which evolves about the simple idea that behavior is controlled by its reinforcing consequences (Skinner, 1938; see also 1948, 1954, 1968, 1973). As outlined in his best-selling *Beyond Freedom and Dignity* (Skinner, 1971), a very, very large segment of everyday human behavior is shaped and controlled by its consequences. Such environmental control is so pervasive, argued Skinner, that the idea of *free will* is a fiction. Everything you do, he proposed, is shaped and controlled by rewards and punishments. *Dignity*, according to Skinner, refers to the seeking of credit and recognition for our accomplishments—recognition we do not deserve since our meritorious good deeds were shaped by outside forces in the first place. In an earlier book, *Walden II*, Skinner (1948) depicted an ideal Skinnerian society in which community members did not bother to say "Thank you" for favors and services. Since the behavior of the good-deed doer had been shaped earlier, he or she really was not responsible for doing favors and therefore should not receive a "Thank you."

Could Skinner possibly have an argument? Let's see if his idea fits. Perhaps you are carefully studying this book in order to score high on a test (a reward) and to receive a high grade (another reward). You wish to avoid a low grade (a punishment). You might be taking this course so that your college will reward you with a degree—a very nice reward. You probably want the degree so you can get a high-status job (a reward) which pays lots of reward. Well, more reward than you're earning now.

There are indeed outside agencies and forces which shape, guide, even "control" our behavior, whether we think we are autonomous or not. Children obey parents and study in elementary school to win approval and avoid censure. High school students may be motivated by such reinforcers as grades, teacher praise, scientific or artistic shows and awards, laws which require school attendance (which include undefined threats), or future college admissions requirements. Eventually we take jobs and fulfill our employment duties in return for money, a reinforcer which may be traded for all sorts of positive reinforcers and discomfort removers. Friendships and love affairs, going shopping, seeing a movie, having your shoes repaired, going to the bathroom, and watching TV are behaviors which also are shaped and maintained by the reinforcing consequences.

Let's say that Skinner is right for many activities and behaviors. At the same time, however, we do exercise our free will, free choices, and independence, and we certainly deserve "thank you's" for favors and recognition for accomplishment.

Intrinsic Reinforcement

We might also mention the concept of **intrinsic reinforcement,** which will be elaborated in Chapter 9. Often, we are motivated to perform some acts for the satisfaction derived from the behavior itself, not for an external reward such as money or a grade. Students sometimes will take classes or read a textbook just for the intrinsic satisfaction of learning. The learning becomes its own reward. Some other behaviors which are intrinsically rewarding are playing games, solving puzzles, completing a challenging task, eating gourmet dinners, or just talking with someone you like. In classroom learning, intrinsic reinforcement (enjoyment) is a very desirable form of reward.

Motivation and Feedback Functions of Reinforcement

Reinforcement actually serves two functions. First, the **feedback** function of reinforcement tells us if we were right or wrong. Second, the **motivational** function of reinforcement strengthens or weakens the tendency to repeat the response. Usually, the two functions are inseparable—a child rewarded for completing a report on time knows that he or she did the correct thing (feedback function); he or she is also pleased by the reward and is more likely to repeat the rewarded behavior (motivational function). It is possible, however, to separate the feedback and motivational functions. A child who is paid one penny for spelling each word—whether or not he or she is right—will continue spelling all week and into Saturday. Unfortunately, without any feedback as to correctness, the spelling ability will not improve. In this bizarre example, the motivational function is left intact; the feedback function is destroyed. Equally bizarre, we could rap the kid's knuckles every time he or she spelled a word correctly. This is feedback about correctness, alright, and the child's spelling might improve, but he or she would not be especially anxious to continue the spelling lesson.

Four Types of Reinforcements and Punishments

It is traditional to distinguish among four combinations of reinforcements and punishments. Basically, the combinations include administering or taking away outcomes which are either rewarding or aversive. To be more specific:

1. Praise, smiles, compliments, high grades, gold stars, coated candies, and diplomas may be *administered* to strengthen such behaviors as paying attention, completing an assignment, or taking a bath. One school system recently announced that Frisbees, yo-yos, and hamburgers would be used to reward school attendance. Critics called it "old fashioned bribery." Learning theorists call it **positive reinforcement.**

2. Such aversive outcomes as embarrassing scoldings, glares, frowns, criticisms, low grades, beatings, or getting rained on may be *removed* by paying attention, stopping the chatter, arriving on time, completing the assignment, or coming in out of the rain. The removal of the unpleasantness strengthens those behaviors. This is **negative reinforcement.**

3. Most any behavior will be weakened by the *administration* of adequately severe punishment, for example, reprimands, low grades, humiliation, arm twisting, and so on. This is **punishment.**

4. Finally, the attractive outcomes listed in contingency type 1 above may be *removed*. This is a form of punishment intended to weaken such unproductive behavior as wandering around the classroom, speaking out of turn, giggling about the teacher's girdle, or fiddling with yo-yos or Frisbees. Psychologists do not have an agreed-on name for this combination, although some call it **punishment II** or **negative punishment.**

Actually, it is common even among psychologists to use the terms *punishment* and *negative reinforcement* interchangeably, although, properly speaking, the two are quite different (compare contingency types 2 and 3).

Primary and Secondary Reinforcement

A **primary reinforcer** is a reward which is desirable for itself, usually to maintain the physiological well-being of the organism. Food, water, pain-avoidance, and sex are the most common examples of primary reinforcers, even though no individual has been known to die from an absence of sex.

A **secondary reinforcer** does not directly remove a physiological deficit. Rather, the reinforcing properties are learned. Some behaviorists assume that secondary reinforcers—such as money, grades, diplomas, or gold stars—acquire their reinforcement value as a result of having been paired with primary reinforcers. For example, money would be a learned or secondary reinforcer because it has been associated with food, comfort, and other pleasures. Chances are good, however, that you have never seen a diploma or gold star directly paired with food, water, sex, or pain-avoidance. Nonetheless, we still must concede that their reinforcement value is learned and that eating money or diplomas does little good.

Social reinforcers, such as praise, smiles, pats on the shoulder, or feelings of success usually are considered secondary (learned) reinforcers.

The argument is that deprivation of social rewards will not disturb the physiological integrity of the human. Many students, in fact, do not seem to need or want social reinforcement from the teacher. Therefore, social reinforcers are not primary reinforcers but secondary, learned reinforcers.

Punishment

As a general rule, beating children is no longer particularly popular as a means of shaping cooperation and learning in the classroom. As another general rule, punishment is one of the most confused and emotionally loaded topics in psychology and education. Let's clarify some problems.

First, punishment can be *physically* painful (spanking, arm twisting, hair pulling, etc.) or *psychologically* painful (embarrassment, sadness, frustration). Second, while physical punishment or extreme psychological punishment may raise a few eyebrows, punishment in the form of withholding rewards (contingency type 4 above) is common and generally not objectionable.

Now consider some of the complexities of using punishment in the classroom:

1. Punishment, such as shouting at Willie Walkabout for leaving his seat every 10 minutes, usually does not eliminate the behavior, just slows it down temporarily (suppresses it). Most often, the undesirable behavior will soon recover, especially with a changed stimulus situation. For example, as soon as the teacher steps out of the room, turns his or her back, or is replaced by a substitute, little Willie again will be hot-footing it to the pencil sharpener or hamster cage.

2. Punishment itself does not show the punishee what the appropriate behavior should be. One principle of behavior modification (Chapter 6) is that alternative desirable behaviors (namely, getting down to business) must be strengthened at the same time the maladaptive behavior (wandering) is weakened. Punishing Willie's wanderings even by acceptable means (calm suggestion, withholding warmth and love) is just half of the task.

3. The teacher's verbal and physical aggression may serve as a pretty poor model for impressionable youngsters. The teacher who screams, "Sit down and shut up! I'll teach you to yell in the halls!" certainly will.

4. Either physical or psychological punishment may result in such nasty side effects as fear or anxiety, either of which will include a very healthy dislike for the teacher and school in general. Such attitudes can lead to further troublesome avoidance and escape behaviors, such as lying, cheating on tests, playing hooky, or dropping out of school entirely. It has been shown that students who like the teacher also like the class. Further, when they like the teacher and the class, students

are more highly motivated and achieve more (Kounin, 1970; see Chapter 10).

5. The effects of punishment may be unpredictable, depending on student personality. Some students accept firm corrections and constructive criticism, while others respond better to positive reinforcers. Also, "punishment" for some students may be just the reinforcing attention they were looking for. Showing off or other disruptive behavior actually might be rewarded and strengthened by glares and reprimands. Also, everybody knows that getting sent to the principal's office permits the offender to see bloody noses, scratched elbows, and secretaries running the ditto machine and intercom. The offender might even get to run errands. Swell punishment.

We will return to these popular topics of punishment, motivation, discipline, and classroom control in Chapters 6, 9, 10 and 18.

Partial Reinforcement Effect

According to a tongue-in-cheek report by Skinner (1959), in his early years of conditioning rats he had to manufacture his own rat pellets with a pharmacist's pill-rolling machine. Since pellet-rolling was a nuisance, Skinner thought he might stretch his pellet supply by reinforcing the rat only for every second, third, fifth, tenth, or even every twentieth bar press. The results of this **intermittent reinforcement** were quite dramatic and have come to be known as the **partial reinforcement effect** (PRE). Intermittent or partial reinforcement leads to:

1. Strong motivated responding, and
2. Slow extinction.

Real-world examples of the partial reinforcement effect are very common. Take gambling. In Las Vegas and Atlantic City, charming little grey-haired ladies will stand for hours patiently pumping nickels into the infamous one-armed bandits. The rewards are irregular both in the frequency of the pay-offs and in the size of the reinforcements, the number of nickels. Other persons lean over the crap tables or sit at roulette or blackjack games quite captivated by the intermittent reinforcements.

Other games are equally overwhelming in their ability to maintain highly motivated responding and tremendous resistance to extinction. The most absorbing American card game is bridge, the downfall of many an undergraduate who should have been studying instead of counting points, overbidding, and going down three in four spades doubled. Of course, sometimes the student makes the bid or grand slam, and this occasional reward keeps him or her involved for many hours. Sports also provide a

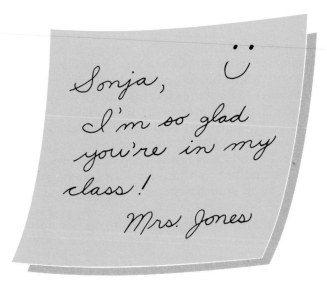

Figure 5.3
Reinforcing note
from Mrs. Jones.

nice partial-reinforcement effect. Even a novice bowler will get an occasional strike, and so the bowling behavior persists. If the game were so difficult the bowler *never* was rewarded, or so easy that he or she *always* got a strike, the novelty would wear off in short order. Other sports and games such as golf, Monopoly, fishing, hide-and-seek, or watching professional football also dispense intermittent rewards guaranteed to motivate persistent responding. And consider the recent uproar about teenagers pumping countless quarters into arcade games—some stealing to support the habit. A schedule of partial, unpredictable rewards strengthens behavior far beyond a 100-percent reinforcement schedule.

In the elementary school, occasional and unpredictable rewards are very effective in creating positive attitudes toward the teacher and toward learning. The occasional round of cookies sent by a thoughtful mother, watching a rocket launch on television, or a surprise note from the teacher (Figure 5.3) can increase the attractiveness of school immensely.

One report (Whitlock, 1966) described a six-year-old boy who was not learning to read. Worse, according to his mother, he had a "fear of words" so strong that he refused even to try to read. In the training program he initially was given one poker chip for each correctly read word presented on a flash card. A jarful of tokens, about 36, earned him the reward of having a storybook read to him; after three jars he could listen to records; for seven jars he could see a cartoon movie. With increasing proficiency the boy was switched to a 2:1 schedule, then 4:1, 20:1 (one page per token), 60:1 (one story per token) and 240:1 (four stories per token). This is called stretching the ratio, or **reinforcement schedule thinning** (Ackerman, 1972, pp. 124–125). Finally, tokens were phased out entirely. After four weeks, about 15 hours, the boy was returned to the regular reading program of his class. Both his actual reading and his attitude toward reading improved immensely. More on token-reinforcement systems in Chapter 6.

Finally, we should note that the partial-reinforcement effect provides a strong argument for using classroom games as a motivating, involving strategy for teaching and learning at any age level.

Superstitious Behavior

Skinner also used principles of instrumental conditioning to explain **super-stitious behavior.** According to one story, Skinner had taught a hungry pigeon to eat from a food hopper. Every 30 seconds the hopper would pop open for 3 seconds, regardless of what the pigeon happened to be doing. Since reinforcement strengthens the behavior it follows, the pigeon developed a ritualistic, stereotyped chain of responses. For example, it would turn sharply to one side, hop back and forth from one foot to the other, and then strut with its head raised high. Sure enough, this strange performance

INSET 5.1

SKINNER'S FAMOUS FOUR REINFORCEMENT SCHEDULES (FR, VR, FI, VI)

B. F. Skinner originally described four basic types of intermittent reinforcement schedules. First, with the **fixed ratio** (FR) schedule the rat (or person) would be rewarded for exactly every, say, fifth response (perhaps a bar press). We would say the rat is "on a 5-to-1 (5 : 1) FR schedule." Second, with the **variable ratio** (VR) schedule the reward might be dispensed on an average of five responses per reinforcement, but sometimes the ratio would be 3 : 1, 6 : 1, 2 : 1, 8 : 1, and so on. Third, with the **fixed interval** (FI) schedule the rat would not receive a reward until the first response after a fixed time interval of, say, 15 seconds. We would say the rat is "on a 15-second FI schedule." The trained rat's usual behavior under the FI schedule is to do nothing during the early seconds of the interval, then press faster and faster until the pellet drops into the dish. Fourth, with the **variable interval** (VI) schedule the average delay time might be 15 seconds, but sometimes the interval is 10 seconds, 19 seconds, 13 seconds, etc.

The ratio schedules and the interval schedules produce the partial reinforcement effect: rapid responding and resistance to extinction.

was rewarded every time with three-seconds' worth of wheat and corn. The rewarded behavior naturally persisted.

In the real world, we find all sorts of superstitious behavior which is (a) accidentally rewarded or which (b) the person thinks will be rewarded. In fact, there is no connection between the particular behavior and the delivery of rewards. Gamblers especially become superstitious about lucky numbers, lucky chairs, left-handed dealers, etc., if these happen to be associated with a string of wins. The ancient Aztecs believed that the Sun God returned each night from west to east through the underworld Land of the Dead, where he must receive nourishment from the hearts and blood of sacrificial victims. Every morning the revitalized rising sun reinforced the periodic slaughter of captives. Throwing flower-decorated six-year-old children into sacrificial wells also was believed to produce a good harvest.

A teacher should at least be aware of the concept of superstitious behavior. One student might come to believe that a front-row seat magically raises test scores, when actually it just reduces distraction and counteracts nearsightedness. Another student may develop a habit of sharpening his or her pencil every five minutes, thinking that math is easier with a sharp pencil. In fact, the trip to the pencil sharpener simply provides a brief, refreshing break.

Teachers themselves develop superstitious patterns of teaching. For example, teacher Gordon Grind might discover that an hour per day of unbearably miserable drill raises spelling scores. Thus reinforced, the teaching behavior persists—despite the availability of more pleasant and even more effective teaching methods.

SOCIAL LEARNING THEORY

Humans are social animals, and much information and skilled performance is acquired through observing, interpreting, and responding in social settings, and through receiving reinforcements and punishments for our responses. Social learning theory analyzes the dynamics and significance of learning by observing and imitating (Bandura, 1977). For example, we watch the coach correctly swing the tennis racket and then try it ourselves. Foreign languages, table manners, surgery, shoe repair, handwriting, diaper changing, and countless other cognitive and motor skills are acquired at least partly through observing, imitating, and receiving feedback (reinforcement). Social learning theory also deals with how we regulate our own behavior by observing and evaluating our own performances. Because of the clear role of reinforcements and punishments in observational learning and in the self-regulation of behavior, social learning theory is quite related to the topic of instrumental conditioning.

Observational Learning

Learning by observing and imitating others (models) is a very efficient method of learning and an effective method for teaching. Bandura (1977) outlined four phases in observational learning: The attention, retention, reproduction, and motivational phases.

Attention is an absolutely critical condition for learning. Normally, the teacher, as a model to be imitated, will be able to control students' attention due to his or her status and expertise—also because the teacher controls rewards and punishments. When the teacher says, "Now pay attention," "Watch closely," "We have a special treat today," or, "This will be on the test," he or she is controlling students' attention. Or attempting to do so. Students' own characteristics—interests, self-esteem, needs, distractibility, etc.—will affect the degree to which they attend to the teacher-model.

When attention has been gained, the effective teacher will make the process of imitation easier by helping students, especially young or learning-disabled ones, to discriminate important cues. For example, "Do you see how just two—not four—sides of the trapezoid are parallel?" or "Be sure to focus the microscope with this large knob." If the number of modeling cues is beyond the information-processing capabilities of the students (as in an involved math formula or a complex equipment assembly), repeated presentations would be required before accurate matching of the teacher's behavior can occur (Bandura, 1969).

The **retention** or storage of a modeled activity will be better if students actively code the teacher's performance into some sort of verbal statement (e.g., "The big knob! The big knob!") or visual imagery (e.g., an image of a trapezoid with the two parallel sides in heavier lines). Rehearsal of the modeled cognitive or motor skill also is a time-tested method of strengthening learning, as we saw earlier in this chapter. Rehearsal may be overt, e.g., practicing drawing trapezoids, or covert, implicitly creating proper trapezoids. Compared with students who passively watch the teacher solve problems or demonstrate equipment, students who actively encode or rehearse are much more likely to retain the modeled performance.

In the **reproduction** phase, the verbal codes or mental imagery guide the actual reproduction of the modeled activity. A high degree of accuracy in learning by imitating a model requires that the activities be overtly enacted and practiced. Particularly with motor skills (e.g., using equipment, handwriting, heart surgery), the mental images of the correct movements must be combined with body-position cues before the motor performance can be performed skillfully. The reproduction phase, incidentally, permits the teacher to evaluate whether or not students have properly imitated all of the component parts in a particular cognitive or motor skill—"Yes Suzy, those two lines are parallel, but now you need two more nonparallel sides for the trapezoid!"

INSET 5.2

IMITATION OF AGGRESSION

In one classic study of the imitation of aggressive behavior, Bandura (1963) divided nursery school children into five research groups. Children in Group 1 watched an adult model physically and verbally attack a large inflated Bo-Bo punching doll. Group 2 saw the same thing on film. Group 3 watched similar violence in a cartoon. Group 4, a control condition, engaged in an unrelated activity. Group 5 observed a calm, subdued, nonviolent adult. Then one-by-one, children were placed in a room with the Bo-Bo doll and were observed through a one-way mirror. You guessed it. The subjects in Groups 1, 2 and 3 imitated the violence, promptly punching Bo-Bo where it hurts. They also sometimes repeated the model's, "Pow, sock 'em!" The Group 4 control subjects showed much less violence, but who can resist punching a punching doll? The Group 5 subjects who watched the subdued model showed the least aggression, although even they got in a few licks.

In the **motivational** phase of observational learning, it is assumed that behaviors learned by observing others will be performed only if it is reinforcing to do so. That is, reinforcements and punishments affect the *performance* of the task, not necessarily the actual *learning* of the observed behavior. Also, in observational learning, reinforcement may be **direct,** as when a teacher praises a student for correctly imitating proper equipment usage or correctly solving a math problem. Reinforcement also may be **vicarious,** as when students see another student lavishly praised for correct performances.

More generally, social learning theory recognizes the role of vicarious reinforcement and punishment in controlling many forms of classroom behavior, not just imitating a model. For example, if the class sees Pete reprimanded for arriving late or speaking out of turn, the observers learn very quickly from the vicariously experienced punishment.

A continuing issue related to learning by imitation is the effect of television violence. Do children learn from watching private-eye or police programs that punching, stabbing, or shooting are good ways to solve problems and "get even"? Even Bugs Bunny and the Road Runner can serve as models of violence and aggression. And then there is the evening news, with wars, murders, robbery, arson, and so on. The Surgeon General's Scientific Advisory Committee on Television and Social Behavior (1972) concluded that for some children, especially those predisposed to violence, watching TV violence is causally related to actual aggressive behavior.

The teacher should keep in mind that he or she is a highly respected and influential model, especially with very young children. In high school, the teacher who swears and boasts of her or his pot-smoking escapades does not promote the cause of good English or a solution to the drug problem.

Self-Regulation of Behavior

With behaviors and performances that are fairly significant—our tennis game, test performances, artistic creations, dieting, interacting with others—we often engage in a form of self-appraisal, evaluating how well we are doing and planning improvements. Bandura (1977) outlined a simple model of the **self-regulation** process which includes three components: (1) observing and (2) judging our performances, and then (3) giving ourselves self-determined rewards or punishments (consequences).

A person who wishes to regulate, for example, how long he or she lectures or how good the basketball or math skills are, must first **observe** the particular self-performances. Observing might involve some measurement and record-keeping—for example, timing one's lecture or recording the number of points scored or the percentage of math problems correctly solved.

Judging, the second component, involves comparing the performance against some standard. Sometimes the standards are internal, as when we rewrite a paper, improve a painting, or work on math problems until we feel they are acceptable. Other standards are learned from models in our social world. For example, we know that a score of 50 percent on a math test or 76 in bowling is not particularly good, while 95 percent or 190 are. Teachers and parents clearly play a significant role in helping children set standards of performance in both academic and nonacademic areas. According to Bandura (1977), "When adults practice and teach leniency, children are self-satisfied with mediocre performance and reward themselves for such attainments" (p. 137).

In Bandura's third step in the self-regulation of behavior, **self-determined consequences,** students might reward or punish themselves by thinking or saying, "I really did great on the chem test!" or "I sure blew that shot!" A person also can reward himself or herself with a movie or a jog in the country after studying hard or with a new shirt for staying on the diet. According to Bandura (1978), people who reward their own behavior ". . . achieve significantly higher levels of performance than those who . . . do not reward their attainments."

BEHAVIORISM AND COGNITIVE PSYCHOLOGY

A Brief
History of
Behaviorism

While some principles of learning can be easily traced to Aristotle, it is John B. Watson who earned the title, "father of behaviorism." Early in this century, Watson's Ph.D research at the University of Chicago involved observing rats as they found their way through a maze for a food reward. Watson complicated their task by first making them either blind or deaf. This research, combined with his knowledge of Pavlov's work, led Watson to form a strong belief that all significant animal and human behavior is made up of muscle or glandular (e.g., salivary) responses to environmental stimuli. He did not deny the existence of mental images, ideas, and feelings, but regarded them as "mere ghosts" with no scientific importance whatever. Thinking, thought Watson, was a matter of subvocal speech—muscle twitches in the throat, larynx, and tongue, a viewpoint which some wags call "muscle twitchism." Watson began a radical new movement in psychology, one which remains influential to this day.

One classic bit of research is Watson's fear-conditioning of little Albert, an infant. Albert initially had no fear of a white rat, and in fact rather enjoyed the furry creature. Researcher Watson began systematically banging an iron bar behind Albert's head whenever he reached for the rat. Following Pavlov's conditioning model, the white rat soon became a conditioned stimulus which elicited a strong fear reaction, the generalization of which caused Albert also to fear Watson's beard, a Santa Claus mask and a fur coat (Watson and Raynor, 1920). (Note: Such harmful research is no longer conducted with humans.)

Another aspect of Watson memorabilia is his famous criticism of the heredity view of intelligence. Watson (1925) argued that intelligence *is* the experiences, response repertoires, and skills which have been learned, claiming:

> *Give me a dozen healthy infants, well-formed, and my own specified world to bring them up in, and I'll guarantee to take any one at random and train him to become any type of specialist I might select—doctor, lawyer, artist, merchant-chief and, yes, even beggarman or thief, regardless of his talents, penchants, tendencies, abilities, vocations, and race of his ancestors* [Watson, 1925, p. 82].

We should point out that while every contemporary psychologist would agree that behavior, skills, and talents are influenced by learning, none would accept Watson's extreme environmental position.

After Watson left his professorship at Johns Hopkins University in the 1930s to take up an advertising career in Chicago, B. F. Skinner immediately became the spokesperson for behaviorism. We already have reviewed Skinner and his ideas concerning the pervasiveness of reinforcements and punishments in controlling behavior. Skinner agreed with Watson that people are products of what they have learned, but he concedes that individual genetic codes also play a role. Representing traditional behaviorism, Skinner then and now argues that psychology, as a science, should concern itself with observable environmental events, observable responses by the organism, and the consequences which follow a given response.

Cognitive Learning Theory

Behaviorism, or S-R psychology, is considered "reductionistic" because complex behavior is reduced to, or explained by, simple principles of conditioning and learning. In contrast with the behaviorist view, psychologists supporting a cognitive approach to learning and behavior recognize that normal humans have goals and purposes and that learning involves comprehension, understanding, thinking, reasoning, making logical inferences, and mentally restructuring ideas and information. Responding directly to the behaviorist position, humanist Abraham Maslow (1970, 1971) argued that humans are conscious and creative free agents, not robots. Generally, cognitive psychologists feel that the reductionistic concepts and principles of S-R psychology are simplistic and inadequate for dealing with the complexity of human learning, thinking, and behavior.

We already have seen one good example of a cognitive theory of learning in Piaget's conception of schemata (Chapter 4). You may recall that mental schemata are Piaget's units of memory. Schemata for things and actions (motor schemata) are formed, modified, and integrated through processes of assimilation and accommodation. Another good example of a cognitive approach to learning is David Ausubel's theory of cognitive structure described in Chapter 8. According to Ausubel, stored information and experience take the form of a branching cognitive structure, with "progressively differentiated" superordinate, coordinate, and subordinate relations among concepts. Learning amounts to "subsuming" new information into the cognitive structure by meaningfully tying it to what you already know. Ausubel's explanation of learning actually is very similar to Piaget's learning process of differentiating and integrating schemata.

A quite different form of cognitive theory is the information-processing approach described in Chapter 7. This orientation tracks the flow of information from the environment to the sensory systems and then to a short-term memory, where information is attended to and interpreted, and then either forgotten, rehearsed, acted on, or stored in long-term memory.

In the 1980s, psychologists and educators draw from both cognitive learning theory (including information-processing theory) and S-R psychology (including social learning theory) to help interpret classroom learning and behavior and to help prescribe strategies for optimal teaching. There is valuable information to be found in both camps.

TO IMPROVE YOUR TEACHING

It truly is important for a person who daily works with children and adolescents to understand the dynamics underlying everyday behavior—for example, principles of conditioning and learning, memory and transfer, social behavior, development, motivation, individual differences, learning disabilities, and so on. This course should help. You should consider taking many additional courses in psychology, educational psychology, and learning disabilities. You may be a teacher for a very long time.

As for the contents of this chapter, the successful teacher should be alert to instances of conditioned fears and aversions, easily acquired (yet difficult to remove) through bad experiences with the teacher or the subject matter. You also can "condition" students' positive feelings toward yourself and your class with pleasantness, fairness, interesting activities, and assignments—perhaps even with punch and cookies. More on effective management procedures in Chapter 10.

Principles of reinforcement are not especially mysterious, but they are effective. The notion that reinforced behavior is strengthened is the single most pervasive principle of behavior in all of psychology. You respond well to social rewards—e.g., compliments from students on a "good class"—and your students also will respond to rewards. Some of the books listed at the end of this chapter spell out in detail how rewards can and do motivate learning and control behavior. You should become acquainted with a variety of "behavior modification" strategies, even if you see yourself as a humanistic teacher bent on teaching personal development, self-esteem, and creativity.

Be aware of the dynamics of punishment—as well as psychologists understand them. Three main points are that (a) punishment may be psychological or physical, (b) there will be side effects, (c) the side effects are unpredictable, depending on the form of punishment and the personality, ability, experience, age, etc., of the student.

Whether teachers are conscious of social learning theory or not, much teaching and learning follows this model. Teaching by imitation should be most effective if you attend to each of Bandura's four phases by: (1) eliciting attention; (b) helping students to form codes or to rehearse the information or skills; (c) allowing practice to perfect an imitated performance; and (d) providing both feedback and motivational reinforcement.

SUMMARY

The purpose of this chapter has been to acquaint you with basic principles of conditioning and learning. The ideas should make you a more informed professional who will better understand some dynamics of some everyday human behavior.

Psychologists assume that most human behavior is learned. Therefore, they seek to understand behavior by studying principles of learning.

Learning theory describes conditions which influence learning, while instructional theory prescribes methods for optimizing learning.

Two basic forms of learning, or conditioning, are classical (Pavlovian) conditioning and instrumental (operant) conditioning. Learning theorists use these concepts to understand thought, language, and behavior, and sometimes to devise teaching methods based on systematic rewards.

Extinction is the cessation of a response; spontaneous recovery is the recurrence of the response without intervening training.

Generalization is responding to a new stimulus the same way you responded to an earlier similar stimulus. Discrimination is responding differentially to two or more stimuli. Similarity makes discrimination difficult.

A classical conditioning formula has been used to attempt to cure bed wetting, drug addiction, and alcoholism. Desensitization therapy is a form of conditioning used to remove phobias.

"Shaping" is Skinner's word for gaining control over an organism's behavior by rewarding responses which come closer and closer to the desired behavior. His book *Beyond Freedom and Dignity* claims that virtually all behavior is shaped and controlled by reinforcement-dispensing agencies (family, friends, church, police, etc.).

Intrinsic reinforcement is reinforcement built into the behavior itself, such as learning for the pleasure of learning or playing Frisbee for the fun of it. In education, it is considered a more desirable form of reinforcement than tangible rewards (M & M's) or even social rewards (praise).

Reinforcement has two functions: It acts as feedback about correctness and it motivates further responding.

There are four formal types of reinforcement contingencies:

1. Positive reinforcement by the administration of a desirable outcome (e.g., candy).
2. Negative reinforcement by the removal of an aversive outcome (e.g., criticisms, getting wet).
3. Punishment by the administration of an aversive outcome.
4. Punishment by the removal of a desirable outcome.

The two contingencies with "reinforcement" in the title (1 and 2) both strengthen the behavior they follow.

Punishment may be physical or psychological. It does not cause forgetting; it just suppresses the punished behavior, usually temporarily. Punishment by itself usually does not demonstrate what the correct behavior should be. The teacher who is quick to verbally or physically abuse is a poor model. The effects of punishment may be unpredictable, usually depending on the students' personal reactions to criticism or other punishment. Some students will enjoy the attention of an angry teacher.

Primary reinforcers are biological necessities, such as food, water, pain-avoidance, and sex. Secondary reinforcers have learned reward value—for example, money, grades, awards, etc.

Intermittent reinforcement, such as occurs in gambling, produces the partial reinforcement effect (PRE)—strong, motivated responding plus resistance to extinction.

Superstitious behavior is behavior which the one doing it thinks will be rewarded, but in fact has nothing to do with producing a reward.

Social learning theory deals with learning by observing others and with the self-regulation of behavior, both of which depend on the reinforcement or punishment of responses. Bandura identified four phases in observational learning (imitation): attention, retention, reproduction, and motivation (reinforcement). In the attention phase the teacher can draw attention to important cues. Retention is facilitated by deliberate encoding or by rehearsal. Accurate reproduction requires practice. Reinforcement in the motivational phase may be direct or vicarious.

J. B. Watson, father of behaviorism, argued that all significant behavior is responses to stimuli. Even thought was considered subvocal "muscle twitches." Watson demonstrated fear conditioning in little Albert, and claimed he could make any randomly selected infant into a doctor, artist, thief, etc. Following Watson, Skinner became the spokesperson for behaviorism.

Cognitive psychologists feel that behaviorism is reductionistic—simplistic, and inadequate to explain complex behavior. Three cognitive theories are: Piaget's cognitive–developmental approach, emphasizing the formation of schemata; Ausubel's cognitive-structure approach; and information-processing theory.

Much can be learned from S-R and cognitive theories of learning and behavior.

TOPICS FOR THOUGHT AND DISCUSSION

1. What sort of conditioned fears or phobias have you seen in or out of classrooms? Do you have any?
2. Think about teachers in your educational background who frequently punished students. Were the punishments subtle or obvious? List some of each.
3. What are the effects of punishments and rewards on student attitudes and behavior in the elementary school? Junior high? High school?
4. Could a teacher design and successfully conduct a desensitization procedure—for example, to remove fear of spiders or math? How?
5. How might a teacher take advantage of (use) the partial reinforcement effect in the classroom? Would this be a form of unethical "behavior control"?
6. Do you think behaviorism of Watson's variety was a help or hindrance in furthering the understanding of the human mind?

PROJECTS

1. If you need a term paper for a psychology course, consider evaluating Skinner's (1971) *Beyond Freedom and Dignity* and/or his *Walden II* (Skinner, 1948).
2. During your student teaching, or any other classroom visit, watch for clear instances in which individual students or the class respond to rewards or punishments. Keep a log.
3. Ask students (even your college classmates) what they like or don't like about any class. You will find that their answers may easily be translated into rewards, punishments, or conditioned aversions (e.g., boring, difficult, too much work, interesting, easy grades).
4. Describe how you would conduct a lesson in a topic you expect to teach on the basis of Bandura's four phases of observational learning. (Begin with some objectives; Chapter 11.)

RECOMMENDED READING

Bandura, A. *Social learning theory.* Englewood Cliffs, N.J.: Prentice-Hall, 1977.

————. The self-system in reciprocal determinism. *American Psychologist* **33,** 1978, 344–358.

Goodwin, D. L., and T. G. Coates. *Helping students help themselves: You can put behaviorism into action in your classroom.* Englewood Cliffs, N.J.: Prentice-Hall, 1976.

Herman, T. M. *Creating learning environments: The behavioral approach to education.* Boston: Allyn & Bacon, 1977.

Malott, R. W. *An introduction to behavior modification.* Kalamazoo, Mich.: Behaviordelia, 1973.

Vargas, J. S. *Behavioral psychology for teachers.* New York: Harper & Row, 1977.

Behavior Modification, Programmed Instruction, and Microcomputers in Education

6

Learning theory in the classroom / Behavior modification: For and against / About behavior modification / Designing behavior-modification strategies / Comment on behavior modification / Programmed instruction / Computer-assisted instruction and microcomputers in education / To improve your teaching / Summary / Topics for thought and discussion / Projects / Recommended reading

LEARNING THEORY IN THE CLASSROOM

Chapter 5 reviewed the main principles of classical and instrumental conditioning. This Chapter will review in more detail the use of behavior-modification approaches to classroom management and teaching that are based on learning theory. We also will briefly review the thinking behind programmed learning and computer-assisted instruction, which also are applications of learning theory. Finally, we will look at a very recent and exciting revolution in education, the use of microcomputers in the classroom.

In recent years, behavior modification techniques have become fairly sophisticated. In the classroom and the clinic, different strategies include the use of models, mental imagery, and self-instructions or "internal dialogue" ("I must pay attention"; "I must speak slowly"; "Relax, take a few deep breaths"). The techniques have been used to assist students or psychiatric patients in dealing with their fears (Johnson and Melamed, 1979) and problems of: learning disability and hyperactivity (Kauffman and Hallahan, 1979); aggression and problem behavior (Goodwin and Mahoney, 1975); self-control and self-esteem (Kanfer, 1977; Meichenbaum, 1977, 1979); and even social isolation (Meichenbaum, 1977). The procedures include such a substantial and deliberate cognitive component, in contrast with traditionally nonmentalistic S-R behaviorism, that the term **cognitive-behavior modification** has become fashionable (Meichenbaum, 1977).

BEHAVIOR MODIFICATION: FOR AND AGAINST

We must mention at the outset that the attitudes of educators toward behavior modification have ranged from "By darn, it really works!" to "Get those damn candy bars outta my class!" Indeed, many fine teachers work hard to promote student interest and effort, using only social rewards such as praise, smiles, grades, peer approval or feelings of accomplishment. They want nothing to do with "bribes" which, they argue, are a lower form of incentive. Note the problems: Do we really want students to feel they should be paid for learning? And what if students come to refuse to learn without payment? "I read two chapters and did six problems, Miss Pickleseed. That'll be exactly one hamburger and 30 minutes of rock music. Here's your change—three jelly beans."

Behavior modification also has been criticized for: not dealing ". . . with the abstractions of life such as aspirations, hopes, needs, disappointments, etc." (Arthur, 1969; Poteet, 1973); ignoring the perpetuation of individualization (Spiro T. Agnew, 1972); being impersonal, manipulative, and mechanistic (Ross, 1967); ignoring the development of attitudes and self-esteem (Poteet, 1973); and being too simple (Homme, 1979).

Naturally, these challenges have been answered. As for bribery, Homme (1979, p. 62) notes that "... all of us ... do what we do because of the anticipated consequences." Regarding the charges that behavior modification is antihumanistic, manipulative, and mechanistic, Homme noted that when students' academic skills are improved by way of behavior modification, their attitudes toward the teacher, the school, and themselves also improve. Are behavior-modification concepts too simple? Well, the basic theory and strategies are indeed simple, but proponents consider that an asset, not a liability.

Behavior modification programs initially were devised for mentally retarded patients in institutions—persons who simply were not interested in traditional classroom reinforcers (grades, praise, success, etc.). However, they were *very* interested in candy, toys, ice cream, hugs, and kisses, and would work hard for those rewards. Some "normal" students or entire classes also will not respond to social rewards—grades and praise simply do not work. An advocate of behavior modification, speaking behavior modificationese, would say that other rewards are successfully competing for control of the students' behavior, or that the usual classroom rewards simply are not important to the students. Behavior modification has caused many students, handicapped and normal, to show tremendous gains in achievement and improvements in behavior when other strategies have failed.

In his own fine book on behavior modification MacMillan (1973) warns that "... the use of tokens should be practiced only after reinforcers higher on the continuum of reinforcers (praise, satisfaction from accomplishments) have proven ineffective. ... a token economy for an entire class of children without serious learning or behavior problems seems difficult, if not impossible, to justify" (p. 187). (For recent reviews of behavior modification see Kauffman and Hallahan, 1979, and Sajwaj, McNees, and Schnelle, 1979.)

Despite some negative sentiment, there remains a strong and even growing interest in behavior-modification techniques, mainly because they often work.

ABOUT BEHAVIOR MODIFICATION

"Behavior-mod" procedures can be very casual or they can be well-planned, administered, and evaluated. At the casual end of the scale, smiles, friendly chats, and even just standing near the student have successfully served as reinforcers for reducing temper tantrums, irrelevant talking and noisemaking (including baby talk), and spelling errors. One junior high school teacher rewarded her class with five minutes of free talking time if they would keep quiet and busy for the rest of the hour. It worked. Another teacher

INSET 6.1

RULES, PRAISE AND IGNORING: WILL THE REAL BEHAVIOR CONTROLLER PLEASE STAND UP?

Using behavior modification in the classroom requires that the teacher plan ahead for such matters as: What rules will be employed? What reinforcers will I use? What punishments (if necessary) will be used? Madsen, Becker and Thomas (1968) summarized these three "crucial elements of classroom control" in three words: *Rules, Praise,* and *Ignoring*. Rules, which may be displayed on the front wall, remind students of acceptable behavior—it's not safe to just assume that children know what the teacher wishes them to do. Praise is used to reward behavior which is in accord with one of the rules. For example, if "Raise hand before speaking" is a rule, students will be praised for raising hands before blurting out. Finally, Madsen *et al.* recommend ignoring students as a means of mildly punishing behavior which violates the teacher's rules.

In two related studies (Becker, Madsen, Arnold, and Thomas, 1967; Madsen, Becker, and Thomas, 1968) the authors first recorded "baseline" misbehavior for five weeks, then applied the Rules, Praise, Ignoring strategy. Misbehavior dropped from 62 percent to 29 percent.

When the authors analyzed their three-barrelled shotgun to find out which element was the most crucial, it turned out that Rules and Ignoring had little effect on the misbehavior. When Praise was added, misbehavior decreased substantially.

Especially in the elementary classroom, Praise cannot be overused.

awarded ice cream cones to her fourth graders who scored 98 percent correct on a weekly spelling test. Spelling accuracy rose dramatically (Poteet, 1973). Play money rewarded cooperation and learning in one math class, even though the funny money was daily returned to the teacher without any "back-up" or "tangible" reinforcers in exchange.

As another example of an informal approach, a teacher may list the class rules on the blackboard (raising hands, listening to directions, completing work on time, etc.). High praise is given for behavior which is in accord with one or more of the rules (Becker, Englemann, and Thomas, 1971; see Inset 6.1). This strategy avoids the dilemma of having children learn what the rules are by getting punished for violating them. With still another informal but effective elementary school strategy, a teacher can wander through the class during seatwork. Each hardworking student is rewarded with a checkmark on a piece of tape stuck to the student's desk or table, along with a comment such as "Gee I like the way you're working!" The children are proud of their checkmarks.

Group-Oriented Contingency Systems

Litow and Pumroy (1975; see also Hayes, 1976) described three types of group-oriented contingency systems which could be used in classroom settings. First, with the **dependent group-oriented contingency system** rewards for the entire class (e.g., extra recess, extra time for talking, gum-chewing, record listening, etc.) can be made contingent on the performance of *one* student. Sammy Sloworker may find that he suddenly has plenty of coaching and encouragement with his math problems—because 25 students don't get their bubblegum unless he finishes on time. Second, in the **interdependent group-oriented contingency system** the rewards for the whole class depend on cooperation and work completion by the whole class. For example, "If every single person completes the six problems by 10:00 A.M., then the class gets 10 minutes of free time." This strategy uses reinforcement, peer teaching, and peer pressure to get results. Finally, with the **independent group-oriented contingency system,** the reward system is in effect for the entire class, but reinforcements are given according to individual performances. For example, "Everyone who scores above 90 percent on the spelling test gets 15 minutes of free time—while the rest of us practice our spelling." It's every man for herself.

Incidentally, free time is one readily available and effective reinforcer which even schoolteachers can afford. (Curiously, if you ask a teacher if he or she has any "free time," the answer will be, "No, I've been busy as a chipmunk all week!") Free time as a reinforcer has been used to increase prosocial classroom behavior (Glynn, Thomas, and Shee, 1973) and academic achievement. It also seems to be effective in a *response-cost* format, in which free time is forfeited for inappropriate behavior (Long and Williams, 1973): "Anyone who is tardy coming in from recess will lose one minute of their free time."

Social, Activity, and Symbolic Reinforcers

Becker, Englemann, and Thomas (1971) distinguish three types of reinforcers which may be used in the regular classroom: *social reinforcers, activity reinforcers,* and *symbolic* (token) *reinforcers.*

Social reinforcers. Social reinforcers may be divided into verbal praise, facial expressions, nearness, and physical contact. Verbal praise can be either **evaluative** or **descriptive.** Evaluative praise refers to the quality or value of the person: "You're a nice person." For classroom management, however, it's best to use descriptive praise, which both informs the student of the correct behavior and indicates that you approve: "I like the way you pay attention, Clementine darling, keep it up."

Facial expressions include smiles, laughs, winks, nods, and expressions of interest. Scowls, sneers, and disgusted muttering are not considered rewarding.

Nearness as a social reinforcer simply means that standing near a child or approaching a group of working students can be a pleasurable event. Physical contact, such as a pat on the shoulder, a hug, or holding a child on the lap also is rewarding—in the lower grades, that is. In high school, the implications are different.

All of these social reinforcers—verbal praise, facial expressions, nearness, physical contact—include *attention*, an extremely potent reinforcer.

Activity reinforcers. In the category of activity reinforcers we find such privileges as listening to music, doing artwork, reading, additional recess or gym, 15 minutes of battling alien invaders on the microcomputer, folding the flag, or just plain "free time." MacMillan (1973) recommends that the teacher point out to the class why the activity reinforcer was awarded: "Morris finished all of his work without talking, so he can read a Dr. Seuss book." This emphasizes to Morris and the rest of the class just what behavior produces what activity reinforcer.

If you can pull it off, Becker et al. (1971) suggest that after children have learned to work for activity reinforcers, you might be able to treat another academic activity as a reinforcer, to whit: "When you finish your writing assignment you can do some math problems." Keep a straight face.

Symbolic reinforcers. The category of symbolic reinforcers refers to the use of tokens or points, later exchangeable for a back-up reinforcer such as a candy bar, toy, free time, etc. Toys, candy, money, or movies are **tangible** reinforcers, which usually are contrasted with the more desirable **social** reinforcers (praise, success, peer approval).

DESIGNING BEHAVIOR-MODIFICATION STRATEGIES

A technically proper behavior-modification program requires attention to usually about eight components:

1. Specifying and describing the undesirable **target behavior.** The target behavior is "the problem," the behavior you wish to modify. For example, Suzy Mousepincher may wander too much.
2. Stating the desirable **goal behavior.** You want to replace the target behavior with the goal behavior. You want Suzy to remain in her seat, at work.

INSET 6.2

THE FAT CHANCE WHEEL: CONTINGENCY CONTRACTING FOR WEIGHT CONTROL

Dr. Brian Iwata, of Western Michigan University, has successfully used behavior-modification tactics that enable participants to control eating, keep records of intake, and attend weekly weight control meetings. The system uses cash rewards plus the threat of public humiliation to shape the shape.

The initial fee was $35 for eight weekly meetings. Participants received a 50¢ Michigan State Lottery ticket for bringing their completed caloric intake charts each week. If the weigh-in showed they lost the agreed-on 1 or 2 pounds, they earned one dollar plus a spin of the Fat Chance Wheel—which paid another $2 to $10!

And if those pudgy rascals missed a meeting without telephoning in an explanation, this embarassing ad went straight to the Kalamazoo Gazette: "____(name)____, where were you? You must be fat! You missed Monday's weight control meeting."

The meetings themselves dealt with such weighty matters as basic caloric needs, nutrition, exercise—and the behavioral control of eating.

The results? One group of six women lost an average of 17 pounds. A second group of seven women lost an average of 8 pounds. One month after the end of the program the pounds were still gone.

3. Objectively measuring the target behavior in terms of frequency of occurrence or duration of occurrence. How often does she leave? How long is the usual expedition?
4. Identifying environmental stimuli which control (elicit) the target behavior. When and why does Suzy wander about the room?
5. Identifying events following the target behavior which might be reinforcing it. Why does Suzy wander? To escape work? For new stimulation?
6. Selecting reinforcers which are reinforcing to the student. What will Suzy work for? Free time? Opportunity to collect papers? A half-hour of BeeGees?
7. Planning and implementing the program.
8. Evaluating the results.

Let's consider each of these eight points.

Specifying the Target Behavior

Formal behavior-modification programs usually are aimed at curing one problem (target behavior) or one student. Tackling more than one problem or one student simply may be too difficult to be done properly. Some examples of target behaviors might be:

- Speaks out of turn.
- Leaves seat too often.
- Does not turn in work, or turns it in late.
- Does not work independently.
- Talks too much, too loud, or makes other noise.
- Causes trouble on the playground.
- Chews pencils, crayons, erasers.
- Stares out of window, fiddles around, doesn't "get down to work."

Incidentally, traditional solutions to these maladaptive or disruptive behaviors have included yelling, threatening, changing seats, giving love and sympathy, talking to the student, talking to parents, sending the student to the principal's office, or sending him or her to the school psychologist. Sound familiar? Are these solutions successful?

Behaviors which make good targets for behavior modification are those that are most disruptive to the student, not just behaviors which happen to irritate the teacher. Sometimes, target behaviors are selected because they disrupt the whole class. They also should be behaviors which, after the intervention, will be supported by "natural" reinforcements—peer approval, teacher approval, or heightened academic success.

The first problem then, is to objectively specify the target behavior. Let's say that Albert Avalanche makes too much noise. You do *not* want to describe the behavior by saying, "That kid drives me nuts!" "He's too noisy." "He's the most active kid I've ever seen." You *do* want to describe objectively and exactly what "makes too much noise" means. For example, you might produce a list including:

- Talks out of turn.
- Deliberately bangs the door shut.
- Stomps his feet.
- Rattles papers.
- Drops books.
- Grinds pencil sharpener with vengeance.
- Coughs and clears throat unnecessarily.

These are specific behaviors we can see. They can be counted. Another observer also would be able to see and count the same noisy activities.

Usually, even an apparently complex and unobjective behavior such as "paying attention" can be defined behaviorally; for example, by such objective specifications as "faces teacher, blackboard, reciting student, or instructional materials, whichever is appropriate."

The target behavior may be a *single* behavior such as "speaks out of turn," "enters late," or "gets out of seat too often." A single target behavior would be the easiest to observe and attempt to modify. However, the target behavior also might be a category of behaviors, as with noisy Albert Avalanche. In his case the target behaviors include talking out of turn, banging doors, stomping feet, rattling papers, dropping books, grinding pencils, and clearing his throat. All would fit into the single target category: makes too much noise.

Specifying the Goal Behavior

Generally, behavior modification takes a positive approach in the sense that an *increase* in a **goal-behavior** is wanted, and so positive reinforcements may be used to strengthen that behavior. The opinion is that rewards are better for everybody's mental health, compared with a negatively oriented punishment program. The goal behavior is inconsistent with, and an alternative to, the problematic target behavior. For example, if the target behavior is "getting-out-of-seat," the goal behavior might be "in-seat working."

Note that most teachers are in the habit of identifying student "problems" as behaviors to be decreased, which in behavior-modification territory implies punishment. With just a little imagination however, the problem or target behavior to be decreased may be recast as a goal behavior to be increased via positive reinforcement. Consider the following magical transformations from target behaviors into goal behaviors:

Target Behavior (Decrease)	Goal Behavior (Increase)
Out-of-seat running around	In-seat working
Interrupting	Raising hand
Making noise	Working more quietly
Turning in work late	Turning work in on time
Daydreaming	Working

In the specific case of Albert Avalanche, who "makes too much noise," the targets would be recast as raises hand, closes door quietly, keeps feet and papers reasonably quiet, uses pencil sharpener properly, avoids unnecessary throat clearing, and avoids dropping *Random House Dictionary* during silent reading.

Measuring the Target Behavior

In a formal behavior-modification program, one needs to gather **baseline data** before starting the intervention program. We need to *measure* what the child is doing and *how often* or *how long* he or she actually does it. The teacher may discover that his or her imagination has been exaggerating how often little Wetsy Betsy really does trot off to the bathroom. A teacher also should not rely on subjective impressions of whether or not an improvement has taken place ("Gee whiz, I don't think she goes so much anymore!") An objectively counted reduction of five trips per day to zero or one is much more convincing.

There are several simple strategies for gathering baseline data. The **rate method** focuses on the number of occurrences per unit of time. With **continuous recording** the time unit could be the entire day. The teacher would tally on a slip of paper the number of times Wandering Willie leaves his seat or the number of times Nelly Needle visits the sharpener. A simple

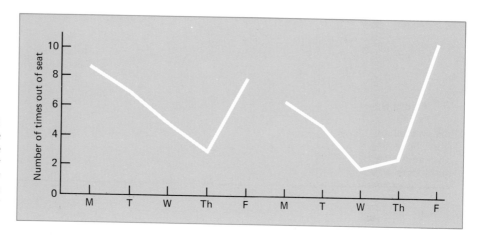

Figure 6.1
Example of rate
method. Figure
shows the number
of times per day
the student was
out of his or her
seat.

two-week graph of Wandering Willie's out-of-seat behavior is shown in Figure 6.1. One week might be adequate; two is better.

If the behavior occurs very often, say more than about 20 times per day, the teacher can use a **time sampling** strategy. For example, Albert Avalanche's perpetual noisiness could be recorded for just one hour or one-half hour per day, say, between 10:30 and 11:00 each morning. The resulting graph generally would take the same form as Figure 6.1.

With some behaviors, such as wandering Willie's out-of-seat excursions, the **duration method**—recording the duration of the behavior—might be more useful than the rate method. He might get out of his seat just once, but not return for two hours. Again, if the behavior does not occur too frequently, the teacher can continuously record the amount of time Willie spends wandering during the entire day. If the behavior occurs too often for the normal two-handed teacher to accurately record, a time-sampling method again could be used. For example, the teacher might record the actual number of minutes spent studying during a 15-minute period in the morning and another 15-minute period in the afternoon. With continuous recording or time sampling, the resulting graph would resemble the one in Figure 6.2.

One variation on the time-sampling, duration technique may be used if the teacher is unable to schedule exactly 30 or 60 minutes per day for regular observation. With this **ratio method** the teacher would record both the duration of the target behavior and the duration of the observation period. The result is easily converted to a percentage (minutes of target behavior divided by minutes of observation) and graphed. For example, the data in Table 6.1 is graphed in Figure 6.3.

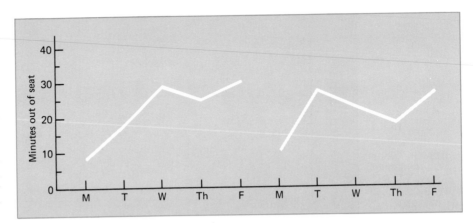

Figure 6.2
Example of
duration method.
Figure shows the
amount of time
the student was
out of his or her
seat over a two-
week period.

As a final four thoughts, measuring target behavior or goal behavior:

1. Will provide objective information which will either support your opinion about a problem, or will tell you if you were underestimating or exaggerating the problem.
2. Might reveal unsuspected patterns of behavior. Note in Figure 6.1 that the frequency of out-of-seat trips for fictitious Wandering Willie was much higher on Mondays and Fridays, a discovery which completely surprised his fictitious teacher.
3. Might suggest ways to alter the behavior. Is there something about Monday and Friday? Does Willie need to use up his energy on these two days?
4. Will indicate, after the treatment is begun, whether the program was successful, when change began, and how successful the program was.

Table 6.1 Example of data recorded when using ratio method

Day	Number of minutes actually studying	Length of observation (in minutes)	Percentage of time spent studying
Mon	5	15	33.3
Tues	3	10	30
Wed	10	20	50
Thurs	9	20	45
Fri	4	5	80
Mon	15	30	50
Tues	4	10	40

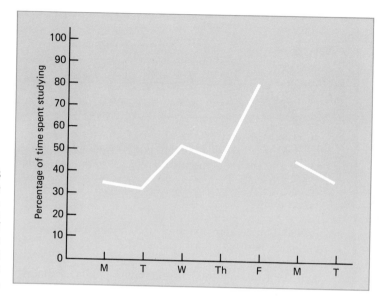

Figure 6.3
Example of the ratio method. Figure shows the percentage of observation time actually spent studying (from data in Table 4.1).

Identifying Stimuli Which Control Target Behavior

What is it that serves as a cue for dashing to the sharpener? Visiting the teacher's desk? Dropping a book? Wandering about the room? Staring out the window? Talking out of turn?

With attention to environmental conditions (the stimuli) that elicit the target behavior (the responses), you might find that the problem children have trouble (a) just before recess, lunch, or the end of the day, (b) just after exercise periods (recess, physical education classes), (c) only during certain subjects, perhaps as an escape from incomprehendable material, or (d) only when friends are watching.

Any trends in the environmental conditions which elicit the target behavior will help the teacher understand the student's problem and better focus the behavior modification effort. (See Inset 6.3.)

Identifying Events Which Follow and Reinforce the Target Behavior

One assumption of behavior-modification theory is that behaviors emerge and are sustained because they are reinforced. There must be a reason for the problem.

Some common reinforcers which support bad habits are:

1. Teacher attention. This can reward frequent trips to the teacher's desk, speaking out, out-of-seatness, being slow to pass along materials, or even smarting off.
2. Peer approval. Clowning may be rewarded with laughter and high status, making any mild reprimand well worth it to your would-be

INSET 6.3

**AN ANALYTIC
BEHAVIOR
MODIFICATION
STRATEGY**

Goodwin and Coates (1976) outlined a behavior modification strategy which is similar to the present eight-step model. Their step 2, however, goes further in helping the teacher understand and cope with the problem behavior. Their four steps are:

1. Select the targets for change.
2. Assess the current environment.
3. Plan and implement a strategy for change.
4. Evaluate the program for change.

Step 2, assessing the current environment, includes analyzing these questions:

a) During what activity do each of the target behaviors occur?
b) What is the teacher doing?
c) What are other students doing (working in pairs, in groups, or alone?)
d) What time of day is it?
e) When during the lesson (beginning, middle, end) do the problems occur?
f) Is the pupil working alone or in a group?
g) What is the pupil's previous experience with this subject matter?

Attention to such matters should indeed help the distraught teacher better understand the problem behavior.

Steve Martin. If the teacher is seen as "the enemy," then aggressive behavior is perceived by peers as courageous.

3. Avoiding an unpleasant task. Wandering or sharpening may serve as an escape from working on an unpleasant assignment; for example, preparing a confusing report, doing confusing problems, or working with friends the student can't stand. Even getting sent to the principal's office may be a welcome escape from a test or an anxiety-loaded oral report.

Identifying the rewards which sustain the target behavior is *very* important. The whole purpose of the behavior-modification program is to alter the reinforcement contingencies which support the target behavior, thereby reducing the high frequency (or long duration) of that behavior.

Selecting Reinforcers Which Are Reinforcing to the Student

Premack Principle. The Premack Principle (Premack, 1965) is one guide to selecting reinforcers. The basic idea is that a preferred (or "high rate") activity such as eating candy, running errands, etc., can be used to reinforce a less preferred (or "low rate") activity, such as staying in one's seat and working independently. You simply make the preferred behavior contingent on performing the less attractive response. Grandma said it all with, "You can't play until you make your bed," or "No dessert until you've eaten your spinach."

The beauty of the Premack Principle is that it opens up a new world of reinforcement possibilities. In addition to the typical activity reinforcers listed earlier (e.g., free time, extra time for music listening, recess, art, reading, gym, or microcomputer games), other reinforcing possibilities might include:

- Five minutes of unrestrained chatter.
- Blowing bubbles with large wads of bubblegum.
- Presiding at the flag raising.
- Sailing paper airplanes.
- Collecting or distributing papers.
- Working crossword puzzles.
- Helping the school secretaries.
- Spinning the teacher in his or her swivel chair.

You can *watch* what the student likes to do, *ask* what he or she likes, or *ask the parents* what he or she likes to do.

Social and tangible rewards. Most elementary school children respond well to social reinforcers—praise, smiles, attention, pats on the shoulder, etc., as described above. Tangible reinforcers may include M & M's, toys, money, playtime, gold stars, peanuts, extended recess periods, or perhaps yo-yo's, Frisbees, and Big Macs. Social rewards are more desirable, if they are effective.

Token reinforcement systems. With a token economy or token reinforcement system, points, check marks, plastic tokens, or glass marbles are awarded for specific studying or rule-following behaviors. These are exchanged for *backup* reinforcers, namely, the "tangibles" listed above.

One particularly good token reward is the *Snoopy Card*, a picture of Snoopy printed on business-card-sized pieces of colored construction paper (Ackerman, 1972). Some students will prefer hoarding the Snoopy Cards instead of trading them in for the back-up rewards.

Ideally, tokens or tangibles are paired with social reinforcers ("Here's your marble, Hortense, you did a swell job!"), since eventually the child should respond to praise, smiles, grades, or feelings of accomplishment without reliance on jelly beans or other tangibles.

INSET 6.4
EVERYBODY RUN AND
SCREAM NOW*

Contingency contracting in the hands of Lloyd Homme has an imaginative and humorous history. In 1963 he was faced with the task of controlling the behavior of three three-year-olds *without* using punishment or tangible reinforcers such as candy or trinkets. Wesley Becker relates what happened:

"The amount of control exercised on the first day can be summarized: none. One child was running and screaming, another was pushing a chair across the floor (rather a noisy chair), and the other was playing with a jigsaw puzzle. Once our scholars discriminated that punishment did not follow these activities (the rate at which this discrimination was made must have set a new indoor record), the response to verbal instruction 'Come and sit down now' was to continue the running and screaming, chair-pushing, and so forth. . . ."

Almost in desperation Lloyd Homme tried to see if a principle set forth by psychologist David Premack might be made to work with these children. In brief, the idea is that any behavior which has a high probability of occurring at time X can be used to reinforce or strengthen any behavior which has a lower probability of occurring at time X. For example, Premack has shown that animals would learn to drink *more water* when water was constantly available, if drinking water gave them an opportunity to run (and running was not otherwise permitted). Running was being used to reinforce drinking water. Most psychologists in the past had only tried to do it the other way: restrict drinking, and use drinking to reinforce running. The beauty of this finding for the teacher is that in order to decide what can be used to reinforce children, she need only observe what they choose to do when given the opportunity and use this activity as the reinforcer.

Lloyd Homme was a good observer. He noted that his children loved to run and scream, push chairs, and play with puzzles.

"We made engaging in these behaviors contingent on the subjects' doing a small amount—very small at first—of whatever we wanted them to do. A typical early contingency was merely for them to sit quietly in chairs and look at the blackboard. This was followed almost immediately by the command, 'Everybody run and scream, now.' This kind of contingency management put us in immediate control of the situation. We were in control to the extent that we were able to teach everything in about one month that we could discover was ordinarily taught in first grade."

From Wesley C. Becker's introduction to *How to use contingency contracting in the classroom*, by Lloyd Homme. Copyright © 1970 by Research Press, Champaign, Ill. Reprinted by permission of Wesley C. Becker and the publisher. The material in quotes is from Lloyd Homme, "Human motivation and environment," *Kansas studies in education*, Lawrence, Kans., 1966.

Punishing target behaviors. The social, token, or tangible reinforcer for performing the desired goal behavior can be accompanied simultaneously by a strategy for reducing the disruptive target behavior. A teacher thus might ignore or withhold rewards for such disruptive behaviors as noise-making or leaving one's seat unnecessarily. Disrespectful behavior might be ignored or swiftly punished, but make sure the punishment is not actually a reward.

Since beating is not particularly fashionable, one recommended punishment procedure is the **time-out** tactic. The theory is that the antisocial behavior will decrease if the disruptive student is removed from the reinforcing environment—usually his or her giggling friends. The isolation period is usually quite short, say two, five or at most ten or fifteen minutes. The time-out area *must* be free of reinforcing stimulation—the principal's office with the friendly secretaries, fascinating duplication machines, and delightful nosebleeds just won't do. Some teachers have simply placed a chair between a file cabinet and the wall (with no window); others have arranged for a stimulation-free time-out room in the school office. A coat hall might work if the disruptee does not steal gloves or take a bite out of each student's lunch.

Implementing the Program

Assume that you have (a) specified and described the target behavior (Albert's noise-making), (b) stated the goal behavior (working on assignments and not making funny noises), (c) measured the problematic target behavior, (d) identified cues that elicit the target behavior, (e) located events which seem to be reinforcing the target behavior, and (f) selected reinforcers which, in

---

INSET 6.5

EFFECTIVE REWARDS IN EXTREME CASES: FOOD, WATER, A TRIP TO THE BATHROOM

In extreme cases, basic physiological needs have been capitalized on in behavior modification. One clinician described to your author a case of "elective mutism"—a child refused to talk in school, although he chatted freely at home. The treatment involved not permitting the student a drink of water or anything to eat unless he *asked* for it. He also could not go to the rest room unless he asked. The procedure was reasonably successful in that he began whispering complete sentences in order to communicate his needs.

fact, Albert really likes. Your plan actually is well along and needs just a few finishing details for implementation.

The behavior modification program normally is a no-secrets-or-subtlety affair: Albert Avalanche would be explicitly told what behavior will be reinforced and why. If the entire class is put on the contingency management plan, the goal behaviors could be posted on the front wall. If tokens are used, the exchange value must be specified and a time for exchanging also will need to be set. Table 6.2 shows one teacher's rate of exchange with the Snoopy cards.

Some behavior modifiers recommend that *all* tokens for all students be cashed in at the end of each day. With this strategy, all students start fresh each morning, with no sandbaggers taking a vacation with their extra tokens accumulated over three months.

You will need a master control sheet for recording the number of tokens given and to whom. If you are working on target behaviors and goal behaviors for individual students, you also will need to continue the measurements exactly as you did during the pre-intervention, baseline period.

Table 6.2 Example of exchange rates for token economy using Snoopy cards

Number of Snoopy cards	Activity
1	Get a drink.
2	Five minutes in library.
3	Ten minutes free reading, art, or game time.
4	No homework in one class.
5	Five minutes extra recess.
6	Chew bubble gum in the morning.
8	Drink pop and chew gum all morning in class.
10	Play games for fifteen minutes.
15	Twenty minutes free art time.
20	Thirty minutes extra physical education.
25	Skip two workbook pages in reading.
26	One hour free reading, art, or game time.
27	Pantomimes for one hour in class.
30	Class playtime for $1\frac{1}{2}$ hours, or no homework in anything for half a day, and get an "A."

From *Operant conditioning techniques for the classroom teacher* by J. Mark Ackerman. Copyright © 1972 Scott, Foresman and Company. Reprinted by permission.

INSET 6.6

DO TOKEN ECONOMIES MAINLY SHAPE THE TEACHER?

That token systems can improve academic work and control behavioral problems is beyond debate. MacMillan (1973, p. 170), however, raises the possibility that such systems are successful primarily because they reinforce good teaching habits. The token economy requires the teacher to clearly spell out the desired behavior, to immediately and frequently reward the behavior positively, and in general to acknowledge student performance. The observed changes in student behavior thus may result from more appropriate teacher behavior.

Evaluating the Results

The outcome of a successful behavior-modification program could be obvious—problem behavior disappears, test grades rise dramatically, attendance becomes near perfect, or all assignments are in on time. However, for scientifically objective evidence of success, a graph of behavior during the intervention is compared with the earlier baseline data (remember baseline data?). You might get something like the decreased target behavior shown in the right portion of Figure 6.4, compared with the left portion.

Figure 6.4 Graph comparing the rate of target behavior before and after the initiation of the behavior modification program.

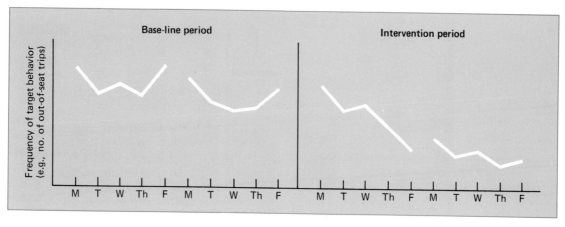

COMMENT ON BEHAVIOR MODIFICATION

The above eight-step procedure was presented in enough detail to acquaint the reader with a reasonably complete behavior-modification program. As we noted however, behavior-mod procedures may be very casual or highly structured, according to the teacher's needs or preferences. The teacher's preference, of course, could be to ignore structured reward systems entirely— for any of the reasons listed earlier in this chapter. A list of books, all small, with further details on the mechanics, advantages, and difficulties of behavior-modification systems appears at the end of this chapter.

PROGRAMMED INSTRUCTION

Programmed instruction is another application of learning theory to teaching. In recent years, American interest in using programmed materials has declined, most likely due to the high attractiveness of competing workbooks, learning centers, audio and video tapes, film strips, microcomputers, and other colorful and interesting educational materials and activities. Interestingly, some foreign countries are successfully using programmed learning.

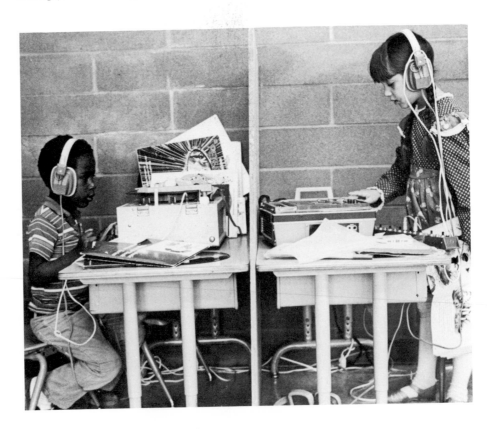

For example, aided by tape recorded text, illiterate adults in Kuwait are learning reading and mathematics (Elerian, 1978). Also, Arabic grammar is taught via programmed techniques to teachers and students in the Syrian Arab Republic (Kalla, 1978).

INSET 6.7

CONTINGENCY CONTRACTING

One form of behavior modification in the classroom involves a written contract; for example:

Date _____

I, _____, hereby agree

to _____

_____

before _____, 19__.

In return, I will receive _____

_____.

_____
Student

_____
Teacher

Homme (1970) lists the essential rules of such a contract as:

1. The contract must be honest and fair. Don't try to extract four hours of math for one jelly bean. The reward should match the effort.
2. The reward should be immediate. Don't offer a movie next June for work done in November.
3. Small frequent rewards are more effective than a few large ones.
4. Administer rewards *after* the performance is completed. First work, then play.
5. The contract must be positive. That is, avoid "You will *not* get punished if your work is done on time."

Some contracts further specify a list of subgoals with promised dates: An outline will be prepared by _____; a map or diagram will be prepared by _____; the final report or project will be completed by _____. Others specify a list of resources: I will consult _____ books, _____ encyclopedias, and _____ other resources (specify) _____.

Despite declining interest, however, programmed materials can be a valuable and worthwhile supplement to your teaching. It also is likely that your future school already will have programmed workbooks available for your use. Therefore we will look briefly at the theory behind programming, the development of programmed materials, and an evaluation of programmed instruction.

The theory behind programmed learning is operant conditioning. In fact, B. F. Skinner himself was responsible for the high interest in programming in the 1960s and early 1970s (Skinner, 1974). A programmed text, or the programmed material in a teaching machine, took the form of a structured sequence of **stimulus** questions to which the learner **responded,** with each response immediately followed by **reinforcing feedback.** A short example of programming is shown in Table 6.3.

INSET 6.8

FROM *WHY WE NEED TEACHING MACHINES*
B. F. SKINNER

Exploratory research in schools and colleges indicates that what is now taught by teacher, textbook, lecture, or film can be taught in half the time with half the effort by a machine of this general type. One has only to see students at work to understand why this is a conservative estimate. The student remains active. If he stops, the program stops (in marked contrast with classroom practice and educational television); but there is no compulsion for he is not inclined to stop. Immediate and frequent reinforcement sustains a lively interest. (The interest, incidentally, outlasts any effect of novelty. Novelty may be relevant to interest, but the material in the machine is always novel.) Where current instructional procedures are highly efficient, the gain may not be so great. In one experiment involving industrial education there was approximately a 25 percent saving in the time required for instruction, something of the order of a 10 percent increase in retention, and about 90 percent of the students preferred to study by machine. In general, the student generally likes what he is doing; he makes no effort to escape—for example, by letting his attention wander. He need not force himself to work and is usually free of the feeling of effort generated by aversive control. He has no reason to be anxious about impending examinations, for none are required. Both he and his instructor know where he stands at all times.

* From *The Harvard Educational Review* 31, 1961, 377–398. Copyright © 1961 by the President and Fellows of Harvard College.

Table 6.3 Example of Programming

Directions: Cover the right (answer) column. Just answer each question, then compare your answer with the printed answer.

1. Programming is a method for individualizing _____.	instruction or teaching.
2. Since programmed instruction is based on the operant conditioning model, there is a stimulus, a response, and a _____.	reinforcement
3. Programming always involves a series of questions. Each question is a s-_____.	stimulus
4. The learner's answer is the r-_____.	response
5. And the printed answer is the r-_____ or "reinforcing feedback."	reinforcement

The important learning principles incorporated in programmed learning are:

1. Learning is individualized, each person proceeds at his or her own rate. Some programs include "branching"—depending on the alternative selected, the student is "branched back" for review or "branched ahead," skipping unnecessary repetitions.
2. Active responding is elicited, which guarantees attention to the task.
3. Reinforcing feedback is immediate. The reinforcement is both informational, in indicating correctness, and motivational, in the sense that it is rewarding to be correct.
4. The material is designed to present small, logically ordered, comprehendible steps in learning. Programs are carefully pretested so that students can maintain a high level of correct responding, above 85 percent. If a difficult spot with many errors is found, more small steps are inserted.
5. Cues or hints for correct responding are systematically "faded out," requiring more and more active recall. This is called **fading**, the "withdrawal of stimulus support."
6. Repetition and review are built into the program.
7. Completion of a program is supposed to be a guarantee of mastery.

Research on Programming

A small mountain of research on programmed learning accumulated during the 1960s and 1970s. With apologies for glossing over details and exceptions, a few prominent conclusions were as follows:

1. Just thinking a response can produce as much learning as actively pushing a button, writing a response, or pointing to a correct alternative (Evans, Glaser, and Homme, 1960; Krumboltz, 1964).
2. Sometimes scrambled frames (questions) are as effective and efficient as logically ordered frames (Brown, 1970; Payne, Krathwohl, and Gordon, 1967). (Presumably this would not be true of complex cumulative material, such as mathematics.)
3. Sometimes self-reinforcement—evaluating our own correctness (Chapter 5)—is as effective as printed informative feedback, at least with simple material.
4. High rates of correctness (85 percent) may be unnecessary. High error rates can indicate weaknesses, challenge students, and be just as effective as low error rates (Goldbeck and Campbell, 1962; Lewis and Pask, 1965).

The important matter, of course, is: Does programmed instruction work better than "traditional" methods? Generally, comparisons of classes taught by programmed material with those taught by "conventional" approaches are mildly supportive but not overwhelmingly so. Lange (1972) reviewed 112 studies: 41 percent favored programming over conventional teaching, 49 percent showed no difference, and 10 percent favored conventional methods. Another review (Jamison, Suppes and Wells, 1974) concluded that programming *is* more efficient than conventional instruction in that learning time usually is reduced.

Generally, programming can be valuable as a drill-and-practice method for teaching well-defined skills and concepts; for example, some math concepts, Spanish vocabulary words, even basic electronics. As a few cautions however, some programs may be dull and repetitious; a given program might be too difficult for slow students, too easy for fast learners; and completion of a program does not necessarily guarantee mastery of the material.

COMPUTER-ASSISTED INSTRUCTION AND MICROCOMPUTERS IN EDUCATION

Computer Assisted Instruction

In the 1960s and 1970s computers were used as sort of an automated super teaching machine called **computer-assisted instruction** (CAI). With most models, TV screens permitted the computer to present pictures, words, diagrams, and even motion pictures, with earphones providing auditory information (e.g., word pronunciations, reinforcing feedback). Often, the Skinnerian format still held: The machine would pose a question (a *stimulus*) by printing it on the TV screen. The student would *respond* by typing an answer or by touching the correct alternative on the screen with a light pen. *Reinforcing feedback* was immediately provided by preprogrammed statements and explanations printed on the screen or spoken through the earphones. Sometimes a smile face on the screen or a merry tune would reward a correct answer; sometimes a pleasant voice would say, "Noooo, that's not correct, try again." The main, but not exclusive, use of CAI was drill and practice, for example, teaching math facts, reading, spelling, foreign languages, geography and history.

CAI permits a unique form of individualization. After a student punches in an identification number, the computer will begin conversing with him or her by name, for example, "OK SUSAN, MY RECORDS SHOW YOU NEED TO WORK ON YOUR 'TIMES' FACTS. IF THAT IS ALL RIGHT WITH YOU TYPE 'YES' AND THE ENTER KEY. OTHERWISE TYPE 'NO' AND THE ENTER KEY." As this statement shows, the computer also can review recent work and decide whether the student needs more practice or can move ahead to the next lesson. Information concerning individual student progress or progress of groups of students can be retrieved by the teacher whenever needed.

Research with computer-assisted instruction has usually produced very positive results. Fletcher and Atkinson (1972) supplemented the regular curriculum of first graders with eight to ten minutes of CAI reading instruction every day for five months. At the end of the year the CAI kids were 5.05 months ahead of other first graders in reading achievement. Jamison, Suppes, and Wells (1974), after some fast arithmetic, concluded that a one-percent increase in the number of CAI sessions of fifth- and sixth-grade children produces a 5.72 percent increase in mathematics achievement scores.

As for student affective reactions to CAI, Hess *et al.* (1970) evaluated the ratings of the computer and the teacher by low-income Mexican-American junior high school students. The computer and the teacher were rated as equally "warm." The computer was rated significantly more fair, better liked, more clear, and easier than the teacher.

A problem with the CAI techniques of the 1960s and 1970s was the cost—quite beyond the budget of even most large schools and school systems. Enter the microcomputer.

Micro-computers and Computer Literacy

Currently, the availability of relatively inexpensive microcomputers is creating a minor revolution in education.* There are new organizations such as the *International Council for Computers in Education* and the *Northwest Council for Computers in Education*; new magazines and journals, such as *The Computing Teacher* and *Creative Computing*; new films, such as *Computers: Challenging Man's Supremacy* and *Now The*

---

* At the time of this writing, a microcomputer which uses programs for teaching (CAI), games, and simulations could be purchased for $399—less than the cost of the school secretary's electric typewriter. A color TV set and the programs (about $25 each) would be extra.

Chips are Down; new books (e.g., Moursand, 1980; Papert, 1981); new companies busily preparing new software programs; new college microcomputer courses; and lots of exciting new computer summer camps (Pierce, 1981). One authority recently suggested that all teachers owe it to their students, their profession, and to themselves to learn about the applications of microcomputers in their particular area (Moursand, 1981). An even stronger statement by one computer camp director claimed, "In the future, those who are not computer literate will be at a terrible disadvantage. Training kids to work with computers is like training them to read—it's that critical!" (Pierce, 1981). There is a call for "universal computer literacy" for both teachers and students.

Computer Literacy for Teachers

There are three main uses of computers in the classroom: for instruction, for simulations, and for games—which may or may not be educational in nature. First, microcomputers can be used for **computer-assisted instruction** just as with the older and larger computers (Perry and Zawolkow, 1982). Again, this sometimes is a drill-and-practice "flashcard" application, with the computer presenting problems, receiving answers, and providing feedback. There are programs (software) for teaching math, reading, spelling, sentence diagramming, grammar, using a library, elementary school biology, high school science, the environment, and many, many more—including teaching about microcomputers and teaching BASIC, the main microcomputer programming language. The programs usually are in the form of "floppy discs"; if you wish to sound as though you know your computers, just call them "floppies." You do not need to learn to write programs. You or a child insert the floppy and turn on the computer. It takes over from there. You can create your own tailor-made exercises by learning to program, or else by working with a programmer. Your local high school can furnish several capable student programmers. The "micros" motivate attention and learning with movement, animation, humor ("Wrong, dummy! Try again"), and sound—beeps, tones, clicks, splats, and even short reinforcing melodies.

Second, **simulations** on microcomputers can be very simple or quite sophisticated. Many simulations are business-oriented. "Lemonade," for example, is a simple program for teaching children to sell lemonade for a profit. "Stock Market" (buying and selling computer-generated stocks) contains more advanced business concepts. Social relations are taught with such software as "Civil War," "Kingdom," or "Warlords." All simulations teach problem solving and decision making by requiring students to formulate and test solutions and then try again.

Third, some computer **games** are about the same as home video games—"Space Defense," "Invaders" and "Road Race," for example. These are fun and can be used as effective classroom rewards (Fisher, 1981). Other games are both educational and enjoyable, for example, "Math Baseball," "Math Darts," and "Hangman" (vocabulary building). "Sargon II" is a sophisticated and unbeatable chess program which seems to teach chess playing by clobbering students game after game. Other, more humane chess and logic problem programs allow the student to select the difficulty level of the computer-opponent, thus individualizing the task.

After students learn to write programs, they can solve many kinds of problems with the microcomputer. For example, one high school student in Eugene, Oregon, wrote a simulation program to help a science teacher demonstrate the blood-chemistry relations between white-cell count, red-cell count, clotting time, and other factors. Another student programmed a microcomputer to predict world conditions in the year 2100, given varying population growth rates, death rates, food supplies, income levels, and so on (Moursand, 1981). Micros can be used to write music, write poetry, and draw. A "Super Talker" (hardware) will permit your computer to talk; for example, it can read words on the screen to children who are learning to read. And the computer never gets mad, and it never plays favorites.

Again, every teacher should investigate the uses of microcomputers in his or her area. The teacher should be acquainted with the capabilities, limitations, and applications of the hardware, and with the availability, quality, and cost of software. The teacher may discover that some subjects

Figure 6.5
This Sunday headline in a Madison, Wisconsin, newspaper reflects the increasing interest in computer literacy in the schools.

can be taught faster, perhaps very enjoyably, with a computer. The teacher also probably will uncover a number of relevant educational games and simulations. New programs—floppies—are rapidly being prepared and marketed.

Computer Literacy for Kids

Computer literacy for students is becoming more and more commonplace, and may soon be expected (Figure 6.5). It takes several forms. First is the awareness level—a simple acquaintance with the local Apple II or TRS-80, using it to play games or learn spelling; second, students can learn about computers—their role in society, their functions, their parts, and how they can be used to learn in school; third, students can learn to program using the BASIC programming language. Many elementary and secondary schools have created computer courses based on these three steps (see Rogers, 1981, for a complete high school computer course outline).

TO IMPROVE YOUR TEACHING

Whatever your attitude toward Skinnerian operant conditioning, behavior modification, and "controlling behavior," always be aware of the powerful effects of rewards and punishments on student motivation, achievement, and attitudes toward the class, the teacher (you), the subject, and school in general. Be especially sensitive to students who are not interested in praise, success, or high grades. They would be prime targets for the use of behavior modification procedures with tangible reinforcers—money, free time, candy, etc.

Keep in mind, however, that you ideally want students to work for social rewards, including praise, peer approval, feelings of success and accomplishment, and of course high grades.

Don't forget the famous Premack Principle. It has changed the perceptions of many psychologists and educators about what a "reinforcer" really is. Whatever a student likes to do can be used to reinforce less preferred activities, such as doing math or writing a report.

Try to become aware of the circumstances which surround and probably trigger and reward undesirable "target" behaviors. Is the student disruptive at a certain time or during a certain subject? Is a particular task especially unpleasant or threatening? Does the disruptiveness occur during teacher-led recitation or during seatwork or small group activities? Is the student rewarded by teacher attention or peer approval? Are there other causes of frustrations? Such an analysis will help point out a solution.

If you believe your class is capable of greater effort or higher levels of performance and achievement, consider using one of the group-oriented contingency systems. Be sure the promised rewards are truly rewarding. Free time is always good, and costs you nothing.

Check with your instructional materials center to find what programmed materials might be available. You may wish to use programmed workbooks as a source of enrichment for fast students, as a remediation device for slow students, or as a means of accelerating your one or two possibly bored gifted students.

By all means become "computer literate." A visit to your local computer store will acquaint you with the equipment and prices, and will allow you to try a game, or a program for teaching reading, math, or Spanish, and perhaps even a simulation. You can pick up a computer magazine or two at almost any drugstore; your college may have a microcomputer course which focuses on educational applications. At your future school, be ready to argue for including a microcomputer or two in the next school budget (you may wish to take your principal to the computer store with you). Also, at the elementary or secondary level, try to have a computer course included in the school curriculum. Usually, the math or science specialists teach the computer courses, order the software, and schedule the use of the machines.

SUMMARY

Behavior modification is the use of rewards and punishments to control behavior. Recent cognitive-behavior modification strategies—often using imagery, self-instructions, or modeling—have been applied to students and adults with learning or personality problems (e.g., learning disabilities, fears, aggressiveness, low self-esteem).

Some educators strongly support behavior-modification techniques in the classroom. Others are strongly opposed, claiming that behavior modification is: a form of bribery; mechanistic, impersonal, manipulative, and simplistic; and indifferent to humanistic and aesthetic matters. However, tangible reinforcers often are effective for students who do not respond to social reinforcers (praise, success, high grades)—for example, retarded, learning-disabled, or emotionally disturbed students.

Group-oriented contingency systems include: (1) making rewards for the entire class contingent on the performance of one student (dependent system); (2) making class rewards contingent on the performance of all students (interdependent system); or (3) making individual rewards contingent on individual performance (independent system).

Behavior mod can be very casual, as in using smiles, praise, or weekly ice-cream cones to reward cooperative and productive behaviors. Behavior mod also can be very systematic and organized, approximately following the steps of:

1. Specifying the problematic target behavior.
2. Stating the more desirable goal behavior.
3. Measuring the target behavior objectively.
4. Identifying cues which elicit the target behavior.
5. Identifying events which follow and reinforce the target behavior.
6. Selecting reinforcers which are reinforcing to the student.
7. Planning and implementing the program.
8. Evaluating the results.

Measuring the behavior in behavior modification may involve continuously recording target behaviors, or using a time-sampling strategy. The frequency or rate method records target behaviors in responses per hour or day; the duration method records the length of time spent engaging in the behavior (e.g., at the teacher's desk).

The Premack Principle is one guideline for selecting reinforcers which are reinforcing to the student: whatever the student likes to *do* (run and scream, listen to rock music, fly airplanes, play basketball) can be used to reinforce less preferred activities (studying).

Reinforcers may be of several types: social reinforcers (including verbal praise, facial gestures, nearness, or physical contact); activity reinforcers (free time, or extra time for recess, gym, art, or music listening); or token reinforcers (points, poker chips, marbles, or Snoopy Cards—all exchangeable for back-up tangible reinforcers). Tangible reinforcers include toys, money, candy, or movies; these are considered inferior to social reinforcers—praise, grades, feelings of success, or peer approval. Time-out was one recommended punishment procedure.

Evaluation usually includes comparing post-treatment rates of behavior with the pretreatment baseline rate.

Programmed instruction is based on the operant conditioning model. Each question is a stimulus; the learner's response is the response; and the printed answer is the reinforcing feedback. Central learning principles in programming include: Learning is individualized; active responses are elicited; reinforcing feedback is immediate; the material is carefully sequenced in small steps; cues are systematically faded out; and repetition and review are built in. Research has questioned some of these presumed principles and advantages of programming. Research on the effectiveness of programmed instruction has been mildly supportive.

Early, expensive computer-assisted instruction (CAI) was essentially a super teaching machine, effectively used for drill-and-practice kinds of learning. Interest in low cost microcomputers is mushrooming. Micros are used for CAI, games, and simulations. Computer literacy for students includes: awareness and exposure; knowledge of computers and their applications; and learning to program. Teachers should become computer literate, learning the uses, limitations, and applications of hardware, and the availability, quality, and cost of software.

TOPICS FOR THOUGHT AND DISCUSSION

1. How can behavior-modification techniques be used to (a) improve motivation, (b) improve achievement, (c) improve attitudes and self-esteem, (d) reduce behavior problems?
2. Are criticisms of behavior mod legitimate? Which ones do you agree or disagree with?
3. What would be the advantages of each of the three types of group-oriented contingency systems—dependent, interdependent, and independent?
4. How important will "universal computer literacy" be in the adult world of present elementary school students.

PROJECTS

1. Outline a behavior-modification procedure for dealing with a behavior problem at the age level you expect to teach. Be sure to follow rules and guides presented in this chapter or elsewhere.
2. Outline a behavior-mod technique for increasing achievement in a subject you expect to teach.
3. Talk with a school psychologist about his or her successes with behavior-modification strategies.
4. If you need a term paper, a good topic would be the pros and cons of (a) behavior mod in the classroom, (b) programmed learning, or (c) microcomputers in education.
5. Outline a computer course for students you expect to teach. See Moursand (1980), Rogers (1981), Papert (1981), and back issues of *The Computing Teacher* and *Creative Computing*.

RECOMMENDED READING Glaser, W. E., and I. G. Sarason. *Reinforcing productive classroom behavior: A teacher's guide to behavior modification.* Washington, D.C.: U.S. Department of Health, Education, and Welfare/Office of Education, National Center for Educational Communications; U.S. Government Printing Office, 1972.

Goodwin, D. L., and T. G. Coates. *Helping students help themselves: You can put behavior analysis into action in your classroom.* Englewood Cliffs, N.J.: Prentice-Hall, 1976.

Herman, T. M. *Creating learning environments: The behavioral approach.* Boston: Allyn & Bacon, 1977.

Homme, L. *How to use contingency contracting in the classroom.* Champaign, Ill.: Research Press, 1979.

Lahey, B. B., and A. E. Kazdin (eds.). *Advances in child clinical psychology.* New York: Plenum, 1979.

MacMillan, D. L. *Behavior modification in education.* New York: Macmillan, 1973.

Moursand, D. *Introduction to computers in education for elementary and middle school teachers.* Eugene, Ore.: International Council for Computers in Education, 1980.

Papert, S. *Mindstorms.* New York: Basic Books, 1981.

Poteet, J. A. *Behavior modification: A practical guide for teachers.* Minneapolis: Burgess, 1973.

Vargas, J. S. *Behavioral psychology for teachers.* New York: Harper & Row, 1977.

Information Processing, Memory, and Transfer

7

Learning and information processing / Sensory register, short-term memory, long-term memory / Mnemonic memory devices / Facilitating memory in the classroom / Transfer / To improve your teaching / Summary / Topics for thought and discussion / Projects / Recommended reading

LEARNING AND INFORMATION PROCESSING

Chapters 3 and 4 explained how a child's stage of development sets limits on his or her capacities for understanding, reasoning, and thinking. This chapter will further explore characteristics and limitations of human thinking, including learning, attention, memory, transfer, problem solving, and even consciousness itself. Together, these critical capabilities have been labeled **human information processing.** These concepts should greatly enhance your understanding of learning and thinking, both in the classroom and out of it. In fact, a thoughtful reading of this chapter is guaranteed to help you understand some of your own thinking patterns, learning capabilities, and memory limitations.

Let's take a simple example of "information processing." You are processing information right now. You are *attending* to these ink marks. You are *recognizing* letter and word combinations and extracting meaning. You can remember exact words for a few seconds (**short-term memory**); after that, you will recall only ideas (**long-term memory**). Now while you are attending to these verbal gems, you probably are ignoring any sounds of an air conditioner, outside traffic, or even someone shuffling papers behind you. These have been *filtered out* by your frankly amazing mechanism of attention—which allows you to concentrate almost completely on one sensory input. You can, of course, switch your attention from one input to another. When you later recall information (for example, from this paragraph), you may find that some ideas are *forgotten*; you also might make up or *construct* information that was not presented at all. All of this is information processing.

We will now take a longer look at information processing—especially attention, memory and transfer—and try to explain how these concepts and principles can be used to improve your understanding of student mental capabilities and perhaps even improve your classroom teaching.

Levels of Information Processing: Conscious and Unconscious

Have you noticed that you can carry on two or perhaps three, four, or five activities at the same time? For example, you can walk across campus, look at the trees, chew gum, and all the while you are talking to a friend about last Friday's exciting movie. A relatively recent theoretical development in psychology, **levels of processing theory,** helps explain the workings of such seemingly complex, simultaneous behaviors.

The core idea is that information processing takes place at several levels simultaneously: a higher "conscious" level and lower "fringe-conscious" and "unconscious" levels. High-level, conscious information processing is limited to one activity at a time—you can talk *or* listen, watch TV *or* read, but you cannot consciously attend to two activities at the same instant. You can quickly switch your attention back and forth from one activity to another, which gives the illusion of attending to two things at once, but it is only an illusion. Some psychologists refer to this attention switching as "time sharing," using as a metaphor the ability of a computer to switch back and forth between different inputs.

Watch your lecturer as he or she tries to write one idea on the chalk board while talking about something else. The person often will make a mistake in the writing, and then break off the speech in the middle of a sentence in order to direct the conscious attention to correcting the error. He or she cannot actively attend to two activities at once.

While your conscious, high-level information processing is attending to one task, your lower fringe-conscious and unconscious levels are handling several tasks simultaneously. Again, you can walk, watch the trees, chew gum, maybe even scratch an itch, all at the same time without missing a word you are speaking or hearing.

Information may be processed at the lower, fringe-conscious and unconscious levels only as long as the input is fully expected—no surprises. In our example, only lower levels of processing are needed to cope with chewing gum, walking, and watching the trees. However, if something unexpected occurs, the information gets passed to a higher, more conscious level of processing in order to cope with the surprising input. In our example, your conversation might easily be interrupted if you should hear screeching tires, see a large owl in one of the trees, bite into a piece of rock, or spot a dime on the sidewalk.

Psychologist Donald Norman (1973, 1976) metaphorically describes levels of information processing as a hierarchy of executives in a bureaucratic organization. If the lowest level executives (perhaps new clerks) can handle the information, no further processing is needed. However, if an unexpected problem arises which the lowest executives cannot cope with, the matter is passed to higher-level executives. That is, the problem is passed to higher, conscious levels of information processing.

One interesting principle of information processing theory is that higher-level, conscious activity is *always* taking place. If you are not attending to one matter, you are attending to another. As you read, you often stop to "think" or daydream. You also will find that your mind wanders when you are listening to a less-than-captivating lecture. In information-processing terms, what truly is happening is that your attention is simply switching from an external focus (reading, listening) to an internal focus (thinking, daydreaming). The conscious activity always is focused on something. In the classroom, a blank stare may mean that a student has shifted his or her attention from you to a new romance or a tennis game. You may regain attention by bursting through the reverie—"Johnny, what do you think about present participles?" "Huh?"

By way of a summary, Norman's (1976; Lindsay and Norman 1977) principles of information processing state that:

1. All incoming information must be processed or accounted for at some level.
2. Higher (conscious) and lower (unconscious) levels of information processing may occur simultaneously, and usually do.
3. Higher level activity (conscious attention) is always taking place.
4. The highest conscious level of processing can deal with only one activity at a time, although attention may be quickly switched to different activities.
5. It is the unexpected, surprising input which is passed to higher levels of conscious attention and information processing.

Maintenance Rehearsal vs. Elaboration Rehearsal

Information not only may be processed at higher (conscious) and lower (unconscious) levels, it may also be processed either superficially or in depth. This distinction is reflected in two types of rehearsal to strengthen memory—**maintenance rehearsal** and **elaboration rehearsal.** With maintenance rehearsal, information may be rehearsed much as we would repeat and repeat a long telephone number. In fact, this is called the "telephone strategy" (Norman, 1976, p. 119). The purpose is simply to keep the numbers in mind long enough to dial them.

Some people believe that this is how we are supposed to learn—by meaningless, rote repetition. It isn't.

On the other hand, information may be processed at a deeper level by elaboration rehearsal, rehearsal which involves searching for meaningful connections—images, ideas, meanings, categories, etc.—with the new material. This is appropriately called the **meaningful-connections strategy** (Norman, 1976) or the **semantic-elaboration strategy** (Craik and Watkins, 1973). The purpose is not to hang on to a few tidbits of information for a few moments, but to integrate the new information with existing knowledge for more-or-less permanent retention. You may note that Piaget (Chapter 4) and Ausubel (Chapter 8) both emphasize that effective learning is a process of relating new information to existing schemata or cognitive structures; that is, engaging in elaboration rehearsal.

Information Processing in the Classroom

In the classroom, levels-of-processing theory tells us that just *one* conscious, high-level activity can occupy the student's attention at any given moment (principle number 4, above). Competing input, known as distractions and interruptions, will interfere with productive learning activities.

Also, principle number 5 tells us that to provide unexpected, surprising input is a sure way to gain attention. As we will see in Chapter 9, learning activities which are novel and surprising will gain attention, arouse curiosity, and motivate students to learn more about the attention-getting phenomena.

Finally, research in depth of information processing has shown that information processed at deeper levels is better learned and remembered. As described above, deeper processing refers to a conscious elaboration of the meanings of the new information. Some methods for stimulating students to analyze and elaborate include:

* Asking thought-provoking questions (Anderson and Biddle, 1975).
* Requiring the application of principles to new examples (Watts and Anderson, 1971).
* Asking questions which require the learner to make inferences.
* Posing questions or problems requiring analysis, synthesis, or evaluation (Kane and Anderson, 1978; see Chapter 11).
* Asking for creative modifications, uses, or improvements (see Chapter 16).

SENSORY REGISTER, SHORT-TERM MEMORY, LONG-TERM MEMORY

The preceding distinction between maintenance rehearsal and elaboration rehearsal brings us to a more traditional distinction between three forms of memory storage: The sensory register (SR), short-term memory (STM), and long-term memory (LTM; see Figure 7.1).

Sensory Register

The most important characteristic of the **sensory register** is its "preattentive" nature. The input to your senses (vision, audition, touch, smell, taste) is stored for a *very* brief period. You have not yet consciously attended to the information. For example, every college student has the frustrating experience of storing the professors' exact words for a couple of seconds. Unfortunately, those pearls of wisdom often fade away (decay) before they can be written down. This is the SR in action. In the auditory SR, the exact words are available for about two seconds (or less). If you do not quickly attend to and perhaps implicitly rehearse the information, it simply is gone. The form of the information in the auditory SR is a literal copy of the auditory input. A clear implication for classroom learning is that if students

Figure 7.1
Sensory register, short-term memory, and long-term memory.

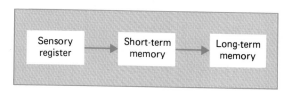

are taking notes, a lecturer must (a) give them time to write down important ideas and (b) write important concepts on the board as he or she speaks. The words will last much longer on the chalkboard than they will in students' auditory SR memories.

In the visual mode, the notion of a sensory register memory device is not very exciting. It's easiest and most accurate to think of the visual SR as the familiar visual afterimage (Sperling, 1960). Remember writing your name in the dark with a sparkler? Seeing spots after staring at a bright light at night? Those fleeting afterimages are a form of storage device, a sort of "memory." Duration usually is only about one-quarter second—and only in the dark. In normal daylight, we do not "see" afterimages nor are we aware of them, since each visual input nicely "erases" the preceding one. There seem to be no educational implications whatever of the visual sensory register. However, our picture of psychological information processing and memory would be incomplete without this brief description of the visual sensory register mechanism.

One can easily conceive of similar sensory register memory mechanisms in other sensory modes, for example, in the senses of taste, smell, and touch. However, science has not yet devised laboratory demonstrations which prove their existence and show the rate of information loss.

To summarize, (a) the sensory register is pre-attentive. By definition, you have not yet consciously responded to, repeated, or otherwise rehearsed the sensory input. (b) The known durations are about one-quarter second (visual) to about two seconds (auditory). (c) It is not possible to maintain information in the SR—for example, by repetition. Any deliberate attention to the input, including attempts to rehearse it, would by definition put the information into the next, short-term memory mechanism. (d) The form of information in the SR is a literal copy, auditory or visual, of the input. (e) The capacity of the SR is quite large, since it is a brief duplicate of whatever is sensed. (f) Forgetting is a relatively fast decay process. (g) Retrieving (recalling) information from the sensory register is a matter of quickly reading, writing, or repeating as much as possible before the fast-fading information is gone.

Short-Term Memory

The **human short-term memory** (STM) is a fascinating device, especially since it intertwines closely with consciousness itself. In fact, the STM sometimes is called the **conscious memory** or the **working memory.** It is most famous for its limited capacity—just seven items, plus or minus two (Miller, 1956).

Unlike information in the sensory register, information in the STM has been attended to, and also may have been rehearsed. As a simple example, let's say you consciously read a seven-digit telephone number from the directory. Unless you repeat it (maintenance rehearsal) or make up associations (elaborative rehearsal), memory loss will be relatively fast. The numbers will be partly lost in 30 seconds or less. How many times have you looked up a seven-digit phone number—and then forgot it before you finished dialing? Add a strange area code and you don't have a prayer.

Forgetting is due mainly to a **decay** process; in about a half-minute, the 7 ± 2 items have faded to about 3 or 4. **Interference** by "competing" numbers also will cause forgetting. For example, if you glance at another phone number before dialing, the first phone number may suddenly be gone—that's interference. Similarly, a child who has just been told to "go to room 251," and then "Oh, yes, pick up 125 pencils in the office," may instantly forget the room number. It was interfered with and lost. Interference will be further discussed in the next section.

In order to extend the 30-second (or less) time limits in STM, you can repeat the information to yourself, as in the maintenance rehearsal strategy described earlier in this chapter. This serves mainly to postpone the forgetting. Actually, if the information is repeated often enough it may become very well learned. That is, the information enters the long-term memory and is later recallable. We would call this **rote memory,** a familiar animal who lives in close proximity to multiplication tables and presidents' names.

The limited capacity feature of short-term memory $(7 \pm 2$ items) applies only to rote, *meaningless* units of information. Therefore, one way to extend the limits of the STM is to group ("chunk," "recode") items into meaningful categories. For example, a nine-item list of names like Mary, John, Max, Don, Maurine, Jimmy, Danny, Doris, and Janice can be grouped or recorded into "three M's," "three D's," and "three J's." Three "chunks" or groups are well within our STM capacity.

There are many other encoding, chunking, or elaborative strategies which may be used to transfer information from our "working" short-term memory to a more permanent long-term memory (Neisser, 1982). Shrewd college students use all sorts of mnemonic memory devices to reduce a long list of ideas to a short, easily remembered list of "chunks" of information. At recall time, known as an essay test, the chunks are recalled, which in turn elicit the associated details. We will be examining some of these devices later in this chapter.

In sum: (a) STM is post-attentive, since you have consciously attended to and perhaps rehearsed the information. (b) The capacity is limited to about 7 ± 2 rote-learned items. (c) The capacity is enlarged by grouping or "chunking" the items into a smaller number of meaningful units. (Chunking also can move information from the STM to the LTM.) (d) Unrehearsed information in STM lasts up to about 30 seconds. (e) Information may be maintained in STM through repetition, or maintenance rehearsal, thus postponing the loss. (f) Forgetting probably is due mostly to a decay process, although interference also is at work in short-term memory.

Long-Term Memory

Our third memory type, **long-term memory** (LTM), should be quite comprehensible since the reader already has plenty of first-hand experience with such a device. Information in the LTM may last from minutes to as long as the person lasts, a century or so for some. There are no known limits to the *duration* of information in the long-term memory. The *capacity* of the LTM also apparently is unlimited. The story of the ornithology professor

INSET 7.1

**EPISODIC AND
SEMANTIC MEMORY**

Psychologist Endel Tulving (1972; see also Roediger and Crowder, 1982) proposed an interesting distinction between two forms of memory: *episodic* and *semantic*. Episodic memory is memory for episodes, events in the person's background such as graduation day, lunch yesterday, or "the last time I saw Harry." This memory storage includes lots of imagery plus spatial and temporal relationships with other autobiographical, personal events.

Semantic memory, heavily verbal, includes one's organized knowledge about words and other symbols, their meanings and referents, the relationships among them, and rules for manipulating words and symbols. For example, you know that Christmas is on December 25, that zebras live in Africa, and that the formula for water is H_2O.

who forgot the name of a bird everytime he learned the name of a new student is not true, although it is moderately amusing.

Information is maintained in LTM largely through its meaningful organization with other information. Where were you at 10:00 A.M. exactly two weeks ago? Can you visualize the outside and inside of the last hotel or motel you stayed in? Can you remember your ninth-grade English teacher's name, face, and the sound of his or her voice? In these examples, and most others, the information to be recalled usually is embedded in a meaningful context. "Where were you at 10:00" is related to the rest of your activities that day, and perhaps to your usual daily schedule. Your last motel is embedded within the memories of your last overnight trip. Details or your ninth-grade English teacher are tied to the school, the room, and other ninth-grade memories.

The form of information in LTM may be visual or auditory (verbal); it also is in the form of tastes, smells, tactile information (remember a wet paw?) and affective feelings (remember being frightened? having fun?).

The process of forgetting in LTM is a matter of some debate. On one hand, our experience and common sense tells us that old memories gradually fade away, a time-related **decay** process. However, forgetting in LTM also may be due to **interference.** Interference most often is due to the presence of confusingly similar, "competing" ideas or information. You probably do not recall the birthday of your best friend in second grade. Is this because of a decay process over a period of years? Or is it because you have "learned" so many birthdays that more recent ones have interfered with the retention of earlier ones? Probably both decay and interference have caused this forgetting. A third cause of forgetting in LTM—loss of accessibility—is explained later in this section.

Interference may be **retroactive** or **proactive.** With retroactive interference, recently learned material interferes with the retention of earlier learned material. For example, say you just looked up a phone number, 251-8662. Before you dial, a friend (?) sticks her head in the door and says "call me tonight at 215-6882." The first number is instantly gone—retroactively interferred with. Proactive interference occurs when earlier learned material interferes with remembering more recently learned, new information. For example, students who recently have learned a list of presidents' names will have trouble soon learning a second list of vice presidents' names, since the first names will proactively interfere with learning the new, more recent ones.

Our present verbal associations and language habits often proactively interfere with the learning of confusingly similar new facts and ideas. For example, a student named Mary Lynn Johnston will be called "Marilyn" or "Johnson" due to similar, interfering associations. Also, proactive interference will slow the learning of a second (or third) language. For example, your phonemic and morphemic rules for speaking English (Chapter 4) are no help at all in remembering that *desamueblado* means "unfurnished" in Spanish or that "now" is *maintenant* in French.

However, we also will experience **proactive facilitation,** in which early learning facilitates the retention of more recently learned material. In learning Spanish, for example, one quickly learns that "much" is *mucho*, "national" is *nacional*, and "vocabulary" is *vocabulario*. Proactive facilitation means about the same thing as **positive transfer** (discussed later in this chapter).

Interference is working daily in the average classroom—working *against* you the teacher. Similar ideas are often confused, and wrong ideas or no ideas at all may be recalled at a later date, For example, in the junior high school, the formula for the circumference of a circle ($2\pi R$) can easily interfere with remembering the formula for the area (πR^2). Similar-looking vocabulary words in a high school German class also readily interfere with each other, *nicht wahr?* In this book *assimilation* and *accommodation* will cause you trouble. Extra effort must be used to draw attention to confusingly similar ideas to ensure that students make the correct discriminations and remember the appropriate concepts and relationships.

Some psychologists have argued that there may be *no* forgetting in long-term memory. The problem, they say, is the inability to retrieve the information—which actually is still in there somewhere but lacks **acces-**

INSET 7.2

FLASH-BULB MEMORY

One interesting form of "instant long-term memory" has been called flash-bulb memory (Brown and Kulik, 1982). When something "big" happens, such as your first hours of kindergarten, your high school graduation, your first kiss, or passing your driving test, the events that surrounded that occurrence are retained exceedingly clearly—as though a permanent flash picture were taken. Do you have a few such flash-bulb memories? Do you recall exactly where you were, what you were doing, who was there, and what was happening around you?

As a teacher, do you think you could create some "flash-bulb" educational experiences? What about exciting field trips, an instructive Hollywood-type movie (e.g., *Gone With the Wind*), or a visit from a mayor, police chief, professional athlete, etc.

sibility. To help distinguish between remembering something and actually recalling (retrieving) it, you can think of memory as a junk box: The stuff can be in the junk box somewhere, but finding it and getting it out is a separate matter.

When we search or scan our junk boxes, the search is guided (unconsciously, of course) by the structure of our associations and categories; they are what make information accessible to us. Recalling the information, then, is a matter of finding the proper associates of the "target" information. As we noted above, information in LTM is maintained through meaningful organization with other information. This means that information which is *not* structurally and meaningfully integrated with other ideas and concepts may not be recalled because there is no access to it—no cues which will help retrieve the buried information.

In sum, then, the main characteristics of long-term memory are that: (a) There is no apparent limit to the duration of long-term memory. (b) There are no apparent limits to its capacity. (c) Information is maintained through meaningful organization with other information in our memory structures. (d) Forgetting is due to any or all of three causes—decay, interference (retroactive or proactive), or loss of accessibility due to the lack of an appropriate cue or "trigger."

The main characteristics of the sensory register, short-term memory, and long-term memory, are summarized in Table 7.1.

Table 7.1 A summary of characteristics of the three memory types

Feature	Sensory register	Short-term memory	Long-term memory
Role of attention	Pre-attentive	Requires attention	Unnecessary, after encoding
Maintenance of information	Not possible	Rehearsal	Through meaningful organization
Form of information	Literal copy, verbal, visual, etc.	Verbal, visual, etc.	Verbal, visual, affective, etc., meaningfully organized
Capacity	Large	7 ± 2	Unlimited
Memory duration	$\frac{1}{4}$ to about 2 seconds	About 30 seconds	Minutes to decades
Causes of information loss	Decay	Decay, interference	Decay, interference, loss of accessibility
Retrieval	Direct readout	Automatic (items are in consciousness)	Retrieval cues, perhaps with memory search

MNEMONIC MEMORY DEVICES

Mnemonic memory devices may be deliberately used to move information from your STM to LTM, from where it later may be retrieved. We all have trouble remembering names, what we were supposed to get at the store, and important facts and concepts for college courses. The possibility that your memory can be improved should be of some interest.

There is no evidence that your memory ability itself can be improved simply through practice, the way piano playing and jogging improve with practice (Norman, 1976, p. 131). Rather, all memory systems teach people to pay attention to the material they want to remember and to organize it. The acts of attending and organizing are roughly what is meant by **coding**, or **encoding**, in memory literature. The organization is essentially a plan for storing the information in such a way that you later can retrieve it from LTM. Three main methods of encoding are (1) **grouping** (or categorizing), (2) the use of **mental imagery**, and (3) **rhyming**.

Grouping

We already have seen how grouping or chunking works. Different ideas are organized into a smaller number of "chunks" or categories. The learner then must try to recall only the category names. Each category name serves as a retrieval cue which elicits the members of the category as associates. As a simple example, let's imagine that fourth-grader Frank Forgetful is supposed to remember the names of 20 animals which his class visited at the Kalamazoo Zoo. His teacher told Frank to organize the animals into four groups, then remember the groups.

"It really wasn't very difficult," recalled Frank, "to remember five kinds of bears (black, brown, polar, Kodiak, and honey), six kinds of hooved animals (deer, elk, moose, reindeer, zebra, and a burro named Milton), seven cats (lions, tigers, leopards, panthers, mountain lions, cheetahs, and bobcats), and two elephants (African, Indian)."

Probably every list of things to be remembered can be organized into meaningful groups, thus encoded for later recall.

Another form of grouping—a strategy familiar to many test-wise college students—involves arranging the *first letters* of to-be-remembered concepts into a single, remembered "word." A high school or college trigonometry student can use the imaginary Indian tribe SOHCAHTOA to remember *sine = opposite/hypotenuse, cosine = adjacent/hypotenuse,* and *tangent = opposite/adjacent.* Also, this section deals with grouping, *imagery* and

---

INSET 7.3

**CONSTRUCTIVE AND
INFERENTIAL PROCESSES
IN MEMORY**

No one remembers exactly what they read. Rather, the reader extracts main ideas—the gist—and remembers those. The reader also *adds to* what he or she remembers: We make *inferences* about information we have read, and we sometimes *construct* information in order to achieve completeness in recall. The process is much like problem solving. We have a natural need to make sense out of our environment, and so we often make logical inferences or we construct information in order to achieve a complete, sensible whole. Consider the sentence: *Frank could come to the party because his motorcycle broke down.* Such a statement leads you, quite logically, to make inferences to explain how a crunched Kawasaki would permit Frank to attend the bash. If you tried to recall exactly everything you did on your fifteenth birthday, you undoubtedly would construct a few ideas to fill in missing facts. We often are not aware of which information is accurately recalled and which is merely constructed in order to produce a balanced and sensible picture of a past event.

rhyming, whose first letters are *g, i,* and *r,* pronounced "gir." Remembering *gir* could help you recall the three main types of mnemonic devices.

A variation of the first-letters strategy involves using an easily remembered sentence. The first letter of each word is a cue for recalling items in a list. For example, *My dear Aunt Sally* would help a first- or second-grade pupil recall the four basic arithmetic operations of multiplication, division, addition, and subtraction.

Imagery

Using mental imagery is another, more colorful method for encoding a list of ideas. There are a number of specific imagery techniques, the most popular of which is the *"one-bun, two-shoe, three-tree"* strategy (Paivio,

1971). This amazing little gimmick allows you to quickly memorize up to 10 ideas, perhaps 10 concepts for a predicted essay exam question, 10 things to get at the grocery store, or 10 things you gotta do today. It all begins with the numbers 1 to 10, and a rhyming "clang" associate of each:

one-bun	six-sticks
two-shoe	seven-heaven
three-tree	eight-gate
four-door	nine-wine
five-hive	ten-hen

Note that this list (a) is easily recalled and (b) stimulates mental imagery. The strategy is simply to incorporate the idea-to-be-remembered into the mental imagery.

For example, let's say you are in a telephone booth without a pencil and your roommate asks you to stop at the local corner store and pick up some cola, a package of marshmallows, a can of tomato soup, a loaf of rye bread, a box of ceral, four apples, six oranges, a can of olives, a small jar of peanut butter and a mouse trap. You carefully integrate each item with the imagery elicited by the numbers, for example, 1-bun (a can of cola in a bun), 2-shoe (a shoe full of marshmallows), 3-tree (a small tree decorated with cans of tomato soup), and so on. The numbers 1 to 10 serve as retrieval cues which trigger the imagery. The list can be recalled backward, forward, or in any other order. The strategy is based on solid information processing theory—attention, organization, and the use of proper associative cues to trigger recall—and it works.

An encoding strategy for remembering names depends partly on mental imagery and partly on word associations. With little or no practice, this technique can help you memorize the names of 20 or 30 students in a few minutes, or the names of a half-dozen strangers to whom you were too-quickly introduced at a party. The "trick" is to pick out an important feature of each person, a feature you will be sure to pick out the next time you encounter him or her. You then associate the name with that feature. If Betty has blond hair, the words "blond Betty" would do the trick. If Oscar has round glasses, the shape "O" should trigger "O for Oscar." If Elizabeth is pretty like a movie star, then "pretty Elizabeth Taylor" would help recall her name. If Joseph has one ear, three arms, and whistles instead of talks, then "just plain Joe" should help keep his name in the long-term memory.

Another imagery-based device includes using a familiar location such as your parent's house (Anderson, 1980). You can easily create a mental image of each room. The ideas to be remembered are systematically incorporated into the imagery of each room. Just as "one-bun" triggers an image of a bun with a can of cola in it, an image of each room will include

INSET 7.4

THE KEYWORD METHOD: USING IMAGERY TO LEARN FOREIGN LANGUAGE VOCABULARY

Recently, several educational psychologists have been studying the usefulness of the **keyword method** for learning the meanings (translations) of foreign language vocabulary words (Atkinson, 1975; Levin, McCormick, Miller, Berry and Pressley, 1982; Paivio and Desrochers, 1981; Pressley, Levin, and Delaney, 1982). Basically, the learner first establishes a stable association between the foreign word and a familiar English word that sounds like part of the foreign word. For example, the Spanish word for duck is *pato*, which could easily be associated with the English "keyword" *pot*. The learner then generates a mental image linking the keyword (pot) with the meaning of the foreign word (duck). In this example, an image of a duck with a pot over his head should do the trick. In one research study (Pressley and Levin, 1978), students who used the keyword method out-performed other students in foreign vocabulary learning by a two-to-one margin!

the image of the to-be-remembered item. A systematic imaginary walk through the house should later produce the ideas in a systematic order. Luria (1982) described a mnemonist who could memorize a list of 70 words by associating each word with an image and storing the image along a familiar roadway which he visualized in his mind. In one test, he recalled such a list perfectly 15 years later.

The first written record of the place or "loci" technique was left by ancient Greek Poet Simonides:

Persons desiring to train this faculty [of memory] must select places and form mental images of the things they wish to remember and store those images in the places, so that the order of the places will preserve the order of the things, and the images of the things will denote the things themselves, and we shall employ the places and images respectively as a wax writing-tablet and the letters written on it. [From Yates, 1966]

The technique was used by virtually every respectable Greek or Roman orator in order to deliver very long, organized speeches with unfailing accuracy.

Rhyming

Our third memory technique, rhyming, does not require mental imagery or grouping. There are several familiar rules serving as memory aids which use a short, rhyming poem to remind us of the correct idea. For example, "*i* before *e* except after *c*" tells us how to spell *receive*, although *chief* is confusing. And which months hath 30 days?

> *Thirty days hath September,*
> *April, June, and November.*

One language arts rule for pronouncing words with double vowels (e.g., *peak*) is:

> *When two vowels go walking,*
> *The first one does the talking.*

The rule works fine for the majority of English words (e.g., *peak*, *main*, *goal*), but *chief* is still confusing.

British children learn a six-word poem which summarizes, in order, the fate of the six wives of King Henry VIII:

> *Divorced, Beheaded, Died,*
> *Divorced, Beheaded, Survived.*

"The principal is a pal" is a semirhyming mnemonic for spelling one troublesome word correctly. It's troublesome because *principle* and *principal* are similar yet a distinction must be made, and so there is interference in remembering which is which. See Bellezza (1981) for a recent review of mnemonic memory devices; Neisser (1982) for descriptions of extraordinary mnemonists.

FACILITATING MEMORY IN THE CLASSROOM

Memory and learning are naturally intertwined. Any principle or strategy for improving learning also improves memory. For example, such basic principles of conditioning as repetition, stimulus-stimulus contiguity, and reinforcement of correct responses are intended to help the student learn *and* remember. However, several principles of teaching and learning specifically attempt to reduce forgetting.

Encourage "Deeper" Processing

Material is remembered better if it is processed in depth. Such processing may include relating the new material to what the student knows, which is one of the single most important principles in this book. Deeper processing occurs when the student *analyzes, synthesizes,* or *evaluates* new ideas, *compares* them to other ideas, *identifies meaningful relationships* among ideas, or is required to *make inferences* or *think creatively* with the information. What do you think of the depth-of-processing idea? Will deeper processing aid learning? Why? How many ways can you think of to encourage deeper processing? How does depth of processing relate to STM and LTM? There, you just processed in-depth depth of processing.

Requiring learning by meaningless rote memory—which remains all too common in our schools—is the best condition for forgetting. Or the worst condition for learning, if you prefer.

Use Review, Repetition to Prevent Forgetting

Memory traces do fade (or decay). Therefore, it is important that material be well-learned, or overlearned, in the first place. Information learned only to the point where it can barely be recalled will soon be at least partly forgotten. Also, interference due to confusion is increased by incomplete initial learning. Review sessions are one appropriate technique. Certainly, teachers should review main concepts and skills before a test. Review also may take the form of applying the concepts and skills in different ways and situations.

Where confusingly similar but conflicting ideas exist, the teacher especially must emphasize the important differences between the concepts so that students can make the proper distinctions. For example, the differences between πR^2 and $2\pi R$ and between *principle* and *principal* should merit a little special emphasis.

Quizzes also serve as a form of review. The quiz itself stimulates recall and repetition; it also provides feedback to the student about what still requires attention. Some educators recommend an ungraded quiz at the beginning of a fall high school course to help identify concepts and skills forgotten over the summer, concepts and skills in need of review and practice.

Emphasize Organization

Virtually everything we know about memory limits, memory structure, and meaningful learning argues the case for systematic and meaningful organization. The concept of chunking tells us that many details may be remembered and recalled if those details are organized into a smaller number of meaningful "chunks." Further, the concept of cognitive structure (Chapter 8) tells us that facts and details are highly forgettable unless anchored to what the learner already knows. The process of organizing material into meaningful categories and relationships serves to anchor (or tie) the new information to cognitive structure, which reduces forgetting.

INSET 7.5

**REPRESSION: IF YOU
DON'T LIKE IT,
FORGET IT**

Sigmund Freud described another mechanism of forgetting: repression. Repression, or *motivated forgetting,* is a process by which unpleasant experiences are conveniently and comfortably forgotten. It happens to everyone, and it makes life much more pleasant.

Freud himself and more contemporary psychiatrists and psychologists have used hypnosis and other techniques to penetrate this ego defense mechanism of repression, and to dredge up forgotten unpleasant experiences.

**Use
Mnemonics
When
Possible and
Appropriate**

There is nothing wrong with using a "trick" to help students learn a rule or principle, or to help them distinguish between two or more similar ideas. Even university medical students use a sing-song poem to learn, in order, the names of 10 vagal nerves; electronics technicians use a dirty ditty to help keep track of the ohm value of color-coded resistors.

**Develop an
Intent to
Learn and
Remember**

Science has discovered that learners who are warned of a recall test (**intentional learning**) retain material better than learners not so warned (**incidental learning**), although both groups are exposed to the same learning activities (Ausubel, Schpoont, and Cukier, 1957). Usually, a conscious intent to learn leads the learner to process the information "in more depth" than learners who do not have this mental set. Goal-setting, incidentally, is a motivational tactic which (a) requires the student to commit himself or herself to mastering particular material or skills, and (b) encourages systematic reviews and study sessions in order to maintain the information or skills (see Chapter 9).

TRANSFER

One of the central purposes of formal education is to teach knowledge, skills, and values of future benefit to the learners and to society. School learning is intended to **transfer** to the real world.

Now, transfer may be **positive** or **negative**. Positive transfer occurs when a learned skill, problem solution or some bit of knowledge helps in coping with a new problem. Learning to use a dictionary, learning to value promptness, learning to multiply, learning about different types of government, learning to paint with the bristle end of the brush—all of these represent skills and knowledge which transfer positively to new problem situations.

Transfer is negative when the training or knowledge interferes with further learning, performance, problem solving or understanding. We will find negative transfer in virtually every educational subject. For example, in language arts rules for conjugating regular verbs can interfere with conjugating irregular verbs. Also, the language habits of foreign and minority students will interfere with learning English morphology (prefixes, suffixes) and sentence construction. In world history, facts surrounding Magellan, Cortez, Balboa, Pizarro, Hudson, and Drake will be difficult to keep straight.

In geography some large American cities (Omaha, Seattle, Miami, Milwaukee) often are incorrectly assumed to be their states' capitals. Even throwing a rock or baseball interferes with learning to throw a football or javelin.

Problem Solving

We often find negative transfer when a rule or solution for one problem is inappropriately applied to solving another, seemingly similar problem. The thinker basically gets nowhere. In mathematics at any level, rules and solution strategies can be incorrectly applied to produce wrong answers. In first-grade arithmetic, children learn to subtract the small number from the large number to find the answer. For example: $\begin{smallmatrix} 9 \\ -5 \\ \hline 4 \end{smallmatrix}$. When more complex problems are presented, such as $\begin{smallmatrix} 2537 \\ -689 \end{smallmatrix}$, many children gleefully apply the same old rule on a digit-by-digit basis—they subtract the little number from the big number and produce the incorrect answer of 2152.

Classic Views of Transfer

Toward the end of the nineteenth century the human mind was seen as a conglomerate of specific *faculties*, such as reasoning, memory, imagination, morality, logic, the "will," and so on. Strengthening these faculties, like building muscles, was thought to require patient, systematic, and very strenuous exercise. This **formal discipline** approach resulted in the memorizing of lengthy Biblical passages in Latin and in heavy doses of mathematics and physics—all intended to strengthen "faculties of the mind."

It doesn't work that way.

Transfer is positive only if the training task is somehow *similar* to the later transfer task. Practice with math problems will transfer positively to later math problems, but will not necessarily strengthen "faculties" of logic and reasoning needed for a career in, say, law or politics. Memorizing Biblical passages in Latin should be helpful for a future career in professional Latin Biblical passage memorizing, but this activity will not strengthen a general "faculty" of memory.

Partly as an overreaction to the formal discipline idea came the notion that *only* practical, applied knowledge and skills should be taught in the schools. After all, the logic went, hasn't research shown that only relevant, practical knowledge and skills transfer to later problem solving? Within this context appeared the **identical-elements** model of transfer proposed by psychologist E. L. Thorndike in 1913. The basic idea was that the degree of positive transfer was related to the number of "identical elements" common to the training task and the new transfer situation. Thus a person who has learned to type can quickly learn to key punch, due to the large number of "identical elements" in the two situations.

The problem with early interpretations of the identical-elements approach was that they led to an extreme overemphasis on applied, practical facts and skills. Since becoming a productive adult does not require training in history, literature, foreign languages, or playing a French horn, many features of a rich, well-rounded education were dropped.

Obviously, the reasonable route is a middle one—a general education which gives each student both practical knowledge and training, yet passes on some of the richness of our world: music, philosophy, botany, history, languages, literature, art, and so on.

Yet another theory of transfer comes from traditional learning theory, the idea of **generalization.** As we saw in Chapter 5, Pavlov in his conditioning studies found that his dogs would salivate juicily to tones which were similar to the training tone (which was paired with the food). A totally different tone would elicit little or no salivation. The generalization idea is basically the same as Thorndike's identical-elements model: If a transfer task (say key punching) is similar to the training task (typing), transfer will be positive. That is, the skill or knowledge will "generalize" to the new situation. The degree of transfer, or generalization, is related to the degree of similarity.

Principles of Teaching for Transfer

Apart from principles for learning and principles for facilitating memory, some recommendations are especially aimed at strategies for teaching skills and information which will transfer.

First, the strongest recommendation is to provide opportunities for application. If a history lesson is supposed to increase understanding of current political problems, then students must actively apply the ideas of the lesson to current political problems.

Second, transfer is best achieved when applications are practiced in a *variety* of situations. Every mathematics text from elementary school through graduate school requires the learner to practice a particular skill (e.g., subtraction, using decimals) with a wide variety of specific problems.

Third, the teacher should emphasize the principles and generalizations. We all forget facts. It is the principles and generalizations which enable the learner to solve new problems, whether in math, music, social studies, or even personal problems.

Fourth, be alert for circumstances of negative transfer. Negative transfer will occur when a new problem seems similar to a familiar problem, but in fact requires a different rule or solution. The teacher should draw students' attention to similar situations which require different solution strategies.

TO IMPROVE
YOUR TEACHING

The main purpose of this chapter is to acquaint you with contemporary ideas about the dynamics of information processing, memory, and transfer. These concepts should increase your understanding of learning, thinking, and memory; they also should help you better arrange learning tasks to facilitate retention and transfer.

Levels-of-processing theory tells us, first of all, that students cannot actively attend to two things at once. If a student is talking, reading, or playing with a puzzle, you and your directions will be "filtered out"—not attended to at a conscious level. Before giving instructions or explaining a concept or skill, you must have everyone's attention—so that it is the puzzle or the book that is temporarily "filtered out," not the teacher.

More important yet is the notion of "deeper processing" as a means of improving learning, understanding and retention. Deeper processing, hence better learning and retention, is elicited when students are asked to, for example, (a) analyze a new concept into component parts, (b) synthesize new ideas into a meaningful whole, (c) evaluate the goodness or truth of a principle, (d) make inferences based on the principle, (e) think creatively about a concept (e.g., thinking of new uses, new applications, consequences, improvements, etc.), or otherwise "think about" the concept or principle.

In this chapter, deeper processing means about the same thing as *semantic elaboration* (integrating the new idea with other ideas) or *elaboration rehearsal* (finding meaningful connections with the new material).

The concept of the auditory sensory register tells us that information presented verbally will be quickly lost, unless the student has a chance to react to it—rehearse it, relate it to other ideas, write it down, or otherwise respond to the verbal message. The most important feature of the STM is its limited capacity—students, and teachers, simply cannot remember more than a handful of unrelated, meaningless units of information (names of cities, planets, raw materials, etc.) without repetition, organization, or both.

To move information from the conscious, temporary limited-capacity STM to the more permanent LTM, the new ideas must be "anchored" to ideas which the students already know ("Now, this flower is a narcissus—it's just like those daffodils except it has white petals, okay?"). Another "elaborative" strategy for encoding new information in LTM is teaching students to group ideas or objects into meaningful categories ("Look, there are four inner planets and five outer planets."). Psychologists call this "chunking." Organizing the material, and explaining the organization, is a form of chunking.

You also should be alert to the possible use of imagery or rhyming techniques to help students retain a rule or a concept. It makes remembering a whole lot easier, compared with requiring repetitious, meaningless rote memory.

In both short-term and long-term memory situations you should be alert to the effects of interference from similar, competing ideas. Invest a little more time helping students discriminate Franklin D. Roosevelt from Theodore Roosevelt, or the State of Hawaii from the Island of Hawaii.

School learning is supposed to transfer. Therefore, any teacher should emphasize applications and implications of new skills and principles. And students should practice a skill in a variety of contexts. Every theory of transfer tells us that the ease of transfer will be related to the similarity of the training task to the transfer tasks. Sometimes, however, transfer will be negative, and the teacher should be alert to such circumstances. For example, learning the musical notes of the treble clef always interferes with learning the notes of the bass clef, with novice musicians.

SUMMARY

Information processing deals with attention, memory, transfer, problem solving, and even consciousness.

"Level of information processing" refers to the idea that incoming information can be "handled" or processed at a conscious level, "fringe conscious" levels, and even unconscious levels—all at the same time.

Some of the main levels of processing principles are: (1) The highest, conscious level of processing—conscious attention—can deal with only one activity at a time, although attention may be quickly switched to other activities. (2) The highest level of processing, conscious attention, is always taking place. (3) It is the unexpected, surprising input which is passed to higher levels of conscious attention.

In the classroom, information processed at a deeper level is better learned. "Deep" processing implies high-level analyses of meanings and relationships. Deeper processing occurs when students are asked to make inferences, to think creatively, to make applications, or to analyze, synthesize, or evaluate the concepts or principles.

Maintenance rehearsal refers to repetition which enables us to retain an exact copy of the information (e.g., a phone number) for a short time. Elaboration rehearsal involves searching for meaningful relationships in order to improve retention.

The sensory register is a brief, afterimage sort of storage device, lasting up to one-quarter second in the visual mode, two seconds in the auditory mode. It is pre-attentive; forgetting is a fast decay process. The short-term memory, limited to the famous 7 ± 2 items, lasts up to about 30 seconds and is post-attentive. Forgetting is due to decay and/or interference. The long-term memory has an apparently unlimited capacity and duration. Forgetting again seems to be due both to a time-related decay process and interference from confusingly similar "competing" ideas.

Chunking or coding allows information to move from the temporary, conscious STM to the more permanent LTM.

In the classroom, interference from confusingly similar ideas is a continuing problem for teachers and learners. Interference may be retroactive, in which new material interferes with the retention of earlier material, or proactive, in which earlier material interferes with the retention of new material.

Recall depends on having appropriate retrieval cues to trigger the associations. Memory searches are assumed to be guided by the structure and organization of our associations and categories. Therefore, meaningless material—not integrated with other ideas and concepts—will be difficult to recall.

Mnemonic devices are deliberate strategies for moving information from the STM to the LTM—from where it may be recalled later by means of appropriate retrieval cues. Three types of mnemonic devices are grouping, using mental imagery, and rhyming.

As for improving retention, any principle or strategy for improving learning also will improve retention; for example, repetition, stimulus-stimulus contiguity, and reinforcing correct responses.

Other recommendations: (1) Encourage "deeper" processing. (2) Use review and overlearning. (3) Emphasize organization and meaningful relationships. (4) Use mnemonics when appropriate. (5) Develop an intent to learn and remember.

Much of the information and skills acquired in school is supposed to transfer to the real world. Transfer from one task or problem to another may be positive (helpful) or negative (a hindrance). Classic theories of transfer include the formal discipline approach of faculty psychology, in which miserable doses of Latin and mathematics were assumed to strengthen "faculties" of, for example, memory and logic. In contrast, the identical-elements approach assumed that the degree of transfer was related to the degree of task similarity, that is, the number of "identical elements" common to the training task and the transfer task. The generalization approach said about the same thing as the identical-elements theory: The greater the similarity, the stronger the generalization.

To strengthen the likelihood of transfer, a teacher might (1) provide opportunities for transfer, (2) practice applications in a variety of situations, (3) emphasize principles and generalizations, and (4) be alert for circumstances of negative transfer—when a new problem requires a different solution than an apparently similar familiar problem.

TOPICS FOR THOUGHT AND DISCUSSION

1. What are some "unconscious" activities that you regularly perform? What surprises cause you to suddenly "pay attention" to what you are doing?
2. What techniques are used in college texts, lectures, labs, etc., to help students learn, understand and retain the subject matter? Do each of these techniques elicit elaboration rehearsal (deeper processing), or just maintenance rehearsal (repetition, rote learning)?
3. Try creating a grouping or "chunking" mnemonic device which will help you recall *all* six sections and all 19 chapters of this book.
4. What could teachers (including professors) do so that lecture information in a verbal sensory register or the short-term memory will not be lost?
5. What are some of the earliest memories in your life? Is long-term memory fairly permanent?
6. Do you have some "flash-bulb" memories?

PROJECTS

1. With a small group of fellow students, brainstorm a list of classroom questions, projects, activities, etc., which should elicit "deeper processing" and therefore better retention of, say, the concepts of *democracy, energy, conservation,* or *nuclear war.*
2. Most teachers have pet "tricks" or "games" to help students learn. Compile a list of these, and see if you can explain the nature of the "deeper processing" involved.
3. With a group of students, discuss memory tricks they use to prepare for exams—you will learn something.

RECOMMENDED READING

Anderson, J. R. *Cognitive psychology and its implications.* San Francisco: W. H. Freeman, 1980.

Bellezza, F. S. Mnemonic devices: Classification, characteristics, and criteria. *Review of Educational Research* **51,** 1981, 247–275.

Ellis, H. C. *Human learning and cognition,* second edition. Dubuque, Iowa: W. C. Brown, 1978.

Neisser, U. (ed.) *Memory observed: Remembering in natural contexts.* San Francisco: W. H. Freeman, 1982.

Norman, D. A. *Memory and attention: An introduction to human information processing,* second edition. New York: Wiley, 1976.

Solso, R. L. *Cognitive psychology.* New York: Harcourt, Brace & Jovanovich, 1979.

A Cognitive Structure View of Learning and Teaching: Ausubel

8

COGNITIVE LEARNING THEORY

In Chapter 5 we briefly mentioned the contrast between behavioristic learning theory—which traditionally deals with the observable stimulus (environment), the response (behavior), and the reinforcing consequences—and cognitive learning theory—which more freely speculates upon the nature of unseen, implicit mental events and structures. The principles and applications of behavioristic learning theory, as these were summarized in Chapters 5 and 6, include a great many ideas which simplify and clarify otherwise complex behavior, and which sometimes prescribe good solutions to many classroom problems. There will be more behavioristic learning theory later in this volume, especially in relation to classroom management and discipline (Chapter 10) and teaching handicapped and disadvantaged learners (Chapter 18).

With "cognitive" approaches to understanding learning, thinking, and behavior, we leave the "S" and the "R" in S-R psychology and plunge inside the hyphen. We look to see how ideas and information are organized in the individual, how the intentions and purposes ("mental sets") of the learner affect learning and memory, how meaningful relations among ideas improve learning, and how the self-discovery of principles also aids learning and memory.

We saw many cognitive-level concepts in Chapters 3 and 4, related to such "mentalistic" matters as personality, identity, egocentrism, moral thinking, cognitive development, transformational grammar, and especially Piaget's concept of mental schemata. We also encountered cognitive concepts in Chapter 7, ideas related to levels of information processing, mental imagery, semantic elaboration, and mnemonic memory tricks. Now, a dedicated behaviorist, or other learning-oriented psychologist, probably could reinterpret or *reduce* these cognitive concepts to a simpler conditioning language. For example, personality traits, eogcentrism, and moral thinking could be defined as particular behaviors of the individual, without regard to mental events; Piaget's schemata might be explained as a network of conditioned associations, as described in Chapter 5. However, the equally dedicated cognitive psychologist would argue that a behavioristic "reductionism" (a) oversimplifies most matters and (b) loses or ignores important complex psychological phenomena—phenomena available only if we accept the complexity of human mental life (Taylor, 1981).

With no offense intended for the short-sighted, narrow-thinking, extremist fanatics in either camp, the most reasonable position for psychologists and educators is a middle one. One should be free to draw explanatory ideas and teaching strategies from either source. Both traditional learning theory and more recent cognitive and developmental models present a wealth of valuable insights into the nature of human learning, thinking, and behavior.

Ausubel's Cognitive Structure Approach

The present chapter is unique in this book in focusing almost entirely upon the ideas and insights of one educational psychologist, David P. Ausubel. Professor Ausubel's theory of learning and teaching continues to have high impact both on academics in their ivory towers and on teacher-practitioners in their classrooms. His concepts present a very intuitively appealing picture of (a) how students learn and (b) how we should be teaching.

The core idea is basically a simple one: "Learning" is a matter of relating new information to what the learner already knows, that is, tying or "anchoring" new ideas to existing cognitive structures. In Ausubel's own words, "If I had to reduce all of educational psychology to just one principle, I would say this: The most important single factor influencing learning is what the learner already knows. Ascertain this and teach him accordingly" (Ausubel, Novak, and Hanesian, 1978, p. iv). Other leading educational psychologists agree. Anderson, Reynolds, Shallert, and Goetz (1977), for example, also argued that what people learn depends largely on what they already know, and that new learning involves the assimilation of information into existing knowledge structures. Piaget's notion that learning is the formation, differentiation, and integration of mental schemata (Chapter 4) is virtually identical to Ausubel's concept of tying new ideas to cognitive structures, or in Ausubel's words, the "progressive differentiation of cognitive structure."

In Ausubel's vocabulary, new ideas are "subsumed" or "anchored" into the learner's cognitive structure. In essence, relating the new material to ideas learned previously makes the new ideas **meaningful.** We thus have several alternative names for Ausubel's theory: It's a **cognitive structure theory,** a **subsumption theory,** a **meaningful verbal learning theory,** or a **meaningful verbal subsumption theory.** Also, since students receive rather than discover, **reception learning** and **meaningful reception learning** are two more names. The remainder of this chapter will elaborate on the concepts mentioned above and on other details of Ausubel's cognitive-structure-based, meaningul, verbal, reception, subsumption theory of learning.

MEANINGFULNESS

Several noted psychologists, including Piaget and Bruner (Chapter 4), have noted that something is "meaningful" if you can relate it to what you already know. As an example, consider the following passage:

> Pteropus *is a member of the* Pteropidae *family of* Megachiroptera. *Unlike members of* Microchiroptera, *Pteropus eats fruit, has a five or six foot wingspan, roosts in trees, looks like a fox, and uses its eyes quite a bit.*

Chances are, you did not learn much from the passage. Six months from now you probably would not remember even seeing the material. It seems self-evident that if you do not "understand" some new concept or concepts, you will neither learn nor remember the material particularly well. Understanding a new idea means that the new idea is meaningful, which means that you can relate this new idea to ideas and information you already have, that is, your existing schemata or cognitive structures.

Let's try the *Pteropus* paragraph again. What if we had introduced the passage by explaining that *chiroptera* is the scientific name for *bats*. You already possess schemata or cognitive structures relating to bats. Now, there are two suborders of bats, the large fruit-eating *megachiroptera* ("mega" = big) and the small insect-eating *microchiroptera* ("micro" = little). The common American Brown Bat is a typical member of the microchiroptera suborder. As you know, it hangs upside down in dark places during the day, and dashes out in the evening for a meal of mosquitoes.

Now read that passage on *Pteropus* again. Since you can now *relate* each item of information to what you already know, it should make sense. It is meaningful and you understand it. Furthermore, you are more likely to remember the information. You also are able to learn and retain additional facts and concepts about *Pteropus*, the Flying Fox of India. *The learnability of new material depends on the ability of the person to relate the material to what he or she already knows.*

Meaningful Learning

There are two main requirements for meaningful learning. First, the learner must have a **meaningful learning set.** That is, the learner must be ready and willing to relate the new ideas to what he or she already knows. This meaningful learning set occurs when students are reminded of related ideas and experiences, and they are made aware that the new ideas should be related to their existing ideas. Science teacher Angela Acorn might remind students about the place of bats in the animal kingdom and about familiar bat facts, thus stimulating a "set" to relate new bat facts (about *Pteropus*) to the already familiar information.

A meaningful learning set contrasts with a rote learning set—which is a predisposition to memorize in an arbitrary, verbatim fashion. More on rote learning later in this chapter.

The second requirement for meaningful learning is that the new material must be **potentially meaningful,** that is, potentially relatable to what the learner already knows. This requirement simply emphasizes that the relevant "anchoring" ideas and experiences must be available in each individual learner. Thus a student who thinks a bat is a grouchy lady or a Louisville Slugger, and knows nothing of insect-eating, night-flying mammals, would not possess the necessary ideas and experiences. Meaningful learning in the sense of relating new material to what the learner already knows will not be possible until the missing information is acquired.

COGNITIVE STRUCTURE

Our past learning and experiences are organized into knowledge structures or **cognitive structures.** A cognitive structure—for example, your cognitive structure related to bats—is comprised both of a *content* and an *organization.* Figure 8.1 might represent a simplified and hypothetical cognitive structure of knowledge about bats. The content is the facts, concepts, principles, ideas, names, places, functions, processes, colors, smells, and so on. The structure is the superordinate, subordinate and coordinate relationships among the various facts, concepts, etc.

Note that the top of the structure in Figure 8.1 includes a small number of broad, inclusive concepts—in this example, *mammals* and *rodents.* These broad concepts are very stable; you could not forget them if you tried. For a given topic, such as bats, there are not very many of the superordinate, inclusive concepts and they have been well-learned over many years. As you proceed "down" the hierarchically organized cognitive structure, the information becomes more specific in the obvious sense of subcategories, sub-subcategories, and sub-sub-subcategories. Any biologist worth his or her stuffed owl would have a highly differentiated and detailed cognitive structure and could tell you all about the eye-color, claw-length, reproduction patterns, habitat habits, scratches, squeaks, and hour-by-hour, season-by-season activities of a variety of bats. These details are both more specific and more likely to be forgotten.

Figure 8.1
Hypothetical cognitive structure, with general, inclusive concepts at the top and differentiated concepts and facts at the bottom.

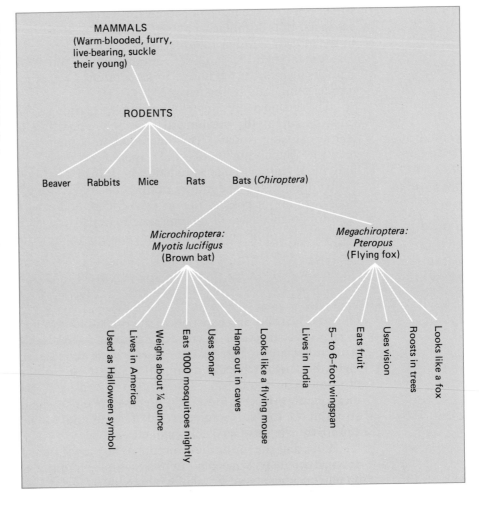

In one summary statement, Ausubel observed that a new concept can be learned and retained only if it ". . . can be nonarbitrarily and substantively related to any appropriate cognitive structure" (Ausubel *et al.*, 1978, p. 38). That is, the new material must be related to ideas already in the existing structure. This is the meaning of *meaningful* and the significance of *cognitive structure.*

Incidentally, it is no accident that the *cognitive structure* in Figure 8.1 closely resembles the example of a *task analysis* described in Chapter 11 (Figure 11.1). Both are based on the content and structure of a particular body of information. Furthermore, the learning of material which has been organized and taught according to a task analysis should produce a cognitive structure which is similar in content and organization to that task analysis. We could even say that a task analysis is a diagram of a cognitive structure, but created for the purpose of logically organizing the sequence and content of instruction.

Learning as Subsumption into Cognitive Structure

The existence of a cognitive structure is the principal factor influencing learning. New material is subsumed or incorporated into an existing structure by anchoring the new ideas to the old. Note that after one reading, our original *Pteropus* passage above probably could not be related to anything you already knew. We have agreed that the material was "meaningless," which is the same as saying it could not be related to an appropriate cognitive structure. However, once we clarified the technical term and said that *Pteropus Megachiroptera* (let's call it the *Flying Fox*) was a *bat*, then immediately an appropriate cognitive structure—a hierarchically organized set of facts and concepts—was available, and the new concepts could be understood and learned. Ausubel would say that the cognitive structure provides "scaffolding" to which to anchor the new information. He would also say that the new information was subsumed into the cognitive structure.

Figure 8.2 illustrates how specific "bat concepts" already in cognitive structure provide anchorage for subsuming the new information.

TEACHING ACCORDING TO SUBSUMPTION THEORY

Let's say you wanted to teach a group of high school students about the amazing Flying Fox fruit bat. Assume that they already know about common American bats. You first would review and discuss crucial parts of the cognitive structure—bats as mammals and rodents, and the size, appearance, sonar capability, eating, and roosting habits of bats—so that students (a) form a meaningful learning set and (b) have the "anchoring ideas" available to both organize and anchor the new material.

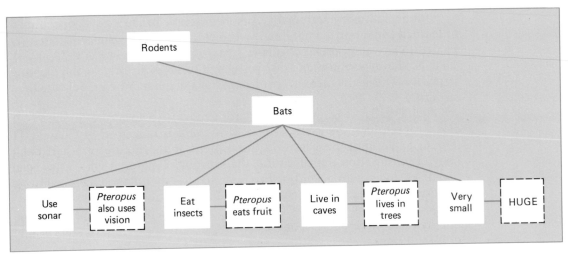

Figure 8.2   New information anchored to ideas in cognitive structure. In this illustration the existing ideas (solid boxes) would serve as comparative organizers for anchoring new ideas (dashed boxes).

Usually, the most reasonable strategy is to first review the more general, inclusive concepts. These are the familiar ideas at the top of the cognitive structure with which all students should be familiar. These *subsumers* provide the anchorage to which the new material may be related. After reviewing the most general and inclusive concepts, one may then introduce more specific topics and concepts, the more differentiated ideas "lower" in the cognitive structure.

Generally, then, meaningful learning in the classroom progresses most efficiently by beginning with the broadest, most general concepts and proceeding from them "downward" to more specific, differentiated topics. This hierarchically organized approach from the general to the specific improves learning in several ways:

1. The familiar and meaningful general concepts have much "explanatory power," which gives meaning to new material that otherwise might be learned by rote memory. For example, if a student knows that *Pteropus* is a bat, that Ganymede is one moon of Jupiter, or that West Germany is a democracy, he or she will instantly understand much about *Pteropus*, Ganymede, and West Germany.
2. Since the meaningful general concepts are very stable (unforgettable), they prove solid anchorage for mooring a boatload of new information. New learning is both more efficient and more unforgettable.
3. The general concepts permit the organization of related facts around a

common theme, and thus help to relate new concepts to one another as well as to the more general anchoring ideas. For example, discussing general concepts of mammals and rodents both anchors *Pteropus* to one's cognitive structure and relates *Pteropus* to rats, mice, hamsters, rabbits, and guinea pigs.

Advance Organizers

We suggested immediately above that a teacher may review and emphasize certain ideas and concepts already in the learners' cognitive structure in order that these subsumers might be available for anchoring the new material. Ausubel calls these special introductory materials **advance organizers** (or just **organizers**). In his words: "The principle function of the organizer is to bridge the gap between what the learner already knows and what he needs to know before he can successfully learn the task at hand" (Ausubel, 1977).

Organizers must be presented in language already familiar to the learner. The organizers are intended to help explain and integrate the new concepts and ideas, and so they themselves must be easily understood.

In many cases, visual illustrations or verbal metaphorical relationships may be used as organizers to anchor the new material to cognitive structure. For example, *pictures* of different bats and bat caves, *comparisons* of bats with mice or with other nocturnal animals, or *contrasts* of bats with birds would help make the new concepts meaningful—and therefore learnable and more unforgettable.

In view of the high visibility and high impact of Ausubel's meaningful verbal subsumption theory, there has been considerable research aimed at evaluating his assumptions and recommendations. Most of this research has been aimed at testing the effectiveness of Ausubel's advance organizers (see Ausubel, 1978).

For example, Mayer (1975a, 1975b, 1978) suggested that advance organizers may be especially important for the learning of poorly organized or unfamiliar (e.g., technical) material. In one study Mayer (1975a) showed that giving an advance organizer prior to learning a new computer programming language produced superior learning and transfer. The 500-word organizer compared a computer to such familiar items as a ticket window, scoreboard, notepad, and so on. In a related study, Mayer (1978) used 24 programmed learning frames to teach computer programming. When the frames were presented in a scrambled order, the subjects with an advance organizer (the 500 words describing computers in familiar terms, plus headings on the frames) learned better than subjects without the organizer. Advance organizers did not help (in fact, they interfered!) when the frames were logically organized. Mayer concluded that organizers serve ". . . as an assimilative context for unfamiliar organization."

INSET 8.1

**THE MANY FACES
OF SUBSUMPTION**

We noted that the highly differentiated facts and details in a cognitive structure are the most easily forgotten (unstable). However, at the risk of wasting paper and ink on too-detailed, too-forgettable facts, let's look at a few forms of Ausubel's meaningful subsumption learning.

1. *Subordinate Learning.* With subordinate learning, the prelearned anchoring idea is at a higher level of generality, abstractness, and inclusiveness than the new idea.

   a) With one form of subordinate learning, *derivative subsumption*, the new information is simply a new example of the higher-level concept. The characteristics of the higher-level concept are not changed. You might think of the new idea as directly "derived from" the higher-level idea. For example, one can learn that a Lhasa Apso is a type of dog without changing one's concept of what constitutes a dog. This sort of learning is comparatively easy.

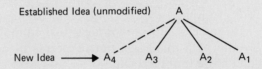

   b) With *correlative subsumption*, the new information again is subordinate to the higher-level concept, but this time the higher-level concept must be modified or extended to incorporate the new idea. One's first exposure to the duck-billed, egg-laying platypus would modify one's concept of *animal*. This type of subsumption is typical of much classroom learning and is considered more difficult than

Interestingly, Lesh (1976) also found that advance organizers aided students in learning a hierarchically organized set of geometry lessons, but did not help with materials having a better integrated, repeated "spiral" organization. Similarly, Schumacher, Liebert, and Foss (1975) found that an advance organizer improved learning when information about U.S. presidents was scattered in six separate paragraphs. The organizer did not help when the information was in a well-organized and integrated passage containing sensible transition phrases. Apparently, organizers are most helpful when organization is needed.

derivative subsumption.

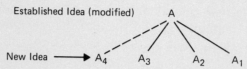

2. *Superordinate Learning.* With superordinate learning, the more specific concepts are the already-learned established ideas and the higher-level concept is the new idea. The established ideas are recognized as examples of the more general concept, and become linked to it. For example, the new realization that rats, mice, rabbits, gerbils, hamsters, guinea pigs, and bats are all *mammals* would be an example of superordinate inductive learning.

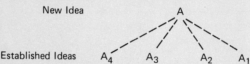

3. *Combinatorial Learning.* With combinatorial learning the new idea is recognized as related to a broad background of relevant ideas, but the new idea has neither a superordinate nor subordinate relationship to the existing ideas. According to Ausubel, most of the *new* generalizations that a student learns in science, math or social studies would be combinatorial relationships among, for example, mass and energy, volume and heat, and supply, demand, and price. Further acquaintance with combinatorially-learned material leads to the development of new superordinate and subordinate relationships.

New Idea ⟶ A · · · · B — C — D ⟵ Established Ideas

Now don't forget any of this.

Perhaps this integrative statement partially explains the *failure* of many studies to show a facilitating effect of advance organizers (e.g., see Ausubel, 1977; Barnes and Clawson, 1975; Mayer, 1975b; West and Fenshaw, 1976). Another reason for organizers failing to improve learning is that the learners simply may not possess the relevant cognitive structures to which potentially meaningful material could be related (Alexander, Frankiewicz, and Williams, 1979).

One good reason that "organizers" is a better term than "advance organizers" is simply that *post* organizers also can aid learning. Alexander,

Frankiewicz, and Williams (1979) content-analyzed instructional material about five cultures (Africa, China, Germany, India, and Mexico) in order to identify "high-level, superordinate concepts" to be prepared as organizers. These general concepts dealt with the shape of the Earth, the notion that people and their basic needs are the same in primitive and modern communities, and the idea that culture is the outcome of a community's attempt to meet those needs. The organizers were presented either visually,

using slides, or verbally, via discussion and questions. Further, the fifth-, sixth-, and seventh-grade subjects who received the organizers received them either before or after a 40-minute presentation on one of the cultures, while control subjects received no organizer at all. The results showed that both verbal and visual organizers improved learning and retention, and that post organizers were about as effective as advance organizers. Post organizers not only permit the organization and anchoring of the concepts, they also give students an opportunity to review the material.

The authors concluded that "When conditions exist whereby students have to learn new and unfamiliar materials without the benefit of a subsumption or organizing construct, the learning that occurs is most likely rote because students probably have to memorize the material verbatim" (Alexander, *et al.*, 1979).

Expository Organizers	Ausubel (1963) identified two main types of organizers, expository and comparative. An **expository organizer** is used when relatively *unfamiliar* concepts and principles are to be taught. Expository organizers have a superordinate, more general relationship to the unfamiliar ideas. They are presented in terms familiar to the learner. The organizers used by Alexander, *et al.* (1979)—the high-level, general concepts about commonalities among communities of the world—were expository organizers, presented before teaching the specifics of new cultures. As another example, say you wish to teach a group of big-city second graders about *Pteropus*, the Flying Fox of India. At present, they know nothing of the little flying mice. One would begin by reviewing higher level, more inclusive concepts—the familiar information already in the learners' cognitive structure. As diagrammed in Figure 8.1, a discussion of the characteristics and definitions of *mammal* and *rodent* should provide the anchorage for meaningfully subsuming more specific information about bats into cognitive structure.

Note that this expository organizer approach would make much more sense than trying to teach, by rote learning, the definitions and characteristics of the Flying Fox to kids who had never heard of a bat—except for Mrs. Grump and her trampled petunias.

Comparative Organizers	By the time they reach elementary school, most children already know about your standard halloween-type bat. Therefore, a **comparative organizer** would provide the necessary meaningful anchorage for the new concept of *Pteropus*. A comparative organizer involves concepts at the *same* level of abstraction as the new material. In our present example, comparative organizers would deal with characteristics of the common American Brown Bat (*Myotis Lucifigus;* see Figure 8.2). There would be a special emphasis

on those characteristics of *Myotis Lucifigus* which distinguish it from *Pteropus:* the size, diet, locale, limited use of vision, and cave-hanging habit. These are concepts to which the new and different characteristics of *Pteropus* will be anchored, as in Figure 8.2.

The emphasis on the *comparative* differences (size, diet, etc.) between the familiar ideas in cognitive structure and the unfamiliar new ideas helps the learner maintain the distinction between the new ideas and the older ones. The new ideas and the old ideas can be confusingly similar. Without the special emphasis of the comparative organizer on the important differences between *Pteropus* and the Brown Bat, the student may end up with the fuzzy impression that some American bats have a six-foot wingspan and are waiting for you at night in your apple tree.

In sum, both the expository and comparative organizers capitalize on the relevant background ideas already in cognitive structure. Both bridge the gap between the old and the new. Both are geared to the appropriate level of inclusiveness and generality. The expository organizer has a superordinate relationship which provides anchorage for the more detailed, differentiated new material. The comparative organizer is at a "coordinate," parallel level, both anchoring the new concepts and providing maximum discriminability between the new and the old.

MEANINGFUL VS. ROTE LEARNING

As we have seen, *meaningful* learning means relating new material to what the learner already knows. Such learning may lead a young scholar to reply, "Oh yeah, it's just like _____, except that _____," or, "Sure it's like what we did yesterday, only _____." This entire chapter is about meaningful learning.

In its most extreme form, rote learning is meaningless memorizing; for example, committing to memory a list of randomly selected Zip Codes. Other rote memorization can be useful: Almost everyone uses multiplication tables at some time; others find it worthwhile to know presidents' names, for example, or the names of all 50 states, scientific names of fish, or the raw materials produced by particular states or countries. Much rote learning occurs in acquiring a foreign language. As you can see by these examples, rote memorizing is not necessarily bad. Indeed, it is a useful and worthy part of school learning. However, rote learning is very, very inefficient: It takes much repetition, and the forgetting rate is very high.

Meaningful learning is much better. It is efficient. It is accompanied by understanding. It aids new learning. It is also more likely to transfer, that is, to be useful in the real world. As we noted in Chapter 7, teaching transferable skills and knowledge is one of the main reasons for formal education in the first place.

DISCOVERY LEARNING AND MEANINGFUL RECEPTION LEARNING

Reception learning. Ausubel's meaningful learning approach is often contrasted with discovery learning. He sometimes refers to his recommended teaching strategy as *meaningful reception learning,* since the student "receives" the entire content of the to-be-learned material in a meaningfully organized, final form. The student need not make independent discoveries of the important concepts and principles, although during the reception learning process students do make discoveries.

Meaningful reception learning implies *expository instruction*—most often with a teacher at the front of the class expositing and attentive students at their desks subsuming this orderly information into their little cognitive structures. Of course, the teaching can include lectures, demonstrations, movies, discussions, and even individual learning from reading, filmstrips, cassettes, records, a microcomputer, a learning center, or other well-organized and structured activities and materials. The student will make discoveries in the course of his or her meaningful reception learning, but the learning activities are deliberately organized for efficient, meaningful subsumption of the information and skills.

Discovery learning. On the other hand, a discovery approach implies individual learning and problem solving, with important discoveries—concepts, rules, principles—made by each student. The learning activities are less likely to include a teacher lecturing. They are more likely to include students working on science projects, researching an integrative report, performing chemistry experiments, selling beads in a make-believe country store, balancing weights on a scale, working out the answers to questions or puzzles, or solving some other problem. Students discover concepts and principles for themselves. They incorporate these principles into their own cognitive structures, using their own language and their own system of categories. According to Ausubel, "After discovery learning is completed, the discovered content is made meaningful in much the same way that presented content is made meaningful in reception learning" (Ausubel *et al.*, 1978, p. 25). That is, the discoverer relates the new discoveries to what he or she already knows, thus anchoring the discoveries in cognitive structure. (Note: Do not take Ausubel's statement to be a kind word for discovery learning. See Inset 8.3.)

Steps in the discovery process. It sometimes is helpful to view the discovery learning process as involving a sequence of four stages (Davis, 1973; Shulman, 1965): (1) *problem sensing,* in which a person initially detects, to his or her discomfort, that some kind of problem or inconsistency exists; (2) *problem formulating,* wherein the person subjectively defines a particular problem and develops his or her own anticipated form of solution; (3) *searching,* in which the individual questions, hypothesizes, gathers infor-

INSET 8.2

**RECEPTION LEARNING
IS NOT THE SAME AS
ROTE LEARNING;
DISCOVERY LEARNING
IS NOT THE SAME AS
MEANINGFUL LEARNING**

A common pair of misconceptions are that (a) teaching in an expository, reception learning fashion leads to rote memorizing and (b) discovery learning is always meaningful learning. To emphasize the distinction between the two dimensions, rote-meaningful and reception-discovery, Novak (1977) and Ausubel, Novak, and Hanesian (1978) present the two-dimensional diagram below. Ausubel's "meaningful reception" notions would be represented in the upper left portion of the diagram. See if you can meaningfully interpret the other eight sections of the illustration.*

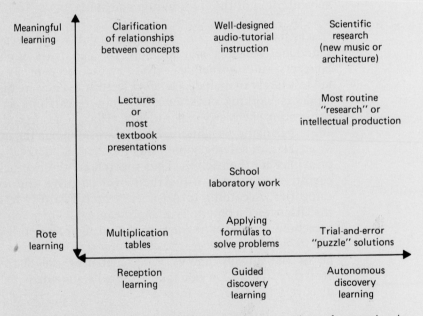

Reception learning and discovery learning are on a separate continuum from rote learning and meaningful learning.

* The illustration is from Joseph D. Novak: *A Theory of Education*. Copyright © 1977 by Cornell University. Used by permission of the publisher, Cornell University Press.

mation, and occasionally backtracks; and (4) *problem resolving*, the final phase in which the person becomes satisfied that he or she has solved the problem or "found out why," thus removing the initial discomfort (or "disequilibrium"). These steps apply to such problems and challenges as researching a topic for a written report, conducting an experiment, or solving an algebra problem. These or similar sets of steps may be taught to students in order to increase their understanding of problem solving and to strengthen their discovery learning and problem-solving skills (Davis, 1973, 1981a; Parnes, Noller, and Biondi, 1977; see Chapter 16).

Claimed advantages. The discovery approach to education has at least a century-long tradition, growing out of the progressive education movement of the late nineteenth and early twentieth century. The idea seemed like a

---

INSET 8.3

A FRIENDLY WORD ABOUT DISCOVERY LEARNING, BY DAVID P. AUSUBEL

Its legitimate uses and advantages have been unwarrantedly extrapolated to include educational goals, levels of intellectual maturity, levels of subject matter sophistication, and levels of cognitive functioning for which it is ill-adapted—and for reasons which derive from sheer dogmatic assertion; from pseudonaturalistic conceptions about the nature and conditions of intellectual development; from outmoded ideas about the relationship between language and thought; from an outmoded overempirical and "inductive" concept of epistemology; from sentimental fantasies about the nature of the child and the aims of education; and from uncritical interpretation of the research evidence.

. . . as the terms "laboratory" and "scientific method" became sacrosanct in U.S. high schools and universities, students were coerced into mimicking the externally conspicuous but inherently trivial aspects of scientific method. They wasted many valuable hours collecting empirical data that, at the very worst, belabored the obvious and, at the very best, helped them rediscover principles that could easily be presented verbally in a matter of minutes. Actually, they learned precious little subject matter and even less scientific method from this procedure.

From Ausubel, D. P., J. D. Novak, and H. Hanesian, *Educational psychology: A cognitive view.* Copyright © 1978 Holt, Rinehart & Winston, p. 523. Reprinted by permission of the first two authors and the publisher.

worthwhile alternative to drills in Latin and memorizing the Old Testament. Famous educator John Dewey's (1933) most famous three words were "learning by doing." Recent claims for the virtues of discovery learning are that (among other things):

- Discovery learning is inherently challenging, rewarding, motivating, and enjoyable.
- Discovery learning teaches skills of problem solving, critical thinking, creative thinking, inquiry behavior, and thinking like a scientist. Such scientific thinking includes independently defining the problem, processing information, generating alternative solutions, and verifying the results. One enthusiastic proponent, Suchman (1961), asserted that, "More basic than the attainment of concepts is the ability to inquire

and discover them independently." Interestingly, learning by discovery is both a teaching *method* and an educational *goal*.

- To really, *really* understand a concept or principle, the learner must discover it for himself or herself. That is, true "meaning" is a product of discovery.
- Discovery learning is more democratic, less authoritarian than expository instruction.
- Discovery learning produces organized knowledge and skills which are better remembered and are more likely to transfer—the "learning" is in a more usable form.

Ausubel, but virtually no one else, takes strong (make it vehement; see Inset 8.3) opposition to these claims. One of his observations is a developmental one. Says Ausubel, learning by doing is a necessary form of learning for elementary school children who need first-hand experiences with concrete materials in order to meaningfully acquire basic concepts. However, the tactic has been inappropriately extended to secondary school students and adults—those capable of meaningful reception learning.

Most educators take a considerably more positive view of the virtues of learning by discovery, supporting the claims we just listed. See, for example, Bruner (1957), Shulman and Kieslar (1966) and Davis (1973).

DISSOCIABILITY: RETRIEVABILITY FROM COGNITIVE STRUCTURE

We already have seen that meaningful learning resists forgetting—the new material is anchored tightly to existing concepts in the conceptual scaffolding, and is available for recall. Ausubel (1963) uses the less-than-lucid term **dissociability**—often misspelled and mispronounced as "disassociability"—to describe the resistance of a concept to forgetting. According to him, a meaningfully learned, well-anchored concept is said to be highly "dissociable" from cognitive structure. That is, it is easily retrieved. If it is not meaningfully learned and not well anchored, it is forgotten. This is to say, the concept is not "dissociable" from cognitive structure; you cannot retrieve it. Overall, Ausubel's theory of meaningful verbal learning nicely integrates the two processes of learning and forgetting into one economical idea—meaningful subsumption with anchoring.

Now, if the reader can close this book and paraphrase the meaning of *dissociability*, he or she can prove that the concept is meaningfully anchored to the rest of his or her cognitive structure. Is dissociability dissociable?

TO IMPROVE
YOUR TEACHING

Your time reading this chapter will have been wasted if you do not incorporate Ausubel's main point into your teaching: Ascertain what the learner already knows, and teach him or her accordingly. This means that any new learning must build on, and be "anchored" to, previous learning. The straight-forward strategy for tying new learning to old learning is the use of advance organizers in introducing the new concepts. You both "remind" students of the necessary anchoring ideas, and prepare them to relate the new concepts to those familiar anchoring ideas. In this way the new ideas are made meaningful, and therefore they are more easily learned and better retained.

The concept of meaningfulness—relatability to cognitive structure—is very important. Too many teachers insist that students memorize concepts by rote repetition, concepts which could be better learned via organizers which make the new ideas meaningful.

There is a role for rote memory, as we noted above, as in memorizing multiplication tables or the names of flowers, chemicals, or historical figures. Even here, however, such strategies as grouping, rhyming, or other mnemonic devices (Chapter 7) can help organize the material into a more *meaningful* form.

Ideally, after learning a particular subject matter a student's cognitive structure should resemble the inherent structure of the subject matter itself (see the example using bats, in Figures 8.1 and 8.2). The fairly obvious suggestion is that a visual diagram of the relationship of new concepts to old concepts is one good form of organizer. Other good organizers are: (a) commonalities or generalizations which tie familiar ideas to new instances; (b) rules or principles which will make a new idea more meaningful; (c) familiar concepts higher in a hierarchically-organized structure, to which the new ideas may be tied; (d) familiar ideas at the same hierarchical level; and (e) other A-V aids (maps, globes, charts, diagrams, pictures, etc.) which relate new ideas to old—i.e., which make new ideas meaningful.

Despite Ausubel's objections, discovery learning tactics are valuable for both elementary and secondary students. Challenging tasks that involve the student are motivating and enjoyable, and they do teach problem solving and research skills. Ausubel is not just whistling *Dixie*, however, when he warns that some teachers may waste time letting students spend an hour discovering a principle which could be adequately explained verbally in 30 seconds. Discovery learning is inherently inefficient as a means of transmitting knowledge. The teacher must be able to distinguish situations where the discovery process has beneficial outcomes from situations where an expository mini-lecture would adequately serve the intended purpose.

SUMMARY

Ausubel's concepts of meaningfulness, cognitive structure, and subsumption learning are important for the understanding of classroom learning and instruction.

Ausubel's theory, which goes by such aliases as "meaningful verbal reception learning," "subsumption learning," a "cognitive structure approach," and other combinations of these terms, is a cognitive theory. A cognitive theory describes implicit mental events and assumes deliberate, conscious purposes or "mental sets," while behavioristic S-R theory traditionally does not.

Meaningfulness refers to the ability of the learner to relate new information to what he or she already knows. With no "substantive relatability to cognitive structure," there is little understanding, little learning and little retention.

Meaningful learning, according to Ausubel, requires (a) a meaningful learning set plus (b) potential meaningfulness (relatability) of the new material; that is, the learner must have the necessary anchoring ideas.

A cognitive structure is one's hierarchically organized set of concepts and ideas related to a given topic. It includes an organization and a content. The broad, general, superordinate concepts are few in number, but well-learned and resistant to forgetting. The detailed sub-sub-subtopics and facts are more quickly forgotten. Ausubel would say they are less stable.

Learning is the subsumption of new information into the existing, appropriate cognitive structure. The cognitive structure provides "scaffolding" for anchoring the new ideas to existing ideas ("subsumers").

Teaching, according to subsumption theory, best proceeds by beginning with broad, familiar concepts, then proceeding to the new, more differentiated material. It is a general-to-specific strategy. The more general, familiar concepts give meaning to the new ideas, provide solid anchorage, and help relate ideas to one another.

Advance organizers, or just organizers, are the introductory, familiar concepts which the teacher wishes to have available for anchoring the new ideas. Expository organizers have a superordinate relationship to the new ideas, and are used when relatively unfamiliar concepts are taught. Comparative organizers are at a hierarchical level similar to that of the new, relatively familiar concepts.

Research on organizers usually, not always, supports their effectiveness, especially when the material is unfamiliar or technical or is poorly organized. Organizers may not be effective if students lack the prerequisite "knowledge structures" to which to anchor the new material. Also, post organizers may be as effective as Ausubel's famous advance organizers.

Meaningful learning is learning with understanding, that is, with relatability to what the learner already knows. Rote learning is the memorization of facts and figures not so related.

Discovery learning requires that each learner discover important concepts and principles for himself or herself. Reception learning, or expository instruction, includes presentation of information in an organized, coherent final form. Four stages in discovery learning are problem sensing, problem formulating, searching, and problem resolving.

Proponents of discovery learning claim that it is motivating and enjoyable, teaches skills of problem solving and scientific thinking, aids understanding, is democratic, and produces better retention and transfer.

Dissociability is Ausubel's term describing strength of learning—or resistance to forgetting, if you prefer. A well-learned idea is said to be dissociable (retrievable) from cognitive structure, while a not-well-learned idea is not retrievable from cognitive structure.

TOPICS FOR THOUGHT AND DISCUSSION

1. Can you think of topics in your college courses that would have been more comprehendible if the instructor had used advance organizers? What types of organizers would have helped?
2. What sorts of advance organizers could be used in teaching elementary students about different forms of government? Fractions? Verbs? Memorizing a poem? Do teachers intuitively use organizers?
3. Under what circumstances (students, subject areas, topics, goals, etc.) do you think discovery approaches (independent projects, library research papers, simulated political events, etc.) are more valuable than expository instruction? When is an expository approach more appropriate?
4. What do you think of the concept of cognitive structure? Does it help make "the mind" more understandable? The process of "learning"? "Teaching"?

PROJECTS

1. For an age group and a topic you expect to teach, create a lesson plan (or an entire unit) which incorporates (a) determining students' current states of knowledge, and (b) advance organizers which tie new concepts to old.
2. Keep a log for one week of all of the sorts of "organizers" which your college instructors seem to use.
3. If you are required to do a teaching demonstration for an educational psychology or curriculum course, incorporate deliberate expository and/or comparative organizers.

RECOMMENDED READING

Ausubel, D. P. *The psychology of meaningful verbal learning*. New York: Grune & Stratton, 1963.

———. Is drill necessary? The mythology of incidental learning. In G. A. Davis and T. F. Warren (eds.), *Psychology of education: New looks*. Lexington, Mass.: D. C. Heath, 1974. Pp. 282–286.

————. The facilitation of meaningful verbal learning in the classroom. *Educational Psychologist* **12,** 1977, 162–178.

Ausubel, D. P., J. D. Novak, and H. Hanesian. *Educational psychology: A cognitive view.* New York: Holt, Rinehart & Winston, 1978.

Bruner, J. S. On going beyond the information given. In *Contemporary approaches to cognition.* Cambridge, Mass.: Harvard University Press, 1957. Pp. 41–69.

Shulman, L. S., and E. R. Kieslar (eds.). *Learning by discovery: A critical appraisal.* Chicago: Rand-McNally, 1966.

MOTIVATION AND CLASSROOM MANAGEMENT

PART IV

Motivation: Theory and Classroom Strategy

9

ABOUT MOTIVATION

Every teacher's number-one problem is motivation. Everything from underachieving and absenteeism to disruptiveness and looting may be seen as problems in classroom motivation. Indeed, if all students were "properly motivated," as displayed by cooperation, attention, interest and a strong desire to learn, the teacher's job would be a much simpler one. In high school and college, it is motivation which determines whether the student stays in or drops out.

In the larger world, and in a broad sense, we can assume that *all* behavior is motivated. In virtually everything you do, you are goaded and guided by forces from within or from the external environment. Small wonder that psychologists have developed a keen interest in motivation—it's a mighty big piece in the jigsaw puzzle of human behavior.

The early part of this chapter will review old and new theories of human motivation. Some of them will be only of academic interest—which assumes that the reader is at least mildly interested in such scholarly matters—while other theories should help the reader to recognize, understand, and even use various forms of motivation in the classroom. The later parts of this chapter will focus more specifically on teaching strategies and principles for stimulating an interest in studying and learning.

Before examining these theories and their classroom relevance, or lack of it, let's review some important principles in motivation: the trait-vs.-state distinction, the energy-vs.-direction concept, and intrinsic vs. extrinsic motivation.

Motivation as a Trait or a Temporary State

Motivation may be seen partly as a stable, enduring **trait** of each person. We all have different interests, different values, and, importantly, different needs for activity and stimulation. You probably have some friends who are compulsive scholars with apparently high needs for success and achievement. Others barely tolerate classwork between beer blasts and tennis games. We also will see later in this chapter that individuals differ dramatically in their needs for arousing, stimulating activities. Some energetic "high sensation seekers" can't wait to climb a cliff, jump from an airplane, or explore the backroads of Brazil. At the other, more peaceful extreme, some people find that reading a good book or tending a quiet lighthouse provide just the right amount of psychological "arousal." The important point is that these individual differences are stable, lasting motivational traits which influence most spheres of a person's life—his or her education, career, hobbies, recreation, and so forth.

There also are temporary situational **states** of motivation. These transient states are due to particularly stimulating or dull events in the environment. For example, a Daffy Duck cartoon normally is a sure-fire way to elicit attention and interest, while a monotone reading of 50

INSET 9.1

EDUCATION'S THREE MOST IMPORTANT CONCEPTS: MOTIVATION, MOTIVATION, MOTIVATION

The concept of motivation runs through virtually all aspects of teaching and learning, and therefore through virtually every chapter in this book. Teacher personality, classroom climate, teacher expectations, accountability, and other facets of teacher-student interaction noted in Chapters 1 and 2 are important because of their effects on student motivation. Also, the problems and challenges in education described in Chapter 1—illiteracy, dropping out, drug abuse, violence, vandalism, and theft—certainly have their roots in motivation, or nonmotivation. Even the developmental concepts in Chapters 3 and 4 implicitly include developmental changes in some forms of motivation, for example, oedipal and Electra "motives" in childhood, the search for identity in the teen years, and the evolving changes in moral thinking throughout the child-to-adult years.

Probably every learning theory and instructional theory and method described in this text has an important motivational component. We find rewards and feedback in behavior modification and programming (Chapters 5 and 6); feelings of success and accomplishment in mastery learning and "direct instruction" (Chapter 12); and motivating concern for others, self-initiated learning, and the development of one's capabilities as part of a humanistic view of education (Chapter 13). It goes without saying that the entire focus of Chapter 10 on classroom management and discipline evolves about motivating children and adolescents to desist from disruption and persist in working. Even Chapter 11, on instructional objectives, includes the central principle that clear, attainable objectives motivate directed learning by students—and directed teaching by teachers.

Education for the gifted and creative also includes important motivational components. Briefly, intellectually gifted students frequently are bored and unmotivated by coursework which they mastered three years ago. They need more demanding challenges. Also, Renzulli (1978; Renzulli, Reis, and Smith, 1981) defines a gifted student as one who is bright, creative, *and motivated* (see Chapter 17). And all of us—some more than others—have creative urges and creative talents begging to be satisfied (Chapter 16).

Chapter 14 treats motivation as one of many sources of individual differences. We find large differences in anxiety, extroversion, and other motivation-related personality and cognitive characteristics. Naturally, Chapter 18, dealing with handicapped children, mainstreaming, and teaching disadvantaged students, is heavily loaded with motivational concepts and strategies.

Motivation is important.

agricultural and mining products of 10 South American countries just might be boring.

It obviously is the state, or environmental, aspects of motivation over which the teacher has most control. The teacher may deliberately choose interesting material, topics, and teaching methods—team games, curiosity-provoking demonstrations, appeals to adventurousness, field trips, role playing, personal problems, etc.—in order to make the classroom an interesting and motivating place. However, the teacher also may have a more permanent effect on students' "trait motivation." For example, if a teacher is able to improve students' attitudes toward the value of learning, raise their educational aspirations, or improve their self-esteem or self-perceptions, those students may well experience a long-term change in their motivational traits. We will see later that a change in perceived causes of success—from external "luck" to internal personal responsibility—also improves students' long-term motivational traits.

Energy vs. Direction

We also can distinguish between **energy** and **direction** in motivation. The idea is simply that any one motive, say hunger, can vary in strength—you can be more hungry or less hungry—and can energize behavior in any of several different "directions." A hungry student might buy a candy bar, skip a 12-o'clock class, get up at 3:00 A.M. for a peanut butter and banana sandwich, or unconsciously gnaw on a pencil or 10 of his or her fingernails. Money, or the desire for it, is another motivator which can vary in intensity and certainly can motivate any number of behaviors, from baby sitting or stealing to earning a college degree or gambling in Las Vegas.

Probably all forms of motivation can vary both in their energy or strength component and in the variety of behaviors which may be stimulated by the particular motive.

Intrinsic vs. Extrinsic Motivation

We say that behavior is **intrinsically** motivated when the goal or reward is intrinsic to the task itself. In education, "learning for the sake of learning" is the best example of intrinsic motivation. Learning or solving problems in order to satisfy curiosity also are examples of intrinsically motivated behavior. More generally, eating for the delight of eating, skiing, playing hopscotch, or getting a backrub would be examples of intrinsically motivated behaviors—the goal is in the task itself.

Extrinsic motivation implies that external rewards and punishments are used to motivate behavior. Tangible rewards such as toys, money, or a longer recess period are extrinsic motivators, and so are grades, smiles, threats, academic awards, and teacher praise. The goal is external to the task itself.

Intrinsically motivated learning is generally more desirable than extrinsically motivated learning (Levine and Fashacht, 1974), although some behaviorists disagree (Feingold and Mahoney, 1975; see also Bates, 1979). Intrinsic motivation also is more difficult to create. Some ideas for stimulating curiosity motivation will be presented later in this chapter.

TRADITIONAL THEORIES OF MOTIVATION

Learning Theory

Motivational concepts in traditional learning theory are not particularly difficult to identify. We saw in Chapters 5 and 6 that much behavior is controlled by rewards and punishments. The rewards and punishments may be considered motivators. Rewards are rewarding and punishments are punishing because they both relate to human **drives.** In Chapter 5 we distinguished between **primary drives,** such as hunger, thirst, sex, and pain avoidance, and **secondary** (or learned) **drives,** such as money, grades, diplomas, or stars on the forehead. *Social rewards,* such as teacher praise or pats on the head, are considered secondary reinforcers. The reasoning is that some students do not respond well to teacher praise or other social rewards. If the need for praise were a primary, physiologically necessary drive, all students would seek praise or other social rewards. Therefore, the reinforcement value of praise must be learned.

We would say that food, water, sex, and physical comfort are **primary reinforcers,** since they satisfy primary drives. Can you guess why money, grades, and diplomas are **secondary reinforcers?** Very good; you're doing just wonderfully!

We earlier noted that all sorts of rewards and punishers are at work in the classroom, leading sometimes to concentrated effort, and sometimes to looting and pillaging (see Chapters 5 and 6). High grades, feelings of accomplishment, teacher praise, and usually peer recognition generally reward academic accomplishment. On the other side of the ledger, peer approval or escape from unpleasant tasks can reward fooling around or disrespectful behavior.

Whatever the reinforcement or punishment, it is effective only because the underlying **needs** exist—needs for attention, for achievement, for self-esteem, for avoidance of pain or embarrassment, or others. When you think of reinforcers and punishments, think also of the needs which will make the rewards rewarding and the punishments punishing.

Psycho-analytic Theory: Sigmund Freud

In Chapter 3 we examined the psychoanalytic ideas of Sigmund Freud as they related to stages of personality development. In this section we will again look at Freudian theory as it relates specifically to human motivation. Indeed, a good part of Sigmund Freud's (1949) psychoanalytic theory dealt with human motives. Most of these motives were assumed to be **instinctive** or **unconscious,** usually both. Two main sources of motivation stem from the **id**—the **libido** or sex urge (hence the term "lust theory")—and aggressive drives. Because the superego (social conscience) will not permit the raw expression of sex and aggressive urges (see Chapter 3), these needs are properly redirected into substitute outlets. For example, creative accomplishments are said to be the product of rechanneled sexual energy. Aggressive drives might find outlets in watching football on TV, in belligerant driving habits, in international political conflicts, in "beating others" on a multiple-choice test, or in disruptive behavior.

Four more motivation-related Freudian concepts are the **Oedipus complex,** the **Electra complex,** the **life wish,** and the **death wish.** As we elaborated in Chapter 3, the Oedipus complex is the notion that the male child, beginning in Freud's "Phallic Stage" (age 3–7 years), loves his mother and hates his father. A dedicated Freudian psychologist or psychiatrist might say that the male student who is aggressively disruptive in school is merely expressing his hostility toward his father by attacking another (safer) authority figure. The Electra complex is the female counterpart. The young girl is assumed to hate her mother and have a passion for her father. Any squabbles between girls and their mothers, or symbolic mothers such as women teachers, are supposed to be due to the unconscious Electra complex.

The interesting attraction of teenage girls to horses (girls outnumber boys three to one as horse owners) is said by psychoanalysts to be due to the Electra complex redirected to this big, strong, muscular, four-footed father symbol.

The unconscious death wish described by Freud may be used to explain the behavior of persons who commit suicide; the life wish accounts for the behavior of those who do not. We all have both a life wish and a death wish, says Freud.

A very valuable and enlightening contribution by Freud lies in his explanation of **ego defense mechanisms.** As we saw in Chapter 3, each of us uses these devices perhaps daily (although unconsciously) to resolve conflicts and protect our self-esteem. While space will not permit a duplication of the definitions and descriptions of defense mechanisms, the list includes repression, denial, projection, reaction formation, displacement, sublimation, rationalization, compensation, identification, and the adolescent defense mechanisms defined by daughter Anna Freud—reversal of affect, withdrawal, asceticism, unwillingness to compromise, and regression (see Chapter 3).

By way of evaluation, we probably should not be too quick to accept the reality of unseen, unconscious, and instinctive drives such as the Oedipus and Electra complexes and the life and death wishes. It is possible that there is a slight tendency for boys to get along better with their mothers and girls with their fathers, but there usually are more direct and enlightening causes of behavior than the Oedipus and Electra complexes or the supposedly sublimated sex and aggressive drives of the id. However, most of the defense mechanisms are too common for us to question their existence. Students (and teachers) will rationalize their poor performances, compensate with other successes, displace their hostilities, and repress their unhappy experiences. We are indebted to Freud for identifying these common psychological devices which motivate behavior.

Need Theory: Henry Murray

A third traditional theory of motivation deals with innate needs. Over 40 years ago Henry Murray (1938) listed no less than 28 "psychogenic needs," sources of motivation said to exist in all of us to greater or lesser degrees (Table 9.1). According to Murray, a need is "... an organic potentiality or readiness to respond in a certain way under given conditions. In this sense, a need is a latent attribute of an organism. ... a more or less consistent trait of personality" (pp. 60–61). Behavior, says Murray, is due to the interaction of inherent needs with the external environment. The environment can either support the expression of a need, or it can interfere with behavior aimed at satisfying needs. For example, the average teacher will support behavior directed toward satisfaction of needs for achievement,

Table 9.1 Murray's 28 psychogenic needs

Need	Definition	Need	Definition
Abasement	(Self-depreciation)	Exhibition	(To attract attention)
Achievement	(To excel)		
Acquisition	(To get possessions)	Exposition	(Teaching)
Affiliation	(Friendship)	Failure Avoidance	(To avoid shame)
Aggression	(To injure)	Inviolacy	(Self-respect)
Autonomy	(Independence)	Nurturance	(Sustaining others)
Blame Avoidance	(To comply)	Orderliness	(Neatness)
Cognizance	(Knowledge)	Play	(Entertainment)
Conservation	(Protecting)	Recognition	(Honors)
Construction	(Creating)	Rejection	(Excluding others)
Contrariness	(To be different)	Retention	(Hoarding)
Counteraction	(Reacting to attack)	Similance	(Copying others)
Defensiveness	(Defending oneself)	Succorance	(Being protected)
Deference	(Following)	Superiority	(Ambition)
Dominance	(Leadership)		

cognizance, failure avoidance, and orderliness, but probably won't do much to encourage satisfaction of needs for abasement, aggression, or rejection (see Table 9.1).

An old joke says that Murray apparently had a strong need to itemize lots of needs. Probably true. Murray's list certainly emphasizes the great diversity of human needs. It is important to note that many of these needs could interfere with healthy classroom participation, for example, needs for abasement or rejection. Some potentially disruptive needs may be rechanneled into constructive outlets. For example, needs for aggression might be guided into team spelling or math competition, needs for play might be directed into educational games, needs for construction and exhibition can find outlets in art displays, music performances, or other exhibitions. Needs for achievement, recognition, and superiority should be working in the teacher's favor continually.

CONTEMPORARY THEORIES OF MOTIVATION

Maslow's Hierarchy of Need Prepotency

Humanist Abraham Maslow (1954) devised a model of human motivation which explains why some needs are dominant at one time, others at another time. Maslow proposed that human motives are **hierarchically ordered** as shown in Table 9.2. His hierarchy begins with basic physiological and security needs and continues through needs for belonging, esteem, knowledge, aesthetic beauty, and is capped by a need for self-actualization. These needs are hierarchically ordered in the sense that the lower-order needs must be met before the higher-level needs will arise. In Maslow's (1968) words, ". . . the single holistic principle that binds together the multiplicity of human needs is the tendency for a new and higher need to emerge as the lower need [is] sufficiently gratified."

To itemize just a few implications and derivations:

1. If a higher-level need conflicts with a lower need, the lower need takes precedence. A starving, cold, hurting, threatened, or rejected student will not worry much about his or her knowledge or aesthetic needs.

Table 9.2. Maslow's (1954, 1971) need hierarchy as modified and interpreted by Root (1970). Each lower level need must be met before a person attends to the next higher need. The first four levels, through Esteem, are considered *deficiency* needs; higher levels are considered *growth* needs.

The ultimate need	*Self-actualization* The need to realize one's potential, to grow into a fully functioning person. Essential for adult mental health.
Aesthetic needs	*Aesthetic needs* Needs for beauty, order, balance and symmetry in all of life.
Achievement, intellectual needs	*Needs for understanding* Needs for knowledge of relationships, processes and systems. Integration of knowledge into theories or broad structures. *Needs for knowledge* Needs for information, skills; needs to know the meanings of symbols and events.
Affiliation, social needs	*Esteem needs* Needs for feelings of self-worth and usefulness. Needs for recognition as a special person with unique and valuable characteristics and abilities. *Belonging needs* Needs for love, belonging, acceptance by a group. Knowing that others want you to be with them.
Physical, organizational needs	*Security needs* Needs to avoid danger, to have things regular, predictable and routine for oneself, one's family and one's friends. *Survival needs* Basic needs for food, water, oxygen, safety; a concern for immediate existence.

2. Lower-level needs, for survival, security, belonging, and esteem, are **deficiency** needs. Deficiencies in these must be met very frequently—daily or even hourly. Higher-level needs, for knowledge, understanding, aesthetic beauty and order, and self-actualization, are **growth** needs, whose fulfillment is necessary for personal growth. Growth needs are less urgent.
3. Frustrated lower needs work against the fulfillment of higher needs. An adult who fears losing his or her job (safety, security), or who fears criticism or loss of esteem, will not "... grow forward ... toward fullness of Self and uniqueness of Self, toward the full functioning of all his capacities, toward confidence in the face of the external world ..." (Maslow, 1954). To humanists Abraham Maslow and Carl Rogers, a fully functioning, self-actualized individual is an independent "forward growing" creative person (Davis, 1981a).

In addition to the clear message that students' lower needs must be met before academic needs will appear, Maslow's hierarchy also has a need-based message about teacher morale and "dedication." Assume that teacher Howie Needum truly needs every need in the Maslow hierarchy. If his teaching job meets his needs for belonging, esteem, and self-actualization, Howie will be a more dedicated, enthusiastic and concerned teacher. However, if teaching is just a job and a paycheck which satisfies only his basic survival needs, Howie will just tolerate his eight-to-four commitment. He will look elsewhere for ways to meet his needs for belonging, esteem, and self-actualization. Perhaps he will join a birdwatchers' group, a travel club, or invest his energy in night school to prepare for a more satisfying career. When people's higher-order needs are not met, they just tolerate the "work"—or they may quit.

Competence Motivation

Harvard psychologist Robert White (1959; Nardine, 1974) observed that children often undertake difficult activities such as tying shoe laces or putting on boots for no other reason than to master the skill itself. Every child, asserted White, is born with a healthy need to become competent in dealing with his or her environment. White argued that primary drives such as hunger, thirst, or pain avoidance cannot reasonably explain such normal infant and childhood behaviors as visual exploration, grasping, crawling, walking, language development, exploring novel objects and places, or actively manipulating and producing changes in the environment. Such behaviors, says White, stem from a biologically determined drive toward increased competence. The child knows what it wants to do, and wants to do it itself—regardless of mistakes, failures, or the fact that Mommy or Miss Jones could do it ten times faster. The concept of **competence**

motivation resembles Maslow's need for self-actualization and his needs to know and understand.

Every teacher should be aware of this built-in drive to develop skills and acquire knowledge. A hasty "Let me do it for you" may cost a small child a small increase in the growth of his or her capabilities and competence. On the positive side, a teacher can capitalize on competence motivation by such prods as, "Let's see if you can . . . ," or "Would you like to learn to . . . ?" Chances are, most students would like to learn to . . . .

Achievement Motivation

We sometimes use the concept of **achievement motivation** to explain the discrepancy between a student's ability, measured by intelligence tests, and his or her actual classroom performance (grades). For example, underachiever Norbert Neverwork may perform below his capacity. He is not particularly success-oriented in the sense of accepting his parents' and school's standards of achievement. Though low in his need for achievement (abbreviated *n Ach*), Norb may be high in needs for affiliation (*n Aff*). His popularity and his cool are more important than a string of "A's" on the old report card. The overachiever is the reverse. His strong desire to excel, along with anxiety about failure, may motivate Carl Compulsive to earn grades which are higher than his aptitude tests would predict. Carl's affiliation needs might be correspondingly weak, since friendships and popularity might run second to an outstanding school record.

The relationship between achievement motivation and academic success is not a simple one, however. That is, students high in *n Ach* do not always perform at higher levels and earn higher grades. The relationship is tempered, for example, when there are conflicts with the teacher or when peer acceptance (social status) is uncomfortably low (Ruhland, Gold, and Feld, 1978; Veroff, McClelland, and Ruhland, 1975).

To complicate matters even more, Veroff (1969) distinguished between two types of achievement motivation in elementary school children. **Autonomously oriented** achievement motivation is based on bettering one's own previous performance. **Social-comparison oriented** achievement motivation is based on comparisons with others. According to Veroff, autonomous achievement motivation develops early, influencing achievement as early as the second grade (Feld, Ruhland, and Gold, 1979). On the other hand, social-comparison achievement motivation develops later (when students begin making such comparisons) and influences achievement at, for example, the fourth- and fifth-grade levels (Ruhland, Gold, and Feld, 1978).

Every student possesses some degree of achievement need. Similarly, all students are motivated to avoid failure. As for the source of these two needs, psychologists David C. McClelland (1976) and John W. Atkinson (1974) point to learning rather than heredity. Parental influence in childhood, they say, is the crucial factor.

Whatever the source, the *relative strengths* of the motive to achieve and the motive to avoid failure result in quite different behavior patterns in the classroom. For example, the child strong in achievement needs (with little fear of failure) prefers tasks of intermediate difficulty. These tasks provide a reasonable chance for success but are sufficiently challenging that the success is worthwhile. In Atkinson's (1974) terms there is a reasonable *probability of success* and a reasonable *incentive value* of that success.

On the other hand, the student whose fear of failure is stronger than his or her need to achieve presents the opposite picture. For that student it is the task intermediate in difficulty which is the most threatening—the reasonable chance for success is a lot less important than the obvious threat of failure. Given a choice, the student motivated by fear of failure usually prefers tasks which are either very easy, guaranteeing success, or tasks which are obviously very hard for anyone. With a difficult task, failure will not be seen as a personal shortcoming, but due to the task itself.

Because of this different reaction to a moderate challenge, ability grouping may affect students high in achievement needs differently from students high in fear of failure. The high *n Ach* students should thrive on the intermediate-level challenges presented to a group of students similar in ability. However, the ability-grouped class and its intermediate difficulty level may be the most threatening to students who fear failure, increasing anxiety and depressing learning (Atkinson, 1974).

McClelland (1965, 1972) proposed several instructional principles aimed at strengthening students' achievement motivation: (a) The instruction must explain the concept of achievement motivation and its importance for success in school and in one's eventual career. Nothing indirect or subtle here. (b) The instruction must realistically convince the learner that, given his or her adequate abilities and talents and the values and realities of society, he or she can and should acquire success-oriented attitudes. (c) The instruction must elicit commitment to specific realistic and worthwhile goals. (d) The instructional atmosphere must support the confidence and individuality of the person. In essence, these points encourage the learner to think as achievement-oriented individuals do, to accept moderate risks, to set realistic and achievable goals, and to feel confident that he or she can achieve these goals.

INSET 9.2

DOES DOODLING REFLECT NEEDS FOR ACHIEVEMENT?

Harvard psychologist David McClelland (1976) proposed with a straight face that one's doodles can reflect the strength of a person's needs for achievement. According to McClelland a person high in *n Ach*: (a) doodles in "dynamic" diagonals (15 degrees off horizontal or vertical), rather than in unimaginative vertical and horizontal lines; (b) uses many "S-shapes," but not long, undulating, multiple waves, which are monotonous; and (c) leaves less than 12 percent unused space at the bottom of the page. For the low *n Ach* person the doodling habits are the opposite: lots of vertical and horizontal lines and long multiple waves, and lots of empty space at the bottom of the page.

Cognitive Dissonance

Leon Festinger's (1957; see also Heider, 1958) **cognitive dissonance** theory mainly explains motivation to change attitudes and opinions. The theory states that whenever ideas are inconsistent with one another, there is a strong tendency to resolve this unpleasant disagreement. For example, let's say your best friend, Donald Dumbkoph, confidently announces that "Higher education is a big waste of time, and that university president of yours is a lazy thief!" The three ideas:

> you like your friend;
> you like higher education and your university president;
> your friend does not like higher education or your university president;

are inconsistent and therefore create an uncomfortable state of cognitive dissonance. Strong (1968) noted that cognitive dissonance may be removed in at least five different ways:

1. You may change your opinion to that of your friend, deciding that your friend must know something that you don't.
2. You may discredit the source, concluding that your friend is ignorant, ill-informed, or both.
3. You may devalue the importance of the whole matter; perhaps with a shrug and a "So who cares?"
4. You may try to change the attitude or opinion of your friend.
5. Finally, you might seek information which supports your original opinion. Whichever of these actions is chosen, the result will bring the inconsistent ideas into a more comfortable, consonant relationship.

In the classroom, children's attitudes are often changed when children encounter conflicting attitudes or ideas presented by persons they admire or respect—namely you, the teacher. The incompatible information causes uncomfortable cognitive dissonance which is removed by a change of attitudes, most often in the teacher's direction. For example, fourth-grade student Sally Snobb might complain about having to dance with Stinky Jones. A discussion of proper manners, rudeness, and hurt feelings would be inconsistent with Sally's attitude, thereby creating cognitive dissonance. The dissonance most likely would be removed by a change in Sally's attitude to a position more in line with that of the teacher. However, the cognitive dissonance also may be removed by a change of attitude toward the teacher ("She doesn't know anything about Stinky Jones!"), which leaves the original bad attitude intact.

Very often, when students' attitudes (e.g., toward drugs, sex, vandalism, or bringing large dogs to class) conflict with attitudes and traditions of the larger society, the resulting cognitive dissonance is removed by discrediting the worth of society's ideas and traditions. Cognitive dissonance is a very powerful motive. We all change our attitudes and opinions toward those credible sources we respect and away from those sources we do not respect.

Attribution Theory

Attribution theory (Bar-Tal, 1978; Bar-Tal, Raviv, Raviv, and Bar-Tal, 1982; Heider, 1958; Weiner, 1979, 1980) deals with how we perceive causes and effects and how we infer motivations from a person's actions. Attribution theory assumes we are rational and that we have a strong need to understand our environment, that is, to understand *why* something occurs. Why did I flunk Botany 101? Why did Zelda Zitt get a higher grade than I did? Why did I receive an "A +" in the chemistry mid-term?

The focus usually is on attributing causation to *internal* factors, especially ability and effort, or *external* factors, such as task difficulty, teacher bias, or just plain luck. Attribution theorist Bernard Weiner (1979; Forsyth and McMillan, 1981) reviewed a number of studies of perceived attributions (causes) of success and failure, producing the three-dimensional model in Table 9.3. According to Weiner, perceived causes of success or failure may be *internal* or *external* to the person, they may be *controllable* or *uncontrollable*, and they may be *stable* or *unstable*. For example, "immediate effort" as a cause of success is internal, unstable, and controllable, while "task difficulty" is external, stable, and uncontrollable. Table 9.3 shows other attributions students frequently make.

Researchers also have concluded that different perceived causes of success or failure lead to different cognitive and affective consequences (Bar-Tal, 1978; Weiner, 1974, 1980). For example, if success is attributed to *ability*, the result should be increased pride and expectations of future successes ("If I did it once, I can do it again"). On the other hand, if success is attributed to *luck*, the result may be decreased pride and an expectation of a change in luck; i.e., poor performance next time ("I was lucky this time, next time I'll probably flunk"). The cognitive and affective outcomes

Table 9.3 Causal attributions for success or failure (from Weiner, 1979)

	Internal		External	
	Stable	Unstable	Stable	Unstable
Uncontrollable	Ability	Mood	Task difficulty	Luck
Controllable	Typical effort	Immediate effort	Teacher bias	Unusual help from others

of the four attributions—*ability, effort, task difficulty,* or *luck*—under conditions of *success* or *failure,* are described in Figure 9.1.

Students also make attributions to teachers. For example, let's say that teacher Harriet Hardnut gives all students "C's," "D's" and "F's." We (and students) would attribute the poor grades to her unfairness, not to the students; that is, the cause of the low grades is due to external factors, not to the internal effort and ability of the students. However, reasonable teacher Ruth Reasonable gives a reasonable number of "A's" and "B's" along with some "C's" and a few "D's." We now infer that the students' grades are due to their own performances—internal ability and effort—and not to the external Ms. Reasonable.

Attribution theory also applies nicely to the making of inferences in interpersonal situations. For example, let's say you are walking down the school hall and motorcycle groupie Theresa Thugg smacks into you. You may attribute the bumping to her obnoxious aggressiveness and send her to the principal's office, or you may infer that it was an accident and do nothing. If you make an "incorrect attribution," you might (a) punish an innocent person, or (b) smile and say "Ooopsy!" to the deliberate offender.

In the 1970s and early 1980s more research dealt with attribution theory than with any other single motivational concept. Some of the more noteworthy findings are:

- Young children tend to attribute their own successes and the successes of others to high ability, high effort, or both (Ames, 1978; Ames and Felker, 1979). These attributions increase achievement motivation and feelings of self-worth.
- Success in competitive situations is especially ego-enhancing; that is, attributions of personal high ability are even stronger (Ames, Ames, and Felker, 1977; Ames and Felker, 1979; Kagan, Zahn, and Gealy, 1977). Performing a task well isn't quite as good as beating out somebody else.
- Attributions become more logical as children get older (Nichols, 1978, 1979). Specifically, children become more likely to attribute success to ability and effort, and less likely to chalk up success to dumb luck. They also come to realize that difficult tasks require more ability than easy tasks.
- Attributions tend to be consistent across different subject matters, especially if the outcomes (success or failure) are the same (Bar-Tal, Raviv, Raviv, and Bar-Tal, 1982).
- Minority students tend to attribute success to task difficulty and luck (external factors; Katz, 1967; Friend and Neale, 1972). External attributions are a form of "learned helplessness."
- With individualized learning programs, students are given tasks that

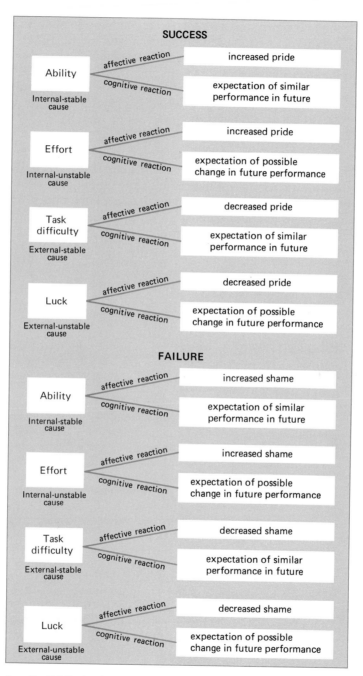

Figure 9.1
Affective and
cognitive
outcomes of
different
attributions under
conditions of
success or failure.

match their abilities. Therefore, success is more readily attributed to ability and effort, and failure to a lack of effort (Bar-Tal, 1978).

- Attributions of college students seem to have a self-serving, ego-protecting function (Arkin and Maruyama, 1979). Thus successful students attribute their stellar behavior to ability and good preparation (internal factors); unsuccessful students attribute their misfortunes to bad luck and tough tests (external factors).

The main educational implication of attribution theory is this: Quite apart from a student's ability, his or her pattern of attributions can have a strong motivational influence on achievement. Therefore, teachers should emphasize and encourage *internal* (especially effort) attributions as the route to success, and emphasize lack of effort as the cause of failure. One study showed sixth-graders could be "retrained" to attribute success to effort instead of to external factors (Andrews and Debus, 1978; see Inset 9.3).

INSET 9.3

PAWNS AND ORIGINS: ALTERING STUDENTS' ATTRIBUTIONS

One problem with underachieving inner-city students is that they feel they have little control over their academic successes and failures. In the language of attribution theory, they attribute their successes to external factors—easy tests and luck—rather than internal factors of ability and effort. DeCharms (1972, 1976; see also Wittrock, 1979) coined the terms *pawns* and *origins* to describe persons who feel they are controlled by others rather than in control of their own destinies.

DeCharms devised his "personal causation training program" to improve motivation and change students' perceived causes of success and failure. DeCharms began by teaching elementary and junior high school *teachers* to perceive themselves as origins—people who feel they are in control of external forces. The teachers, in turn, taught students to believe that they too should think as origins, taking individual responsibility for their learning and, indeed, for their destiny.

Over a three- or four-year period, the program increased the motivation of both teachers and students. Also, language skills and math improved substantially.

Curiosity and Arousal: Intrinsic Motivation

Daniel Berlyne (Day and Berlyne, 1971) pointed out that the most desirable form of motivation occurs when the goal is **intrinsic** to the task itself. As we noted above, eating for the pleasure of eating, solving problems for the goal of removing curiosity, and studying for the satisfaction of learning are examples of intrinsically motivated behavior. In contrast, studying in order to earn a high grade or a Frisbee, or eating spinach because Mom makes you, would be instances of **extrinsic** motivation because the motivators are external to the behavior itself.

Arousal is a key concept in Berlyne's theory of intrinsic motivation. A state of arousal may be due simply to a startling noise, to confusing words or blurred pictures, to some emotionally loaded stimulation (a snarling dog or sexy pictures), or, importantly, to some incident which challenges the wits or stimulates curiosity. Physiologically, an increase in one's state of arousal can include an increase in muscle tension, a change in heart rate or respiration, and perhaps an increase in perspiration. Very high levels of arousal—due to fear, anxiety, loud TV, or whatever—are unpleasant and will lead to behavior aimed at reducing the stimulation. On the other hand, moderate increases in arousal usually are enjoyable.

Psychologically, the moderately aroused person is mentally alert—with focused attention, a store of information available, and an increased ability to make fine discriminations (Berlyne, 1961). Clearly, the student is best prepared to learn under an intermediate level of arousal, neither too high nor too low.

Curiosity is a particularly attractive form of arousal, or intrinsic motivation, since the teacher can deliberately stimulate curiosity in order to motivate learning. According to Berlyne, curiosity stems from a conceptual conflict. You may be reminded of cognitive dissonance theory, which assumes that conceptual conflict motivates behavior (or attitude change) aimed at removing the conflict. You probably already have been looking at the incongruous Elephish (named Gerald) in Figure 9.2. Were you curious? The degree of conceptual conflict will determine the level of arousal, and therefore the amount of exploratory and information-seeking behavior necessary to remove the conflict. You probably also read the caption to Figure 9.2 (information-seeking behavior) in an effort to understand Elephish Gerald.

Some types of conceptual conflict which may be deliberately used to arouse curiosity and learning are these (Berlyne, 1961):

1. *Doubt* is a conflict between tendencies to believe and disbelieve. Difficult-to-believe ideas (for example, the idea that male seahorses get pregnant) will probably arouse information seeking and learning aimed at removing this conflict.

Figure 9.2
Elephish Gerald,
an incongruous
stimulus.

From Day, H. I., and D. E. Berlyne. Intrinsic motivation. In G. S. Lesser (ed.), *Psychology and Educational Practice*. Glenview, Ill.: Scott, Foresman, 1971. Reproduced by permission.

2. *Contradiction* is a conflict between, for example, attitudes and beliefs of students and opposite statements proposed by the teacher. For example, "when is it good to be greedy?" should pique a little thought.

3. *Perceptual incongruity* is an internally inconsistent sensory input, such as the Elephish. Surprising chemical or physics demonstrations often produce perceptual incongruity.

4. *Conceptual incongruity* is information about events or objects which contain incompatible elements; for example, "Alaskan palm trees" or "South American penguins."

5. *Confusion* (or *ambiguity*), as we all know, stems from unclear ideas or incomplete information. Confusion usually arouses behavior aimed at simplifying the ambiguous matter at hand.

6. *Novelty*, like incongruity, also contains a degree of unexpectedness and uncertainty which stimulates interest and curiosity. For example, unusual clothes, weapons or other artifacts, or "strange" behavior patterns should stimulate curiosity about another culture.

State-and-trait arousal. Thus far we have treated arousal as a *state*, a temporary condition due to environmental stimulation. A very enlightening concept mentioned earlier in this chapter is arousal as a *trait*—an enduring characteristic which differs among individuals. Indeed, there are very large variations in students' levels of arousal. Some students lead relatively quiet lives, both inside and outside the classroom. A game of gin or a TV show is excitement enough. Others seem constantly to lead thrill-seeking, high-risk, adventurous lives, perhaps in traveling the globe alone, sky-diving, skiing, mountain climbing, or even stealing cars. (See Inset 9.4.) As we will see in Chapter 16, creative productivity is another outlet for energetic, arousal-seeking persons (Davis, Peterson, and Farley, 1973; Farley, 1981).

INSET 9.4

ARE YOU A SENSATION SEEKER?

Zuckerman (1979) developed the *Sensation Seeking Scale* to measure individual differences in the tendency to seek or avoid stimulating, "psychologically arousing" activities. A few of his test items are:

1. A. I would like a job which would require a lot of traveling.
   B. I would prefer a job in one location.
2. A. I am invigorated by a brisk, cold day.
   B. I can't wait to get into the indoors on a cold day.
3. A. I often wish I could be a mountain climber.
   B. I can't understand people who risk their necks climbing mountains.
4. A. I dislike all body odors.
   B. I like some of the earthy body smells.
5. A. I sometimes like to do things that are a little frightening.
   B. A sensible person avoids activities that are dangerous.
6. A. I would like to try parachute jumping.
   B. I would never want to try jumping out of a plane, with or without a parachute.
7. A. I prefer friends who are excitingly unpredictable.
   B. I prefer friends who are reliable and predictable.
8. A. A good painting should shock or jolt the senses.
   B. A good painting should give one a feeling of peace and security.

From Zuckerman, M. *Sensation seeking: Beyond the optimal level of arousal.* Hillsdale, N.J.: Lawrence Erlbaum, 1979. Copyright © 1979 by the American Psychological Association. Reprinted by permission of the author and publishers.

Optimal arousal theory. According to "optimal arousal theory" (Berlyne, 1961; Farley, 1981), each of us functions more comfortably at some personally optimal intermediate level of psychological arousal. Furthermore, due to differences in our trait levels of arousal, each of us will take different actions to achieve and sustain that optimal arousal level. Thus some will seek relatively quiet lives while others look for adventure.

Cognitive Drive: Ausubel

In Chapter 8 we reviewed the main principals of Ausubel's (1974, 1977) cognitive structure theory of classroom learning, a sensible and defensible viewpoint. The approach explains learning as a process of subsuming new material into a learner's cognitive structure by meaningfully relating or "anchoring" new concepts to ideas already in that cognitive structure.

As for motivation, Ausubel, Novak, and Hanesian (1978) emphasize that motivation can be an *effect* of learning as much as a *cause*. Students may very well be unmotivated, initially. However, if they are taught effectively—according to principles of meaningful subsumption theory, of course—the satisfaction derived from learning will motivate further learning. Ausubel, Novak, and Hanesian called this process **cognitive drive,** a very desirable form of intrinsic motivation which amounts to the desire for knowledge as an end in itself.

GOAL-SETTING CONFERENCES

We are all much more efficient and motivated when we have clear, attainable goals. For example, you might decide that after classes you must pick up your sweaters at the laundry, make a 4:00 o'clock hair styling appointment, read two chapters of this educational psychology text, and be ready for dinner at 6:15 sharp. You understand what must be done, you do it, and the rewards—clean sweaters, neat hair, relief from I'm-getting-behind anxiety, and relief from hunger—strengthen the habit of systematically planning what must be done.

In an elementary school organization structured for individualized education, goal-setting conferences have been marvelously effective in motivating learning (Klausmeier, Jeter, Quilling, Frayer and Allen, 1975). Children have scored great gains in arithmetic achievement, basic reading skills (word decoding) and in independent reading. At least as important has been the striking improvement in attitudes; the children began taking pride in their reading and arithmetic achievement and they enjoyed their extracurricular reading. Would you believe that many children in one goal-setting program independently, without teacher encouragement, began setting realistic goals for themselves in other subject areas? Or that they continued their goal-setting (and high achievement) after the formal teacher-child goal-setting conferences ended? Further, the goal-setting conference strategy seems to be effective in both central city and suburban schools (Klausmeier, *et al.*, 1975).

The goal-setting conferences in arithmetic, reading skills, and other basics require an individualized instructional program. However, the dramatically successful conferences for motivating children to read independently may be incorporated into virtually any classroom. Therefore, we will describe these conferences. (More detailed information is available in Klausmeier, *et al.*, 1975).

Goals of the Conferences

The purposes of the conference are: (a) to help the child learn to set realistic achievement goals; (b) to motivate the child to increase his or her nonclassroom recreational reading; (c) to improve reading skills; and (d) to foster positive attitudes toward outside reading.

Preconference Planning

The goal-setting conferences are held weekly, usually lasting only about 10 minutes. The conferences may be conducted by a teacher, an instructional aide, a student teacher, or a volunteer adult.

If not all students can participate, the first step will be student selection. Students who are average or below-average readers and who do no outside reading would be prime targets. However, good readers who do little outside reading also are good candidates for the conferences.

As for books, Klausmeier *et al.* (1975) recommend a stack of about 60 paperbacks for every 25 conference students. The selections should include humor, fiction, biographies, and source books on a variety of topics (horses, skiing, astronomy, travel, how-to books, etc.). The conference will require a regular, predictable weekly meeting time and place. Ideally, conferences are held in a nondistracting private room during the child's independent study time (if any). For the first conference, it is efficient to meet with the children as a group in order to discuss the purposes and scheduling of the conferences. In one Milwaukee school, conferences were held in the aide's work room. The children prized the conference time so much they actually made and hung a "Do Not Disturb" sign on the door.

Holding the Conferences

A step-by-step, word-by-word strategy for conducting the goal-setting conferences would run about like this (from Klausmeier *et al.*, 1975):

Beginning the meeting.
1. Show that adults enjoy reading by actually reading as the child arrives.
2. Greet the child pleasantly.

Conducting the conference.
1. Review the purpose of the conference, in case the child has forgotten.
2. Look at the child when either of you speak, and speak slowly and clearly.
3. Discuss with the child his or her interest in reading and the particular reading he or she has done during the past week.
4. Praise the child for the amount or variety of reading, for improvement in reading skills, and for meeting (or progressing toward) the goals.
5. Be pleasant throughout the session.
6. Keep records of what the child reads, and inform the child of his or her progress from week to week.
7. Provide lots of appealing books and magazines at a suitable reading level.

Closing the conference.
1. Help the child choose books which are of interest.
2. Make sure the books are of an appropriate level.
3. Help the child set a goal for the amount of reading he or she will complete by next week.

Theory Behind Goal-Setting Conferences

The strategy for conducting goal-setting conferences is based on these four time-tested principles of motivation and learning: (1) modeling correct attitudes; (2) goal setting; (3) providing feedback; and (4) providing reinforcement.

Modeling correct attitudes. The adult must model positive attitudes toward outside reading by, of course, visibly reading. The child will be impressed to find the adult engrossed in a copy of *Moby Dick, Return of the Native,* a copy of the *New Yorker,* etc. The adult may discuss books he or she has read, show pictures of great people reading books, or explain how reading is valuable in different occupations. The idea is to subtly convince the child that reading is good and that good people read.

Goal setting. Setting a goal implies making a commitment—indeed, a virtual promise to try hard to reach that goal. Cognitive dissonance (remember cognitive dissonance?) would occur if the child were to make a commitment and then fail to follow through. Furthermore, the child gains in feelings of self-esteem by personally deciding part of his or her own educational activity. The child, then, not the well-meaning adult, must set the reading goal.

The adult's role is to keep the goals realistic enough to assure success, but still challenging to the student's ability—not too easy, not too difficult. The adult also must keep in mind that different children need different types of goals. For example, some children need a general improvement in reading; others may read only certain types of books and need breadth; still others may choose books which are too easy for them. As they gain experience, children become more independent, more responsible, and more accurate in setting reasonable achievement goals.

Providing feedback. Students need to know what they did right or wrong and what to do about it next time. At the goal-setting conferences the adult (a) reviews what goals were set the previous week, and (b) asks the child what was actually done. The adult has a nice opportunity to provide feedback regarding goal attainment, and how realistic the goals were, with such positive comments as "Gosh, Roselyn, you really knew what you could do—three books promised and three books read!" or "Maybe you gave yourself too much last week, Jimmy. Should we take on a little less this time?" The feedback helps children learn to set reasonable, achievable goals independently.

Providing reinforcement. Providing feedback and providing reinforcement are closely intertwined. Therefore, telling Sarah Striver "You did a good job" both informs her that she did the right thing and motivates her to do more of the same. However, for special emphasis on developing good attitudes, the adult must praise warmly and generously for accomplishing the goal, or even for progressing toward it, and for mastering new vocabulary words. Especially praise effort, even if goals were not met.

With positive reinforcement, the child should form positive attitudes toward independent reading, toward the conferences, and toward goal-setting itself as a good way to get things done.

CLASSROOM MOTIVATION: SELECTED PRINCIPLES

In Inset 9.1 at the outset of this chapter we noted that motivation, like learning itself, runs throughout virtually every topic in education and therefore virtually every chapter in this book. It would be space consuming and redundant to review all of the motivational concepts and implications which appear in this text. There are, however, some recommendations for stimulating classroom motivation which seem to be time-honored favorites with educational psychologists. Some of these appear elsewhere in this chapter or this volume, others do not.

1. Make learning objectives as explicit as possible. Clear goals encourage learning.
2. Maximize successes by using goals and objectives which are challenging but realistically attainable.
3. If students can help in selecting goals, on either a classroom or an individual basis, they automatically commit themselves to achieving these goals.
4. Capitalize on existing interests and motivation.
5. Avoid cut-throat competition. It creates failure, frustration, and feelings of low worth for the less able scholars. Competition *is* a legitimate and

INSET 9.5

**SENECA FALLS
CONVENTION:
JULY 1848**

Whoever said learning can't be fun never reconstructed the Seneca Falls convention of 1848, probably the first formal women's rights conference in America. In 1980 a class entitled *Women In American History* at Middleton High School in Wisconsin put on the conference. Speaking as one parent who watched the show, it was a glorious success. All of the speakers and almost everyone else were dressed to the hilt in the latest 1848 fashions—usually mother's long dress and shawl—with hair done up in a bun and sporting a pair of granny glasses, scrounged from somewhere. Every enthusiastic speaker was "in character," most, in fact, were more than a little hammy. Each one delivered exactly the same speech presented 130 years earlier by her (or his) simulated character. Audience participation also was in character, and the spontaneous speakers were fiery and dedicated. They'd had enough of this legitimized slavery called American Womanhood.

What better way is there to learn the feelings, attitudes, and actions of early women leaders, such as Lucretia Mott, than to hear it from Lucretia herself? Or better, to become Ms. Mott for a few moments.

A reward probably was not necessary, but nonparticipating students earned extra points for dressing up and for contributing to the discussions of the resolutions which followed the formal speeches.

effective form of motivation. It can be used effectively in individualized instruction where students compete against themselves, or else in team competitions, particularly in educational team games.

6. Educational games? Games are motivating. For example, there are word games for developing reading skills with youngsters, history and math games for the junior high school student, and political and economic simulation games for high school students (see Inset 9.5).*

7. Make material meaningful, in the Ausubelian sense of relating new material to what students already know. Meaningful ideas will hold interest much better than confusing, meaningless information.

---

* Many games are free, for example, Spelling Baseball (with teams, correct spellings equal a base hit, incorrect spellings spell O-U-T. A little imagination can extend the baseball game to math problems or to questions about social studies reading). There also are many commercial educational games for all ages. One excellent source book is *Games for Growth* by Gordon (1970). Many computer games and simulations are enjoyable and educational (Chapter 6).

8. Use reinforcement. Reinforcement—in the form of success, praise, smiles, recognition, or other social rewards (or if necessary in the form of tangibles such as extra recess, a treat or a new pencil)—is a proven motivator. Verbal reinforcement or praise is a Great Good. Practice saying "Excellent!" "Good work!" or "You're doing wonderfully, Kim!" Writing praise on tests and papers is another good way to reward and motivate students.

9. Capitalize on curiosity, suspense, exploration, and discovery learning. There are many forms of "discovery learning." However, the common thread among these is the delightful intrinsic motivation which arises from an energizing, arousing challenge. Many schools provide interest-arousing art, reading, science, or other learning centers for students to explore and use.

10. Generally, arrange learning tasks which are appropriate to each student's level of ability. A steady diet of stress, failure, and frustration is not especially motivating. Feelings of success increase motivation.

11. Provide models of proper social and educational behavior, models which show self-control and persistence. The models can (or should) be the teacher, along with older students, exemplary students in the class, or famous persons or characters such as the Little Engine that Could.

12. Capitalize on students' needs for achievement. Sometimes, as noted in our earlier section on achievement needs, students' needs to achieve are obscured by stronger needs to avoid failure.

TO IMPROVE
YOUR TEACHING

Successful teaching and learning certainly evolve about the problem of motivation. Motivated students care about classroom activities, they pay attention, and they try to succeed. The concepts in this chapter should increase your sensitivity to important motivational concepts and principles. For example, the trait-state distinction warns you that some students will be innately more enthusiastic and attentive than others; the "state" concept implies that you will have considerable control over the interest value of your classes. The intrinsic-extrinsic distinction emphasizes the role of feelings of success, learning for the sake of learning, and the use of curiosity, challenge, games, etc., to intrinsically motivate learning. Extrinsic rewards, especially high grades and praise, also are known to support effort and achievement.

As we have seen (and will see) elsewhere in this book, students do respond to rewards and punishments. The rewards might be academic success; they might be peer praise and esteem for shoving a teacher down the stairs. A teacher should be sensitive to student needs, needs which predict just what will be reinforcing.

Murray's need theory and Freud's psychoanalytic approach are not especially prescriptive of specific, sound educational practices. They do call our attention to the very great variety of needs and wants that students bring to the classroom. You will soon discover that some students have very strong needs for achievement and recognition, others for affiliation, and still others for aggression and dominance. Some needs will make your job easier, some will make it harder. Freud, of course, also describes his insightful defense mechanisms. Do not be surprised when students generate fanciful "reasons" for their behavior, or when they compensate or repress to handle ego-threatening situations. We all use these devices.

The message in Maslow's need hierarchy is simple, yet profound. A student's deficiency needs (survival, security, belonging, esteem) must be met before attention may be fully devoted to growth needs (knowledge, understanding, beauty, and self-actualization). It also is worth repeating that a teacher also has growth needs which must be met, preferably by increasing his or her knowledge, skill, and self-satisfaction in being a super teacher.

One of the more interesting aspects of achievement motivation theory is the distinction between students motivated by needs to achieve and students motivated to avoid failure. They have different personalities and far different approaches to classroom learning. The fear-of-failure student, as we will see in Chapter 13, functions best in a threat-free situation where he or she can compete against his or her own previous accomplishments (e.g., in individualized learning approaches).

McClelland's recommendations for increasing student needs for achievement—convincing the learner that achievement is important and that he or she can reach worthwhile goals—is very similar to the attribution theory approach to student motivation. Teachers can and should convince students that success and failure are attributable to internal factors—especially effort—rather than external factors (task difficulty and luck). DeCharms's effort to teach elementary and junior high school students to think like "origins" instead of "pawns" is a convincing demonstration that motivation and achievement can be improved by teaching students that *they* are the causes of their successes and failures.

Arousal theory also gets right to the heart of classroom motivation and learning. *Psychological arousal* and *attention* are virtually synonymous.

Students who are "aroused" are alert, attentive, able to make fine discriminations, and just plain ready and willing to participate and learn. The concept of arousal says much about the value of creating high interest, curiosity, challenging activities, and so forth. We will see in Chapter 10 that high interest also is a main solution to problems of classroom management.

Goal-setting conferences are one effective way to motivate learning, if instruction can be individualized. The key feature is eliciting a commitment—publicly setting a goal—which the student then feels obligated to meet. The strategy could be used when the entire class is on an individualized strategy, say, for teaching math. Goal-setting conferences also could be used when students are individually selected for remedial instruction, for enrichment activities, or for exploring a biological or geological problem as part of a gifted program.

SUMMARY

Psychologists assume that all behavior is motivated, which makes motivation a rather important topic. It is every teacher's number-one concern.

Motivation may be viewed as an enduring individual trait or as a temporary state. The teacher mainly controls temporary motivational states; however, more permanent traits may be altered by changes in self-esteem, aspirations, attitudes, or attributions.

Any one motive has an energy or strength component which is different from the direction component. Direction refers to the variety of behaviors which any one motive may "energize."

Extrinsic motivation involves external rewards such as money, points, grades, or praise. With intrinsic motivation the pleasure derives from the task itself, such as eating, skiing, or learning for the sake of learning.

Three traditional forms of motivation theory are found in learning theory, psychoanalytic theory, and "need" theory. Learning theory includes the use of rewards and punishments to motivate behavior. What is rewarding or punishing depends on student needs.

Freud's main sources of motivation are the sex and aggressive instincts, both part of Freud's *id*. Also, the Oedipus and Electra complexes supposedly motivate, for example, a boy's aggression against his father or a substitute "father figure." Freud's ego defense mechanisms are common psychological devices for protecting our "self" or "self-esteem."

Henry Murray's 1938 list of 28 psychogenic needs includes an explanation for just about any sort of observable human behavior. His list emphasizes the variety of needs students will bring to the classroom.

Turning to more contemporary theories of motivation, Maslow's need hierarchy begins with low-level survival and security needs (deficiency needs) and progresses to higher-level needs for knowledge, understanding, aesthetic beauty and order, and self-actualization (growth needs). The lower needs must be met before higher needs emerge, which tells us that hungry or fearful children or adults will not be particularly concerned about needs for knowledge or self-actualization.

The concept of competence motivation emphasizes that every child is born with a strong need to develop talents and skills—to become competent in dealing with the environment.

Achievement motivation includes the familiar ideas of underachieving and overachieving. With some students, the motivation to avoid failure will be stronger than the motivation to achieve success. Principles and programs for strengthening achievement motivation focus on getting students to think as high achievers think—to acquire a "success orientation" and to set realistic and worthwhile goals.

Festinger's theory of cognitive dissonance tells us that when two ideas or attitudes are inconsistent with each other, there will be a strong motivation to remove the uncomfortable state by changing one's attitudes or behavior.

Attribution theory deals with perceptions of cause-effect relationships. A flurry of recent research and theory focuses on attributing success and failure to external factors (task difficulty, luck) or internal factors (ability, effort). Different attributions (perceived causes) for success and failure produce different cognitive and affective results.

Curiosity motivation (Berlyne) is a form of intrinsic motivation. Curiosity is arousing, and the aroused person is alert, attentive, his or her store of information is more available, and he or she is better able to make fine discriminations. Curiosity is aroused by a conceptual conflict due to doubt, contradiction, incongruity, confusion, ambiguity, or novelty. "Optimal arousal theory" assumes that each of us seeks a personally comfortable level of arousal—leading some to be arousal-seekers, others to be arousal-avoiders.

Ausubel's concept of cognitive drive assumes that the satisfaction derived from successful learning will motivate further learning.

Goal-setting is an effective motivational device. In the schools, goal-setting conferences motivate independent reading or other academic accomplishments. The strategy is based on modeling the correct behavior (e.g., reading), eliciting the goal-setting commitment, providing feedback on progress, and providing warm reinforcing praise for accomplishments.

A list of principles of classroom motivation included:

1. Use explicit objectives.
2. Use goals and objectives which are challenging but realistic, ensuring a meaningful success.
3. Use student goal-setting.
4. Capitalize on existing interests.
5. Avoid cut-throat competition in which only a few can "win."
6. Use educational games.
7. Make material meaningful in the sense of "nonarbitrary substantive relatability to cognitive structure" (Chapter 8).
8. Use reinforcement: praise, smiles, recognition, feelings of success, etc.
9. Capitalize on curiosity, exploration, and discovery.
10. Arrange tasks appropriate to student abilities, thereby avoiding frustration and failure.
11. Provide (or be) models of self-control and persistence.
12. Capitalize on natural needs for achievement.

TOPICS FOR THOUGHT AND DISCUSSION

1. Look over Murray's list of 28 psychogenic needs. How would you rate yourself on each need? Which are your strongest? Your weakest? Try rating a political figure, say the Ayatollah Khomeini.
2. How might each need be capitalized on in the classroom?
3. What might be some good strategies for changing students' perceived causes of success and failure (attributions) from external sources (luck, task difficulty, unfair teachers) to internal sources (ability, effort)? Would the strategies differ for elementary and secondary students?
4. How might students' achievement motivation be increased in the grade and subject you expect to teach?
5. How might competence motivation be capitalized on, say, in a language arts, science, or art course?
6. How would goal-setting conferences be different for low-ability, low-achieving students, compared with (a) average or (b) gifted students? Consider goals, strategies, materials, etc.

PROJECTS

1. Outline a lesson plan based on curiosity motivation. Include a curiosity-provoking arousing demonstration or a challenging problem. What are your goals? How will you introduce the problem? Will you lead a discussion or let students, independently or in small groups, research the topic? What will be the follow-up discussion or activity? How will you evaluate the learning?
2. Outline a goal-setting strategy for teaching science to 12 gifted elementary school children, two from each grade (1–6). Outline another goal-setting strategy for teaching math to gifted junior and senior high school students. Reread the goal-setting section of this chapter for ideas.

RECOMMENDED READING

Bar-Tal, D. Attributional analysis of achievement-related behavior. *Review of Educational Research* **48,** 1978, 259–271.

DeCharms, R. *Enhancing motivation: Change in the classroom.* New York: Irvington, 1976.

Gordon, A. K. *Games for growth: Educational games in the classroom.* Chicago: Science Research Associates, 1970.

Klausmeier, H. J., J. T. Jeter, M. R. Quilling, D. A. Frayer, and P. S. Allen. *Individually guided motivation.* Madison: Wisconsin Research and Development Center for Cognitive Learning, 1975.

Weiner, B. A theory of motivation for some classroom experiences. *Journal of Educational Psychology* **71,** 1979, 3–25.

————. *Human motivation.* New York: Holt, Rinehart & Winston, 1980.

Classroom Management and Discipline

10

ABOUT CLASSROOM MANAGEMENT

If every student spent all day quietly working away at academic tasks, you would probably conclude that the entire class was sick. There always will be disruptions in the classroom. Most problems will be routine minor ones, caused by normal, well-adjusted students—talking, laughing, chewing gum, clowning, forgetting pencils, being late, moving about the classroom, or fooling around instead of working. Other problems will be severe, such as vandalism, refusal to work, racial tensions, hostility toward the teacher, truancy, popping pills and puffing pot, obscene language and gestures, and so on.

As a general rule, teachers who are competent, organized, and well-prepared will have fewer management and discipline problems. Also, teachers who are able to minimize the management and discipline problems tend to be successful in their teaching. Management skills and techniques are especially critical for the beginning teacher. First of all, failure to control the classroom will hardly promote serious instruction and learning. Also, the ability to control a classroom—quite apart from teaching skill—can weigh heavily in the evaluations and ratings of new teachers. Many idealistic beginning teachers have been driven from the classroom by continual problems with students.

Causes of Disruptiveness

There are many causes of student disruptiveness, some simple and correctable, others more deeply rooted. In the first category is *boredom*. Classwork may not be sufficiently captivating—and with nothing else to do, the talking, clowning, and poking begins. Clowning and poking also are good releases of *tension*, caused partly by *frustration*. Some classwork requires considerable intellectual effort and strain, perhaps in a subject in which the student has no interest. Also, some teachers may be too strict. Mom or Dad may appreciate a martini, a coffee break, or a movie to release tension. In the classroom, junior might wander, sail an airplane, or rip the soap dispenser off the washroom wall. Peer recognition and approval for being a clown or for defying the teacher also can be a relatively simple cause of misbehavior.

Turning to deep-rooted, more troublesome causes of disruptiveness, we find such problems as:

- Poverty and alienation
- Parental rejection
- Low ability, producing frustration
- Irrelevant curriculum
- Crowded and impersonal schools
- Peer traditions of rebellion and defiance

About three students in 10 have at least mild emotional or adjustment problems; one in 10 has severe problems (Clarizio and McCoy, 1976); a few will be psychotic or psychopathic. Boys are three times more likely to have adjustment problems than are girls. (Problems of emotional disturbance will be explored in Chapter 18.)

Some Solutions: Classroom Management

The best solution to many classroom behavior problems is a preventive one—avoid the opportunities and incentives for misbehavior before they happen. **Classroom management** refers to motivating students to work at their assignments and to learn. It includes dealing with problems in such a way as to minimize interference with regular classroom activities. Classroom management requires skills and techniques that go beyond "being warm and patient," "creating good rapport," and "making the learning interesting." Among other tactics, the teacher concerned with good classroom management will:

- Establish clear and reasonable rules, but as few as possible.
- Establish positive expectations and a good working relationship.
- Let students know that they are accountable for their behavior and their assignments.
- Keep students engaged in learning or other activities, avoiding satiation and boredom.
- Plan for smooth and efficient transitions between activities.
- Plan for interest and variety.
- Arrange the room for continual teacher surveillance.
- Let students know that teacher knows what is going on.
- Remove stimuli—materials or friends—which set off clowning, talking, poking.
- Ignore minor undesirable behavior, not reinforce it with attention.
- Use humor or threats before using punishment.

Socializing Students vs. Teaching Content

It is true that neither psychotherapists nor correctional institutions have been brilliantly successful in dealing with severe behavior disorders or delinquency. Yet somehow Ms. Normal Teacher, equipped with her B.A. in education, is expected to cope with and perhaps even cure such difficulties. One dilemma common to the classroom is focusing efforts on either *student socialization* or *teaching content*. Some teachers feel that helping students to overcome their problems and take a more positive, constructive approach to life is far more critical than teaching academic content. Others have little interest in student socialization and prefer to invest their efforts in teaching academic skills and knowledge. Actually, of course, a judicious blending of the two is appropriate for most classes.

Student socialization and personal development problems are more prominent in grades 5 through 10 (especially 7 through 10). These, of course, are the years of adolescence. A teacher who is particularly interested in student social and personal development might find these grades to be challenging and rewarding. On the other hand, a teacher who wishes to focus on instruction and avoid socialization problems may choose to teach at the early elementary level, before problems begin, or the late secondary level, where severe problem students have been selectively screened out.

PRINCIPLES AND TECHNIQUES

"Withitness," Overlapping, and Ripple Effects: Kounin

One of the most thorough research efforts aimed at identifying (a) effective principles of classroom management and (b) characteristics of good teacher-managers is the five-year work of Jacob Kounin (1970). One of the most important traits of good classroom managers was labeled **"withitness"**—the ability of a teacher to demonstrate that he or she knows what is going on. That is, a teacher must communicate to students that he or she "has eyes in the back of his or her head." Kounin actually measured withitness by videotaping classes in progress. Teachers were given a low withitness score if the *target* of a request to "desist" was the wrong student or the *timing* of the request was incorrect. For example: Alice and Jack are whispering; Charlie joins in and starts to giggle and then turns to Fred; Fred says something to Janet—and finally our low-withitness teacher, Ms. Cucamonga, says, "Janet, please stop talking and get busy on your algebra problems!" In this case, both the target and the timing were wrong, and the message to the students was that Ms. Cucamonga did not know what went on. A high-withitness teacher would have more quickly nailed the correct targets, Alice and Jack, before the deviancy spread to other students.

"Overlapping" is another principle of effective classroom management. Basically, overlapping is the handling of two classroom activities at once—especially, attending to deviancy without disrupting on-going learning activities. For example, let's say that Mr. Georgia is working with a microcomputer group when across the room Grant and Lee begin sword fighting. A low-overlapping Mr. Georgia promptly stops the computer group and asks Grant and Lee to reach a truce and return to their reading. A more effective overlapping teacher might have said, "Jan, you show Bill how to log on," and then turned to squelch Grant and Lee. With overlapping, neither deviancy nor any other type of interruption is permitted to interfere with learning.

Other instances of overlapping might involve two instructional activities. For example, a teacher might be supervising math work when a student walks up to ask about a new vocabulary word. If the teacher handles both tasks at once, instead of neglecting one to attend to the other, this is overlapping.

Are withitness and overlapping truly important for effective management? Kounin (1970) obtained scores on deviancy rates and ratings of task involvement. Sure enough, with 49 first- and second-grade classrooms, teachers high on withitness and overlapping also showed lower deviancy rates and greater student task involvement in both recitations and seatwork. Withitness and overlapping themselves were highly related, so that a teacher with "eyes in the back of his or her head" (withitness) also was better able to deal with two matters at once (overlapping).

Kounin's **ripple effect** should come as no big surprise. With kindergartners through college students as subjects, Kounin found that when a teacher corrects the misbehavior of one student, others who witness the reprimand also are affected. They would conform more and misbehave less. For example, a kindergarten correction such as, "Suzy, please stop talking and pay attention," would cause other students to be quiet and pay attention. Many would even sit up straighter!

Smoothness and Momentum	A teacher changes learning activities quite frequently. Sometimes the change is physical, as when the students move from their seats to a reading circle. Sometimes the change is psychological, as when the class switches from a spelling quiz to mathematics. In either case, the movement can be smooth and efficient or it can be slow and unnecessarily disruptive. Activity transitions provide a super opportunity for student rowdiness and misbehavior.

Kounin's (1970) concept of **momentum** refers to keeping the class moving on academic activities, or "the absence of slowdowns." A related concept is **smoothness,** which is the absence of teacher behaviors that break up the continuity of an on-going lesson or disrupt transitions between activities. Three types of teacher behaviors which disrupt momentum and smoothness—*flip-flops, fragmentation,* and *dangles*—are described in Inset 10.1. Research by Kounin (1970) showed that the smoother the movement between and within activities, the greater the work involvement and the lower the deviancy.

A recent study by Arlin (1979) confirmed that transitions between classroom activities are indeed disruptive. Observing students in grades one through nine, from lower to upper-middle SES levels, Arlin found that during transitions students' off-task behaviors—including talking, hitting, throwing things, making obscene gestures, making silly faces, dueling with clarinets, etc.—occurred at a rate which was double the regular classroom rate. Having confirmed the problem, Arlin listed several recommendations for improving smoothness and momentum during transitions:

1. Early in the year, children can be drilled, for example, in quietly putting books back on the shelf or calmly going to the gym. If students know what they are expected to do during a transition, they usually will do it peacefully.
2. Plan ahead for transitions. For example, instead of permitting students to madly dash for materials before instructions are completed, they can be told to listen first, then pick up materials second.
3. Don't make children wait. One teacher with a reputation for good discipline gave this experienced advice: "Always make sure the kids . . . have something in their hands so they can't throw anything. Never let kids wait longer than a minute for anything. You can't bog down or you'll pay for it!" (Arlin, 1979)

INSET 10.1

FLIP-FLOPS, FRAGMENTATION, AND DANGLES: HOW NOT TO TEACH

Kounin (1970; Kounin and Doyle, 1975; Kounin and Gump, 1974) identified several bad teaching habits which can disrupt momentum and smoothness during a transition from one activity to another or during a single lesson activity.

With *flip-flops,* a teacher ends one activity (spelling), begins a second activity (math), then flops back to the first activity: "How many spelled all of the words correctly?"

Fragmentation is the unnecessary breaking up of an activity into jerky steps, for example, asking students to join a reading group one at a time: "Mary, you come and take this seat. Fine. Now Fred, you come and sit there. Janet, now you stand up and come over here," etc., etc.

With *dangles,* the teacher starts the class on one activity, then suddenly reacts to a different matter, leaving the class dangling. For example, Ms. Kantwate might ask Jean to stand up and read a paragraph, then says "My goodness, Richard King isn't here today. Does anyone know if Richard is ill?" Jean and the rest of the class are left dangling. According to Kounin, a "stimulus bound" teacher cannot resist reacting to any stimulus which pops into his or her field of attention, even if the entire class is left dangling and waiting to continue.

**Group
Alerting**

Consider the following two sets of instructions to a class:

"Margaret, how much is 11 plus 12?"

"How much is 11 plus 12 (teacher looks around the room), Margaret?"

Although noticeably similar, the first instruction singles out Margaret to think about and solve the problem. The rest of the class need not be alert; they can relax and wait until their name is called. The second instruction, however, has a strong **group alerting** effect—nobody knows who will be called on and so everyone must keep on their toes and be ready to respond. The same situation would arise if, say, students in a reading circle were called on *in order,* so that beginning with Chrissy, everyone knows exactly when they will need to begin thinking. We would have a more alert group of readers if each reciter were selected in a more random fashion.

Group alerting, then, refers to keeping all children alert and attentive, not just the one who is reciting (Kounin, 1970). Generally, any strategy which alerts nonperformers that they could be next will keep students on their proverbial toes. For example, the teacher can:

- Randomly call on different reciters, so that no one knows who will be next ("Let's see now, who can I call on next . . .").
- Require the class to recite in unison ("Okay class, what's the right answer?").
- Ask for a show of hands by all who know the correct answer.
- Alert nonreciters that they might be asked to find mistakes made by the reciter ("Everybody watch Egbert and then tell me whether he does it right or wrong").
- Alert nonreciters that they might be asked about the reciter's content ("After Bill reads I'm going to ask questions to see who was listening").

Teachers who maintain high group alerting also elicit higher work involvement—and less deviancy (Kounin, 1970).

SATIATION VS. VARIETY: PROGRAMMING FOR INTEREST

The science of psychology discovered some time ago that repetition and lack of variety leads to satiation and boredom. In the classroom, bored little hands are likely to raise the devil. Some signs of satiation and boredom are: frequent and longer pauses in seatwork; looking around the room and out the window; and any number of "escape" activities—fiddling with paper clips, sharpening pencils, disturbing neighbors, drawing on or scratching the desks, writing notes, and so on. On the other hand, satiation occurs more slowly when students feel they are making good progress and when the challenge, variety, interest value, or some other attractiveness feature is strong. By itself, length of time at a task does not necessarily produce boredom, lower task involvement, and therefore deviancy.

There are a number of effective methods for programming variety and challenge into the teaching routine.

Variety in Activity and Content

A change in learning activities and content may be very small or very large and refreshing. For example, a switch from copying spelling words to copying sentences does not entail a particularly substantial change in the activity—students remain in the same spot copying things with a pencil. On the other hand, a change from copying spelling words to watching a thought-provoking science demonstration in another part of the room involves a change in content, a change in location, a change in intellectual function, a change in teacher function, a change in props and materials, a change in group configuration, a change in student activities and responsibility, and a change in the child's overt behavior. We will look more closely at some of these sources of variety, interest and challenge.

Variety in Level of Thinking

Different learning tasks elicit different types and levels of intellectual functioning. In increasing order of interest and challenge:

1. Some tasks require only attention and a little effort, such as listening or copying.
2. Others may require rehearsal or use of a simple skill, such as coloring, simple addition, or oral reading.
3. Still other tasks will require comprehension and understanding—for example, answering questions or otherwise recalling recently learned material.
4. A task might even require thought and decision making, such as solving arithmetic story problems, categorizing, or solving puzzles.
5. Finally, students might be asked to analyze, synthesize, or evaluate (Chapters 11, 19) or to think creatively (Chapter 16).

The point is that the more challenging and engaging the task is, the higher will be the task involvement and achievement, and the lower will be student deviancy (Kounin, 1970; Rosenshine, 1971, 1979).

Props and A-V Aids

As with level of thinking, it also is possible to categorize props and audiovisual aids according to the degree of interest or arousal which is usually stimulated. At the routine-and-repetitious end are pencils, paper, and everyday books. Slightly more interesting are props which, though generally available, are not used regularly: maps, charts, academic games, song books, and the like. Still more attention getting are unique, one-of-a-kind educational props such as phonographs, movie or slide projectors, videotape players, and perhaps new learning centers, microcomputers, microscopes and so on. Satiation and boredom should decrease with a larger variety of props and with the use of more interesting props.

Group Configuration, Student Activities and Responsibilities

The teacher can work with an entire class, a subgroup, or with individual students. Such changes in group configuration, along with the changes in the associated activities and responsibilities, can provide refreshing variety.

For example, some *large-group* activities can include:

1. Lectures, explanations, demonstrations by the teacher.
2. Teacher-led discussions.
3. Question-and-answer recitations; unison responses.
4. Sending students to the blackboard.
5. Presentations by individual students, student groups, panels or committees; debates.
6. Presentations via movies, videotapes, slides, film strips, audiotapes, records, etc.
7. Team games, simulations, role playing (Charles and Stradskler, 1973).
8. Brainstorming sessions.
9. Field trips.

Some *small-group* activities can include:

1. Discussions of right and wrong test answers.
2. Reading in groups.
3. Planning panel or committee presentations or debates.
4. Planning and constructing projects.
5. Conducting experiments.
6. Working together at learning centers.
7. Attending in small groups to videotapes, records, etc.
8. Using spelling, math, or language flash cards.

Some *individual* learning activities can include:

1. Seatwork—math, reading, art, etc.
2. Individual library research projects.
3. Working at learning centers.
4. Exploring bulletin boards, maps, displays, etc.

INSET 10.2

**SATIATION
+ AROUSAL SEEKING
= DEVIANT BEHAVIOR**

In Chapter 9 on motivation, we discussed the concept of *optimum arousal level*. Basically, each of us seeks to maintain a certain level of psychological arousal or "activation." If the environment (read: the lesson) gets tiresome and does not provide the necessary stimulation, normal human beings—little ones and big ones—will generate their own stimulation in order to raise their sagging arousal levels. Activities which raise arousal levels can include simply daydreaming or doodling with a pencil; they also can include sailing airplanes, flipping paper clips, talking, or disrupting neighbors.

As we saw in Chapter 9, there are very great individual differences in optimum arousal levels and, consequently, in arousal-seeking tendencies. For example, juvenile delinquents are very high in arousal seeking—there's nothing as pleasant as stealing a few tires, breaking some windows, or mugging a helpless person. On the other hand, students who are nervous, anxious, and perhaps withdrawn may welcome longer sessions of nonstimulating, repetitive tasks.

The teacher should remain aware of the great individual differences among students in their tolerance for boredom and needs for stimulation.

Location

Finally, a change of location also can reduce satiation. Students can work at their desks, around a table, in a reading circle, at a display or learning center in the classroom, around the teacher, or outside the classroom in the IMC, music room, art room, or gymnasium. Field trips, too, present a refreshing and memorable change of pace.

OTHER MANAGEMENT PRINCIPLES AND IDEAS

Getting Started with a New Class

Sometimes hardened, experienced teachers will advise the newcomer to "get tough" immediately and perhaps ease up later. "Don't smile until Christmas" is frequent advice. This is fine if you wish to become "the enemy," establishing perhaps a year-long relationship of alienation, mistrust, and hostility. Good and Brophy (1977) seem to have a better idea in recommending the early establishment of likeability, credibility, respectability, trustworthiness, and being a generally attractive, worthwhile person. They recommend communicating to the students that:

- You enjoy teaching, both the instruction and the personal interaction.
- You look forward to getting to know each student individually.
- You are willing to help not only with subject matter, but in any way you can.
- You expect to teach the subject matter successfully and to help each student go as far as he or she can.
- You are a teacher, not a disciplinarian; certain behaviors will be expected, others will be forbidden.

Of course, your credibility requires that your behavior be consistent with these guides.

Rules   You must convey to the group that you intend to retain control—and that you mean what you say. You will need rules which are simple and clear, and you must enforce them for all students. The children should understand that the rules will help them and the teacher work together as a team. If

the rules are violated, the teamwork is disrupted and time is wasted. The specific rules will depend mainly on the grade level you teach and the general level of rebelliousness in a class. Obviously, rules for first graders will be different from rules for junior high or high school students. Also,

Table 10.1 Math department—grading criteria

I. BEHAVIOR AND CLASS PREPARATION

A. Bring a pencil, notebook and your math book to class every day.
B. Do not talk unnecessarily or disrupt class activities.

FOR BREAKING RULES A OR B YOU WILL RECEIVE AN X.

1st X—warning
2nd X—warning
3rd X—grade lowered one level (B+ to B)
4th X—grade lowered, again
etc. . . .

II. GRADES

Complete and hand in assignments on time. Late work will receive a lower grade. No overdue work will be accepted once the unit test is given.

Daily work, homework and class participation = $\frac{1}{4}$ of grade
Quizzes = $\frac{1}{4}$ of grade
Tests = $\frac{1}{2}$ of grade

III. TARDINESS

You are expected to be in class on time. If you are tardy three or more times per quarter your grade will be lowered one level (B+ to B).

IV. ATTENDANCE

Regular attendance in math class is absolutely necessary for any student wishing to master the material presented. During the course of the year, however, there may be special circumstances which cause a student to miss one or more class periods. As a department we have outlined the following guidelines for you to follow in the event that you must miss a class.

A. Illness—you will be allowed one day for every day that you are absent to complete the missed work. If you miss more than two days you are *strongly* urged to call a classmate for your assignments or to contact the school office so that your teacher can leave the necessary materials for pick up in the office.
B. Field trips, films, dentist/doctor appointments, music or athletic events, etc. If at all possible, arrange to do these activities outside of class time. If you must miss class be sure to notify your teacher *in advance*. You will *not* be given an extra day to make up work. Missed assignments will have to be completed during your study hall or at home. You will be expected to have the work necessary for class the next day. Do not expect your teacher to spend extra time reteaching the material you missed.
C. Vacations—see your teacher in advance for all work you will miss.
D. Unexcused absences—you will not be allowed to make up any work you miss due to unexcused absences.

rules for college-bound middle-class students will be different from the rules for a group of budding thugs.

Generally, Good and Brophy (1977, p. 79) recommended that rules be *broad, flexible,* and *few in number.* Rules such as "Disruptive behaviors will not be tolerated" or "We will be courteous at all times" are sufficiently broad that no long, depressing lists of *do's* and *don't's* should be necessary. As for flexibility, situations change and the teacher and his or her rules must sometimes bend. For example, throwing things may be outlawed, but if Dotty tosses Jim a needed eraser there is no need for a reprimand simply because "a rule is a rule is a rule." Unreasonable enforcement of picky rules is a common source of conflict between many teachers and their students.

One set of rules used in a middle-class suburb of Madison, Wisconsin, appears in Table 10.1. Note that this list includes both general rules and clear, specific penalties for violating the rules.

The Physical Classroom: Design for Peace

Some room arrangements are more conducive than others to manageability. Basically, seating should be arranged to maximize attention and minimize disruption. The teacher should face the class, whether seated at his or her desk or standing. Students also should face the teacher at times when attention is expected. When students are working in small groups, a circle or oval pattern of chairs facilitates communication. If several groups are working at once, they should be maximally spread out to reduce disruptions and distractions.

Traffic patterns too should be analyzed. Are main entrance and exit routes wide enough and free of obstacles? Can students get to the bookshelves and pencil sharpener without tripping over Orville the snake or stepping on someone's lunch or art project?

PUNISHMENT

Punishment was discussed briefly in Chapters 5 and 6 in conjunction with principles of conditioning and behavior modification. We noted in Chapter 6 that punishment:

- Can be physically or psychologically painful.
- Often just represses—temporarily slows down—the misbehavior.
- Presents a model (of aggression) for young students to imitate.
- Has unpleasant side effects, such as fear, anxiety, or hostility.
- Effects may be unpredictable, depending on student personality.

In 1977 the Supreme Court upheld the use of corporal (physical) punishment in the schools, although three states (Maryland, Massachusetts, and New Jersey) specifically prohibit it. Before smacking a kid, however, you will want to consider not only the points just listed, but the reactions of parents, school board members, your principal, other students, other teachers, and perhaps your conscience. A calm, professionally prepared teacher should have other alternatives prepared in advance, so that a rash slap or shaking need not even be considered.

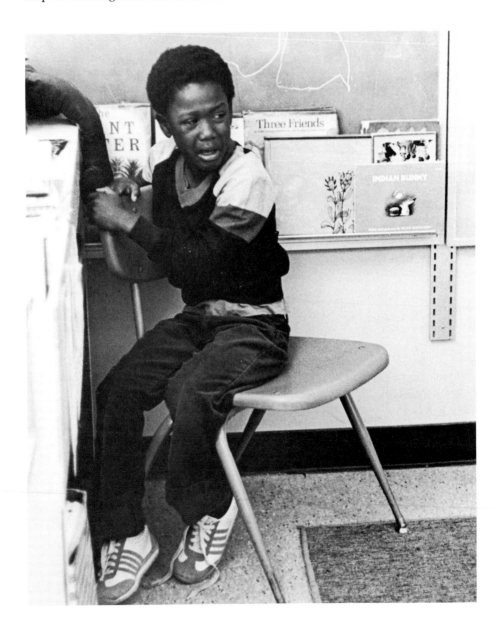

Punishment should be considered a last resort for controlling misbehavior or disruptiveness—to be used if all else fails. Too often the punishment backfires, producing even stronger resentment, hostility, mistrust, and aggressiveness.

Ignoring, Vicarious Learning, Humor

For many minor rule infractions, such as not paying attention or speaking out without raising hands, one time-tested strategy is to **ignore** the offense and reward the correct behavior. This behavior-modification approach should teach Bobby Blurtwell that speaking out or interrupting others will get him nowhere, while the correct behavior of raising his hand produces good results. Be warned, however, that the ignoring strategy at first may cause an increase in the disruptiveness—just as you might raise your voice when ignored by a store clerk.

The teacher also can shape Blurtwell's behavior through a **vicarious learning** or modeling procedure (Chapter 6). He or she can reward other students for behaving properly: "I like the way Freddy raises his hand before speaking. That's how we do things in school." Such a comment should communicate to Blurtwell that his behavior will not produce good results.

A **humorous response** to a rule infraction may also do the trick: "You have a lovely voice Bobby, but I'd rather not hear it until I call on you. Is that a deal?" Such a response conveys the message, but everyone stays pleasant and unperturbed.

Use Threats First, Then Punish with Punishment That Punishes

Again, punishment is a last resort. The second-to-last strategy is threats of punishment. The teacher should explain (a) that the student's behavior is making impossible for the class to continue working, (b) that the student is responsible for causing problems for himself, and (c) that you the teacher are disappointed that the student will leave no alternative. Your own credibility requires that the threat be carried out if the student continues to misbehave.

One reason the student may continue to misbehave is that "punishment" often does not punish. Some students may enjoy baiting the teacher until he or she blows up and gives an impromptu speech on good manners and proper conduct. To their friends, they're heroes. Also, for students who thoroughly dislike you and your damn school, getting suspended is more of a two-week vacation than a remorseful lesson in good citizenship. They may even take pride in having forced you and your principal to take such drastic action.

The point is that the teacher should analyze any punishment to make certain that it does, in fact, stimulate regret, fear or remorse, and that it will lead to better behavior. Most important, the punishment must stop the misbehavior.

INSET 10.3

TIME OUT!

In Chapter 6 we mentioned the time-out punishment strategy. It is one which is acceptable to most parents and principles and usually is effective in calming down a rowdy scholar. Basically, the student is sent to a stimulation-free area or time-out room for 2, 5 or perhaps 10 or 15 minutes. The time-out area *must* be free of high-interest stimulation—no windows, no secretaries to watch, no lunch bags to plunder, no attractive posters or calendars. The student is to clam down and meditate on his or her behavior, not receive a refreshing change of scenery. A hasty "Billy, go out into the hall until you can act your age!" may provide Billy with a rewarding brief vacation from classroom pressures and responsibilities. The misbehavior may be inadvertently strengthened, not weakened.

Problem-Centered Negotiations and Investigations

Good and Brophy (1977, p. 90) point out that many students who will not respond to either positive appeals or punishment will agree to change their ways in a negotiated settlement. The teacher arranges for a private discussion, probably after school. The teacher can ask the student for his or her explanation of the misbehavior. He or she then provides feedback in terms of the teacher's emotional reactions ("I get very upset that you won't let me teach my class") and the effects on the rest of the class ("You disturb everyone and keep them from reading and doing their lessons"). The problem-centered discussion should be honest and open and have a "no-lose" character—the agreement should be satisfactory to both parties with no loss of face and with no obvious winner or loser. You, of course, will win if the negotiated truce works.

Occasionally, problems will arise among students (for example, accusations of theft) which require investigation. It is important for the teacher to establish a reputation for fairness. Students also must learn that if they misbehave, they *will* have to deal with you face-to-face. The discussion should be private, it should include only those involved, and it should have a problem-solving focus—what is the problem and how shall we resolve it.

Each student must be given an uninterrupted opportunity to present his or her side of the story. The teacher also should try to help students understand the motives and perceptions of the other person. Often, the students can be brought to realize that what they perceived as an infringement on their rights was actually a misunderstanding. If someone is guilty of a crime (theft, obscenities, shoving, etc.), they should leave the meeting understanding that the punishment or reprimand is due to their own behavior, not the teacher's hostility or personal dislike for them. Hopefully, the student should be ashamed, embarrassed, and unlikely to repeat the offense.

MANAGEMENT AND DISCIPLINE IN DISADVANTAGED NEIGHBORHOODS

In rough neighborhoods, student rebelliousness can mean physical danger for the high school teacher and even the junior high school teacher. On September 2, 1979, the CBS television news show "60 Minutes" described teaching conditions in some extraordinarily rough New York City and Los Angeles schools. The show was titled "Violence in the Schools." Many teachers had been beaten, stabbed, or shot; some had died; and one woman teacher was raped in her classroom at knifepoint. Most teachers were fearful of physical attacks, and their personalities had changed drastically as a result of this anxiety. They were nervous, had trouble sleeping, many had continual diarrhea (an anxiety symptom), and many had difficulty in relating well to their spouses and children. Women teachers in one New York City school always used the elevator and never the stairs—they were afraid they would be shoved down the stairs and injured. Confrontations with students were avoided because (a) all other students would side with the culprit, no matter how bad his or her behavior, or (b) the student might be armed. You do not win in such circumstances. For many students, the teachers were "the enemy," and the school was a prison.

It is important to point out that the schools represented in the TV show were the newsworthy ones, and not the typical inner city schools. The majority of schools in disadvantaged neighborhoods are filled with decent kids who study, learn, and attend football games just like students in any other part of town.

Testing the Teacher

In virtually any classroom, a teacher's authority will be tested. With disadvantaged children the tests will come quickly: How much talking will he or she tolerate? Can I get away with bursting in five minutes late? Can I wear my sunglasses in class? Can I take a nap? Can I get away with disrupting the whole class when I stomp and chatter to the pencil sharpener? The disruptive students are hoping the teacher will fail in his or her attempts to cope with them. At the same time, however, they will lose respect for the too-tolerant teacher and probably will feel more insecure in the classroom. Also, the students who are watching usually are hoping the teacher will handle the rascal properly. If not, they too will lose respect for the teacher and may reject and eventually turn against him or her (Ornstein, 1969a). The teacher cannot afford to fail.

INSET 10.4

ARE YOU A BOOMER, MAVERICK, ENTERTAINER, OR SECULAR INTELLECTUAL?

There is no one perfect teaching style and no one perfect teacher personality. In his work with teachers of the poor, Frank Riessman (1969) described eight different teacher styles that worked well with disadvantaged children.

1. The *fussy and compulsive* teacher teaches things over and over and is very concerned that everyone understands the material. The compulsiveness seems to create the order and structure that disadvantaged children like.
2. The *boomer* shouts in a strong voice, "I'm here to teach you, you're going to learn, and there is no nonsense in this classroom." The boomer sets the rules early, and the students quickly learn not to overstep the bounds. Students may not like the boomer, and some psychologists would label him or her hostile, but he or she uses that hostility effectively and students learn.
3. The *maverick* is convinced that ideas are meant to stir people up, and so he or she is always presenting difficult questions and disturbing ideas. The maverick is as surprised and curious as his or her students with each new discovery. It is this fresh, inquiring quality that comes through to the maverick's eager students.
4. The *coach* is informal, earthy, and may even be an athlete. He or she is physically expressive in front of the class, and many disadvantaged students relate quickly and comfortably to the high level of activity and motion.
5. The *quiet one* is about the opposite of the coach, yet equally effective. His or her sincerity, calmness, and dignity pervade the classroom and command both respect and attention.
6. The *entertainer* is colorful, melodramatic, and not afraid to have fun with the kids. He or she tends to be inventive, and actively involves the students in engaging learning experiences.
7. The *secular* teacher is relaxed, informal, sometimes has lunch with the students, and might even use the students' bathroom. He or she is comfortable with the students, and they respond well.
8. Finally, the *secular intellectual* shows his or her genuine interest in knowledge and in its transmission to young people. He or she has broad interests, for example, in all kinds of music—not just socially proper classics. The secular intellectual might take a sincere interest in learning hip language or minority culture from his or her students.

Which of these styles fit you best? Could you role play all of them? If you were a disadvantaged student, to which style would you respond best?

Guidelines for Classroom Management in Disadvantaged Neighborhoods: Ornstein

New York City psychologist Allan Orstein (1969a) itemized nearly two dozen rules and procedures for controlling classroom rowdiness and improving learning. While Ornstein specifically had difficult-to-teach, disadvantaged students in mind, the list contains good ideas for classroom management for other students as well. Says Ornstein, "Some of the rules . . . seem almost too basic for explanation. Yet my experience is that they are far from rudimentary." The reader should recognize several ideas already presented in this chapter.

1. The first rule is to have rules. (Guidelines for preparing rules were presented above.)
2. Train students to enter the room in an orderly fashion. Do not allow them to walk around or socialize; they are there to learn.
3. Keep a clean and attractive room. Gaping closet doors and disarrayed papers and chairs set a tone of disorder. Change pictures and bulletin boards. All of this shows you care.
4. Be certain you have everyone's attention before you start. Require 100 percent attention, and don't wait for an offender to pay attention when he or she feels like it.
5. Be consistent with your class routine. Many students do not cope well with changes.

6. Get to know the students early in the term. Don't let them think they are shielded by anonymity. You also need to know the difficulties and limitations of each person.

7. Hold students accountable. Students must realize that they cannot get away with poor preparation. Challenge the student who walks in late or does not do homework, but do not humiliate him or her.

8. Speak softly. Do not shout. Try not to get excited.

9. Be clear with instructions. Give one instruction at a time. Make sure your instructions are understood and executed before issuing another one.

10. Aim to have full class participation. Teach students to show respect for one another by listening to one another.

11. Be aware of undercurrents of behavior. As you teach, try to watch what everyone is doing. Do not turn your back on the class. Call on a disruptive student to answer questions or to go to the board.

12. It may be appropriate to keep students in their seats and not permit wandering. You may wish to prohibit students from coming to your desk. If students remain in their seats, discipline problems will be

INSET 10.5

**REDUCING RACIAL
TENSIONS: ARONSON'S
JIGSAW METHOD**

Racial tensions exist even in the elementary school. Black children associate with black children, Mexican-American with Mexican-American, and white with white. Sometimes, the tensions explode into violence. Now, it is a long-standing principle of social psychology that competition for a mutually exclusive goal produces hostility, while cooperation for a group goal produces strongly positive group feelings and interpersonal liking. Psychologist Elliot Aronson and his colleagues (Aronson, Blaney, Sikes, Stephan, and Snapp, 1975) sought to reduce racial tensions with a learning strategy that requires cooperation among children of different ethnic ancestry. These particular children had been forced into the same school by a new busing policy.

With Aronson's *jigsaw technique,* an upper-elementary class is divided into mixed-race groups of about six students each. The children are told that in one hour they will have a test to see how well they have learned, for example, about the life of newspaper publisher Joseph Pulitzer. Each of the six students is given one paragraph covering a different aspect of Pulitzer's career. To do well, each student must read his or her own paragraph and reduced. Do not permit students to abuse hall passes with frequent "emergencies."

13. Depend on interest to maintain order. A bored class is potential trouble. Keep students engaged in meaningful activity.

14. Be friendly but maintain a proper psychological distance. It's fine to take a joke and to be an entertainer. However, if you are too friendly, some children may perceive you as "soft" and take advantage of you. They prefer to keep the teacher on a different level.

15. Be consistent with discipline. Do not be lenient one day, strict the next. Do not punish one student, not another. All threatened punishments must be carried out.

16. Do not threaten. You can make your point by the way you look at an offender or touch him or her. If you do threaten, don't make impossible threats ("Stop that or I'll have you expelled in 10 minutes!"). You lose face with such warnings.

17. Be flexible. Some children need guidance, not discipline. Others need both. Some excitable students must be handled after class; others can be dealt with on the spot.

---

then explain the contents to the others. Cooperation and interdependence is the only route to success.

Aronson's research included in the experimental groups 76 black students, 41 Mexican-Americans, 177 Anglos, and 1 Oriental; in the control group 9 blacks, 20 Mexican-Americans, 50 Anglos, and 2 Orientals. The results were fairly dramatic:

1. Children in the experimental groups became friendlier toward *individuals* of other races with whom they had worked. (Unfortunately, the liking did not seem to extend beyond individuals to other members of a given racial group.)
2. Most children using the puzzle method (but not the black children) acquired more positive attitudes toward school; children in the control group actually became more negative.
3. The experimental children gained in self-confidence and self-esteem.
4. Grades for children using the puzzle technique improved, while grades of the control children declined.

Teachers reported that the changes in attitudes and self-concepts and the improved classroom atmosphere were very impressive—and they intended to continue using the jigsaw method to reduce racial tensions.

18. Always work with the individual offender. It causes resentment and shows you can't cope if you punish the whole class because somebody tossed a pickle at the map. (You were supposed to face the class, remember?) Try to invoke peer disapproval by explaining that "some selfish person is disrupting the class." Watch who they look at.
19. Try to handle all discipline yourself. You admit defeat and surrender authority when you send Peter Pickletosser to the principal.
20. Never make an offense personal. Try to make disruptions appear aimed at the class ("Peter, you're ruining it for the class!"). Also avoid public arguments—they just make a hero of the debater. ("Pete, let's talk after class.")
21. Be certain to dismiss the class. Students should work to the end of the class; they should not start packing up and combing their hair five minutes before the bell. However, they are in no mood to work after the bell. One good gesture is a "Have a good day" right after the bell rings.

TO IMPROVE
YOUR TEACHING

Present your message to students on the first day of class. Let them know that you look forward to getting to know each student, that you are there to help and to teach, and that they will be accountable for both coursework and behavior.

Also, prepare and present the set of classroom rules you will need. The specific rules will vary according to grade level, subject matter, and student populations. Use the example in Table 10.1 for ideas, although it may be too long and detailed. Generally, the fewer rules the better. Also, look over Ornstein's recommendations for classroom management. There are plenty of ideas for rules in his list.

Keep in mind the idea of "withitness." When you begin teaching, you will want to develop the habit of knowing what everyone in the room is doing—and letting them know that you know what they are doing.

Overlapping, smoothness, and momentum also reduce behavior problems. You will want to devise your lesson plans and activities so that transitions are smooth and efficient, with minimal opportunity for disruptiveness.

In your recitation sessions, keep in mind the group-alerting concept—let everyone know that he or she could be called on next. Do not let 26 students start daydreaming, passing notes, or talking because they know that student number 27 is the one who must be ready to perform.

Remember also that boredom produces deviancy, deviancy aimed at breaking the monotony and raising "arousal levels." Plan for variety and interest. You can vary content, location, type of intellectual function (thinking activity), teacher function, A-V aids, group configuration, and especially student activities.

Plan ahead, too, for your punishment problems, including negotiations with unruly students and investigations into student problems. You do not want to be caught unprepared when some form of discipline or investigation clearly is in order. Be ready to ignore minor infractions; respond by rewarding correct behavior. Humor also can get the message across without a scene.

Be ready also for students to test your tolerance. Some will need a clear message early in the year regarding what you will and will not tolerate.

SUMMARY

Some classroom disruptions are routine and minor, others are severe and intolerable. Disruptiveness may be caused by boredom, frustration, peer recognition for being a hero, or by deeper problems of poverty, alienation, low ability, irrelevant curriculum, impersonal schools, or peer traditions of defiance. A few students will have severe problems, including psychosis.

The best solution to disruptiveness lies in preventing trouble before it happens, which is precisely what classroom management is about.

Good management will include reasonable rules, positive expectations, accountability, planning for interest and variety, smooth transitions between activities, continual surveillance, control of stimuli which trigger clowning or other disruptiveness, and using threats carefully.

Student socialization is especially a problem during the adolescent, junior high school years.

Kounin identified many principles of good classroom management and many characteristics of effective teacher-managers. "Withitness" is letting students know that you know what is going on. "Overlapping" is the ability to attend to two events at once. The "ripple effect" is the quieting effect on students who only witness a culprit being reprimanded or requested to desist.

Kounin's momentum is the "absence of slowdowns" during transitions between activities. Smoothness is the absence of teacher behaviors which break up continuity within or between activities. Smoothness and momentum can be disrupted by flip-flops, fragmentation, and dangles. Sometimes, teacher interruptions are due to "stimulus bound" reactions—impulsively reacting to an immediate irrelevant stimulus.

Three suggestions for improving smoothness and momentum are as follows: (1) Drill children in making peaceful transitions between activities; (2) plan ahead for smooth transitions; and (3) don't make children wait.

Group alerting is keeping everyone on their toes, expecting to be called on next.

Research shows that withitness, overlapping, smoothness, momentum, and group alerting all are related to task involvement and an absence of deviancy.

Satiation and boredom can be reduced by varying the type and level of student thinking, props and A-V aids, group configurations, student activities and responsibilities, and activity location.

It is important to get the class off to a good start by informing students that you enjoy teaching, you are willing to help, you expect to teach the material, and certain behaviors will be expected, others forbidden. Rules will help; they should be simple, broad, flexible, and few. You should always face the class. Traffic patterns should minimize disruption.

Punishment should be a last resort, since it may increase the resentment. Ignoring minor deviations and rewarding good behavior can shape proper conduct. Using vicarious learning (rewarding another student's good behavior) and humor also can teach proper behavior.

Threats, used before punishment, should tell the student that he or she is responsible and that you will have no choice. The punishment should be analyzed to make sure that it punishes, not rewards, deviant behavior.

Private no-lose negotiations with a student also can bring peace. Investigations of inter-student problems should be private, fair, and aimed at pinpointing a misunderstanding or making the culprit feel embarrassed or ashamed.

A few schools in disadvantaged neighborhoods pose physical dangers for "the enemy." That's you. Students will test the teacher's authority.

Ornstein listed 21 guides for classroom management. These included firm rules, an attractive classroom, requiring attention, a consistent routine, getting to know students personally, accountability for assignments, keeping calm, keeping track of everyone's behavior, prohibiting wandering, maintaining high interest, maintaining psychological distance, consistent discipline, flexibility, and others.

TOPICS FOR THOUGHT AND DISCUSSION

1. Kounin advises variety to reduce satiation and boredom. Ornstein recommends a consistent routine "because many of these children cannot cope with change." Is there an inconsistency in these viewpoints?
2. How many ways can you think of to reduce boredom and increase interest?
3. Which theories of motivation (Chapter 9) are most helpful in providing ideas for classroom management?
4. How would you, as a junior high school teacher in a potentially dangerous area, cope with your teaching job? How could you best help the students—by teaching academic content, socialization, or both?

PROJECTS

1. Prepare a set of rules for a class of disadvantaged first-grade children. What considerations, potential problems, expectations, etc., must be covered?
2. Outline a set of rules for an eighth-grade science class. Do the rules in Table 10.1 provide suggestions?
3. When practice teaching, ask teachers about the management and discipline "tricks" they find helpful. Be sure to ask what *not* to do as well. Prepare a list.
4. Outline threat-and-punishment procedures for every possible contingency you can think of at the grade level you expect to teach.

RECOMMENDED READING

Aronson, E., N. Blaney, J. Sikes, C. Stephan, and M. Snapp. Busing and racial tension: The jigsaw route to learning and liking. *Psychology Today* **8** (9), 1975, 43–50.

Glasser, W. *Schools without failure.* New York: Harper & Row, 1969.

Good, T. L., and J. E. Brophy. *Looking in classrooms,* second edition. New York: Holt, 1978.

Kounin, J. S. *Discipline and group management in classrooms.* New York: Holt, Rinehart & Winston, 1970.

Ornstein, A. C., and P. D. Vairo (eds.). *How to teach the disadvantaged.* New York: David McKay, 1969.

TEACHING: THEORY AND METHOD

PART V

Setting Classroom Objectives

11

About instructional objectives / Educational outcomes: four models / Writing instructional objectives / Objections to objectives / Task analysis / Taxonomy of educational objectives: cognitive domain / To improve your teaching / Summary / Topics for thought and discussion / Projects / Recommended reading

ABOUT INSTRUCTIONAL OBJECTIVES

An **instructional objective** describes what the student should be able to do after the instruction. The term **behavioral objective** often is used interchangeably, since the effects of instruction (new knowledge, skills or attitudes) are to be reflected in the students' visible *behavior*, for example, on a test, in a completed paper or project, or in some other demonstration of a skill. In Chapter 12, which deals with instructional theories and models, we will see that preparing a clear statement of instructional objectives is an integral step in many strategies for effective, efficient teaching. In fact, the concept of preparing instructional objectives, in combination with Bloom's **Taxonomy of Educational Objectives** for the cognitive domain (discussed later in this chapter and in Chapters 17 and 19), has had a profound effect on educational thought and practice throughout the world (Seddon, 1978).

As we will see later, however, there are strong criticisms of behavioral objectives. The main complaint is that preparing precise behavioral objectives can have a constraining, limiting effect on both teachers and students. That is, teachers may resist excursions into unplanned but beneficial topics because ". . . they are not in the objectives." Similarly, students may confine their educational interests and efforts only to meeting the teacher's prepared list of specific objectives. Criticisms and cautions will be reviewed in more detail after the case in favor of preparing and using instructional objectives has been presented.

Advantages for the Teacher

The first and most obvious advantage of outlining one's instructional objectives is to *aid instructional planning*. If the teacher knows exactly where he or she wants to go, it will be a lot easier to get there. The organization and content of lectures, discussions, demonstrations, films, readings, reports, projects, and other individual and group activities will be planned according to the statement of instructional objectives. As a corollary to this better planning benefit, a definite set of objectives helps keep the teacher on target. A teacher who has a clear picture of what skills and behaviors are to be learned is much less likely to waste time on completely irrelevant topics and activities.

The second benefit to the teacher is in *evaluating learning*. When objectives are used, testing and evaluation will be much more structured and sensible, since the objectives themselves suggest the form and content of the evaluation. For example, one objective of Ms. Luna Landing's science class might be: "Without looking at a diagram of the solar system, students should be able to sketch the solar system, showing planet names, approximate sizes, and approximate distances from the sun." Is there any ambiguity regarding how this objective should be fairly evaluated? Evaluation is based squarely on the objectives.

For the Student	Explicit objectives provide tremendous *structure* and *guidance* for the student. If the student knows exactly what he or she will be expected to do, study time and effort will be directed with notable efficiency. The student knows what to look for and how he or she is supposed to reproduce it. In research with college students, Duchastel (1979; Duchastel and Brown, 1974) demonstrated that a clear set of objectives does indeed play an orienting role. In studying written material about nuclear breeder reactors, specific objectives such as: "Be able to give three reasons why breeder reactors are seen as attractive sources of energy," caused students to selectively attend to and learn the target information.

Without objectives to explain the goals of the instruction, many students will assume they are supposed to memorize facts. Actually, the teacher may want students to synthesize facts in order to deduce, for example, the unique astronomical and geological conditions for life on Earth.

Instructional objectives also have a subtle *motivational* effect. When a student, or anyone else, clearly understands what must be done, there is motivation to attack the chore, wrap it up, and get on with something else. With some teaching strategies, students will work hard to meet the stated objectives so that they can work on projects of their own—which they are free to do as soon as they reach the stated objectives.

There are indeed clear advantages to informing students of *what* the teacher is trying to teach and *how* the information or skill will be evaluated.

For Parents	Speaking as one, it's refreshing and enlightening to see exactly what information and skills one's children are learning, particularly since the names of courses do not describe the details of the course content.

For Principals and Other Administrators	Education in general, and sometimes specific schools and teachers, are criticized for (a) teaching irrelevant concepts and skills, (b) teaching in ineffective or abstract ways which do not promote learning, retention, and transfer, or (c) failing to properly evaluate what was taught. A solution which grew out of these accusations has been labeled **competency-based** or **performance-based education,** and is based directly on the use of instructional objectives (see Chapter 1). The statement of objectives announces publicly what the school system, district, school, or teacher intends to teach, and therefore what the students are expected to learn. The objectives are viewed as "competencies" for which students may be held accountable. Some cities will not permit a student to graduate from high school if he or she has not passed the appropriate competency tests. In the 1980s, competency testing remains a lively issue.

As we saw in Chapter 1, the concept of accountability also may be applied to teachers, who may lose their jobs if students do not master the stated instructional objectives.

EDUCATIONAL OUTCOMES: FOUR MODELS

One sometimes subtle difference between school systems, schools, principals, and even individual teachers is their emphasis on different sorts of major educational outcomes. As one attempt to simplify this problem, Mitchell and Spady (1978) described four different educational models, each with a different emphasis on what the instructional objectives and the end product (the student) should be.

The first outcome-based model, **competency-based education** (Chapter 1), emphasizes the achievement of technical competence. The important educational outcomes are seen as those with high economic or social utility. Instruction is thus organized around high academic achievement, with defined certification standards. Students are (hopefully) motivated to work hard in order to meet the standards and thus to qualify for real future opportunities.

A second type of outcome-based approach is **development-based education.** This is basically a humanistic approach (Chapter 13) which combines intellectual development with affective development. Students are motivated (hopefully, still) by natural curiosity, a sense of adventure, and most importantly by the promise of enhanced personal effectiveness. School programs emphasize awareness (e.g., of social problems and issues), concern for others, personal identity, pride in excellence, and quality of educational experiences. The development-based education model forms the base of most alternative and free schools and elementary schools.

A third outcome-based model is **social-integration-based education.** Here, social integration, acculturation (of minorities), and involvement of students in the larger social milieu are seen as the important educational outcomes. In shorter words, the goals are (a) eliminating racial stereotypes and bigotry and (b) helping students assume positive and productive social roles. Elements of this orientation may include multicultural teachers, bilingual or bicultural instructional methods, integrated classrooms, and not letting Archie Bunker types give guest lectures. Students learn to associate personal growth with becoming productive, worthwhile citizens, participating in and making a contribution to the social order. Indeed, the motivation for student learning is each student's desire to form a positive personal identity, to feel that he or she is an attractive person of high worth.

A fourth outcome-based approach is called **social-responsibility-based education.** This model most closely applies to a successful military school. The focus is on the development of each student's sense of personal responsibility for his or her own conduct in relation to the values of the larger social system. Academic achievement thus plays third fiddle to good citizenship, positive attitudes, and loyalty to the social system. The impact of a social-responsibility orientation will be the creation of closely structured classrooms and tightly organized schools (e.g., military academies) and even the use of "disciplinary specialists" who, shall we say, heighten awareness of conduct norms. Student motivation is based on status, recognition, and prestige, which are awarded in relation to the degree of loyalty to and respect for the social standards.

WRITING INSTRUCTIONAL OBJECTIVES

As we have seen, an instructional objective is a statement which describes what the student should be able *to do* after the period of instruction. The emphasis is on the changed behavior, the *terminal performance*, the capacity of the student to demonstrate his or her learning. Therefore, statements of instructional objectives traditionally use action-oriented verbs such as *names, lists, draws, differentiates, solves, identifies, chooses, illustrates, makes up an example of, describes, selects, marks, circles, reads orally, arranges*, and others.

A teacher who is preparing specific instructional objectives which describe terminal performances would not use fuzzy, unobjective, nonbehavioral, nonvisible verbs such as "understands," "knows," "grasps," "appreciates," or even "learns." These nonbehavioral verbs may be used in statements of broad, general instructional objectives (described below), but such verbs do not clearly specify observable terminal performances. The highly specific behavioral objectives describe behaviors which are definite evidence that students do learn, understand, appreciate, etc.

Robert Mager, most famous for his little book *Preparing Instructional Objectives* (Mager, 1962, 1975), emphasizes three points in writing objectives:

First, the statement must describe what the student will *do* to demonstrate achievement; that is, it must describe the student's terminal performance. The focus is on proper *verb* selection. Remember all those action-oriented verbs above?

Second, the statement should include important *conditions* under which the student will demonstrate his or her competence. This is not particularly confusing. It refers to such restrictions as:

"Without using a map, . . ."
"In just 15 minutes, . . ."
"By Friday morning, . . ."
"Using any reference, . . ."
"Without peeking at the book, . . ."

Third, the statement should include the *acceptable level of performance* that is expected. Some sample performance criteria, which include important conditions of performance, might be:

"In 30 minutes, solve the 10 problems on page 12 with 80 percent accuracy."

"Without looking at a map, reproduce the New England states without omitting a single state, even Rhode Island."

"Be able to spell the 50 words on the list with no more than one error."

"By Friday, be able to summarize, without notes, two theories (not just one) of how the asteroid belt between Mars and Jupiter was created."

If students are provided with a detailed list of behavioral objectives which includes a description of the *conditions* of the expected terminal performance and the *criteria* for evaluation, then in some cases the teacher may need to do little else (Mager, 1975).

General and Specific Objectives

Thus far, we have described instructional objectives primarily as being very specific and concrete, each objective describing a specific terminal performance. Virtually always, however, *specific* behavioral objectives should be tied to more *general* educational objectives and goals. There has been a tendency for teacher trainees, teachers, and curriculum writers to produce long lists of behavioral objectives—sometimes to the point of absurdity. Actually, neither the length of the objectives list nor the explicitness of the objectives guarantees high quality or appropriateness. Specific objectives should be related to general goals, goals which probably cannot and should not be phrased in a concrete behavioral form (e.g., "Understands basic Spanish vocabulary," "Appreciates democracy," "Has mastery of fraction and decimal operations").

Also, parents and principals may be more interested in general objectives ("Understands ecological balance in Southwest deserts") than specific ones ("Lists eleven lively lizards living in northern Arizona").

Norman E. Gronlund, in his own little book *Stating Objectives for Classroom Instruction* (Gronlund, 1972, 1978), recommends stating a *general* objective first, followed by *specific* objectives which would give evidence of mastering the general objective. For example:

Understands scientific principles

1. States the principle in his own words.
2. Gives an example of the principle.
3. Identifies predictions that are in harmony with the principle.
4. Distinguishes between correct and incorrect applications of the principle.   [Gronlund, 1972, p. 17]

Note that the general principle or objective uses a properly fuzzy, nonbehavioral verb (understands), while the specific objectives use verbs which describe what the learner is to do (i.e., he or she must state, give an example, identify, distinguish). Gronlund also advises us to "Be careful not to omit complex objectives (for example, critical thinking, appreciating) simply because they are difficult to define in specific behavioral terms" (Gronlund, 1972, p. 17). This statement eases us gracefully into the next short topic.

Expressive Objectives

Eisner (1969) recognized the limited nature of most performance-based objectives and invented a cure: the **expressive objective.** These are used to describe situations in which the teacher anticipates an "educational encounter." The expressive objective does not specify a clear, behaviorally defined objective, but describes a "loose" situation in which students will explore issues or grapple with problems. While instructional objectives describe what *should* be learned, expressive objectives deal with what *could* be learned, including attitudinal or emotional outcomes, such as empathy or feelings of compassion. Expressive objectives may be preplanned, as in a postmortem discussion of a movie. They also may occur spontaneously, as when a discussion of Egypt turns into a lively debate about "ancient astronauts" who might have built the pyramids, Stonehenge, and the Easter Island heads. Expressive objectives increase one's flexibility and legitimize complex instructional activities which do not have definite behavioral outcomes.

OBJECTIONS TO OBJECTIVES

The positive side of instructional objectives looks pretty good. To summarize, the use of instructional objectives:

1. Helps teachers plan and conduct instruction.
2. Helps teachers fairly evaluate learning.
3. Helps students efficiently use their time and energy.
4. Helps keep parents informed as to what is really being learned.
5. May provide a clear basis for performance-based education and accountability.

A partial list of unswerving supporters of the benefits of educational objectives reads like a list of *Who's Who* in educational psychology: Robert Gagné (1967), Robert Glaser (1967), Robert Mager (1968), James Popham (1969, 1973), David Krathwohl and Benjamin Bloom (Bloom, Englehart, Furst, Hill, and Krathwohl, 1956).

However, not all teachers nor all educational psychologists are impressed, and the criticisms of behavior-based instructional objectives have been quick and from the heart. For example, it has been rumored that using clearly stated and behaviorally defined objectives is unrealistic, unimaginative, ineffective, inhuman, impractical, inflexible, short-sighted, aimed at trivial learning, and just plain unnecessary. Feelings are fairly strong, and some very important issues and values are at stake. We will briefly look at some of the main criticisms and some capsulized responses to the criticisms.

1. *Behavioral objectives can deal only with trivial outcomes of learning, those easy to measure and which may have little long-range educational value.* The response to this criticism is that, as described above, thoughtfully prepared behavioral objectives—which may indeed seem overly specific and trivial—should be related to more general, superordinate educational goals. Long lists of highly specific objectives should not be prepared as isolated ends in themselves.
2. *Some instructional goals do not lend themselves to statements of behavioral objectives: for example—aesthetic goals (e.g., in art, music, drama); process goals (e.g., critical thinking, problem solving, creative thinking); affective and humanistic goals (e.g., honesty, patriotism, confidence and initiative, concern for mankind).* The counterargument is that with a little effort and ingenuity, most instructional goals can be prepared as behavioral objectives—and the teacher is better off for doing so (Popham, 1969). Also, the use of expressive objectives (Eisner, 1969; see above), essentially inviting students to explore unstructured issues, was designed for situations demanding broader, more complex, even affective outcomes.
3. *Using behavioral objectives encourages students to restrict their interests and attention to the stated objectives, and discourages them*

from expanding their horizons with a broader approach to education (Atkin, 1968; Raths, 1971). If teachers and students perceive the teaching-learning process only as meeting the teachers' specific behavioral objectives, this argument could be a sound one. However, the use of behavioral objectives should not prevent flexibility in teaching, nor the individualization of some projects and assignments in accord with students' needs and interests. Also, most strategies for individualizing instruction routinely use objectives to structure individual student work (Chapter 12). In this sense, objectives promote flexibility and individualized education.

4. *Using behavioral objectives prevents teachers from following up potentially valuable teaching opportunities because those opportunities "... are not in the objectives."* A reasonable teacher should not be improperly enslaved by a long list of objectives. A well-prepared teacher has a ready set of instructional activities, but should be flexible enough to alter the plans if a different instructional opportunity arises—especially one related to general instructional goals. Objectives are intended to reduce irrelevant, off-target wandering, but should not prevent worthwhile educational sidetracks.

5. *Behavioral objectives are unnecessary; many fine teachers do very well without them (Jackson, 1966). Besides, a good teacher will encourage different accomplishments and outcomes from different students.* The response to this criticism is simply that clear objectives can help good teachers become better teachers by improving their planning, encouraging active learning in students, and clarifying the evaluation procedure for everyone.

6. *Behavioral objectives are dehumanizing and encourage conformity.* Proponents of objectives would argue that clarifying and structuring what is to be done by teachers and students in fact humanizes the educational process. Also, using objectives treats the learner as a competent human being capable of guiding a good portion of his or her own learning.

Generally, and in spite of the rebuttals, this list of criticisms should be interpreted as a warning regarding some of the pitfalls of behavioral objectives. The preparation and use of behavioral objectives does not guarantee improved teaching. Objectives can be a tremendous instructional aid, but if misused they can be a limitation and a detriment to good teaching practices.

Are Objectives Effective? The Research   One frequent criticism is that behavioral objectives simply do not produce the claimed miracles: Teachers who use objectives do not produce better learning than teachers who do not. In fact, research on the value of using objectives has produced mixed and conflicting results. For example, Duchastel and Merrill (1973) reviewed 50 studies, with half showing a positive effect and the other half . . . well, showing no damage done due to using objectives.

In a recent article reviewing the effects of using behavioral objectives, Melton (1978) appears to have determined why some research shows positive effects (e.g., Dalis, 1970; McNeil, 1967; Rothkopf and Kaplan, 1972) and other studies do not (e.g., Cook, 1969; DeRose, 1970; Tiemann, 1968). After examining both successful and unsuccessful efforts to increase learning by using objectives, Melton identified several circumstances in which providing students with objectives may *not* aid learning.

1. Students may not be aware of the objectives; or if they are, they may ignore the objectives or not bother to read them. It is not enough simply to provide the students with the objectives; the students must attend to them, read them, and be sufficiently interested to be guided by them.
2. The objectives may be too general or too ambiguous to be of specific help in guiding learning. Dalis (1970) found that clear, precisely stated objectives improved learning much more than did vague objectives.
3. If the objectives are extremely difficult, most students will not master them—and so there will be no difference in performance between students who are provided with objectives and students who are not. Sensible enough. It works the other way too: If the learning objectives are too easy ("You will learn to spell *cat, dog* and *go* to a criterion of 100-percent accuracy"), then everyone will master the task and again the availability of precise objectives will make no difference.
4. If students are very conscientious and highly motivated, they will achieve the teacher's objectives with or without a specific list of them.

In view of the mixed results of the research, and the criticisms and cautions listed previously, the conclusion seems to be that (a) using specific behavioral objectives can indeed provide direction and promote efficiency for both teachers and students, but (b) under some circumstances, or if they are misused, behavioral objectives may have no effect—or may even have detrimental (mainly limiting) effects—on the education of children and adolescents.

TASK ANALYSIS

As with most other scholarly areas of interest, the topic of instructional objectives can quickly become as complex as your interest and patience will allow. One recent article, for example, presented mathematical analyses of Bloom's six levels of instructional objectives—to determine whether their structure fit a "simplex," "circumplex" or "radex" model (Seddon,

1978). Most practicing teachers probably don't care very much. This section, however, will deal with a development in instructional objectives which seems more immediately useful in the classroom: Task analysis. The next section will look at Benjamin Bloom's famous and influential *Taxonomy*

of Educational Objectives: Cognitive Domain (Bloom, 1974; Bloom, Englehart, Furst, Hill, and Krathwohl, 1956).

Task analysis is one systematic approach to formulating objectives and organizing instruction. According to Gagné (1977), the most important feature of task analysis is breaking down major objectives into component objectives. One thus begins with the ultimate instructional goals and, working backwards, successively divides these objectives into component, prerequisite subskill objectives. The teaching process begins with the practice and mastery of each component subskill, perhaps in isolation. When the component skills are learned, the teacher progresses to more complex levels of the task analysis by either combining the component skills into more complex skills or adding new component skills which are needed for the higher-level, more complex objective. An example of a task analysis will be presented shortly.

A broader task-analysis approach to formulating objectives and organizing instruction includes the use of four guiding questions:

1. How is mastery defined?
2. What "cues" regulate students' performances? What cues do experts use? Are there problems in discriminating the proper cues?
3. Is there a hierarchy of prerequisite subskills which must be mastered? Can the hierarchy be outlined?
4. Can the learning task be subdivided into subskills without distorting performance? What do experienced performers do?

These questions can be very helpful in organizing objectives and instruction in most subject areas, for example, language learning, typing, mathematics, physics, music, athletics, and others.

As an example, let's say that eighth-grade typing teacher Barbara Backspace wishes to do a task analysis of typing skills. She might *define mastery* (Question 1) as the ability to:

- Type simple material at a rate of 40 words per minute with no more than three mistakes per page.
- Neatly type business letters in three different forms.
- Neatly correct mistakes.

In thinking about *stimulus cues* (Question 2) that regulate performance (those that experts use plus those that are potentially confusing), Ms. Backspace notes that these cues consist of the verbal material to be typed, the "feel" of the keys, cues which indicate that the paper is in straight, and cues which show where the next letter will be typed. She also notes that experts depend heavily on the "feel" of the keys, and that experts use whole words, not individual letters, as cues to trigger the motor response of typing. Potentially confusing cues could arise from keys rarely used (x and z) or from keys difficult to reach (6 or 0). These may require special practice.

As for a *hierarchy* of prerequisite subskills (Question 3), Ms. Backspace realizes that there are a lot of subskills involved in fluent, neat typing. She decides to draw a tree diagram to help show which subskills are prerequisite to which (see Figure 11.1).

In subdividing each more complex objective into component subskills, it is best to look for subdivisions of subskills which will *not distort* the final performance (Question 4). For example, pressing the shift key would be integrated with typing capital letters, not practiced as a separate subskill. Also, typing numbers would be integrated with typing words, so that the typing of an address could be performed smoothly. There always are important interdependencies among subsets of subskills.

In sum, a thoughtful task analysis encourages the teacher to (a) define "mastery," (b) identify important cues and consider their discriminability, (c) identify necessary subskills and sub-subskills (this is the key step in any task analysis), and (d) segment the learning tasks into meaningful subdivisions. The awake reader should detect right away that task analysis can indeed be very useful in formulating learning objectives for both the main instructional goals and the prerequisite subgoals and in organizing the sequence and content of the instructional activities themselves.

Figure 11.1   Example of a tree diagram in task analysis.

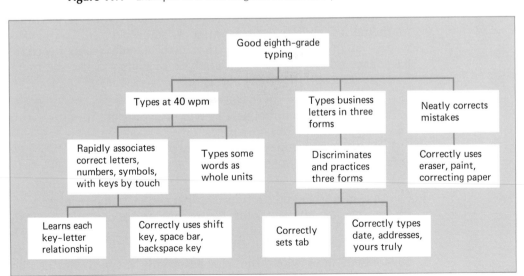

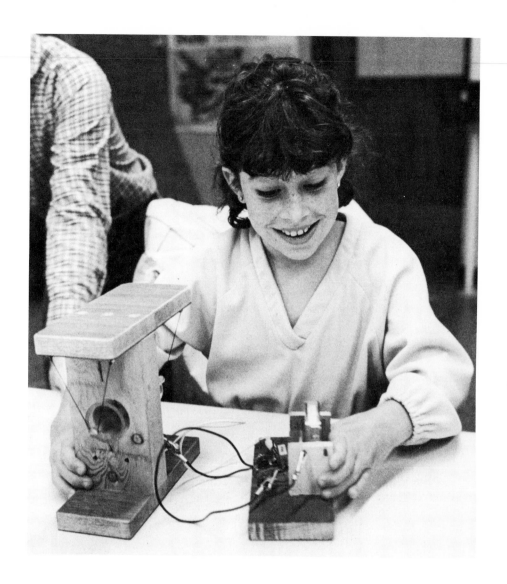

TAXONOMY OF EDUCATIONAL OBJECTIVES: COGNITIVE DOMAIN

No discussion of educational objectives would be complete without the **Taxonomy of Educational Objectives: Cognitive Domain** (Bloom, 1974; Bloom, Engelhart, Furst, Hill, and Krathwohl, 1956; see also Furst, 1981), popularly known as Bloom's Taxonomy. There also is a taxonomy for the affective domain (which will be described in Chapter 13) and another for the psychomotor domain (see Inset 11.1).

Bloom's taxonomy has had an international impact on education, primarily by drawing attention to **higher-level thinking skills** which should be taught and evaluated. The taxonomy thus serves as a guide for the preparation of instructional objectives; it helps dictate teaching strategies

INSET 11.1

TAXONOMY OF EDUCATIONAL OBJECTIVES: PSYCHOMOTOR DOMAIN

Educational psychologists have created three taxonomies of educational objectives, one in the cognitive domain (Bloom and his associates, (1956), one in the affective domain (see Chapter 13; Krathwohl, Bloom, and Masia, 1964), and one in the psychomotor domain (Kibler, Barker, and Miles, 1970). As with the taxonomies in the cognitive and affective areas, the purpose of the taxonomy of psychomotor objectives is to help the teacher prepare objectives, plan instruction, and evaluate learning.

The taxonomy includes four main types of motor behavior which are partly hierarchical, in the sense of one being a necessary (and developmental) prerequisite to the next. That is, *gross motor behavior* developmentally precedes, and is a prerequisite for, *fine motor behavior*. Also, psychomotor communicative acts proceed from *nonverbal communication* to *speech behaviors*. The three or four subcategories of psychomotor skills within each of the four main categories also generally are hierarchically ordered, from simpler prerequisite skills to more complex ones. The taxonomy:

Taxonomic classification	*Examples*
1.00 Gross Body Movement	
Objectives here emphasize strength or speed in gross movement, although some coordination with eyes or ears is required	
1.10 Movements Involving Upper Limbs	Throwing a baseball 50 feet; accurately serving a volleyball
1.20 Movements Involving Lower Limbs	Running a 50-yard dash in 10 seconds
1.30 Movements Involving Two or More Body Units	Swimming a backstroke one pool length; dribbling a basketball across the floor
2.00 Finely Coordinated Movements	
Objectives here require coordination of movement patterns or sequences with eyes and/or ears	

2.10 Hand-Finger Movement	Zipping a zipper blindfolded
2.20 Hand-Eye Coordination	Typing 40 words per minute
2.30 Hand-Ear Coordination	Tuning a uke to a piano
2.40 Hand-Foot Coordination	"Throwing" a pot on a potter's wheel; kicking a football 50 feet
2.50 Combinations of Coordinated Movements	Making three out of four basketball lay-up shots; driving a car smoothly

3.00 Nonverbal Communication Sets

Objectives here involve communicating messages without words

3.10 Facial Expressions	Can show surprise, joy, fear, and disgust
3.20 Gestures	Can convey simple message with hands; can act as referee using only hand signals
3.30 Bodily Movement	Can express message in dance; can pantomime a simple episode (stepping on a cat at 2:00 A.M.)

4.00 Speech Behavior

Objectives here involve speech production, for example, in language learning, public speaking or drama

4.10 Sound Production	Can produce vowel and consonant sounds
4.20 Sound-Word Formation	Can pronounce Spanish words correctly
4.30 Sound Projection	Can be understood at the back of the auditorium
4.40 Sound-Gesture Coordination	Can effectively use gestures in a speech, dramatic role, or song

The taxonomy of psychomotor objectives is not as useful nor as well known as the taxonomy of cognitive objectives. The taxonomy of affective objectives lies somewhere in the middle in popularity and usefulness.

Adapted from Kibler, R. J., L. L. Barker, and D. T. Miles, *Behavioral objectives and instruction*. Copyright © 1970 by Allyn and Bacon, Inc. Used with permission.

and student activities aimed at different levels of objectives; it also helps guide the evaluation of learning (see Chapter 19).

The six main levels of the taxonomy describe progressively higher levels of cognitive activity, from transmitting facts, figures, definitions, and rules at the *knowledge* and *comprehension* levels to expecting students to *apply, analyze, synthesize* or *evaluate* that information at higher levels. Table 11.1 lists the six main levels of the taxonomy, along with examples of student activities associated with each level.

Table 11.1 Taxonomy of educational objectives: cognitive domain.

Category	Examples
Knowledge	Defining terminology, symbols Recalling facts, names, examples, rules, categories Recognizing trends, causes, relationships Acquiring principles, procedures, implications, theories
Comprehension	Rephrasing definitions Illustrating meanings Interpreting relationships Drawing conclusions Demonstrating methods Inferring implications Predicting consequences
Application	Applying principles, rules, theories Organizing procedures, conclusions, effects Choosing situations, methods Restructuring processes, generalizations, phenomena
Analysis	Recognizing assumptions, patterns Deducing conclusions, hypotheses, points of view Analyzing relationships, themes, evidence, causes and effects Contrasting ideas, parts, arguments
Synthesis	Producing products, compositions Proposing objectives, means, solutions Designing plans, operationss Organizing taxonomies, concepts, schemes, theories Deriving relationships, abstractions, generalizations
Evaluation	Judging accuracy, consistency, reliability Assessing errors, fallacies, predictions, means and ends Considering efficiency, utility, standards Contrasting alternatives, courses of action

From Metfessel, N. S., W. B. Michael, and D. A. Kirsner. Instrumentation of Bloom's and Krathwohl's taxonomies for the writing of educational objectives. *Psychology in the Schools* **6**, 1969, 227–231. Reprinted by permission.

The level of cognitive complexity which you specify in your objectives will influence both your instructional activities and your evaluation of learning. Is your goal to have students memorize names and facts? This is often appropriate, as when learning multiplication tables or capital cities. Other times you will want students to apply principles or theories, analyze relationships, synthesize concepts or generalizations, or evaluate alternative ideas or courses of action.

As a general rule, a teacher moves from objectives and learning activities at the knowledge level to objectives and learning activities at progressively higher levels. Classroom questions (see Inset 11.2) which initiate discussion can be nicely tailored to the increasing cognitive complexity reflected in the taxonomy. As an example of the way in which questions can elicit increasingly complex learning and thinking, consider:

Knowledge: What is meant by *satellite*?
Comprehension: What is the relationship between a satellite and its planet?
Application: How would scientists place a satellite in orbit?

INSET 11.2

WHAT KINDS OF CLASSROOM QUESTIONS?

Sanders (1966) prepared a 176-page book entitled *Classroom Questions: What Kinds?* which describes how teachers can use questioning to strengthen skills at all levels of Bloom's taxonomy (cognitive domain). For example:

Knowledge   What do the Navajo Indians call their (traditional) houses? With what materials do the Navajos make their houses? What is the meaning of *wickiup? Wampum?* Why do desert dwellers know little of the outside world?

Knowledge questions require students to recognize or recall facts, definitions, generalizations, main points, points of view, and central issues. Some facts and definitions are ends in themselves, possessed by all literate members of a culture. Other facts serve as building blocks for higher levels of learning and thinking. The teacher should continually ask himself or herself, "What facts deserve emphasis? What facts are necessary for further learning?"

Comprehension   Define *revolution* in your own words. Is the climate of Rockport, Maine, the same as that of Frostproof, Florida? Compare English socialism with Russian communism.

Comprehension questions or activities usually require students to translate information into another form (pictures, charts, maps, models, outlines, summaries, or paraphrasing) or to interpret relationships (e.g., cause and effect, estimating degrees of similarity, comparing ideas or cultures).

Application   Why does Suzy have a high temperature? Which political principles apply to the government of Iran? Write and type a business letter. Prepare a profit-and-loss statement for Company X.

Analysis: What factors would cause a satellite to crash into its planet?
Synthesis: How would satellites such as the moons of Jupiter affect one another?
Evaluation: Is it a good idea to put so many satellites in orbit? Explain.

In recent years, Bloom's taxonomy has served as a guide for developing activities for programs in gifted education (see Chapter 17). The assumption is that these talented students have both the capability and the need to function at the higher taxonomic levels. Also, as we will see in Chapter 19, Bloom's taxonomy can help the teacher construct multiple-choice test items which can evaluate learning at any of the six levels.

Application questions often require students to use knowledge, principles, and skills to solve problems. They will be successful with application questions only if prepared for them.

Analysis   Is the reasoning in the quotation sound or unsound? Explain. Are these syllogisms true and valid? What does the author mean by "poverty and deprivation"?

Analysis activities are important, yet often ignored by teachers. Analysis activities can include examinations of statements and logical fallacies, inductive and deductive reasoning, and the analysis of semantic meanings of words.

Synthesis   Make up as many interesting titles for this story as you can. How many hypotheses can you suggest that would explain why tropical countries seldom developed a high level of civilization? How can our community attract new industries?

Synthesis questions can elicit imaginative and original thinking, the derivation of relationships, the formation of hypotheses, the planning of courses of action, or the designing of a research experiment.

Evaluation   Should church and state be separate? Are labor unions too powerful? Is the book well written? Has Greece or England developed the most valuable ideas?

Implicitly or explicitly, evaluation questions require students to establish standards or values and then match an object or idea against those standards. Evaluation questions may be used to have students assess the quality of something, to consider controversial or even hypothetical issues, or to evaluate courses of action.

TO IMPROVE
YOUR TEACHING

Be objective conscious. When planning a unit of instruction, prepare a list of worthwhile instructional objectives. For ideas, review any district-wide or system-wide statements of goals and objectives. Look also at lists of objectives which may appear in student textbooks and/or in teachers' manuals which accompany your texts. List general objectives, which may be in a general, nonbehavioral form, and then list specific behavioral objectives under each general objective. Ideally, objectives should include the conditions under which the performance will be demonstrated and the acceptable criterion level.

The use of expressive objectives will allow you to include educational experiences or "encounters" which seem potentially valuable, but which do not permit the formulation of explicit behavioral outcomes. For example, "We will discuss the value of the field trip," or "We will explore the implications of the movie on nuclear energy."

And don't keep your objectives a secret. Research has proven that students who have a list of the desired instructional outcomes more efficiently direct their efforts toward meeting those objectives. However, informing students of the learning objectives is not likely to improve studying and learning if students simply ignore the objectives—they must not only be aware of the objectives but also be sufficiently interested in the material to work toward them. Also, objectives will not improve student studying and learning if they are too general: Objectives must be clear, concrete, and specific, describing what the learner should be able to *do* at the end of instruction. Further, your carefully created objectives won't be a great asset if the goals are either too difficult or too easy in the first place. The objectives should be challenging, but attainable.

Be especially conscious of the potentially limiting effects of using behavioral objectives—which can restrict the teacher from beneficial departures from the planned objectives, and which can lead students to define their education as "meeting the teacher's specific list of objectives." Do not ignore humanistic, aesthetic, or personal development goals because they are difficult to state in a behavioral form. Some unthinking teachers have become slaves to lists of objectives; don't you become a victim.

As for using a task analysis, you may or may not wish to invest long hours in dissecting your subject matter into prerequisite skills and subskills. However, principles of task analysis do draw our attention to important teaching problems and considerations. For example, we should continually be aware of the importance of prerequisite subskills. As obvious examples, pupils who cannot add or read will be unable to multiply or learn from written text. We also should be conscious of cues which elicit correct responses (cues experts use) and cues which elicit errors, helping students to make the distinctions. Some examples might be correctly reading ambiguous words (tough vs. through), discriminating similar concepts (communism vs. socialism), correctly using a lathe in a machine shop, or correctly fingering C# on a saxophone.

One of the most important concepts in this chapter, and perhaps in the entire book, is Bloom's taxonomy of educational objectives. Be certain that you grasp the full impact of the taxonomy, the notion that your objectives and your teaching must include higher-level skills—application, analysis, synthesis, and evaluation—as well as the more common lower levels of knowledge and comprehension. The idea is simple but powerful in its impact on educational thinking and practice.

SUMMARY

Instructional objectives help the teacher plan both instruction and evaluation. Clear objectives help the student use his or her study time efficiently. A statement of objectives also informs parents what really is taught. Objectives also may form a basis for competency-based (performance-based) education and accountability.

If instructional objectives are stated in behavioral terms, describing precisely what the learner should be able to do after the instruction, they are called behavioral objectives.

Robert Mager recommends that each behavioral objective include (a) what the student will do after instruction (the terminal performance), (b) the conditions under which the student will demonstrate his or her competence, and (c) the acceptable level of performance.

Norman Gronlund suggests that classroom learning requires general instructional objectives (stated in nonbehavioral terms), each followed by specific behavioral objectives which give evidence of achieving the more general objective.

Expressive objectives may be used to plan unstructured "educational encounters," such as movie discussions or spontaneous debates about educationally relevant issues.

Critics of instructional objectives mainly claim that: (a) Objectives can deal only with trivial forms of learning that are easy to measure. (b) Some goals (aesthetic, process, affective, and humanistic) cannot be stated as behavioral objectives. (c) Behavioral objectives restrict students. (d) Strict adherence to planned objectives causes teachers to pass up good educational opportunities. (e) Behavioral objectives are unnecessary. (f) Behavioral objectives are dehumanizing and encourage conformity.

Research shows that providing students with lists of objectives promotes efficient study habits and better learning about half of the time. Stated objectives do not improve learning (a) when students ignore them, (b) when they are too general or ambiguous, (c) if the learning goals are too easy or too difficult, or (d) if students are highly motivated to achieve.

It was concluded that behavioral objectives can promote efficiency for teachers and students, but may have limiting effects if misused.

Task analysis is a strategy for preparing objectives and organizing instruction by working backward from the ultimate instructional goal, preparing a hierarchy of prerequisite skills and subskills. Task analysis also requires that the teacher define exactly what is meant by "mastery" and determine what "cues" will regulate performance.

Finally, Bloom's *Taxonomy of Educational Objectives: Cognitive Domain* was designed as an aid to preparing objectives and instruction. Six major levels of the taxonomy describe progressively "higher" forms of learning and cognitive activity: knowledge, comprehension, application, analysis, synthesis, and evaluation. Objectives and classroom activities, including teacher questions, may be designed for any of these levels.

TOPICS FOR THOUGHT AND DISCUSSION

1. What is your opinion of behavioral objectives? Look over the criticisms and the claims. Are there real dangers?
2. Is it possible to list clear objectives for courses in music appreciation, pottery, art history, and acting?
3. Think about a recent or current college course you are taking. Are the objectives clear? Do you know exactly what the instructor expects you to be able to do at the end of the course?
4. In relation to that college course in Question 3, is the instructor teaching at a knowledge-and-comprehension level? Or does he or she also expect some application, analysis, synthesis, and evaluation?
5. In schools you have visited (e.g., as a student teacher), do all teachers use objectives?

PROJECTS

1. Practice preparing a set of general and specific behavioral objectives for a unit you eventually will teach. You will need to include the *conditions* under which the performance will be demonstrated (e.g., "without looking at a map") and the criteria of acceptable performance (e.g., "to a level of 80 percent accuracy").
2. Try writing some "expressive" objectives to describe the desired outcomes of a field trip to an art gallery, attending a concert, seeing the movie "Gone With

the Wind," or discussing a recent political event (a revolution, an invasion, political corruption, etc.). Expressive objectives deal with what *could* be learned from exploring meanings, implications, or possible applications, elaborations, and modifications.

3. Practice writing objectives at all of Bloom's taxonomic levels for a topic or unit you expect to teach.

4. Whether you are male or female, try creating a task analysis for baking a cake. What component skills and subskills are prerequisite for baking a cake? Create a flow-chart (hierarchy of boxes and arrows) which includes a detailed analysis of exactly what the novice baker must be able to do before he or she can master a higher-level component skill.

RECOMMENDED READING

Burns, R. W. *New approaches to behavioral objectives.* Dubuque, Iowa: W.C. Brown, 1977.

Gagné, R. M. *The conditions of learning,* third edition. New York: Holt, 1977.

Gagné, R. M., and L. J. Briggs. *Principles of instructional design.* New York: Holt, Rinehart & Winston, 1974.

Mager, R. F. *Preparing instructional objectives.* Palo Alto, Calif.: Fearon, 1962.

————. *Goal analysis.* Belmont, Calif.: Fearon, 1972.

Popham, W. J., and E. L. Baker. *Systematic instruction.* Englewood Cliffs, N.J.: Prentice-Hall, 1970.

————. *Criterion-referenced instruction.* Belmont, Calif.: Fearon, 1973.

Sanders, N. M. *Classroom questions: What kinds?* New York: Harper & Row, 1966.

Theories and Models of Instruction

12

ABOUT THEORIES AND MODELS

"Model" and "Theory"   In psychology and educational psychology, the term **model** has two main meanings: First, *model* is used to mean "little theory," and is meant to explain a relatively limited aspect of behavior in some specific topic area. For example, we speak of "models of memory," "models of problem solving," the "conditioning model," the "generative grammar model," and "models of instruction." These "little theories" contrast with such broad, comprehensive sets of concepts and principles as Freud's psychoanalytic theory (Chapter 3) or Skinner's behavioristic learning theory (Chapter 5).* Second, *model* is used in the metaphorical sense, in which a psychological process is assumed to have an analogical correspondence with a simpler, more comprehendible phenomenon. Especially, information processing models use the computer as an analogy to human information input, storage, matching, decision-making, retrieval, alternate response modes, and so forth.

With either meaning of model, contemporary psychologists and educational psychologists quite comfortably use the terms **theory, model,** and **theoretical model** virtually interchangeably. Thus we may speak of "Kohlberg's moral development theory" or "Kohlberg's moral development model," "Ausubel's cognitive structure theory" or "Ausubel's cognitive structure model," and in this chapter, "instructional theories" or "instructional models."

Functions of Theories and Models   Any theory, model, or theoretical model performs several valuable functions. First, a theory or model helps *simplify* a complex phenomenon so that normal human beings can more easily understand and deal with the matter. Examples are countless. In this book, reinforcement theory (Chapters 5, 6, and 18), Kohlberg's theory of moral development (Chapter 3), Piaget's cognitive development model (Chapter 4), attribution theory and cognitive dissonance theory (Chapter 9), and others (see Inset 12.1) are theories or models which help clarify complex and confusing phenomena. Second, due to the simplification function, a theory or model also allows us to *explain* and therefore to *predict* what will happen under certain circumstances. For example, reinforcement theory tells us that behavior which persists probably is sustained by some form of reward or avoidance of punishment. Piaget's theory explains why children cannot deal with highly abstract or theoretical concepts.

Third, a theory or model provides a *language* and a *point of view* for thinking about or describing a phenomenon. In Chapter 8, for example,

---

* Skinner preferred the word *system* to *theory*. He felt that psychology should concern itself with "low order" relationships among stimuli, responses, and consequences, not with more abstract "theoretical" relationships. See Skinner (1959).

Ausubel's concepts of *meaningful learning, cognitive structure, anchoring,* and *subsumption* gives us both a language and a point of view for conceptualizing effective classroom learning. Humanistic and affective educational models in Chapter 13 present an entirely different viewpoint on the goals of teaching and learning. Fourth, a theory also provides *guidance* for dealing with problems. Learning theory, for example, makes fairly clear recommendations for increasing motivation (use rewards) or for coping with discipline problems (remove supporting rewards). Ausubel's theory, Kohlberg's theory of moral development, and Bloom's taxonomy all provide guidance for selecting the content and sequence of instruction.

Teaching is fantastically complex. It is influenced by large differences in (a) teacher personalities, (b) preferred teaching styles, (c) subject matter requirements, (d) student age and ability, (e) student motivation and personality, (f) available media and facilities, (g) district and state goals, guidelines, and requirements, and so on. It is our view that the literate professional teacher should be armed with a large inventory of theoretically

INSET 12.1

OTHER MODELS AND THEORIES OF INSTRUCTION

We should note that other models and theories which serve as instructional guides appear in almost every chapter of this text. Most notably, Kohlberg's moral developmental model (Chapter 3), Piaget's cognitive development model (Chapter 4), learning theory and behavior modification (Chapters 5, 6, and 18), memory, transfer, and information-processing models (Chapter 7), the discovery learning model and Ausubel's cognitive structure theory (Chapter 8), motivation theories and models (Chapter 9), classroom management principles (Chapter 10), behavioral objectives and Bloom's taxonomic model (Chapter 11), affective and humanistic models (Chapter 13), creative development models (Chapter 16), programming models for gifted and talented education (Chapter 17), and instructional models for learning disabled and handicapped students (Chapter 18).

The uniqueness of the models in this chapter is that they, along with Ausubel's theory and discovery learning, are known primarily as "instructional theories." The others listed above are recognized first as developmental theories, learning theories, motivation theories, and so on. Just as with the theories and models in this chapter, however, they serve to simplify complex phenomena, allow explanations and predictions, provide a language and a point of view, and provide guidance in planning instruction.

sound teaching strategies. From this bag he or she can make an informed choice of methods or materials suited to a given subject, to particular students, or for a desired outcome.

Consider the following questions: How are instructional objectives selected? How exactly are objectives related to instruction and to evaluation? Is the goal the transmission of verbal facts and concepts? Is it teaching motor skills or attitudes? What internal events take place during attention and learning? Can instruction be built around these internal information processing activities? Will the teacher be satisfied with a "normal distribution" of achievement, or does the teacher want every student to achieve mastery? The theories and models in this chapter suggest answers to these and other practical, everyday classroom problems.

This chapter will focus on four models of instruction: (1) the Popham and Baker (1970, 1973) goal-referenced instructional model; (2) Gagné's (1974, 1977) outcomes, events, and conditions of learning; (3) the mastery model of instruction (Bloom, 1971, 1973; Carroll, 1971); and finally (4) a very recent development, Rosenshine's (1979) direct instruction approach. These models are not particularly related to each other, although the first three do depend heavily on the use of objectives. Each position has its own point of view and its own recommendations for improving teaching and learning.

THE POPHAM AND BAKER GOAL-REFERENCED INSTRUCTIONAL MODEL

James Popham and Eva Baker (1970) proposed a fairly straightforward **goal-referenced instructional model.** "Goal referenced" is an insider's catch word which means that instructional objectives (Chapter 11) play a central part in the teaching process.

According to Popham and Baker, "Effective instruction . . . [is] . . . an ability to bring about desirable modifications in the abilities and perceptions of the learner" (1970, p. 10). From this viewpoint, beginning teachers should not ask "What shall *I* do?" The important question is "What do I want my *students* to become?" The emphasis clearly is on what students should be able to do after instruction—that is, on behavioral objectives.

As we saw in Chapter 11, with clear objectives the teacher has a definite picture of the competencies and skills which students should acquire. Such information is of direct help in the selection of instructional strategies and activities. Namely, the teacher can plan opportunities for the learners to practice those skills and competencies specified in the objectives. The teacher need not select activities just to fill time.

Another advantage of a goal-referenced instructional model is that it can provide clear guides for evaluating and improving one's instructional methods. Quite simply, if objectives were not met, a change in strategy is in order. If students do demonstrate the behaviors and skills in the objectives, the instructional strategy need not be totally overhauled. The teacher may, however, extend, improve or elaborate the present set of objectives.

Popham and Baker's goal-referenced model includes four steps or operations (Figure 12.1): (1) specifying objectives in behavioral form; (2) pre-assessing students' current status with respect to those objectives; (3) designing and conducting instructional activities; (4) evaluating students' achievement of the objectives.

Specifying Objectives

To save repetition, paper, and ink, let's assume that by now you basically know what a behaviorally stated **instructional objective** is. This section will elaborate on objectives and outline some of Popham and Baker's guides for selecting objectives.

Behavior and products. First of all, there are only two ways to behaviorally operationalize instructional goals: We can describe the learner's **behavior** or his or her **products.** With learner behavior, the teacher must record or evaluate the activity *while it happens.* For example, the instructor might evaluate a speech, a panel report, running speed or endurance, individual contributions to a discussion, or perhaps even student "self confidence." With learner products—such as tests, term papers, reports, a science project, or a chocolate cake—the teacher has more time for the evaluation. Most objectives and evaluations deal with products: tests, papers, or projects.

The learner's interests. Popham and Baker suggest a three-part framework for selecting objectives, the learner, society, and the subject matter. As for the learner, it could be helpful to know (a) student ability, (b) achievement in the subject thus far, (c) student needs, and (d) student interests. ". . . it is obvious to anyone who ever learned anything that learning becomes more exciting when one is vitally concerned with the goals that have been selected" (Popham and Baker, 1970, p. 52). Students in a science class might be interested in space travel; history or social-studies students might have an honest interest in slavery and the Civil War; band students might like to play Led Zeppelin rock.

Society's objectives. "Society" also has a few objectives in mind, for example, good citizenship, knowledge of our culture, and mastery of basic skills. Also, since society seems to change, the ability or readiness to cope with change could lead to important specific objectives. Society also expects students to be able to write a business letter and to think critically about advertisements, political promises, and used car promotions. And students also ought to (society has lots of "ought to's") be aware that cigarette smoking, drugs, booze, motorcycles, and social diseases are hazardous to their health.

The subject matter. The subject matter itself, of course, is a direct source of instructional objectives. Popham and Baker especially recommend the identification of major, key concepts in a field. Such core material provides a stable framework to which students may anchor more detailed facts and concepts. The thoughtful planner also will continually check to see if material is either trivial or out-of-date.

Pre-assessment

The main purpose of the **pre-assessment** operation, the second phase of the Popham and Baker model, is to determine whether students already possess the competencies listed in your objectives. A pretest can use items similar or identical to items in the post-test. If most students already possess the objectives to be taught, then everybody's time would be wasted. However, if students do badly on a pretest but very well on a post-test, the teacher can rightfully take credit for modifying the students' skills and behaviors.

A slightly different form of pretest also can indicate whether students have the necessary prerequisite skills for the forthcoming instruction. In this pre-assessment, the teacher does not ask if students already know the material, but whether they have retained the necessary prerequisite skills and information from earlier coursework.

Instruction

The third step of Popham and Baker's model is **instruction,** an immensely complex topic but one simplified by the use of objectives. An underlying theme is the **principle of appropriate practice,** which requires that the teacher provide opportunities to practice the skills, knowledge, or behavior specified in those objectives. In Popham and Baker's (1970) words, ". . . the more appropriate practice activities a teacher can build into an instructional sequence, the more likely the learner will be to achieve the objectives" (p. 83). This is goal-referenced instruction.

In Chapter 11 we noted that students should be aware of the teacher's objectives so that study time and effort can be efficiently focused on the right goals. In addition to focusing study efforts, a discussion of the class objectives also has motivational effects. The discussion of objectives will include an explanation of *why* the particular objectives are worth achieving. Intuitively, an understanding of why a learning objective is important should elicit a stronger commitment to reaching that object; the learning would have a purpose.

Many different specific instructional strategies are available—lectures, discussions, demonstrations, individualized learning, movies, field trips, projects, one-to-one tutoring, and so on. Selection from among these should be based on considerations of student interest and motivation and appropriateness to the objectives, along with such matters as available time, expense, acceptability to parents and the school board, and so on.

Evaluation

The fourth step, **evaluation,** is aimed at determining the degree to which the objectives were achieved. We noted above that objectives may involve either a *behavior* or a *product*. In evaluating behaviors such as an oral presentation, participation in group discussions, or dribbling a basketball, an appropriate recording system must be devised. If a test—one form of

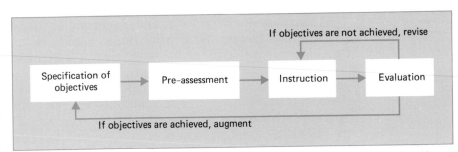

Figure 12.1
The Popham and Baker goal-referenced instructional model.

From Popham, J. W., and E. L. Baker, *Systematic Instruction*. Copyright © 1970, p. 17. Reprinted by permission of Prentice-Hall, Inc., Englewood Cliffs, N.J.

product—is used, the test questions should focus specifically on the behaviors described by the objectives. This is **criterion-referenced testing—** the teacher has a very clear idea of what skills or knowledge (the criteria) are to be evaluated. Importantly, each student's score is interpreted relative to that absolute. Also, the teacher hopes that everyone will earn a high score, demonstrating mastery of the instructional objectives.

The teacher who accepts the Popham and Baker goal-referenced instructional model would *not* be interested in **norm-referenced testing,** which aims at producing a wide "bell-shaped curve" distribution of scores (Chapter 19). With norm-referenced testing, a student's score is interpreted relative to other students' scores (e.g., Leo DaVinci scored 10 points below the group mean and gets a "D"; Al Einstein scored 2 standard deviations above the mean and gets an "A").

As shown in Figure 12.1, when your criterion-referenced test shows that objectives are not met, revision of the instructional practices is in order.

LEARNING OUTCOMES, EVENTS IN LEARNING, AND CONDITIONS OF LEARNING: ROBERT GAGNÉ

Educational psychologist Robert Gagné, who speaks absolutely no French, has produced a fairly involved model of school learning. As with other theories and models of learning, this one can simplify and clarify some important features of learning and teaching, and can provide some good guidelines for improving learning. Unfortunately, Gagné's (1977) most recent book requires 339 pages, with small margins and very few illustrations, to adequately present the fine points of the model. With apologies to Gagné, and as a warning to the reader, the following necessarily will be "streamlined."

As an advance organizer, the model includes three main components. First are Gagné's (1972) five types of **learning outcomes.** These are sometimes called learned *capabilities*, because once the outcomes are achieved the student logically possesses new capabilities. The outcomes also may be thought of as goals or *objectives.* Anything any student could ever learn in a classroom is classifiable as one, or a combination, of these five learning outcomes: (1) verbal information; (2) intellectual skills (e.g., classifying, rule-following); (3) cognitive stretegies (e.g., for regulating one's own attention or remembering); (4) attitudes; and (5) motor skills.

The second component, **events of learning,** is an information-processing model which describes the instant-by-instant phases in a single, simple learning event, from sensory input through short-term and long-term memory to the overt response. We talked about information processing in Chapter 7.

The third component of the model is **conditions of learning,** which divides neatly into **internal** conditions and **external** conditions. Internal conditions for learning are the prerequisite skills and information—Ausubel's cognitive structures—to which new information is anchored. External conditions for learning consist of—instruction. We will look at Gagné's five outcomes of learning, the information-processing events in learning, and then tie it all together with a discussion of instructional "conditions" which relate "outcomes" to "events."

Outcomes of learning

Verbal information, Gagné's first outcome of learning, corresponds to the knowledge level of Bloom's taxonomy of cognitive objectives (Chapter 11). It includes facts, concepts, names, principles, generalizations, and ". . . knowledge about the world and its people, about historical events and trends, about the culture of a civilization as represented in its literature and art, and about current and practical affairs of life" (Gagné, 1974, p. 52). Viewing verbal information as a *learned capability* implies that the learner is able to *state*—verbalize, write, type, diagram, or otherwise represent—what he or she has learned. The information may not be totally remembered as "words," since we all have internal mental images, attitudes, spatial relationships, etc., but the learner must be able to verbally state the information. Verbal information is a prerequisite for further learning in the sense that, for example, a student cannot compare and evaluate systems of government unless he or she has information pertaining to democracies, houses of parliament, monarchies, dictatorships, and so on.

Intellectual skills, Gagné's second learning outcome, refers to the capabilities of (a) *discriminating* among similar objects or ideas, (b) classifying objects or ideas into *concept* categories, (c) following a *rule* (as in chemistry or math), and (d) *solving problems.* These intellectual skills are considered hierarchically ordered in the sense that each skill, (a) through (d), is a prerequisite for the next higher skill. That is, one must be able to make simple discriminations before one can classify concepts; one must have the necessary concepts with which to form rules; and one must have a repertoire of rules in order to solve problems.

As a simple example, a child must be able to discriminate dogs from cats, ducks, and beavers before he or she can master the concept category of *dog.* The concept of *dog* might combine with the concept of *bite* to form the rule *dogs bite.* This rule would combine with other rules (e.g., *ropes prevent travel*) in order to solve the problem "How do we prevent Snoopy from attacking the mailman?"

In earlier years (Gagné, 1964, 1968), these intellectual skills were well known as Gagné's hierarchy of different types of learning, from simple to complex.

Cognitive strategies, the third type of learning outcome, are internal capabilities which the learner uses to guide or manage his or her attending, learning, remembering, and problem solving. The learner learns *how* to attend, learn, recall, or solve a type of problem. Other learning theorists use the terms "self-management behaviors" (Skinner, 1968), "executive control processes" (Greeno and Bjork, 1973), or strangely enough, "cognitive strategies" (Bruner, 1971) to describe these self-guiding behaviors.

The important point about cognitive strategies is that becoming an effective independent learner depends strongly on acquiring these cognitive strategies for managing one's own process of learning.

Attitudes, learning outcome number four, are notably easier to explain. As we will see in Chapter 13, all aspects of school include likes, dislikes, needs, fears, preferences, values, self-concepts, and so forth. Such attitudes are clearly an important (affective) outcome of classroom learning.

Motor skills make up the final, straightforward outcome of learning or learned capability. Many, but not all, classrooms deal with such motor skills as printing and writing, using rulers or laboratory equipment, typing, shooting a basketball, driving a car, or welding a boat trailer.

Events of Learning: The Information-Processing Model

The second component of Gagné's theory, **events of learning,** is an information processing model with lots of boxes and arrows. This model (Figure 12.2) describes the phases or processes involved in a "single act of learning." Since we already have grappled with this sort of model in Chapter 7, perhaps a brief explanation will wrap up this aspect of Gagné's thinking.

We begin at the left side of Figure 12.2: Stimulation from the *Environment* activates our sensory *Receptors.* Patterns of visual, auditory, tactile information are then stored in the *Sensory register* "memory" (see Chapter 7) for just one or two seconds, at most. A process of selective perception and attention quickly moves important aspects of the information into a *Short-term memory*, which has a retention duration of about 20 or 30 seconds. Once the information has entered the Short-term memory, two things can happen. (1) For an immediate response, the information in the STM is input directly into a *Response generator*. This hypothetical device selects the mode of response (verbal, motor) and its pattern, producing an organized performance by the *effectors*. "Effectors," the traditional opposite of Receptors, are simply hands, feet, speech apparatus, or any other muscle system that has an effect on the Environment—which puts us back at the left side of Figure 12.2 where we began. (2) Information in STM also can go into Long-term memory, from where it later may be dredged up to activate the Response generator and Effectors, which react to the Environment.

Consider an example of how the system works: You just telephoned your local hardware store to find out what time they close that evening. The clerk (Environment) emits a string of vocal sounds which your Receptors hear as "Well, Monday and Friday we're open until 9:00. Today is Wednesday so we close at 6:00." These exact words rattle around in your head (Sensory register) for a second or two. You attend to, and perhaps transform, the important part of the message, "6:00 o'clock," which is stored in Short-term memory and transferred to Long-term memory. Your Response generator leads you to grab (with Effectors) your coat, checkbook and car keys and zip off to buy some wallpaper paste. Next week, at 7:00 P.M. on

Figure 12.2
Gagné's information-processing model. See text for explanation.

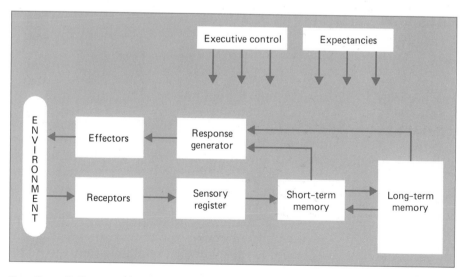

Wednesday, your roommate says, "Let's go to the hardware store for some coat hooks." You recall the meaning, the essence of the earlier information from LTM, and your Response generator leads your vocal Effectors to say, "Forget it. They close at 6:00. Let's go out for pizza instead." To which your roomie's Effectors respond, "Great, I'll hang my sweater on a pepperoni!"

Executive control processes and *Expectancies* are previously learned "processes" and thus are part of the LTM. They affect all of the other boxes and arrows. For example, selective perception is controlled by these processes; also, the selection of information to be stored in LTM and the mode and pattern of the Effectors are determined by Executive control processes and Expectancies.

The Parts Assembled: Outcomes, Events, and Conditions

The three components of the model—the five outcomes of learning, the information-processing events in learning, and the internal/external conditions for learning—are tied together about as follows. The planning of instruction requires attention to the *expected* outcomes or goals of learning. Gagné's five outcomes, you recall, are a type of instructional objectives. Planning instruction also requires attention to the prerequisite simpler skills and knowledge—the *internal conditions of learning*. Gagné's *external conditions of learning*, alias *instruction*, consist of a sequence of instructional steps aimed at accommodating the different phases of information processing.

Figure 12.3 lists eight instructional events, each of which ". . . is designed to influence one or more of the internal processes of learning" (Gagné, 1974, p. 118).

Instructional Events, or External Conditions of Learning

Let's briefly take it from the top.

1. *Activating motivation.* This initial instructional event is directed at arousing interest, perhaps by stimulating curiosity, appealing to student interests, creating a challenge, or by eliciting achievement needs or other motives (see Chapter 9). Are you interested in this theory which could help you better understand learning and instruction and become a better teacher?

2. *Informing the learner of the objectives.* Informing students of the instructional objectives establishes an expectancy of what is to come. This also is partly motivational in nature. Just think, when you finish this section of your text, you will be able to explain how Gagné's outcomes, events, and conditions all fit together in one big integrated theory of learning and instruction.

3. *Directing attention.* Selective attention and perception requires that the learner's attention be appropriately directed. Something like, "Look at this map of Alaska," or "Listen to how we say '*Chez moi*'," is all that is meant here. As you read this section, be sure to look at Figures 12.2 and 12.3 for reference.
4. *Stimulating recall.* In order to anchor the new ideas to previous learning, the previous learning must be made available. "Remember how . . . ," or "Remember what . . . ," are simple but good examples of stimulating recall. Remember what Ausubel said about advance organizers, cognitive structure, and anchoring (Chapter 8)?
5. *Providing learning guidance.* Providing learning guidance is intended to help transform, for example, verbal information into a form in which

Figure 12.3
Relations between steps in simple learning and instructional events.

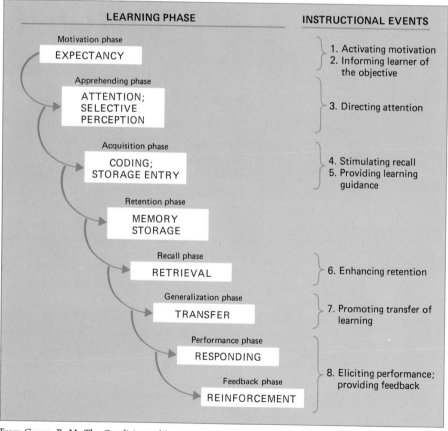

From Gagne, R. M. *The Conditions of Learning.* Copyright © by Holt, Rinehart and Winston, Inc. Reprinted by permission of Holt, Rinehart and Winston, CBS College Publishing.

it can be stored in long-term memory. For the learning of verbal
information, providing a meaningful context or using prompts are two
of Gagné's examples of guiding learning for encoding and storage. For
the learning of a new intellectual skill, such as a new geometry rule,
learning guidance will include stimulating recall of necessary prerequisite rules and guiding their arrangement into the new sequence.
Guiding the acquisition of a motor skill will involve such things as
modeling the proper stance or racquet swing.

Pictures, diagrams, etc., are great devices for guiding learning to
facilitate "coding and storage entry." Chances are, you wouldn't want
to teach students what a camel or a locomotive is without using
pictures.

In Gagné's model, Figures 12.2 and 12.3 should help you encode
information for storage. Also, don't forget that there are just three main
parts of the theory (*outcomes*, information processing *events*, and
internal/external conditions), which should be easily encodable for
long-term storage.

6–7. *Enhancing retention* and *Promoting transfer of learning.* In Chapter 7
we discussed some principles for promoting retention and transfer. As
two examples, Gagné recommends spacing reviews and using a variety
of examples to aid both retention and transfer to new learning tasks.

Also, information well anchored to previous learning (cognitive structure) is better retained and more available for transfer to a new situation.

Gagné's theory should be "anchorable" to information processing ideas—including sensory registers and short-term and long-term memories (Chapter 7)—and Ausubel's cognitive-structure subsumption theory of learning (Chapter 8).

8. *Eliciting the performance; providing feedback.* After students have learned verbal information or an intellectual or motor skill, the natural next step is a demonstration of the learning outcome. The performance would be followed by reinforcing feedback as to the correct or appropriateness of the verbal information, intellectual skill, motor skill, or other outcome of learning.

Well, what do you think about Gagné's theory of instruction, which required 20 years for its evolution into the present form?

ACADEMIC ENGAGED TIME AND DIRECT INSTRUCTION: BARAK ROSENSHINE

This section deals with the no-nonsense discovery that academic achievement is higher when students spend more time working on academic tasks. This seemingly self-evident truth has been the focus of a flurry of classroom research in very recent years, and has generated considerable interest and excitement in educational research circles. What's so startling about the discovery that students who work more also learn more? Not much, except that it has taken educational researchers about a half century of sifting through teacher characteristics and behaviors in order to arrive at this profound-but-not-so-profound conclusion (see, e.g., Peterson and Walberg, 1979).

And furthermore, this apparently strong relationship between time-on-task and achievement currently is leading some educators to take long, hard second looks at a few other "self-evident truths" concerning such liberal principles as:

- Student choices in seating, work groups, and learning activities are good for motivation and learning.
- Teacher-centeredness and teacher-directedness are not as desirable as student-centered learning (Chapter 13).
- Quiet, orderliness, and drill create a bad learning environment.
- Inquiry and discovery procedures promote high achievement.
- Educational games motivate interest and learning (Chapter 9).
- Teachers should promote higher-level thinking (analysis, synthesis, evaluation; Chapter 11).

With the present emphasis on "teacher-led controlled practice," the reader might wonder about such humanistic and affective matters as motivation, attitudes toward school, self-esteem, and creativity. We will return to these after a lengthier look at Rosenshine's (1979) "academic engaged time" and "direct instruction."

Background

For several decades educational researchers have asked—and researched—some pretty simple questions: What teacher characteristics and behaviors produce high achievement? What learner characteristics and behaviors relate to high achievement? Naturally, the answers were not simple. Explorations of the effects of teacher attitudes, personality, and even preservice training were a disappointment. Perhaps "flop" would be closer to the truth. In a 1963 review, educational psychologist Nathan Gage concluded that "These studies have yielded disappointing results: correlations that are nonsignificant, inconsistent from one study to the next, and usually lacking in psychological meaning" (Gage, 1963, p. 118). A few pages later in the same *Handbook of Research on Teaching*, Getzels and Jackson announced, "Despite . . . a half century of prodigious research effort, very little is known for certain about the relation between teacher personality and teaching effectiveness" (Getzels and Jackson, 1963, p. 574).

After another decade had passed, University of Illinois researchers Barak Rosenshine and N. E. Furst (1971, 1973) were beginning to zero in on the true determiners of student achievement. They surveyed about 15 years of fairly intense research on teacher and student behavior and produced a list of ". . . 10 variables which had the best research history or which seemed the most promising for future research" (Rosenshine, 1979).

1. Clarity of the teacher's presentation.
2. Enthusiasm of the teacher.
3. Variety of activities during the lesson. This factor was *negatively* related to achievement, that is, a greater variety of learning activities was related to lower achievement. It seems that a simultaneous potpourri of student-selected activities (remember student choices?) can produce disorder, inattention, and lower achievement.
4. Task-oriented and businesslike behaviors in the classroom.
5. Amount of content which is covered by the class. The "amount of content covered" is closely tied to the amount of time in which the student is actively engaged in learning the content.

Of the ten items in this list, 4 and 5 were easy winners as predictors of student achievement in academic areas, usually reading and math.

The reader should appreciate the simple, elegant truth which was beginning to surface in the 1970s: The more time the students spend on academic engagement, and therefore the more content which is covered, the higher the academic achievement will be. In clear agreement, leading educational researcher F. J. McDonald (1976) reported, "If students have not been taught . . . some . . . content or procedure, they simply do not do well on those portions of the test relevant to that topic."

The remaining five variables in the 1971 list, as with the first three, have not proven as profoundly related to achievement as items 4 and 5.

6. Teacher acknowledgement and encouragement of student ideas during a discussion. This teacher variable naturally is most important when there are discussions, that is, with older and more mature students.
7. Criticism of the student. This teacher behavior properly relates negatively to student achievement, that is, the more of item 7, the lower the achievement scores.
8. The use of structuring comments at the start of and during a lesson. (The reader should be reminded of Ausubel's advance organizer concept, Chapter 8.)
9. The use of a variety of types of questions. (The reader should be reminded of the different levels of instructional objectives in the cognitive domain as discussed in Chapter 11. Different questions require different levels of thinking.)
10. Probing of student responses by the teacher.

Rosenshine (1979) dismissed items 8 through 10 with, "Such variables have not yielded particularly notable (research) results and have not been studied systematically." This conclusion certainly could be debated. In any event, Rosenshine's most significant points are made in items 4 and 5, to which we now return.

Academic Engaged Time

By now the reader should have some feel for the meaning of Rosenshine's new phrase, **academic engaged time**. Academic engaged time is closely related to the concept of *attention*, since *engagement* implies directing one's full attention to the task at hand. As we noted above, academic engaged time also is closely tied to the amount of *content covered*, since one tends to cover more content when one spends more time attentively engaged with that content. *Time-on-task* also may be used interchangeably with academic engaged time, since it is quicker to pronounce when spoken and saves nine letters when written.

Now that we know that *attention* and *amount of content covered* functionally mean about the same thing as *academic engaged time*, we can look at a summary quote by Rosenshine: "These two variables of (amount of) content covered and student attention have yielded the highest and most consistent correlations with achievement gain of any of the classroom

variables studied to date. The message is: What is not taught and attended to in academic areas is not learned" (Rosenshine, 1979).

In presenting the details of research and reviews of research, Rosenshine reported moderately strong statistical correlations between attention and achievement in 16 separate research studies. This relationship is stronger than the relationship of student achievement to *any other* student or teacher behavior studied.

Allocated Time

It's important to note, noted Rosenshine, that time merely *allocated* for content coverage is not the same as actual academic *engaged* time. The distinction seems obvious and even trivial, except that teachers always work with time allocated while academic engaged time is actually the critical determiner of learning. One teacher might allocate 30 minutes for reading and by insisting on high engagement actually get 25 minutes of time on task. Another teacher with a looser ship might allocate 45 minutes, but only get 20 minutes of engaged reading. The distinction between time allocated and time engaged is worth remembering.

Of course, a teacher need not—indeed, cannot—maintain highly motivated, attentive on-task working at all times. Looking at activities for the entire day, second-grade researchers Filby and Marliave (1977) found that an average of 122 minutes (two hours) were allocated to all academic activities (reading, math, science, social studies). Of this, academic engagement consumed an average of about 89 minutes, or 73 percent. The rest of the day is invested in such nonacademic matters as collecting money, distributing materials, lining up, quieting down, taking breaks, taking seats, story time, art time, music time, milk time, waiting time, free time, and time for feeding Nellie Goldfish and Bert Guinea Pig. The total day was divided about 43 percent for academic matters, 57 percent for those nonacademic essentials.

The picture for the fifth grade was about the same, with about 48 percent of the day allocated to academic matters, 52 percent to distributing and collecting materials, music, basketball, hamsters, and so on. Of an average of 154 minutes allocated for academic subjects, about 115 were spent in active on-task engagement, or 75 percent.

Direct Instruction

The term **direct instruction** has been coined to refer to those activities which promote academic engaged time, and therefore relate to "making progress in reading and mathematics" (Rosenshine, 1979). According to Professor Rosenshine, in direct instruction:

- The teacher controls instructional goals.
- The teacher selects material appropriate for the student's ability level.

- The teacher paces the instructional activity.
- Direct instruction deals with academic matters.
- Goals are clear to the students.
- Allocated time is sufficient.
- Content coverage is extensive.
- Student performance is monitored.
- Interaction is structured, but not authoritarian.
- The atmosphere is academic, but also convivial.

Within this enlightened framework of academic engaged time and the direct instruction which promotes it, Rosenshine (1979) itemized another list of four classroom variables related to classroom organization and management. His enthusiasm is reflected by the promise, "The choice of instructional variables . . . is illuminating and shows how far we have progressed in the last few years."

1. *Academic focus.* First, we must define a "successful teacher" as one who produces high-achieving students. With this definition, research strongly suggests that successful teachers tend to be task-oriented—determined that their students *will* learn. For example, in a study of 150 first-grade and third-grade Project Follow Through classrooms, Stallings and Kaskowitz (1974) concluded that, sure enough, when more time was spent on math and reading activities, academic achievement was higher. Achievement was negatively related to the amount of classroom time spent on stories, arts and crafts, play, puzzles, toys, child-selected work groups, and even academic games.

In this study and others, ". . . no nonacademic activity yielded positive correlations with reading and mathematics achievement" (Rosenshine, 1979).

2. *Teacher-centered instruction.* Teachers who produce high achievement tended to be stronger leaders. They are the center of attention, they are businesslike, and they direct activities. They do not give students choices, they do not make students the center of attention, nor do they organize learning around student problems.

3. *Grouping students for learning.* Now it might seem that working with just one or two students should promote achievement. The problem is that the other 25 troops must at the same time be unsupervised.

The research seems to show that when students work in groups without adult supervision, achievement tends to be lower (Soar, 1973). The reason: Academic engaged time seems to run from about 68 to 73 percent of the total group time. This contrasts sharply with the higher achievement of closely monitored groups, whose engaged time is about 95 percent of the total group time (Filby and Marliave, 1977; Fisher, Filby, and Marliave, 1977).

Reasons Rosenshine (1979), the large group permits closer supervision of all students. The students therefore spend more time on academic tasks, and so academic achievement tends to be higher.

4. *Factual questions and controlled practice,* and *higher-order questions.* An interesting and slightly amusing picture emerges from research on "question levels." Bloom's taxonomy (Chapter 11) implicitly suggests that teachers should emphasize higher-level thinking skills, such as analysis, synthesis and evaluation, not just lower-level factual knowledge. Achievement tests, however, typically evaluate the mastery of factual knowledge or related skills.

So what happens to achievement when the teacher asks single-answer factual questions (which serve as **controlled practice,** which translates as academic engaged time) compared to when she or he asks higher-level questions, many of which request opinions or interpretations? The strategy of asking lower-level factual questions, and providing low-level factual feedback, can lead to higher achievement in basic arithmetic and reading skills (Stallings and Kaskowitz, 1974). Conversely, asking high-level open-ended questions may either depress achievement scores (Soar, 1973) or may be unrelated to achievement scores (Gall, Ward, Berliner, Cahen, Crown, Elashoff, Stanton and Winne, 1975; Winne, 1979). Again, high-level questions often do not relate closely to the academic content—especially the content of the achievement test.

Affective Focus

We promised to return to (a) the effects of more direct instruction and (b) less openness and student choice on affective and humanistic matters—self-esteem, motivation, creativity, and attitudes toward school.

First of all, with a strong task orientation there actually seems to be a *gain* in many of these traits, not a loss. High-achieving classrooms, which also are high in task orientation and academic engaged time, tend to be warm and pleasant, and the teacher tends to know and care about each student (Filby and Cahen, 1977; Rosenshine, 1979; Tikunoff, Berliner, and Rist, 1975). Furthermore, it should not be surprising to find that high achievement also is related to high self-esteem (Abt Associates, 1977; Covington and Beery, 1976; see Chapter 13).

Solomon and Kendall (1976) studied 30 suburban fourth-grade classes, many of which were characterized by considerable permissiveness and openness—students planned classroom activities following their own interests. These classrooms also were characterized by shouting, rowdiness, disorderliness, low academic achievement, lower creativity, lower self-esteem, and poor inquiry and writing skills. Effective teachers typically are high on *both* academic and affective orientation. The notion that strong academic orientation implies a forbidding atmosphere simply is not true.

Second, despite his clear commitment to direct instruction and academic engaged time, even Professor Rosenshine agrees that a sensible classroom should have a balance of no-nonsense academic engagement along with student-centered, open activities. Some examples might be art, hobbies or crafts, music, discussions, field trips, individual projects, exploration and discovery, and so on—all those enjoyable activities which may or may not contribute to hard-line academic achievement test scores.

MASTERY LEARNING: INDIVIDUALIZED INSTRUCTION

The **mastery model** of instruction assumes that nearly all students are capable of high achievement—that is, of mastering the material—if they are given sufficient opportunity (time) to learn and if they are aided when they have difficulties. According to mastery expert Benjamin Bloom (1971, 1973, 1976), mastery procedures allow about 80 percent of the students to attain a level of learning that is typically reached by only about 20 percent of the students. Thus the concept of mastery learning is having a very dramatic and positive influence on educational philosophy and classroom practice.

The basic mastery learning strategy is not complex. It is an individualized learning approach. Each student works at his or her own pace on a relatively small segment of material. When ready, he or she takes a short diagnostic test. If the test indicates that the skills are mastered, he or she proceeds to the next assignment. If the skills are not mastered, some form of remediation—to be followed by retesting—is in order. A more specific example of a district-wide mathematics mastery program will be elaborated below.

By this time in your college career, you probably are aware of bell-shaped curves and "normal distributions" of scores, since many instructors of large undergraduate courses assign grades on this basis (see Chapters 14 and 19). For illustration, and with implications for mastery learning, assume that a class of 25 students is "normally distributed" with respect to intellectual ability—some are well above average, some are well below, but most are near the middle. Then all students receive the same *amount* and the same *quality* of instruction. What happens on the achievement test? You guessed it. Some students score well above average, some score well below, but most are near the middle. Generally, intelligence test scores and grades are fairly strongly related.

This means that students' grades are at least partly fixed even before they enter the learning situation. Such a circumstance is not particularly fair to the student who learns at a slower pace.

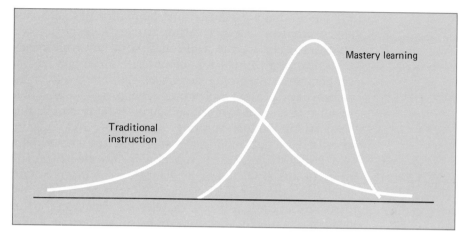

Figure 12.4
Distribution of achievement under traditional instructional conditions and under mastery learning.

Under the mastery model, student intellectual ability will still remain normally distributed. It's a fact of life. However, the amount of time allowed for instruction and the nature of the instruction will be individualized, and the large majority of students will be able to achieve at high levels of mastery (Figure 12.4). Furthermore, the correlation between aptitude and achievement will drop to nearly zero, as it should (Block, 1971b).

Diagnostic Tests

There are a variety of specific procedures for implementing mastery learning. However, virtually all strategies will involve **diagnostic tests,** sometimes called *formative tests* or *diagnostic progress tests.* They also are often called pretests and post-tests. The tests are not used for assigning class grades. They serve only to assess what has been learned and what remains to be mastered. The construction of the diagnostic tests requires serious attention to (a) specific instructional objectives and (b) what criterion of achievement constitutes "mastery" of a given topic. Traditionally, 80 percent correct on, say, a math test indicates adequate mastery of the skills, and the student is permitted to proceed to the next material.

The teacher usually will have to divide a course into smaller segments—perhaps book chapters, sets of math problems, or some other well-defined units—in order to give students a clear, short-term goal. At present, there are some published materials based on a mastery approach to individualized learning. Naturally, these already are subdivided into smaller units with diagnostic tests and learner prescriptions already prepared. Two examples are the *Individually Guided Science* and *Individually Guided Mathematics* materials published by Addison-Wesley.

Given that a diagnostic test pinpoints areas of weakness or confusion, a key problem lies in creating attractive activities which will motivate students to accept the additional work and time necessary to remediate their learning difficulties. Bloom (1971) emphasized that the design of supplementary learning activities can creatively challenge the teacher committed to mastery learning. Bloom (1971) and Block (1971a) recommended the use of two-person buddy systems, small group problem-solving sessions, individual tutoring, workbooks and programmed instruction, alternative texts, audio tapes and cassettes, and perhaps academic games and puzzles. One tested solution is for the teacher (or other adult) to examine the student's performance on the diagnostic test, then tutor the student on the spot. Alternatively, the teacher may have the student review parts of the same (missed) material or refer to other texts or workbooks dealing specifically with the troublesome concepts and skills.

A District-Wide Mathematics Mastery Program

The Middleton-Cross Plains school district in Wisconsin has received considerable publicity for its original and very effective elementary mathematics mastery program. It requires no specially written math books or materials. It does require a drop or two of ingenuity.

The curriculum is divided into topics and subtopics which approximately correspond to traditional sections and chapters of most elementary school math books. In the fifth and sixth grades, for example, the math curriculum includes addition, subtraction, multiplication, division, estimation (rounding), fractions, decimals, percents, and geometry. There usually are 10 lessons for each topic, but sometimes fewer, sometimes more. Each classroom has about a half-dozen different textbooks and workbooks available, with multiple copies of each. Most will be at grade level, but a few will be available at the next higher and lower grade level.

Each student takes a pretest, for example, with "Percents 1." If he or she scores over 80 percent correct, the lesson is considered mastered and the child moves right to the pretest for "Percents 2." If the student scores below 80 percent, he or she is given a "Road Map." The Road Map directs the student to selected pages or perhaps a chapter in one or more of the available books. The student does the required problems. According to one 11-year old authority, your author's daughter Sonja Davis, "Each Road Map can take five minutes to a month!" Sonja is prone to exaggeration.

When the Road Map (a lesson) is finished, the student takes a post-test, which is very similar to the pretest. The tests are always 10 or 20 problems long, which makes the definition of "80 percent correct" very clear. (Try defining "80 percent correct" with six or seven problems!) With a score over 80 percent, the student proceeds to the pretest for the next lesson.

If a student scores below 80 percent after completing the Road Map, the next step is designed on the spot by the sensitive, caring teacher. The student may be asked only to correct his or her errors on the post-test. This minor assignment may clearly prove that the student has mastered the objectives and therefore should proceed to the next pretest. If the student is more confused, the teacher-in-charge-of-Road-Maps will select a page or two of extra problems geared specifically to the child's weakness.

Will the child pass the post-test on the second try? Not necessarily. According to mastery expert Sonja Davis, "I flunked Decimals 1 four times! There was one kind of problem I just couldn't get." At worst, after several sorties into additional small assignments, the skills will be mastered and the post-test will be passed *summa cum laude.*

It is not at all unusual for students to pass a pre-test without doing the particular Road Map assignments. In addition to handling the managerial duty of administering pre- and post-tests and handing out Road Maps, the teachers also teach. A Review Group of a half-dozen or so students will be convened to be taught a new kind of problem. ("I want to meet with people in Fractions 6 through 10.") The teacher meets with the small group for usually 10 to 30 minutes to teach the new skills—which will enable some students to pass a future pretest on the first attempt.

Now, one hypothetical problem with a completely individualized instructional program is that the fast students can get further and further ahead, while the slower learners get further and further mired in confusion. In the present example of mastery learning, the teachers also hold Review Groups to help students who are getting behind. ("I want to meet with people in Division 1 and 2.") With a small group of just five or six, the teacher can ask the students what problems each is having. He or she also can review with the students the skills necessary for a future lesson.

By the end of the school year, different students will "land" in different topics. A few will have mastered the most advanced geometry Road Maps while others will have mastered less sophisticated lessons. Overall, however, achievement runs very high for all students—and in a noncompetitive, nonthreatening atmosphere.

Results of Mastery Learning: Cognitive and Affective

The most exciting feature of mastery learning is its effects, both cognitive and affective (Bloom, 1971, 1976, 1977). We have already noted that mastery procedures typically permit about 80 percent of the students to perform at a level normally achieved by only 20 percent. Naturally, this increased competence better prepares the student for further learning, particularly in cumulative subject areas such as mathematics. As some research examples of mastery effectiveness: A fifth-grade arithmetic class of "advantaged" students changed from 19 percent A and B grades to 75 percent A's and B's when mastery procedures were used (Kersh, 1970); an eighth-grade mathematics class also climbed to 80 percent A's and B's when a mastery strategy—lists of objectives, formative tests, specific prescriptions for using the text, notes, and handouts—was adopted (Collins, 1970); even a graduate university course in test theory changed student achievement from 30 percent A's to 80 percent A's when a mastery model was adopted (Airasian, 1967). Stinard and Dolphin (1981), teaching a college anatomy and physiology course, found that a mastery approach was especially effective for students with weak science backgrounds.

On the affective side, consider how greatly the feelings of frustration, failure, inadequacy, and even humiliation are reduced when achievement is high. Indeed, a student's entire self-concept may be altered as he or she acquires the ability—under mastery conditions—to achieve both high grades and public recognition of his or her academic achievement. As reinforcement theory would tell us, students do, in fact, actually begin to like previously difficult subjects, since these subjects are now sources of strong, positive rewards. Also, the abolition of low grades fosters a healthy classroom attitude of cooperation for the benefit of all, instead of competition for the scarce rewards.

INSET 12.2

**IS MASTERY LEARNING
NEW? THE 1922
WINNETKA PLAN**

In 1922, Carleton Washburne and his associates reported a successful individualized mastery program in Winnetka, Illinois. The strategy was similar to present ones. First, the criteria of mastery were defined in terms of specific instructional objectives. Second, self-instructional materials were organized into carefully sequenced learning units designed to teach the desired objectives. Learning was completely self-paced, with students taking whatever time was needed to master each unit. Third, when ready, students took a diagnostic test (ungraded) at the end of each unit. Mastery of a given unit was a prerequisite for proceeding to the next unit. Finally, if the diagnostic test reflected learning difficulties, supplementary learning activities were prescribed which enabled students to attain the unit objectives.

Isn't mastery learning an exciting new idea?

TO IMPROVE
YOUR TEACHING

This chapter presented four instructional models: the Popham and Baker goal-referenced model; Gagné's outcomes, events, and conditions model; Rosenshine's direct instruction and academic-engaged-time model; and the Bloom and Carroll mastery model. The most sensible approach to actually using this information in your teaching is to pick what you like, what appears valuable and helpful from each viewpoint, and then to incorporate the information or strategy into your teaching.

From Popham and Baker, for example, we find potentially valuable idea sources for preparing instructional objectives—student interests, society's objectives, and of course the subject matter itself. The concept of pre-assessment—to determine whether students already have mastered your objectives and/or whether they possess the prerequisite skills and knowledge—also could be a valuable idea. Their principle of appropriate practice certainly should be followed, and the use of criterion-referenced tests also is sensible.

Gagné's many concepts and principles and guidelines can indeed be overwhelming. Gagné has been developing and integrating these ideas for at least 20 years, and he is not finished yet (see, for example, Gagné and White, 1978, for even more involved developments in his thinking). His "outcomes" taxonomy draws attention to, apparently, all possible objectives and outcomes of teaching—verbal knowledge, intellectual skills, cognitive strategies, attitudes, and motor skills. It very well could be helpful to remain aware of these possible outcomes when designing objectives and planning instruction. It also may be valuable to look again at how Gagné ties instructional steps ("external conditions of learning") to each step in the information processing sequence ("events in learning"; Figs. 12.2 and 12.3). Certainly learning does begin with motivation and attention, "stimulating recall" is virtually identical to Ausubel's important concept of advance organizers, and an emphasis on promoting both retention and transfer definitely is justifiable.

Rosenshine's million-dollar breakthrough would be very amusing, because of its obvious simplicity, if it were not for the profound importance of the idea. The more time spent working ("academic engaged time") and the more content covered, the higher the achievement test scores. Rosenshine also gives us a new perspective on the educational value of, for example, student-selected activities, discovery-learning procedures, small-group activities, educational games, variety in learning tasks, and even the use of higher cognitive questions (Chapter 11). Rosenshine himself resolves this dilemma of promoting academic engagement and "direct instruction" vs. relaxed and perhaps more enjoyable classroom activities: *Both are needed.* Achievement levels will suffer if the entire day is spend in "open" activities; attitudes and morale will suffer if 28 noses are bent to the grindstone for the whole day.

Mastery learning is intuitively appealing—learning is individualized, and average achievement levels are raised substantially. You should agree also that a student's grade should not be fixed by his or her academic ability, a good part of which he or she was born with (Chapter 15). Mastery approaches seem to work very well indeed—especially with mathematics and science instruction, but also in such areas as teaching English (Block, 1971b, pp. 124–126). If you teach in the elementary school, you should seriously consider such a strategy, even if you have to design the procedure yourself (see the Middleton-Cross Plains plan in this chapter). The simplest mastery plans include only diagnostic tests, to be passed at a predetermined (usually 80 percent) level, which follow a small unit of (usually) self-instruction. Mastery strategies have been found effective in junior and senior high school math classes and in college courses in statistics, physics, biology, anatomy, psychology, educational psychology, and philosophy (Block, 1971b; Stinard and Dolphin, 1981).

SUMMARY

Instructional theories and models, like theories and models in any discipline, (a) simplify complex phenomena, (b) permit explanation and prediction, (c) provide a language and a point of view for thinking about instruction, and (d) provide guidance for organizing instructional activities.

The Popham and Baker goal-referenced instructional model includes four steps or operations: (1) specifying objectives; (2) pre-assessing students' knowledge of the objectives and their prerequisite skills and knowledge; (3) designing and conducting the instruction, which includes the principle of appropriate practice; and (4) evaluating achievement of the objectives, usually with a criterion-referenced test. Testing also may be used to evaluate the instruction and assign grades.

Objectives can include learner behaviors (as in a class presentation) or most often, products (tests, papers, projects). In selecting objectives, which amounts to selecting a curriculum, Popham and Baker recommend considering (a) the students' abilities, achievement, needs, and interests, (b) society's goals of education, and (c) the subject matter.

As presented here, Gagné's most recent instructional theory includes (1) outcomes of learning, or learned capabilities, (2) events in learning, and (3) conditions of learning.

The five outcomes of learning exhaustively include everything a person could learn in a classroom: (a) Verbal information includes facts, names, principles, or other mostly verbal knowledge. (b) Intellectual skills include hierarchically ordered discriminating, learning concepts, learning rules, and solving problems. (c) Cognitive strategies are self-management strategies for attending, encoding, remembering, recalling, and problem solving; skills needed for self-directed independent learning. (d) Attitudes are affective outcomes. (e) Motor skills are motor outcomes.

Gagné's events of learning consist of an information-processing model of a single learning event: stimulation of sensory receptors, storage in a sensory register, attention to important details and retention in a short-term memory, encoding in long-term memory, and generation of a response via the effectors. Executive control processes and expectancies, both part of LTM, control information-processing events.

Instruction, Gagné's external conditions of learning, is a sequence of steps aimed at accommodating each of eight steps in information processing and learning, from activating motivation through eliciting the performance and providing feedback. Internal conditions of learning were prerequisite skills and information.

Educational researcher Barak Rosenshine reviewed decades of research on teacher and student characteristics related to high achievement. Reviews in 1971 and 1973 suggested that "task-oriented behaviors" and "amount of content covered" seemed to be consistently related to high achievement. These were combined into the concept of *academic engaged time*—the amount of time attentively engaged in learning the academic content—the single most powerful predictor of student achievement of all student and teacher variables studied.

Direct instruction promotes academic engagement. The teacher selects the academic material and the goals, and paces and monitors student performance. The atmosphere is academic but convivial, not authoritarian. Teachers who elicit high achievement are task-oriented, are strong leaders, and are the center of attention; they closely monitor work groups; and they ask lower-level questions which serve as controlled practice on to-be-tested knowledge.

Teachers in task-oriented, high-achieving classes also are strong in their humanistic concern for the success and self-esteem of individual students. A classroom with a balance of high academic engagement and student-centered "open" activities is probably most sensible.

The mastery learning model of instruction assumes that most students are capable of high achievement if they are given sufficient time (opportunity) and assistance. In contrast, when all students receive the same amount and quality of instruction, achievement will be substantially determined by ability.

Usually, instruction is mostly individualized, with diagnostic tests given after short-term units of work. Usually, a student who gets 80 percent correct is judged to have mastered the material and proceeds to the next unit. One Wisconsin elementary school mastery math program uses pretests, Road Maps (assigned problems), post-tests and, if necessary, careful individualized remediation.

Mastery strategies usually result in higher achievement and beneficial affective rewards (confidence, self-esteem).

TOPICS FOR THOUGHT AND DISCUSSION

1. Is the Popham and Baker model a "good" (complete, sufficient, appropriate) one to follow for instructional planning? Can you find shortcomings, for example, instructional situations or activities for which it is inappropriate?

2. Which of your college courses seem to adhere to the "principle of appropriate practice" in helping train you and prepare you for exams? Explain.

3. What do you think of the Popham and Baker guidelines for selecting instructional objectives—based on student interests, society's goals and the subject matter? Do most teachers follow these guides without consciously realizing it?

4. Which parts of Gagné's model seem most enlightening in helping to clarify or simplify the process of learning and/or teaching? Could you use any, most, or all of this model in planning your instruction? Explain.

5. In view of Rosenshine's direct instruction and academic engaged time concepts, do you think "free" or "alternative" high schools are a mistake? Why or why not?

6. Could mastery learning be used in all subject matters at all levels? Explain.

PROJECTS

1. Locate a mathematics, science, or social studies textbook series in your education library for the grade you expect to teach. Using a book at grade level, plus one text one year above and one text one year below, design a mastery-based unit of instruction. You will need a diagnostic test and assignments for each small instructional unit.

2. Observe a classroom for a morning or an afternoon. Keep a record of the amount of time spent in direct instruction by the teacher, total academic engagement, and "other" activities. What proportion of the total time was spent on academic tasks? Was the balance sensible? What proportion of the academic time was spent in actual academic engagement? Should it have been more or less?

3. Prepare a lesson plan following the four steps in the Popham and Baker model. Use a grade level and subject matter appropriate to your future teaching plans.

RECOMMENDED READING

Block, J. H. *Mastery learning: Theory and practice.* New York: Holt, Rinehart & Winston, 1971.

Bloom, B. S. Recent developments in mastery learning. *Educational Psychologist* **10,** 1973, 53–57.

_____. *Human characteristics and school learning.* New York: McGraw-Hill, 1976.

Furst, E. J. Bloom's taxonomy of educational objectives in the cognitive domain: Philosophical and educational issues. *Review of Educational Research* **51,** 1981, 441–453.

Gagné, R. M. *Essentials of learning for instruction.* New York: Holt, Rinehart & Winston, 1974.

_____. *Conditions of learning,* third edition. New York: Holt, Rinehart & Winston, 1977.

Popham, W. J. *Criterion-referenced instruction.* Belmont, Calif.: Fearon, 1973.

Popham, W. J., and E. L. Baker. *Systematic instruction.* Englewood Cliffs, N.J.: Prentice-Hall, 1970.

_____. *Classroom instructional tactics.* Englewood Cliffs, N.J.: Prentice-Hall, 1973.

Rosenshine, B. Content, time and direct instruction. In P. L. Peterson and H. J. Walberg (eds.), *Research on teaching: Concepts, findings and implications.* Berkeley, Calif.: McCutchan, 1979.

Humanistic and Affective Education

13

ABOUT HUMANISM AND AFFECTIVE LEARNING

To many educators, this chapter on the intertwined topics of humanistic education and the affective domain could be the most significant chapter of the entire book. It deals with values and attitudes that shape students' lives. It deals with whether or not students think of themselves as worthwhile, success-oriented human beings. It deals with human meanings, human understandings, and human relationships and experiences.

Humanistic Education

Humanistic education is a philosophy. It is a way of looking at students interacting with teachers, with other students, and with all humankind. A basic assumption is that the feelings and perceptions of students, especially their self-concepts, are at least as important in the educational program as the acquisition of knowledge and skills. To many, humanistic matters are much more important than scholastic matters. In the words of humanist Arthur Combs (1975), "We can live with a bad reader; a bigot is a danger to everyone." Combs also observes that modern education must do better than produce graduates with cognitive knowledge and skills. We must have humane individuals who contribute to society, who behave responsibly and cooperatively, who care about their fellow citizens, and who become loving fathers and mothers.

The humanistic teacher thus is concerned with the personal development of each student. This orientation especially includes the development in students of: (1) a healthy self-concept built on self-acceptance and self-valuing; (2) a strong sense of identification with and concern for the feelings and welfare of others; (3) self-actualization, which means the "fully functional" realization of one's capabilities, or becoming what one is capable of becoming; and (4) an attitude of self-motivated, self-initiated learning for the intrinsic enjoyment of learning. Other goals of humanistic education include: (5) the development of creative abilities, (6) the fostering of students' sense of responsibility, and (7) the teaching of positive and constructive values.

Humanistic teaching is said to be *learner-centered,* that is, the focus of education should be on the healthy development and education of the student. According to some humanists, modern education is far too teacher-centered, with too much emphasis on a standard curriculum, instructional objectives, and the necessity for all students to meet the teacher's curriculum requirements.

The Affective Domain

The affective domain in education shares many of the concerns of the humanist philosophy. It focuses on student attitudes and values (e.g., honesty, democracy, fair play), feelings and emotions (e.g., anxieties, frustrations, hostilities), "character," personality, prejudices, personal philosophies, self-concept and self-esteem, personal and social adjustment, and mental health in general. One finds affective behavior in any school situation—or anywhere else, for that matter (Ringness, 1973). Yet strangely enough, there is precious little affective learning content in the curriculum. Most teachers are not well informed in the dynamics of affective learning. They also may not realize the influence they might have in shaping these vital dimensions of student personality and behavior. It also is true that both students and teachers usually are rewarded for academic gains, not for affective and humanistic progress.

The purpose of this chapter is to explain the case for humanistic and affective education, to increase the reader's understanding of these topics, and to present a sample of instructional techniques designed to foster

affective and humanistic growth. Accordingly, we will look first at some specific values which the prospective teacher may wish to teach. Then we will examine the taxonomy of affective objectives, which both explains the development of attitudes and values and presents a sequence for preparing objectives and teaching attitudes and values. A section on conditioning describes more dynamics regarding the development of attitudes, fears, and other emotions. Following an itemized description of humanist Carl Rogers' principles of humanistic education, we will look at the significance of students' self-concept and self-esteem—and the measures students will take to protect these valuable assets. Finally, a description of the humanistic teacher will be followed by a section presenting a sample of classroom activities for helping students understand their feelings and emotions and for strengthening humanistic traits of students at all age levels.

Affective and humanistic virtues should not replace traditional curricular knowledge and skills, but they should be given some class time.

SOME VALUES WORTH TEACHING

Depending on the particular community, students have many opportunities to acquire maladaptive or even self-destructive values—for example, appreciation for successful lying, cheating, stealing, sitting on the curb drinking wine, or using heroin or other hard drugs. Surveys among slum youngsters have shown that many of them admire, respect, and hope to emulate the pimps, prostitutes, and drug dealers whose fine clothes and air-conditioned Cadillacs are clear testimony to their "success" in American society.

Davis (1983) compiled a short list of values which seems worth teaching to students at the elementary or secondary level:

Honesty
Not cheating
Not stealing or shoplifting
Not vandalizing
Not lying
Returning things

Keeping promises
Trustworthiness
Understanding and respect for
   police

Rights of Others
Respecting rights of fellow students, teachers, friends, family members, business owners
Accepting and respecting individual differences
Friendliness

Listening
Helping others
Empathizing with others' problems
Not hurting others
Not playing tricks on others

Energy, Environment
Conserving electricity, gas, coal, wood, metals, paper, school supplies, etc.

Caring for property, own and others'
Not being a messy person

Manners
Asking
Waiting
Sharing
Doing favors
Being courteous
Being considerate with older

people, handicapped persons, fellow students, the teacher, the family
Behaving properly in public; on the bus, in stores, restaurants, theatres, etc.

School, Work Habits
Paying attention
Promptness
Following directions
Industriousness, perseverance
Using time wisely

Doing neat work
Accepting leadership or participant roles
Valuing education
Observing safety rules

Personal Development
Accepting responsibility
Accepting consequences
Valuing physical health, hygiene
Compassion for fellow humans
Developing one's talents to the fullest
Valuing good friends

Self-respect, pride
Earning respect from others
Controlling one's temper
Courage, honor, patriotism
Appreciation for beauty
Deep sense of democracy, fair play

There is no good reason why the development of such important affective, humanistic matters should be left to chance.

TAXONOMY OF AFFECTIVE OBJECTIVES

In Chapter 11 we briefly reviewed the *Taxonomy of Educational Objectives: Cognitive Domain*. The purpose of that taxonomy was to help teachers prepare objectives (which guide instruction, student studying, and evaluation) in areas of academic content. To help clarify objectives in the affective domain, Krathwohl, Bloom, and Masia (1964) created the *Taxonomy of Educational Objectives: Handbook II, The Affective Domain* (see Table 13.1). As in the cognitive domain, the purpose of the taxonomy of affective objectives is to provide a guideline for identifying objectives and for structuring the teaching of affective concepts.

INSET 13.1

**IDENTITY,
CONNECTEDNESS,
AND CONTROL**

Newberg (1977) reduced the problem of affective education to three basic clusters of human concerns: identity, connectedness, and control. *Identity* is the concern reflected in such questions as: "Who am I?" "Am I a worthy person?" "What do I value?" "Does my body serve me well?"

The concern for *connectedness* evolves around relationships with other people: "Do others like me?" "How do I make contact with other people?" "How can I build relationships with others that are mutually satisfying?" "Where is my place in the world?"

The concern for *control* or effectiveness appears in such questions as: "How can I take charge of my life?" "What can I really accomplish?" "Can my behavior make a difference at home, in school, in the world?"

A "concern" is a preoccupation or a need that causes people to feel uneasy, anxious, or insecure. These three groups of concerns—identity, connectedness, and control—lie at the heart of the Affective Education Program in Philadelphia (Newburg, 1977), and could serve as the basis for any humanistic teacher's effort to build better students.

The entire system is hierarchically organized, with five major steps ranging from a simple, passive reception of affective information (Level 1) to an extensive overhaul of the subject's personality, values, and lifetime commitments (Level 5). Each of the five stages contains two or three substages which also are ordered. The main theme is that normal attitude development—and therefore a sensible teaching sequence—follows approximately the steps in the taxonomy.

For example, let's say that elementary school teacher Conscience Hartfelt wishes to teach compassion and concern for the less fortunate. According to Level 1, **Receiving,** Hartfelt would simply expose students to problems of pain, poverty, and suffering and to the proper humanitarian attitudes. She wants students to become *aware* of such problems and *willing to receive* pertinent information.

In Level 2, **Responding,** the learner has now formed an opinion—he or she is unquestionably against poverty, pain and suffering—and does something about it. At first, students simply accept the teacher's attitudes. Following this *acquiescence* phase comes a self-initiated willingness to explore the problem and possible solutions. For example, students might search out information on the magnitude of the problem, or explore federal, state, or church programs for the needy.

With Level 3, **Valuing,** the appropriate attitudes have become more and more accepted as genuine personal values, and the student's behavior is consistent with those values. The student no longer laughs at the pencil-selling derelict. He or she buys all the pencils and then gives them back, or at least leaves a big tip. The student identifies with the attitude and feels committed to personal action.

At Level 4, **Organization,** the value of compassion is internalized. In the present example, the learner makes clear judgments about the respon-

Table 13.1 Taxonomy of educational objectives: Affective Domain. The arrows on the right-hand side of the table reflect the portion of the taxonomy relevant to some commonly used affective terms (adjustment, attitude, value, appreciation, interest).

1.0 Receiving	1.1 Awareness
	1.2 Willingness to receive
	1.3 Controlled or selected attention
2.0 Responding	2.1 Acquiescence in responding
	2.2 Willingness to respond
	2.3 Satisfaction in response
3.0 Valuing	3.1 Acceptance of a value
	3.2 Preference for a value
	3.3 Commitment
4.0 Organization	4.1 Conceptualization of a value
	4.2 Organization of a value system
5.0 Characterization by a value complex	5.1 Generalized set
	5.2 Characterization

(Right-hand arrows label ranges of the taxonomy: Adjustment, Value, Attitudes, Appreciation, Interest)

From *Taxonomy of educational objectives: The classification of educational goals: Handbook II: Affective domain,* by David R. Krathwohl et al. Copyright © 1964 by Longman, Inc. Reprinted by permission of Longman, Inc., New York.

sibility of the haves to the have-nots. The attitudes become integrated with other values regarding, for example, education, government, life goals, and the directions American society should take.

With Level 5, **Characterization by a value complex,** the attitude and value systems essentially become a permanent philosophy of life and perhaps even a career, for example, in social work or welfare programs.

Note that the continuum in Table 13.1 follows the development of a single attitude or value. Thus the formation of any one of the several dozen values listed above would begin with simple exposure to the value. The person so exposed would then accumulate more information, internalize the value, integrate that value with other values, and perhaps make a lifelong commitment.

Of course, borders between categories and subcategories of the taxonomy are not distinct, they gradually shade into each other. Also, the taxonomy is politically neutral—negative values of racism, greed, or fascism would follow the same development as more positive attitudes.

AFFECTIVE LEARNING IN CLASSICAL AND INSTRUMENTAL CONDITIONING

In Chapter 5 we explained how emotional responses can become associated with particular school subjects, teachers, or school in general. Classical conditioning tells us that "things which occur together tend to become associated." Since punitive teachers and classrooms are paired with feelings of fear, anger, hostility, resentment, failure, anxiety, depression, and/or humiliation, these emotional responses may be elicited as virtual conditioned reflexes to school-related stimuli. Even *thoughts* of school may elicit negatively-toned conditioned reactions.

From a conditioning point of view, the best countermeasures are preventive ones—try to prevent negative emotions from becoming associated with school in the first place. Also, just as anxiety or hostility may be conditioned, pleasant emotions—joy, excitement, discovery, friendship, success, pleasure—also may come to be associated with classroom learning. Affective specialist Ringness (1973) pointed out that a cheery, attractively decorated school with interesting equipment, media, and other materials can help stimulate responses of pleasure, interest, and effort. The teacher also can be a pleasant "stimulus," aided by such traits as cheerfulness, enthusiasm, friendliness, a sense of humor, and a willingness to accept students as worthwhile individuals.

The instrumental conditioning model also has answers for the teacher of alienated, anxious, hostile, or apathetic students. Chapters 5 and 6 described such reinforcers as candy, prizes, extended recess periods, a few minutes' worth of loud chatting or gum-chewing, praise, tokens, head-pats, and so on, and how these can be used to motivate cooperation and learning. Behavior modification strategies can lead to a noteworthy improvement in study habits, attitudes toward school, and self-control. Thus the reinforcers not only "control" the classroom behavior, but often improve students' evaluations of themselves and their teachers (Ringness, 1973, p. 77). The term *humanistic behaviorism* (or behavioristic humanism) is used to describe the use of operant conditioning for humanistic ends.

CARL ROGERS' PRINCIPLES OF HUMANISTIC EDUCATION

Psychologist Carl Rogers is a very respected, authoritative person in the area of humanistic education. In his *Freedom to Learn*, Rogers (1969) presented a summary list of principles which may help "... set students free for self-initiated, self-reliant learning." For example:

1. *Human beings have a natural potential for learning.* Says Rogers, we are born with a natural curiosity about our world which creates an eagerness to discover, to know, and to understand.

2. *Significant learning takes place when the subject matter is perceived as relevant to the self.* Rogers estimates that if school material is seen as relevant for the "... maintenance or enhancement of his own self, ..." students could learn in one-third to one-fifth of the usual amount of time. (Could this be?)

3. *Learning which involves a change in self-organization—in the perception of oneself—is threatening and tends to be resisted.* In this principle, Rogers refers mainly to the learning of new attitudes and values which threaten currently held beliefs and thus the self-concept. For example, doper Darlene Downerz may resist information on the dangers of certain drugs, since Darlene's self-concept includes being a "with it" pill-popper. Teachers too, says Rogers, have their beliefs threatened when they are asked to ignore shaggy hair or indecent blouses. After all, if the students are *right*, then the teacher must be *wrong*.

4. *Those learnings which are threatening to the self are more easily accepted when external threats are at a minimum.* As we will see in the next section, the fear-of-failure student cannot perform well when his or her self-worth is continually on the brink of being demolished by low grades, criticism, or other public demonstrations of inadequacy. Rogers recommends (a) a supportive environment, (b) individualized instruction with some degree of student self-evaluation, and (c) no insulting grades. The poor student may become a more self-actualized, capable person if he or she can begin at his or her own level of achievement—from which every small step is accompanied by feelings of progress, achievement and success.

5. *When threat to the self is low, experience can be perceived in a differentiated fashion and learning can proceed.* If a learner feels personally secure or "psychologically safe," he or she will be better able to discriminate and learn in the sense of progressive differentiation described in Chapter 8.

6. *Much significant learning is acquired through doing.* As we saw in Chapter 8, learning by doing (or discovery learning) is not particularly efficient when compared with expository instruction. However, doing and discovering is virtually guaranteed to be a highly meaningful, memorable, and educational event. Rogers suggests placing students in direct confrontation with social, ethical, moral, and even personal issues. For example, heated discussions of drugs, discrimination, thievery, cheating, women's rights, or military service will plunge students into significant problems they are currently facing.

7. *Learning is facilitated when the student participates responsibly in the learning process.* When students help decide their own course of learning—choosing topics, formulating problems, selecting resources, and living with the consequences of these decisions—learning is more

meaningful and motivating than when students feel they must do as they are told.

8. *Self-initiated learning which involves the whole person—feelings and intellect—is the most lasting and pervasive.* Rogers describes this "whole person" learning as a "... 'gut-level' type of learning which is profound and pervasive." It often happens in the personal discovery of a self-generated idea, in the learning of a difficult cognitive or motor skill, or in the act of an artistic creation. In these, the whole person "lets go" and becomes totally involved in the learning experience.

9. *Independence, creativity, and self-reliance are all facilitated when self-criticism and self-evaluation are basic and evaluation by others is of secondary importance.* According to Rogers, all children and adolescents must evaluate their own behaviors, so that each may decide what standards of excellence are appropriate for him or her. The child or adolescent who depends entirely on the evaluations of others may remain permanently dependent.

10. *The most socially useful learning in the modern world is the learning of the process of learning, a continuous openness to experience and incorporation into oneself of the process of change.* Rogers suggests here that the survival of our culture requires an attitude of *changing.* Indeed, change is a prominent fact of modern life, and individuals must be comfortable with the notion that continuous new learning is necessary in such a world.

SELF-ESTEEM AND SELF-WORTH THEORY

In our competitive American way of life, it is common for feelings of personal competence and self-esteem to be tied very closely to experiences of success. With adults, there are many types of success experiences which reinforce feelings of adequacy and self-esteem. A person not only has job success, but success as a husband, mother, church member, bridge player, home decorator, union member, fisherperson, golfer, tennis player, beer guzzler, gourmet cook, driver-of-expensive-car, and so on. Unfortunately, with children it is primarily feedback from school work and the teacher that tells each child whether he or she is a capable, worthwhile human being.

Self-Concept and Self-Esteem

Before examining the details of Covington and Beery's (1976) perceptive and sometimes provocative **self-worth theory,** let's look at a list of principles and research-based conclusions pertaining to the development of a student's self-concept and self-esteem.

1. Developing a positive self-concept is an important educational goal. This goal is reflected, for example, in major programs for disadvantaged students, such as Head Start and others (Graham and Hess, 1965; Smiley, 1967). Improving the self-concept may be seen either as a goal in itself or as a means of stimulating higher academic achievement (Bloom, 1977; Rubin, Dorle, and Sandidge, 1977; Scheirer and Kraut, 1979).

2. The self-concept is multifaceted. A person perceives such separate aspects as an academic self, a social self, an emotional self, and a physical self (Jordon, 1981; Shavelson, Hubner, and Stanton, 1976; Shepard, 1979).

3. The self-concept also is organized, relatively stable, and, importantly, evaluative in the positive/negative sense. It is the evaluative dimension which relates to mental health: With a positive self-evaluation, a person essentially says, "I see myself, and I like what I see" (Shepard, 1979). Rogers (1949) proposed that mentally healthy people see their "actual self" as similar to their "ideal self."

4. According to the "mirror theory" (Gecas, Calonico, and Thomas, 1974), the self-concept is a product of the reflected assessments of others.

5. The self-accepting student is self-understanding. The student is aware of strengths and weaknesses, yet still values himself or herself. The self-rejecting student considers himself or herself of little worth, and may have other symptoms of maladjustment (Shepard, 1979).

6. Failure in academic settings can lead to "shame and distress" (Covington and Omelich, 1979), since such negative feedback prevents students from maintaining feelings of competence. Worse yet, failure despite great effort is even stronger evidence of low ability and therefore maximizes "shame" (Covington and Omelich, 1979; Kelley, 1973; Kun and Weiner, 1973).

7. The self-concept is protected when excuses are constructed for explaining why the effort did not produce success. The reader may recognize this phenomenon as rationalization (Chapter 3).

8. A student's self-esteem and pride are greatest when his or her success at a difficult task is seen as due to both high ability and high effort (Covington and Omelich, 1979).

Self-Worth Theory: Covington and Beery

In one of the finest little educational books ever written, *Self Worth and School Learning,* Covington and Beery (1976) explained that the scarcity of rewards in the typically competitive classroom exposes many students to failure and threats of failure. Note the penetrating logic: (a) Feelings of self-esteem and self-worth are a highly treasured commodity; (b) low ability can mean low worth as a person; (c) failure can mean low ability; and so

(d) failure (or even the possibility of failure) is very threatening to self-esteem and self-worth. The upshot is that, as we will see, students faced with potential failure will develop and cling to defense strategies which protect their valuable egos. Unfortunately, most of these strategies work against legitimate high achievement and success.

The success-oriented student. In Chapter 9, we distinguished between students motivated by needs to achieve and students motivated by needs to avoid failure. The achieving, success-oriented student may be described quickly; the other character will take a little longer.

The **success-oriented** student usually succeeds. This person's history of success naturally inspires confidence in his or her own ability. He or she has succeeded in the past and therefore has the ability to succeed in the future. When failure occurs, it is attributed to lack of effort, not lack of ability, and so failures are used constructively to clarify shortcomings and prepare better for next time. As Covington and Beery (1976, p. 21) nicely put it, "The person has temporarily fallen short of a goal, and has not fallen short as a person." Success-oriented students thus develop confidence in their abilities, a sense of responsibility for their actions, and feelings of control over their environment. They are content with themselves, and life is something between a piece of cake and a bowl of cherries.

The failure-oriented student. Many sudents are motivated not by needs for success, but by strong needs to avoid failure. Such students tend to doubt their abilities. *The real threat, however, is that the doubts might be confirmed.* Since ability is tied so closely to one's self-perceived value as a person, the **failure-oriented** student becomes proficient at tactics which prevent failure, or at least a sense of failure. Unfortunately, those tactics which protect these students' feelings of self-worth greatly reduce their chances for real success.

Defense mechanisms. A failure-threatened student might deliberately *underachieve.* Unable to get away with avoiding school work altogether, he or she puts in just enough effort to squeak by. Naturally, this student's ability and ego are not threatened by this borderline performance since, after all, he or she did not really try. The teacher might say, "Craven is unmotivated!" Actually, Craven is very highly motivated—to protect his self-respect. There is another bonus which reinforces underachieving. If Craven gets lucky and does very well, say, on a test, this may be taken by him and by others as the highest evidence of ability: doing well without trying.

In college this **defensive underachieving** produces the "Gentleman's C" syndrome. No true gentleman or highbrow lady would knock himself or herself out competing for a high grade. Of course not. Think of the humiliation and destroyed self-concept if his or her best effort still merited a low grade. The solution: Take an effortless C and maintain the illusion of intellectual superiority. Conveniently, the illusion cannot be confirmed or disconfirmed. Small wonder there are so many ladies and gentlemen on campus.

Another ego-protection strategy is **defensive goal setting**—for example, setting goals unrealistically high, say about the A+ level. Such ambitious goal setting may appear irrational for a student of average or below average ability. However, it is very rational in protecting against a sense of failure: It's no disgrace to fall short of an impossibly high performance standard.

A variation of defensive goal setting involves establishing a very wide distance between one's highest expected achievement level and the lowest acceptable achievement level: "I'll get something between a D+ and a B+." Such a wide *confirming interval* makes success, and therefore failure avoidance, a lead-pipe cinch (Birney, Burdick, and Teevan, 1969).

Still another defensive strategy is to set the goal too low: "I modestly expect a mere C−." Craven thus guarantees himself success, albeit a trivial and meaningless one. He reaps an added bonus in appearing modest to his peers.

If failure avoidance becomes combined with strong needs to achieve, the result may be a compulsive, driven over-achiever. Again, with feelings of self-worth equated with success, this individual makes more and more demands upon himself or herself in order to sustain a very high level of achievement. High achievement means high ability means high worth.

It is characteristic of the failure-oriented student to attribute failures to external causes: "The test wuz unfair," "My baby sister ate the assignment."* Curiously enough, he or she also may not take credit for honest successes. A high grade or a well-done project implies the ability and therefore the *obligation* to continue high quality work. This may be very threatening to a failure-avoiding student. Therefore, successes will be attributed to such external sources as luck, an easy exam, or capricious grading, but not to personal competence.

Scarcity of classroom rewards. The main cause of a failure orientation is the scarcity of classroom rewards. Students often are required to play against one another for successes (high grades, teacher approval), and there usually is not a lot of room at the top. In order to compete for a fair share of the successes and recognition, below-average students are forced into the

---

* *Attribution theory,* which deals with perceived causes (e.g., attributable to the individual or to the external environment), was described in Chapter 9. *Locus-of-control theory,* which also deals with attributing successes and failures to oneself (internal locus of control) or to external factors (external locus of control) will be described in Chapter 14.

predicament of setting *personal* achievement goals according to stringent *classroom* standards. When their performance is publicly compared against that of more able students, feelings of failure are usually inevitable. The fault is not with the students, but with the inappropriate and unfair standards: For some to succeed, others must fail and lose dignity and self-respect. Competition for high classroom grades and recognition is motivating only for students who think they can win. Students who are forced to compete but feel they have little chance of winning become disillusioned and discouraged (Combs, 1975).

Unfortunately, the very fact that rewards for high achievement are scarce serves to increase the psychological value of those rewards, thus increasing the heat of the competition. Small wonder some students are forced to raise their defenses to avoid failure, frustration, and self-doubt.

Individualization of instruction. One solution to the sorts of self-defeating, self-perpetuating defenses against failure described above is to restructure both the definition of success and the allocation of rewards. There are many systems of individualized instruction in which success and individual excellence include meeting and exceeding one's *own* standards, without requiring that someone else fail. These strategies usually permit students to set both their own goals and their own pace of learning. Aspirations are always just ahead of current performance, not so high as to be unreachable, yet not too low to guarantee a trivial success. (One example is given below; see also Chapters 9, 12, and 18 for more ideas for individualization.)

According to Covington and Beery (1976), when students are not competing, they will set reachable, realistic goals, and these provide both the best challenge and the best conditions for a satisfying success. It is important to note that with individualization, students not only control their own objectives and rate of learning, but their own rates of meaningful successes and nonthreatening failures.

Let's look at one simple but ingenious and successful example. Alschuler (1969, 1973) described a competitive, boring fifth-grade math class. Every day, yesterday's homework was reviewed, new material was explained, and more homework was assigned (sound familiar?). The result was success for some, but plenty of defensive failure dodging for others. The simple success-oriented alterations were as follows:

1. Students worked at their own rate on a chapter-by-chapter basis. When ready, they took a proficiency test at the end of each chapter.
2. They were paid—in play money!—for the number of correct problems.
3. Critically, they were required to estimate the percentage of problems they expected to get correct—with dollars subtracted for setting goals unrealistically low *or* high.

INSET 13.2

**TUTORING: AFFECTIVE
AND ACADEMIC
BENEFITS FOR THE
TUTOR**

A basic principle of role theory is that the enactment of a particular role will produce changes not only in a person's behavior, but in that person's attitudes and self-perceptions as well. Basically, the role player assumes the prestige, authority, and feelings of competence and esteem associated with a particular role (Allen, 1976; Allen and Feldman, 1976). Now let's consider little Loretta Lonormal, an insecure, anxious, low ability, and low achieving sixth-grade student. Imagine she is invited to help one or two first graders with their reading. Nothing complicated, she just needs to help them with word decoding and word meanings when they make a mistake or have a question.

From little Loretta's point of view, she has been singled out, specially chosen to do an important job; she will have the responsibility for another person's learning. She thus will be playing the role of teacher—clearly a responsible, authoritative role associated with high prestige and high competence (Gartner, Kohler and Reissman, 1971). Little Loretta should begin to feel good about herself. She also will learn some new skills, which further increases feelings of competence.

The system thus rewarded realistic goal setting along with academic performance.

The results? Would you believe the average math achievement level climbed nearly three grade levels in one year? These previously apathetic students voluntarily worked on their math over weekends, missed very few assignments, and demonstrated an honest liking for the "unpleasant" subject of math.

The important elements of the success-oriented, student-centered structure were that:

1. Goal setting was realistic; goals were reachable yet challenging.
2. The objectives and steps in the learning process were clear, permitting the teacher to teach to the objectives and allowing the learner to concentrate his or her efforts.
3. Success depended on effort, something which even students of lesser ability could control.
4. The "work" included an element of play, a form of intrinsic motivation.

Many systems of individualized instruction, including contingency management and mastery learning, incorporate most of the above concepts

Research supports the positive effects of tutoring on the tutor's self-esteem and attitudes toward school. In a study by Robertson (1972), fifth-graders tutored other fifth-graders three days per week for two months, after which they showed better self-concepts and better attitudes toward reading and teaching. High school students, in a study by Cairns (1972), also showed a more positive self-image and better attitudes toward attending school after a tutoring experience. Gartner, Kohler, and Reissman (1971) and Roddy (1980) review extensive anecdotal and experimental evidence that tutoring does indeed improve the tutor's self-esteem and attitudes toward school.

Tutoring also has produced academic gains with fifth-grade tutors (Robertson, 1972), seventh- and eighth-trade tutors (Lippitt and Lippitt, 1968), and high school tutors (Cloward, 1967; Morgan and Troy, 1970). Not too surprisingly, the tutors also improve in their ability to work with others (Gartner, Kohler, and Reissman, 1971).

In special cases, such as when tutoring handicapped children, the adult trainer should: (a) train the tutors in, for example, simple behavior modification (rewarding) skills; (b) prepare the tutors for the unresponsiveness of severely disturbed children ("but he won't even look at me!"); and (c) reward the tutors' efforts with praise and perhaps a Certificate of Merit (Kerr and Strain, 1978; Roddy, 1980).

(see Chapters 6, 12, and 18). However, Covington and Beery warn that students may be unprepared for the necessary self-initiated, autonomous governing of their own time and resources. Naturally, the failure-oriented students need the autonomy most, but are least prepared for self-management. Some training in the study habits and skills necessary for self-directed learning may be necessary.

The payoff, however, might be heightened achievement, better attitudes toward school, and a healthier self-concept—all of those swell things we've talked about in this important affective domain of education.

THE HUMANISTIC TEACHER

Let's assume for the moment that you are convinced that a humanistic concern for both academic development and students' feelings and self-esteem is the way to go. How do you become a more learner-centered, humanistically oriented teacher? Easy—just change your personality.

The humanistic teacher should try to cultivate a more self-actualized, fully functioning self. According to Pine and Boy's (1977) very nice book *Learner Centered Teaching: A Humanistic View* (appropriately published

by the Love Publishing Company), a humanistic teacher first must be comfortable with herself or himself as a real, worthwhile person. He or she should be able to accept and respect himself or herself, and not be terribly threatened by anxieties and insecurities. A warm and secure teacher will reflect that warmth and security and will communicate this basic humanism to others (Pine and Boy, 1977, p. 4).

These authors compiled a list of characteristics of humanistic teachers, based on the thoughts of such humanists as Carl Rogers, Abraham Maslow, Arthur Combs, and Earl Kelly. The self-actualized, humanistic teacher:

1. *Thinks well of himself or herself.* He or she has a good self-concept.
2. *Is a whole, unified, and integrated person.* The honesty and genuineness of the humanistic teacher dissolves any conflict between the "real"

self and the "role" self, between the "inner" person and the visible "outer" person.

3. *Thinks well of others.* The humanistic teacher likes and accepts other people, and functions well in cooperative relationships.
4. *Sees himself or herself in the process of "becoming."* The humanistic teacher, as with other self-actualized persons, is continuously "forward growing," learning, exploring, and changing.
5. *Develops and lives by humanistic values.* The humanistic person is honestly concerned with the welfare of fellow human beings and with the betterment of the human community.
6. *Takes risks, sees the value of mistakes.* As a creative, adventurous innovator, the humanistic teacher is willing to take risks, to try something new. Importantly, he or she is personally secure enough to profit from mistakes instead of being threatened by the errors.
7. *Trusts himself or herself.* Humanistic teachers have confidence in their own feelings and intuition and trust their own decisions and reactions.
8. *Is open to experience.* A self-actualized person by definition is open to viewpoints of others and to his or her own inner feelings. He or she is not defensive but is open and responsive to both internal and external sources of experience and information.
9. *Is initiatory.* The self-actualized, humanistic teacher exercises control over his or her life and environment, and is more creative than reactive. He or she also not only accepts change, but initiates needed changes.
10. *Is responsive, vibrant, and spontaneous.* The humanistic teacher tries to live optimistically and energetically. The spontaneity and vitality includes a sensitivity to the needs and feelings of others.

HUMANISTIC AND AFFECTIVE TEACHING METHODS

Apart from their arguments for (a) humanistic attitudes and personalities in teachers and (b) educating students to be concerned, self-actualized, self-initiated "whole" human beings, until a decade ago humanist authors had very little to say about *what* and *how*—exactly—students should be taught. In recent years, however, a number of teaching strategies and fine workbooks have offered help to the humanist teacher who wants to know what to do and how to do it. This section will briefly describe a few strategies and materials: values clarification, sensitivity and awareness training, socio-drama, Eberle and Hall's (1975) *Affective Education Guidebook*, and Davis' (1983) *Good Person Book.* Space will hardly permit a thorough description and analysis of these tactics; the self-initiated seeker after wisdom and truth will have to go to the sources listed at the end of this chapter for more complete and detailed information.

INSET 13.3

**BECOMING A
HUMANISTIC TEACHER:
ROGERS**

Humanist Carl Rogers (1969, 1974) itemized what the humanistically inclined teacher should do to promote student self-actualization, feelings of self-worth, student-initiated learning, and other humanistic values.

1. The teacher sets the climate of optimism and trust in the class.
2. The teacher helps clarify the reasons for and purposes of the class, and the purposes of the students in the class.
3. The teacher tries to use the motives and interests of each student to motivate significant individual learning.
4. The teacher organizes and makes available the widest possible range of learning resources.
5. The teacher accepts both the intellectual and the personal, emotional sides of students.
6. The teacher is alert to expressions of deep feelings.
7. The teacher tries to recognize and accept his or her own limitations and feelings.

**Values
Clarification**

In the words of noted psychoanalyst Lawrence Kubie, "The child's fifth freedom is the right to know what he feels . . . and [to] put into words all the hidden things that go on inside. . . ." Further, at home and at school the child's normal development is distorted by "the conspiracy of silence" (Newburg, 1977). As the name suggests, **values clarification** (VC) is one technique for helping students discover and understand their own values— a strategy for ending the conspiracy of silence. Such an understanding should lead to a new self-confidence, a feeling of inner security, a sense of strength and potency, and a sensitivity to the feelings of others.

The basic, three-part activities in VC are:

1. *Choosing.* Selecting beliefs and behaviors from among a set of alternatives.
2. *Prizing.* Publicly affirming that these are values and behaviors which the student believes in and cherishes.
3. *Acting.* Behaving consistently and repetitively in accord with the clarified values.

Simon, Howe and Kirschenbaum (1972; see also Purpel and Ryan, 1976; Simon and Massey, 1973) present no less than 79 VC strategies. One of

Table 13.2 Are you someone who . . . ?

A	B	C	Are you someone who:
			1. Likes to break the curve on an exam?
			2. Likes to stay up all night when friends visit?
			3. Will stop the car to look at a sunset?
			4. Puts things off?
			5. Will publicly show affection for another person?
			6. Will do it yourself when you feel something needs doing?
			7. Will order a new dish in a restaurant?
			8. Could accept your own sexual impotence?
			9. Could be satisfied without a college degree?
			10. Could be part of a mercy killing?
			11. Is afraid alone in the dark in a strange place?
			12. Is willing to participate in a T-group?
			13. Eats when you are worried?
			14. Can receive a gift easily?
			15. Would steal apples from an orchard?
			16. Is apt to judge someone by his or her appearance?
			17. Would let your child drink or smoke pot?
			18. Watches television soap operas?
			19. Could kill in self-defense?
			20. Needs to be alone?

From Sidney Simon and Sara Massey, Values clarification, *Educational Leadership*, May, 1973. Reprinted with permission of the Association for Supervision and Curriculum Development. Copyright © 1973 by the Association for Supervision and Curriculum Development. All rights reserved.*

their favorites involves a list of attitudes and behaviors. The question is asked "Are you someone who . . . ?" and the student checks, *yes* (A), *maybe* (B), or *no* (C). (See Table 13.2.) Such action helps clarify what the student feels strongly about, is neutral toward, or is opposed to.

In one variation, each student in a group of three has a copy of the form in Table 13.2. In colum A, each student checks characteristics and values which describe himself or herself. These marks are folded out of sight and the form is passed to another member of the group, who places checkmarks in column B—trying to guess the items checked by the first person (i.e., guessing the first person's values). Again, answers are folded

* For information about current Values Realization Materials and a schedule of nation-wide training workshops, contact Sidney B. Simon, Old Mountain Road, Hadley, MA 01035.

out of sight and the forms are passed to the remaining person—who uses column C to try to guess which items were checked by the first person. When the three forms are returned to their original owners, each person has his or her own ratings plus the guesses of the other two. The three then

---

INSET 13.4
CLASSROOM MEETINGS

The name *classroom meetings* is most closely associated with William Glasser (1969, 1974). In their original form, Glasser's three types of classroom meetings were directed toward both academic and affective/humanistic ends. The students and the teacher of a class meet, in a tight circle, at least once per week and as often as every day. The meetings are open-ended and nonevaluative.

In the **social-problem-solving** meetings the concern is with students' social behavior in school (for example, truancy) and sometimes at home. In the early grades students discuss such problems as individual and group responsibility. Always, the focus is on solving the problem, not finding fault or determining guilt.

In the **open-ended** meetings, students discuss any thought-provoking question related to their lives, questions which also may be related to the classroom curriculum. In lower grades, the teacher may have to make the connection between the discussion topic and the curriculum; in higher grades the students can bridge the gap.

The **educational-diagnostic** meeting is always directly related to what the class is studying. For example, if the formal lessons deal with the Constitution, the discussion can center on the meanings of personal freedom, privacy, and the role of the police.

Newburg (1977) outlined a slightly different set of classroom meetings. A *sharing* meeting is essentially a "show and tell" opportunity for children. They display and describe their hobbies, skills, and interests. In a *plans* meeting, a small group meets for up to an hour to organize plans for some project they intend to accomplish. With a *problems* meeting, an individual student requests help from the teacher, a small group, or the entire class in dealing with a pressing personal concern. The group brainstorms possible solutions to the problem.

Classroom meetings of either the Glasser or Newburg variety have proven effective in solving important student and school problems, in eliciting commitments to personal improvement (e.g., less truancy), in teaching students that education is related to the outside world, and in teaching students that others care about them, that their ideas and opinions are worthwhile, and that they can contribute to a discussion and solve problems by using their brains.

discuss the agreements and inconsistencies in terms of the messages and impressions we send and how these are interpreted by others. The group members consider their own values and what kind of people they are, plus other people's perceptions of the values and opinions they hold.

Simon and Massey (1973) note that the traits in Table 13.2 represent just a few of the hundreds of possibilities. In an exercise which further clarifies feelings and self-understanding, students can have a rousing time brainstorming other lists of, usually, 20 traits per list (e.g., "Blushes at a compliment," "Talks loudly when nervous," and so on). Adolescents might create a list of traits for the question, "I am looking for someone who is . . . ." Checking these traits will clarify what one values and cherishes in a "special partner" and in life.

Other VC strategies by Simon, Howe, and Kirschenbaum (1972) again require conscious choices and public affirmation. For example, with their Strategy 5 students line up on one side of the room or the other according to whether they identify more with a Volkswagen or a Cadillac. They pair off with another who made the same choice and compare reasons for the decision. Strategy 42 requires students to write a letter to an editor of a newspaper or magazine, publicly expressing their beliefs on an issue. The Simon *et al.* book will lead you through all 79 exercises for clarifying values, building self-concepts, and increasing sensitivity to the feelings of others. For a review of the effectiveness of VC, see Lockwood (1978). Are you someone who will investigate these ideas for humanistic teaching?

Sensitivity and Awareness Training: Magic Circle

While adult sensitivity sessions can become vicious and devastating, the **Magic Circle** technique is quite safe and beneficial. In the Magic Circle, children learn ". . . how to be more effective, why people are sometimes happy or unhappy, how to feel good about themselves, and how to get along with others" (Lefkowitz, 1972). The Magic Circle helps children develop an awareness of their good and bad feelings, their good and bad thoughts, and their good and bad behaviors. In complete agreement with the "conspiracy of silence" mentioned above, Palomares and Rubini (1973) noted that children are often not allowed to accept and understand their own feelings. For example, when frightened, they are told there is nothing to be afraid of. When they feel pain, they are told to smile and be brave. They must conclude that what they really feel is both unique to them and unacceptable to adults. Palomares and Rubini describe one kindergarten student who, after a Magic Circle session, ran home bubbling with excitement: "Guess what, Mom? Fanny and Kathy and Paul are afraid of the dark, too. I'm not so silly after all!"

The procedure begins with a group of from seven to twelve children, with the number of boys and girls nearly equal. The remainder of the class can either observe or work quietly on some other project. The three ground rules are:

1. Anyone who wants to speak gets a chance to do so.
2. To speak, a person must raise his hand and be called on by the leader. (The teacher will be the leader until students are practiced enough to fill that role themselves.)
3. Everyone must listen, and must be able to show he or she has listened by being able to repeat what was said.

The children and the leader form a circle. The teacher-leader explains the rules, describes the procedure, and introduces the topic for the day. For example, "The subject for today's magic circle is 'I felt good when . . . .' Who would like to start?" Student Dizzy Daremore might reply, "I felt good when I rode the roller coaster with my arms in the air." The leader might ask *why*, and Dizzy might explain that he felt thrilled, brave, and proud of himself. The teacher might ask, "Who can tell me why Dizzy felt good on the roller coaster?" This provides feedback to little Dizzy, in addition to assuring attention. The leader then continues with, "Who else would like to tell us about something that made them feel good?"

Some Magic Circle topics are:

- I felt good (or bad) when . . . .
- A pleasant (or unpleasant) thought I have is . . . .
- Something I can do (or wish I could do) is . . . .
- I made somebody feel good (or bad) when I . . . .
- Somebody made me feel good (or bad) when they . . . .

Lefkowitz (1975) recommends starting out with the positive form of these problems, trying the negative forms after some experience. He also recommends that the teacher:

1. Be accepting.
2. Invite shy children to participate.
3. After every third or fourth speaker, ask someone to review what has been said.
4. Limit sessions to about 20 minutes.
5. Thank each child for his or her contributions.
6. Before ending, help children review and summarize what they learned— the points about why people are sometimes happy and sad, how to feel good about themselves, and how to get along with others.

Sensitivity Modules

Once upon a time, there was a teacher in an all-white, eleventh-grade social studies class in a middle-class suburb of New York City. The teacher (we'll call him Robert Reality) told his class all about poverty, claims of police brutality, welfare, and lots of other not-so-wonderful things that happen to other people in other places. Mr. Reality felt that his comfortable and well-fed students somehow could not truly relate to those kinds of problems. So teacher Robert Reality invented the very first **Sensitivity Modules** (Kirschenbaum, 1975).

"Look, gang," said Mr. Reality, "I want you to get *involved*. I want you to discover the *real* world with *real* people and tune in to some *real* understanding."

So in the next two weeks, each student had to do two projects. After each project, they were to discuss their experiences in class. Here's a list of some of the projects:

1. Wear old clothes and sit in the waiting room of the State Unemployment Office. Listen, observe, talk to people, read the announcements, etc.
2. Attend a service in a store-front church.
3. Go to magistrates court and make a list of the cases. How are the defendants treated?
4. Sit in a maternity ward of a city hospital that handles welfare patients. Talk to anyone there.
5. Live for three days on the money a welfare mother receives to feed a son or daughter your age.
6. Take a seat in line at a community health center. Observe the attitudes of the staff. Talk to the patients.
7. Compare the prices of the same brands and models of TV sets and radios at your suburban department or discount store with the prices of the same merchandise in an inner-city credit store.
8. In January or February, turn off your heat and spend the night in a cold house.

Kirschenbaum (1975) notes that comparable sensitivity modules can be constructed for classes of minority students. As the reader might guess, such experiences generate powerful feelings. But yes, there is some risk involved in some of the experiences. Risk should not be eliminated, however, since it is central to the experience of true and deep feelings—even if they are unsettling (Kirschenbaum, 1975). At the same time, students should not be sent into places where they would be dangerously unwelcome.

Sociodrama

Sociodrama is a technique for giving students a more clear picture of a problem by having them live the situation. It can change attitudes quickly and profoundly. It does not require professional training, for example, in psychotherapy.

Three preliminary ground rules are that:

1. The class should generally have a cooperative group feeling and should be interested in an accurate portrayal and understanding of the issue to be explored.
2. The students should have some knowledge both of the situation and the person they are to role play.
3. The sociodrama should not be an end in itself, but a supplementary instructional means.

Michels and Hatcher (1975) describe one example of sociodrama dealing with cheating. Now, every student and most parrots can memorize those three little words, "cheating is wrong, cheating is wrong, cheating is wrong, aaarrk!" Sociodrama helps students empathetically understand the matter from the point of view of the several people involved.

Six students might play the roles of teacher, the student caught cheating, the accessory student who passed him or her the answers, the tattle-tale student who blew the whistle, the principal, and the mother of the culprit. There are no scripts, no rehearsals (or very short ones), and the production may last just five or ten minutes. The players may trade roles for another go-around, or other students in the class may take a role. Before the session and the issue is concluded, the class is asked for its reactions to the emotional involvement and the different viewpoints of the players, for example, "What were your feelings (or reactions)?" or "Were any important points overlooked?" (See Michels and Hatcher, 1975, for more details regarding the teacher's role in selecting topics and organizing and conducting the sociodrama sessions.)

Exercises in Affective Education: Eberle and Hall

One especially nice workbook jammed with exercises for humanistic and affective teaching is *Affective Education guidebook* (Eberle and Hall, 1975; see also their *Affective Direction: Planning and teaching for thinking and feeling*, Eberle and Hall, 1979). Their *Mini-Speech* strategy probably is based on the Magic Circle approach. Students select a topic (perhaps drawing one blindly), and then give a two- to four-minute speech which expresses and elaborates their feelings about the topic. Some topics are:

- I get real angry when . . . .
- I think I'm pretty good at . . . .
- Compared to most people, I'm different because . . . .
- I like people that . . . .

- I am embarrassed when . . . .
- Getting along with another person is easy if . . . .
- If I could do it over, I would . . . .
- My feeling are easily hurt when . . . .

Class discussion can follow each Mini-Speech.

With the *What It's Like* exercise, students clarify and identify their feelings and learn that their behavior can make other people feel good or feel uncomfortable. The strategy is basically one of class discussion. Students are encouraged to tell "What it's like" when:

- People yell at you.
- Someone tells you that you have done something very well.
- Somebody doesn't do what they said they would.
- You get a gift you didn't expect to get.
- You don't have to get up to go to school on Saturday morning.

Students and teachers can make up more "what it's like" questions or reverse the roles of the current questions (e.g., "What's it like to yell at people?").

The *How Else* exercise helps students think of a variety of ways to express feelings, and gives them practice expressing those feelings. In groups of four to six, students try to think of "the right words and gestures" to convey feelings. Consider these feelings:

- You bug me.
- I wish you would be quiet.
- I do not agree with you.
- I like you.
- I trust you.
- I need to know how you feel.
- I would like to spend more time with you.

First, students practice making these statements to others in the group. Second, they think of alternative ways to verbalize the feelings. Third, they practice expressing the feeling without using words.

The Good Person Book: Davis

In his *Good Person Book*, Davis (1983) describes how specific values may be taught using eight general teaching strategies. For example, with the *brainstorming* approach, students would be asked to "Think of all the ways you can to show friendliness in the classroom." Or with reverse brainstorming, "List all the ways you can think of to hurt someone's feelings." With

the *empathy* strategy, students are asked to imagine themselves in another role. For example, "What would it be like to be a very old person with no family and little money? How would you feel? What would you do?" With the *metaphorical thinking* approach, students make comparisons—for example, "How is a messy person like an out-of-tune piano?" or, "How is someone who loses his or her temper like a pinball machine?"

With the *mental-visualization* approach, students relax and shut their eyes while the teacher leads them through a value-loaded mental experience.

For example, students relax and shut their eyes while the teacher reads the following: "Imagine a classroom where none of the children pay attention or listen to the teacher (pause). The teacher is at the board trying to explain an arithmetic problem (pause). One student is making airplanes (pause). Another is scratching his sore ankle (pause). Three more are talking about a new Steve Martin movie (pause). . . ." And so on. After the experience, the students may discuss the values and feelings involved, such as the purpose of school, the value of math, the feelings of the teacher, and so on. In the *creative thinking* strategy, a "What would happen if . . . ?" approach is used; for example, "What would happen if everybody always cheated everybody else?"

The *questioning* approach is basically a class discussion of value concepts, for example, "What is rudeness?" or, "What is a good person?" With the *problem-solving* approach, an issue is identified (such as wasting time) and students consider each of the steps: (1) What is the problem and why is it a problem? (2) What can be done? What are some solutions? (3) What are the consequences of each of the solutions? Finally, with *role playing* the teacher sets simple scenes and asks students to play roles which require the expression of feelings, as described earlier in this chapter.

TO IMPROVE
YOUR TEACHING

Since you are relatively grown up, educated, and possessed of intelligence, common sense, and a middle-class sense of values, you probably are convinced that the humanistic and affective concepts in this chapter are good and desirable, just like apple pie and the flag. Younger people, however, particularly in non-middle-class neighborhoods, may possess none of these traits. None. They need help in understanding and appreciating themselves, in clarifying and accepting basic values of honesty and respect for others' rights, and in becoming motivated to develop their own capabilities. One key concept is *self-actualization.* Another is to end the "conspiracy of silence" that prevents students from understanding themselves, their feelings, and their values.

A recent local newspaper column described how teenagers stole three automobiles worth approximately $15,000, and proceeded to play demolition derby until the autos were scrap iron. No qualms about grand theft; no empathy for the rights of others. Who is to blame?

This chapter should increase your awareness of some of the specifics of the affective, humanistic movement in education. That is, you should become more sensitive to conditions which violate these principles and to conditions which promote feelings of success, self-esteem, self-actualization, and good values. Bloom's taxonomy of affective objectives should help you understand the course of development of an attitude or value, and it suggests a teaching sequence. Rogers' principles of humanistic education also provide general guides for a more humanistic, affectively oriented classroom. You will need to decide for yourself which of Rogers' recommendations are sensible for your own teaching, and which are not.

The very nice Covington and Beery description of the significance of a student's self-worth, and his or her efforts to protect it, should be enlightening. Some students avoid the continual battering of failure and feelings of low worth by simply dropping out—and becoming a useful and respected worker in a factory, dime-store, construction company, or something of the sort.

You should look over the traits of a humanistic teacher and decide whether they fit you, or whether you should (or can) alter your attitudes, personality, and teaching style to fit that description. You probably do not have far to go.

Finally, you might take a closer look at the teaching strategies described in this chapter, and hopefully take a longer look at some of the references listed at the end. Regardless of what grade or what "type of students" you eventually will teach, you owe it to those students to include training in basic values in your curriculum. No teacher enjoys hearing about a former student being sent to prison or becoming a street walker. Perhaps a few hours, over a year's time, discussing honesty, personal development, and "what life's all about" could have made the difference.

SUMMARY

Humanistic and affective education is concerned with students' feelings, emotions, attitudes, values, self-esteem, responsibility, concern for others, creative development, self-directed learning capabilities, and—most significantly—self-actualization.

One list of seemingly teachable values (Davis, 1983) fell into the categories of honesty, rights of others, manners, energy/environment, school and work habits, and personal development.

The *Taxonomy of Educational Objectives: Affective Domain* provides a guide for preparing affective objectives and therefore for teaching attitudes and values. The taxonomy includes the five stages of receiving, responding, valuing, organization, and characterization by a value complex.

Both negative and positive emotional reactions may be acquired through what is basically a classical conditioning process. It is best to try to make the classroom elicit feelings of pleasure, excitement, friendship, discovery, and success in the first place. Behavior modification strategies have been used to make the classroom a more rewarding situation.

Humanist Carl Rogers' principles of humanistic education emphasized the following: students' natural curiosity and desire to learn; the importance of relevant curriculum; the effects of threats to the self; learning by doing; student participation in deciding the student's course of learning; learning and discovery involving feelings and intellect; self-evaluation and self-criticism; and an attitude favoring change and continuous new learning.

Self-esteem is important to everyone. Children are strongly influenced by feedback from schoolwork, which tells them whether they are capable, worthwhile human beings.

Eight principles are summarized pertaining to the development of the self-concept and self-esteem: Developing a good self-concept is a worthwhile educational goal; the self-concept is multifaceted, organized, and evaluative; the self-concept reflects (mirrors) the assessment of others; self-acceptance implies self-understanding; failure creates feelings of shame (especially after high effort); excuses reduce shame; and pride is greatest when success is attributed to high ability and effort.

According to self-worth theory, the success-oriented student has a history of succeeding, which inspires confidence and feelings of high self-worth. Failure is attributed to lack of effort.

The failure-oriented student may use defense strategies, since failure threatens valuable feelings of self-worth. The failure-oriented student may deliberately underachieve, set goals unrealistically high, use a wide "confirming interval," set goals very low, or compulsively overachieve. The failure-oriented student may blame external sources for his or her failure, and may avoid taking credit for successes because they imply an obligation to do better.

The main cause of a failure orientation is the scarcity of classroom rewards due to competitive grading systems. Individualization of instruction may permit all students to set reachable goals, thus assuring worthwhile successes and feelings of self-worth.

The humanistic teacher should be warm, secure, and self-actualized. Some traits of a humanistic teacher are: thinks well of himself or herself; is an honest, genuine, integrated person; thinks well of others; is in a continual process of changing and "becoming"; lives by humanistic values; profits from mistakes; trusts himself or herself; is open to experience; is an initiator of change; and is responsive, spontaneous, energetic, and optimistic.

Some humanistic teaching strategies include values clarification, classroom meetings, the Magic Circle awareness/sensitivity procedure, sensitivity modules, sociodrama, and the use of workbooks prepared by Eberle and Hall (1975, 1979) and Davis (1983). All of these strategies aim at helping students acquire positive attitudes and values, clarifying emotions and values, and helping students understand the viewpoints and problems of others.

TOPICS FOR THOUGHT AND DISCUSSION

1. What values and attitudes do you think should be taught in middle-class elementary schools? Middle-class secondary schools? In elementary and secondary schools in economically disadvantaged areas?
2. Whose fault is it when big-city teenagers commit major crimes, such as auto theft, burglary, or murder? Take an hour and brainstorm some solutions to this apparently "unsolvable" problem.
3. Can you think of high school or college courses which violate Rogers' principles of humanistic education? Which principles?
4. Have you ever taken evasive action to avoid feelings of failure and low worth? What did you do?

PROJECTS

1. Outline in detail a few hours' worth of affective/humanistic lessons and activities for the grade level you expect to teach. Be specific about the objectives, the strategy, and any follow-up discussion.
2. Look over the ideas for sensitivity modules listed in this chapter. Brainstorm, alone or in a group, another 15 or so which would be appropriate for high school students in an area you know (perhaps your own high school).

RECOMMENDED READING

Alschuler, A. S. *Developing achievement motivation in adolescents.* Englewood Cliffs, N.J.: Educational Technology Publications, 1973.

Brown, G. I., M. Phillips, and S. Shapiro. *Getting it all together: Confluent education.* Bloomington, Ind.: Phi Delta Kappa Educational Foundation, 1976.

Brown, G. I., T. Yeomans, and I. Grizzard (eds.). *The live classroom: Innovations through confluent education and gestalt.* New York: Viking Press, 1975.

Canfield, J. W., and H. C. Wells. *100 ways to enhance self-concept in the classroom.* Englewood Cliffs, N.J.: Prentice Hall, 1976.

Covington,. M. V., and R. G. Beery. *Self-worth and school learning.* New York: Holt, 1976.

Davis, G. A. *The good person book: Affective and humanistic education.* Cross Plains, Wis.: Badger Press, 1983.

Eberle, B., and R. Hall. *Affective education guidebook: Classroom activities in the realm of feelings.* Buffalo, N.Y.: DOK Publishers, 1975.

————. *Affective direction: Planning and teaching for thinking and feeling.* Buffalo, N.Y.: DOK Publishers, 1979.

Glasser, W. *Schools without failure.* New York: Harper & Row, 1969.

Howe, L. W., and M. M. Howe. *Personalizing education: Values clarification and beyond.* New York: Hart, 1975.

Newburg, N. A. *Affective education in Philadelphia.* Bloomington, Ind.: Phi Delta Kappa Educational Foundation, 1977.

*Pine, G. J., and A. V. Boy. *Learner-centered teaching: A humanistic view.* Denver, Colo.: Love Publishing Co., 1977.

*Read, D. A., and S. B. Simon (eds.). *Humanistic education sourcebook.* Englewood Cliffs, N.J.: Prentice-Hall, 1975.

Rogers, C. R. *Freedom to learn.* Columbus, Ohio: Charles E. Merrill, 1969.

Simon, S. B., L. W. Howe, and H. Kirschenbaum. *Values clarification.* New York: Hart, 1972.

* Contain extensive lists of books, articles, organizations, films, and you name it dealing with humanistic education.

INDIVIDUAL DIFFERENCES

PART VI

The Nature of
Individual Differences

About individual differences / The psychometrician's
view of individual differences / Individual differences in
personality and cognitive style / To improve your
teaching / Summary / Topics for thought and
discussion / Projects / Recommended reading

14

ABOUT INDIVIDUAL DIFFERENCES

Throughout this text we have emphasized primarily the commonalities in the abilities, characteristics, and behavior of people. Students are indeed alike in many ways. At the same time, however, no two are identical. Students differ in appearance, temperament, anxiety, honesty, intelligence, styles of learning, styles of perception, ways of thinking, rate of development, dexterity, coordination, conformity, creativity, economic background, values, motives, interests, dimples, pimples, and anything else any psychologist has ever cared to measure or evaluate.

The field of psychology specializing in individual differences traditionally has been called *differential psychology;* more often, the field is just called **individual differences** or "ID's." The oldest and still most popular ID topic is intelligence (Chapter 15). Two other important individual differences are creativity (Chapter 16) and giftedness (Chapter 17). This chapter will begin with a review of selected measurement concepts in individual differences—so you will be able to think like a differential psychologist. After this foray into abstract, formal operational thinking we will look at some important individual differences in personality, motivation, and "cognitive styles," all of which shape the way we think, learn, perceive, and behave.

Aptitude by Treatment Interactions

The newest, most enlightening (and yes, fashionable) form of ID research in education deals with **aptitude by treatment interactions,** or "ATI research." This approach attempts to coordinate individual differences (aptitudes) with particularly effective instructional procedures (treatments). For example, perhaps highly anxious students function best in a structured teaching situation, while low-anxiety students might blossom with more flexible, discovery-oriented strategies. One recent study showed that high-ability and low-ability children learned geometry better in small groups, but medium-ability children learned better in large groups (Peterson, Janicki, and Swing, 1981).

The two main types of ATI are shown diagrammatically in Figure 14.1. (This illustration might be most clear to readers high in spatial ability.) In the left portion, students with Aptitude A_1 do poorly in Teaching Condition 1, but much better in Teaching Condition 2. Vice versa, Aptitude A_2 students do well in Condition 1, but poorly in Condition 2. This type of aptitude by treatment interaction, in which instructional methods affect two types of students in opposite ways, is fairly rare. ID researchers call this form of ATI a "disordinal" interaction. With our other type of ATI in the right half of Figure 14.1, students with Aptitude B_1 do equally well under either teaching condition, while B_2 students do well only under Teaching Condition 1. This type of "ordinal" ATI is relatively common.

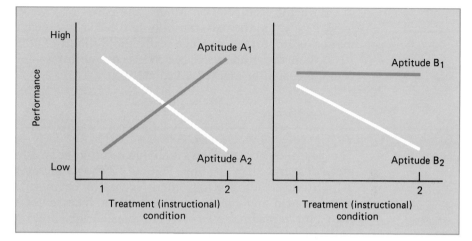

Figure 14.1
Two types of
aptitude by
treatment
interactions, the
criss-cross
"disordinal" ATI
and the diverging
"ordinal" ATI.

For example, bright students may learn equally well in lecture and independent discovery conditions, while less capable students may learn best from the structured lectures.

Once an aptitude by treatment interaction is found, there are three ways the information may be used to match different student aptitudes with different instructional (treatment) conditions. The first strategy, called the **Capitalization Model,** capitalizes on the student's academic strengths (Cronbach and Snow, 1977, pp. 169–171) or personality characteristics. For example, if a student is an independent, hard-working achiever, then a course arranged for independent productivity would capitalize on this personality type. A more conforming student might learn better in a structured teaching situation. Either teaching condition capitalizes on particular strengths or personality factors.

A second way to match instructional conditions to individual differences is the **Compensation Model,** in which the instructor tries to compensate for student weaknesses. The approach is about the same as giving Granny a pair of false teeth—the treatment does for the learner what the learner cannot do for himself or herself. For example, if the student is a poor reader, then material is presented via a tape recorder; if the student is deficient in organizing material for learning, it is organized for him or her. Tracking, the currently unpopular (for good reason) method of grouping according to IQ scores, also would be an example of compensating for deficiencies. Note that the compensation strategy accommodates a weakness, but does not cure it.

With the **Remediation Model,** the particular weakness in knowledge or skill is strengthened—the hole is filled in. Remediating gaps in information is important, but not really too difficult. The real challenge is to strengthen the students' basic skills and abilities—for example, reading comprehension or mathematical abilities.

THE PSYCHOMETRICIAN'S VIEW OF INDIVIDUAL DIFFERENCES

The psychometrician views individual differences as variation around a mean or average. For example, Figure 14.2 shows a hypothetical distribution of fictitious reading achievement scores of Levin's (1977) 24 imaginary round-headed and square-headed children. The scores range from 0 to 6, with a mean reading score of 3. The distribution shows differences between individuals—that is, **interindividual differences.**

We also have differences within an individual—**intraindividual differences** in attention, motivation, distractibility, concentration, fatigue, or anything else that makes us score higher one time and lower the next. These *internal factors* which lead to intraindividual variation are related to some *external factors* such as noisy test conditions, time pressure, or the particular content or form of the test. Such external factors may heighten anxiety or distractibility and cause intraindividual variation in scores from

Figure 14.2
Representation of individual differences in reading achievement scores in a class of 24 children.

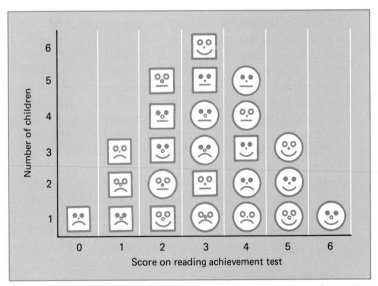

From Levin, J. R. Learner Differences: Diagnosis and Prescription. Copyright © 1977 by Holt, Rinehart and Winston. Reprinted by permission of Holt, Rinehart and Winston, CBS College Publishing.

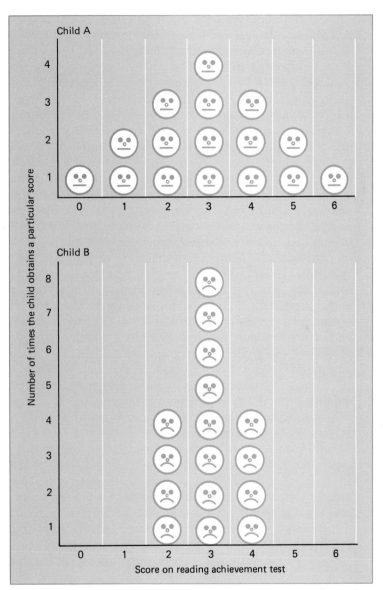

Figure 14.3
Representation of relatively large (Child A) and relatively small (Child B) intraindividual differences.

one test administration to the next. Figure 14.3 shows how round-headed Child A scores anywhere from 0 to 6 (average is 3) on 16 administrations of the reading achievement test. Round-headed Child B shows less intra-individual variability, with scores varying only from 2 to 4 (average still is 3).

Reliability and Validity

The psychometrician uses the term **reliability** to describe the accuracy or consistency of a test. Reliability coefficients range from .00 (no consistency) to 1.00 (perfect consistency).* Imagine that 100 students took a test of logical reasoning in January and then again in February. If each student produced *exactly* the same score on both occasions, we would say the test has high reliability (reliability coefficient = 1.00). If every person produced a score totally unrelated to his or her earlier score on the same test, we would say the scores are unreliable (reliability coefficient = .00). Most often, a respectable test will show a moderately high reliability coefficient, perhaps ranging from .70 to .90. More crude research tests, and many teacher-made tests, may show *test-retest reliabilities* of only .50 or so.†

Low test reliability—that is, low consistency from time A to time B—definitely is not a big asset for purposes of (a) reaching research conclusions or (b) assigning course grades. For example, let's say that Roberta Researcher wishes to determine whether student anxiety level is related to achievement in high school chemistry. If her test of anxiety (the *Nervous Student Inventory*) is unreliable due to poor test items, her anxiety scores will be inaccurate. Her research conclusion of "no relationship between anxiety and achievement" might be due entirely to worthless, inconsistent scores on the anxiety test. Similarly, if Tom Teacher makes up a social studies test which nobody can understand or which is unrelated to the stated objectives, the grades based on these unreliable test scores will be arbitrary and unfair.

Describing reliability is like dropping just one shoe; the other shoe is **validity**—the ability of a test to measure what it is supposed to measure. When Roberta Researcher created her *Nervous Student Inventory*, was she certain the test *really* measured anxiety? Are test scores related to other anxiety measures? If her test is invalid, her research conclusions could be dead wrong, because the *Nervous Student Inventory* actually might have nothing to do with student anxiety. Similarly, if Tom Teacher's social studies test doesn't really measure mastery of the material—that is, if the test is invalid—his grades again will be unfair.

Reliability and validity are related to the extent that a test that is *not* reliable is *not* valid. This is sensible enough. Tests whose scores are inconsistent, inaccurate, and generally raggedy-andy can't very well be valid

---

* Reliability coefficients are statistical correlations—e.g., between test scores in January and February (test-retest reliability). The meaning of correlation coefficients is described later in this chapter and in Chapter 19.

† Other forms of reliability are *alternate forms reliability*, the correlation between scores on Form A of a test and the same students' scores on Form B of the test; and *internal consistency reliability*, the degree to which all test items are measuring the same characteristic (e.g., anxiety or mastery of math).

measures of whatever it is they were supposed to measure. But the reverse is not necessarily true—a test that *is* reliable *may or may not* be valid. That is, the test may be measuring something with high consistency—but that something may not be what the test is supposed to measure. More abstractly: Reliability is a necessary but not sufficient condition for validity.

Generally, **identification variables** such as height, weight, eye color, or waist size are measured very reliably. The only sources of inaccuracy would be slight differences in measuring devices (most tape measures stretch) and differences between persons doing the measuring (Levin, 1977). Usually there are no validity problems, since stretching a tape around the waist or stepping on a bathroom scale are clearly valid measures of waist size or weight. However, **behavioral variables** such as anxiety, intelligence, reading achievement, and others are less accurately (reliably) measured. The individual may score differently from one assessment to the next due to internal factors (concentration, fatigue, motivation, etc.) or external factors (distractions, ambiguous test items, intimidating examiners, etc.). Measures of behavioral variables also are less valid than measures of identification variables—it simply is not easy to construct a definitely clear measure of an unclear trait (anxiety, intelligence, reading achievement, and many more described below).

Group Differences

Differential psychologists are interested in group differences as well as in individual differences. Remember the round-heads and square-heads of Figure 14.2? Did you happen to notice that the round-heads tended to score higher on the reading achievement test? (Look again.) The 24 heads in Figure 14.2 are graphed separately in Figure 14.4. Sure enough, the scores of square-heads range from 0 to 4 with a mean of 2; the scores of the round-heads show they are eggheads. The truth is, the imaginary round-heads were given two months of fictitious training with a make-believe reading program. Even after this hypothetical training, however, the two groups still overlapped in reading scores.

The notion of *overlap* is important in considering group differences. For example: School A, in a rich neighborhood, may be known to have children with high *average* academic ability; School B, in a poor neighborhood, may have children with a lower *average* academic ability. However, there inevitably will be a large overlap in academic ability, so that some rich kids from School A may have ability scores as low as any in School B, and some poor kids from School B will have ability scores as high as any in School A. With any ability or trait, the differences among students within a school always will be much larger than the differences in mean scores between two schools.

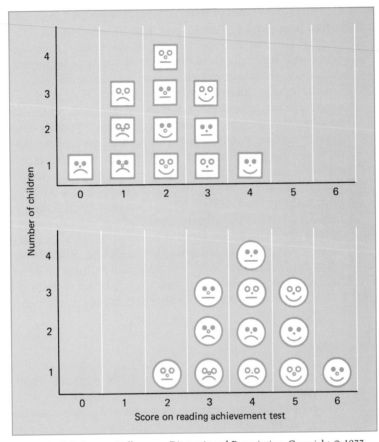

Figure 14.4
Representation of inter- and intragroup differences: distribution of reading achievement scores in a classroom consisting of 12 square-heads and 12 round-heads.

From Levin, J. R. Learner Differences: Diagnosis and Prescription. Copyright © 1977 by Holt, Rinehart and Winston. Reprinted by permission of Holt, Rinehart and Winston, CBS College Publishing.

Correlation

At the same time however, the variable of "school" (School A or B) may be related to the variable of academic ability. That is, the two factors are *correlated* so that very generally, variation in one factor (school) is associated with variation in a second factor (reading achievement).

Let's return to Levin's 24 round-heads and square-heads and look at correlation coefficients in context of individual differences. In addition to the imaginary reading achievement test, the students also took a pretend spelling test. Is there a correlation between scores on the reading test and scores on the spelling test? Figure 14.5 shows reading scores and spelling scores plotted together in a "scattergram." The position of each head reflects both a student's score on the reading test (horizontal axis) and his or her score on the spelling test (vertical axis). The tendency for the heads to be "scattered" from the lower left corner to the upper right corner means that, overall, higher reading scores are associated with higher spelling scores. Since the two measures tend to vary together, we would say there is *covariation* between the two measures—i.e., the measures correlate. A specific formula for computing correlation coefficients appears at the end of Chapter 19. For now it is enough to note that correlation coefficients range from -1.00 (a perfect negative relationship—the *more* of this, the *less* of that) to $+1.00$ (a perfect positive relationship—the *more* of this, the *more* of that). A correlation coefficient of .00 indicates no relationship. The scattergram in Figure 14.5 shows a moderate correlation of .54. The larger the correlation coefficient, the stronger the relationship between the two

Figure 14.5
Representation of the relationship between reading achievement and spelling scores in a classroom of 24 children.

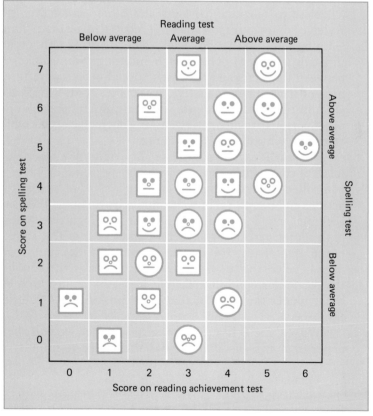

From Levin, J. R. Learner Differences: Diagnosis and Prescription. Copyright © 1977 by Holt, Rinehart and Winston. Reprinted by permission of Holt, Rinehart and Winston, CBS College Publishing.

variables—and the more accurately we can predict one score given the other.* Thus, if boys' weights correlate .90 with how much weight they can lift in their gym class, we would be able to predict any boy's weight-lifting ability pretty well by knowing his weight. However, if a correlation coefficient is only .54 (Figure 14.5), accurate prediction is difficult: The heads that scored 4 on the reading test scored 1, 3, 4, 5, and 6 on the spelling test. A correlation of .54 thus shows general trends, for example, heads that are below average in reading are likely to be below average in spelling. Specific predictions for any one head are not likely to be accurate.

INDIVIDUAL DIFFERENCES IN PERSONALITY AND COGNITIVE STYLE

There are a number of interesting personality traits and cognitive styles which educational psychologists are trying to (a) measure, (b) understand, (c) relate to biographical facts and other personality traits and cognitive styles, and, most importantly, (d) relate to classroom conditions for optimal learning and instruction. Every student brings his or her personality and thinking styles to school each morning. Sometimes there is a good fit between the traits and the instructional tasks, sometimes there is not. The present list is not exhaustive. It includes traits which have attracted some amount of attention due to potential importance. The future may produce other personality characteristics and cognitive styles which may have equal or greater educational significance.

Personality traits are personality traits. We will look at (a) anxiety, (b) locus of control (the degree to which a person feels he or she is "externally" controlled by others, chance, and fate instead of by his or her own "internal" actions and talent), (c) introversion-extroversion, (d) sensation seeking (thrill seeking), and (e) masculinity-femininity. **Cognitive styles** are habitual ways of thinking, perceiving, and sometimes acting. The emphasis is on the form of the mental activity, not the content. For example, a person may have an impulsive cognitive style which interferes with school work regardless of the particular content area. We will look at just two cognitive styles, (a) the tendency for global or analytical thinking, and (b) reflective or impulsive thinking.

With some traits it's a toss-up whether we call them cognitive styles or personality traits. In particular, the reflective-impulsive, locus-of-control,

---

* Statistically, the squared correlation coefficient produces the *coefficient of determination*, the proportion of a student's score on Test B "determined" or "fixed" by his or her score on Test A. Thus a correlation of .90 tells us that 81 percent of a person's score on Test B is determined by his or her score on Test A. The remainder is due to random (internal or external) factors.

and sensation-seeking characteristics could be considered either cognitive styles or personality traits. The reader who can accept this fuzziness probably has a high tolerance for ambiguity, another personality trait (or cognitive style).

Anxiety

Anxiety as a personality trait is a more-or-less continual state of vague worry, nervousness, or apprehension which seems to be unrelated to any specific known cause. There are large individual differences in anxiety levels. Some children and adults are absolutely unflappable—nothing seems to worry or upset them. Others seem to live in a state of borderline terror. They may appear jumpy, self-conscious, timid, high-strung, often blushing, and so on. Most of us, of course, are somewhere in the middle, generally at ease but nervous during times of stress, such as when taking exams, speaking to a group for the first time, or visiting our friendly neighborhood dentist.

Anxiety is a form of motivation. As with other forms of arousal and motivation (Chapter 9), performance (for example, on a test) is best at an intermediate level of anxiety. If the student is too calm, sleepy, and disinterested, he or she is unlikely to give his or her best performance. Conversely, extreme jitters or fear will disrupt test taking, a musical performance, or a class presentation. With test taking, high anxiety tends to blot out details of earlier learned information. Only the strongest, most dominant ideas will be remembered. With a musical performance, a good case of jitters will interfere both with the ability to concentrate and with the execution of the fine motor responses. Under moderate anxiety, the senses are sharpened, information is available, irrelevancies are "filtered out," and motor responses are quick and precise. The inverted U-shaped function relating anxiety to performance appears in Figure 14.6.

Cronbach and Snow (1977) note that anxiety may be *facilitative*—some people do their very best under lots of pressure. Most often, though, *debilitative* anxiety is the norm—performance deteriorates under high pressure.

We may speak of **trait anxiety,** an enduring personality characteristic, or **state anxiety,** a temporary and transient form of anxiety due to immediate circumstances (e.g., taking a test, speaking in front of a class, or getting drilled and extracted). Both trait and state anxiety may be measured with tests. Table 14.1 shows items similar to those used for measuring trait and state anxiety in children. Scores on the two types of anxiety test are "moderately highly" related, with correlation coefficients around .60 (Sarason, Lighthall, Davidson, Waite, and Ruebush, 1960). Table 14.2 presents a dozen items similar to those in an adult-level trait-anxiety questionnaire.

We noted that high anxiety—state or trait—will interfere with test taking (Figure 14.6). One fairly obvious implication is that test performance

Figure 14.6
Inverted U function relating performance to level of anxiety.

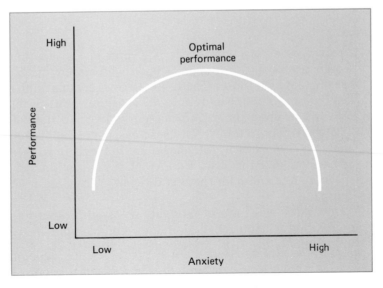

Table 14.1 Questions measuring trait and state anxiety in children

	Item	Very much	Some	Not At All
Trait anxiety	I am a shy person.	____	____	____
	I often worry about making mistakes.	____	____	____
	I worry about what other people think of me.	____	____	____
	I cry easily.	____	____	____
	I am unhappy.	____	____	____
	I often get upset at home.	____	____	____
	I am secretly afraid of things.	____	____	____
	It's hard to fall asleep.	____	____	____
	It's hard to make up my mind.	____	____	____
	I worry a lot.	____	____	____
State anxiety	*Right now* I am: Nervous	____	____	____
	Scared	____	____	____
	*Happy	____	____	____
	Mixed-up	____	____	____
	*Cheerful	____	____	____
	*Calm	____	____	____
	Jittery	____	____	____
	*Relaxed	____	____	____
	Troubled	____	____	____
	*Satisfied	____	____	____

* Negatively related to anxiety

should improve if the teacher can reduce high anxiety to a more moderate level.

A perhaps less obvious implication of the inverted U-shaped relationship between anxiety and performance is that the student very low in anxiety may need a boost in arousal level—perhaps an engaging challenge—in order to learn and perform at an optimal level.

Generally, highly anxious students do not do their best under time pressure or in unstructured learning environments. Careful instructions, practice sessions, and warmth and support tend to reduce anxiety, improve learning and performance, and make the students happier learners.

Table 14.2 Adult anxiety test items

Item	True	False
I am embarrassed easily.	——	——
I am more nervous than most people.	——	——
I wish I could be more happy.	——	——
I cry very easily.	——	——
I have more fears than most people.	——	——
I am self-conscious.	——	——
I often think I am no good at all.	——	——
I have many nightmares	——	——
I have diarrhea once a month or more.	——	——
I often blush.	——	——
I sweat easily.	——	——
I am hungry most of the time.	——	——
My feelings are easily hurt.	——	——

The keen reader may have noticed that we already have discussed some aptitude-by-treatment interactions relating to anxiety: High-anxiety students do better under reduced stress (less time pressure, less threat, more certainty in procedures, more warmth and support); low-anxiety students may be more stimulated and challenged by the reverse conditions. Matters are not this easy. Ability level also may interact with anxiety, so that low-ability students are more likely to become anxious than high-ability students. Thus, with students of any level of trait anxiety (low, medium, or high), a difficult or ambiguous task will stress the low-ability students more than students of high intellectual ability.

Regarding possible causes of anxiety, there are several explanations. Physiologically, it seems that the activation of certain brain structures releases hormones into the bloodstream which cause increased heart rate, muscle tension, trembling, sweaty palms, and dry mouth (Morris, Davis, and Hutchings, 1981). As for theory, you may recall that Freud attributed anxiety to unconscious conflicts (such as between the *id* and the *superego*) or to the Oedipus or Electra complexes (Chapter 3). Also, as noted by Erikson, psychosocial conflicts of trust vs. mistrust, industry vs. inferiority, intimacy vs. isolation, initiative vs. guilt, etc. (see Chapter 3) will produce anxiety or neurosis if they are not resolved in a healthy fashion.

In sum, student anxiety level is a very important personality trait of which the teacher should remain aware. Very high or very low anxiety will interfere with learning and performance. Time pressure, high task difficulty, or ambiguity and lack of structure will be disruptive for the highly anxious student (Dowaliby and Schumer, 1973; Grimes and Allensmith, 1961; Spielberger, O'Neil, and Hanson, 1972). Cognitive behavior modification strategies—which involve self-instructions ("Now calm down, take it easy, don't get upset.")—have been used to help students control, for example, mathematics anxiety (Brown and de Bronac-Meade, 1982; Meichenbaum, 1977).

Locus of Control

The locus-of-control concept is based on the assumption that the way we behave is influenced strongly by our perceptions of causal relationships between ourselves and our environment (Heider, 1958). As we saw in conjunction with attribution theory (Chapter 9), some individuals tend to attribute their successes and failures to such external sources as chance, "fate," the teacher, or others. These people are said to be high in **external control.** On the other hand, people high in **internal control** tend to feel that they have more control over their destinies. Their successes and failures are seen as due to their own abilities, skills, and effort (Rotter, 1966; Weiner, 1980). Typically, of course, our lives are influenced by both internal factors (abilities, interests, motivations, etc.) and external factors (freeway jams, difficult coursework, inflation, poor job market, etc.). Nonetheless, there are reliable differences in this trait of locus of control—and the person who believes academic success and success in life are due to luck, "the breaks," and biased teachers and bosses will behave much differently from the person who attributes success to one's own ability and hard work.

Items similar to those in a children's locus-of-control-test appear in Table 14.3. Adult locus-of-control test items are shown in Table 14.4. The items are not particularly mysterious—one either attributes one's fortunes to oneself or to external forces (luck, chance, the teacher, etc.).

In school, the student who is very high in external control may tend to blame everything and everybody for a bad showing: "The test was unfair"; "I didn't have time to study"; "I've been sick"; and so on. As we saw in Chapter 13, such claims may serve as defense mechanisms which protect feelings of self-worth. Importantly, if the student does not see effort as a route to success, he or she is not likely to take that route.

The student high in internal control will have the opposite attitude—he or she is personally responsible for his or her actions and generally is in control of his or her failures and successes. Since success is attributed to effort, this student is motivated to exert the effort. High school and college students high in internal control also are more likely to believe they can change "the system" through their own actions, and therefore are more

Table 14.3 Items similar to those in a children's internal-external locus of control inventory. Is it worth taking the test, or won't it do you any good anyway?

Item	Yes	or No
Are some people just born lucky?	Y	N
Do you think that parents usually listen to what their children say?	Y	N
When people are mean to you, is it for no reason at all?	Y	N
Do you believe that wishing can make things happen?	Y	N
Is it nearly impossible to change your parent's mind?	Y	N
Do you usually feel that you have little to say about what your family does?	Y	N
Do you usually feel that it is impossible to change your teacher's mind about something?	Y	N
Do you believe that teachers usually listen to what their students have to say?	Y	N
Do you believe that planning ahead makes things turn out better?	Y	N
Do you think that it doesn't pay to try hard, since things never turn out right anyway?	Y	N

likely to picket, protest, and boycott (Carlson, 1975; Lefcourt, 1972, 1976; Rotter, Chance, and Phares, 1972; Weiner, 1980).

There has been much recent research with this fascinating trait of internal-external locus of control. Some educationally relevant findings are that:

- Older children are more internal than younger children (Lefcourt, 1972).
- Middle-class children are more internal than lower-class children (Lefcourt, 1972).
- Students high in internal control are likely to be high achievers (Lefcourt, 1976), especially males (Nowicki, Duke and Crouch, 1978), and have high educational goals (Lao, 1970).
- High achievement may cause internal thinking, or internal thinking may cause high achievement (Lancaster, 1974).
- Some students will accept blame for failures (internal control) but not accept credit for successes (external control), and vice versa (Newhouse, 1974; Nowicki and Strickland, 1974).
- Internally controlled children have better self-concepts; externally controlled children are more punitive toward themselves and others (Bryant, 1974).
- Learning-disabled children are higher in external control (Chapman and Boersma, 1979).

Table 14.4 Items similar to those in an adult internal-external locus of control inventory. Pick the alternative which best describes you. Do you control your own destiny, or are you a sock in the laundromat of life?

Item

1. _____ Many misfortunes are due to bad luck.
   _____ Many misfortunes are due to the mistakes people make.

2. _____ One of the main reasons for war is that people are not interested in politics.
   _____ We will always have wars, no matter what people do to try to prevent them.

3. _____ Teachers are not unfair to students.
   _____ Students' grades are strongly influenced by accidental happenings.

4. _____ Heredity is largely responsible for personality.
   _____ Experiences are largely responsible for personality.

5. _____ The average person can influence government decisions.
   _____ There is not much the "little guy" can do about running the world.

6. _____ Getting what I want has nothing to do with luck.
   _____ Often, we might as well make decisions by flipping a coin.

7. _____ Getting to be the boss depends on luck and being in the right place first.
   _____ Promotions and success depend on ability; luck has nothing to do with it.

8. _____ I often feel I have little influence over the things that happen to me.
   _____ I cannot believe that luck or chance plays an important role in my life.

The sensitive teacher should be aware of the personality dimension of internal-external locus of control. There could be occasions when a folksy lesson on (a) personal achievement, (b) responsibility for actions, (c) positive expectations from oneself, or (d) spitting in the eye of fate and bad luck might be of value to students too high in external control.

Introversion and Extroversion

These characteristics need little explanation. Some students always seem to be the center of attention, through clowning, boisterousness, or simply outgoing friendliness or leadership talent. **Extroverts** are interested in social life and in matters outside themselves. **Introverts** tend to be the anxious, jittery types we described under the anxiety heading above. They tend to be interested in their own feelings and thoughts; they definitely do not wish to be the center of attention, as in speaking to the class or taking the lead role in the school play. Items similar to those from an adult introversion-extroversion scale appear in Table 14.5. A children's introversion-extroversion scale is very similar (Eysenck, 1965).

Table 14.5 Items similar to those in an introversion-extroversion scale. For your extroversion score, score 1 point for "Yes," except for items 3, 11 and 12, which receive 1 point for "No."

Item	Yes or No	
1. Are you generally carefree?	Y	N
2. Would you do most anything on a dare?	Y	N
3. Do you usually prefer reading to meeting people?	Y	N
4. Do you sometimes play pranks?	Y	N
5. Can you easily put life into a dull party?	Y	N
6. When shouted at, do you shout back?	Y	N
7. Do others think of you as "lively"?	Y	N
8. Are you fairly self-confident?	Y	N
9. Do you frequently long for excitement?	Y	N
10. Do you often do or say things without stopping to think?	Y	N
11. Is it difficult to enjoy yourself at a lively party?	Y	N
12. Are you quiet when you are with other people?	Y	N

Cronbach and Snow, in their book on ATI, mention that "American anxiety is a composite of British neuroticism and introversion" (1977, p. 410). This statement refers to the moderate correlations between anxiety test scores and neuroticism test scores of British pyschologist Hans Eysenck. Also, the British researchers themselves often refer to neuroticism as "anxiety" (Cronbach and Snow, 1977, p. 410). We may conclude then, that the traits of introversion, anxiety, and neuroticism are partly the same trait. Therefore, much of the above section on anxiety also would apply to the topic of introversion.

As for ATI specifically involving introversion-extroversion, two studies concluded that extroverts are more motivated by blame than by praise (Kennedy and Willcutt, 1964; Thompson and Hunnicutt, 1944). The opposite was true for introverts, who responded better to praise. In the classic Thompson and Hunnicutt study, sixth-graders were performing a simple cancellation task, such as crossing-out verbs or the letter "e." For several days the teacher wrote either "good" or "poor" on the worksheets. Sure enough, the discouraging words stimulated performance of extroverts, depressed performance by introverts. When often was heard an encouraging word, the effect was opposite: introverts improved, extroverts worsened. Most likely, the secure extroverted personality can comfortably use blame or constructive criticism to improve behavior. The shaky, defensive ego of the anxious introvert is likely to become more distraught by criticism but responds well to warmth and support.

Several studies compared college extroverts with introverts using programmed materials in either an inductive discovery approach (examples first, rule later) or a deductive approach (rule first, examples later). The training difference was mainly in the sequencing of the program content. Generally, the more stable extroverts learned better in the inductive, discovery programs than in the more structured deductive sequences. Introverts learned more in the deductive programs than with the discovery-oriented inductive materials (Lieth, 1969; Lieth and Wisdom, 1970).

One speculation was that the high drive of anxious, introverted students helped them in the passive deductive types of programs (Cronbach and Snow, 1977, p. 421). Do these conclusions hold for younger learners? Why yes, say Leith and Trown (1970). A total of 128 pupils from 11 to 13 years old worked for four weeks on programmed materials in vector algebra. Again, extroverts did better with their discovery, inductive program. Introverts did better with the deductive materials.

Generally, as with the related anxiety concept, structure and support seem to help the insecure, defensive introverted student. The extrovert can take criticism and responds positively to less structured, challenging learning tasks, such as the discovery learning procedure.

Sensation Seeking

Sensation seeking or arousal seeking (Zuckerman, 1979; Zuckerman, Kolin, Price, and Zoob, 1964) is a relatively new dimension of personality, and certainly an interesting one. In Chapter 9 we described sensation seeking in conjunction with arousal theory. Some people, high in sensation seeking, seem to be continually interested in excitement, danger, risk, and other arousal-raising thrills. According to arousal theory, they are compelled to raise their arousal level to a more personally comfortable, optimal level (Berlyne, 1961). They appear to have a high, bubbly energy level. Others seem to consciously avoid such activities. The items of Zuckerman's (1979) *Sensation Seeking Scale* speak for themselves (see Chapter 9). The high-sensation seeker is more likely to be interested in flying a plane or jumping out of one, climbing a mountain, skiing, traveling in foreign countries or exploring new cities, camping instead of moteling, and so on. The person low in sensation seeking definitely is not interested in such high excitement and risk-taking. High-sensation seekers tend to be extroverts; low-sensation seekers tend to be more introverted and, therefore, more anxious. No big surprises here.

What may be surprising are strong relationships between (a) sensation seeking and creativity and (b) sensation seeking and juvenile delinquency. Davis (1975, 1981) and Farley (1980) have confirmed that creative college students tend to score high in sensation seeking. In fact, one study (Davis, Peterson, and Farley, 1973) showed the *Sensation Seeking Scale* (SSS) to be a better predictor of creativity than two creativity tests. Chapter 16 will summarize some reliable characteristics of the creative personality, which will include a high energy level, risk taking, spontaneity, curiosity, and self-confidence—some of the same traits measured by the SSS.

Interestingly, juvenile delinquents also score high in sensation seeking (Farley, 1980). It seems that stealing hubcaps, fighting, getting high, breaking windows, burglary, and assaulting teachers are not really the cup of tea for anxious, introverted, low-sensation seekers. High-sensation seekers also are more likely to use drugs (Kaestner, Rosen, and Appel, 1977) and alcohol (Segal and Merenda, 1975). Motivation psychologist Farley (1973, 1980; Farley and Sewell, 1976) proposed that the sensation-seeking tendencies of delinquents could be rechanneled into constructive, creative outlets—a new national resource!

Sensation seeking, then, correlates positively with energy level, creativity, delinquency, drug and alcohol use, extroversion, and absence of anxiety. The teacher will see students who are more energetic and who seem to need more excitement than quiet, sensation-avoiding students. The energy clearly must be directed into acceptable outlets, such as creative activities, or it will appear in unacceptable forms—noise, attention getting, disruptiveness, or perhaps even law breaking.

Masculinity, Femininity, and Androgyny

An even newer concept is Bem's (1974, 1975) concept of the **androgynous personality.** Traditionally we think of masculinity and femininity as opposite ends of a continuum, with most males at one end and most females at the other. Not so, says Bem. Masculinity and femininity should be seen as independent dimensions of personality. Thus a person could be high on both, low on both, or high on one and low on the other. According to Bem, the male who strongly accepts the stereotyped role of the he-man macho male is not particularly well-adjusted. He won't accept feminine interests or behaviors such as knitting or even petting a kitten. The macho male also tends to be less intelligent and less creative. Ditto for the too-feminine female whose blanket acceptance of the female social role will not permit masculine attitudes or behaviors. She also tends to be less intelligent, less creative, and more anxious—insecure about herself and her "proper" social role.

Enter the hero: The Androgynous Person, well-adjusted, self-accepting, intelligent, creative, and able to leap short buildings with no help at all. The androgynous person is willing to accept both masculine and feminine traits and behavior patterns. He might be a football player, but he is willing to play a flute, sew on a button or, like Rosey Grier of the Los Angeles Rams, do nice needlepoint. Similarly, in addition to feminine characteristics, the androgynous female will accept traditionally masculine traits and

Table 14.6 Sample items from the Bem Psychological Androgyny Scale.

Masculine Items	Feminine Items
Self-reliant	Yielding
Independent	Cheerful
Athletic	Shy
Strong personality	Affectionate
Has leadership abilities	Sensitive to the needs of others

Reproduced by special permission of the publisher, Consulting Psychologists Press, Inc., from the *Bem Sex Role Inventory*, by Dr. Sandra Bem, copyright © 1978.

behaviors—aggressiveness, career orientation and an interest in sports. Table 14.6 presents part of Bem's androgyny scale. How would you score? How would General Patton have scored? How would Cinderella score?

We should note that there are important cultural and socioeconomic factors influencing androgyny or the lack of it. For example, in many Arab and Spanish-speaking countries, adherence to masculine and feminine sex roles is strongly reinforced. Also, members of lower SES groups tend to be more rigid in sex-role learning and acceptance.

At present there appear to be no obvious educational implications of a student's sex role—masculine, feminine or androgynous—except as these might relate to mental health. The evidence thus far suggests that, in Western society, the macho male or too-feminine female may be unreasonably committed to the traditional social role. The androgynous personality, on the other hand, seems to be more secure and better adjusted.

Field Dependent Thinking and Field Independent Thinking

The cognitive styles of **field-dependent** thinking and **field-independent** thinking make up one of the most researched characteristics in psychological and educational literature (see Witkin, Moore, Goodenough, and Cox, 1977). This dimension sometimes is called *global* vs. *analytical thinking*, or else *field articulation*. Field dependence or field independence is reflected in how people perceive, in their styles of thinking, their sociability, their choice of careers—and how they interact in the classroom.

Individuals differ greatly in their ability to perceive analytically—to break down or "articulate" a complex perceptual field into component parts. The field-dependent person, or global thinker, tends to be less analytical, less attentive to detail. The perceptual field is seen as an integrated whole which resists being taken apart. The field-independent or analytical thinker more easily separates (articulates) a complex whole into its parts. He or she is less influenced by the initial structure and more easily makes judgments independent of the immediate perceptual field. Everyone is located at some point on a continuum from high field dependence to high field independence, with most of us somewhere in the middle. There are not just two distinct classes of people, although the following discussion sometimes may sound that way.

Tests of field dependence and field independence. The classic tests of field dependence and field independence should help make the distinction between them more clear. With the rod-and-frame test, a rotatable rod is mounted in the center of an also rotatable frame. Both are tilted at strange angles (see Figure 14.7). The apparatus usually is mounted inside a barrel-shaped container to remove all vertical and horizontal visual cues. The person's task is to judge when the rod is rotated to a perfect vertical position—despite the conflicting orientation of the frame. The more field-independent person successfully separates the part (rod) from the field (frame) and adjusts the rod close to a perfect vertical, using body orientation cues. The field-dependent person is strongly influenced by the frame and has difficulty orienting the rod to a true vertical position.

A similar situation is the body adjustment test. A small room contains a chair, and the room and chair may be tilted independently. The task is

Figure 14.7
Rod-and-frame test. With no external or horizontal cues, the subject attempts to align the rod to a perfect vertical, ignoring the distracting frame.

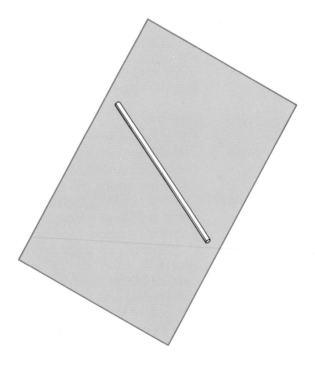

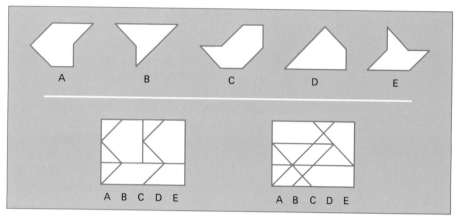

Figure 14.8
Sample item from the Hidden Figures Test. Which one of the simple figures is embedded in which one of the complex figures?

to adjust the chair to an upright position, ignoring the conflicting room (field). Some astonishingly field-dependent persons will neatly align the chair with the room even at an angle of 35 degrees, and calmly agree, "This is the way I sit when I eat dinner," or, "This is the way I sit in class" (Witkin, Moore, Goodenough, and Cox, 1977). These people usually do better with their eyes shut. The more field-independent types will adjust the chair close to a perfect upright with eyes open.

A third task, this time a paper-and-pencil one, is the Hidden Figures Test (HFT). The person is given a series of complex figures and must locate simple figures embedded in the complex figures (see Figure 14.8). While it appears to be a drastically different sort of challenge, the HFT, like the rod-and-frame test and the body adjustment test, requires the individual to perceptually separate the individual parts from the complex whole. Thus the field-dependent or global thinker will take longer to complete the HFT, just as he or she tended to align the rod with the tilted frame and the chair with the tilted room. However, with all three tasks the field-independent thinker tends to analyze details, to perceive objects as discrete from their background, and to generally analyze and impose structure.

Traits of field-dependent and field-independent persons. The field-dependent person tends to be more socially oriented, a trait which shows up in an interesting variety of circumstances. First, the dependent person is "dependent" on social cues for his or her own self-definition. That is, the self-concept of the field-dependent person is heavily influenced by cues and feedback from others. The field dependent person is thus more affected by praise or blame (Ferrell, 1971). According to Witkin, *et al.* (1977), field-dependent people develop a keen "social radar" for detecting thoughts and attitudes. For one thing, they tend to look at faces, which is a very good way to detect feelings. Under conditions of ambiguity, they depend more on the opinions of others than do the field-independent types; that is, they may be quicker to conform (see Inset 14.1).

In addition to being sensitive to social cues and influenced by the attitudes and judgments of others, field-dependent people tend to like people and to like being with people. Apparently, people also like them. Compared with field independents, field dependents have been perceived as more considerate, tactful, warm, affectionate, and socially outgoing (Witkin, et al., 1977). The field independent person, on the other hand, may be perceived as more socially insensitive, cold, distant, impersonal, and—of course—independent.

It's not too surprising to find that field-dependent students lean toward college majors and careers that are relatively nonanalytical and people oriented—for example, elementary education, social work, counseling, nursing, teaching in the social sciences, selling, personnel work, school administration, and the ministry. On the other hand, field-independent students lean toward majors and careers which permit use of those analytical, structuring talents: mathematics, physics, chemistry, biology, engineering, art, architecture, medicine, and teaching mathematics or science.

INSET 14.1

THE AUTOKINETIC EFFECT

You may have noticed how a solitary evening star appears to drift about in the sky. A fixed point of light in a darkened room also seems unable to hold still. This is the *autokinetic* effect, a perceptual phenomenon which can be influenced by suggestions from others.

Linton (1952) permitted college students to write down their estimates of how far a light (which was actually stationary) moved in each of a series of trials. Following this, the experimenter's confederate by pre-arrangement verbally gave very large estimates of the light movement. Sure enough, field-dependent subjects were more influenced by the stooge. They showed larger increases in their judgments than did the field-independent subjects. This study showed field-dependent college students to be more readily influenced by others. It also showed that you can't always believe experimental psychologists.

Classroom effects of field dependence and field independence. The general tendency of field-independent persons to analyze and impose structure gives them an advantage over the field-dependent learner in unstructured learning situations (Davis and Frank, 1979; Frank and Davis, 1982). When instructional material is not clearly organized, field-dependent thinkers need more explicit instructions—for example, definite learning objectives or clear problem-solving instructions. They may be less able to analyze and synthesize (Frank and Davis, 1982).

Now, it is not only students who differ in field dependence-independence; teachers do also. The socially oriented field-dependent teacher tends to favor interaction with students, as in class discussions. The more impersonal, field-independent teachers tend to prefer lecture or discovery methods (Wu, 1968). Also, the field-independent teacher is more likely to punish students or to criticize students who perform below capacity (Witkin, *et al.*, 1977). The field-dependent teacher, who relies on social feedback for his or her own self-concept, is less likely to antagonize those whose feelings and opinions are so valuable.

It's important to note that both field-dependent and field-independent teachers can be good, effective teachers, although their teaching styles will differ. The socially oriented field-dependent teacher will use discussion and personal conversation to develop rapport and a warm learning environment. The field-independent teacher may be less student centered, but may be strong in organizing learning experiences and in guiding student learning.

Finally, a group of interesting findings show that when the cognitive style of the teacher does not *match* the cognitive style of the student, (a) the teacher and the student may like each other less (DiStefano, 1970; Gaeta, 1977), (b) the teacher may give lower grades (James, 1973; Saracho, 1982); and (c) students learn less (Packer and Bain, 1978).

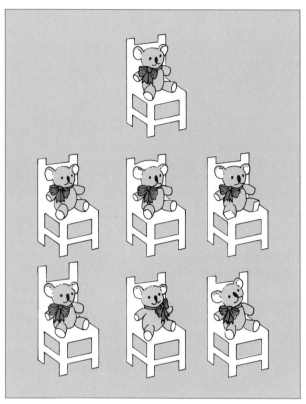

Figure 14.9
Sample item for the Matching Familiar Figures Test. Which of the six lower figures matches the top "standard" figure?

From Kagan, J., B. Rosman, D. Day, J. Albert, and W. Phillips, Information processing in the child: Significance of analytic and reflective attitudes. *Psychological Monographs* **78**, 1 (Whole No. 578), 1964. Copyright © by the American Psychological Association. Reproduced by permission of the first author and the publisher.

Impulsivity and Reflectivity

Have you noticed how some people generally are more quick to react and therefore more likely to make mistakes? Others respond more thoughtfully, taking more time but making fewer errors. The first type thinks impulsively, and the second type thinks reflectively. The main test of **impulsivity-reflectivity** is Kagan's (1965; Kagan, Rosman, Day, Albert, and Phillips, 1964) *Matching Familiar figures* (MFF) Test (Figure 14.9). The subject simply chooses which of several familiar figures (in this case, a teddy bear in a chair) matches the "standard." Subjects who respond faster and make more errors than the average are classified as impulsive. Reflectives both respond slower and make fewer errors than the average.

We should note that reflectiveness probably is related to analytical thinking, which is related to field independence. That is, the reflective

INSET 14.2

DOES REFLECTIVENESS
RUB OFF?

Using the *Matching Familiar Figures Test* (MFF), Yando and Kagan (1968) identified 10 first-grade teachers as impulsive and 10 as reflective. A total of 160 first graders took the MFF in the early fall and again in the late spring. Does the teacher's style influence the students' style? Apparently so, since students of reflective teachers slowed down their spring response times much more than students of impulsive teachers. Unfortunately, the error scores did not improve. This leaves us somewhere, but it's difficult to tell where.

person who takes more time before responding probably is analyzing the details and structure of the task, a habit which should reduce mistakes.

Research on impulsivity-reflectivity has shown that reflective children perform better on tasks of inductive reasoning (Kagan, Pearson, and Welch, 1966) and memory (Kagan, 1966). Of most importance, reflectives also do better in general school work (Messer, 1970). One interesting finding is that although creative children tend to be reflective, creative adolescents and adults tend to be more spontaneous and impulsive.

It would seem that accuracy and therefore reflectiveness is more desirable than making mistakes through impulsiveness. Appropriately enough, researchers have explored several strategies for training habits of reflective thinking. There are at least four approaches, each quite different from the others. With the first strategy, impulsive students simply are required to wait 10 or 15 seconds before responding. This approach seems to force those who think impulsively to think a little longer and to inhibit their impulsiveness. With a second approach, impulsive students observe how a model correctly takes time to analyze and respond to the task (Debus, 1970; Ridberg, Park, and Hetherington, 1971). Many impulsives in these studies did imitate the appropriate reflective behavior.

With a third approach, experimenters have tried to improve the "detail scanning" and "pattern comparison" habits of impulsive children (Butter, 1979; Egeland, 1974). Butter, for example, used the MFF test itself to train nine-year-old boys to make careful comparisons among pairs of alternatives: "We want to find the difference between these two designs first and then go back to look at the one on top to see which one is more like it." Finally, with the fourth strategy, Meichenbaum and Goodman (1971) used a clinical self-instructional approach—they taught impulsive children to tell themselves to slow down. While working math problems, the children were given visual reminder cards containing such statements as, "Stop and listen," "Look and think," "Think before answering," and "How did I do?" Responding slowed and accuracy improved.

The cognitive styles of impulsivity and reflectivity are indeed important. In many cases, it seems that students' error-producing impulsiveness may be at least partly curable.

TO IMPROVE
YOUR TEACHING

No one has to tell you that people are different and that your future students will be different. In fact, most chapters in this book deal with individual differences in one way or another. The chapters on personality and moral development, affective learning, motivation, creativity, intelligence, giftedness, and the disadvantaged learner all focus on variations in important learner characteristics. Other chapters on behavior modification, programmed learning, mainstreaming, instructional theory, teaching methods, and strategies for individualizing also emphasize different strokes for different folks. This chapter has tried (a) to explain how an educational psychologist views individual differences and (b) to summarize some important personality and cognitive style traits that have educational implications.

At the very least, an understanding of the individual differences described in this chapter and others will help you understand what makes your students tick. You will be a more informed professional, and this information will help you to make more sophisticated judgments about students' learning problems and possible remedies. For example, ATI research, while admittedly still in a primitive stage of matching thinking styles with ideal teaching methods, clearly recommends that students who are anxious, introverted, or low in ability will function best in structured learning situations. For them, the absence of structure and direction may be disturbing.

A sensitivity to the locus-of-control trait might enable you to perform a fine service for "external" students who feel they have no control over their academic successes or their outside lives. As we saw in Chapter 13, part of humanistic education includes strengthening students' feelings of personal responsibility. They must learn that with effort they can achieve both in school and in the real world. They must not continue to blame the

teacher, the school, bad luck, or bad relatives for their shortcomings. Internal thinking is necessary for high achievement.

An awareness of reflectivity-impulsivity also will permit you to improve students' habits of thinking and responding. We reviewed several strategies which could induce an impulsive student to slow down and reduce mistakes: modeling the correct "conceptual tempo," teaching students to instruct themselves to slow down, or with some tasks perhaps teaching scanning and comparison strategies. A habit of reflective thinking is clearly more adaptive in school and in the real world than a habit of error-producing impulsiveness.

The sensation-seeking trait is another important individual difference. High sensation seekers can cause you and themselves plenty of trouble if their energies are not directed into proper channels—perhaps athletics, independent projects, creative outlets, leadership roles, or some other energy-consuming activities.

As for field dependence and field independence, both thinking styles are adaptive—the world has plenty of room for both, and there is no need to try to change this student thinking style. You should, however, be aware of your own and your students' tendencies toward field dependence or field independence. According to research, socially oriented field-dependent teachers favor close interactive teaching methods and are less likely to be punitive than the more impersonal and analytic field independent teachers. Also, field-dependent students are more affected by criticism from the teacher, prefer socially oriented coursework and careers, and are more conforming. It also seems that when the teacher's field dependence-independence differs from the cognitive style of the student, they may not get along well.

You will see these personality and cognitive style traits in your students. You should be ready to recognize them, understand them, and respond to them appropriately.

SUMMARY

People, including students, differ from each other in any physical or psychological trait that anyone has ever cared to measure.

Aptitude-by-treatment interaction (ATI) research attempts to coordinate individual differences (aptitudes) with particular instructional conditions (treatments). With the *Capitalization Model*, the teacher capitalizes on the student's particular strengths, personality, or preferred learning style. With the *Compensation Model*, the student's weakness is catered to. With the *Remediation Model*, the weakness in knowledge or skill is remediated.

The psychometrician is interested in interindividual differences and intraindividual differences. Internal factors which cause intraindividual variation (e.g., changes in motivation or concentration) may be related to external factors (e.g., time pressure or distractions).

Test-retest reliability refers to the consistency of test scores from one administration to a second administration. Reliability coefficients range from .00 (no consistency) to 1.00 (perfect consistency). Test validity, with coefficients also varying from .00 to 1.00, describes the ability of a test to measure what it is supposed to measure.

The measurement of identification (physical) variables is usually reliable and valid. The measurement of behavioral variables often suffers from questionable reliability and validity.

When two variables are related, such as IQ scores and grades, we say the factors are "correlated" or there is "covariation" between the two measures.

There are large differences in anxiety level. As a general rule, learning and performance are optimal at an intermediate anxiety level. The concept of *facilitative* anxiety means that some students perform best under high stress, which is *debilitative* for most of us. *Trait anxiety* is an enduring personality characteristic; *state anxiety* is a temporary condition due to immediate circumstances. ATI research suggests that high-anxiety students perform best under reduced stress, while low-anxiety students may need a challenge (e.g., time pressure, a difficult or uncertain task) for optimum performance.

With locus of control, students high in external control attribute their successes and failures to external factors: chance, luck, the teacher, or bad weather. Students high in internal control feel they have control over, and responsibility for, their successes and failures. Internal control is necessary for high achievement.

Introversion/extroversion is another common dimension of personality. Research suggests that extroverts can comfortably use blame or criticism to improve their performance. Introverts, easily upset by criticism, may respond better to praise. Introverts, who also tend to be high in anxiety, need structure in school learning.

Students also differ greatly in sensation-seeking tendencies. High-sensation seekers tend to be more creative. Juvenile delinquents also tend to be high-sensation seekers. Low-sensation seekers tend to be more anxious and more introverted.

Androgyny is the acceptance of both masculine and feminine characteristics. The androgynous person is usually better adjusted, more intelligent, more creative, less anxious, and more self-accepting than the he-man male or the too-feminine female, both of whom accept the cultural sex-role stereotype.

Field independent (analytic) thinkers tend to analyze a complex "perceptual field" into its component parts. Field dependent (global) thinkers are less attentive to detail, perceiving the "field" as a unified, integrated whole. The three research instruments for measuring field independence-dependence are the rod-and-frame test, the body adjustment test and the hidden (embedded) figures test. The field-dependent person is more socially oriented and more likely to choose a people-related career. The field-independent thinker is less social, more likely to choose a career which will use analytic talents.

Field-dependent teachers tend to favor interaction with students, as in discussion methods. Field-independent teachers may favor impersonal lectures or discovery methods. The field independent teacher also is quicker to criticize or use other punishment. Some research has shown that teachers and students like one another better if they match in field dependence or independence.

Finally, students may differ in impulsivity and reflectivity. Impulsives respond too fast and make errors; reflectives take more time and make fewer errors. Research has suggested that the desirable reflectiveness tendency probably can be taught. Four strategies were: (a) requiring a 10 or 15 second delay before the student can respond, (b) modeling reflective behavior, (c) training students in scanning and comparing, and (d) teaching students to self-instruct.

TOPICS FOR THOUGHT AND DISCUSSION

1. Can you think of your own past teachers who were high in anxiety and/or introversion? What were the effects on (a) teaching and (b) interacting with students?
2. Can you think of strategies for improving students' (a) internal control, (b) reflectiveness, or (c) androgyny?
3. What might be some outlets for high school students who are high-sensation seekers? What about elementary level students?
4. Should a field-dependent person become romantically involved with a field-independent person? Why or why not?

PROJECTS

1. When student teaching, practice rating students on anxiety, internal-external locus of control, introversion-extroversion, sensation seeking, androgyny, field dependence-independence, and reflectivity-impulsivity. Which traits seem to "go together"?
2. When student teaching or visiting a school, ask one or two teachers how they deal with (a) anxious, introverted students, (b) extroverted sensation seekers, (c) impulsive students, or (d) external students who blame everybody and everything except themselves.

RECOMMENDED READING

Bem, S. L. The measurement of psychological androgyny. *Journal of Consulting and Clinical Psychology* **42,** 1974, 155–162.

Kagan, J., B. L. Rosman, D. Day, J. A. Albert, and W. Phillips. Information processing in the child: significance of analytic and reflective attitudes. *Psychological Monographs* **78,** (1, Whole No. 578), 1964.

Lefcourt, H. M. *Locus of control: Current trends in research and theory.* Hillsdale, N.J.: Lawrence Erlbaum, 1976.

Levin, J. R. *Learner differences: Diagnosis and prescription.* New York: Holt, Rinehart & Winston, 1977.

Spielberger, C. D. (ed.). *Anxiety and behavior.* New York: Academic Press, 1966.

Tyler, L. E. *The psychology of human differences,* third edition. New York: Appleton, 1965.

Witkin, H. A., C. A. Moore, D. R. Goodenough, and P. W. Cox. Field-dependent and field-independent cognitive styles and their educational implications. *Review of Educational Research* **47,** 1977, 1–64.

Zuckerman, M. *Sensation seeking: Beyond the optimal level of arousal.* Hillsdale, N.J.: Lawrence Erlbaum, 1979,

Intelligence

15

ABOUT INTELLIGENCE

What Is Intelligence?

We all have a personal conception of what intelligence is—the ability to learn quickly, solve problems, understand complex and abstract issues, and generally behave in a reasonable, rational, and purposeful manner. Definitions by noted scholars probably will not improve your present conception very much.

David Wechsler designed the *Wechsler Intelligence Scale for Children—Revised* (WISC-R; Wechsler, 1974) and the *Wechsler Adult Intelligence Scale* (WAIS; Wechsler, 1955), which are among the most widely used individually administered intelligence tests. He defines intelligence as "... the aggregate or global capacity of the individual to act purposefully, to think rationally, and to deal effectively with his environment."

Lewis Terman—who in 1916 helped produce the first American intelligence test, based on the French Binet tests (described later in this chapter)—defined intelligence simply as the ability to carry on abstract thinking.

In a book entitled *The Meaning of Intelligence*, Stoddard (1943) sifted through 40 years of literature and put together a definition which includes most everything:

> *Intelligence is the ability to undertake activities that are characterized by (1) difficulty, (2) complexity, (3) abstractness, (4) economy, (5) adaptiveness to a goal, (6) social value, and (7) the emergence of originals, and to maintain such activities under conditions that demand concentration of energy and a resistance to emotional forces.*

Some professors and text writers have thrown up their hands and accepted Boring's (1923) early and circular definition: Intelligence is "what intelligence tests test." We would not define *running ability* as "what a stop watch measures" or *rain* as "what a rain gauge measures." Boring's definition tells us only that intelligence is difficult to define. As we will shortly see, both the *number* of intellectual abilities and the *nature* of those abilities remain in hot dispute into the 1980s (see Carroll and Maxwell, 1979, for a recent review; also Sternberg, 1980).

The IQ-Testing Rebellion

Throughout the 1970s and continuing into the 1980s, intelligence testing in the schools has become less and less popular. In fact, some school systems have banned the routine, mass administration of intelligence tests entirely. The question was simply whether intelligence testing was doing more harm than good.

As we saw in Chapter 2, the IQ-testing rebellion was partly, if not entirely, initiated by the highly publicized Rosenthal and Jacobson (1968) research which seemed to show that teacher expectations can become self-fulfilling prophecies.* That is, the biased teacher may be quite willing to accept effortless and poorly done assignments because, after all, the low IQ score indicates that the student is not intelligent enough to do any better. The teacher's low expectations not only lower the student's level of academic achievement, they also lower the student's self-esteem and level of aspirations. Students easily pick up the teacher's attitudes and begin to think of themselves as stupid and incapable (Braun, 1976).

Now, in the 1930s, 1940s and 1950s tracking or ability grouping was common. The noble thought was that instruction could be tailored to student capabilities—classes of fast students could go faster, classes of slow students could go slower. Naturally, intelligence tests were needed to help decide who was fast and who was slow. The Rosenthal and Jacobson research, valid or not, served to confirm the suspicions of some educators and public officials that the not-so-noble outcome of tracking was a near-permanent branding of some students as village idiots (Kamin, 1975). It was not surprising that a great many school systems eliminated intelligence testing and tracking almost entirely.

Contemporary Uses of Intelligence Testing

Presently, and even in school systems banning the wide-scale administration of intelligence tests, there are several situations in which intelligence testing remains common and potentially valuable. First, as we will see in Chapter 17, there is a strong resurgence of interest in educating the gifted. Whatever the grade level, intelligence testing plays a central role in most such programs in the selection of intellectually gifted students. Second, intelligence tests are frequently used by school psychologists who are attempting to understand the problems, anxieties, and frustrations of a student who might be learning-disabled, underachieving, emotionally disturbed, disruptive, possibly retarded, and so on (Chapter 18). The tests thus help select students for special education programs or, in some cases, for institutionalization. Third, intelligence tests are used for student counseling, especially in helping students select educational programs and even careers. Finally, there are preschool intelligence tests, most notably the *McCarthy Scales of Children's Abilities* (McCarthy, 1972) and the *Wechsler Preschool and Primary Scale of Intelligence* (Wechsler, 1967), which school psychologists profitably use to assess development and maturational factors important for school success in the primary grades (Salvia and Yesseldyke, 1978).

---

* Even though the Rosenthal and Jacobson research has been partially (some say entirely) discredited, the reaction of the public and many school administrators in many cities was to ban intelligence testing.

A Brief
History of
Intelligence
Testing:
Galton and
Binet

Historically, it was the Englishman Sir Francis Galton, a younger cousin to Charles Darwin, who is credited with the earliest significant research and writing devoted to intelligence and intelligence testing. In the late 1800s, Galton, considered the father of intelligence testing, believed that intelligence was related to the keenness of ones' sensory equipment— vision, audition, reaction time, etc. His intelligence testing efforts therefore involved, for example, tests of visual and auditory acuity, reaction time, tactile sensitivity, and so on. Importantly, having been highly impressed by cousin Charles' *Origin of Species*, Galton reasoned that evolution would favor persons with keen senses. Therefore, he concluded that one's sensory ability—intelligence—was due to natural selection and heredity. The hereditary basis of intelligence seemed to be confirmed by his observations, reported in his most famous book *Hereditary Genius* (Galton, 1869), that distinguished men often appeared in succeeding generations of distinguished families. Galton initially overlooked the fact that members of distinguished, aristocratic families also inherit a superior environment, wealth, privilege, and opportunity—incidentals which make it much easier to become distinguished.

Galton also is noted for conducting the first twin studies aimed at distinguishing genetic from environmental (learned) components of intelligence (described later). Incidentally, Galton himself was reading at age two and one-half and writing well at age four. Terman (1917) estimated Galton's IQ at 200 on the basis of the tasks Galton could perform at particular ages.

Modern intelligence tests, however, had their roots in Paris in the 1890s. Alfred Binet, aided by Theophile Simon, was hired by government officials in Paris to devise a test to identify which (dull) children would not benefit from regular classes, and therefore would be placed in special classes to receive special training. Someone had perceptively noticed that teachers' judgments of student ability were biased by such traits as docility, neatness, social skills, and others. Some children were placed in schools for the retarded because they were too quiet, too aggressive, or had problems with speech, hearing or vision. A direct test of intelligence was badly needed.

Binet tried out a number of tests that failed. It seems that normal students and dull students were *not* particularly different in (a) hand squeezing strength, (b) hand speed in moving 50 centimeters (almost 20 inches), (c) the amount of pressure on the forehead which causes pain, (d) detecting differences in hand-held weights, or (e) reaction time to sounds or in naming colors. But when he turned to measuring the ability to attend, memory, judgment, reasoning, and comprehension, Binet began to get results. The tests would separate children judged by teachers to differ in intelligence.

One of Binet's significant contributions was the notion of **mental age—** the concept that children grow in intelligence, and that any given child may be intellectually at the proper stage for his or her years or may be measurably ahead or behind. A related notion is that at any given age level, children who learn the most do so partly because of greater intelligence.

Following on the heels of Binet's work, Lewis Terman supervised the modification and Americanization of the Binet-Simon tests, producing in 1916 the grandfather of all American intelligence tests, the *Stanford-Binet Intelligence Scale* (described below). It was revised in 1937 and again in 1960. In 1972 new norms were published, based on a sample of 2100 children, including black children and Spanish-surnamed children. The test itself remained almost identical to the 1960 edition.

INTELLECTUAL ABILITIES: WHAT KINDS AND HOW MANY?

We noted at the outset of this chapter that there remains a lively dispute regarding both the *nature* and the *number* of basic intellectual abilities (see, for example, Carroll and Maxwell, 1979; Sternberg, 1980). The Stanford-Binet test produces a single intelligence quotient (IQ) score, reflecting a basic, general, intellectual ability. Other positions described in this section argue for two, five, 120, or an unknown number of "specific abilities" or "components of intelligence."

"g" Factor and "s" Factors and Primary Mental Abilities In his two-factor theory of intelligence, Charles Spearman argued in 1927 for a **"g" factor** (general intelligence) plus many **"s"** (specific) **factors.** Spearman assumed that each task we perform requires abilities that are specific to that particular task. The "g" factor permeates all intellectual tasks; it is the general ability that is common to all specific tasks.

L. L. Thurstone (1938) examined interrelationships of ability tests and concluded that there was not just one single general ability. He devised Thurstone's *Primary Mental Abilities* (PMA) test battery (T. G. Thurstone, 1963; Thurstone and Thurstone, 1962) which measured five primary mental abilities:

1. *Verbal meaning:* The ability to understand ideas expressed in words. Measured by picture vocabulary items at young age levels, verbal vocabulary at higher levels.
2. *Number facility:* The ability to work with numbers and quantitative problems rapidly and accurately.
3. *Reasoning:* The ability to solve logical problems.
4. *Perceptual speed:* The ability to recognize differences and similarities between objects and symbols quickly and accurately.
5. *Spatial relations:* The ability to visualize objects and figures rotated in space.

The Thurstone model of primary abilities emphasizes the simple truth that some students will be better scholars with verbal materials and concepts, others are strong in quantitative reasoning (but may not be very articulate), while still others might have strengths in reasoning, perceptual speed, or spatial relations. The reader who is high in spatial relations and reasoning may wish to visualize a single person's profile of ability scores, with a different score for each primary ability.

The discrepancy between Spearman's "g" and "s" approach and Thurstone's five primary mental abilities is not difficult to resolve if we insert one level of abilities between Spearman's "g" and "s" levels. That is, we may think of *groups* or *classes* of specific abilities, such as verbal abilities (reading, vocabulary, comprehension, etc.), mathematical abilities (computational skills, mathematical reasoning, etc.), spatial abilities (visualizing rotations of objects, recognizing similarities and differences, etc.), and so forth. Thurstone's Five primary mental abilities thus may be viewed as groups of Spearman's "s" abilities. Some scholars strongly endorse three levels of abilities or intellectual factors: A general factor, group (or class) factors, and specific factors (Sternberg, 1980).

Guilford's Structure of Intellect Model

If Thurstone's five different abilities are not enough, how about 120? J. Paul Guilford argues for the existence of 120 separate intellectual abilities. These are made up of all possible combinations of four Contents, five Operations, and six Products ($4 \times 5 \times 6 = 120$). Guilford's **Structure-of-Intellect** model is shown in Figure 15.1.

Figure 15.1
J. P. Guilford's Structure-of-Intellect model.

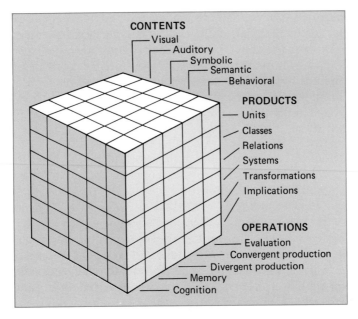

CONTENTS
— Visual
— Auditory
— Symbolic
— Semantic
— Behavioral

PRODUCTS
— Units
— Classes
— Relations
— Systems
— Transformations
— Implications

OPERATIONS
— Evaluation
— Convergent production
— Divergent production
— Memory
— Cognition

Operations are intellectual activities or processes—what a person does with information. Guilford's five cognitive operations include *cognition* (discovery, recognition, awareness, comprehension), *memory*, *divergent production* (generation of a variety and quantity of ideas), *convergent production* (reaching a single best solution), and *evaluation*.

Contents refers to the types of information upon which the operations are performed. Guilford's four contents are *figural* (visual, spatial), *symbolic* (e.g., letters, numbers, words, musical or mathematical notations), *semantic* (especially word meanings, but also picture meanings), and *behavioral* (nonverbal human interactions). Finally, Guilford's **Products** refers to the form in which the information may occur: *units, classes, relations, systems, transformations,* and *implications.* This products dimension of the model is hierarchical in the sense that units combine into classes, classes form relations, relations make up systems, and so on. The scholarly reader interested in the two or three tests that define each of the 120 factors in the *Structure of Intellect* model can see Guilford (1967, 1977).

Crystallized and Fluid Intelligence

Another two-part conception of intelligence is Cattel's (1963, 1971; Horn and Cattel, 1966, 1967; Horn, 1978, 1979) distinction between **crystallized and fluid intelligence.** Crystallized intelligence is mainly one's accumulated store of knowledge and experiences. It is measured mainly by tests of vocabulary and information. Crystallized intelligence naturally increases over the life span as we gain knowledge and experience, although there is a not-surprising decline in old age. Fluid intelligence is one's ability to reason, discriminate, and think abstractly. Consequently, this form of intelligence is measured by tests of reasoning and abstract thinking, such as the *Raven's Progressive Matrices* (Raven, 1958). Fluid abilities are said to peak somewhere between the ages of 18 and 38.

One interesting recent line of research has been an effort to train fluid intelligence—reasoning and abstract thinking—with elderly populatioons (Labouvie-Vief and Gonda, 1976; Panicucci and Labouvie-Vief, 1975; Plemons, Willis, and Baltes, 1978; Willis, Blieszner, and Baltes, 1978). The usual strategy has been to train these subjects in problem-solving rules and logical thinking strategies using problems similar to those on tests of fluid intelligence. The Labouvie-Vief and Gonda (1976) procedure, however, was to teach their elderly subjects to use self-instruction ("I'll keep calm") to control anxiety during testing. It worked.

Incidentally, while many psychologists and nonpsychologists glibly attribute lowered IQ scores in the elderly to "mental deterioration" (senility), it is difficult to determine what portion of the lowered IQ scores is due to an actual lowered intellectual ability and what proportion is due to lowered test-taking motivation, debilitative test anxiety, or sensory or even motor impairment (vision, hearing, writing, speaking, etc.).

Componential Theory of Intelligence

The most recent addition to the intelligence-theory family is the **componential** theory of intelligence (Pelligrino and Glazer, 1979; Sternberg, 1980, 1981). The approach is most closely related to information processing theory (Chapters 7, 12); in fact, the authors speak of "processes" instead of "abilities." According to Sternberg (1980), components of intelligence can be classified according to *function* (what the component does) and *level* (whether the componemt has a high-level planning and decision-making function or a lower level specific process function).

The five kinds of *functions* include:

1. *Metacomponents:* High-level planning and decision-making processes used, for example, to define a problem that needs solving and to select the lower-order components needed to carry out the solution.
2. *Performance components:* The processes which implement the plans laid down by the metacomponents. For example, they combine elements into a new solution, compare the solution to the problem requirements, and then physically produce the solutions.

INSET 15.1

CATTELL 1978: A HIERARCHICAL CONCEPTUALIZATION OF HUMAN ABILITIES

The search for the structure and content of human intelligence is continuing—probably indefinitely. In one recent development, Hakstian and Cattell (1978) analyzed interrelationships among the 20 primary abilities measured by their Comprehensive Ability Battery (Hakstian and Cattell, 1975; see also Cattell, 1971). This first factor analysis produced six main underlying abilities. When the interrelationships among these six abilities or "factors" were further reduced, three basic global abilities appeared. The overall result was a hierarchical conceptualization of human intelligence in which each of the 20 primary abilities was related to one (or more) of the six more general abilities; and in turn, one (or more) of these six were subsumed under one of three even more general abilities.

The three final abilities were: (1) *Original fluid intelligence*, made up of numerical and spatial abilities, reasoning, memory, and perceptual speed; (2) *Capacity to concentrate*, comprised of visualization abilities, mechanical ability, memory, and perceptual speed; and (3) *School culture*, which includes crystallized intelligence (knowledge and experience), a general retrieval capacity (which includes ideational fluency and originality), and perceptual speed.

(continued)

The entire hierarchical organization might best be presented diagrammatically:

Original Fluid Intelligence

 Fluid Intelligence
- Spatial ability (two-dimensional figures)
- Numerical ability (computation)
- Inductive reasoning (letter series)
- Perceptual speed (evaluating symbol pairs)

 General Perceptual Speed
- Speed of closure (recognizing incomplete words)
- Spelling (identifying misspellings)
- Word fluency (anagram problems)
- Perceptual speed

 General Memory Capacity
- Associative memory (rote memory of design-number pairs)
- Meaningful memory (memorizing noun-descriptor pairs)
- Numerical ability (computation)

Capacity To Concentrate

 General Visualization Capacity
- Aiming (making fine pencil marks)
- Representational drawing (reproducing figures)
- Mechanical ability (automotive, electrical, mechanical principles)
- Spatial ability (two-dimensional figures)

 General Memory Capacity
- Associative memory
- Meaningful memory
- Numerical ability

 General Perceptual Speed
- Speed of closure
- Spelling
- Word fluency
- Perceptual speed
- Span memory

School Culture

 General Retrieval Capacity
- Ideational fluency (listing attributes of nouns)
- Originality (synthesizing two objects)
- Esthetic judgment (abstract design preferences)

 Crystallized Intelligence
- Verbal ability (vocabulary, proverbs)
- Mechanical ability (automotive, electrical, mechanical principles)

 General Perceptual Speed
- Speed of closure
- Spelling
- Word fluency
- Perceptual speed
- Span memory

Is intelligence as simple as an IQ number?

3. *Acquisition components:* The processes involved in learning.
4. *Retention components:* The processes which retrieve previously learned information.
5. *Transfer components:* The processes used in applying information in new situations.

The classification of components by *level* resembles the three-level distinction made earlier among general, class, and specific factors in intelligence. We already noted that *metacomponents* (comparable to Spearman's "g") comprise the highest level "control processes," which plan and direct thinking and reasoning activities. *Class* components, the next level, are "moderately general" processes such as making inferences or applying particular strategies to new problems—processes applicable to a subgroup of specific tasks. Finally, *specific* components (comparable to Spearman's "s" factors) are processes used to perform specific single tasks.

The component theory of intelligence provides a slightly different perspective on the meaning of intelligence. Instead of focusing on students' verbal and nonverbal abilities, the component approach emphasizes differences in the effectiveness of students' intellectual components—differences in their capacities to carry out thinking processes. According to this point of view, students thus would differ in their high level (metacomponent) processes which define problems and select lower level processes, and in their (class and specific) processes which perform the needed learning, retention, and transfer activities.

THE INTELLIGENCE TESTS

The WISC-R   The *Wechsler Intelligence Scale for Children-Revised* (WISC-R; Wechsler, 1974) is individually adminstered and is used with persons from age 6 to 16 (see Figures 15.2 and 15.3). The test was standardized on a sample of 2200 children, including whites, blacks, Mexican-Americans, Puerto Ricans, American Indians, and orientals represented in about the same proportion as they appear in the American population.

Figure 15.2
Sample items of the Wechsler Intelligence Scale for Children— Revised (WISC-R) test kit.

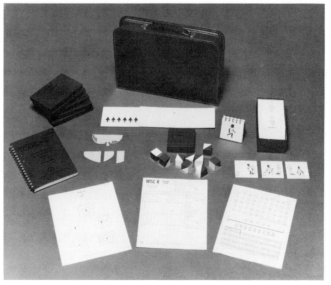

Photo provided by, and used with permission of, The Psychological Corporation.

Figure 15.3 Summary Record Form for the WISC-R.

WISC-R RECORD FORM

Wechsler Intelligence Scale
for Children—Revised

NAME _____ AGE _____ SEX _____

ADDRESS _____

PARENT'S NAME _____

SCHOOL _____ GRADE _____

PLACE OF TESTING _____ TESTED BY _____

REFERRED BY _____

WISC-R PROFILE

Clinicians who wish to draw a profile should first transfer the child's *scaled* scores to the row of boxes below. Then mark an X on the dot corresponding to the scaled score for each test, and draw a line connecting the X's.*

	Year	Month	Day
Date Tested	____	____	____
Date of Birth	____	____	____
Age	____	____	____

VERBAL TESTS — Information, Similarities, Arithmetic, Vocabulary, Comprehension, Digit Span

PERFORMANCE TESTS — Picture Completion, Picture Arrangement, Block Design, Object Assembly, Coding, Mazes

Scaled Score boxes

Scaled Score		Scaled Score		Scaled Score
19	• • • • • •	19	• • • • • •	19
18	• • • • • •	18	• • • • • •	18
17	• • • • • •	17	• • • • • •	17
16	• • • • • •	16	• • • • • •	16
15	• • • • • •	15	• • • • • •	15
14	• • • • • •	14	• • • • • •	14
13	• • • • • •	13	• • • • • •	13
12	• • • • • •	12	• • • • • •	12
11	• • • • • •	11	• • • • • •	11
10	• • • • • •	10	• • • • • •	10
9	• • • • • •	9	• • • • • •	9
8	• • • • • •	8	• • • • • •	8
7	• • • • • •	7	• • • • • •	7
6	• • • • • •	6	• • • • • •	6
5	• • • • • •	5	• • • • • •	5
4	• • • • • •	4	• • • • • •	4
3	• • • • • •	3	• • • • • •	3
2	• • • • • •	2	• • • • • •	2
1	• • • • • •	1	• • • • • •	1

*See Chapter 4 in the manual for a discussion of the significance of differences between scores on the tests.

NOTES

	Raw Score	Scaled Score
VERBAL TESTS		
Information	_____	_____
Similarities	_____	_____
Arithmetic	_____	_____
Vocabulary	_____	_____
Comprehension	_____	_____
(Digit Span)	(_____)	(_____)
Verbal Score	_____	
PERFORMANCE TESTS		
Picture Completion	_____	_____
Picture Arrangement	_____	_____
Block Design	_____	_____
Object Assembly	_____	_____
Coding	_____	_____
(Mazes)	(_____)	(_____)
Performance Score	_____	

	Scaled Score	IQ
Verbal Score	_____	*
Performance Score	_____	*
Full Scale Score	_____	

*Prorated from 4 tests, if necessary.

Printed in U.S.A.

Twelve subtests are divided into six *verbal* and six *performance* tests. The six subtests within each group are designed to measure interrelated intellectual abilities. The verbal battery includes tests of information, comprehension, arithmetic, similarities, vocabulary, and digit span. The performance tests include picture completion, picture arrangement, block design, object assembly, coding, and mazes. The digit span and mazes tests are not used with normal children, leaving a battery of 10 subtests most often used. The verbal and performance IQ scores combine into a *full-scale* IQ, with a mean of 100 and a standard deviation of 15. ("Standard deviation" is a measure of variability, defined later in this chapter and in Chapter 19.)

One of the advantages of the WISC-R is that the nonverbal performance tests will enable a spatially or mechanically oriented person—perhaps a potential artist or superb mechanic—to score very well. For example, Daryl Diesel might produce a verbal IQ score of 96 and a performance IQ of 120, for a full-scale IQ score of about 112—well above average.

In addition to the three IQ scores, a skilled examiner making observations of the child can use the WISC-R testing situation to diagnose such traits and behaviors as reactions to stress, coping with failure, the use of defense mechanisms, the child's approach to intellectual tasks, persistence, and perhaps others.

The Revised Stanford-Binet

The *Revised Stanford-Binet Intelligence Scale* (Terman and Merrill, 1960), like the WISC-R, is individually administered. The test evaluates **mental age** (MA) from age 2 through 14. After age 14, four remaining levels are Average Adult and Superior Adult I, II, and III.

From ages 2 through 4 there are six subtests of increasing difficulty for each half year of development, each subtest representing one month of mental age. From ages 5 through 14, there are six subtests for each year of development, with each subtest representing two months of mental age.

Figure 15.4 shows some of the objects used in the *Stanford-Binet* to measure IQ's of young children. Verbal items are used with older children and adults. For example, at the six-year level some items might be:
"A bird flies; a fish _____."
"An inch is short; a mile is _____."
A question from the seven-year level asks, "What's the thing for you to do when you've broken something that belongs to someone else?"

To determine a person's mental age, or MA, the examiner begins at a level at which the person passes all six subtests and proceeds to a level at which he or she passes no tests. For illustration, let's say that little Wendy Wizard is exactly 10 years and 2 months old, or 122 months of age. She passes all of the subtests for age 11 plus seven more subtests from the age 12, 13, and 14 levels. She passes no tests at the age 15 level. Since each of the seven subtests is worth two months of mental age, her total mental age is $132 + (7 \times 2) = 146$ months.

In the 1916 and 1937 editions of the *Stanford-Binet* test, a person's IQ score was computed by the formula

$$IQ = \frac{\text{Mental age}}{\text{Chronological age}} \times 100.$$

With this **ratio IQ** approach, Wendy's IQ score would be $\frac{146}{122} = 1.20 \times 100 = 120$. The problem with the ratio IQ score is that intellectual growth begins to slow down at about age 13; adults usually do not increase their mental age at all from year to year. Therefore, beginning with the 1960 edition, **deviation IQ** scores were used. A deviation IQ reflects a person's score in relation to a larger, normal distribution of scores—the bell curve. For any age group, the distribution of raw mental age scores is converted into standard scores with a mean of 100 and a standard deviation of 16.

As a brief explanation, Figure 15.5 shows a bell curve—lots of scores in the middle which systematically tail off in both directions. For any given

Figure 15.4
Stanford-Binet Intelligence Scale
(Form L-M) test kit.

Used with permission of the Riverside Publishing Company.

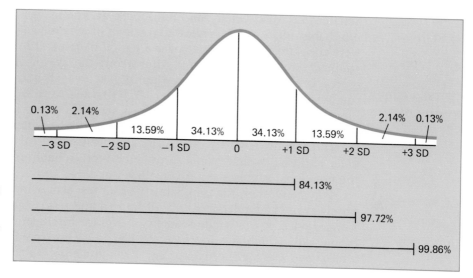

0.13%   2.14%

13.59%   34.13%   34.13%   13.59%

2.14%   0.13%

−3 SD   −2 SD   −1 SD   0   +1 SD   +2 SD   +3 SD

84.13%

97.72%

99.86%

Figure 15.5
Theoretical
normal
distribution of
scores, alias the
bell curve.

raw MA score, the perfect bell curve (or normal distribution) tells us (a) exactly the person's position in standard deviation units above or below the mean, and (b) the person's exact percentile rank relative to others in the same age category. Thus a person whose raw score is exactly one standard deviation above the mean would rank at the 84.13 percentile (see Figure 15.5) and would have an IQ score of 116. Prepared tables permit the easy conversion of any raw MA score into an IQ score for a person in any age group. (The WISC-R also uses deviation IQ scores.)

Group Tests   In addition to the individually administered WISC-R and Stanford-Binet IQ tests, there are several carefully developed group intelligence tests. As the reader might surmise, wide-scale, routine IQ testing virtually always involves group tests. It's cheaper. Some of the better known tests are the *Lorge-Thorndike Intelligence Test*, the *Differential Aptitude Tests*, the *General Aptitude Test Battery*, the *SRA Primary Mental Abilities Tests*, the *California Test of Mental Maturity*, the *Henmon-Nelson Test of Mental Ability*, the *Otis-Lennon Mental Ability Test*, the *School and College Ability Tests* (SCAT), and the *Kuhlman-Anderson Intelligence Tests*. The *Buros Mental Measurements Yearbook* is a standard source for information on tests and testing.

Individual IQ tests—the WISC-R and the Stanford-Binet—are more accurate than group tests, particularly at high and low levels of intelligence.

Stability of IQ Scores

Science has discovered that IQ scores at young age levels are rather unreliable. Bloom (1964) reviewed research in which IQ's of the same people were measured several times over a period of years. The results of several studies were quite consistent. After about the age of 10, individuals' IQ scores correlated highly with their IQ scores at maturity (correlation coefficients about .85). Below age 10, IQ scores were less and less stable. Bloom concluded that intelligence test scores begin to be stable at about age 5 through 7 and are highly stable by age 10. This increased stability of IQ scores could be partly due to the emphasis on verbal test content with older children, which seems to produce more reliable measurement than the nonverbal subtests at early age levels.

For the teacher, the unreliability of IQ test scores means that those IQ numbers in the students' files will be less and less accurate in lower and lower grades. A first-grade student of average intelligence might score 90 on one day, which is below average, and 112 a few months later, which is well above average. Even after age 10, a student's IQ scores occasionally will fluctuate as much as 20 points due to changes in motivation, testing conditions, or peculiarities of particular test items.

THE USEFULNESS OF IQ SCORES

We already have noted that some schools and school systems have discontinued wide-scale group intelligence testing, since the results often have been used to the students' disadvantage (Kamin, 1975). We also have noted that IQ tests currently are useful in: helping to understand the problems of learning-disabled, underachieving, emotionally disturbed, and possibly retarded students; selecting candidates for gifted or special education programs; educational and career counseling; and assessing preschool readiness. The fact is, intelligence tests *do* generally predict success in school as measured by grades. Perhaps this successful prediction is partly due to the fact that grades are determined by similar sorts of tests.

The question has been raised, however, as to whether IQ tests predict anything *but* school success. Correlations between job or career success and IQ scores have been notoriously low, usually zero. The school grades themselves also show little or no relationship to success as, for example, a factory worker, bank teller, or air traffic controller. Wallach (1976) reviewed research dealing with the relationship of academic aptitude tests and professional achievement, concluding:

> *Above intermediate score levels, academic skills assessments are found to show so little criterion validity as to be questionable bases on which to make consequential decisions about students' futures. What the academic tests do predict are the results a person will obtain on other tests of the same kind.*

It is true that "job success" is difficult to define and measure (e.g., "good teaching" has many definitions). With questionable measures of "job success," correlation coefficients between these measures and IQ scores or grades cannot be very high. Perhaps more importantly, McClelland (1973) noted that in the real world of work, the social competence skills needed for success (perhaps punctuality, motivation, pleasantness, thoroughness, etc.) are not the sorts of skills measured by intelligence tests or by school grades (see also Zigler, 1970, 1973; Zigler and Trickett, 1978).

RACIAL DIFFERENCES IN INTELLIGENCE?: JENSEN

In 1969, Berkeley psychologist Arthur Jensen achieved instant unpopularity with his *Harvard Educational Review* article, "How Much Can We Boost IQ and Scholastic Achievement?" In 129 pages he presented data and arguments supporting a genetic basis for racial differences in IQ scores. Said Jensen: Anatomical differences between races have been found wherever the scientist has looked; it would be strange indeed if the brain alone were exempt from this generalization (Jensen, 1969, 1973a, 1973b, 1974). Now, it is acceptable to argue that intelligence is largely inherited. Indeed, in the next section we will present evidence that it is. However, it is not acceptable to propose that racial group differences in average tested IQ scores are due more to biological differences than to environmental factors. This unacceptable attitude has been nicknamed *Jensenism*.

Jensen's writings stimulated both strong protest and a renewed interest in the traditional nature-vs.-nurture controversy. Jensen himself has been harassed, insulted, catcalled, hissed, picketed, and threatened with severe beatings about the head and face. He also has garnered strong support from some respectable psychologists. Most notably, Harvard Professor Richard Herrnstein, writing in *Atlantic* (September 1971), reviewed research on the relative importance of heredity and environment and concluded that 80 to 85 percent of the variability in intelligence is due to genes. Another eminent psychologist, Hans J. Eysenck of the University of London, arrived at about the same conclusion (Eysenck, 1971).

It is true that many studies have shown IQ scores of black children to be an average of 10 to 15 points lower than the average for whites (Shuey, 1966). Critics of Jensen's hypothesis, who support an environmental explanation of the IQ test score differences, have pointed out many reasons why lower SES, black, and other minority children may not score well on IQ tests (Klineberg, 1963; Longstreth, 1978; Trotman, 1977, 1978). Among the most recurrent arguments:

- Intelligence tests were designed by middle-class whites for middle-class whites. (In fact, earlier editions of the Stanford-Binet test itself used children from the relatively privileged Stanford, California, area.) Lower-class and minority children simply have not had an opportunity to acquire the skills necessary to perform well on the tests.

- Lower-class and minority children may not be motivated to do well on the tests.
- Nonwhite children may not respond well to white test administrators.
- Nonwhite children may lack self-confidence and self-esteem.
- A subculture language, such as black English, works against success in intelligence tests, especially with items assessing vocabulary or verbal comprehension.
- IQ tests do not measure the talents and experience of "street-smart" children who learn, reason, and solve problems very effectively in a challenging and sometimes threatening environment.

Supporters of the environmental position also have looked over the 300-year history of blacks in America, noting that 200 of those years were spent in slavery. Since Emancipation, blacks have faced widespread and systematic discrimination in economic, educational, social, and political matters. One outspoken critic of Jensenism, Nathan Gage (1972), pointed out that blacks have been

> . . . insulted, impoverished, made fearful, and instilled with self-hatred. In short, it would be difficult for psychologists, using what research has yielded concerning factors affecting cognitive functioning and development, to plan an environment better designed to harm the average intelligence of an experimental group consisting of about a 10 percent sample of the nation's population.

INSET 15.2

IMPLICATIONS OF THE RACIAL DIFFERENCE HYPOTHESIS

There are at least three undesirable implications of Jensen's racial difference hypothesis:

First, efforts to raise the intellectual level of minority children through early intervention programs will not succeed over the long run.

Second, instead of searching for ways to improve instructional efforts, the children themselves may be blamed for educational failures.

Third, a disproportionate number of minority members will be forever relegated to lower occupational levels, higher unemployment, a second-class role in society, and a smaller slice of the Good Life pie.

Clearly, differences in test scores can reflect native racial differences only if environmental differences are absent, a condition which has not yet been met (Gage, 1972). It is interesting to note that the World War I *Army Alpha* test showed the average IQ score of black soldiers from several northern states to be higher than the average IQ scores of white soldiers from certain southern states. Intelligence and IQ scores can be depressed by deprived or different environments, economic suppression, social values and pressures, poor educational opportunities, deficits in motivation and achievement needs, and many other factors. It also is true that no school or home environment approaches the ideal, and no child approaches his or her full capacity for achievement.

HEREDITY AND ENVIRONMENT: TWIN STUDIES

Neither a strict "nature" nor a strict "nurture" position will explain individual differences in intelligence. It is uniformly accepted in modern psychology and educational psychology that both environment and heredity play a role, and a legitimate academic challenge has been to determine the relative contributions of each. It is important to note that this continuing effort arose independent of—and long before—the Jensenism issue. Indeed, Sir Francis Galton himself grappled with the same issue, and was the first to use the same basic twin studies method.

The logic to twin studies runs about like this: Since identical twins come from a single ovum fertilized by a single sperm cell, they have absolutely identical genetic composition.* For various reasons, identical twins sometimes are split up at birth and raised in separate family environments. Now, if these twins raised separately show identical intelligence test scores, we would be forced to conclude that environment counted nothing and that heredity alone determined intelligence. On the other hand, if IQ scores of twins raised separately are completely uncorrelated, we would have to conclude that heredity meant nothing and that intelligence was due solely to each twin's environment.

You can do about the same thing if you happen to have IQ scores for adopted children, their foster parents, and their biological parents. If the IQ scores of adopted children correlate highly with the IQ scores of the real parents, but are unrelated to the IQ scores of their foster parents, we would have to conclude that intelligence is due to heredity, not environment. Vice versa, if the adopted children's intelligence was related to the intelligence of the foster parents, but not their biological parents, we would deduce that intelligence was due solely to environment, not at all to heredity.

---

* One glitch, mentioned in Chapter 3, is that if same-sexed fraternal twins happen to look alike, it is impossible to determine whether they are identical or fraternal.

INSET 15.3

**DOES REACTION TIME
MEASURE IQ?: YES,
SAYS JENSEN**

Earlier in this chapter we noted that Alfred Binet rejected reaction-time measures as reliable estimates of intelligence. In recent years, however, Arthur Jensen has been exploring the usefulness of reaction time as a measure of Spearman's pure "g" (general intelligence) with apparently promising results (Anonymous, 1978; Jensen, 1982). Jensen used a black light panel with a "home button" and up to eight button/light combinations. Starting with his or her finger on the home button, the subject was required to quickly push a button under whichever light flashed on. Electronic timers measured the time between the light flash and lifting the finger off the home button (reaction time, RT), and the time between leaving the home button and punching the button under the light (movement time, MT). According to Jensen, "The reaction time but not the movement time parameters are significantly correlated with scores on standard intelligence tests in adults, and both the RT and MT parameters are correlated with intelligence in children and retarded adults."

Jensen proposes that pure intelligence (g) may be related to how fast brain cells recover from discharging—the rate of oscillation from ready to unready to ready. If a person has a rapid oscillation (or recovery) rate, then the brain cells can respond more quickly and more often, and more cells will be available for reasoning and learning.

Says Jensen, if the test is valid it has several advantages: It is free from cultural or knowledge influences, it requires no learning, and scores are not affected by trying harder or by relaxing. A major drawback is that the RT measure ". . . is highly unstable from day to day . . ." That is, a subject may turn in quite different RT (IQ) scores from one day to the next. Yes, that could be a problem.

As you might guess, the matter is not quite so neat and simple. The issue is complicated, for example, because: (a) intelligence is never due entirely to environment or heredity, but both; (b) fraternal twins may be misidentified; (c) intelligence measures are not perfectly accurate; (d) there are uncontrolled differences in family emphases on academics and achievement; and probably other problems. Nonetheless, researchers have tried to overcome (or live with) such difficulties by identifying at least nine situations of decreasing genetic and environmental similarity (Erlenmeyer-Kimling and Jarvik, 1963; Jensen, 1969; Skodak and Skeels, 1949):

1. Identical twins raised together
2. Identical twins raised separately

3. Fraternal twins, same sex
4. Fraternal twins, opposite sex
5. Ordinary siblings raised together
6. Ordinary siblings raised separately
7. Foster parents and foster children
8. Unrelated children raised together
9. Unrelated children raised separately

As shown in Figure 15.6, correlations between IQ scores decrease with decreases in *both* genetic similarity and environmental similarity. By statistical means, researchers concluded that intelligence is determined about 75–80 percent by heredity, 20–25 percent by environment. Note in Figure 15.6 that the correlation between IQ's of identical twins raised separately (Category 1) is high, about .75, but climbs to .87 if the twins

Figure 15.6
Median correlations of IQ scores. The median is the central score (in this case, a correlation coefficient) in a distribution of scores.

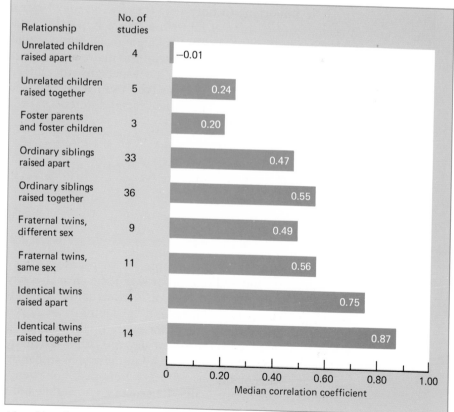

Adapted from Jensen, A. R. How much can we boost IQ and scholastic achievement? *Harvard Educational Review* **39**, 1969, 1–123.

were raised together. Similarly, IQ's of ordinary siblings raised separately (Category 6) are fairly strongly correlated at about .46, but the relationship climbs to about .54 if the siblings live under the same roof. Most variation then, is due to heredity, but a goodly share is due to environment.

While, as we noted, virtually all twin studies were conducted before and independent of the Jensen race matter, Jensen and others nonetheless have attempted to use the data to their own advantage. And what have the scholars of the racial difference and the environmental camps decided as a result of the twin studies? Actually, their minds were already made up, and they were not about to be confused by evidence which, conveniently, could be interpreted either way. The scholar committed to a racial-difference position can readily point to the large chunk of IQ variation due to genetics and claim strong support for his or her views. The environmentalist won't quibble about some genetic influence, but will happily point to the clear evidence that a good environment *will* raise IQ scores—and will call for more effort and more programs to strengthen intellectual skills of disadvantaged children.

It is important to note that the "twin study" research does indicate that heredity is three or four times more important in determining differences in intelligence within the single racial group studied—American and British whites. However, in view of the many environmental influences on IQ test scores (noted above), and especially the total failure to equate environments of different races, the twin-study data does not support a position of genetically determined racial differences, i.e., Jensenism.

TO IMPROVE
YOUR TEACHING

The main purpose of this chapter is to increase your understanding of "intelligence" and "IQ scores." It should be clear that psychologists do not agree on the number and type of intellectual abilites, although most will go along with the idea of a general "g" factor of intelligence. It should also be clear that a student's IQ score easily might be 5 or 10 points higher or lower if measured on a different day or with a different test. There is no intelligent reason to "brand" an IQ number on a student's forehead, forever classifying him or her as "gifted," "retarded," or even "average." In the elementary grades especially, IQ scores are unstable and unreliable.

Despite lack of agreement on definitions or types of intelligence, IQ tests can be profitably used in conjunction with the judgment and experience of the teacher, counselor, social worker, school psychologist, or special education teacher. Your author recently encountered an information sheet on a student in a *gifted* education program—with a tested IQ of 85. The student, a fine artist, would not have been selected if undue weight had been placed on that (low) IQ number. An intelligence test also might uncover a bright but unmotivated underachiever or a talented minority student, either of whom a teacher might assume is not talented or capable.

Finally, we should emphasize that all teachers have an obligation to work with whatever children come their way—majority, minority, foreign or domestic—and to help each student learn and develop his or her talents as far as possible.

SUMMARY

The definitions of intelligence by experts are not much different from our existing conception—the ability to learn quickly, solve problems, understand abstract issues, and behave rationally.

Intelligence testing and tracking have been banned in many school districts due to the damaging effects of "branding" some students as incapable. The Rosenthal and Jacobson expectancy research was instrumental in fueling the IQ testing rebellion.

Intelligence testing is useful in selecting students for gifted programs; for understanding students with anxieties, learning disabilities, or emotional disturbances; for identifying students for special education classes or even institutionalization; for educational and career counseling; and for assessing preschool readiness.

Sir Francis Galton, father of intelligence testing, believed that intelligence was related to sensory acuity and was inherited.

Frenchman Alfred Binet published (in 1905) the first intelligence tests, designed to identify dull children who would not benefit from regular schooling. Binet's tests were based on the mental-age concept. Lewis Terman modified the tests for American use, publishing the first edition of the Stanford-Binet Intelligence Scale in 1916.

Psychologists do not agree on the nature or number of basic intellectual abilities. The Stanford-Binet test produces a single "general intelligence"

IQ score. Spearman proposed a general intelligence "g" factor plus specific intellectual "s" factors. Thurstone devised the Primary Mental Abilities test to measure five primary mental abilities: verbal meaning, number facility, reasoning, perceptual speed, and spatial relations. Thurstone's five primary mental abilities may be viewed as groups or classes of Spearman's "s" abilities.

J. P. Guilford's structure-of-intellect model describes 120 separate intellectual abilities, made up of all possible combinations of four contents, five operations, and six products.

Cattell's two-part conception of intelligence includes crystallized intelligence (knowledge and experience) and fluid intelligence (ability to reason, think abstractly, discriminate). Crystallized intelligence continually increases; fluid intelligence peaks between ages 18 and 38. Some research has sought to increase the fluid intelligence of elderly people.

The componential theory of intelligence, related to information processing theory, classifies components of intelligence according to function (metacomponents, performance components, and acquisition, retention, and transfer components) and level. Metacomponents, the highest level, are involved in direct planning, decision making, and the selection of lower level components; class components are moderately general processes applicable to several tasks; specific components are processes used to perform specific tasks.

The WISC-R is used with children from 6 to 16, producing verbal, performance, and full-scale (deviation) IQ scores. Such traits as reactions to stress, persistence, coping with intellectual tasks, etc., also may be informally assessed.

The Revised Stanford-Binet Intelligence Scale produces a mental age score, which, divided by chronological age (in the 1916 and 1937 editions), produced an intelligence quotient: $IQ = MA/CA$. For those above the age of 14, the test discriminates four adult levels. Beginning with the 1960 edition, a deviation IQ is produced, based on the (normal) distribution of scores at each age level.

In addition to these individual tests, there are many group intelligence tests which are used for evaluating large numbers of students. The individual tests, the WISC-R, and the Stanford-Binet, are more accurate.

After age 10, IQ scores are quite stable. Below 10, they are progressively more unreliable.

IQ scores predict school success fairly well, probably because both are assessed by similar sorts of tests. However, IQ scores seem to have little validity for predicting job or career success, which require additional social competence talents and habits (motivation, pleasantness, punctuality, etc.).

Arthur Jensen proposed that racial differences in average IQ scores have a genetic basis. Critics have argued that minority children's IQ scores are depressed because: They have not had the (environmental) opportunity to learn the skills necessary to perform well on tests designed for middle-class whites; minority children may be unmotivated; they may not respond well to white test administrators; subculture language differences interfere; IQ tests do not measure "street smart" talents.

Since environmental conditions between races have never been equal, the effects of race on IQ scores have never been fairly evaluated.

Twin and adopted-children studies suggest that intelligence is determined about 75–80 percent by heredity, 20–25 percent by environment.

TOPICS FOR THOUGHT AND DISCUSSION

1. Would American education be any different if IQ tests were never invented? How?
2. How do you think the personality and cognitive style factors described in Chapter 14 would affect IQ test scores—especially anxiety, locus of control, impulsive/reflective thinking, and field independent (analytic) thinking?
3. How should we teach elementary students of various intellectual abilities? Secondary students? How would motivational differences influence these strategies?
4. Have you known students who at first appeared "dumb," but later turned out to be very bright? Can you explain your changed opinion?

PROJECTS

1. Visit with your school psychologist. Have him or her show you the various popular IQ test kits and record forms. Find out *exactly* how IQ is measured.
2. Check the records of older students who might have two or three IQ scores on file. Is there much variability among the scores? Which tests were used?
3. Ask your school psychologist, counselor, and special education teachers how they interpret and use IQ scores. Do they seem to agree on the meaning and rational use of IQ testing?

RECOMMENDED READING

Carroll, J. B., and S. E. Maxwell. Individual differences in cognitive abilities. *Annual Review of Psychology* **30**, 1979, 603–640.

Crawford, C. George Washington, Abraham Lincoln, and Arthur Jensen: Are they compatible? *American Psychologist* **34**, 1979, 664–672.

Gage, N. L. IQ, heritability, race differences, and educational research. *Phi Delta Kappan* **53**, 1972, 308, 312.

Jensen, A. R. How much can we boost IQ and scholastic achievement? *Harvard Educational Review* **39**, 1969, 1–123.

Kamin, G. *The science and politics of IQ.* New York: Halstead Press, 1975.

Sattler, J. M. *Assessment of children's intelligence.* Philadelphia: Saunders, 1974.

Sternberg, R. J. Factor theories of intelligence are all right all most. *Educational Researcher* **9** (8), 1980, 6–13, 18.

Zigler, E. The effectiveness of Head Start: Another look. *Educational Psychologist* **13**, 1978, 71–77.

Zigler, E., and P. K. Trickett. IQ, social competence, and evaluation of early childhood intervention programs. *American Psychologist* **33**, 1978, 789–798.

Creativity

16

ABOUT CREATIVITY

As with the concept of intelligence, most of us have a personal idea of what "creativity" is. In art galleries we see creative paintings and sculptures. We read classic and modern books creatively written by talented authors. We see brilliantly creative movies. Every year produces more and more innovative consumer products—trash mashers, Weed Eaters, home computers and TV games, wristwatches with built in alarm clocks, stop watches, and calculators, and synthetic motor oil good for 25,000 miles between changes. Closer to home, we also see award-winning science projects in the high school, sensitive poetry produced by junior high adolescents, and original, technically good artwork lining the halls of every elementary school.

We would agree that these are examples of creativity, and that creativity is a good thing to have around.

Self-Actualized Creativity

There is another form of creativeness which is not quite so obvious. Humanists Abraham Maslow (1971) and Carl Rogers (1962) refer to it as **self-actualized creativity**—the mentally healthy tendency to live all aspects of one's life in a flexible, open, original, and creative fashion. In this sense, creativity is a lifestyle, a personality trait, a way of perceiving the world, a way of interacting with other people, and a way of living and growing. Living creatively is developing your talents, tapping your unused potential, and becoming what you are capable of becoming. Being creative is exploring new places and new ideas. Being creative is developing a sensitivity to problems of others and problems of humankind. The self-actualized creative person may be a superb homemaker, an innovative business person, a fine mechanic, or a clever defensive end.

Most of what was said about humanistic teaching and learning in Chapter 13 applies to self-actualized creativeness—positive self-concepts, self-motivation, fully developed and used talents, humanistic and empathetic concern for the feelings and welfare of others, and an understanding of one's own attitudes, feelings, and viewpoints. Maslow (1968) noted that self-actualization includes an ever-increasing move toward unity, integration, or "synergy" within the person. Tying self-actualization to creativity, Rogers (1962) wrote, "The mainspring of creativity appears to be the same tendency which we discover so deeply as the curative force in psychotherapy—*man's tendency to actualize himself, to become his potentialities*. . . . the urge to expand, extend, develop, mature—the tendency to express and activate all the capacities of the organism. . . ."

The creative person, then, is more than a predictable source of innovative and zany ideas. He or she is a well-adjusted, independent, forward-growing and adventurous individual who is living a fuller and more self-actualized existence. You do not have to produce highly visible, widely recognized

creative products in order to consider yourself an innovative, energetic, artistic, and creative person.

THE CREATIVE PERSON

The Nature-Nurture Problem: Can Creativity Be Taught?

One continuing issue regarding creativity is the nature-nurture one—are you born creative, or is creativity the result of a favorable, nurturing environment? As with intelligence, the answer is *both*. Some individuals—most visibly the Einsteins, DaVincis, Picassos, Beethovens, George Washington Carvers and Madame Curies—clearly are born with superior creative abilities and talents. However, there seems to be no doubt that, within limits, some amount of creativeness can be taught and learned (Davis and Bull, 1978; Edwards, 1967; Parnes, 1978, 1981; Torrance, 1979). Unlike the intelligence issue, there have been no twin studies or foster child studies aimed at determining what proportion of creativeness is due to heredity and what proportion is due to learning.

What is taught when you "teach creativity" will be described later in this chapter.

Creativity and Intelligence

There are two main viewpoints regarding the relationship of creativity and intelligence. The first position is simply that creativity and intelligence are moderately strongly related. The intuitive evidence is that (a) no major creative accomplishments of worldwide significance have emerged from the legions of our mentally retarded citizens, while (b) outstanding creative contributions usually—not always—are produced by reasonably bright people. Research evidence with school children and adolescents confirms that, sure enough, as children grow older they become smarter. They also produce better quality poetry, artwork, and science projects and they score higher on most tests of creativity, especially divergent thinking tests (e.g., listing unusual uses for a brick). There is a good argument for a moderately strong relationship between creativity and intelligence.

The second viewpoint is the preferred one: the *threshold* concept. The argument is that over the wide range of intelligence, from mental deficiency through the normal ranges to the genius levels, there certainly is a positive and moderately strong relationship between creativity and intelligence. However, at higher levels of intelligence—namely, above a "threshold" of IQ = 120—there is no relationship at all. That is, above an IQ of 120, neither a person's IQ score nor college grades will predict his or her level of creativeness.

Personality and Motivational Characteristics

Psychologists have taken many long looks at creative people in order to understand the sorts of characteristics that might contribute to a person's creativeness. Is creativity just intelligence? Intelligence plus motivation? Do special childhood or biographical circumstances play a role? Is it personality traits? Or are creative people so individualistic and nonconforming that each one has nothing in common with any other creative person? Also, is there any reason why a creative artist should resemble a creative executive or a creative scientist?

The single most extensive examination of traits of creative people took place at the University of California, Berkeley, in the 1950s. Psychologists Frank Barron (1969, 1978) and Donald W. MacKinnon (1978) identified nationally recognized creative architects, writers, and men and women mathematicians. The names were selected by nominations from faculty in Berkeley's Departments of Architecture, English, and Mathematics. The creative persons were observed informally over a three-day weekend. They also took intelligence tests, personality tests, divergent thinking tests, and filled out biographical inventories. The results from this study and others showed that while creative people may be nonconformists, they certainly have a lot in common.

We first should acknowledge that not all of the following characteristics apply to all creative people. There simply are too many forms of creativity and creative persons to make such a generalization. However, given this scientific caution, a brief list of recurrent traits of highly creative people would run about as follows (Davis, 1975, 1981a; Davis and O'Sullivan, 1980). Creative people often are:

- Aware of their creativeness
- Independent
- Self-confident
- High in risk taking
- High in energy level
- Enthusiastic
- Spontaneous
- Adventurous
- Curious
- Playful, childlike
- Humorous and witty
- Artistic
- Aesthetically inclined
- Idealistic
- Reflective
- Attracted to the mysterious, complex, and asymmetrical

When you think about it, most of these traits are not too surprising. Most highly creative people are consciously aware of their creativeness. They are in the habit of doing things creatively and they like being creative. If asked, they will modestly admit that, yes indeed, they probably are more creative than the average person.

The creative person also is high in self-confidence and independence and is more willing than the average to take a creative risk. These are essential traits. The innovative person must dare to differ, make changes, stand out, challenge traditions, make a few waves and bend a few rules. Creative people tend to have an internal locus of evaluation rather than being swayed too easily by external influences and opinions. In view of this independence and innovativeness, the creative person risks (a) failure, (b) criticism, (c) embarrassment, (d) the distinct possibility of making himself or herself look like an idiot, or (e) all of the above.

Creative people usually have a very high energy level—a certain enthusiastic zest and a habit of spontaneous action. The creative person may get caught up in seemingly simple problems, perhaps working well into the night on an exciting project. The creative artist, writer, researcher, business person, engineer, or advertising executive often becomes totally immersed in his or her ideas and creations, literally unable to rest until the work is complete.

A related trait has been called sensation-seeking or arousal-seeking, which was discussed in Chapters 9 and 14 as a form of intrinsic motivation. The *Sensation Seeking Scale* itself (see Chapter 9) may be a better measure of creativeness than some creativity tests, according to a study by Davis, Peterson, and Farley (1973). In their research with college students, creative individuals were much more likely than the average to say that they would like to:

- Take up skiing.
- Parachute from an airplane.
- Try mountain climbing.
- Be hypnotized.
- Work in a foreign country.
- Explore strange cities without a guide.

And they preferred:

- Camping to a good motel.
- To jump right into a cold pool, instead of dipping a toe first.
- Bright colors in loud modern art over subdued traditional paintings.

The sensation-seeking trait reflects adventurousness, a high energy level, and a tendency toward risk-taking.

The creative person also has strong curiosity, a childlike sense of wonder and intrigue. He or she may have a history of taking things apart to see how they work, exploring attics, libraries, or museums, and a general strong urge to understand the world.

An especially frequent creative trait is a good sense of humor, which is first cousin to the ability to take a fresh, childlike, playful approach to a problem. Many discoveries, inventions, and artistic creations are the result of "fooling around" with ideas, playing with strange possibilities, or perhaps turning things upside down or inside out. A favorite comment is that the creative adult is essentially a perpetual child—the tragedy is that most of us grow up (Fabun, 1968).

The creative person usually will rate himself or herself high in artistic qualities—whether he or she can draw or not. This person tends to be more conscious of artistic considerations. He or she also has aesthetic interests—interests in concerts, plays, art galleries, antique shows, Masterpiece Theatre on Educational TV, scenic views on the freeway, and so forth. A pattern of idealism and reflectiveness also is common. The creative person, more than the average, may ponder his or her role in the world. What's life about? Why am I here? What should I do with my life? Is money important?

It is a sad fact that creative students—those young people with the greatest potential for contributing to the world—are overrepresented in the ranks of high school and college drop-outs. Do they ponder too much their role in the universe and the university? Do they realize that their creative needs simply are not met in an environment which demands acquiescence and conformity?

Finally, the creative person is attracted to the mysterious and the complex. One test, the *Barron-Welsh Art Scale* (Welsh and Barron, 1963; see Inset 16.1) has repeatedly shown that creative persons prefer smudgy, complex, asymmetrical drawings over simple, balanced drawings (Barron, 1969). Interestingly, creative persons also tend to be strong believers in

INSET 16.1

ARE YOU SIMPLE AND BALANCED? OR COMPLEX AND SMUDGY?

The *Barron-Welsh Art Scale* (Welsh and Barron, 1963) is a set of 80 drawings, some simple and balanced and others complex and asymmetrical. Artists tend to like the complex and asymmetrical and to not like the simple and balanced. Interestingly, so do more creative people. Some patterns similar to those in the Art Scale have been created below.

___ like ___ don't like   ___ like ___ don't like

___ like ___ don't like   ___ like ___ don't like

such psychical and mysterious matters as extrasensory perception, mental telepathy, precognition, astral projection (an out-of-body experience), flying saucers, and spirits and ghosts (Davis, Peterson, and Farley, 1973). Perhaps creative individuals simply have livelier imaginations, or perhaps they are more open and receptive to fantastic possibilities. Or maybe they are in tune with vibrations the rest of us do not sense. Many creative persons have reported mystical experiences (Mark Twain, for example) and many feel they possess psychical capabilities. One familiar example is Orson Welles, creator of the 1938 radio show *The War of the Worlds*, which scared the daylights out of millions of Americans, and the movie *Citizen Kane*, usually rated as the best movie ever made. Welles frequently demonstrates his psychical abilities on live TV shows. He also is a good magician, suspiciously enough.

Negative Creative Traits

So far, the creative personality looks pretty good. Unfortunately, creative children and adolescents may show some habits and dispositions which can upset a normal parent or teacher, and perhaps the rest of the class as well. For example, the independence and self-confidence noted above can become stubbornness and resistance to teacher domination. Their general unconventionality may include an indifference to conventions, such as arriving on time or being courteous. Other swell traits are uncooperativeness, assertiveness, capriciousness, cynicism, low interest in details, and perhaps some sloppiness and disorganization with unimportant matters. There also may be tendencies toward questioning laws, rules, and authority in general, and toward being egocentric, demanding, or sometimes emotional, temperamental, or withdrawn (Smith, 1966).

When Sammy Stubborn or Ingrid Independent show some of these upsetting characteristics, the teacher might consider the possibility that the symptoms are part of a larger picture of original, questioning, independent creativeness. Appropriate creative outlets for these creative traits and needs could help.

Biographical Characteristics

The topic of creativity traits also includes biographical factors, which may be of two sorts: subtle and not-so-subtle. Not-so-subtle factors are simply the person's history of creative activities. Logically enough, a person whose background is filled with unusual hobbies (such as collecting horse bones, red tennis shoes or spider webs, or doing impersonations or magic shows), artistic accomplishments, theatrical performances, scientific inventions, and so on, is probably creative. A person who has been creative in the past very probably will continue to be creative in the future.

INSET 16.2

**A HIGH SCHOOL AND
ADULT CREATIVITY
INVENTORY**

The Group Inventory for Finding Interests II (GIFFI II) test (Davis and Rimm, 1980) is a 60-item inventory which assesses personality traits and biographical factors usually associated with creativeness. Most of the items are taken directly from a college-level test which has proven beyond a reasonable doubt to measure creativeness (Davis, 1975; Davis and Bull, 1978). Below are a few sample items, plus a comment on the creative trait assessed. Davis and Rimm have published similar inventories for measuring creative potential in the junior high school (GIFFI I; Rimm and Davis, 1979) and the elementary school (GIFT; Rimm and Davis, 1976, 1980, 1982; see Chapter 17).

Indicate the extent to which each statement applies to you, or the extent to which you agree with the statement. Mark your answers on your score sheet according to the following scale.
a) No
b) To a small extent
c) Average
d) More than average
e) Definitely

Subtle biographical correlates of creativity include background facts which are a bit more surprising. Schaefer (1970) found that creative high school students were more likely to have friends younger and older than themselves, rather than the same age. The creatives also were more likely to have lived in more than one state and may have traveled outside the USA. Interestingly, the creative students more often reported having an imaginary childhood playmate. Also, high school girls who were creative in writing were more likely to own a cat.

Cultivating a More Creative Personality

Many of the traits listed above probably can be changed in a more creative direction. For example, one might consciously try to cultivate curiosity and wider interests, begin attending more concerts and plays, and visit more art galleries and museums. One's adventurousness might be increased by exploring new places and trying new activities. Perhaps even one's sense of humor, independence, and internal locus of control can be sharpened.

I have a very good sense of humor. (Sense of humor)
I have always been active in drawing or painting. (Artistic; art experience)
I would like to get a pilot's license. (Sensation seeking)
I would like to explore new cities alone, even if I get lost. (Sensation seeking; curiosity)
I enjoy thinking of new and better ways of doing things. (Originality)
I am very curious. (Curiosity)
I tend to become childishly involved with simple things. (Curiosity; playfulness)
I am quite original and imaginative. (Self-rating of creativeness)
I have had many hobbies. (Wide interests; many hobbies)
My mother visits art galleries and museums. (Creative parents)
I have composed or arranged music. (Creative activity)
I have performed music with school or community groups. (Aesthetic, creative activity)
My father has (or had) scientific hobbies. (Creative parents)
I have been active in photography or film-making. (Creative hobby)

Most importantly—and the focus of every creativity training course—one's creativity consciousness and one's willingness to try to use creative talents certainly can be strengthened.

THE CREATIVE PROCESS

There are several ways to look at the process of creativity. This section will review, first, sets of steps and *stages* in creative problem solving; second, the creative process as a *change in perception*; and finally, personal and standard creative thinking *techniques*—strategies for deliberately producing new ideas and idea combinations.

Steps and Stages

The Wallas Model. The most traditional—which could mean "most old"—analysis of stages in the creative process was originated by Wallas (1926). There are four steps.

Preparation.   Preparation includes clarifying and defining the problem, gathering relevant information, and becoming acquainted with innuendos, implications, and perhaps unsuccessful solutions.

Incubation.   Incubation may best be viewed as a period of "preconscious," "fringe-conscious," or perhaps even "unconscious" mental activity which takes place while the thinker is (for example) jogging, watching TV, playing golf, eating pizza, walking along a seashore, or even sleeping. Guilford (1979) suggested that incubation takes place during reflection or during a pause in action, and that some people are simply more reflective than others.

Illumination.   Illumination is the "Aha!" or "Eureka, I've found it!" experience.

Verification.   Verification is checking the solution, in case your Eureka turns out to be a vacuous idea.

The reader may note that these stages resemble steps in the classic scientific method: State the problem, propose hypotheses, plan and conduct research, and evaluate the results. Note also that the stages are not an invariant sequence. Some stages may be skipped or the thinker may backtrack to an earlier stage. For example, the process of defining and clarifying the problem (preparation) may lead directly to a good illuminating idea. Or if the verification confirms that the idea won't work, the thinker may be recycled back to the preparation or incubation stage.

The Creative Education Foundation stages. A more contemporary and perhaps more useful set of stages is outlined by Sidney Parnes, President of the Creative Education Foundation, Ruth Noller, and Angelo Biondi in their *Guide to Creative Action* (Parnes, Noller, and Biondi, 1977). These five steps are useful because they guide the creative process—they tell you what to do at each immediate step in order to eventually produce one or more creative, workable problem solutions. Another unique feature is that most of the steps involve, first, a *divergent* phase in which lots of ideas are divergently generated and, second, a *convergent* phase in which only the most promising ideas are selected. You will shortly see how it works.

These stages could guide a high school creative thinking session which (a) teaches stages in the creative problem-solving process, and (b) gives students some exposure to a rousing, productive, and probably humorous creative thinking experience.

The five stages—preceded by the problem "mess"—are shown in Figure 16.1. Let's say you have a problem: Your junior high school grounds are filthy—students casually toss away candy and burger wrappers, school papers, old tennis shoes, and pop cans without aiming for the available trash cans.

Fact finding.   You begin by divergently listing lots of facts related to the problem. For example, students are not motivated to keep the grounds clean; school pride is low; students or others will work for rewards; and so on. The list of ideas is then convergently narrowed to a few facts which might be especially productive.

Problem finding. In this stage the thinkers first divergently list many different statements of the apparent problem. This can be done by looking at the problem in different ways. For example: In what ways might we motivate students to want to keep the grounds clean? What incentives might we use to motivate neatness? How can we increase school pride? How can we make a game or contest of cleaning up the grounds? What student groups could we entice to clean up the grounds for us? And so on. The list is then reduced to the most promising definitions.

Idea finding. In the idea-finding phase, the individual or group lists as many ideas as possible for the particular problem(s) selected, then again narrows the list to the most promising.

Figure 16.1
A five-step analysis of the creative problem-solving process devised by Parnes, Noller, and Biondi.

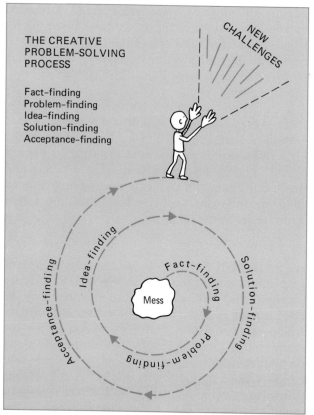

From Sydney J. Parnes, Ruth B. Noller, Angelo M. Biondi, *Guide to Creative Action*. Copyright © 1977 Charles Scribner's Sons. Reprinted with the permission of Charles Scribner's Sons.

Solution finding. Solution finding is the evaluation phase. It may involve, first, divergently listing criteria for evaluating solutions (e.g., cost, acceptability, workability, etc.) and then, second, convergently selecting the most important criteria. The ideas listed in the idea-finding stage are evaluated according to these selected criteria.

Acceptance finding. This stage involves implementing the ideas identified above. In some cases this stage also may include "selling" the idea, for example, to the principal, the students, the teachers, and perhaps others.

A two-stage analysis. Often, creativity in art, writing, music, photography, or in product invention or science seems to involve just two fairly clear steps (Davis, 1981a):

The big-idea stage. This is a stage of fantasy in which the creative person is looking for a new, exciting idea, perhaps for an art or photography project, a term paper, a research study, or a business enterprise.

The elaboration stage. After the big idea is found, a stage of reality—work—begins. The idea must be developed and elaborated in order to arrive at the final creative product. The artist must assemble his or her materials, do preliminary sketches, and create the final work. The research scientist or business entrepreneur also must organize the details and carry out the work necessary to implement her or his big idea.

The Creative Process As a Change In Perception

The process of creation frequently involves a change in perception—a new way of looking at something, seeing a relationship that was not there before, or perceiving new implications, new meanings, new applications, or new combinations. The process often is literally a perceptual one in the sense of looking at one thing and suddenly discovering something else.

To help yourself experience first hand this process of creative discovery, try the exercise in Figure 16.2.

Personal Creative Thinking Techniques

Every creatively productive person uses special techniques to produce new perceptions and new relationships (Davis, 1981b). Often, the techniques are so well-learned and habitual that the thinker may be unaware that a systematic strategy is being used. The artist or photographer, for example, may develop favorite styles or topics which he or she anticipates will produce a pleasing, creative result. The writer of poetry, novels, or even textbooks will mentally juggle words, phrases, and sometimes metaphors until an effective combination is found. A decorator learns to arrange carpets, furniture, wallpaper, paint, and drapes—balancing this with that, adding or subtracting something else—to produce a unique and esthetically pleasing product. The architect or the designer of clothes or jewelry may wander through a museum, finding creative inspirations from the Civil War period, from China, from Rome, from the Incas, from Nigeria, from Ancient Egypt, and so on.

As some additional specific examples, Einstein used his famous mental experiments—such as fantasizing a trip through space in an elevator at the speed of light—to produce new perceptions, new relationships, new ideas. Picasso deliberately dissassembled faces, people, musicians, etc., and then put them back together in a more imaginative arrangement. Picasso also is known for his "periods," when his artistic perceptions were evidently inspired by definite sources. He had, for example, his harlequin period, his blue period, his African period, and others.

All 15 of Franz Liszt's Hungarian Rhapsodies were taken from folk tunes of Hungarian Gypsies. Tchaikovsky also built folk tunes into symphonies. In one case, Tchaikovsky used a folk tune as the basis for his *Marche Slav*, and composer Cesar Cui used the same tune for his *Orientale*. Contemporary composers still borrow tunes. For example, how many rock versions of Beethoven's Fifth Symphony have you heard?

Figure 16.2 What is the main picture in this mess? After you find it, see if you can find (a) a flying pig, (b) an Al Capp Lil' Abner character with a snaggle lower tooth, and (c) a woman with her hair in a bun reclining on a sofa (she's in white). After you find these easy (?) ones, look for (d) the Road Runner, (e) Harry Belafonte, (f) Jesus, and right next to Jesus (g) a lady with a bouffant hairdo. Did you hear yourself quietly yelling "Aha!" or "Oh!" or "Eureka, I've found it!"? The figures are outlined at the end of the chapter.

From Sydney J. Parnes, Ruth B. Noller, Angelo M. Biondi, *Guide to Creative Action*. Copyright © 1977 Charles Scribner's Sons. Reprinted with the permission of Charles Scribner's Sons.

Figure 16.3
Personal creative thinking technique of transferring ideas from one context (Peter Pan) to another (John Anderson's presidential campaign). It is basically metaphorical thinking.

Reprinted by permission of Mike Peters and the Dayton Daily News.

Political cartoonists frequently use a technique of deliberate metaphorical thinking. Metaphorical thinking refers to transferring ideas from one situation to a new context, thus producing a new relationship—often an amusing one. Figure 16.3, for example, presents a cartoon in which ideas from Peter Pan were metaphorically transfered to John Anderson's 1980 political campaign.

Davis (1981b) listed several strategies a teacher might use to help students develop personal creative thinking techniques. First, since such techniques logically would develop in the course of doing creative things, students might become more involved in such inherently creative activities as art, photography, creative writing, acting, journalism, research, or other esthetic or professional activities requiring creative thinking and problem solving. Second, teachers also can provide direct instruction in creative thinking techniques, for example, in artwork, creative writing, or in conducting science experiments. As we will see in Chapter 17, many programs in gifted education provide opportunities for students to develop personal creativity techniques, for example, through mentor programs and apprenticeships, special art or theatre classes, work-student programs, field trips, and professional instruction in summer and Saturday programs.

Standard Creative Thinking Techniques

Every adult-level creative thinking course includes instruction in creative thinking techniques—deliberate methods for producing new combinations of ideas. One lively workbook, *Imagination Express* (Davis and DiPego, 1973), has incorporated these techniques into a form suitable for about the seventh grade. Space will not permit a thorough elaboration of the fine points of using these techniques; the interested reader is encouraged to see Davis (1973, 1981a, 1981b). Most of the procedures—particularly brainstorming—are basically simple enough to be (a) taught to older students as techniques developed by professionals to increase their creativeness, and (b) practiced in class as creative thinking exercises.

Brainstorming. Brainstorming is an effective, simple procedure which in a school setting may be used for either practicing creative thinking or for solving some pressing school problem, such as high absenteeism, messy school grounds, drug problems, bicycle thefts, raising money, selling play tickets, and so on.

The main principle of brainstorming is *deferred judgment*—idea evaluation is postponed until later. There must be no criticism during the thinking session itself. Any sort of criticism or evaluation simply interferes with the generation of imaginative ideas, and the purpose of any brainstorming session is to generate a long list of possible problem solutions.

Brainstorming rules are quite simple (Osborn, 1963):

1. *Criticism is ruled out.* This is deferred judgment. It helps achieve the receptive, creative atmosphere so essential for uninhibited imaginations. Rogers calls this *psychological safety.*
2. *Freewheeling is welcomed.* The wilder the idea the better. This rule clearly supplements the deferred judgment principle (rule 1). It is very possible that a crazy, far-fetched idea could lead to something imaginative yet workable.
3. *Quantity is wanted.* This principle reflects the purpose of the brainstorming session: to produce a long list of ideas. The seemingly sensible rationale is that with a large number of ideas, there is a greater chance of finding good ideas.
4. *Combination and improvement are sought.* This lengthens the idea list. Actually, during the session students will spontaneously "hitchhike" on each other's ideas, with one idea inspiring the next.

It's easy to run a classroom brainstorming session. The teacher would begin by discussing creativity and creative ideas, which leads to brainstorming as one method which stimulates creative thinking. The rules would be discussed, a problem selected (such as "how to make more money," or "how to turn the classroom into a foreign planet"), and a volunteer idea recorder would write ideas on the blackboard. The teacher-leader's role is easy. He or she often asks, "Anyone else have an idea?" Or the teacher might specifically ask the quieter students if they have ideas they wish to contribute. With a little experience, students can lead the sessions.

The brainstorming session, which usually lasts just 20 to 40 minutes, may be followed by an idea evaluation session. Your class may simply agree on the cleverest or most useful ideas, or you can help them brainstorm criteria for idea evaluation—Will it work? Does it cost too much? Will parents, etc., go for it? The idea evaluation stage would be most important if your class intends to present the school principal with one or more blue-ribbon solutions to a current school problem.

One interesting variation of brainstorming is called *reverse brainstorming.* The strategy is to list all of the ideas you and your class can to make the problem *worse.* For example, how can we run up the school electric bill? How can we increase truancy? How can we make parents stay away

---

INSET 16.3

IDEA SQUELCHERS

It's bad enough to be uncreative. It's worse to squelch other people's creative thinking. This list of *idea squelchers* was modified for education by Warren (1974), based on a list published in 1958 by Clark in his book *Brainstorming.* You would never make any of these comments, would you?

We've never done it that way before . . .
I just know it won't work . . .
We've tried that before . . .
We're not ready for it yet . . .
What will the parents think?
Somebody would have suggested it before if it were any good . . .
We're too small for that . . .
We're too big for that . . .
We have too many projects now . . .
It has been the same for 20 years, so it must be good . . .
Won't we be held accountable?
The Board will faint . . .
That's not our job . . .
I'll bet some professor suggested that . . .
It won't work in our neighborhood . . .
But we have to be practical . . .
It's not in the plan . . .
There are no regulations covering it . . .
It's not in the curriculum . . .
It'll mean more work . . .
Our people won't accept it . . .
Etc.
Etc.
Etc.

from the Parents' Night exhibits? Or with a group of teachers, how can we stifle creative thinking in the classroom? Reverse brainstorming usually brings home what everyone is doing wrong.

Attribute listing. Compared with the brainstorming approach, attribute listing is a more specific technique for generating new ideas. The creator of this technique, Robert Crawford (1978), claimed that "Each time we take a step we do it by changing an attribute or a quality of something, or else by applying that same quality or attribute to some other thing."

There are thus two forms of attribute listing: *attribute modifying* and *attribute transferring.* With attribute modifying, the thinker lists main attributes (characteristics, dimensions, parts) of the problem object, then thinks of ways to improve each attribute. For example, students in a high school interior design course could break down a living room into its "attributes" of (1) wall coverings, (2) floor coverings, (3) drapery, (4) furniture, (5) wall decorations, and (6) lighting, and then list lots of specific ideas under each category.

The strategy may be used with any sort of problem which has identifiable attributes—for example, writing stories (with attributes of characters, settings, plots), designing playground equipment (with attributes of climbing things, swinging things, bouncing things, sliding things), and others. For classroom exercises, students can invent new types of breakfast cereals or candy bars. They first list the important attributes (size, shape, color, flavor, name, packaging, etc.), then list specific ideas under each attribute.

With the attribute-transferring strategy, attributes from one situation are transferred to another situation. Attribute transferring is identical to metaphorical thinking, the personal creative thinking technique used by cartoonists, composers, architects, clothes designers, and others described earlier in this chapter. As an example of a classroom application, if students wanted to design some truly creative, memorable displays for a parents' night or open house, they could transfer attributes (ideas) from a carnival, a circus, Disneyland, a farmers' market, a funeral parlor, a Frankenstein or Star Wars movie, McDonald's, and so on. Ideas from these or other settings could provide the inspiration for some very imaginative booths or displays.

Classroom exercises with the attribute-listing procedures will be fun; the students will learn two effective creative thinking techniques; they will receive practice stretching their imaginations; and they will learn that they are able to think of clever new ideas. Their creativity consciousness also will be increased.

Morphological synthesis. This is a simple extension of the attribute-modifying procedure (Allen, 1962; Davis, 1973). Here, specific ideas for one attribute or dimension of a problem are listed along one axis of a matrix.

Ideas for a second attribute are listed along the other axis. Plenty of idea combinations are found in the cells of the matrix. One example of a sixth-grade morphological synthesis problem (mercifully called the "checkerboard method" in *Imagination Express*) appears in Figure 16.4. The kids had a swell time inventing new sandwich spreads, many of which are not too revolting.

Idea checklists. Sometimes, you and your students can find a checklist which suggests solutions for problems. For example, the Yellow Pages of a

Figure 16.4 A sixth-grade Milwaukee class used the morphological-synthesis method to generate 121 zany ideas for creative sandwiches. Can you find a tasty combination? A revolting one? If you added a third dimension, with five types of bread, how many total ideas would you have?

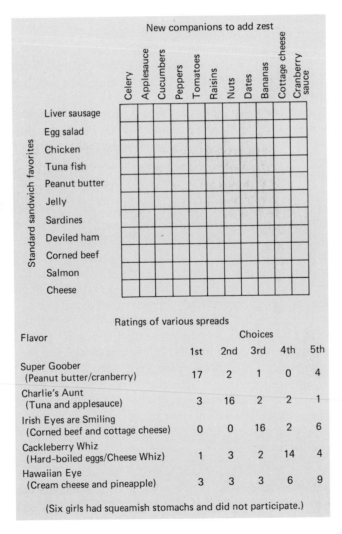

Ratings of various spreads

Flavor	Choices				
	1st	2nd	3rd	4th	5th
Super Goober (Peanut butter/cranberry)	17	2	1	0	4
Charlie's Aunt (Tuna and applesauce)	3	16	2	2	1
Irish Eyes are Smiling (Corned beef and cottage cheese)	0	0	16	2	6
Cackleberry Whiz (Hard-boiled eggs/Cheese Whiz)	1	3	2	14	4
Hawaiian Eye (Cream cheese and pineapple)	3	3	3	6	9

(Six girls had squeamish stomachs and did not participate.)

phone book often are used as an idea checklist for problems like "Who can fix my TV?" or "Where can I get a haircut?" A high school counselor might use the Yellow Pages or the want ads for ideas on career counseling. Books about China, Sweden, the middle ages, etc., have provided countless suggestions for classroom decorations.

Some idea checklists have been designed especially for creative problem solving (see Davis, 1973). The most popular of these is Alex Osborn's (1963) "73 idea-spurring questions." The list is guaranteed to stimulate ideas for such classroom brainstorming exercises as "How can we build a better mousetrap (or backpack, bicycle, or playground equipment)?" In abbreviated form:

- *Modify?* New color, motion, sound, odor, form, meaning?
- *Magnify?* What to add? Greater frequency? Stronger? Higher? Longer? Thicker? Duplicate? Multiply? Exaggerate?
- *Minify?* What to subtract? Smaller? Condensed? Miniature? Lower? Shorter? Lighter? Omit? Split up? Understate?
- *Substitute?* Who else instead? What else instead? Other ingredient? Other material? Other process? Other power? Other approach?
- *Rearrange?* Interchange components? Other pattern? Other sequence? Transpose cause and effect?
- *Reverse?* How about opposites? Turn it backward? Upside down? Reverse roles?
- *Combine?* How about a blend? An assortment? Combine units? Combine purposes? Combine appeals? Combine ideas?

Synectics Methods. Synectics, taken from the Greek *synecticos*, means the joining together of apparently unrelated elements—a good definition of a creative idea. The synectics methods were originated by Wiliam J. J. Gordon, former school teacher, horse handler, salvage diver, ambulance driver, ski instructor, sailing schooner master, college lecturer, and pig breeder. [The outcome of the pig project was ". . . a lot of bone and not much bacon, but they were the fastest pigs in the East" (Alexander, 1978).] Gordon also worked with creative thinking groups, an experience which led him to identify strategies which creative people use unconsciously. These strategies have been made conscious and teachable in a form for adults (Gordon, 1961) and children (Gordon, 1969). His workbooks, *Making It Strange, Books 1–4* (Gordon, 1974) give children first-hand experience with the fascinating synectics problem-solving methods: direct analogy, personal analogy, and fantasy analogy.

With the **direct analogy** method, the thinker—of any age—is asked to think of ways that similar problems are solved in nature by animals, birds, flowers, insects, worms, snakes, and so on. For example, if students wanted to think of ideas for conserving energy, they would ask how animals, birds,

flowers, etc., keep warm in winter without furnaces or electric blankets. Virtually any sort of problem can be creatively attacked using the direct analogy method.

With the **personal analogy** method, the thinker achieves new perspectives on a problem by becoming part of the problem. To give students practice in the personal analogy method, one of Gordon's (1974) "be the thing" exercises went about like this: Imagine you are a piece of bubble gum. You are sitting quietly in your box with your gum friends on the shelf of a corner candy store. A little boy walks in, places three cents on the counter and points at you. How do you feel? What are your thoughts?

Some classroom exercises might be: If you were a door, what would it feel like to be slammed all the time? Or imagine you are a highway; how do you feel about people dumping their pop cans and other trash on you?

With the **fantasy analogy** method, the problem solvers think of fantastic, far-fetched, perhaps "ideal" solutions which might lead to creative, yet practical ideas. For example, students can work on such problems as: How can we get the hallways to keep themselves free of litter? How can we get parents to want to attend our Open House? How can we make school lunches into Thanksgiving banquets for 25¢ each?

The synectics methods have given professional problem solvers some good ideas—for example, for a NASA space-suit closure, a space feeding system, *Pringles* potato chips, the trash masher, electric knife, disposable diapers, and many others. The strategies can be used in the schools either as (a) creativity exercises or (b) perhaps for older students, as material for lessons in techniques of creative thinking.

TEACHING FOR CREATIVE DEVELOPMENT

The importance of creative development, as self-actualization, was emphasized at the outset of this chapter. We also already have made suggestions for exercises, activities, and other content which could increase students' creativity consciousness, increase their understanding of creativity, and through practice strengthen creative thinking skills and abilities. The main points have been as follows:

- Creative personality traits might be deliberately strengthened, for example, by developing an interest in esthetic and cultural matters, exploring new places and activities, and especially by developing a creativity consciousness.
- Stages in the creative thinking process can be taught to secondary students both to increase their understanding of creativity and to provide practice with the stepwise approach to creative problem solving.
- Personal creative techniques would develop in the course of doing creative things (art, writing, theatre, science, etc.) and through instruction by teachers or professionals.
- Students of any age can practice brainstorming, which not only provides exercise in thinking creatively, but implicitly stresses the importance of a receptive, creative atmosphere.

Other techniques—attribute listing, morphological synthesis, idea checklists, and the synectics methods—all serve to increase students' understanding of creativity, provide practice in creative thinking, and change attitudes and awareness in a more creative direction (e.g., attitudes of receptiveness to, appreciation for, and valuing of creative thinking).

In this section we will briefly summarize, or reemphasize, related strategies for strengthening creativeness at all levels. One model for creative development, which describes four stages in becoming a more creative person and summarizes an instructional sequence for teaching a unit on creativity, is summarized in Inset 16.4.

The Creative Atmosphere

The most critical consideration in stimulating creative thinking is maintaining a **creative atmosphere.** A creative atmosphere is mainly a matter of attitudes. We noted earlier that Rogers emphasized psychological safety as a prerequisite for creativeness; a creative atmosphere is a psychologically safe one. Osborn's brainstorming also is based on a noncritical, nonevaluative, receptive atmosphere where fresh and even wild ideas may be safely proposed. The creative personality too, includes a conscious readiness to

---

INSET 16.4

BECOMING MORE CREATIVE: THE MODEL AUTA

Davis (1981a; Davis and O'Sullivan, 1980) outlined a taxonomy of creative development which describes (a) the process of becoming a more creative adolescent or adult, and therefore (b) an instructional sequence for teaching a course or unit on creative thinking. The model AUTA includes four sequential parts: an *Awareness* of creativity; a deeper *Understanding* of the nature of creativity; the acquisition of *Techniques* for creative production; and, finally, a humanistic increase in the *Actualization* of one's potential.

Awareness.   The first step in becoming more creative involves an increase in one's "creativity consciousness." Most people simply do not think about creativity or becoming more creative. The learner must appreciate the contribution of creativity to one's personal development—for developing one's talents, for self-actualization, for mental health, and simply for getting more out of life. The learner also should grasp the role of creative innovation in the development of civilization and in solving society's present and future problems.

Understanding.   There is a large body of information which will contribute to one's understanding of creativity and creative behavior. Space will not permit a complete summary, but some important topics and issues are: (a) characteristics of the creative person; (b) the nature of the creative process; (c) theories of creativity; (d) the nature of creative abilities; and (e) tests of creative potential. Some of these topics are summarized in this chapter.

Techniques.   The development of creative thinking techniques involves (a) developing personal creative thinking techniques, and (b) learning to use "standard" creative thinking methods, as described in this chapter.

Actualization.   The true goal of creative development is self-actualization—the full development of one's capabilities and potential. The self-actualized creative person is mentally healthy, well-adjusted, open to new ideas and experiences, shows concern for fellow human beings, is a self-initiated learner, and takes a flexible, creative approach to all aspects of life.

think creatively, and a receptiveness to the innovative ideas of others. You may wish to look again at the idea squelchers presented earlier. They typify precisely what a creative atmosphere and a creative person are *not*.

A creative atmosphere is thus a safe atmosphere in which creativity is encouraged and rewarded. It is an ancient principle of psychology that rewarded behavior will persist and become stronger, while punished or ignored behavior will disappear. Creativity is no exception.

The Model AUTA.

Illustration by R. O. Swinehart, Discover Design, Carnegie-Mellon University. Reprinted by permission.

The Importance of Understanding Creativity

Creativity consciousness and a predisposition to think creatively will take a giant step forward when those involved—you or your future students—know more about the topic. The purpose of this chapter, in fact, is to increase your awareness of creativity and your understanding of the topic. In the classroom, it is helpful to do creativity exercises, learn about creative people, have brainstorming sessions, and design creative art, science, and writing projects. However, such training will have more impact if the learners are directly helped to understand creativity and its importance for personal development and for the betterment of society.

A few lessons on creativity might include such topics as:

- The importance of creativity to self and society.
- Biographies and characteristics of creative people.
- The nature of creative ideas as modifications and combinations of other ideas.
- Techniques of creative thinking—brainstorming and others.
- The nature of the creative process: stages, changed perceptions, metaphorical thinking.
- Creativity tests, which may be taken and explained.

Of course, the teacher must tailor the level of the discussion to the age and abilities of the students.

Esthetic, Scientific Involvement

Football players are given lessons, exercises, and practice to develop their appropriate skills. So are violin players, computer programmers, bus drivers, and used-car salespeople. Our bear-trap logic suggests that creative talent in art, writing, drama, music, science, and other areas will be strengthened if students have experience in these activities.

Most schools provide opportunities for involvement in some creative, esthetic activities. The teacher interested in encouraging creativeness can work to expand the opportunities. Are music, science and art programs adequate? Are supplies and instruction available for all? Are students encouraged by all teachers to become involved? Do students realize that art and drawing supplies and handicraft materials can be purchased? That hobby stores carry microscopes, telescopes, bug and butterfly kits? That libraries have books on just about any hobby or creative interest one could think of?

Exercises in Creative Thinking

There are a great many strategies for stimulating creative thinking in the classroom. Most of these are based on the assumption that creative imagination—like skills of arithmetic, typing, or shooting baskets—can be strengthened with practice.

Over the years, creative education leader E. Paul Torrance has devised dozens of exercises aimed at strengthening simple and complex creative abilities. Many of the exercises in this section stem directly or indirectly from his creative writings (see Torrance, 1979; Torrance and Myers, 1970). The teacher can:

- Pose provocative questions for the entire class as a whole and lead the brainstorming.

- Divide the class into two-, three-, or four-person problem-solving teams who work on the same problem and then report creative solutions to the class.
- Create brainstorming groups of eight to twelve members who follow brainstorming procedures and report their list of ideas (or best ideas) to the class.

What would happen if?   The old standard open-ended, creativity-stimulating question is the "What would happen if . . ." approach. Normally, an unlikely event is proposed and students deduce or create real or far-fetched consequences. The strategy can be used with absolutely any subject matter.

- What would happen if it were against the law to sing?
- What would happen to world agriculture if an atomic explosion caused the earth's axis to shift 50° and Brooklyn became the North Pole?
- What would American life be like if the Revolutionary War had been lost?
- What would we do without numbers? Without geometry? Without algebra? Without calculus? ("Celebrate" is not the right answer.)
- What would happen if the only musical instruments were drums?
- What would happen if vaccines were never discovered?

Product improvement.   Another type of open-ended question asks students to think of improvements for common products—pencils, desks, classrooms, bicycles, pianos, typewriters, calculators, and so on. This type of exercise is about as versatile as the "What would happen if . . ." approach.

Posing problems, paradoxes.   Problems and paradoxes are intrinsically interesting and challenging. Sometimes the problem or paradox will require *solutions*, as when brainstorming such problems as:

- How can we make school more interesting?
- How can bicycle thefts be eliminated?
- How can the school (family) light bill be reduced?
- What could we buy or do for parents for Christmas/Hannukah for under five dollars?
- Mr. Jones, 50 years old, hates his boring job as a night watchman but has no special training. What should he do?
- How could we get a hippopotamus out of the bathtub?
- Improved medical technology has created an enormous population of elderly people who consume food and energy and require care. Is this a problem? What are solutions?
- What is wrong with the Communist principle that individuals exist only to serve the state?

INSET 16.5

TORRANCE TESTS OF CREATIVE THINKING

The *Torrance Tests of Creative Thinking* (Torrance, 1966) measure creative abilities of *fluency* (number of ideas), *flexibility* (number of different types or categories of ideas), *originality* (uniqueness), and *elaboration* (number of embellishments). Exercises similar to Torrance's subtests are presented below. Spend a few minutes on each one. Are you fluent? Flexible? Original? Are you elaborate?

Directions: Make a meaningful picture out of each of the nonsense forms below. Try to be original. Give each one a name.

Directions: List as many unusual uses as you can for discarded rubber tires.

_____   _____

_____   _____

_____   _____

_____   _____

_____   _____

_____   _____

_____   _____

Other types of problems and paradoxes challenge students to find *explanations*, for example:

- The grass behind a southern Wyoming billboard is lush green. Why?
- The principal unexpectedly announces that gym classes are cancelled for two weeks. What are some explanations?
- Ten paintings were discovered missing from the art gallery on Monday morning, but there was no sign of a break-in. How could they have disappeared?

Encouraging future projection.   How will governments function in 200 years? What about food? Travel? Housing? Leisure activities? Education? Energy? War? Such questions require the learner to think originally and divergently, to extrapolate, to transform knowledge, and to make deductions and inferences.

TO IMPROVE
YOUR TEACHING

We devoted a lot of space at the outset of this chapter to describing characteristics of creative people. The purpose of this was to enable you to identify creative children and adolescents when they appear in your classes. While they all will differ from "regular" students and from each other, most of them will show such traits as high energy, curiosity, adventurousness, nonconformity, and a good sense of humor, and they also will have creative hobbies and interests. As a teacher, your own "creativity consciousness" will include being aware of creative students, their needs, and their problems. The creative students may or may not be the bright and cooperative "teacher pleasers."

Creative talents of all students should be recognized and encouraged, not left to chance development or even squelched. Both you and your students, of course, must realize that there is a time for conformity—with assignments, rules, and regulations—and a time for unconventionality and creative expression.

For all students at all levels, much can be done to encourage creative development. The topic of creativity can be presented and discussed (see the model AUTA in this chapter). Students can become involved in creative activities—art, writing, drama, music, science, photography, and others. Independent research projects—which strengthen many creative and problem-solving skills—may be assigned. You also may wish to try out some creative thinking techniques—especially brainstorming, attribute listing, and the synectics methods of direct analogy, and—if your class really gets "into it"—perhaps personal analogy. Creative men and women in history also may be discussed—their attitudes, abilities, courage, and their problems. (Even Galileo had to keep quiet to avoid jail!) Most critically, create an atmosphere that is psychologically safe and creative, one where students will truly feel comfortable in suggesting and exploring new ideas and new activities.

Learn more about creativity. See some of the references at the end of this chapter. Write to publishers of creativity training materials and ask for a catalog (one suggestion: DOK Publishers, 71 Radcliffe Road, Buffalo, New York 14214).

SUMMARY

Creativity is all around us, for example, in new consumer products and in esthetic creations in the schools.

Humanists Abraham Maslow and Carl Rogers speak of self-actualized creativeness, the mentally healthy tendency to do everything in a flexible, innovative fashion.

Creativity, like intelligence, is due both to heredity and to learning.

Two views of the relationship between creativity and intelligence are that (a) they are moderately strongly related, and the preferred viewpoint (b) they are related only up to a threshold IQ of about 120, above which there is no relationship between creativity and intelligence.

Research by Frank Barron and Donald MacKinnon at Berkeley indicates that the creative personality usually included traits of independence, self-confidence, risk-taking, high energy, high "sensation seeking," curiosity, artistic interests, a sense of humor, an attraction to the complex and mysterious, an awareness of one's creativeness, and others.

In school, creative children may show some troublesome characteristics: stubbornness, resistance to domination, indifference to conventions (rules), uncooperativeness, cynicism, capriciousness, egocentrism, temperamental emotionality, and perhaps sloppiness or disorganization with unimportant matters.

Biographical traits of creative people may be unsurprising or subtle. For example, a background of creative accomplishments and unusual hobbies and interests is not unexpected. However, having a childhood imaginary playmate, owning a cat, preferring friends younger and older, and living in more than one state are more subtle correlates of creativeness.

Some creative personality traits probably can be strengthened.

The creative process is viewed in three ways: as a set of stages in creative problem solving; as a change in perception; and as techniques for creative thinking.

The most traditional set of creative problem solving stages is Wallas' 1926 sequence of preparation, incubation, illumination, and verification. Five stages suggested by Creative Education Foundation leaders Parnes, Noller, and Biondi (1977) are fact finding, problem finding, idea finding, solution finding, and acceptance finding. Each stage includes first a divergent phase, then a convergent phase.

A simple two-stage analysis includes a "big idea" or fantasy stage, followed by an elaboration or reality stage.

The creative process also can include a change in perception—a usually sudden perception of new relationships, new meanings, new applications, or new idea combinations.

Personal creative thinking techniques are developed and used by every creatively productive person. They may develop such techniques in the course of doing creative things, or by taking instruction from teachers or professionals.

Standard creative thinking techniques include: brainstorming, a group (or individual) procedure based on deferred judgment; attribute listing, including the two substrategies of attribute modifying and attribute transferring; morphological synthesis, the matrix method; and using idea checklists.

William J. J. Gordon's synectics methods include: (1) direct analogy, looking for ways similar problems are solved in nature; (2) personal analogy, finding new perspectives by becoming part of the problem objects or processes; and (3) fantasy analogy, thinking of far-fetched, perhaps "ideal" solutions.

The model AUTA includes four steps in personal creative development: Awareness of the importance of creativity; increased Understanding of creativity; acquiring Techniques of creative thinking; and finally, increased self-Actualization.

Teaching for creative development includes: encouraging the acquistion of creative personality traits and interests; teaching and practicing stages in creative problem solving; and practicing brainstorming and other creative thinking techniques.

We especially emphasized the importance of: (1) a creative atmosphere; (2) helping students understand creativity and creative thinking; (3) providing involvement in esthetic and scientific activities; and (4) practice with imagination-stretching exercises—such as "What would happen if . . .", product-improvement exercises, posing problems and paradoxes, and encouraging future projection.

TOPICS FOR THOUGHT AND DISCUSSION

1. Look over the list of personality traits of creative people. Which traits fit you and which do not? Should you try to strengthen these creative traits or not?
2. Examine the model AUTA closely. Could you develop a unit on creativity at the grade level you expect to teach on the basis of this taxonomy?
3. What would happen if all school administrators, all teachers, and all students become highly "creativity conscious"?
4. Virtually all creative thinking courses teach the creative thinking techniques described in this chapter. Would the mastery of these procedures make you truly "more creative"? Why or why not?

PROJECTS

1. In a group discussion with your classmates, evaluate the importance of "creative attitudes," the creative atmosphere, and "psychological safety." Does everyone know some rigid uncreative persons? Teachers, principals, or perhaps professors?
2. Have a group of teachers or education majors brainstorm the problem: How can we stifle creativity in the classroom? After the session, point out that *all* of the ideas listed are common school practices!
3. For a required paper for this or another education or psychology course, review tests of creativity—their reliability, validity, and usefulness for different age groups.
4. Ask teachers in different subject areas how, and if, they try to strengthen creative thinking skills. Keep a log of activities and a list of useful curriculum materials.

RECOMMENDED READING

Davis, G. A. *Psychology of problem solving.* New York: Basic Books, 1973.
———— *Creativity is forever.* Cross Plains, Wis.: Badger Press, 1981a.
———— Personal creative thinking techniques. *Gifted Child Quarterly* **25,** 1981b, 99–101.
Davis, G. A., and G. DiPego. *Imagination express: Saturday subway ride.* Buffalo, N.Y.: DOK Publishers, 1973.
Davis, G. A., and J. A. Scott (eds.). *Training creative thinking,* reprinted edition. Huntington, N.Y.: Krieger, 1978.
Fabun, D. *You and creativity.* New York: Macmillan, 1968.
Feldhusen, J. F., and D. J. Treffinger. *Creative thinking and problem solving in gifted education.* Dubuque, Iowa: Kendell/Hunt, 1980.
Gordon, W. J. J. *Making it strange.* Books 1–4. New York: Harper & Row, 1974.
Koberg, D., and J. Bagnall. *The universal traveler.* Los Altos, Calif.: William Kaufman, 1976.

Lee, J. M. and C. J. Pulvino. *Educating the forgotten half.* Dubuque, Iowa: Kendell/ Hunt, 1978.

Parnes, S. J. *The magic of your mind.* Buffalo, N.Y.: Creative Education Foundation, 1981.

Parnes, S. J., R. B. Noller, and A. M. Biondi. *Guide to creative action.* New York: Scribner's, 1977.

Smith, J. A. *Setting conditions for creative teaching in the elementary school.* Boston: Allyn & Bacon, 1966.

Torrance, E. P., and R. E. Myers. *Creative learning and teaching.* New York: Harper & Row, 1970.

Torrance, E. P. *The search for satori and creativity.* Buffalo, N.Y.: Creative Education Foundation, 1979.

Solutions to ambiguous figures in Figure 16.2

The cow

Popeye

Dogpatch person

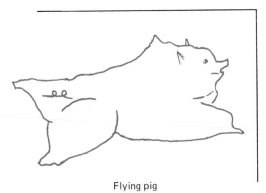

Flying pig

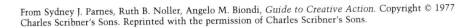

Solutions to
ambiguous
figures in Figure
16.2 (continued)

Napping lady

Road runner

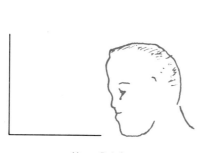

Harry Belafonte

Jesus
Lady with bouffant hair

Education of the Gifted and Talented

17

THE GIFTED AND THE TALENTED

In recent years many educators have taken a renewed interest in the gifted child, and for very good reason. Somewhere in those thousands of elementary and secondary schools sit tomorrow's musicians, senators, research scientists, artists, engineers, executives, and other political, scientific, cultural, and business leaders. It seems like a good idea to help these gifted people get started—to identify them and to provide them with the guidance, materials, and facilities necessary to help them cultivate their budding talents.

We owe it to these young people to help them develop their capabilities to the fullest, to help them become what they are capable of becoming. We also owe it to society to prepare our most talented young people to grapple with the problems of today and tomorrow. There are and will be countless challenges in need of creative solutions—problems of overpopulation, hunger, disease, political conflicts, energy shortages, resource shortages, inflation, and prejudice and discrimination, to name a few of the more obvious difficulties. Never has the world needed more talented and creative problem solvers.

The renewed interest in education for the gifted is easy to justify. Some critics, however, have suggested that the present deluge of new programs, organizations, books, and journals for the gifted is simply a fad—one which recurs every 20 years (Sputnik, in 1957, spurred the last flurry of interest in special programs for gifted students). The pendulum of public interest and government support, they say, swings back and forth between programs for the disadvantaged and handicapped and programs for the gifted and talented. Many educators, however, are convinced that the present focus on educating the gifted is sufficiently crucial that it is here to stay (Renzulli, 1980). Ideally, programs for both populations of special students—the disadvantaged/handicapped and the gifted—will continue to receive the attention and support they both deserve.

Are G/T Programs Undemocratic? Elitist?

We may as well wrestle with one issue right away. Virtually every time a program for gifted and talented (G/T) children is discussed, someone will ask, "Is it fair to give *these* kids special treatment?" Or you might hear, "These kids will succeed without help—why not help the ones who really need it?" Or even, "If these kids can't succeed on their own, they're sure not very gifted (chuckle, chuckle)!" There are charges of **elitism**—aiding only the (intellectually) elite—and unfair and undemocratic practices. "Wouldn't *all* kids benefit from such a program?" "Isn't it undemocratic to single out the most able and talented students and devote extra time and money to making them even *more* superior?"

The response to these criticisms is straightforward: Gifted children and adolescents have special talents and potential; it is unfair to them not to

provide special services which permit them to develop their capabilities. It is a basic democratic principle that every person should have an opportunity to progress as far as his or her talent and motivation will allow. It therefore is an undemocratic disservice to prevent gifted and talented youth from developing their capabilities.

We also might note that there are special classes and special teachers for students with learning disabilities, emotional problems, or just reading deficiencies. Project Head Start and Project Follow Through, for example, will and should continue. We might easily argue that gifted students are "special students" with special learning needs which also must be accommodated.

WHO IS GIFTED? WHO IS TALENTED? THE DEFINITION ISSUE

The problem of defining who is gifted or talented is not so simple that an office secretary, charged with locating "the top 5 percent," can simply flip through files to find the top 15 IQ scores among the school's 300 students. Especially, a school's definition of "gifted and talented" is intimately related to the kind of identification procedures that are used. In fact, the identification procedures used will define just who is gifted and who is talented for that particular program.

The Marland U.S.O.E. Definition

A widely accepted definition of giftedness was prepared by Sidney Marland (1972), then Commissioner of Education, for a U.S. Office of Education publication entitled *Education of the Gifted and Talented*:

> *Gifted and talented children are those identified by professionally qualified persons who by virtue of outstanding abilities are capable of high performance. These are children who require differentiated educational programs and services beyond those normally provided by the regular school program in order to realize their contribution to self and society.*
>
> *Children capable of high performance include those with demonstrated achievement and/or potential ability in any of the following areas:*
>
> *1. General intellectual ability*
> *2. Specific academic aptitude*
> *3. Creative or productive thinking*
> *4. Leadership ability*
> *5. Visual and performing arts*
> *6. Psychomotor ability**

The six categories are fairly self-defining. **General intellectual ability** (note that it is number one on the list) refers to the highly visible child who is extremely bright. He or she scores high on IQ tests, learns easily,

---

* A 1978 revision of this definition is virtually identical to the 1972 version, except that "psychomotor ability" was excluded. These gifted students—athletes—normally are well provided for without special congressional endorsement.

INSET 17.1

**AN ARGUMENT FOR
EQUALITY**

Kurt Vonnegut in *Harrison Bergeron* wrote a spoof on equality:
    "The year was 2081, and everybody was finally equal. They weren't only equal before God and the law, they were equal in every which way. Nobody was smarter than anybody else. No one was better looking than anyone else." [Equality was enforced by giving handicaps to people who were outstanding in various ways. Those who could dance well had to wear sandbags on their feet; those who were good looking had to wear a mask. Intelligence?] "George, while his intelligence was way above normal, had a little metal handicap radio in his ear. He was required by law to wear it at all times. He was tuned to a government transmitter. Every 20 seconds or so, the (government) transmitter would send out some noise to keep people like George from taking unfair advantage of their brains."

Excerpted from "Harrison Bergeron" from the book *Welcome to the Monkey House* by Kurt Vonnegut Jr. Copyright © 1961 by Kurt Vonnegut Jr. Originally published in *Fantasy and Science Fiction*. Reprinted by permission of Delacorte Press/Seymour Lawrence.

understands complex issues, has a large vocabulary and high verbal fluency and generally seems to get a lot out of educational experiences.

Specific academic aptitude refers to strong talent in just one or a few areas, for example, mathematics, social studies, biology, botany, astronomy, creative writing, and so on.

Creative or productive thinking is basically the ability to produce lots of original, imaginative ideas. "Productive" thinking may be contrasted with "reproductive" thinking—which is the ability to learn and memorize nonoriginal information and "reproduce" it on a test. The creative student usually will show many of the creative personality traits described in Chapter 16—independence, curiosity, a high energy level, artistic and esthetic interests, a good sense of humor, and a willingness to fantasize and play with ideas.

Leadership ability is the apparently natural talent of some students to lead, direct, and perhaps dominate others. Leadership talent also includes traits of responsibility, self-confidence, flexibility in thought and actions, sociability, and likability.

Talent in the **visual and performing arts** includes various forms of artistic ability (painting, drawing, sculpting, lettering, photography, pottery, and miscellaneous types of handicrafts) along with music, dance, and drama.

As for **psychomotor ability,** every high school and most junior high schools already have programs for talented students. They are called the football, basketball, baseball, and track teams, and sometimes swimming, hockey, tennis, and gymnastic squads.

Athletic programs present one ideal model for programs for the gifted. Participating students receive expert training; they are provided with high quality expensive equipment; they meet with others of similar outstanding talent; and they do not hide nor hold back their talents—in fact, they encourage one another to perform at their absolute best.

Renzulli's Three-Ring Model

Renzulli (1977; Renzulli, Reis, and Smith, 1981) criticizes the U.S.O.E. definition for ignoring the critical role of motivation. On the basis of studies of persons who have made significant contributions to society (Renzulli et al., 1981), Renzulli defines a gifted student as one who is (a) high in **creativity,** (b) high in **task commitment** (motivation), and (c) above average—but not necessarily outstanding—in **ability** (intelligence). (See Figure 17.1.)

Taylor's Multiple-Talent Totem Poles

Psychologist Calvin W. Taylor enjoys making the issue of "Who is gifted? Who is talented?" as disturbing as possible. From Taylor's viewpoint, almost everyone is gifted and talented. He may be right. It's a virtual certainty

Figure 17.1
Renzulli's three-ring model of giftedness. Gifted students are defined as those who are high in creativity and motivation and above average in intelligence.

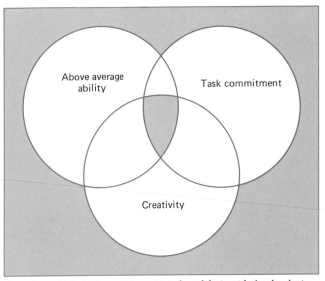

Above average ability

Task commitment

Creativity

From Renzulli, J. S. *The enrichment triad model: A guide for developing defensible programs for the gifted and talented.* Wethersfield, Conn.: Creative Learning Press, 1977. Reprinted by permission.

Figure 17.2
Taylor's Multiple Talent Totem Pole. The important point is that if you look at a large variety of gifts and talents, virtually every child will be above average—perhaps even outstanding—in something. Who is gifted? Who is talented? Almost every student.

that you, the reader, have one or more special areas of skill, information, or interest—special strengths that most people do not have. Do you play an instrument well? Sing? Play a good game of bridge? Chess? Do you tie flies? Speak a foreign language fluently? Cook exotic dishes with gourmet skill? Fix mufflers? Understand computers or the stock market? If we dig—and probably not too far—we will find that virtually every student has special gifts and talents. According to Taylor, the question becomes: How many types of giftedness can your program tolerate?

In a recent article entitled "How Many Types of Giftedness Can Your Program Tolerate?" Taylor (1978) described his famous **totem poles** (Figure 17.2). The idea is fairly straightforward. If we use the traditional *academic ability* (IQ, achievement) talent for selecting gifted students, Ann—who is at the top of the academic totem pole in Figure 17.2—is the natural choice. However, if *creativity* also is considered, Steve is the most outstanding. If we look at *planning* (organizing, designing) talents, little Randy heads the top of the pole. For *communicating*, Kathy is the most talented. Who should be selected for a G/T program? It's not an easy question, says Taylor.

CHARACTERISTICS OF GIFTED STUDENTS

Intellectual, Personality, Motivational, and Avocational Traits

In order to help teachers recognize, identify, understand, and work with gifted and talented students, several scholars have itemized intellectual, personality, motivational, and avocational characteristics which these students often show. Of course, not all traits characterize all gifted and talented students.

Fox (1979) summarized these cognitive/intellectual characteristics of gifted students:

1. They learn at a faster pace.
2. They master higher levels of content at an earlier age.
3. They handle abstract concepts with greater understanding and insight.
4. They may be outstanding in some areas, but quite average in others.

Supplementing Fox's list, Pulvino, Colangelo and Zaffran (1976; Perrone, Karshner, and Male, 1979) and Maker (1982) listed these personality and behavioral characteristics. Gifted students:

1. Have an unusually advanced vocabulary; are effective in spoken and written communication.
2. Have a rich reading background.
3. Possess a large storehouse of information on a variety of topics.
4. Show a wide range of interests, or in exceptional cases a heavy concentration on one.
5. Are keen observers; usually "see more" than others.
6. Spend time beyond usual assignments or schedules on things that interest them, special projects of their own.
7. Perform significantly above grade level in school subjects, and usually receive good grades.
8. Give refreshing twists to even old ideas.
9. Have rapid insight into cause-effect relationships.
10. Show little patience with routine procedures and skills.
11. Ask penetrating questions, particularly about causes and reasons; like to seek answers to problems and puzzles.

James J. Gallagher (1975a), noted expert on the gifted, reviewed a number of studies, conducted mainly in the 1960s, which concluded that gifted students typically are superior to average students in:

Truthfulness	Resourcefulness
Happiness	Maturation
Purposiveness	Moral reasoning and judgment
Judgment	Protectiveness

Self-sufficiency	Internal locus of evaluation
Independence	Personal adjustment
Dominance	Responsibility
Originality	Good work habits
Creativity	Achievement
Inventiveness	

It is interesting that Gallagher's list seems to describe a self-actualized person (Chapters 13, 16)—one who is creative, mentally healthy, self-initiated, high in moral reasoning, and who is developing his or her capabilities to the fullest.

A study of Merit Scholar finalists, studied as college seniors, showed them to be less religious, less conventional, and more concerned with freedom from supervision—an interesting point for educators (Nichols and Davis, 1964; see Gallagher, 1975b). When selecting adjectives which described themselves, they frequently chose: Intellectual, dominant, forceful, idealistic, rebellious, moody, lazy, witty, and cultured. Would you enjoy a roomful of students who see themselves as forceful, rebellious, moody, and lazy? How about intellectual, idealistic, witty, and cultured?

One G/T program director said that his students:

- Have an irresistible desire to devour a subject. They may, in fact, become a bit arrogant about being an expert on a particular topic.
- Set high standards for themselves. They may become so self-critical that they may not feel successful at anything.
- Resist routines at school and home, such as spelling drills, chores, TV rules, or bedtime.
- Are serious minded, interested in world affairs, the meaning of life, and other adult topics.
- Need to make observations, establish cause-effect relationships. They seek order, structure, consistency.
- Are sensitive to values, such as honor and truth.
- Are sensitive and empathetic to people, situations, and circumstances, such as underdog causes and liberal political positions—both of which may upset parents.
- Are intolerant of ignorance, including that of teachers or other authorities.

Terman's Gifted Students

No description of characteristics of gifted students would be complete without a brief description of the famous Terman research. Indeed, the most studied group of gifted people in the world are the subjects in Lewis Terman's longitudinal study of 1500 gifted children—800 boys and 700 girls. As a brief background, in the 1920s Terman and Melita Oden (1925, 1947, 1951, 1959) used the Stanford-Binet test, which he helped develop (Chapter 15), to identify his subjects. All were selected by scoring 140 or higher, the upper one percent. The ensuing field studies in 1927–1928, 1939–1940, and late 1950s, interspersed with occasional mailings, traced the personal and professional doings of the subjects for over half a century. The work is being carried on by Terman's survivors (e.g., R. R. Sears, 1977; P. S. Sears, 1979; P. S. Sears and Barbe, 1977).

One of the main findings pertaining to personality was the fact that Terman's kids were *better* adjusted and healthier than the average student. The myth of brilliant students being undersized, weak, unpopular, disturbed, neurotic, one-sided in their abilities, or emotionally unstable simply was not true. They were not only well adjusted in childhood, but showed a below-average incidence of suicide and mental illness as adults.

Terman and Oden (1951, pp. 12–14) summarized the main characteristics of their gifted children as follows:

1. The average member of our group is a slightly better physical specimen than the average child.
2. For the fields of subject matter covered in our tests, the superiority of gifted over unselected children was greater in reading, language usage, arithmetical reasoning, science, literature, and the arts. In arithmetical computation, spelling and factual information about history and civics, the superiority of the gifted was somewhat less marked.
3. The interests of gifted children are many-sided and spontaneous, they learn to read easily and read more and better books than the average child. At the same time, they make numerous collections, cultivate many kinds of hobbies, and acquire far more knowledge of plays and games than the average child.
4. As compared with unselected children, they are less inclined to boast or to overstate their knowledge; they are more trustworthy when under temptation to cheat; their character preferences and social attitudes are more wholesome, and they score higher in a test of emotional stability.
5. The deviation of the gifted subjects from the generality is in the upward direction for nearly all traits. There is no law of compensation whereby the intellectual superiority of the gifted tends to be offset by inferiorities along nonintellectual lines.

What happened to Terman's geniuses? Unfortunately, it was not fashionable in the '20s, '30s, and '40s for women to get excited about a career. Depending on your comedian, a woman's place was in the oven (Woody Allen) or the maternity ward. One female Terman subject reported,

"When it came time to go to college, it was deep depression for the family. Of course, my brother went to college, but not I" (P. S. Sears, 1979). Nonetheless, Terman's girls did produce one gifted poet, one talented actress and author of a successful broadway play, and ". . . successful novelists and journalists" (Terman and Oden, 1951).

Many (not all) of the 800 fellows, however, made a big splash:

> *The achievement of the group at midlife is best illustrated by the case histories of the 800 men, since only a minority of the women have gone out for professional careers. By 1950, when the men had an average age of 40 years, they had published 67 books (46 in the field of science, arts, and the humanities, and 11 books of fiction). They had published more than 1400 scientific, technical, and professional articles; over 200 short stories, novelettes, and plays, and 236 miscellaneous articles on a great variety of subjects. They had also authored more than 150 patents. The figures on publications do not include the hundreds of publications by journalists that classify as news stories, editorials, or newspaper columns, nor do they include the hundreds if not thousands of radio and television scripts. . . . The level of education attained by this group was over ten times that expected of the general population (Terman and Oden, 1951, pp. 33–34).*

Incidentally, according to Renzulli (1981), the main distinction between Terman's males who achieved eminence and those who did not was a difference in creativity and motivation, since both groups were equal in intelligence. This argument, of course, support's Renzulli's case for defining a gifted student as one who is high in ability, creativity, *and* motivation (see Renzulli's three-ring model in Figure 17.1).

PLANNING A PROGRAM FOR THE GIFTED AND TALENTED

In planning an eduational program for gifted and talented students at any grade level, sooner or later you the planner will need to attend to these five concerns:

1. Needs assessment.
2. A written philosophy and rationale (and perhaps a written plan).
3. Identification procedures.
4. Instructional plans.
5. Program evaluation and modification.

Teachers and administrators frequently begin with step (3) or (4), and then fill in with the other steps as the problems arise. However, life will be much simpler if you attend to the problems in the above order.

Needs Assessment

The basic problem in the needs-assessment stage is to clarify what the heck you are doing and what needs to be done. You should begin by determining the *present status* of gifted education in your district, city, or even state. You might ask:

- What is being done at present?
- What does the superintendent and the school board think about G/T programs? (Some will oppose them.)
- Is there a written policy? A state plan?
- Is there a G/T coordinator in the district or state central office?
- Are there interested teachers? Parents? Parent groups?
- Most importantly, what are the needs of the gifted and talented students in your school?

Your needs-assessment stage can include some firm preliminary decisions regarding:

1. Who the program is for, and the identification methods and criteria (issues and strategies are discussed below).
2. The scope and content of the program, including acceleration and enrichment strategies, grouping and individualization plans (some options will be discussed below), and curriculum development.
3. Assignment of leadership roles.
4. Teacher inservice training plans, including visits to other G/T programs.
5. Plans for creativity and other personal development and "process" (e.g., scientific or critical thinking) activities.
6. Program evaluation.

A Written Philosophy and Rationale

Everyone—parents, administrators, the school board, other teachers—will want to know what you are doing and why, especially if you ask for money or for released time for one or more teachers. Your philosophy statement should include the *reasons* for the program and the program *objectives*. An excellent guide for preparing a statement of philosophy or a written plan is Kaplan's (1974) *Providing Programs for the Gifted and Talented*. As a sample of the possible content of a philosophy-and-goals statement, consider the following reasons and objectives:

- "For the minority of children at the upper end of the mental ability continuum the regular educational program is inappropriate . . . the plight of the highly able pupil is often ignored and left unchallenged" (Kaplan, 1974, p. 34).
- "The gifted and talented represent a group of students whose learning style and thinking dimensions demand experiences which are outside the educational mainstream" (Kaplan, p. 8).
- Our objectives are: to provide ". . . appropriate learning experiences which incorporate the academic, psychological and social needs of these students" (Kaplan, p. 8).

- To include "... administrative procedures and instructional strategies which afford intellectual acquisition, thinking practice, and self-understanding" (Kaplan, p. 8).
- To provide G/T students with an educational environment that will provide the greatest possible development of their abilities, thus enabling them to realize their contributions to self and society.
- To provide opportunities that will develop self-awareness, personal strengths, and social responsibilities beyond those in the regular school program.
- To provide gifted children with the opportunity to explore personal interests through independent study and community involvement.
- To provide experiences which develop the higher cognitive operations of analyzing, synthesizing, divergent production, and evaluation.
- To provide activities and experiences that will stimulate critical thinking, comprehension, competency, and creativity.
- To include strong components of basic skills, career awareness, sex-equity, and multiethnic experiences.

INSET 17.2

**PREPARING
A WRITTEN PLAN**

Kaplan (1974) presented an eleven-point description of a written plan for G/T programs. Such a plan formalizes the program—and indicates in black and white exactly what the program is to accomplish and how these goals are to be met. The plan thus can serve as a guide for evaluating how well the program achieves its objectives. The written plan should be sufficiently clear and detailed that it answers virtually any question without interpretation by the program developers. The eleven elements are:

1. Population and enrollment.
2. Descriptive summary.
3. Philosophy, goals, and objectives.
4. Identification procedures.
5. Organization patterns: prototypes, facilities, time allocation.
6. Curricular opportunities: activities, techniques, materials.
7. Differentiation from regular school program.
8. Accountability of personnel.
9. Supportive services: inservice, consultants, auxiliary personnel.
10. Budgetary allocations.
11. Evaluation processes.

- To foster awareness of self and others.
- "The good of any program for the gifted should be to provide meaningful experiences in the most efficient and effective way in order to maximize learning and individual development and to minimize boredom, confusion, and frustration" (Fox, 1979).

Your statement of philosophy and goals also must include at least a brief description of the identification procedures—your definition of *who* is gifted—and an overview of the educational program. An extended and detailed philosophy and rationale statement can serve as a "written plan" for your program, a plan which should answer almost any question anyone could ask (see Inset 17.2).

Identification   A **multiple-talent** approach to giftedness (see the U.S.O.E. definition and Taylor's Multiple Talent Totem Poles, above) is almost universally accepted. Gifts and talents involve more than just a high IQ score and/or high grades. The following list of identification methods reflects a multiple-talent orientation

- Group intelligence tests (Chapter 15)
- Individual intelligence tests (Chapter 15)
- Achievement tests (standardized and teacher-made)
- School grades
- Creativity tests (Chapter 16)
- Teacher nominations (see Martinson, 1974)
- Parent nominations
- Peer nominations
- Self-nominations
- Motivation rating scales (Renzulli, Hartman, and Callahan, 1975)
- Leadership rating scales (Renzulli *et al.*, 1975)
- Product evaluations

Virtually all programs use some combination of these, weighted in various ways. Of course, the particular identification procedures used must match the goals of the program. For example, a program may focus strictly on mathematics acceleration, art, music, or science projects; or it may be a program capable of individualizing learning for any bright, energetic student.

Whichever methods and criteria are used, at least three problems or issues may arise. First, if teacher nominations are used (and they almost always are), teachers may nominate "teacher pleasers" for participation—punctual, cooperative, dutiful, hardworking, neat, smiling, and at least moderately intelligent students. Teachers may ignore a more brilliant or creative, but slightly obnoxious, gifted student.

Second, ability tests may identify a very bright underachiever. His or her teachers may argue against selecting this person, since "he/she is not very gifted in my class!" Third, both tests and teachers may not recognize

---

INSET 17.3

**THE REVOLVING DOOR
IDENTIFICATION
MODEL: RENZULLI**

The Revolving Door Identification Model of G/T education leader Joseph Renzulli (Renzulli, Reis, and Smith, 1981) seems to be a highly rational approach to the selection of and programming for gifted and talented students. Typically, students are selected in the early fall for participation in a special program. For example, if the district budget and guidelines allows for five percent of a school of 250 students to participate, about 13 students will be selected in September. They are "in," and the other bright, creative, and energetic students will be "out" for the entire year.

With the Revolving Door plan, a Talent Pool is identified on the bases of both objective data (intelligence tests, achievement tests, grades, creativity tests, and so on) and subjective evaluations. The Talent Pool comprises about 25 percent of the school population; in the present example, about 63 students. The previous "13 students" is redefined as "13 slots." Now, whenever a teacher detects a student who is above average in intellectual ability, creative, and highly motivated to work on an independent project, that student (after review) is shuttled to the G/T resource room to be aided and supervised by the G/T resource specialist.

When the student completes his or her project—perhaps a study of hummingbird migration, the making of a film, the writing of a play, or research on the disappearance of dinosaurs—he or she (a) steps aside so another gifted student can fill the slot and work on a project, (b) develops a more advanced project on the same topic, or (c) develops an interest in a new project. With (b) or (c), the student is reconsidered along with others in the Talent Pool for permission to work in the resource room.

The RDIM capitalizes on Renzulli's three-ring definition of giftedness—above average ability, creativity, and high motivation (task commitment). Only students from the Talent Pool are selected, and only if they show all three qualities. Also, since the selection procedure is a continuous one, teachers must remain alert all year for candidates for the program; identification is not finished in September, as with other G/T strategies.

The Revolving Door model will be a widely accepted and adopted identification and programming plan in the 1980s.

gifted minority, disadvantaged, or handicapped students. We often do not look for gifted students in such populations.

As a final identification note, the characteristics of gifted students described above also should help a teacher identify children and adolescents who are good candidates for a G/T program.

INSET 17.4

**WHO KNOWS
WHO'S WHO?**

One way to identify gifted children is to ask the kids in the class—they know who's who. The Milwaukee Public School System created a structured peer nomination form which seems to ask: Who has a lot of information (1)? Who does school work quickly and easily (2)? Who is creative (3, 5)? Who is a leader (4)?

You simply tally up who has the most votes in each category. A student who is outstanding in *all* categories is a good prospect for your G/T program.

Directions to Teacher

Read the following statements to your class:

a) "Each of you has been asked to assist in an information gathering survey for the Milwaukee Public Schools."
b) "Please take out a sheet of paper and a pencil."
c) "Number your paper from 1 to 5."
d) "Please answer each question that I will read with the *complete* name of one student in our class."
e) "Pick someone whom you think is the best choice and not just your friends."
f) "You can pick the same person for more than one question if you think that person is your best choice."

Questions

1. If a person from outer space wanted someone in your class to tell him about different things on earth, who do you think could tell the most?
2. What student in class can complete his or her work and still have time to take part in other activities?
3. Who says things in class that are most original, things that you never thought of before?
4. If kids didn't have to go to school, what student in your class could talk you into going?
5. Who do you think might invent or make something that no one ever made before? (This is the person you might ask to help you write a poem or play, or help you make something for a school science fair.)

Educational Programs: Acceleration Strategies

As the name directly implies, the gifted student in an **acceleration** plan proceeds at a faster pace than his or her age-mates—"... to a higher level of content, and to more abstract and evaluative thinking" (Fox, 1979). To help clarify the distinction between acceleration and enrichment, acceleration plans are those which result in advanced credit or advanced placement. Acceleration strategies usually do not involve great financial expense. In fact, money may be saved by accelerating gifted students through and out of an elementary or secondary school. Some acceleration strategies are:

1. Early admission to kindergarten, first grade, junior or senior high school.
2. Early admission to college.
3. Advanced placement or subject skipping. For example, first- or second-year high school students might be placed into junior- or senior-level math, chemistry, physics, botany or composition classes.
4. Credit by examination. This is similar to advanced placement. The student earns credit for the skipped classes by scoring sufficiently high on relevant examinations, thus reducing the number of required semesters for graduation.
5. Grade skipping.
6. College courses taken by junior or senior high school students (see Inset 17.5).
7. University correspondence courses, an option which might appeal to talented high school students who do not have a nearby college.
8. Telescoping* with homogeneously grouped gifted classes. Especially useful in the junior high school, these classes cover three years' content in two years. Such classes also can provide greater depth and breadth of coverage. They also may include special opportunities for self-directed study, work with a community professional (mentor), or other creative development activities.
9. Telescoping high school requirements into three years. This may be done by "... reducing or eliminating electives, earning credit by examination, skipping grade levels in some subjects but not others, taking college or summer courses outside of school, and combinations of all of these" (Fox, 1979).

Educational Programs: Enrichment Strategies

Often **enrichment** programs include far too much fun and games ("That's enough finger-painting, kids—let's build an igloo and then practice tic tac toe!"). Gallagher (1975b), Fox (1979), and Renzulli (1977) recommended that for enrichment activities to be valuable, they should: (a) help students see

---

* *Telescoping* refers to "grade skipping" without missing any significant curriculum content by condensing three years' work into two, or perhaps four years' work into three. Items 8 and 9 describe the two main telescoping strategies (Fox, 1979).

INSET 17.5

STANLEY'S STUDY OF MATHEMATICALLY PRECOCIOUS YOUTH (SMPY)

The best-known example of accelerating bright secondary students into college-level mathematics courses is Julian C. Stanley's (1979a) SMPY program, the Study of Mathematically Precocious Youth, at Johns Hopkins University. On the basis of very high SAT-M scores (Scholastic Aptitude Test-Mathematics) obtained in an Annual Mathematics Talent Search, seventh, eighth, and ninth grade students begin taking ". . . special mathematics classes, usually taught by a college professor . . ." at Johns Hopkins.

"Since 1972, SMPY has seen hundreds of youths take college courses for credit before becoming full-time college students. The cumulative gradepoint average of the group is 3.6, well above the requirement for being placed on the Dean's List at Johns Hopkins" (Stanley, 1979a; see also Stanley, 1979b; Solano and George, 1976). The SMPY program has served as an exemplary model for other mathematics and science acceleration programs.

relationships among facts and ideas; (b) encourage original and creative thinking; (c) provide an opportunity to work through complex problems and issues; or (d) develop higher-level thinking skills.

Some enrichment options are:

1. Mainstreaming the gifted. There are circumstances in which the gifted child must be taught by the regular teacher in the regular class, for example, when a school has no formal G/T program. Some strategies are: (a) individual tutoring; (b) diagnostic-prescriptive teaching, in which individual objectives and curricula are based on a diagnosis of particular strengths and weaknesses; (c) self-directed research projects; and (d) learning centers (see 4, below).

2. Field trips to museums, art galleries, concerts, factories, aquariums, planetariums, geological formations, and so on.

3. Pull-out programs, in which gifted elementary students are "pulled out" for from one hour to one afternoon (or day) per week, usually to work on special projects (e.g., a newspaper, individual research projects) or to engage in personal development activities (e.g., creative thinking, critical thinking, evaluation exercises, problem solving, moral thinking exercises, values clarification, sensitivity and awareness, etc.).

4. Learning centers. There are many commercially available table-top learning centers designed for individual enrichment experiences. Creative teachers also may design their own. In some cases, entire buildings or large portions of buildings are designated as "learning centers" and are used as resource rooms, work rooms for special projects, or classrooms for special classes or seminars.

5. Self-directed research projects. These are explained below in conjunction with Renzulli's Type III enrichment.

6. Special classes. Especially in the junior or senior high school, special classes may be created in one or two subjects (advanced botany, physics, organic chemistry, computer programming, jewelry making, music writing, etc.) or in all subjects.

7. Extra classes. A fast-learning gifted high school student might be counseled into exchanging his or her "open" hour for something more challenging, e.g., calculus, physics II, etc.

8. Magnet schools, satellite schools. In large cities, one high school may be designated as a school for sciences and/or engineering, another as a school for drama and dance, another as an art school, and so on. Students attend the high school matching their interests, needs and talents.

9. Special schools. In large cities an entire elementary school may be designated as a school for gifted students, who are bused in from all corners of the area. One such school, the Golda Meier School in Milwaukee, is staffed by enthusiastic teachers who offer training in foreign languages, piano, and other enriched and accelerated areas.

10. School-within-a-school. With this option, the gifted and talented students in a school attend special classes taught by special teachers for part of the day, but mix with the rest of the students for nonacademic subjects (e.g., physical education, study hall, manual arts) and sports and social events.

11. Summer institutes, Governor's schools. One expensive alternative is the Governor's school concept, a form of live-in summer school in which gifted and talented students receive specialized training from professionals. Art, creative writing, music, mathematics, physics, and computers are some frequent foci. A strong plus for the Governor's school concept is that students from all areas of a state—including disadvantaged communities—meet with other students and professionals who have similar talents and interests.

12. Mentor programs, internships. This plan takes advantage of professional talent in the community. Virtually any artist, musician, executive, museum director, business manager, actor, newspaper editor, journalist, printer, mortician, researcher, doctor, lawyer, or police chief is fair game. The student spends a few hours per week with the mentor, receiving personal training and learning about the glories and pitfalls

of the particular profession. A formal internship might include being paid for services (e.g., in a printing shop) while learning about the business.

13. Career education. Career education can take many forms. It can include coursework in areas of professional interest, such as writing, archeology, statistics, journalism, psychology, and so on. It can include mentor programs and internships. It can include information on opportunities and needed training. Career education also can include strong contributions from counselors who help students understand their strengths, their weaknesses and their interests. Career choice can be a difficult problem for students with many talents and many interests (Sanborn, 1979). Career education is especially complicated for women, and may include such problems as (a) encouraging them not to suppress "unfeminine" talents, (b) dealing with a possible conflict between female-domestic roles and professional roles, (c) informing them of the importance of advanced mathematics to some college majors and careers, and (d) learning about legal rights regarding educational and vocational opportunities (Wolleat, 1979).

14. Saturday programs. Saturday (morning) programs can include special classes in art, science, computers, or other high interest topics that will encourage energetic learners to sacrifice one of their two days of rest.

Enrichment Triad Model: Renzulli

Gifted educator Joseph Renzulli (1977; Renzulli and Smith, 1978) has attracted considerable attention in the field of G/T education with his **Enrichment Triad Model.** The model includes three sequential but qualitatively different steps: Type I activities are *general exploratory activities* designed to acquaint students with a variety of topics and interest areas. Type II training group activities deal with the *development of thinking and feeling processes,* for example, scientific methods, self-awareness, and creativity. Type I and II activities are appropriate for all students, not just the gifted ones (Renzulli, 1977). Type III activities, appropriate for gifted students, focus on the *investigation of real problems*—actual research on problems " . . . that are similar in nature to those pursued by authentic researchers or artists in particular fields" (Renzulli, 1977).

Figure 17.3, inspired by a Los Angeles freeway sign, shows that (a) the three activities are interrelated, and (b) most of the time and effort of gifted students should be invested in Type III activities.

We noted above that Renzulli defined gifted students as those who are high in motivation and creativity, and at least above average in intelligence. It is this combination of traits which enables them to successfully carry out Type III enrichment activities (Renzulli, 1977; Renzulli, Reis, and Smith, 1981).

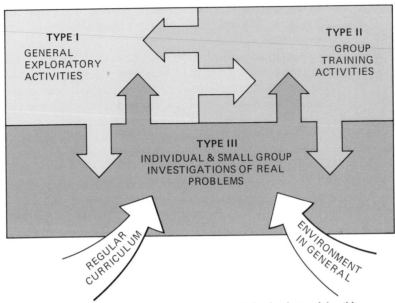

Figure 17.3
Renzulli's
enrichment triad
model.

From Renzulli, J. S. *The enrichment triad model: A guide for developing defensible programs for the gifted and talented.* Wethersfield, Conn.: Creative Learning Press, 1977. Reprinted by permission.

Type I enrichment. Type I activities, general exploratory experiences, are intended to expose students to a wide variety of topic areas, to give them ideas for later Type III projects. Some students already will have long-standing interests or hobbies which are well suited for Type III projects. In these cases the exploratory Type I activities will serve mainly to broaden the students' scope of interests.

Type I enrichment includes both a well-stocked resource center and field experiences in which the gifted students meet dynamic people involved in creative and problem-solving endeavors—artists, actors, engineers, museum and art gallery curators, TV show directors, business leaders, and so on.

Type II enrichment. The purpose of Type II training activities is to strengthen "thinking and feeling" processes—skills, abilities, attitudes, and strategies—which should enable all students to better deal with a variety of problems in different topic areas. The thinking and feeling skills are especially important for the advanced independent work (Type III enrichment) of the gifted students.

Some affective concerns are sensitivity, awareness, and social responsibility training, values clarification, and self-concept development (Chapter 13). Other cognitive processes and skills might include creative thinking, problem solving, critical thinking, and discovery learning; Bloom's objectives of application, analysis, synthesis, and evaluation (Chapter 14); and library and research skills.

Renzulli recommends that the process activities be related to students' interests or topic areas. For example, Cheryl Shutterbug might solve problems, create, analyze, and evaluate within her pet area of photography.

We might mention that many G/T programs focus *exclusively* on the sort of process activities listed in Renzulli's Type II enrichment. A danger, note Renzulli and Smith (1978), is that too much emphasis on process activities may be at the expense of individual projects which truly develop independent-research, problem-solving, and creative skills. Which brings us to Type III enrichment.

Type III enrichment. With Type III activities, the gifted young person becomes an actual researcher investigating a real problem or an artist developing original works. Students thus should act as *producers* of knowledge or art, not *consumers* of information. That is, they should not simply do more math problems or consult more encyclopedias and textbooks and write more reports.

The types of topic areas and projects are virtually unlimited, and could include anything from aeronautics, agriculture, antipollution, archeology, and astronomy to set design, silk screening, transportation design, weaving, and zoology. Whatever the project, the student plays an active part in formulating the problem and designing the research or artistic methods. The teacher serves as a "guide on the side," helping to clarify the problem and recommending information sources or community experts for guidance.

Outlets for creations. It is very desirable for students to have an audience for their Type III research results or creative product (Renzulli, 1977). Gifted students are product-oriented—they wish to show their accomplishments, to inform and perhaps influence a particular audience. Renzulli suggests that such local organizations as historical societies or science or dramatic groups might be suitable audiences. Children's magazines and newspapers routinely publish children's writings and research summaries. There may be community, city, state, or national children's art shows or science fairs which also could be good outlets for the children's products. (If such shows are not available, think about starting some.) Local newspapers also like a human interest story, and good publicity definitely will not hurt your G/T program.

Program Evaluation

You, your board of education, and your school district will need to evaluate the "success" of your gifted program; you also will need information allowing you to revise and improve the program. If you wish to be technical, the term **formative evaluation** is used to describe evaluation based on continuous feedback, information used to modify and improve the program while it is in operation (Renzulli and Smith, 1979). **Summative evaluation** is concerned with overall program effectiveness—its success or lack thereof.

Depending on the type of program and the type of objectives, evaluating success (summative evaluation) may be relatively *easy* or relatively *difficult*. Beginning with the "easy" category, the criteria for success of most acceleration strategies is virtually self-evident. Did the students succeed in the advanced classes? Did they perform well in their college or correspondence courses? Were there any drawbacks in letting Herman skip a grade? Or permitting Matilda to enter kindergarten at age four?

Enrichment plans which result in a *bona fide* product, such as a report of a research project, a school newspaper, a poetry book, an environmental impact study, artwork, etc., also provide easy program evaluation data: There is a clear change in student skills and performances which most likely would not have taken place without the G/T program (Renzulli and Smith, 1979). Some other readily available (easy) criteria of success can be found in records of, e.g., number of history, philosophy, or science books read, the amount of time spent at the microcomputer, pottery wheel, or in the executive's office, or the number of chemistry or physics experiments completed.

It gets "difficult" to evaluate the success of a program when the focal goals are improving creativity, self-awareness, self-concept, decision-making, reasoning, analyzing, synthesizing, evaluating, social responsibility, critical thinking, intrinsic motivation, sex-equity and multiethnic experiences—all of which are, in fact, stated objectives of G/T programs described in the Fall, 1979, issue of the *Gifted Child Quarterly*. The difficulty of evaluating such affective and process objectives is compounded by the fact that many programs outline different goals and objectives *for each student*. Some program planners have used creativity tests in an effort to evaluate changes in creative potential; others have used personality and self-concept tests to evaluate any improvement in self-awareness, self-concepts, or social and interpersonal attitudes. The problem, as stated by Renzulli (Renzulli and Smith, 1979), is: "... standardized tests of cognitive and affective abilities may fail to yield valid information about student growth. ... Selecting and constructing appropriate data gathering instruments is perhaps the most difficult aspect of evaluating programs for the gifted and talented."

In your author's experience, one effective and productive strategy for evaluating the success of training programs is the direct approach—*ask* the persons involved (teachers, students, parents) for their opinions. Although their answers may be biased, due to personal involvement in and commitment to the program, valuable ideas and suggestions still can be elicited by asking such questions as:

- Do you feel the program was a success? Explain.
- Do you feel the students' communication (speaking, writing) skills have improved as a result of the program?
- Do you feel the students are now much better informed about their research topic areas as a result of the program?
- Do you feel the student's creative thinking habits and skills have improved?
- Do you feel the students have more self-confidence as a result of the program?
- What do you like best about our special program?
- What do you like least about our program?
- Can you suggest changes?

Such direct questions can provide a wealth of straightforward feedback regarding the perceived successes and shortcomings of the program. Renzulli (1975) provides rating scales and checklists which may be used by students, teachers, parents, the school board, or an evaluation team to evaluate strengths and weaknesses of G/T programs.

Finally, we should note that some outside persons—the principal, members of the school board, the district superintendent, parents—may evaluate the results of your program strictly according to the statement of philosophy and rationale or other written plan. They will ask such questions as: Were the identification procedures sensible, effective, and fair? Were the instructional strategies carried out as planned? What happened to the trip to American Popcorn and Kidney Research facility? Did students really become independent learners, thinkers, creators, and problem solvers? Were skills of analysis, synthesis, evaluation, critical thinking, and divergent thinking really strengthened? Were mentor/professionals in the community used as planned? Were the evaluation and modification procedures carried out as planned? If not, why not?

Such questions clearly serve as a means of "controlling" or "checking up on" the program leaders, and may easily be perceived as threatening.

DESIRABLE CHARACTERISTICS OF TEACHERS OF THE GIFTED

Before you volunteer to organize your school's G/T program, and agree to teach in a pull-out program, or an advanced class, or to serve as the resource specialist, you may wish to consider characteristics which make for good teachers of gifted and talented students. First, it is helpful (but not essential) if the teacher is highly gifted, talented and/or creative. This facilitates communication with and understanding of gifted children and adolescents. Second, the teacher also should be sufficiently secure and confident to work with students who may be more intelligent, quicker at reasoning and making inferences, more creative, or more artistic than the teacher is.

Finally, the teacher should be dedicated to teaching, energetic, and enthusiastic about developing or improving a program and working with gifted and talented students. There is a lot of planning and administrating to be done; and students will need guidance and training with projects and activities that the teacher will have to learn about for the first time.

TO IMPROVE YOUR TEACHING

In Chapter 16 we recommended that you become creativity conscious. Now, we suggest that you add "gifted conscious." The school you eventually join, whether an elementary or junior or senior high school, may or may not have programs and plans for gifted students. If they do not, you may wish to discuss the matter with other teachers, school counselors and psychologists, the principal, and perhaps even district administrators. A careful rereading of this chapter, plus some of the recommended readings, will enable you to propose informed identification and programming alternatives. You also should be able to prepare a written philosophy and rationale, and eventually a complete written plan.

If your school does have a G/T program, you should be in position to extend and improve it. You might examine the selection procedures to see if they are sensible, defensible, and fair. No matter what the current identification criteria are, some talented children probably are excluded. Look especially at the disadvantaged, minority, or handicapped students to see if gifted ones have been overlooked. Suggest that parents be asked about participation by their child—who might be gifted and creative only in spare-time hobbies at home.

Also, whatever the current program plan, it can be extended. If your elementary school has a Friday afternoon pull-out program, suggest grade skipping, subject skipping, a telescoped plan, special classes (this will cost!), or a Saturday art or science class. If your junior or senior high school handles gifted students simply by letting them self-select more challenging math, chemistry, or art classes, you might suggest college course work (which will take some organizing), college correspondence courses, telescoping into a three-year plan, early college admission, or a mentor or internship plan.

Gifted students should not be held back. You will be in a position to help them develop their intellectual, creative, affective, and social capabilities.

SUMMARY

There is a growing interest in special programs for gifted and talented children. Such training benefits the G/T children and society. It is undemocratic and unfair to prevent these students from realizing their potential.

The Marland U.S.O.E. definition of giftedness includes: (1) general intellectual ability, (2) specific academic aptitude, (3) creative or productive thinking, (4) leadership ability, (5) verbal and performing arts, and (6) psychomotor ability.

Renzulli defines giftedness as including above average intelligence, high creativity, and high motivation (task commitment).

Taylor's Multiple Talent Totem Pole concept suggests that every student in the class will be above average—perhaps even outstanding—in something.

There are many identified traits of gifted students. Some especially recurrent ones are: high achievement, high creativity, high energy, wide interests, creativity, independence, dominance, high moral reasoning and values, internal locus of evaluation; the ability to learn faster and to higher and more abstract levels; and better personality adjustment. The students also may be self-critical or arrogant about their expertness, intolerant of ignorance, and may resist routines.

Terman's 1500 gifted (IQ = 140+) students were better looking, better adjusted, more trustworthy, and higher achievers in school and in careers. More males achieved at higher levels than females, due to the social framework of the '30s, '40s, and '50s.

Planning a gifted program requires attention to:

1. Needs assessment, including an analysis of the current status of G/T education in your area and a listing of what needs to be done— identification procedures, inservice training, acceleration and enrichment plans, curriculum materials, evaluation plans, and especially an analysis of the needs of the gifted and talented students.
2. A written philosophy and rationale, including reasons for and objectives of the program, plus an overview of the entire program.
3. Identification procedures, which (based on a multiple-talent approach) may include: Intelligence, achievement, and creativity tests; grades; nominations by teachers, parents, peers, or gifted students themselves; ratings on motivation, leadership; and product evaluations.

Attention must be paid to the problems of overselecting "teacher pleasers," underselecting minority, disadvantaged, and handicapped students, and underselecting bright underachievers who score high on intelligence tests.

Renzulli's Revolving Door Identification Model recommends a continuous selection and participation process during the school year.

4. Programming plans. For acceleration (advanced credit or placement), these may include early admission to kindergarten, first grade, junior or senior high school, or college; subject or grade skipping; credit by exam; college courses; and telescoping.

   For enrichment, they may include mainstreaming, field trips, pull-out programs, learning centers, research projects, special classes, magnet schools, special schools, schools-within-a-school, Governor's schools, mentor programs, career education, and Saturday programs.

5. Program evaluation, which may be easy (as in reviewing the effects of acceleration or evaluating the worth of students' projects), or difficult (as in evaluating improvements in self-concepts, creativity, or other higher-level thinking skills). Participants, teachers, or parents may be asked for their opinions. Outsiders may evaluate how well the written plans were carried out.

It is desirable for teachers of the gifted and talented to (a) be gifted, talented, and/or creative, (b) be secure and confident, and (c) be dedicated and energetic.

TOPICS FOR THOUGHT AND DISCUSSION

1. Are programs for the gifted unfair? Can you see both sides of the issue?
2. Imagine that an average student wishes to take the "special class" in science or computer programming. The principal insists the course is reserved for the "top 10 percent." What do you do?
3. Are all students talented, as C. W. Taylor says? Does this raise questions and problems for the selection process?
4. Marland's 1972 U.S.O.E. definition includes gifts and talents in six areas. Renzulli claims gifted students are those high in intelligence, creativity, and motivation. Is there a serious discrepancy here? Can you resolve it?
5. Which acceleration or enrichment strategies would be most suitable for the grade level or subject matter you expect to teach? Would these be financially feasible?

PROJECTS

1. When doing your student teaching or otherwise visiting a school, ask about their G/T identification and programming policies. Ask embarrassing questions, such as "Why aren't you using other identification strategies as well?" or "Have you considered other [name some] programming alternatives?"
2. Brainstorm specific activities, for example, for an elementary school pull-out program.
3. Do a literature search on identification strategies, individualizing instruction for the gifted, program plans, or evaluating gifted programs.

4. Locate groups in your state who are interested in promoting education of the gifted—parent groups, educator groups, state and district coordinators, or others. These can be a good source of future social support, possible funds, and information.

5. Do a survey of G/T programs in your city, county, or state.

RECOMMENDED READING

Barbe, W. B., and J. S. Renzulli. *Psychology and education of the gifted*, second edition. New York: Irvington, 1975.

Clark, B. *Growing up gifted*. Columbus, Ohio: Charles E. Merrill, 1979.

Colangelo, N., and R. T. Zaffran (eds.). *New voices in counseling the gifted*. Dubuque, Iowa: Kendall/Hunt, 1979.

Gallagher, J. J. *Teaching the gifted child*, second edition. Boston: Allyn & Bacon, 1975.

Gifted Child Quarterly **23** (Fall), 1979. Special issue on local projects.

Helman, I. B., and S. G. Larson. *Now what do I do?* Buffalo, N.Y.: DOK, 1979.

Kaplan, S. *Providing programs for the gifted and talented*. Ventura, Calif.: Office of the Ventura County Superintendent of Schools, 1974.

Maker, C. J. *Curriculum development for the gifted*. Rockville, Md.: Aspen, 1982.

Renzulli, J. S. *The enrichment triad model: A guide for developing defensible programs for the gifted and talented*. Mansfield Center, Conn.: Creative Learning Press, 1977.

Renzulli, J. S., S. M. Reis, and L. H. Smith. *The revolving door identification model*. Mansfield Center, Conn.: Creative Learning Press, 1981.

Williams, F. E. *Classroom ideas for encouraging thinking and feeling*. Buffalo, N.Y.: DOK, 1970.

Mainstreaming and the Education of Exceptional Children

Prior to 1969, the teacher of a "regular" class filled with "regular" children did not worry much about coping with and teaching mildly handicapped children. A child who could not function in a regular class was referred to specialists for diagnosis and likely placement in "special ed" classes. The school psychologist, the speech teacher, the reading specialist, and the special education teachers were trained and paid for such services. Since the **Mainstreaming Act** of 1969 (Public Law 94-142), more and more handicapped children are appearing in regular classes to be taught by regular teachers, many of whom have not been ready for the special educational, adjustment, and social challenges often presented by exceptional students. Today's teachers must understand the various handicaps, and must possess strategies for teaching these children.

WHO ARE EXCEPTIONAL CHILDREN?

According to Kirk (1972), "The educationally exceptional child is one who deviates from the normal child in mental, physical, and/or social characteristics to such an extent that he requires a modification of school practices or educational services in order to develop to his maximum capacity." This definition includes both the gifted and talented (Chapter 17) and students who have handicaps—learning disabilities, mild retardation, emotional disturbance, or social maladjustment; hearing, vision, speech, or language impairments; or orthopedic, neurological, or health impairments.

In this chapter we will look first at the background, details, and some issues and problems of PL 94-142. Then we will review some of the main symptoms and problems of three categories of handicapped students, the learning disabled, mildly retarded, and emotionally disturbed, along with recommendations for teaching them. We also will look at the PL 94-142 mandated Individualized Education Program, which must be prepared for each handicapped student.

MAINSTREAMING

Public Law 94-142 is the Education for All Handicapped Children Act (see Inset 18.1). Its most famous three words are **"least restrictive environment,"** which must be provided for every child. It extends the right of all handicapped children to a "free and appropriate" public education; and access to a nonsegregated mainstream of American education. The "least restrictive environment" is the regular classroom. Public Law 94-142 has caught a lot of educators unprepared, from school superintendents and deans of teacher-training programs to principals, teachers, and support personnel in the

INSET 18.1

**EXCERPTS FROM THE
EDUCATION FOR ALL
HANDICAPPED
CHILDREN ACT
(PL 94-142)**

"A free public education will be made available to all handicapped children between the ages of 3 and 18 by no later than September of 1978 and all those between 3 and 21 by September of 1980 . . .

"For each handicapped child there will be an 'individualized educational program'—a written statement jointly developed by a qualified school official, by the child's teacher and parents or guardian, and if possible by the child himself . . .

"Handicapped and nonhandicapped children will be educated together to the maximum extent appropriate . . .

"Tests and other evaluation material used in placing handicapped children will be prepared and administered in such a way as not to be racially or culturally discriminatory, and they will be presented in the child's native tongue . . .

"There will be an intensive and continuing effort to locate and identify youngsters who have handicaps . . .

"The States and localities will undertake comprehensive personnel development programs, including inservice training for regular as well as special education teachers and support personnel and procedures will be launched for acquiring and disseminating information about promising educational practices and materials coming out of research and development efforts."

schools. The Education for All Handicapped Children Act requires local school districts to enroll handicapped children. It requires detailed accountability of the local school district to state and federal agencies. The Act requires a multidimensional assessment and an Individual Education Program (IEP; described later in this chapter) for each handicapped child.

The implementation of a "least restrictive learning environment" requires a common understanding by personnel at all levels of public education. It requires changes in attitudes toward handicapped children by educators who are misinformed or who have feelings of guilt or fear regarding these children. There is much more involved than learning a new batch of instructional tricks. There are administrative, legal, political, psychological, and financial dimensions to the problem.

In the words of University of Wisconsin Education Dean John Palmer, "The impact on the daily professional activity of teachers and other school personnel is dramatic, if not traumatic" (unpublished memo to School of Education Faculty, January 1978).

Roots of PL 94-142: The Supreme Court

In 1896 the United States Supreme Court ruled that a Louisiana law requiring separate railway accommodations for blacks and whites was constitutional. This was the famous, or infamous, "separate but equal" decision in the case of *Plessey* v. *Ferguson*. It set the stage for 60 years of segregation in education. Not until 1954, in *Brown* v. the *Board of Education of Topeka, Kansas*, did the Supreme court change its mind. In this case, the Supreme Court decided that separate facilities are "inherently unequal," and such a policy has no place in American education.

It does not take a lot of imagination to view separate schools and separate classes for the learning disabled, mildly retarded, and mildly emotionally disturbed as a form of segregation—the placing of certain students into restrictive environments. Mainstreaming and PL 94-142 constituted court-ordered desegregation, which moved these children into "least restrictive environments"—the regular classroom. Kaufman, Gottlieb, Agard, and Kukic (1975) reported that at least 36 cases in state and federal courts have been aimed at guaranteeing the handicapped child (a) the right to an education, (b) the right to appropriate treatment, and (c) the opportunity for appropriate placement.

Public Law 94-142 led to such dramatic changes in American educational practices that issues and problems were certain to arise. Especially, one researchable question was: Does mainstreaming work better than special education classes? That is, do the educational and emotional benefits outweigh the liabilities? Also, what problems do teachers have in the mainstreamed classroom? And what are the reactions of parents of handicapped children?

Special Classes vs. Mainstreaming: Which is More Effective?

Obviously, the idea behind special classes for exceptional children was that specially trained teachers and smaller classes would lead to superior academic achievement. Also, it was considered unfair or even cruel to require these children to compete in regular classrooms. Said L. C. Quay (1963) ". . . regardless of outcome, special class placement is important from a humanitarian point of view . . . [for it] prevents frustration and feelings of inferiority from undue competition." These were, and sometimes are, the professional opinions of special educators. Dunn (1968), however, reported that segregating special students has not produced the level of academic and social development which had previously been expected. Affleck (1975) also concluded that *not one* research study has shown that special students do, in fact, achieve at a higher level in special classes than in regular classes.

However, if we look at the other side of the coin, Lowenbraun and Affleck (1976, p. 7) reported that there also is no conclusive evidence that integration—mainstreaming—is superior to placement in special classes. Zigler and Muenchow (1979) similarly concluded that "To date, the data on the merits of educating retarded children with their nonretarded peers is simply inconclusive. Academically, it appears that mainstreamed retarded children fare no better or worse than children in special classes."

Social Acceptance and Self-Concept Development

Research on the social problems of handicapped students, which usually focuses on mildly retarded children and adolescents, most often (but not always) shows some amount of rejection by "normal" students. Bryan (1978) and Hoffman (1976) explained that some handicapped children—for example, mildly retarded, physically handicapped, or emotionally disturbed students—may visibly differ from peer group norms. Apparently, a "normal" child tends to feel that association with an atypical peer threatens the normal child's social image within his or her norm group (Mannheim, 1980). Several studies have shown that handicapped and emotionally disturbed

INSET 18.2

THE EFFECTS OF LABELS

We understand very well the stigma attached to labeling a child as emotionally disturbed, learning disabled, or mentally retarded. The labels lead to rejection and sometimes cruel treatment by peers. The labels also lead to negative expectations and to self-fulfilling prophecies by teachers (Chapter 2).

Exceptional-child expert Nicholas Hobbs (1975, p. 11) put the case even more strongly: "Categories and labels are powerful instruments for social regulation and control, and they are often employed for obscure, covert, or hurtful purposes: to degrade people, to deny them access to opportunity, to exclude 'undesirables' whose presence in some way offends, disturbs familiar custom, or demands extraordinary effort."

On the positive side, identifying the difficulty of a troubled student tells the teacher, school psychologist, and special ed teacher a great deal about the nature of the child's problem. The "label" also leads to ideas for treatment or remediation, ideas which have proven successful in past similar cases.

The clear dilemma is that although labeling a child as handicapped opens doors for special services and special funds, it also opens the door to discrimination and hurtful treatment.

children frequently are rated as the "least liked" in the classroom (Bruininks, 1978; Lansdown and Polak, 1975; Novak, 1974; Richardson, 1962, 1971). Burton and Hirshoren (1979) further found that the greater the severity of the problem, the greater the degree of social rejection.

In fact, mainstreamed students sometimes are brutalized by other students—for example, by name calling or other insults, along with social exclusion (Iano, Ayers, Heller, McGettigan, and Walker, 1974; Zigler and Muenchow, 1979). Now, daily social rejection by one's peers is not the most constructive feedback to use in forming a healthy self-concept. Students with personality or learning difficulties or physical handicaps easily sense the rejection—especially if it includes teasing. The social rejection lowers the atypical child's self-image and feelings of personal integrity (Bryan, 1978; Chiland, 1976; Halverson and Victor, 1976). The rejection also creates feelings of social inadequacy in comparison to others, which may lead to two possible coping strategies: Either withdrawal and isolation or else an impulsive striving to gain acceptance (Halverson and Victor, 1976).

There are, however, inconsistencies in the reports of the effects of mainstreaming on the self-concepts of handicapped children. Walker (1974), for example, reported no substantial changes in self-concepts due to mainstreaming. Budoff and Gottlieb (1976) found improved self-concepts among mainstreamed exceptional children. Strang, Smith, and Rogers (1978) helped clarify the conditions in which mainstreaming may help or hinder the development of a positive self-concept. They found that children mainstreamed on a half-day basis used other special education students as a comparison group, and thus showed improved self-concepts. On the other hand, students mainstreamed on a full-day basis compared themselves with regular students and showed a worsening of self-regard.

Overall, considering both academic and social-emotional development, a recent review by Meyers, MacMillan, and Yoshida (1980) simply concluded: "There appears to be no unambiguous answer to the primitive question of whether segregated or integrated placement is better." Zigler and Muenchow (1979) nailed down the problem a little more specifically: "Much more work is needed to determine . . . which children with which handicaps benefit from mainstreaming, (and) also what the environmental nutrients are that promote full development."

Some Complaints By Teachers

Many teachers feel the mainstreaming plan simply does not work. Some reasons:

- Instead of getting six hours of special attention in special education classes, taught by trained special education teachers, mainstreamed students receive only one or two hours of such special attention. Many

INSET 18.3

REQUIRED COOPERATION: ONE SOLUTION TO POOR SOCIAL RELATIONSHIPS

The usual teaching strategy of "treating everyone alike" does not necessarily lead to improved social relationships between normal and exceptional students (Forehand and Ragosta, 1976; Slavin, 1979). One potentially useful solution might be found in the longstanding principle of social psychology that group cooperation increases mutual attraction among group members and reduces prejudice (Allport, 1954). In a series of studies, Slavin and Madden (1979) created multiracial learning teams in which members worked together and were rewarded according to their group performance. Friendship choices on sociometric questionnaires reflected fairly dramatic increases in cross-racial friendship selections. A similar study by Johnson, Rynders, Johnson, Schmidt, and Haider (1979) showed that positive interactions among retarded and normal junior high students increased when five-person teams had a common goal—increasing the *team's* bowling score by 50 points in one week. When members of other teams were instructed to increase their *individual* scores by 10 points, or were given no instructions at all, interactions between retarded and normal students remained low.

parents have worked hard and long to obtain special classes and special services for their child, and mainstreaming has taken those classes and services away.

- Teachers may feel they are being set up to fail. They already have "normal" children who are not doing particularly well—and PL 94-142 is presenting them with children who have even greater difficulties.
- They sometimes have to prepare two lessons.
- They worry about discipline problems.
- Mainstreaming, they worry, might disrupt the potential of the regular class to be an effective learning environment.

LEARNING DISABILITIES

Very many children have learning disabilities. One estimate is from three to seven percent of the entire school population (Kirk and Kirk, 1971); another estimate is from one to three percent (Bureau for the Education of the Handicapped, 1979).

The Learning Disabilities Act of 1969 includes this definition of learning disability:

> *Children with special (specific) learning disabilities exhibit a disorder in one or more of the basic psychological processes involved in understanding or in using spoken or written language. These may be manifested in disorders of listening, thinking, talking, reading, writing, spelling, or arithmetic. They include conditions which have been referred to as perceptual handicaps, brain injury, minimal brain dysfunction, dyslexia, developmental aphasia, etc. They do not include learning problems which are due primarily to visual, hearing, or motor handicaps, to mental retardation, emotional disturbance, or to environmental disadvantage.*

It is very important to note the emphasis on separating learning disabilities from problems of retardation, emotional disturbance, or being disadvantaged. Students who are retarded, emotionally disturbed, and disadvantaged may have learning disabilities, but it is accurate and proper to consider the problem of learning disabilities as distinct from these other handicaps. Be aware, however, that a child's learning disability—especially if it is in understanding spoken language, speaking, writing, doing arithmetic, reasoning, or concentrating—may very well prevent him or her from performing well on an intelligence test, although the child actually may be of normal or above average intelligence.

The Learning-Disabled Child
First of all, no two learning-disabled children are alike. What they do have in common is a pattern of underachievement: There is a discrepancy between the level of school performance expected (based upon their tested or apparent potential) and the performance actually demonstrated. According to one expert (Ross, 1977), whenever a case of noteworthy underachievement occurs, "... in the absence of other reasons, the existence of a learning disability should be considered" (p. 43). The underachievement pattern may be uneven, with the student achieving up to potential in some areas, but not in others (Bryan and Bryan, 1975; Coles, 1978; Hammill, 1978).

Hallahan and Kaufman (1978) listed 10 types of problems which seem to recur with learning-disabled students. In order of frequency, beginning with the most common:

1. Hyperactivity
2. Perceptual-motor impairments
3. Emotional lability (instability, changeability)
4. General coordination deficits
5. Disorders of attention

6. Impulsivity
7. Disorders of memory and thinking
8. Specific learning disabilities: reading, arithmetic, writing, spelling
9. Disorders of speech and hearing
10. Equivocal neurological signs and electroencephalographic (EEG) irregularities

Kirk and Kirk (1971), noted for their *Illinois Test of Psycholinguistic Ability*, the test battery most often used by psychologists to diagnose learning disabilities (Coles, 1978), presented another list of characteristics of learning disabled children:

- Difficulty in sensory-motor or perceptual-motor learning
- Difficulties with visual or auditory perception
- Language disorders
- Problems in forming concepts
- Memory problems (especially with things that look or sound alike)
- Short attention span
- Maturational lag
- Emotional problems, including low self-esteem
- Difficulties in learning social skills (lack of sensitivity to people; poor understanding of social situations)

One recent analysis of learning disabilities describes impairments in two main areas, **psychological processes** and **language** (Blake, 1981; Hallahan and Kauffman, 1976; Haring and Bateman, 1977). The psychological-processes area is further subdivided into *intellectual functions* and *inhibitory functions*. Impairment in intellectual functions can include:

- Problems in *memory*—for example, difficulties recalling either visual material or auditory input.
- Problems in *perception*—for example, difficulties discriminating critical features of objects so they can be identified, or difficulties separating a foreground picture from its background (visual agnosia).
- Problems in *conceptualizing*—that is, working with abstract common characteristics which are the basis for grouping objects.
- Problems in *thinking*—for example, using ideas to reason, solve problems, or plan activities.

Impairment in inhibitory functions includes: *distractibility*, an inability to focus or control attention; *hyperactivity*, an inability to control activity; *low frustration tolerance*, proneness to become angry or cry with minor frustrations and difficulties; and *perseveration*, an inability to stop or inhibit responses.

The second main impairment area, *language,* includes a list of disabilities not only in the language area, but in related mathematical and motor
control areas as well. A particular learning-disabled child may have one or
more than one of these disabilities:

- *Receptive aphasia,* difficulty in understanding (decoding) spoken lan-
  guage.
- *Expressive aphasia,* difficulty in speaking (encoding language).
- *Total aphasia,* difficulty speaking or understanding language.

- *Hyperlexia,* using words with little or no understanding of them.
- *Anomia,* difficulty in naming objects
- *Dyslexia,* an inability to read (other names for this common problem are *alexia, bradylexia, strephosymbolia, congenital symbolamblyopia,* and *word blindness*).
- *Dysgraphia,* an inability to write (also called *agraphia*).
- *Dyspraxia,* difficulty in making intended movements, for example, catching a ball.
- *Dyscalculia,* an inability to do arithmetic or use numbers (also called *acalculia*).

Causes of Learning Disabilities

Frankly, no specific causes of learning disabilities have been completely confirmed. There are, however, at least three main possibilities. Arguments for a **brain damage** hypothesis are based on the fact that some brain-injured war veterans demonstrated many of the same symptoms as learning-disabled children: hyperactivity (with inattention and low tolerance for frustration), aphasia, and perceptual and conceptual problems. The assumption of brain damage includes the extra assumptions that (a) there was a biological or traumatic injurious cause (perhaps a prenatal Rh-factor incompatibility, malnutrition, oxygen deprivation at birth, or injury during birth), (b) the effect is irreversible, (c) medical care is needed anyway, and (d) the child has limited potential (Hallahan and Kauffman, 1978; Ross, 1977).

The problem with the brain-damage hypothesis is that neurological examinations of learning-disabled children virtually *never* show any structural defects (Hallahan and Kauffman, 1978). Since brain damage could not be detected, according to this argument, the damage must be very minimal, and so the terms "minimal brain damage," "minimal brain dysfunction," and "minimal cerebral dysfunction" were quite popular into the 1970s.

The proponents of a **genetic** cause of learning disabilities point out that at least one learning disability, dyslexia (inability to read), tends to recur in some families. Also, there is a greater likelihood of both identical twins being dyslexic than both fraternal twins (Blake, 1981).

The third viewpoint claims that **early environmental deprivation** prevents certain perceptual, linguistic, and other brain processes and functions from developing on schedule. Also, inhibitory processes—leading to hyperactivity—are said to be not properly learned, as they would have been in a "normal" environment.

At present, the most sensible and informed position is to admit ignorance: We do not know if learning disabilities are due to brain damage, genetics, early environmental deprivation, some combinations of these, or as yet undiscovered causes. One interesting explanation of the cause of—and treatment for—hyperactivity appears in Inset 18.4.

INSET 18.4

CAN A CHANGE IN EATING HABITS CONTROL HYPERACTIVITY?: THE FEINGOLD DIET

Ben F. Feingold, M.D., claims that over five million bright, physically sound children in the United States suffer from hyperkinesis—hyperactivity. Based upon his pioneering research at the Human Resources Institute of Boston University, Dr. Feingold concluded that in the majority of cases hyperactivity is due to eating food additives, namely synthetic food coloring, artificial flavorings, and preservatives (Feingold, 1975; Feingold and Feingold, 1979). Some of the specific culprits are soft drinks, fruit punches, powdered drinks, chocolate milk, candy, bubble gum, cake, cookies, ice cream, popsicles, hot dogs, ketchup, margarine, some breakfast cereals, and even some antihistamine cough syrups. Feingold noted that virtually all children's medicines and vitamins are artificially flavored and colored—probably curing one problem while causing another.

After Feingold's conclusions were publicized, some parents informed him

Hyperactivity, Amphetamines, and Methylphenidate

A great many learning-disabled children, perhaps 50 percent, are hyperactive, which means they also are unable to maintain attention over a normal time span. Strangely enough, **stimulant drugs** such as amphetamines (Dexedrine and Benzedrine) and methylphenidate (Ritalin) have a *calming* effect on many (not all) hyperactive children. The children usually settle down, they are less aggressive, and they are better able to concentrate on the learning task. Small wonder that after this discovery was popularized in the 1960s many parents and teachers were asking physicians to prescribe (usually) Ritalin for hyperactive students.

The United States Office of Health, Education, and Welfare made a report (described in the *APA Monitor*, April 1971) that seemed to support the use of the drugs. The report noted that about three percent of all school age children suffer from ". . . minimal brain dysfunction and hyperkinesis." Further, "Stimulant medications are beneficial in only about one-half to one-third of cases in which trials of the drug are warranted. In these successful cases . . . the drugs improve the child's attention, learning and social abilities . . . and there is no evidence to show that the proper use of amphetamines . . . leads to subsequent addiction in later life." The report properly recommended diagnosis by a physician and close supervision of that, indeed, during the Christmas holidays and after birthday parties their hyperactive children became "irritable," "uncontrollable," "turned on," "raving maniacs," or "whirling dervishes." Many had been on Ritalin drug programs for years; all were stigmatized by the labels "minimal brain damaged," "hyperactive—learning disabled," or "neurologically handicapped."

Under Feingold's supervision, dozens of children were put on diets which eliminated or restricted the intake of these foods. The improvements usually were early (e.g., two weeks) and dramatic. Said Feingold (1975, p. 71), "The best estimate, based on careful records, is that 50 percent have a likelihood of *full* response, while *75 percent can be removed from drug management*" (italics mine). Some failures were due to parents who did not adhere to the prescribed diet; other failures were due to children who flatly refused to cooperate or who were urged by peers to indulge in candy or soda pop. Even one candy bar on Monday could set off hyperactivity lasting until Wednesday or Thursday. In one successfully treated case, a 10-year-old boy had been sedated daily and placed in a learning disabilities class. After the diet change, he not only was taken off drugs but was switched to the class for gifted students.

All in all, Feingold's diet may be a valuable and effective alternative to drugs.

the treatment—including the caution that children must not be responsible for taking their own pills.

There have been many problems in treating hyperactive children with drugs, and the trend is rapidly disappearing. As examples of these difficulties:

- While they help some children, they make others worse. In many cases they have no effect at all.
- The dosage must be adjusted by the physician for each child. By the time the physician receives reports from teachers about a reduction in hyperactivity, the child's increasing dosages may be so high as to interfere with thinking and problem solving (Ross, 1977, p. 55).
- Sometimes, low dosage levels improve learning but do not reduce the hyperactivity. Naturally, the dosage is increased until the hyperactivity is reduced—at which time the beneficial effects on learning may have disappeared. A teacher or parent who chooses between a quiet child and a learning child may prefer the quiet child.
- Often, Ritalin has been used to diagnose "minimal brain dysfunction." The reasoning: Ritalin reduces hyperactivity in MBD children; therefore, if Ritalin reduces hyperactivity in Busy Bonnie, Busy Bonnie must

be an MBD child. The logical fallacy is that Ritalin might reduce activity levels in normal children as well. We don't know—we never give Ritalin to normal children.

- Critics have claimed that thousands of active children were being drugged into docility and submission, and that educators were creating large numbers of drug addicts.
- Imagine a child who has suffered adult complaints and criticisms for years. Suddenly she discovers that the little green pills improve her work and please those adults. She may become psychologically dependent on the drug—attributing her improvement to the medication, not to her own diligence and achievement.
- There are side effects. One common one is reduced appetite, resulting in ". . . a suppression of growth in both weight and height" (Ross, 1977, p. 57). Another side effect is heartbeat irregularity.

The weight of the evidence does *not* encourage the use of stimulant drugs for reducing hyperactivity.

INSET 18.5

THE PLIGHT OF B. BRADFORD

Bradford Bradford is a learning-disabled fifth-grader, but nobody knows it. What his teacher and parents *do* know is that Brad won't sit still, won't listen, cannot seem to read very well, doesn't understand math, hates school, and doesn't get along with other children. In fact, he prefers to insult or spit on them, rather than be friends. He irritates his classmates, aggravates his teachers, and completely befuddles his parents, who often respond, "He's always been like that." Remedial reading and math efforts have failed. He's labeled a "problem child," but even this fine label doesn't seem to help Brad either. Brad blames the teacher ("She doesn't like me!"), the other students ("Nobody likes me!"), and sometimes his brain ("There's something wrong with my brain!"). He does have a rather unique ability to predict the future ("What's the use of trying, I'm going to fail anyway!"). The teacher blames Brad's parents ("They never make him mind!") or Brad ("He's just not trying and he won't pay attention!"). The Bradfords blame the teacher ("She doesn't try to understand Brad—you see he's always been like this!") or the genes of Mr. Bradford, who also had trouble paying attention and learning to read, and used to insult and spit on other children.

TEACHING LEARNING-DISABLED CHILDREN

Teaching learning-disabled children may take two forms, attempting to remediate (cure) the learning disability and/or working around the learning disability to teach the student the usual academic content. Most often, efforts are made on both fronts.

Remediation of Learning Disabilities

Detailed prescriptions for remediating learning disabilities are far beyond the scope of this survey text (see Blake, 1981; Hallahan and Kauffman, 1976; Hammill and Bartel, 1978; Haring and Bateman, 1977; Kirk and Kirk, 1971; Reynolds and Birch, 1982; Ross, 1977). However, as an example of some methods, Kirk and Kirk (1971) outline both general and specific strategies for remediating learning disabilities identified by their *Illinois Test of Psycholinguistic Ability* (ITPA; Kirk, McCarthy, and Kirk, 1968). Some general teaching strategies for learning-disabled children were:

- Start the remediation very early, at preschool age.
- Individualize instruction.
- Focus training on the deficient skills and abilities.
- Remediate prerequisite deficits first. For example, letter identification would be a prerequisite to reading and would be trained first.

Kirk and Kirk (1971, p. 135) also describe very specific remediation strategies for disabilities identified by ITPA subtests. As just one example, the child with an auditory reception problem:

- May not recognize and identify sounds.
- May not have developed a listening attitude.
- May have difficulty attaching meaning to words.
- May not understand consecutive speech.

To remediate the first possible problem, three exercises were: (1) Drop keys and a block; have the child note the different sounds. (2) Have the child name everyday sounds, perhaps recorded by other children. (3) Have the child recognize a sound embedded in background noise. Exercises aimed at other problems identified by the ITPA are equally detailed and specific.

Other programs and strategies for strengthening specific learning disabilities are, for example, the *Frostig Program for the Development of Visual Perception* (Frostig and Horne, 1964), the *Karnes Early Language Activities Program* (Karnes, 1975), the *MWM Program for Developing Language Abilities* (Minskoff, Wiseman, and Minskoff, 1975), *Building Spelling Skills With Dyslexic Children* (Arena, 1968), and *Building Number Skills With Dyslexic Children* (Arena, 1972).

Instructional Procedures

The particular teaching methods for any learning-disabled student depends both on the nature of the disability and on the objectives for that particular student. For example, if a student is dyslexic, the teacher might use tutors to read to the student, or use audio or video tapes to present the academic content.

A group of **stimulus control** strategies have been designed for use with hyperactive children (Blake, 1981; Cruickshank *et al.*, 1961; Ross, 1977). For example, very plain, undecorated, distraction-free rooms have been recommended. Since these children have trouble focusing on essential aspects of a classroom, the plan was to remove nonessential aspects. (Sometimes, plain cubicles have been constructed for hyperactive students.) Also, in order to both increase structure and reduce mental or physical wandering, teachers have closely directed student learning activities. Special materials also may help students focus attention on the relevant features. For example, in teaching handwriting, heavy black lines or colors may be used to emphasize where the student should write and where he or she should stop. In teaching reading, special books present only one line at a time; in teaching arithmetic, only one problem per page may be presented. Also, for hyperactive, manipulative students, devices with moving parts have been recommended, such as using an abacus to teach arithmetic (Blake, 1981).

Behavior modification strategies, using token or tangible reinforcers (Chapter 6), also have proven effective in teaching hyperactive, learning-disabled children (Prout, 1977). Behavior modification strategies initially were designed for use with exceptional children.

MILDLY MENTALLY RETARDED

Psychologists identify two categories of retardation. With **familial** retardation, the mental deficiency simply runs in the family—Dad and Aunt Henrietta had the same problem. On the other hand, the subnormality may be due to a **neurological** or biochemical problem (e.g., brain damage at birth or a nutritional deficiency), which is not characteristic of close relatives.

As we saw in Chapter 15, intelligence test scores are (approximately) normally distributed in a bell-shaped curve. There is no clear demarcation between normal and retarded. Nonetheless, lines must be drawn somewhere, and currently IQ scores between 55 and 69 define the mildly (or educable) mentally retarded category (EMR). Individualized intelligence tests (WISC; Revised Stanford-Binet) have a mean of 100 points and a standard deviation of 15 points. This indicates that an IQ of 69 is two standard deviations below the mean; 55 is three standard deviations below the mean. A quick look ahead at Figure 19.2 in Chapter 19 will confirm that 2.14 percent of the population (the human race) will be in this category—between two and three standard deviations below the mean. These children will be in the public schools, in "special ed" classes for part of the day and mainstreamed into your regular class for part of the day.

Now, IQ scores do not tell us everything we need to know about a potential candidate for special education services. Indeed, a child who scores 75 or 80 may share many of the learning and behavioral difficulties of

INSET 18.6

THE "SPECIAL ED" TEACHER

As a teacher in a mainstreamed regular classroom, you will have students who have earned various handicap labels. The labels, despite their stigmatizing and possibly ostracizing effects, often are a legal step necessary for the extra funds needed for extra services. Extra services? The extra services mainly are those of the special education teacher. While the exact duties and obligations will vary, the special education teacher:

1. Is responsible for processing all referrals from teachers. He or she also holds conferences with each teacher to discuss the action to be taken on each referral.
2. Is responsible for the diagnosis, program planning, and evaluation of each special student.
3. Prepares all reports necessary, both for outside agencies and for within-school purposes.
4. Teaches two or more special education classes, for example, in reading or math, planned in conjunction with the regular teachers.
5. Reports to the parents of each special education student (a) regarding the initiation and termination of special programs and (b) at regular reporting times. These parent conferences usually are held four times per year; two of them are attended by the regular teacher.

The teaching methods of the special education teacher will include:

- Individualized instruction, since each child will have his or her own special needs and problems.
- Behavior modification strategies.
- Adaptation of materials for special educational purposes.
- Use of the services of other specialties, namely, the school psychologist and the speech and language teachers.

As a teacher in a regular classroom which contains educationally handicapped, mainstreamed students, you may need to perform some of these same duties and use some of these same teaching strategies.

children in the 55–69 class, and therefore may be referred for diagnosis and possibly special services. Many states and school districts review deficits in academic, social, or physical functioning, along with IQ scores, in determining eligibility.

McCandless (1964, pp. 192–193) recommended that a child is a possible candidate for special services if the teacher observes the following:

- The child is significantly behind his or her age mates in academic acquisition. The child is a slow worker, and shows little evidence of being able to generalize what he or she learns.
- The family is poor. The vast majority of mildly mentally retarded individuals come from low socio-economic stratas of society, where lack of early stimulation sometimes produces children who are academically retarded compared to their middle-class age mates.
- With some forms of organic retardation, both physical and mental development is delayed. The child is smaller than other children, coordination is poor, and babyish, or inappropriate social behavior is frequent.

In a middle-class school, such children will be dramatically obvious. In a lower-class school, it will be more difficult to isolate deficient children. According to Lowenbraun and Affleck (1976, p. 11), the teacher should ask herself or himself if present educational services are failing to help the possibly retarded child.

EMOTIONALLY DISTURBED CHILDREN

In addition to the learning disabled and mildly retarded, another population of handicapped children is the **emotionally disturbed** (ED). You may recognize this category by some of the more specific labels:

- Behaviorally disordered
- Emotionally maladjusted
- Emotionally immature
- Emotionally inadequate
- Delinquent
- Sociopathic
- Character disordered

Who Are Emotionally Disturbed Students?

Now, none of us are perfect and a great many children display minor adjustment problems in school. Some students seem to avoid group play; others seem to need constant reassurance from the teacher; many are shy; a few have difficulty settling down to work; a teenage girl may refuse to undress in her gym class; and others cannot seem to be prompt or cannot control speaking out. Such problems are not cause for alarm. The alarm should sound, however, if the maladaptive behavior becomes more severe. One rule of thumb is that a teacher should make referrals if the student's behavior (a) interferes with his or her own academic progress, or (b) interferes with the learning of others.

It is a fact that most emotionally disturbed, disruptive students are boys. The reasons for this sex difference are not clear. Learning probably plays a significant role, since aggressive behavior is often accepted (even reinforced) with boys. Genetic factors, however, need not be excluded. Chapter 3 reviewed evidence supporting the heritability of many personality traits. Most likely, both learning and genetic factors are involved.

Hewitt and Jenkins (1946) analyzed case histories of "problem children" and identified three main syndromes. Students in the **unsocialized aggressive behavior** category were the classroom aggressors, bullies, and fighters who might bite other students (elementary school) or punch the teacher (junior high school). Students in the second category, **socialized delinquent,** have lots of possibilities for deviant behavior: They can steal from the teacher's desk, disrupt others by slamming doors or dropping books, pull the wings off trapped houseflies, meow like a cat or grunt like a pig, drink the poster paints, urinate on the playground, tell fantastic lies, remove pages from books, and sneak peeks into the girl's wash rooms and locker rooms. You find a rule, they'll break it. Finally, in the **over-inhibited child** category are the excessively withdrawn students; the shy, timid, withdrawn, self-conscious, passive, and likely-to-play-alone children.

More recent classifications produce about the same groups. Peterson (1964) used a two-group classification: (1) conduct problems (aggressive behavior) and (2) personality problems (withdrawn behavior). Bullock and Brown (1972) identified four factors: (1) aggressive/acting out, (2) withdrawn, (3) tense/anxious, and (4) irresponsible/inattentive.

One case history described by Stephans (1977) appears in Inset 18.7. Severe disturbance such as this usually will land students in special classes for part or all of the day, or even in special schools.

Teaching and Treatments

Some classroom management (discipline) techniques for controlling disruptive students appear in Chapter 10. Lowenbraun and Affleck (1975) recommend that these types of techniques be tried before children are referred—and labeled—as emotionally disturbed. Even if a child is referred, he or she most likely will not be removed from your class. Unless the problem is severe, the child simply will receive additional services while remaining in the regular class. You will not get off the hook quite so easily.

Treatments for emotionally disturbed children will involve both (a) the modification of the behaviors which interfere with learning and (b) the modification of the school environment. ED children generally do better in

INSET 18.7

**CASE HISTORY OF AN
EMOTIONALLY
DISTURBED BOY**

Stephans (1977) reported a case history of a severely emotionally disturbed sixth-grade boy named Kurt.

Kurt, a twelve-year-old, was placed in a full-time special class for behaviorally disruptive students as a result of his misbehavior in a regular sixth-grade class. When Tony Rodriquez, the school psychologist, received a referral to evaluate Kurt, he began by talking to his sixth-grade teacher, Mr. Hall. He had anticipated his visit and had an anecdotal record of Kurt's misbehavior over a seven-day period. It follows.

Fri., Sept. 24
Sat on top of bookcase to catch flies.
Broke all pencils in room.
Spread corn around room.
Tore book apart at noon.
Went on the fire escape.

Mon., Sept. 27
Tore pen apart.
Drank ink and smeared it all over.
Dismissed from gym for failure to behave.
Spit on floor of room.
Exposed himself before girls and urinated on floor.

Tues., Sept. 28
Put boys' gym equipment into toilets.
Smashed girls' lunchpail in cafeteria.
Swore openly in the classroom.
Ran through cafeteria lines until he was made to sit on stool there.
Took money from one of the girls.
When girls went to gym, he went to restroom, kicked lunchpails, and tore geography books. Girls also said he was standing in front of frosted windows.
Marked two new desks with crayolas.
Ran on the highway three times.
Chased neighbor's ducks.
Turned the gas pumps on behind the school.
Spit on cafeteria windows.
Continually running and yelling in halls.
Disturbing classes.

Wed., Sept. 29

This morning he ate almost half an apple at his desk until I took it away from him. I had to get after him several times for talking aloud.

I had missed candy several times from my desk drawer. More was missing today when I returned from lunch. Another boy in the class told me that when he came back to the room from lunch he saw Kurt taking candy from the drawer of my desk.

During the afternoon he was noisy, talked all the time, did not mind, threw his paint shirt up on top of the tall cupboard so he had an excuse to climb up after it, sharpened the paint brush handles while I was helping someone else. In general, he was just impossible!

Thur., Sept. 30

He was noisy, talking at the top of his voice even when I was trying to explain something to the whole group. He refuses to do most of the work even on his own ability level unless someone is working with him most of the time.

Friday., Oct. 1

Kurt bent a pair of school scissors which were supposed to be in my drawer. He had them without permission. He was unlocking the heater with them when he bent them. He crawled up on the window sill, up on top of the cupboard on the west side of the room, down into the sink and back to the floor. He said, "Just make me," when I told him to be quiet. I have to lock the door to keep him out of the room if he finishes his lunch before I do. He talked loudly or yelled many times today. I did not count them. He gets other boys to misbehave with him.

Mon., Oct. 2

Kurt yelled or talked loudly many times when he did not get my individual attention. When I told him to zip his zipper, he pulled it down farther and showed himself to other children. He came in after lunch with a grasshopper which I made him throw out the window. He got out of the door before I could stop him and brought the grasshopper back to the room. He put it in a girl's desk. Out the window again went the grasshopper. Kurt slipped out once more and got it, but out the window it went again. About a half hour later he said he was sorry and would not do those things again.

Mr. Rodriquez decided it would be advisable for him to observe Kurt and also to obtain additional descriptions of his behavior. The following are behaviors recorded by Mr. Rodriquez during two observation periods.

First Observation: Time — 90 minutes
Talked incessantly, very loud, in class.

(continued)

INSET 18.7 (*continued*)

Broke up several pencils for no apparent reason.
Punched the teacher when he was correcting him.
Climbed into the cupboard and shut the door on himself.
Climbed up on the window sill.
Climbed up on the window sill, across the cupboard, down into the sink, and back to the floor.

Second Observation: Time — 50 minutes
Said, "God damn you," when the teacher tried to correct him. Took scissors from the teacher's desk without permission. Stole candy from the teachers' desk.

Three days elapsed between the first observation, which was during reading instruction, and the second observation. In addition, Mr. Rodriquez discussed Kurt's behavior with the building principal.

The principal reported that Kurt was new to the school in September, having moved to the community from another state. His report card indicated he had been a C and D student last year and had satisfactorily completed fifth year work. He also said that during the first week of school Kurt had been reported by the school patrol for climbing onto the trunk of the mailman's car and taking a short ride unnoticed by the mailman.

an environment which is highly stable, structured, and predictable. A carefully structured school program therefore is essential (Lowenbraun and Affleck, 1975). Also, contingency management (behavior modification) often is effective for motivating learning. In some cases, drug therapy has been used, just as with hyperactive learning-disabled children.

INDIVIDUALIZED EDUCATION PROGRAMS (IEP's)

PL 94-142 mandates the preparation of an **Individualized Education Program** (IEP) for each student classified as handicapped. The program is to be prepared jointly "... by a qualified school official, by the child's teacher and parents or guardian, and if possible by the child himself ... " The "qualified school official" is a member of the Local Education Agency (LEA) or an Intermediate Education Unit (IEU) who is qualified to supervise specially designed instruction to meet the needs of handicapped students.

Kurt had been referred to the office on other occasions during the first few months of the school year. He was referred by a teacher who had observed Kurt spit on another boy in the hallway.

The playground supervisor complained that he swears at her. Mr. M, physical education teacher, refuses to have Kurt in class because he will not do anything he is told or even sit down and be quiet while he is giving directions.

The bus driver has been in complaining that she cannot do anything with Kurt on the bus. As an example, one day Kurt was hanging from the waist up out the window while the bus was moving down the highway. He also has been using obscene language on the bus.

Finally, Mr. Rodriquez administered an individual test of intelligence and standardized achievement tests to Kurt with parental permission. He found him to have a measured IQ of 109. Reading achievement was at the beginning third grade level (3.1) and arithmetic at middle fifth grade.

It was recommended to the special education team that Kurt be placed in the special adjustment class at Main Street Elementary School.

From T. M. Stephans *Teaching Skills to Children With Learning and Behavior Disorders.* Columbus, Ohio: Charles E. Merrill, 1977. Reprinted by permission of the author and publisher.

In addition to these participants, possible consultants may include any of the following: a psychologist, speech pathologist, social worker, school nurse, physical therapist, guidance counselor, curriculum specialist, vocational rehabilitation counselor, audiologist, ophthalmologist/optometrist, or others (Swanson and Willis, 1979). Overall, the IEP serves as a guide for managing the (a) testing, (b) placement, (c) instruction, and (d) procedural safeguards which each student needs (National Advisory Committee on the Handicapped, 1976; Torres, 1977).

The IEP itself will include:

1. The handicapped student's present levels of performance—for example, as determined by reading or vocabulary tests, intelligence tests, personality tests, psychiatric evaluations, and informal observations and reports by teachers, parents, school psychologists or others. Rating forms, such as the *Referral Form Checklist* or the *Developmental Therapy Objectives Rating Form*, may be used by teachers, parents, or

others to help identify problems related to aggression, attention, confidence, honesty, carelessness, emotional control, self-help skills, and so on (Blake, 1981).

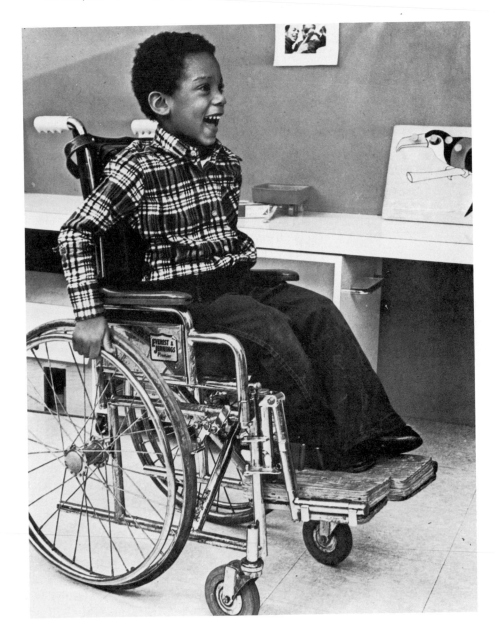

2. Annual goals, including short-term instructional goals. For example, a long-term goal for a student with socialization and communication problems might be "To participate in classroom routines"; a related short-term goal might be "To participate verbally and physically in music, games, and sports activities without adult intervention." These goals would eventually result in such specific instructional activities as doing calisthenics with the class, playing rhythm instruments in unison with others, and so on.

3. Specific educational services to be provided. The description of specific education services may include special placement in *residential schools* designed for students with specific handicaps (blindness, deafness, retardation), special preschool programs, or, of course, special education classes for the retarded, physically handicapped, emotionally disturbed, learning disabled, or vision or hearing impaired. The description of educational services may include such special teaching strategies as behavior modification, individual tutoring, or the use of special equipment, e.g., wheelchairs, special amplifiers for the hearing impaired, braille or magnifying machines for the visually impaired, or communication boards for students with severe speech handicaps. Standard teaching methods also may be listed—for example, teacher presentations, group work, individual projects and assignments, mastery learning, AV materials, field trips, and others.

4. Extent to which the student will be able to participate in regular educational programs. Will the student be in the special education class all day? Only for "home room"? Which classes can the student attend with "regular" students?

5. The projected date for initiation and the anticipated duration of the services.

6. Appropriate objective criteria and the evaluation procedures. (Evaluations at any time may result in a review and revision of the IEP, if appropriate.)

7. A schedule for determining (at least on an annual basis) whether instructional objectives are being achieved.

Accountability We noted earlier in this chapter that PL 94-142 "...requires detailed accountability of the local school district to state and federal agencies." Actually, this accountability only demands that the program be proper and adequate, and that all involved persons make good-faith efforts to assist each child in achieving the specified goals. Teachers and others are not "held accountable" if the child fails to meet the goals. Parents, however, specifically have the right to complain and to ask for revisions if they feel the good-faith effort is not being made (PL 94-142, Sec. 121a.349).

TO IMPROVE
YOUR TEACHING

In view of today's "mainstreaming consciousness," it is possible that your college or one nearby offers a course specifically in mainstreaming. You may wish to take it. If there is none, try to take more than the minimum number of credits in your behavioral-disabilities or learning-disabilities area. It is likely you will be able to use all of the professional training you can get.

Remain very aware of the distinctions between children who are learning disabled, retarded, emotionally disturbed, economically disadvantaged, or members of a minority group. Become acquainted with the tests and behavioral cues which the school psychologists, the counselors, and the reading specialists use to diagnose learning problems. Try to not allow learning-disabled students to be labeled as retarded or emotionally disturbed and sent to special classes where they will receive help for the wrong problem. Also, try to not allow economically disadvantaged students to be labeled as retarded, emotionally disturbed, or learning disabled and sent to "special ed" classes unless the diagnosis is accurate and the need is real. You may need to educate the principal, other teachers, or parents regarding the complexities of and distinctions among different forms of handicaps (learning disabilities, retardation, and emotional disturbance, for example).

Try to arrange cooperative activities which require the regular and mainstreamed students to work together. In most cases such interaction produces a positive change in attitudes. You need not let unthinking students get away with teasing, insulting, or otherwise brutalizing mainstreamed students. Lessons in humanity from you, the principal, or parents may be in order.

If you discover that some hyperactive children in your school are taking Ritalin, you might wish to be a hero and discuss the difficulties and very serious side effects with the teachers, principal and parents. The parents can talk to their doctor. All should appreciate your informed concern for the children.

Be prepared to work with one or two mildly retarded children who may be mainstreamed into your class. Try not to resent the extra preparation; look at the matter from the child's perspective. Should he or she have contact *only* with other retarded children and special education teachers?

Also, be prepared to cope with some rowdy, possibly emotionally disturbed children. Have some tactics ready. Understand classroom management principles (Chapter 10) thoroughly.

Do not lose or forget about the withdrawn children who never raise their hands and never ask for help. They need love and understanding and attention.

SUMMARY

Exceptional children are those who are gifted and talented and those who are handicapped. The handicap may be a learning disability, emotional disturbance, retardation, or social maladjustment; a physical impairment of hearing, vision, speech, or language; or other orthopedic, neurological, or health impairment.

Public Law 94-142 requires that handicapped children have access to a nonsegregated "mainstream" of American education, that is, that they be placed in the "least restrictive environment"—the regular classroom. The Act requires the preparation of an Individualized Education Program for each child. Public Law 94-142 has administrative, legal, political, psychological, and financial implications.

The history behind the mainstreaming law began with the 1896 *Plessey* v. *Ferguson* case, which ruled that "separate but equal" (segregated) railway accommodations were constitutional. In 1954 the case of *Brown* v. the *Topeka Board of Education* ruled that segregated facilities were inherently unequal and therefore unconstitutional. Public Law 94-142 essentially outlawed the segregation of handicapped children.

Evidence seems to indicate that handicapped children do not achieve better in special classes, contrary to the opinion of special education experts. However, as yet there is no clear evidence that mainstreaming improves achievement either.

Handicapped students are often rejected, sometimes brutalized by "normal" students. The rejection sometimes leads to poor self-concepts.

Two coping strategies are withdrawal or striving to gain acceptance. Some studies, however, show no change or improved self-concepts.

The problem of which circumstances of mainstreaming help which children with which handicaps is not yet settled.

Some teachers have complained that: With mainstreaming, special services are taken away from some handicapped children; they already have plenty of students with learning problems; they may have to prepare two lessons; and the learning of the regular students may be disrupted.

Two estimates set the number of learning-disabled children at from one to three percent or from three to seven percent. Learning disabilities

are distinct from problems of physical handicaps, retardation, emotional disturbance, or environmental disadvantage.

One common characteristic of learning-disabled children is underachievement in one, a few, or many areas.

One taxonomy describes learning disabilities as impairments in psychological processes (intellectual functions—memory, perception, conceptualization, thinking; and inhibitory functions—hyperactivity, distractibility, low frustration tolerance, perseveration) or language (receptive or expressive aphasia, hyperlexia, anomia, dyslexia, dysgraphia, dyspraxia, dyscalculia).

The causes of learning disabilities are unknown. Three hypotheses are brain damage, heredity, and early environmental deprivation.

Stimulant drugs, especially Ritalin, were often prescribed for hyperactive children in the 1960s and into the 1970s. Serious problems and issues (side effects, psychological dependency, "drugging kids into submission") mitigate against using such drugs.

Teaching learning-disabled children can include trying to remediate the learning disability, or working around the disability to teach usual academic content. Remediation recommendations include starting very early, individualizing instruction, and focusing on deficient skills and their prerequisites. Many programs and materials have been designed to remediate learning disabilities.

Instructional procedures must consider the nature of the disability and the learning objectives. Stimulus control strategies reduce effects of hyperactivity (common to 50 percent of LD children); behavior modification techniques also have proven effective.

Retardation may be familial or neurological. IQ scores between 55 and 69, between two and three standard deviations below the mean, define the mildly mentally retarded category (EMR). Information pertaining to academic, social, and physical functioning also is used in making referrals.

Three frequent traits of EMR children are: significant deficits in academic work; a low SES background; and sometimes physical and emotional immaturity.

Many children display adjustment and behavior problems. Emotionally disturbed children would be referred for special services if the poor behavior interferes with the student's own academic progress or with the academic work of others. Various classifications of emotionally disturbed children primarily include aggressive, delinquent, and withdrawn behavior.

Emotionally disturbed children are treated by modifying the student's behavior (e.g., with behavior modification) and modifying the school environment (e.g., by increasing structure). Classroom management strategies also help.

Individual Education Programs (IEP's) are management plans for the testing, placement, instruction, and protection of handicapped children. The IEP—designed by a school official, the teacher, parents, perhaps the child, and perhaps professional consultants—includes: (1) present levels of performance, (2) annual and short-term goals, (3) educational services to be provided, (4) extent of participation in regular programs, (5) initiation and duration dates, (6) evaluation procedures and criteria, and (7) an evaluation schedule.

The local school district is held accountable for providing an adequate program, not for student failure.

TOPICS FOR THOUGHT AND DISCUSSION

1. Which children with which handicaps do you feel are most likely to benefit from mainstreaming? Consider achievement, self-concept, and social skills.
2. Let's assume you join a school faculty which routinely sends learning-disabled children to special classes for (a) the mildly retarded or (b) emotionally disturbed. What should you do? What will happen if you do it?
3. Why are disadvantaged and minority children overrepresented in the ranks of those labeled "learning disabled"? According to the definitions and descriptions in this chapter, are they really "learning disabled"?
4. What are some effects of labeling? Can you think of some first-hand examples?
5. Can you think of effective techniques for increasing the social acceptance of mildly retarded or other handicapped students?

PROJECTS

1. During your practice teaching (or some other time) arrange to chat with the school psychologist and, separately, the special education teacher. Ask their opinions on the (a) causes, (b) diagnosis, and (c) treatment of different kinds of learning disabilities. Ask the same questions about emotionally disturbed children.
2. For this or another class, prepare a report reviewing methods and materials for teaching learning-disabled students.
3. Visit a "home" for retarded children. Meet the children. Ask administrators if PL 94-142 has affected any of their activities. Ask if children have benefitted.
4. Practice preparing an individualized education program (IEP), based on a hypothetical or real handicapped child.

RECOMMENDED READING

Blake, K. A. *Educating exceptional pupils.* Reading, Mass.: Addison-Wesley, 1981.

Hallahan, D. P., and J. M. Kauffman. *Introduction to learning disabilities: A psychobehavioral approach.* Englewood Cliffs, N. J.: Prentice-Hall, 1976.

Gearheart, B. R., and M. W. Weishahn. *The handicapped child in the regular classroom.* St. Louis: C. V. Mosby, 1976.

Hammill, D. D., and N. R. Bartel (eds.). *Teaching children with learning disabilities and behavior disorders.* Boston: Allyn & Bacon, 1978.

Kirk, S. A. *Educating exceptional children*, second edition. Boston: Houghton-Mifflin, 1972.

Haring, N. G., and B. Bateman. *Teaching the learning-disabled child*. Englewood Cliffs, N. J.: Prentice-Hall, 1977.

Reynolds, M. C., and J. W. Birch. *Teaching exceptional children in all America's schools*. Reston, Va.: Council for Exceptional children, 1982.

Ross, A. O. *Learning disability: The unrealized potential*. New York: McGraw-Hill, 1977.

Swanson, B. M., and D. J. Willis. *Understanding exceptional children and youth*. Chicago: Rand McNally, 1979.

Torres, S. *A primer on individualized education programs for handicapped children*. Reston, Va.: Foundation for Exceptional Children, 1977.

Turnbull, A. P., and J. C. Brantley. *Mainstreaming: Developing and implementing individualized education programs*, second edition. Columbus, Ohio: Charles E. Merrill, 1982.

Evaluation: Test Construction and Interpretation

19

ABOUT TESTING

Throughout your college years you have been tested up one side and down the other—multiple-choice tests, matching tests, true-false tests, fill-in-the-blank tests, short-answer essay tests, and occasionally a full-blown "long-answer" essay test. The obvious reason for the tests is that the instructor, including your present one, is required to assign grades. In order to do this, he or she uses tests to evaluate how well you have mastered the material. There are other reasons for tests in college, too. One is to motivate learning. Frankly, it's a form of fear motivation called *test anxiety*. As with any other form of anxiety, it is an unpleasant state which you are motivated to remove—how else but by studying until you feel more comfortable about the matter. Needless to say, some students are more anxious about tests than others. A third reason for college tests, a slightly more subtle one, is to provide feedback to the instructor about the effectiveness of his or her teaching. If a large number of students clearly misunderstand the same concept or skill, chances are good that the teaching of that concept or skill was not very good.

As we will see shortly, assigning grades, motivating learning, or evaluating instruction are just three uses of tests. There are several additional purposes for testing in the elementary and secondary schools, and each use requires slightly different considerations in the construction of the test.

Before turning to the various functions and purposes of tests, we need to add a few concepts to our working vocabulary. Some were presented earlier.

Reliability

As we saw in Chapter 14, **reliability** refers to the accuracy or consistency of a test. Test reliability is evaluated, and expressed, by a **correlation coefficient.** "Correlations" also were in Chapter 14. Correlation coefficients reflect the degree of relationship between two sets of scores. When used to assess reliability (and validity), correlations range from .00 to 1.00. As a general guideline to evaluating correlations (or reliability coefficients):

.00 to .20 is low.
.20 to .40 is moderately low.
.40 to .60 is fair.
.60 to .80 is good.
.80 to 1.00 is excellent.

The formula for a correlation coefficient appears at the end of this chapter.

There are three main types of reliability: **test-retest** reliability, **equiv-alent-forms** reliability, and **internal-consistency** reliability. With all three types, poor (unclear, imprecise, inconsistent) test items will lower the reliability coefficient.

Test-retest reliability. With test-retest reliability, the *same test* is administered to the *same group* with an intervening time interval—sometimes a few days, sometimes a few years. The reliability coefficient is the correlation of the first set of scores with the second set of scores. This coefficient will reflect changes in the testing procedure and in the day-to-day stability of the students' responses. Reasonably enough, the longer the intervening interval, the lower will be the reliability coefficient.

Equivalent-forms reliability. Equivalent-forms reliability involves the administration of *two forms* of the same test during the same administration period. The two forms are intended to be equivalent in the sense of measuring the same abilities or knowledge. The reliability coefficient is the correlation between scores on "Form A" and scores on "Form B." The reliability coefficient will indicate the degree to which the two forms measure the same abilities; that is, the degree to which the two sets of test items are in fact equivalent.

Internal-consistency reliability. Internal-consistency reliability is the degree to which different parts of a test measure the same abilities. Put another way, this reliability coefficient reflects the degree to which all items in the test measure the same abilities. The most common internal reliability coefficient is based on the *split-half* method—students' scores on even-numbered items are correlated with their scores on the odd-numbered items. A high correlation (high reliability) means that most or all of the items are measuring the same skill or ability (e.g., mastery of the subject matter), and you can have confidence that grades based on these scores are probably fair. A low correlation means the reverse.

You are much more likely to evaluate internal-consistency reliability than either of the other two. This is because test-retest and equivalent-forms reliability require a deliberate research approach: students either retake the same test at a later date, or else take two forms of the same test during the same administration period. Internal-consistency reliability requires only the usual single administration of a single test.

Validity

As we saw in Chapter 14, test **validity** is the extent to which a test measures what it is supposed to measure. That is, do the test results serve their intended purpose? For example, a spelling test is clearly a valid measure of the ability to spell those words. The same test may or may not be a valid measure of "spelling ability in general." There are three conceptually different kinds of validity (American Psychological Association, 1974): **content validity, criterion-related validity** and **construct validity.**[*]

---

[*] Psychologists and others also speak of "face validity," the degree to which a test simply "looks like" it should measure what it is intended to measure.

Content validity. Content validity is the important one in devising classroom tests. It refers to how well the test content represents the content of the material (or the skills) the students were to master. Does a particular history test adequately (validly) sample the information students were to learn? Asking students to list the names of Lincoln's sisters probably would not be a valid assessment of mastering important Civil War events.

The important point is *sampling.* A test always includes just a sample of the many questions which could be asked. Content validity is the degree (low, medium, high) to which the sample of questions used on a text adequately represents this larger universe of possible questions (Gronlund, 1977).

Criterion-related validity. Criterion-related validity refers to the ability of a test to predict performance on some other relevant *criterion* measure. For example, a creativity test has criterion-related validity if it accurately measures how creatively students perform in their art, science, or creative-writing activities. In this case, the criterion measure might be the teachers' ratings of the "creativeness" of students' projects. We speak of **concurrent validity** when both measures—the test and the criterion—are obtained at about the same time. For example, ability test scores in one file may be used to predict grades in another file. The criterion-related validity is **predictive** if the test scores are used to predict future performance. For example, scores on a newly developed creativity test administered at the beginning of the school year might be used to predict teacher ratings of student "creativeness" six months later.

With either type of criterion-related validity—concurrent or predictive—correlation coefficients normally would be used as an index of the degree of relationship between the test scores and the criterion measures.

Construct validity. Many psychological traits or abilities are referred to as *constructs*. We can't *see* intelligence, mechanical aptitude, anxiety, or creativity; they are considered hypothetical qualities or constructs. Tests which are designed to measure these traits or abilities have **construct validity** to the extent that they truly evaluate these constructs. This is no easy matter, since the constructs themselves, obscure rascals that they are, defy direct measurement. According to Gronlund (1977), about the best you can do in construct validation is to make predictions that would be consistent with the assumptions underlying a test, and then see if the data agree with the predictions.

For example, let's say you are developing a creativity test which assesses personality traits and biographical characteristics associated with "creativeness" (a construct). You might predict that:

- Items would have high internal consistency (reliability), since all items are supposed to measure the same construct.
- Students who are outstanding in creative art, creative writing, creative science ideas, or other forms of creativity should score higher than average on the test.
- Test scores should correlate positively with scores on other established creativity tests.
- After a creativity course or training program, scores should increase.

If these hypotheses are supported, the construct validity of a creativity test would be supported. Similar sets of predictions could be made to establish the construct validity of tests of anxiety, critical thinking, or mastery of Russian.

Norm-Referenced Tests, Criterion-Referenced Tests

We saw this pair of concepts in Chapter 12, in conjunction with the Popham and Baker criterion-referenced instructional model. With **criterion-referenced testing** the teacher wishes to evaluate which knowledge and skills each student has mastered, without regard to the scores of other students. It is quite all right—even desirable—for all students to master all concepts and skills.

Norm-referenced testing is used to produce a relative ranking of students, which is rather difficult to do if all students score 100 percent on a test. The test must be difficult enough to produce a distribution of scores.

The terms "criterion-referenced" and "norm-referenced" refer mainly to the interpretation of the test scores. The same test can be interpreted as norm-referenced or as criterion-referenced. For example, on a geography test Ferdie Magellan correctly answered 18 out of 20 questions (criterion-referenced interpretation), scoring higher than 67 percent of his class (norm-referenced interpretation). It is best, however, if a test is constructed for its intended interpretation. Especially, norm-referenced tests should include items of average difficulty (see below) in order to produce a wide distribution of scores. Criterion-referenced tests must include items that are directly relevant to the desired learning outcomes, whether they are easy items or not (Gronlund, 1977).

INSET 19.1

BUILDING A CRITERION-REFERENCED OR NORM-REFERENCED TEST

Measurement expert Norman E. Gronlund (1977, pp. 15–16) outlined some specifics to be considered in designing criterion-referenced (CRT) and norm-referenced tests (NRT).

Objectives
NRT: Objectives may be general or very specific.
CRT: Objectives tend to be very specific and detailed.

Learning Outcomes
NRT: Usually, a wide range of outcomes is covered, with just a few items per outcome.
CRT: Usually, a limited area of outcomes is covered, with a larger number of items per outcome.

Test Items
NRT: Selection items—multiple-choice, true-false, matching—are preferred.
CRT: Many kinds of items may be used; there is less dependence on selection items.

Reliability
NRT: Traditional reliability estimates are appropriate (e.g., split-half).
CRT: Traditional reliability estimates are not suitable, due to a (likely) lack of score variability.

Item Writing
NRT: Items should be written so as to discriminate among students who have different degrees of mastery.
CRT: Items should be written to describe student performance on specific learning tasks.

Intended Use
NRT: Used for end-of-unit or end-of-course summative testing (and grading). Also used for advanced placement.
CRT: Used primarily in readiness, formative, and diagnostic testing, as in mastery learning or other individualized teaching strategies.

Item difficulty is an important consideration in developing any test, but especially a norm-referenced test. Item difficulty is quantified simply in terms of the decimal fraction (or percentage) of students who answer the item correctly: In a class of 24, if only 6 students answer a particular multiple-choice question correctly, the difficulty level is $\frac{6}{24}$ or .25 or 25 percent. If the question is, "What color is an orange?" the "difficulty" level would be 1.00 or 100 percent.

When the difficulty of an item is exactly .50, that item achieves its maximum ability to discriminate between students who do possess the knowledge and skills being measured and students who do not. If *every* item on a test has a .50 difficulty level, two things happen: (1) A normal distribution of scores (bell curve) is produced, and (2) the total test achieves its maximum ability to discriminate among students. (See the section on Item Analysis later in this chapter.)

TYPES OF TESTS

Now that you know all about reliability, validity, norm-referenced and criterion-referenced testing, and item difficulty level, we can discuss four types of tests: (1) **placement tests**; (2) **formative tests**; (3) **diagnostic tests**; and (4) **summative tests**. The four types are intended for four different purposes.

Placement Tests

Placement tests would be used at the beginning of instruction. They are used to provide the teacher with two types of information:

1. *Entry skills:* Do students possess the information, skills, and abilities needed for the instruction?
2. *Entry performance:* Have students already achieved the intended objectives of the instruction?

To evaluate *entry skills* the test must include one or, preferably, more items assessing each prerequisite entry behavior (information, skill, or ability). For example, a test of English grammar might be given at the beginning of a French class—to insure that students understand the meaning of *noun, pronoun,* and *present tense verb.* Items typically are easy, and the test is criterion-referenced.

To evaluate *entry performance* the test should include items covering a representative sample of the unit objectives. For example, at the beginning of a unit on multiplication, you would want to find out if students already can multiply three-digit or four-digit numbers accurately. What about five-digit or six-digit numbers? With one decimal place? Two? Three?

Placement tests can be of graduated, increasing difficulty to assess entry skills and entry performance. To find out exactly what each student can do, placement test items have a wide range of difficulty and are norm-referenced.

In some individualized instructional strategies, placement testing (pre-testing) is used to determine whether a student can skip a particular assignment. If he or she already has the information and skills, he or she moves on to the next pretest. With this type of placement test the items would evaluate *all* or most of the lesson objectives.

It's often true that if a teacher has worked with a group of students for some time, he or she may be well acquainted with each student's entry skills and entry performance. In this case, placement testing may be entirely unnecessary.

Formative Tests

Formative tests are used during instruction, usually in conjunction with a mastery-learning or other individualized teaching method. The test covers a limited amount of material. The purpose of the test is to provide feedback on learning progress both to the students and to the teacher. For example, with the individualized elementary math program described in Chapter 12, students took a post-test at the end of each "road map" (directions for doing problems in different books). With an 80-percent correct score, both students and teachers are pleased and the child goes on to the next assignment.

Such a formative test should evaluate *all* of the unit or lesson objectives, or at least the most essential ones. Items are criterion referenced and their difficulty level will match the difficulty level of the unit objectives—they could be easy or not-so-easy.

Diagnostic Tests

Diagnostic tests are used to identify (diagnose) specific learning difficulties. For example, is little Joey's difficulty in multiplication due to an inability to "carry"? A failure to learn elementary multiplication tables? A basic mathematical learning disability (dyscalculia, remember dyscalculia?)?

The diagnostic test normally includes a large number of items in a specific area, with slight variations from one item to the next so that specific types of errors can be pinpointed. The items would be based on common sources of learning difficulties. For example, if you think Joey can't carry, then a number of variations of carrying problems would be used. Items usually are easy.

Often, a student's performance on a formative test will provide diagnostic information on learning problems. Other times, a professional learning-disabilities specialist with special tests will be needed for a proper probe of learning problems.

Summative Tests

These are the ones you get in college at the end of a unit or course. The purposes are to determine how well each student has achieved the intended objectives and, of course, to assign grades. The summative test also provides information on the effectiveness of instruction in general and in specific areas.

The items should have content validity—they should be based on a representative sample of course objectives. Also, the items usually have a wide range of difficulty. There should be plenty of medium-difficulty questions, since these are the best discriminators between who has and who has not mastered the material. Usually, the test is norm referenced; the instructor normally wants a wide distribution of scores. Occasionally, the test is criterion referenced and the instructor is happy to have everyone earn a high score.

TYPES OF TEST ITEMS

The six main types of test items divide into two categories, (1) **selection items,** which require the student to recognize and select the correct alternative, and (2) **supply items,** which require the student to recall and supply the answer. The six item types are:

1. Selection items
   a) Multiple-choice
   b) True-false
   c) Matching
2. Supply items
   a) Essay, extended response
   b) Essay, restricted response
   c) Short-answer (word or phrase) and completion (fill-in-the-blank)

Tests made up of selection-type items (multiple-choice, true-false, matching) and short-answer and completion items are often called **objective tests** because the questions are highly structured and the answers are either right or wrong—as objectively evaluated by the scoring key. As you might guess, the three selection-type items are "slightly more objective" than the short-answer and completion items. Essay tests have been called **subjective tests** because a student's score depends on the teacher's intuitive (subjective) evaluation of the answer.

The test should use the item type which is most appropriate for measuring the desired learning outcomes (Gronlund, 1977, p. 10). The extended-response essay question (for example, "Describe the teacher's role in mainstreaming") is not especially useful for evaluating the mastery of

specific facts and concepts, since the student may or may not use the specific ideas in his or her response. On the other hand, the extended-answer essay test can be quite useful in evaluating such complex outcomes as the ability to organize, synthesize, select relevant material, evaluate, or create.

The restricted-response essay question (for example, "Describe three ways to lower gas prices") would be more useful than the long-answer essay for evaluating the understanding of facts and concepts, but less useful for evaluating "the ability to organize" or "the ability to select relevant material." The short-answer and completion types of questions are almost entirely limited to measuring the recall of specific facts and ideas.

The highly structured selection questions (multiple-choice, true-false, matching) can be used very flexibly to evaluate simple or complex learning outcomes—the mastery of facts, principles, applications, interpretations, and so on. As examples, a true-false question can present a proposition which the student must interpret or evaluate as correct or wrong. Matching questions can present a set of principles and examples or terms and definitions to be matched. Multiple-choice items can be used to evaluate knowledge of facts, examples of a principle, applications of a theory, or other skills and information.

TAXONOMY OF EDUCATIONAL OBJECTIVES AS A TEST CONSTRUCTION GUIDE

As we saw in some detail in Chapter 11, Bloom's *Taxonomy of Educational Objectives: Cognitive Domain* draws attention to six main categories of learning outcomes: (1) knowledge, (2) comprehension, (3) application, (4) analysis, (5) synthesis, and (6) evaluation. The categories are hierarchically organized in order of increasing complexity from the simple recall of facts and concepts (knowledge) to judging the value of an idea, theory, event, or phenomenon (evaluation). Not all of these outcomes will be covered in a particular unit or course or, therefore, in a given test. Formative tests, for

Table 19.1 Taxonomy of educational objectives: cognitive domain, with examples of action verbs for each category

Taxonomy category	Sample verbs for describing learning outcomes
Knowledge	Identifies, names, defines, describes, lists, matches, selects, outlines
Comprehension	Classifies, explains, summarizes, converts, predicts, distinguishes between
Application	Demonstrates, computes, solves, modifies, arranges, operates, relates
Analysis	Differentiates, diagrams, estimates, separates, infers, orders, subdivides
Synthesis	Combines, creates, formulates, designs, composes, constructs, rearranges, revises
Evaluation	Judges, criticizes, compares, justifies, concludes, discriminates, supports

Table 19.2 Table of specifications, specifying content, outcomes, and numbers of test items

Content	Knowl-edge	Compre-hension	Applica-tion	Analysis	Synthesis	Evalua-tion	Total number of items
Exceptional children	1	1		1	1	1	5
Mainstreaming	2	1	1			1	5
Learning disabled children	1	2	1	2			6
Intellectual processes, language	1	1			1		3
Hyperactivity and Ritalin		1		1		2	4
Teaching LD children			2			1	3
Mildly mentally retarded	1	1		1		1	4
Emotionally disturbed children		1	1	1		2	5
IEP's	1	1	2	1	1	1	7
Total number of items	7	9	7	7	3	9	42

example, most often evaluate knowledge outcomes (terms, facts, rules, procedures), comprehension outcomes (interpretations, extrapolations) and application outcomes (using the information). Summative tests, however, can include items based on all six of the taxonomy categories.

A summary form of the taxonomy, along with the kinds of action verbs (behaviors) used to state objectives for each category, appears in Table 19.1.

Table of Specifications

One systematic way to prepare a test—if you happen to be a systematic person—is through the use of a **table of specifications** (Gronlund, 1977, pp. 27–32). The table will help you relate the content of your course or unit to the types of (Bloom's) learning outcomes. It also helps you balance the number of test items devoted to each topic and each outcome level. Table 19.2 presents a sample table of specifications based on most of the main topics in Chapter 18.

WRITING TEST ITEMS

Multiple-Choice Items

The reason you have taken so many multiple-choice tests in college is that the multiple-choice test is such a darn good evaluation device. Multiple-choice items can be written (and most often are) to evaluate simple knowledge outcomes; they also can be written to evaluate complex learning, such as the ability to interpret, classify, predict, identify relationships, analyze, synthesize, or evaluate.

The multiple-choice item includes a *stem*, which may be either a question or an incomplete statement. The four or five alternative answers include the correct answer plus three or four *distractors*. The purpose of the distractors is to fool students who don't know the material as well as they should. Many of the following guidelines are designed to minimize cues which help the shrewd test taker eliminate distractors and pick the correct response without knowing a thing about the subject matter. Multiple-choice items should be based on important objectives, they should be easily understood, they should be answerable only by those who have achieved the objectives. Some guidelines:

1. Each item should measure an important outcome (objective) of learning.
2. The stem of the item should present a clear problem in simple language. Complex, poorly stated, partially irrelevant, or ambiguous stems may confuse even knowledgeable students.
3. Be sure to emphasize any negative wording you use in the item stems. If students overlook the negative aspect of a stem, they will NOT answer correctly. Generally, it is better to use positively stated stems.
4. Be sure that the correct alternative is clearly the best answer. Check each distractor to make certain that good students could not defend any of them as the correct answer.
5. Be sure that all alternatives are grammatically consistent with the stem. The correct answer is always grammatically consistent with the stem—it's those distractors you have to watch. Especially be careful about ending the stem with "a" or "an"—the correct answer will never be "an declaration of war" or "a exclamation point."
6. Avoid similarity of wording in the stem and in the correct answer. It provides an obvious cue to the correct alternative.
7. Avoid stating the correct alternative in stereotyped, textbook language. The testwise student will select that answer because it seems vaguely familiar, whether he or she understands the material or not.
8. Always avoid using absolute terms (always, all, never, none, etc.) in distractors. The correct answer never uses absolutes. Often, the correct answer may use qualifiers, like *may, often, usually,* etc.
9. Make the distractors seem plausible and appealing to uninformed test takers. Some suggestions for increasing the credibility of distractors are:
   a) Make the distractors equal in length and complexity to the correct response.
   b) Use common errors or misconceptions as distractors.
   c) Have as many "good sounding" words in the distractors as in the correct answer, words like *important, accurate*. Also, you can use

words in distractors which are common associations of words in the stem (for example, if *science* is in the stem, *laboratory* could be used in a distractor).

10. Avoid using "all of the above." If a student recognizes at least two correct answers, he or she can deduce that "all of the above" must be the correct alternative.

11. Randomly vary the position of the correct alternative. Testwise college students know that alternative "b" is used more than others. Any other pattern also will be detected, for example, never having the same alternative correct more than twice in succession or avoiding alternative "a."

12. Be sure items are independent. Sometimes the answer to one question will accidentally appear in the stem or alternatives of another question.

13. Make sure the difficulty level is appropriate to the test purpose. If the test is criterion-referenced—to evaluate the mastery of certain outcomes—items generally are relatively easy. If the test is norm-referenced—intended to produce a spread of scores—items will be more difficult.

14. With any test, start with easier items at the beginning. This increasing order of difficulty has a desirable motivational effect and prevents weaker students from "bogging down" on a tough question early in the test period (Gronlund, 1977, p. 105).

We noted above that multiple-choice questions can be used to evaluate complex learning outcomes as well as simple knowledge objectives. At Bloom's *Application* level, for example, the correct alternative can be an example of the correct application of a principle or a procedure; distractors would be inappropriate applications. At the *Analysis* level, students can be asked to recognize correct relationships, organizing principles, or inferences. Outcomes of *analysis, synthesis,* or *evaluation* may be evaluated by providing students with a map, chart, graph, description of an experiment, law, paragraph, poem, etc. A series of multiple-choice questions then would ask students to detect relationships, synthesize different facts, recognize unstated assumptions, or recognize unwarranted conclusions or inferences.

As a general rule, multiple-choice items are considered the best means of evaluating simple or complex learning outcomes; they mostly avoid common problems of essay tests (limited information sampled, subjective grading). They also are preferred to true-false questions. One reason is that a true-false test will be less reliable (less accurate, less consistent) than a multiple-choice test, given that both tests have equal numbers of items. Gronlund recommends that the test-maker (you) begin by writing multiple-choice items, then switch to true-false (or another item type) when the subject matter or learning outcome makes it desirable to do so.

True-False Items

One situation which lends itself especially well to a true-false format is when students are to learn a list of characteristics or properties—for example, 12 traits of a creative person. If you constructed six multiple-choice questions with five alternatives (one correct answer, four distractors), you would need to make up 24 (6 × 4) distractors. You also would sample students' knowledge of just six traits. With a true-false format, you could list about nine traits plus about eight or nine distractors (not 24!) and ask students to identify which traits are, and which are not, characteristic of creative people.

As some guidelines for constructing true-false items:

1. Use just one central idea, not several. It saves ambiguity and confusion.
2. Word the statement clearly so that it can unambiguously be judged true or false. Short statements in simple language will help you measure the intended learning outcome—and not just measure students' reading and comprehension abilities (Gronlund, 1977, pp. 55–56).
3. Avoid using negatives, since the "not" is frequently overlooked. Especially avoid using double negatives, which often are not unambiguous.
4. Avoid clues to the correct answer, such as using absolutes (always, never, all, or none). Length also can be a clue—longer statements tend to be true, short statements false.
5. Use about equal numbers of true and false statements. The usual tendency is to use too many true statements, which tells the sharp guesser: "When in doubt, guess 'true'."

Matching Items

Matching items are basically modified multiple-choice items. Instead of the four or five alternatives being listed under each stem as in multiple-choice questions, the series of related stems (called *premises*) are listed on the left, and the common set of response alternatives is listed on the right. As a few guidelines for constructing matching items:

1. Each matching item should include homogeneous material, since all responses must be plausible alternatives for each premise. Matching items thus are suitable for evaluating the learning of theorists and their theories, scientists and their discoveries, books and authors, historical events and dates, etc.
2. Place the brief responses (alternatives) on the right, to save reading time. For example, the longer theories could appear as premises on the left, the alternate names of the theorists on the right.
3. Use a larger or smaller number of responses than premises, and/or allow responses to be used more than once. Such manipulations make uninformed guessing more difficult. Make sure students understand that answers may be used more than once.

Short-Answer, Completion Items

The short-answer and fill-in-the-blanks questions are the only form of *objective* test item in which students supply, not select, the correct response. These items can involve direct questions ("Who is buried in Grant's tomb?") or a fill-in-the-blank form ("_____ is buried is Grant's tomb"). Short-answer and completion questions are generally considered an inferior type of test item, mainly because it often is difficult to phrase questions so that exactly one answer is correct. For example: "_____ freed the slaves" might elicit "Abe Lincoln," "President Lincoln," "Honest Abe," or "The guy on the penny." Along with subjective decisions about misspelled words, there generally is more subjectivity in scoring completion items than multiple-choice items.

However, for occasions where you wish students to *recall* (not recognize) specific information, this type of item may be quite appropriate. Some guidelines:

1. Try to state the item so that only a single answer is possible. This is not especially easy. Use simple, clear and precise wording—and hope that it is simple, clear, and precise to the reader.
2. Direct questions usually are more clear than incomplete statements, but not always.
3. Students should be asked to supply important words or concepts, not "and," "the," or "because."
4. Avoid clues to the correct answer, such as ending the statement with "a" or "an" or using longer blanks for longer words.

Essay Tests

With essay tests, the student is free to decide how to approach the problem, what information to use, and how to organize the answer. Essay tests thus are best suited for evaluating the ability to produce, integrate and express ideas (Gronlund, 1977, p. 76). In regard to Bloom's taxonomy, essay tests are best for evaluating *synthesis* and *evaluation* outcomes. They also are good for assessing *comprehension*, *application*, and *analysis*.

There are serious weaknesses. First, since only a few questions can be used, just a small sample of the students' achievement actually can be evaluated. An unlucky student may study the wrong material. Second, writing skills—spelling, grammar, punctuation, handwriting, organizing ability, writing speed—tend to influence the score. The story in Inset 19.3 demonstrates how a fluent bluffer sometimes can garner a good grade. A third and related problem is the subjectivity of the scoring. Research has shown that (a) grading standards shift as the instructor reads more and more papers, (b) different raters assign different grades, and (c) the same rater may assign a different grade when reevaluating an essay test after a period of time (Coffman, 1971).

INSET 19.3

FAKING AN ESSAY EXAM

One problem with essay tests is that the fluent, fast-thinking student often can bluff himself or herself into a few extra points. One tale, probably distorted in the retelling, describes how a college test bureau sent a clever student with special writing skills into a mid-term examination to see how well he could do on an essay test with absolutely no preparation. The main question called for a critical evaluation of a novel that the student had not read. His answer started out somewhat as follows: "This is not the best novel I have ever read, but neither is it the worst. It has some real strengths, such as the detailed attention given to the development of the main characters. On the other hand, some of the minor characters have not been developed as fully as they might be. . . ." His evaluation continued along this vein. The paper was returned at the next class meeting, along with this comment by the professor: "This is the best evaluation of this novel I have ever read."

With **restricted-response** essay questions, the teacher places limits on the subject matter and form of the answer. For example, the instructor might ask students to "list reasons," "define," "describe the steps in _____," or "itemize the main results of Dr. Heffner's 1976 research with bunnies." While such questions can evaluate fairly specific outcomes at the comprehension, application, and analysis levels, they usually are not good for synthesis and evaluation outcomes (Gronlund, 1977, p. 79).

It is the **extended-response** question which permits the integration and evaluation of ideas and the development of problem solutions. Students may be asked to give reasons, describe data, explain relationships, formulate conclusions, design a method, defend a position, plan a strategy, compare two viewpoints, criticize a theory, evaluate an idea, and so on. It usually is appropriate to begin the question with "explain," "compare," "describe," "relate," "contrast," "analyze," "criticize," "evaluate," or "why."

A few guidelines for constructing essay tests are:

1. Use essay questions only to evaluate complex outcomes of learning. Knowledge and comprehension outcomes can be measured more reliably with objective tests.
2. Design each question to elicit one or more well-defined outcomes. The question will not elicit the complex outcomes unless it is carefully worded to do so.

3. Provide ample time for answering. Teachers who give too many questions in the allowable time are evaluating writing speed as much as anything else. If you wish to sample many learning outcomes, don't use an extended-answer essay test. Also, indicating the amount of time to be spent on each question will help structure the test and will improve the quality and sensibility of the results.

4. Grade all answers to one question before moving to the next question. Each answer is more likely to be judged on its own merits if it is compared with other students' answers to the same question. There is a positive or negative "halo effect" in grading essay tests, such that a swell answer to Question 1 will bias the teacher to see the answer to Question 2 as better than it really is. And vice versa, a bad answer to Question 1 will lead the teacher to expect (and perceive) a bad answer for Question 2.

5. To increase scoring reliability, have two persons grade each answer. Use the average score as the basis for grading. This procedure is most critical if students' tests are used for important decisions, e.g., special opportunities or awards.

6. Grade anonymously. You need not wear dark glasses and a big hat, but you should not look at students' names before reading the essay answers. The obvious problem is a positive or negative halo effect. "So this is little Hank Kissinger's paper. I bet it will be _____, as usual."

ITEM ANALYSIS

A critical consideration in test construction is whether or not your test items are "working" as they should. The main purpose of an **item analysis** is to help you build better questions for the next time around. Some simple procedures will tell you everything you ever wanted to know about the effectiveness of each of your test questions.

Norm-Referenced Test Items

In evaluating the worth of test items intended to produce a wide distribution of scores, you would be interested in at least three points: (a) What is the difficulty level of an item? Is it too easy? Too difficult? (b) Does the item discriminate between prepared students and weaker students? Or could the correct response be due to good guessing or chance? (c) Are all of the distractors (in multiple-choice questions) actually distracting somebody? Or are some too easily eliminated?

Item analysis information not only helps you improve the items, but it provides a basis for post-mortem class discussions of the test results. Easy questions can be skipped over, with discussion time devoted to apparently difficult questions (topics). Items which do not discriminate (that is, in which correct responding is unrelated to mastery of the material) can be pointed out to students as defective—and not defended as "fair questions." Popular but incorrect response alternatives can be analyzed and explained.

As an example, let's say you have 27 students in your class who just took a multiple-choice test on American history. You have scored the tests. You would select the nine students with the highest total scores (top one-third) and the nine students with the lowest total scores (bottom one-third). Put the remaining nine tests in your lower left-hand drawer under your apple; we won't need them.

For each test item, count the number of students in the *top* group who selected each alternative. Ditto for the *bottom* group. Your data will look something like:

Item 11	A	B	C*	D	E
Top 9	0	2	7	0	0
Bottom 9	2	2	2	3	0

*Correct alternative

As we saw earlier, **item difficulty** is simply the proportion of students who answer the item correctly, including top and bottom students. In this case nine students (7 + 2) answered correctly, and so the difficulty level is

$\frac{9}{18}$ or .50 or 50 percent. A higher percentage figure will reflect an easier item. Item difficulty figures also can be based on the result from the whole class, not just the top and bottom thirds.

The **item discriminating power** refers to the ability of an item to discriminate in the same way that the entire test does. That is, do the top third of the students tend to answer the item correctly? And do the bottom third tend to miss the item? An eyeball examination of the item analysis may be all that is necessary. In the above example, seven of the nine top students answered correctly. This item is working fine. It is possible (a) for no more top students than bottom students to answer an item correctly, or worse (b) for *more* bottom students than top students to get the item correct. In either case, the item is defective and should be returned for warranty repairs or replacement.

If you like numbers, an **index of discrimination** may be computed by, first, subtracting the number in the bottom group who answered correctly from the number in the top group who answered correctly. (The resulting difference should be a positive number; it could be zero or a negative number.) This difference is divided by the number of students in *each* group—nine in our example. Thus our index of discrimination for item 11 would be:

$$\frac{7 - 2}{9} = \frac{5}{9} = .56.$$

If all students in the top group answered correctly and all students in the bottom group answered incorrectly, the index of discrimination would be a perfect 1.0. Witness:

$$\frac{9 - 0}{9} = \frac{9}{9} = 1.0.$$

Test of your logic: With *all* of the top students answering correctly and *all* of the bottom students answering incorrectly, we would have a *difficulty level* of 50 percent. That is, half of the students answered correctly, half incorrectly. Only in this circumstance can discrimination power approach 1.0. This is why measurement folks recommend that item difficulty levels should be 50 percent in order to maximize discrimination power in norm-referenced tests.

The effectiveness of the various distractors can be evaluated simply by visually comparing the numbers of top and bottom students who select each distractor. A good distractor will fool more students from the bottom group than the top group. In our example, alternative B misled as many top students as bottom students; alternative E didn't fool anybody. B and E do not work very well; A and D are fine, since bottom students chose them but not top students.

Criterion-Referenced Test Items

Since criterion-referenced tests include items which are deliberately easy, and the teacher is not interested in a wide spread of scores, the traditional item analysis (above) usually is not appropriate. The teacher now is asking: Is the item measuring the effects of instruction? For example, if *all* students can answer a question before and after instruction, the question does little good. Vice versa, if *no* student can answer the question before or after instruction, the item again tells you nothing about reaching the objectives. A good item would be missed before the instruction but answered correctly in a post-test.

An index of *sensitivity to instructional effects* (Kryspin and Feldhusen, 1974, p. 166) can be computed with the formula:

$$S = \frac{R_A - R_B}{T}.$$

Where S is sensitivity to instruction, R_A ("right after") is the number of students answering the item correctly after instruction, R_B ("right before") is the number of students answering correctly before instruction, and T is the total number of students answering the item both times. Obviously, to use the formula you must give the test to the same students both before and after instruction. The resulting sensitivity index values will range from zero (bad item) to 1.0 (ideal item). As an example of a "fair" item:

$$S = \frac{19 - 7}{24} = .50.$$

A "good" item:

$$S = \frac{23 - 1}{24} = .92.$$

INTERPRETING TEST RESULTS

There are a number of standard concepts used to interpret test results. Most of these assume a normal distribution of test scores, that is, scores on norm-referenced tests. It is a virtual certainty that sooner or later you will feel like an idiot if you do not (a) understand these concepts and (b) know where to look up the formulas after you forget them. Where? In this book, of course.

Grade Equivalent Scores

Grade equivalent scores are scores reported in terms of grade level. For example, a grade equivalent score of 5.2 would be the average score of a fifth-grade student in the second month of the school year. Grade equivalent scores are only found with published tests—for example, in reading. You find the grade equivalent score simply by looking up a raw score in the test publisher's table which converts raw scores to the grade equivalent score.

Percentile Rank

A widely used index of a student's relative standing on a test is the **percentile rank.** It indicates what proportion of the class (or other students who took the test) scored lower than a given student. For example, if student Clarence Carthug scored "at the 67th percentile," it means that 67 percent of the students who took the same test scored lower than Clarence.

Tables for converting raw scores to percentile ranks often are included in publisher's test manuals. You can easily compute your own by the formula:

$$\text{Percentile rank} = \frac{\text{Number of students with the same or lower score}}{\text{Total number of students taking the test}}.$$

For example, in his class of 27 English students, Clarence scored higher than 18 of them in a test of long division. Thus:

Percentile rank = $\frac{18}{27}$ = 67%.

Keep in mind that since test scores tend to cluster in the middle (remember the bell curve?), the difference between the 50th and the 51st percentile may be 1 test point. At the extremes, however, scores get spread out and so the difference between the 2nd and 3rd percentile (or 98th and 99th percentile) could be 10 points or more.

Range

The **range** of scores is simply the difference between the lowest and the highest scores. For example, if the lowest score is 21 and the highest 57, the range of scores is 36 points. It's also proper to say, "The scores ranged from 21 to 57."

Median

The **median** is the score of the central person in the distribution. If there are an even number of persons, the median is the midpoint between the two central scores. For example, if 10 scores on the Simpleton Spelling test are:

21
21
20
18
16
15 ← median = 15.5
13
13
13
13

the median is 15.5—half the students scored below the median, half above.

The advantage of using a median, instead of using an average (mean) score, is that extreme scores do not receive undue weight. For example, if five teachers earn $12,000 per year and a sixth earns $50,000 (tutoring Murgatroyd Moneybags's children), the "average" salary is $18,333—which hardly represents anybody's actual income. The median salary, of course, would be $12,000, a figure which better represents the typical teacher in the group.

Mode

The **mode** is the most frequently obtained score in a distribution. In the distribution of scores on the Simpleton Spelling Test (above), the mode or modal score would be 13—more students received a score of 13 than any other score. You eventually will hear the phrase "bimodal distribution," which is a distribution with two modes. For example, one group of students may score very high, another group may score very low. In such a case neither the median score nor the average (mean) score accurately represents the score of the typical student.

Mean

The **mean** is the average score. If there are 10 scores, add them up and divide by 10.

The mean, median, and mode all are referred to as "measures of central tendency," since they all may be used to describe the typical performance of a group of students. If a distribution is "normal" (bell shaped), the mean, median, and modal score will be the same. If a distribution is *skewed*, with, say, high scores scattered off into the sunset, then the mean, median, and mode will be related as shown in Figure 19.1. One mnemonic device for

Figure 19.1
Mean, median, and mode in a skewed distribution.

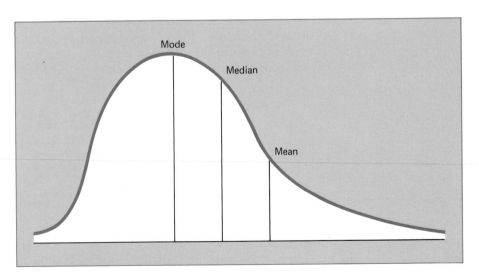

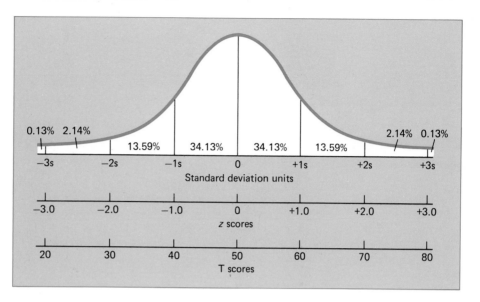

Figure 19.2
A normal
distribution,
showing the
percentage of the
population in
each segment of
the distribution,
standard
deviations,
z-scores, and
T-scores.

remembering the relationship is that the mean, median, and mode are in alphabetical order as you go "up the hill."

Standard Deviation

We met the **standard deviation** in Chapter 18 in conjunction with the normal distribution. The standard deviation is basically a measure of score variability, in the sense that a test with a standard deviation of 3 points shows less score variability than a test with a standard deviation of 25 points. You will most often encounter the standard deviation in discussions of norms of published tests. For example, a published reading comprehension test might report a mean of 40 and a standard deviation of 6. Such information is extremely helpful in interpreting the significance of any student's score.

For example, if Sam scores 40 on the test, this tells you his performance was exactly average in comparison with the norming group (whose scores make up the test norms). A score of 34 by Polly tells you that she scored one standard deviation (6 points) below the mean. Reference to Figure 19.2 tells you that about 84 percent (50 + 34.13) of the norming group scored higher than Polly's 34. A little more thinking lets you know that Polly's score of 34 is at the 16th percentile.

It is not difficult to compute a standard deviation, especially if you have a $10 pocket calculator. The formula is:

$$sd = \sqrt{\frac{\Sigma d^2}{N}}$$

where

sd = standard deviation,

Σ = sum of,

d = difference between each score (X)
and the group mean (M),

$d^2 = (X - M)^2$,

N = number of scores,

$\sqrt{}$ = square root sign.

Let's run through a short example:

Score (X)	$d(X - M)$	d^2
30	−10	100
32	−8	64
32	−8	64
35	−5	25
39	−1	1
40	0	0
41	1	1
43	3	9
45	5	25
45	5	25
47	7	49
51	11	121
480		484

$$M = \frac{480}{12} = 40.$$

$$sd = \sqrt{\frac{484}{12}} = \sqrt{40.33} = 6.35.$$

With these 12 scores, we find a mean of 40 and a standard deviation of 6.35.

A short-cut method for computing a standard deviation was devised by Diederich (1973):

$$sd = \frac{\text{Sum of high sixth} - \text{Sum of low Sixth}}{\frac{1}{2} \text{ the number of scores}}.$$

Will it work? In our example:

$$sd = \frac{(47 + 51) - (30 + 32)}{\frac{1}{2}(12)}$$

$$= \frac{98 - 62}{6} = \frac{36}{6} = 6.00.$$

The short-cut standard deviation of 6.00 is close enough to the proper standard deviation of 6.35 to justify using it instead of the longer formula. Especially if your $10 calculator does not have a square-root button.

Standard Scores

A glance at Figure 19.2 will quickly unravel the mystery of the **z-score.** A z-score is simply a score converted to standard deviation units. Thus if Polly's score of 34 is one standard deviation below the mean, her z-score is -1.00. This simple formula is:

$$z = \frac{X - M}{sd} = \frac{34 - 40}{6} = \frac{-6}{6} = -1.00.$$

We would say that the z distribution has a mean of 0 and a standard deviation of 1.

Another standard score is the T-score, which has a mean set at 50 and a standard deviation of 10 (Figure 19.2). Polly's raw score of 34 is converted first to a z-score of -1.0, then to a T-score of 40. You can see that, for Polly:

$$T = 50 + 10z$$
$$T = 50 + 10(-1.0) = 40.00.$$

Some standardized test norms will report T-scores.

Stanines

One statistic which is becoming increasingly popular in education is the **stanine,** an abbreviation of "standard nines." There are nine stanine groups, and each stanine is one-half of a standard deviation (Figure 19.3). A student's standing on a particular test is identified according to which stanine he or she is in. Thus Polly's score of 34, one standard deviation below the mean,

Figure 19.3
Stanine scale, showing percentages in each stanine and the relationship to the standard deviation scale.

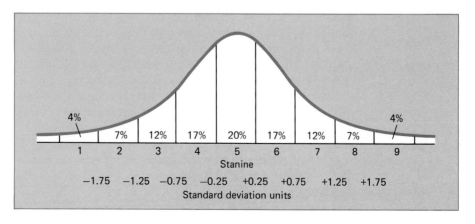

would put her in the third stanine (Figure 19.3). A particular student's stanine group can be found by reference either to the standard deviation units or to the percentile rank. For example, Polly's percentile rank of 16 also puts her into the third stanine (Figure 19.3). The percentage figures in Figure 19.3 also will tell you what proportion of the class to expect in each stanine, *if* the scores are normally distributed.

TO IMPROVE
YOUR TEACHING

When you use standardized tests or when you make up your own tests, pay attention to matters of reliability and validity. Some published tests actually have fairly *low* reliability and validity, despite a pretty appearance and a reputable publisher's name on them. It is not fair to classify students (e.g., as anxious, creative or gifted) or assign grades with an unreliable or invalid test.

You also must keep in mind that a formative test used in individualized instruction is a criterion-referenced test—a different animal from a summative, norm-referenced test used at the end of a course to assign grades.

Most teachers ask factual type questions. Keep in mind that we also should be teaching, and testing for, higher-level cognitive objectives— applications, analyses, syntheses, and evaluations. A table of specifications will help you keep track of both the topics covered and the cognitive level of the thinking involved.

Remember too that objective questions should be simple and clear and should measure important outcomes. Emphasize "NOT" and keep multiple-choice alternatives grammatically consistent with the stem. Also, avoid accidental cues to the correct answer—such as using absolutes in wrong alternatives, or putting the answer in another question somewhere else in the test. With essay tests, remember the *many difficulties:* Only a small sample of knowledge is evaluated, and scores can be biased by students' verbal fluency, spelling, neatness, and bluffing ability—and students' names.

As for item analyses, university professors with large classes do these routinely in order to see which questions are "working" and which are not. You can (should) do the same thing with a class of 25 in order to confirm to yourself that your questions are doing their intended job. Finally, you also will find that at least some of the statistics—means, medians, modes, standard deviations, stanines, percentiles—will be very handy in summarizing your group's performance and communicating that performance to others.

SUMMARY

As we saw in an earlier chapter, reliability refers to the accuracy or consistency of a test. Three types of reliability estimates, all quantified by using correlation coefficients, are test-retest reliability, equivalent-forms reliability, and internal-consistency reliability. The latter usually involves the split-half method. Poor items will lower all three.

Validity is the ability of a test to measure what it is intended to measure. This chapter described content validity (the degree to which the test items accurately represent the content of the material studied), construct validity (the degree to which the test measures unseen psychological constructs, such as intelligence or anxiety), and criterion-related validity (predictive and concurrent).

You also should understand by now the difference between a norm-referenced test, used to produce a wide distribution of scores (which may be thought of as "norms" for grading, if it helps), and criterion-referenced tests, used to evaluate the mastery of specific learning objectives or "criteria." Criterion-referenced test items might be used in placement testing, in evaluating entry skills and entry performance, in formative evaluation, or in diagnostic testing.

Item difficulty level, the proportion of students answering correctly, is an important consideration in developing norm-referenced tests for summative evaluation and in constructing criterion-referenced tests.

College tests are mainly norm-referenced summative tests, used at the end of a unit or course to (a) assign grades, (b) motivate learning, and (c) provide feedback on the effectiveness of instruction.

Selection items are multiple-choice, true-false, and matching items. Supply items are short-answer (word or phrase), completion (fill-in-the-blanks), restricted-response essay and extended-response essay. The essay questions are considered subjective tests; all others are objective (in reference to scoring). Multiple-choice items generally are considered superior for most purposes.

The different item types are useful for evaluating different sorts of outcomes. Extended-answer essay questions are most suited for evaluating complex learning outcomes, for example, at the higher levels of Bloom's taxonomy. Restricted-answer essay questions are good for evaluating the recall and understanding of concepts. Short-answer and completion items are almost entirely limited to evaluating the recall of specific facts. All selection items—multiple-choice, true-false and matching—may be used to evaluate simple or complex outcomes.

A table of specifications helps you relate the content of your unit to the level of complexity of the outcome, using Bloom's taxonomy as a guide.

Suggestions were outlined for constructing each type of test item. Some recommendations were to (a) have each question measure an important outcome, (b) write questions in simple, clear, unambiguous language, (c) emphasize any negative wording, or avoid negatives altogether, (d) avoid clues to the correct answer (such as using absolutes, using longer correct answers), (e) avoid giving the answer to one question in another question, (f) make sure the difficulty level is appropriate to the test purpose, (g) provide ample time to answer essay questions, and others.

Item analysis tells you whether your test questions are working as they should. With norm-referenced test items you can look at difficulty level, ability to discriminate between good and poor students, and the effectiveness of each distractor. With criterion-referenced tests the item analysis tells you if students tend to miss the question before instruction, but answer it correctly after. If so, it is a good item.

Statistical concepts included under the heading of test interpretation were (a) grade equivalent scores, (b) percentile rank, (c) range, (d) median, (e) mode, (f) mean, (g) standard deviation, (h) standard scores, and (i) stanines.

TOPICS FOR THOUGHT AND DISCUSSION

1. Admission to G/T programs often is based on intelligence test scores, grades, creativity test scores, teacher recommendations, and sometimes parent recommendations. Which of these "measures" would be highest in reliability? Which lowest? Why?

2. For grading purposes, college courses usually use norm-referenced testing. Is criterion-referenced testing ever used in college? Should it be used more?

3. Since most measurement experts argue that multiple-choice test items are the "best," under what circumstances would you use other kinds of test items? Could a multiple-choice test be used in those cases?

4. In college courses in which you have taken essay exams, do you think the grading has been biased? If so, by what factors? Should the instructor have used essay questions?

PROJECTS

1. Find two or three published test manuals for evaluating, for example, math skills, reading comprehension, or intelligence (see the school psychology, counseling psychology, or learning disabilities staff at your school or college). Read the information on reliability, validity, and group norms. How do the tests compare? Are the students in the norm group comparable to the students in your local schools? Is this important?

2. Practice computing all of the statistics in this chapter. (This is the only way you will feel comfortable with them.)

3. When you next visit a school, talk with one or two teachers at the grade level you expect to teach about the statistics (e.g., means, medians, modes, standard deviations, percentiles, etc.) they find most helpful and actually use.

RECOMMENDED READING

Bradley, J. I., and J. N. McClelland. *Basic statistical concepts: A self-instructional text.* Glenview, Ill.: Scott, Foresman, 1963.

Chase, C. I. *Measurement for educational evaluation.* Reading, Mass.: Addison-Wesley, 1974.

Gronlund, N. E. *Measurement and evaluation in teaching,* third edition. New York: Macmillan, 1976.

———. *Constructing achievement tests,* second edition. Englewood Cliffs, N.J.: Prentice-Hall, 1977.

Terwilliger, J. S. *Assigning grades to students.* Glenview, Ill.: Scott, Foresman, 1971.

APPENDIX TO CHAPTER 19: COMPUTING A CORRELATION COEFFICIENT

You may never in your lifetime experience an overwhelming urge to compute a correlation coefficient. On the other hand, you might wonder how students' scores on your test relate to their scores on other tests, their tested IQ, their pretest, their grades in another class, etc. The correlation coefficient is one of the most useful statistical devices since Euclid invented geometry.

It is not really that difficult. Let's say 10 students have taken Test A and Test B and you wish to determine the correlation (r) between scores on Test A and Test B. Scores on A will be "X's" and scores on B will be "Y's." The formula is:

$$r = \frac{N\Sigma XY - \Sigma X\Sigma Y}{\sqrt{[N\Sigma X^2 - (\Sigma X)^2][N\Sigma Y^2 - (\Sigma Y)^2]}}$$

where

$$
\begin{aligned}
N &= \text{Number of pairs of scores,} \\
\Sigma &= \text{Sum of,} \\
XY &= \text{Each } X \text{ multiplied by its } Y, \\
\Sigma XY &= \text{Add up the cross products (of each } X \text{ times its } Y), \\
\Sigma X\Sigma Y &= \text{The sum of all the } X \text{ scores multiplied by the sum of all the } Y \text{ scores,} \\
X^2 &= \text{Each } X \text{ score squared,} \\
\Sigma X^2 &= \text{Add up the } X^2\text{'s,} \\
\Sigma X &= \text{The sum of the } X \text{ scores,} \\
(\Sigma X)^2 &= \text{The sum of the } X \text{ scores, which is then squared,} \\
Y^2 &= \text{Each } Y \text{ score squared,} \\
\Sigma Y^2 &= \text{Add up the } Y^2\text{'s,} \\
\Sigma Y &= \text{The sum of the } Y \text{ scores,} \\
(\Sigma Y)^2 &= \text{The sum of the } Y \text{ scores, which is then squared.}
\end{aligned}
$$

I believe we're ready.

Student	Test A X	Test B Y	X^2	Y^2	XY
Al	5	8	25	64	40
Bob	5	9	25	81	45
Carla	6	7	36	49	42
Doris	8	10	64	100	80
Ed	9	12	81	144	108
Fred	9	12	81	144	08
Gloria	10	11	100	121	110
Harriet	11	9	121	81	99
Irv	13	16	169	256	208
Jack	14	22	196	484	308
	$\Sigma X = 90$	$\Sigma Y = 116$	$\Sigma X^2 = 898$	$\Sigma Y^2 = 1524$	$\Sigma XY = 1148$

Plugging in the numbers we have:

$$r = \frac{(10)(1148) - (90)(116)}{\sqrt{[(10)(898) - (90)^2][(10)(1524) - (116)^2]}},$$

$$r = \frac{11480 - 10440}{\sqrt{(8980 - 8100)(15240 - 13456)}},$$

$$r = \frac{1040}{\sqrt{(880)(1784)}},$$

$$r = \frac{1040}{\sqrt{1,569,920}} = \frac{1040}{1252.97} = .83.$$

GLOSSARY

Academic engaged time. Amount of time students are actively engaged in task-oriented studying (Rosenshine). A good predictor of achievement. See *Direct instruction.*

Acceleration. Moving gifted, fast-learning students into higher levels of achievement, usually through promotion or advanced placement, special classes, college courses, telescoped programs, or early admission to kindergarten, first grade, high school, or college. To reduce confusion with "enrichment," acceleration programs are defined as strategies which result in advanced credit or placement.

Accommodation. Altering cognitive structure to fit a new concept (Piaget). See *Assimilation.*

Accountability. In education, a philosophy in which students or teachers or both are held accountable for student achievement. Students may be required to pass minimal competency tests; teachers may be penalized if the students do not.

Achievement motivation (n Ach). The need to achieve. It may be outweighed by a conflicting need to avoid failure (McClelland).

591

Activity reinforcer. Letting students do rewarding things, for example, with extra recess or gym time, talking time, free time, or 15 minutes of rock music.

Adolescence. Begins at puberty—age 10–17 for girls, 12–18 for boys—with its dramatic physical changes. Some main features of adolescence are sexual development and interest, some self-consciousness, and the formation of a more-or-less stable adult identity.

Advance organizer (or just Organizer). Introductory material in the form of background information which the learner already knows (Ausubel). An *expository organizer* is composed of concepts at a hierarchically higher, more general level and is used with learning relatively unfamiliar new material. A *comparative organizer* is composed of concepts as the same hierarchical level and is used with relatively familiar new material.

Affective domain. Deals with attitudes, values, feelings, emotions (fears, hostilities, etc.), tastes, prejudices, personal philosophy, personality, self-esteem, personal and social adjustment, and mental health.

Allocated time. Time allowed for learning, which may differ from time engaged in learning.

Amphetamines. Dexedrine and Benzedrine, stimulant drugs used to (strangely enough) calm hyperactive children. See *Ritalin.*

Anchoring. "Tying" new ideas to ideas already in cognitive structure (Ausubel); i.e., making the new material meaningful. Advance organizers are intended to do this.

Androgyny. Accepting both masculine and feminine attitudes and behaviors (changing a tire; mixing baby formula), rather than accepting the traditional sex role stereotype (Bem).

Animistic thinking. Tendency to attribute life to inanimate objects, such as streams, the sun, etc. (Piaget).

Anomia. Language disability in which the child has difficulty naming objects.

Anxiety. Vague worry, nervousness, or apprehension without a specific known cause. Anxiety may be *facilitative,* motivating studying and test taking, or *debilitative,* interfering with needed concentration and performance.

Aphasia. *Receptive aphasia* is difficulty understanding spoken language. *Expressive aphasia* is difficulty speaking. A learning-disabled child may have one or both.

Aptitude by treatment interactions (ATI). The examination of the effectiveness of different teaching methods (treatments) for different types of student personality, ability, or cognitive style (aptitudes).

Arousal. An alert mental state, including increased muscle tension and a change in heart rate. Considered by Daniel Berlyne to be a necessary state for learning. May be stimulated by curiosity, leading to the term *curiosity motivation.*

Assimilation. Altering or reinterpreting new concept to fit cognitive structure (Piaget). See *Accommodation.*

Associative networks. The conception of mental life as webs of interrelated associations among words, ideas, symbols, images, etc.

Attribute listing. Robert Crawford's creative thinking technique(s) of (a) modifying important problem attributes or (b) transferring attributes from one situation to another.

Attribution theory. Heider's explanation of our motivation to understand cause-

and-effect relationships. Students may attribute performance to internal (ability, effort) or external (luck, task difficulty) causes (Weiner). See *Locus of control.*

AUTA: A model for creative development. A model which describes the steps through which one proceeds in becoming a more creative person: An Awareness of the importance of creativity; an Understanding of the topic; learning Techniques of creative thinking; an increase in self-Actualized creativeness.

Authoritarian leadership style. Situation in which the teacher-leader decides all policies and procedures. Future activities are kept unclear. Standards for praise and criticism also are ambiguous. See *Classroom climate.*

Baseline data. Rate of undesirable target behavior before behavior modification intervention, usually responses per hour or per day (frequency method) or minutes of target behavior per day or per observation session (duration method).

BASIC. The basic microcomputer programming language.

Basic school, Middle school, Transition school. Former U. S. Commissioner of Education Ernest L. Boyer's recommendation for restructuring America's schools. Basic schools teach basic skills; middle schools focus on contemporary issues plus traditional disciplines; transition schools provide specialized training which accommodates individual differences in talents and goals.

Behavior and products. Two types of objectives (Popham and Baker). Behavior might be a speech, a contribution to a discussion, a demonstration of an attitude, or the demonstration of a motor skill (e.g., using a lathe). Products refers to tests, papers or projects.

Behavioral genetics. The study of genetic influences on mental and some behavioral characteristics, such as intelligence, retardation, mental illness, and personality.

Behavioral objective. Instructional objective stated in terms of what the learner must *do* to demonstrate his or her learning.

Behavioral variables. Cognitive and performance characteristics which are difficult to measure reliably, such as intelligence, anxiety, or reading ability. See *Identification variables.*

Behaviorist. Traditionally, a psychologist who believes that psychology, as an objective science, should be concerned with observable environmental stimuli, measurable responses, and reinforcement contingencies. Reference to unobservable mental events (ideas, images, purposes, etc.) should be avoided. B. F. Skinner and, earlier, John B. Watson, are both behaviorists.

Behavioristic view of language. A traditional conditioning-oriented interpretation of language learning based upon forming associations, viewing sentences as stimulus-response word chains, reinforcement, punishment, and modeling.

Body adjustment test. A measure of field dependence-independence (Witkin). A person in a tilted room tries to adjust his or her tilted chair to a perfect upright position.

Brainstorming. Popular group-think strategy based on the deferred-judgment principle—no criticism or evaluation during the brainstorming session itself. Originated by Alex Osborn, founder of the Creative Education Foundation.

Branching program. In programmed learning, according to which multiple-choice response is selected, fast learners are "branched ahead," slow learners may be "branched back" for review. See *Linear program.*

Brown v. Topeka Board of Education. The 1954 case making segregation illegal.

Capitalization model. An ATI strategy which capitalizes on a student's academic strengths or personality characteristics—for example, a hard-working "loner" might be given independent projects. See *Compensation model* and *Remediation model.*

Chromosomes. Rodlike structures containing one's genetic blueprint for physical and some mental characteristics. They contain thousands of genes.

Classical conditioning. The idea that two stimuli presented together tend to become associated, such as Pavlov's dog's *bell* and *meat*, or *salt* and _____. Five synonyms are Pavlovian conditioning, contiguity learning, stimulus-stimulus learning, signal learning, and respondent conditioning.

Classroom climate. Psychological atmosphere which influences student attitudes and effort, based mainly on teacher attitudes and leadership patterns. The classic Lewin, Lippett and White boys club research studied the effects of authoritarian, democratic and laissez-faire leadership styles (Chapter 2).

Classroom management. Methods of running a classroom for minimizing disruption, maximizing effort.

Classroom meetings. Informal, nonevaluative, open-ended meetings dealing with social, personal and educational problems (Glasser). Newburg (1977) extended the concept to sharing (show-and-tell) meetings, project-planning meetings, and personal problem-solving meetings.

Cognitive dissonance. Festinger's notion that when two ideas or two attitudes are inconsistent, an uncomfortable mental state is created which motivates one to remove the dissonance by changing one's attitudes or thinking.

Cognitive drive. Ausubel's notion that successful learning motivates further learning. A form of intrinsic motivation.

Cognitive learning theory. A theory which describes unobservable mental events and processes. Ausubel's concepts of "cognitive structure" and "subsumption learning," Piaget's "mental schemata," and information-processing theory definitely are cognitive, not behavioristic, concepts.

Cognitive strategies. Gagné's self-management skills of attending, encoding for retention, and problem solving. Independent learning requires the acquisition of these cognitive strategies.

Cognitive structure. Internal representation of a hierarchically organized body of information and experiences. Ausubel's cognitive structure is equivalent to Piaget's differentiated schemas. See *Progressive differentiation.*

Compensation model. An ATI strategy in which the teacher "does for the learner what he cannot do for himself." For example, if a student is a poor organizer, the material is organized for him or her. See *Capitalization model* and *Remediation model.*

Competence motivation. Robert White's theory that children, especially, have built-in needs to develop skills and become competent (or capable) in dealing with their environment.

Competency-based education. Accountability system in which students must demonstrate minimal competencies (objectives) before they are permitted to graduate from high school or, in some cases, move to the next higher grade. Evaluation is by competency testing or "taking competency tests." Also, one of four of Mitchell and Spady's (1978) outcome-based educational models, this one emphasizing high academic achievement and technical competence, which lead to real future opportunities.

Componential theory of intelligence. Newest intelligence theory which analyzes intellectual ability into component processes which differ in function (e.g., acquisition components, retention components) and in level (metacomponents, class components, specific components).

Computer-assisted instruction (CAI). The use of computers as super teaching machines.

Computer literacy. In microcomputer circles, a popular phrase referring to a practical knowledge of computers by teachers and students.

Concrete operations. Piaget's third stage of cognitive development (age 7–11), characterized by thinking with representations of concrete objects; thinking before acting; the ability to conserve; and the ability to classify, leading to lots of collections.

Concurrent validity. A form of criterion-related validity. The relationship of scores on one test to scores on a criterion measure obtained at about the same time. See *Predictive validity.*

Conditioned stimulus (CS), Conditioned response (CR). A conditioned stimulus is a neutral stimulus (e.g., a bell) which, after pairing with an unconditioned stimulus (UCS; e.g., food), elicits a conditioned response (e.g., salivation).

Conditions of learning. Gagné identifies internal and external conditions of learning. Internal conditions are prerequisite skills and information. External conditions means instruction, which is designed according to a sequence of information processing "events" of learning.

Confirming interval. In goal setting, the distance between highest expected achievement and the lowest acceptable achievement. Failure-oriented students may set wide intervals in order to avoid feelings of failure.

Conservation. Ability to realize that volume, mass, weight, and number do not change with simple alterations in appearance (Piaget).

Conspiracy of silence. Lawrence Kubie's phrase describing the failure of parents and teachers to help students understand and verbalize their feelings.

Construct validity. Degree to which a test measures psychological traits (e.g., anxiety, creativity) which cannot be measured directly. Difficult to determine.

Content validity. The degree to which the test content represents the content of the material students were to learn; or how well the particular test items represent the larger universe of possible test items.

Continuous recording method. In behavior modification, the method of recording occurrences of target behavior whenever they occur in a given day. Used when fewer than about 20 responses (e.g., unnecessary trips to teacher's desk) per day are emitted. Contrasts with *time sampling* method.

Correlation coefficient. Numerical figure representing the degree of relationship between two variables on a scale from -1.00 to $+1.00$. A positive correlation means "the more of this the more of that"; a negative correlation means "the more of this the less of that." A zero (.00) correlation means no relationship; a correlation of 1.0 or -1.0 indicates a perfect relationship. When used to assess reliability and validity, correlations run from .00 to $+1.00$.

Correlational research. Research which determines interrelationships among factors (or variables). Does not demonstrate which factors cause which other factors. See *Experimental research, Observational research.*

Creative personality. Attitudes, values, motivations, and other dimensions of personality which contribute to creativity. Self-confidence, risk taking, curiosity, humor, high energy, sensation seeking, artistic interests, and a "creativity consciousness" are some of the most recurrent traits.

Creative thinking techniques. *Personal* creative thinking techniques (Davis, 1981a, 1981b) are individual strategies developed by every creatively productive person to generate new ideas or produce creative products. *Standard* creative thinking techniques, taught in virtually every creative thinking course and text, include brainstorming, attribute listing, morphological synthesis, idea checklists, and the synectics methods.

Criterion-referenced test. Test used to evaluate the mastery of objectives, especially in placement testing and formative evaluation. Items may be easy; a wide distribution of scores is unnecessary. See *Norm-referenced test.*

Criterion-related validity. The ability of a test to predict performance on a criterion measure. Criterion-related validity may be concurrent or predictive, depending on whether the criterion measure was obtained at the same time or later.

Critical period. In Chapter 4, the phenomenal language-learning ability of the child, who is a "linguistic genius" from age 2 to 6 or 7.

Crystallized intelligence. One's accumulated store of knowledge and experiences which increases over the years (Cattell). See *Fluid intelligence.*

Dangles. Interrupting the class with an irrelevant question or comment (Kounin). The class is left "dangling." See *Smoothness.*

Death wish, Life wish. Conflicting motives to die or live, says Freud.

Decay. A forgetting mechanism; the fading of information in the sensory register, short-term memory, or long-term memory with the passage of time. See *Interference.*

Decentering. Piaget's term for the young child's gradual understanding of a world apart from the self; a reduction in egocentrism.

Deeper processing. Analysis of meanings and relationships. *Semantic elaboration,* one form of deeper processing, is the eliciting of related images and meanings of a sensory input. Deeper processing improves memory.

Defense mechanisms. Psychological devices for removing conflicts, reducing tension, and protecting one's self-concept. First identified by Freud, they include repression, denial, projection, reaction formation, displacement, sublimation, rationalization, compensation, and identification.

Defensive goal setting. Setting unrealistic goals (too high or too low) to protect against feelings of failure.

Deferred imitation. Delayed copying; e.g., mixing a cake a few hours after watching mommy do it.

Democratic leadership style. Situation in which activities are determined by group decision. The group leader assists, encourages, clarifies alternatives, and explains the basis for praise. See *Classroom climate.*

Dependent group-oriented contingency system. In behavior modification, rewards for the entire class depend on the performance of one student; e.g., "If Nancy finishes, we all hear the Beatles." See both the *Independent* and the *interdependent group-oriented contingency systems.*

Dependent variables (measures). What the experimenter measures in experimental research; usually test scores.

Descriptive praise. A form of praise which describes the desirable behavior being rewarded; e.g., "I like the way you're working." Contrasts with *Evaluative praise.*

Desensitization. The removal of conditioned fears, phobias, and hostilities by having persons engage in the emotion-provoking activity without the fear or anger being elicited.

Development-based education. An educational orientation which emphasizes humanistic and affective goals, including concern for others, personal identity, and quality educational experiences (Mitchell and Spady, 1978).

Deviation IQ. A person's intelligence test score in relation to a normal (bell-curve) distribution of test scores. See *Ratio IQ, Intelligence quotient.*

Diagnostic tests. Tests used to identify specific learning problems. The tests usually consist of a large number of similar items in a specific area, for example, "carrying" in multiplication problems.

Differential psychology. Traditional name for the field of psychology concerned with individual differences.

Direct analogy. Technique for finding creative ideas by asking how animals, birds, insects, plants, etc., have solved similar problems. One of the *Synectics methods.*

Direct influence. A form of Flanders "teacher talk" classroom interaction behavior. The teacher talks and talks, for about 85 percent of the class period. See *Indirect influence.*

Direct instruction. Teacher activities which promote academic engagement, and therefore high achievement (Rosenshine). See *Academic engaged time.*

Discovery learning. The use of unstructured (or partly structured) problems, materials, experiments, etc., requiring each learner to discover for himself or herself the important ideas, rules, concepts, or principles. Its claims of being more motivating, more meaningful, more transferable, and less authoritarian than expository instruction are criticized by Ausubel.

Discrimination, generalization. Discrimination is learning to respond differentially to two or more stimuli (which may be similar). Discrimination is considered the opposite of generalization, which is responding in the same fashion to two or more stimuli (which may be similar).

Dissociability. Ausubel's term for the "retrievability" of information from cognitive structure. If well-learned, the information is said to be "dissociable" from cognitive structure.

Distractors. Incorrect alternatives in multiple-choice items. They should be sufficiently plausible that unprepared students will select them instead of the correct alternative.

Divergent and convergent associations. With divergent associations, one stimulus, such as a word, elicits several responses or associations. With convergent associations, it is the reverse; several stimuli all elicit the same response.

Divergent thinking. Producing lots of unusual ideas for an open-ended problem. Contrasts with *convergent thinking,* finding one correct answer for a problem.

DNA (Deoxyribonucleic acid). Complex molecules in the double helix (spiraling ladder) shape which carry coded genetic information. "Growth" takes place by unzipping down the middle, then selecting chemicals to build identical molecules.

Down's Syndrome (Mongoloidism). A common, inherited form of retardation. Down's Syndrome children show particular physical characteristics (flattened skull, round face, short stature, and others).

Duration method. In behavior modification, a method of recording the amount of time spent in a target behavior (e.g., at the pencil sharpener). Contrasts with *Frequency* (rate) *method.*

Dyscalculia (acalculia). Arithmetic disability.

Dysgraphia (agraphia). Writing disability.

Dyslexia (alexia, word blindness). Inability to read.

Dyspraxia. Difficulty in making intended movements.

Early childhood. Period from 18–24 months to 5–6 years; it includes the development of self-care and school readiness skills.

Ego. According to Freud, that part of the personality which is in contact with reality and which copes with the real world in a rational manner.

Egocentrism. In the preoperational stage, the inability to take another person's perspective (Piaget).

Elaboration rehearsal. Finding related ideas, meanings, associations to improve retention of an idea or concept. See *Deeper processing, Maintenance rehearsal.*

Electra complex. Female counterpart of Oedipus complex; a girl's attraction to her father and dislike of her competitor mother (Freud).

Embedded figures test. A test requiring the person to locate a simple geometric figure "embedded" in a more complex figure (Witkin). Measures field dependence-independence.

Embryonic period. In prenatal development, from about two weeks after conception to eight weeks. Basic body parts are identifiable and internal organs begin to develop. Embryo is very susceptible to damage, especially neurological.

Emotionally disturbed children. Children who are aggressive, delinquent, or excessively withdrawn.

Enactive. Bruner's first, infant-level form of mental representation, based on sensory and motoric activities. See *Iconic, Symbolic.*

Energy and direction in motivation. The related ideas that (a) any one motive may vary in intensity, or energy, and (b) any one motive may be satisfied in a number of different ways, or directions.

Enrichment. In the education of the gifted and talented, activities designed to strengthen both "process" skills (e.g., self-awareness, creativity, reasoning, scientific thinking, etc.) and skills and knowledge in particular interest areas (e.g., photography, computers, etc.). May include research projects, field trips, pull-out programs, learning centers, special classes, special schools, mentor programs, summer and Saturday programs, and others.

Enrichment triad model. Joseph Renzulli's model of programming for G/T children. Type I enrichment includes exploratory activities; Type II includes the development of thinking and feeling processes; Type III includes investigations of real problems. Types I and II are considered desirable for all students. Type III is suitable only for G/T children, due to their high creativity, motivation, and intelligence.

Entry performance. The results of a placement test used to determine whether students already have achieved the intended instructional objectives.

Entry skills. The results of a placement test used to determine whether students have the prerequisite abilities, skills, and information needed for the instruction.

Equilibration. The restoration of equilibrium by solving a disturbing problem or understanding a new experience (Piaget).

Equivalent-forms reliability. Degree to which two forms of a test are measuring the same abilities; quantified as a correlation coefficient.

Erikson's developmental stages. Eight "psychosocial" stages across the lifespan, each including a crisis which will be resolved in a mentally healthy or a mentally unhealthy fashion. The first five are similar, but not identical, to Freud's five stages. Erikson adds adulthood, middle age, and old age.

Essay test. There are two types. The type calling for an *extended response* is a long essay test—perhaps one-half hour per question. It is useful for measuring such complex outcomes as the ability to organize, select relevant material, synthesize, and evaluate. The type calling for a *restricted response* requires shorter, more structured responses; e.g., "List five reasons for classroom testing."

Evaluative praise. Generally lauding the quality or decency of a student; e.g., "You're a nice person." See *Descriptive praise.*

Events of learning. In Gagné's model, an information-processing analysis of a simple learning event. The model includes receptors, a sensory register, short-term memory, long-term memory, a response generator, effectors, and executive control and expectancies which supervise everything.

Expectations. Preconceptions about student abilities which influence teaching effectiveness, student effort and self-esteem, and therefore student learning and skill development. Known in education circles as the *Pygmalion effect* (Rosenthal and Jacobson).

Experimental research. Research which, in the simplest case, involves an experimental group which receives a "treatment" and a control group which does not. Differences in subsequent average performance scores usually allow the experimenter to infer that the treatment caused the group differences. See *Correlational research, Observational research.*

Expressive objective. Objectives which may apply to spontaneous educational situations in which it is impossible to write precise behavioral objectives (e.g., "We will discuss the meaning of the film").

External factors. Environmental sources of test score variability, such as noises, time pressure, or the particular test content. *Internal factors* are sources of score variation within a person, such as changes in motivation, attention, or fatigue.

Extinction. Cessation of a conditioned response, usually because of discontinued reinforcement.

"Faces." Our personality. Our *social face* is a personality mask we put on to impress others, to present ourselves well. Our *personal face* is how we see ourselves. Our *real face* is our true personality.

Factor analysis. Statistical procedure which reduces a large number of intercorrelations to a few basic, underlying dimensions or factors.

Faculties. The antiquated idea that the mind was composed of, e.g., faculties of memory, logic, reasoning, morality, humor, etc. See *Formal discipline.*

Fading. The systematic withdrawal of stimulus support (hints) in programmed learning, requiring progressively more active recall.

Failure-oriented student. The student who doubts his or her own ability and avoids threatening situations which could confirm that fear.

Fantasy analogy. Technique for producing creative ideas by looking for far-fetched or "ideal" problem solutions. See *Synectics methods.*

Fetal period. In prenatal development, from eight weeks to birth; characterized by growth and development of body parts and organ systems.

Field dependence. A cognitive style reflecting a tendency to perceive "wholes" rather than "parts," to be influenced by the perceptual field, and to generally be less analytical (Witkin). The field-dependent person tends to have a more social orientation.

Field independence. Reverse of field dependence. Other names for field dependence-independence are *global-analytical thinking* and *field articulation.*

Filtering. The automatic ignoring of some sensory inputs (e.g., air-conditioner noises) while attending to others (the lecturer's voice).

Flip-flops. A disturber of *smoothness.* When changing classroom subjects, the teacher flops back to the previous subject; e.g., "Put away your math, open your social studies texts—how many of you got all the math problems correct?"

Fluid intelligence. The ability to reason, discriminate, and think abstractly (Cattell). Fluid intelligence seems to peak somewhere between the ages of 18 and 38. See *Crystallized intelligence.*

Formal discipline. A theory of transfer, or an educational philosophy, based on the idea that exercises in mathematics and memorization strengthen "faculties" of logic, reason, memory, etc.

Formal operations. Piaget's fourth, adultlike stage of cognitive development (beginning between age 11–14), characterized by symbolic ability; "metathinking"; accurate perceptions of space, time, reality; idealism; self-consciousness; strong conformity to fads.

Formative test. Test used during learning to assess student progress; used especially in mastery learning or other individualized instructional strategies. See *Summative test.*

Fragmentation. Unnecessarily breaking up class *momentum*; e.g., by having students pick up a worksheet at the front of the room one person at a time (Kounin). See *Momentum.*

Frequency (or Rate) method. In behavior modification, recording the number of target behaviors emitted per unit of time; for example, 25 trips per day to the pencil sharpener. See *Duration method.*

Freud's developmental stages. Five "psychosexual" stages said to be critical for personality development: Oral (trust), anal (independence), phallic (sexual identity), latency (coping, mastery) and genital (identity). From Freud's psychoanalytic theory.

"g" factor. General intellectual ability (Spearman). The "s" factors are "specific" or "special" abilities needed to perform specific tasks. It usually is assumed that "g" represents whatever is common to the specific "s" factors.

General objectives. Gronlund's suggestion that advanced, complex learning requires broader, nonbehavioral general objectives (e.g., "understands scientific principles"), each followed by specific behavior objectives (e.g., "Gives an example . . .," "Identifies predictions . . ."). The specific behavioral objectives provide concrete evidence that the broader, general objective has been met. Probably every specific behavioral objective should be tied to general objectives and goals.

Genotype. Genetic make-up. See *Phenotype.*

Germinal period. First two weeks after conception, characterized mainly by cell division and attachment to the uterine wall.

Gifted, talented students. Students who are capable of unusually high achievement and performance, and who need special attention to help nurture their abilities. See *Marland's U.S.O.E. definition of giftedness; Three-ring model of giftedness.*

Goal Behavior. In behavior modification, behavior which is to be strengthened; for example, attending to business instead of tripping off to the pencil sharpener. See *Target behavior.*

Goal-referenced instruction. Popham and Baker's instructional model built around using clear objectives (goals). The four-step model includes: (1) specifying objectives, (2) pre-assessment, (3) instruction, and (4) goal-referenced evaluation.

Goal-setting conferences. An individualized instructional strategy consisting of weekly 10-minute goal-setting meetings. Elicits commitment and achievement (Klausmeier). Based on motivational concepts of modeling, setting goals, providing feedback, and reinforcement.

Good teachers. Teachers who are effective, respected, and well-liked. See *Humanness.*

Grade equivalent score. Score reported in terms of grade level; e.g., 6.3 would be the average score of students in the sixth grade, third month of the school year.

Group alerting. Keeping the entire class attentive and ready to recite; e.g., by selecting students randomly and having others watch for mistakes (Kounin).

Grouping. One memory device involving the deliberate organization or "chunking" of facts into meaningful groups for later recall. Grouping or chunking extends short-term memory limits.

Hardware. With computers, the machinery and equipment itself; i.e., the computer, a TV screen, a printer, a "Super Talker," etc. *"Software"* refers to programs for computer–assisted instruction, games, and simulations.

Hidden curriculum. Unwritten routines, policies, and teacher expectations and feelings which a student must learn in order to be successful in school.

Hierarchy of fears. A list of frightening stimuli ranked from least to most terrifying. Used in desensitization therapy.

Holophrase. One-word utterances which convey the information of a complete phrase or sentence; e.g., "Juice!"

Humanness. As applied to good teachers, being reasonable, fair, easy to relate to, humorous, understanding, trusting, liking students, and admitting to having feelings, having imperfections, and making mistakes.

Hyperactivity. High activity level, including a reduced ability to attend or concentrate. It may include low impulse control and low tolerance for frustration.

Hyperlexia. Using words with little or no understanding of them.

Iconic. Bruner's second mode of representation: mental images. See *Enactive, Symbolic.*

Id. Freud's instinctual part of the personality, mainly sexual and aggressive, which operates unconsciously, irrationally, and seeks immediate gratification.

Identical elements. Thorndike's theory of transfer which stated that the degree of transfer from one task to another is related to the number of elements the two tasks have in common, i.e., the number of "identical elements."

Identification variables. Objective human characteristics such as height, weight, age, eye color, or even income level which may be reliably measured. Contrasts with *Behavioral variables.*

Identity, connectedness, and control. Newburg's three clusters of student concerns. Identity deals with "Who am I?"; connectedness evolves around relationships with other people; control relates to feelings of ability and effectiveness.

IEP. Individualized education program, a management plan for each handicapped student which includes a description of present performance, annual and short-term goals, educational services to be provided, participation in regular programs, initiation and duration dates, and evaluation criteria and schedule.

Imagery. Mental images, which may be used in different forms of memory devices. See *Mnemonic memory devices.*

Imaginary audience. A form of adolescent egocentrism in which the adolescent believes that everyone else is concerned about the adolescent's appearance and behavior. See *Personal fable.*

Impulsivity and reflectivity. Tendency to respond too quickly and make errors (impulsive) and the tendency to take more time and make fewer errors (reflective). Usually measured by the *Matching familiar figures test.*

Independent group-oriented contingency system. A group-oriented system in which the same reinforcement contingencies are in effect for everyone, but rewards are earned individually for individual performances; e.g., "Anyone who gets 90 percent correct can play with the hamster for five minutes." See both the *Dependent* and the *Interdependent group-oriented contingency systems.*

Independent variable(s). What the experimenter manipulates in an experimental study. For example, type of training could be one independent variable; sex or age of subject might be other independent variables.

Index of discrimination. An item analysis method for quantifying item discriminating power. See *Item discriminating power, Item analysis.*

Indirect influence. A form of Flanders' "teacher talk" classroom interaction behavior; the teacher solicits ideas and opinions, administers praise and encouragement, and helps clarify student feelings. See *Direct influence.*

Individualization. Teaching strategies which permit setting individual, reachable goals, thus providing a good challenge and good conditions for success experiences.

Infancy. Period from birth to about 18–24 months; ends about when the child begins speaking in short phrases.

Instrumental conditioning. Conditioning following a stimulus-response-reinforcement formula; the use of rewards and punishments to control behavior. Operant conditioning and stimulus-response (S-R) learning are synonyms.

Intellectual skills. In Gagné's model, hierarchically ordered learned capabilities: making discriminations, forming concept classes, following rules, and solving problems.

Intelligence quotient (IQ). Mental age divided by chronological age, multiplied by 100. This conception is mostly replaced by the deviation IQ. IQ scores are measures of intelligence, with average IQ = 100. See *Deviation IQ, Ratio IQ.*

Interdependent group-oriented contingency system. Rewards for the entire class depend on the performance of the entire class; e.g., "If you all finish by three o'clock, we'll see a movie." See both the *Dependent* and the *Independent group-oriented contingency systems.*

Interference. Forgetting due to competing input, which usually is similar but conflicting. Interference may be *retroactive,* with new information interfering with the recall of earlier learned information, or *proactive,* with earlier information interfering with the retention of later learned information. See *Decay.*

Interindividual differences. Variation between people, often creating a "normal" distribution. "see *Intraindividual differences.*

Internal consistency reliability. Degree of relationship between different parts of a test, expressed, for example, by a correlation between scores on even-numbered vs. odd-numbered items (split-half method). An index of test accuracy.

Internal factors. Sources of test score variation within a person, such as changes in motivation, attention, or fatigue. See *External factors.*

Intraindividual differences. Variation in a single person's scores from one testing time to the next. See *Interindividual differences.*

Intrinsic and extrinsic motivation. With intrinsic motivation, the goal is in the activity itself, such as learning for the sake of learning or playing tennis for the built-in enjoyment. Extrinsic motivation implies working or studying for external rewards—money, toys, extra recess, or playing tennis only for trophies.

Introversion-extroversion. You know this one—the extremes are the classic nervous wallflower and the boisterous attention-getting boor.

Intuitive phase. Second stage (age 4–7) of Piaget's properational stage of cognitive development. It is often considered a transitional period before the next (concrete operational) stage, since some behaviors give the appearance of concrete operational thinking.

Item analysis. Method for determining whether each test item is "working" properly. Difficulty level, item discriminating power, and effectiveness of distractors usually are examined.

Item difficulty level. Proportion (percentage) of students answering an item correctly. Used in *Item analysis.*

Item discriminating power. The ability of an item to discriminate between prepared students (who should answer correctly) and ill-prepared students (who should miss the item). May be quantified with the *Index of discrimination* formula.

Jensenism. The notion that racial group differences in average IQ scores are largely due to genetic differences. Stems from writings by Arthur Jensen.

Jigsaw method. A strategy for forcing students (e.g., of different races) to cooperatively work together. Each member of the six-person team has one piece of information (e.g., a paragraph); the team will be tested on all information in one hour.

Junk-box model of memory. The metaphorical notion that memory is like a junk box. The information may be in there, but finding it and getting it out is another problem. Emphasizes the distinction between remembering and recalling (or retrieving).

Kohlberg's stages of moral development. Six sequential stages in the development of moral thinking. There are two stages each within the three larger stages of preconventional thinking (responding to rewards and punishments) conventional thinking (conformity to expectations and rules), and postconventional thinking (determination of universal principles; recognition that rules can be changed).

Laissez-faire leadership style. Leader is passive, leaving complete freedom to group members, and friendly; does not evaluate performance. See *Classroom climate.*

Language impairments. Learning disabilities involving aphasia, dyslexia, hyperlexia, anomia, or dysgraphia. Dyscalculia and dyspraxia also may be included, although they are not strictly linguistic.

Law of contiguity. Aristotle's law of thought emphasizing that events (stimuli) occurring at the same time tend to become mentally associated; about the same as classical conditioning.

Law of effect. E. L. Thorndike's classic idea that responses producing a good effect (satisfiers) will be strengthened, and responses that produce a bad effect (annoyers) will be weakened.

Learner-centered teaching. Teaching with an emphasis on the humanistic personal development of the learner. The term often is used interchangeably with *humanistic teaching.* Contrasts with "teacher-centered" or "curriculum-centered" teaching.

Learning disability. Impairment of psychological processes or language. See *Psychological processes, Language impairments.*

Learning outcomes. Gagné's term for goals and objectives; sometimes called *learned capabilities.* Includes the categories of verbal information, intellectual skills, cognitive strategies, attitudes, and motor skills.

Least restrictive environment. Phrase used in Public Law 94-142, the mainstreaming law, meaning the regular classroom.

Levels of processing. The idea that "unconscious" or "lower-level" activities (walking, fiddling with car keys) can take place at the same time as "higher-level" conscious activities (talking, writing, reading, or thinking).

Linear program. Form of programmed learning in which every learner proceeds through the same questions (frames) in the same order. See *Branching program.*

Linguistic competence. A child's language ability; what he or she knows or understands. See *Linguistic performance.*

Linguistic performance. The language which the child actually produces, which typically is at a less sophisticated level than his or her *Linguistic competence.*

Locus of control. The tendency to attribute successes and failures to one's own efforts and abilities *(internal locus of control)* or to such outside factors as luck, fate, unfair teachers, easy or difficult tests, etc. *(external locus of control).* See *Attribution theory.*

Long-term memory (LTM). Your storehouse of remembered experiences and information. It seems to be unlimited in capacity and duration.

Magic circle. A civilized form of children's sensitivity training. Children form a circle and respond to open-ended questions such as "I felt good when . . . ."

Mainstreaming. Placing handicapped (exceptional) children in regular classes for at least part of the school day. Mandated by Public Law 94-142.

Maintenance rehearsal. Simple repetition to forestall forgetting in short-term memory; sometimes called the "telephone strategy." See *Elaboration rehearsal.*

Marland's U.S.O.E. definition of giftedness. Six categories: (1) General intellectual ability, (2) specific academic aptitude, (3) creative or productive thinking, (4) leadership ability, (5) visual and performing arts, (6) psychomotor ability.

Mastery learning. Instructional model in which time is allowed for all (or most) students to achieve at high levels. Usually includes individualized instruction and diagnostic tests.

Matching. The process of recognizing an object or event by matching it against existing "schemata." See *Schema.*

Matching familiar figures test. A measure of impulsivity-reflectivity which requires the person to choose which of several similar drawings exactly matches the standard. Scored for response time and errors.

Mean. Average score.

Mean length of utterance (MLU). Roger Brown's average sentence length, which is a better measure of children's language development than age. Ranges from 2.0 (Stage 1) to 3.5–4.0 (Stage 5).

Meaningful learning. According to Ausubel, meaningful learning requires (1) a meaningful learning set and (2) potential meaningfulness (relatability) in the new material. See *Subsumption.*

Meaningful learning set. A conscious readiness to relate new material to existing ideas.

Meaningfulness. A new idea is meaningful if the learner can relate it to what he or she already knows; that is, it has "nonarbitrary substantive relatability to cognitive structure" (Ausubel).

Median. Score of central person in a distribution (or midpoint between two central persons).

Metathinking. Thinking about thinking, as in evaluating beliefs or ideals or thinking about intelligence.

Mnemonic memory devices. Memory "tricks" which essentially move information from STM to LTM for later recall; includes the use of appropriate cues or "triggers." See *Grouping, Imagery, Rhyming.*

Mode. The most frequently obtained score in a distribution. Also called "modal score."

Model. In psychology and educational psychology, (a) a "small theory" dealing with a limited segment of behavior, or (b) a set of concepts with a metaphorical relationship to another phenomenon (e.g., information-processing models are metaphorically related to computers). In current usage, *model* is virtually interchangeable with *theory*. See *Theory*.

Model of instruction. An explanation of instruction which simplifies, allows prediction, provides a language and a viewpoint, and provides prescriptive guidance.

Momentum. Keeping the class moving, uninterrupted by *Fragmentation* or *Overdwelling* on a minor incident (Kounin). Related to *Smoothness*.

Morphological rules. Linguistic rules for combining morphemes (units of meaning) into words; e.g., *biplane* is allowed, *bidog* is not.

Morphological synthesis (Checkerboard method). Creative thinking technique in which ideas for one aspect of a problem are listed on one axis of a two-dimensional matrix; ideas for a second dimension are listed along the other axis. Idea combinations are found in the cells.

Multiple-talent totem poles. Imagine a totem pole made up of kids, with the smartest at the top progressing down to the least intelligent at the bottom. A second talent totem pole is based on creativity, highest to lowest; a third is based on communication (speaking, writing) skills, etc. With enough talents examined, virtually everyone is above average or "gifted" in something (Taylor).

Need hierarchy. Maslow's notion that needs are hierarchically ordered, such that the lower-level "deficit" (e.g., physiological, safety) needs must be met before we attend to higher-level "growth" (e.g., self-actualization) needs.

Need theory (Psychogenic needs). Henry Murray's now-classic notion that we have at least 28 innate "psychogenic" needs or motives. The strength of each need varies greatly among individuals.

Needs assessment. The first step in developing a G/T program. It requires an analysis of the current status of education programs for the gifted in the district, city, or state, and a listing of what needs to be done to implement a program.

Negative creative traits. Personality traits of some creative children which teachers will not like. For example, some may be stubborn, assertive, cynical, temperamental, disorganized, emotional, and indifferent to conventions—such as showing up on time or being courteous.

Negative reinforcement. Removing aversive outcomes; e.g., scoldings, glares, insults, low grades, or getting frostbitten. The removal of these strengthens (reinforces) behavior; e.g., cooperating, studying, or coming in out of the cold.

Negotiations. In classroom management, a private problem-centered discussion with a disruptive student. Teacher's feelings, the student's explanation, and a no-lose mutually acceptable agreement are discussed openly.

Norm-referenced test. Test of average difficulty level used to produce a wide distribution of scores, perhaps for assigning grades. Creates a relative ranking of students. See *Criterion-referenced test*.

Oak School Experiment. The famous study by Rosenthal and Jacobson which purportedly demonstrated that high teacher expectations could raise student IQ scores.

Object permanence. The tendency of a sensorimotor child to look for a hidden object; it implies the existence of mental imagery (Piaget).

Objective tests. Tests whose scoring does not involve subjective teacher judgment: multiple-choice, true-false, matching, and short-answer (word or phrase), and completion tests.

Observational learning. Learning by observing and imitating others. Bandura includes the four phases of attention, retention, reproduction, and motivation (reinforcement). Reinforcement may be *direct,* as when the learner is rewarded for correctly matching the model's behavior, or *vicarious,* as when observers learn by seeing others rewarded or punished. Observational learning is part of social learning theory.

Observational (naturalistic) research. Research in which information is obtained by observing the natural behavior of students and teachers in classrooms. Behavior recording scales are often used. See *Correlational research, Experimental research.*

Oedipus complex. A boy's romantic and sexual attraction to his mother and dislike of his competitor father, says Freud. The *Electra complex* is the girl's attraction to her father, with a dislike for mother.

Open words, Pivot words. Open words are a small number of frequently used words (e.g., *more, see*) which are combined with pivot words (usually nouns; e.g., *milk, truck, ball*), producing such phrases as "see milk," "see truck," "see ball."

Openness to experience. A willingness to accept inner feelings, and an energetic interest in exploring new activities and ideas.

Optimal arousal theory. The notion that each of us seeks a comfortable level of arousal; achieved by sensation-seeking activities by some, excitement avoidance by others (Berlyne).

Overdwelling. Spending too much time on some minor rule infraction or deviancy (Kounin). Breaks up *Momentum.*

Overlapping. Ability to handle two events at once (Kounin). Especially, the ability to cope with a minor disruption without disrupting the ongoing lesson or activity: "Mary, keep reading. Bill, sit down, please, you've sharpened 10 pencils this morning."

Partial reinforcement effect (PRE). Strong motivated responding and strong resistance to extinction. It is caused by irregular or intermittent reinforcement, as in gambling, bowling, watching professional football, playing bridge, or in educational games and puzzles.

Pawns and origins. DeCharm's terms for people who feel they are controlled by external factors and people who feel they control their own behavior and destinies. Relates closely to *Attribution theory.*

Percentile rank. Indicates percentage of students scoring lower than a given person.

Person-situation theory. An approach to personality and behavior which argues that a person's behavior depends upon both his personality and the particular situation; i.e., behavior is variable instead of consistent. Contrasts with *Trait theory.*

Personal analogy. Creative thinking technique in which new perspectives and ideas are found by imagining oneself to be part of the problem; e.g., "What's it like to be a smooth-working zipper?" See *Synectics methods.*

Personal fable. The adolescent's strong belief in his or her uniqueness; i.e., the feeling that no one can possibly understand how the adolescent thinks or feels. A form of adolescent egocentrism. See *Imaginary audience.*

Phenotype. Observed and measured traits and behavior. See *Genotype.*

Phenylketonuria (PKU). Inherited enzyme deficiency causing retardation.

Phonological rules. Linguistic rules for combining vowel and consonant sounds (phonemes); e.g., *cl* is allowed, *qz* is not.

Placement test. Test administered at the outset of instruction to determine whether students (a) already have achieved the objectives (*entry performance*), or (b) possess the necessary *entry skills* (abilities, prerequisite information).

Plessey v. Ferguson. The 1896 "separate but equal" United States Supreme Court decision legalizing segregation.

Positive reinforcement. Administering desirable outcomes; e.g., points, money, smiles, high grades, or candy. These strengthen (reinforce) behavior.

Predictive validity. A form of criterion-related validity. The ability of test scores to predict a future performance; usually expressed as a correlation coefficient. See *Concurrent validity.*

Premack principle. The idea that whatever a student likes to do (e.g., fly airplanes, chew gum, chatter for 10 minutes, spin the teacher in his or her chair) can be used as a reinforcer to strengthen what the student does not like to do (sit quietly and attend to business).

Premises. In objective tests, the stems of matching items, which are arranged at the left of the page.

Preoperational phase. First two years (age 2–4) of preoperational stage (Piaget). Includes characteristics listed under *Preoperational stage,* below.

Preoperational stage. Piaget's second stage of cognitive development (age 2–7 years). Often subdivided into a preoperational phase (age 2–4) and an intuitive phase (age 4–7). Characterized by considerable language growth, egocentrism, animistic thinking, and failure to conserve.

Primary drives. Physiological deficit types of needs, such as hunger, thirst, pain avoidance, sex. These needs are met by *Primary reinforcers,* food, water, etc.

Primary mental abilities. Thurstone's notion that there are (usually) five distinct mental abilities (verbal meaning, number facility, reasoning, perceptual speed, and spatial relations).

Primary reinforcement. A reward which is necessary for the physiological equilibrium and well-being of the organism. The most popular ones are food, water, pain-avoidance, and sex. See *Primary drives.*

Product development research. Research aimed at field-testing and improving an educational strategy or curriculum material.

Progressive differentiation. Refers to the tree-like form of a cognitive structure, with a few general, superordinate concepts and a larger number of specific subordinate ideas (the branches and twigs; Ausubel).

Psychological processes. In Chapter 18, intellectual functions (memory, perception, conceptualizing, thinking) and inhibitory functions (hyperactivity, distractibility, low frustration tolerance, perseverance) which may be involved in learning disabilities.

Public law 94-142. The Education for All Handicapped Children Act (1969) which, among other things, mandated mainstreaming and the preparation of IEP's.

Punishment. Administering aversive stimulation, such as scoldings, glares, beatings, or low grades. These weaken behavior. Removing desirable outcomes (points, smiles, high grades, recess) is another form of punishment intended to weaken undesirable behavior.

Range. The difference between the lowest test score and the highest score.

Ratio IQ. The ratio of mental age to chronological age; i.e., (MA/CA) × 100. Used in the 1916 and 1937 editions of the *Stanford-Binet* test. See *Deviation IQ*, *Intelligence quotient*.

Ratio method. In behavior modification, the proportion (percentage) of the "time sample" spent on goal behavior. For example, in a 30-minute recording period, 67 percent (20 minutes) may have been spent studying.

Reception learning. A general term for Ausubel's expository instruction approach. It implies that the learner receives information in a final form from an instructor, rather than discovers it for himself or herself.

Recursive thinking. "I know that you know that I know"; a formal operational level of perspective taking.

Reductionistic. In this book, the notion that behaviorism attempts to explain complex human behavior by interpreting it in terms of simple conditioned responses and related concepts. The term implies that this approach is simplistic and inadequate.

Reliability. The accuracy or consistency of a test. Three types are equivalent forms, test-retest, and internal consistency reliability, all quantified by correlation coefficients.

Remediation model. An ATI strategy in which deficiencies are corrected. See *Capitalization model, Compensation model*.

Response-cost format. Behavior modification contingency in which a reward such as free time is forfeited for misbehavior.

Revised Stanford-Binet Intelligence Scale. Latest revision of the 1916 Stanford-Binet intelligence test, which was based on the historic Alfred Binet intelligence tests. Produces a single IQ score.

Rhyming. A mnemonic device sometimes used in learning simple rules (e.g., "*i* before *e* except after *c*").

Ripple effect. The not-too-surprising discovery that witnesses to a reprimand tend to be better behaved after the (vicarious) experience (Kounin).

Ritalin (methylphenidate). Stimulant drug most commonly used to calm hyperactive children.

Rod-and-frame test. A measure of field dependence-independence. The person tries to align a rod to a perfect vertical, independent of the tilted frame surrounding the rod.

Role expectations. In teaching, role expectations are the formal job requirements plus the additional duties and obligations that come with the territory.

Rules. An essential factor in classroom management. They should be simple, general, clear, flexible, and few in number. Students must know what is expected and what will not be tolerated.

Satiation. Too much of one task or topic; lack of variety. Produces boredom which leads to deviancy. Can be avoided by variety in teacher activities, A-V aids, group configurations, student activities and responsibilities, location of student work, etc.

Schema (Schemata). Internal organization of experiences and concepts. Piaget also speaks of "looking schema," "grasping schema," and "sucking schema." We may speak of a person "having a schema" for books, Florida, or virtually any other organized concept or experience. See *Matching*.

Secondary drives. Drives which are learned, such as needs for money, gold stars, grades, diplomas, or even praise. The goal objects (money, grades, etc.) are *secondary reinforcements*. Social reinforcers, such as smiles and praise, are considered secondary reinforcements because they are not critical for the physiological integrity of the person.

Selection items. Multiple-choice, true-false, and matching items. Students recognize and select the correct answer. Contrasts with *Supply items*.

Self-actualization. Becoming a "fully functional" person, one who uses all of his or her abilities to become what he or she is capable of becoming. Self-actualization includes having a good self-concept, being open to experience, and having humanitarian attitudes.

Self-actualized creativity. The mentally healthy tendency to do everything in a flexibile, creative way (Maslow).

Self-esteem, self-worth. One's evaluation of oneself, a very important consideration. Failure in school implies low ability, which threatens feelings of self-worth.

Self-regulation of behavior. The observing and judging of one's own behavior, and the providing of self-determined consequences (rewards, punishments). A part of social learning theory.

Sensation seeking. The attraction to exciting, arousing activities, such as skiing, camping, mountain climbing, or travel.

Sensitivity to instructional effects index. A form of item analysis used with criterion-referenced tests; reflects the proportion of students who missed the item before instruction, but who answered it correctly after they received instruction.

Sensitivity modules. Activities for learning first-hand about the problems and feelings of less fortunate persons. For example, perhaps in old clothes, visiting unemployment offices, welfare agencies, etc., talking directly to the poor people with the problems.

Sensorimotor stage. Piaget's first stage of cognitive development (age 0–2 years). Begins with reflexive behavior, ends with initial language, and is characterized throughout by improving sensory-motor coordination.

Sensory register. A brief, sensory afterimage type of "memory" or storage device, lasting about two seconds in the auditory mode, $0-\frac{1}{4}$ second in the visual mode. It is "preattentive."

Sex differences. Apparently sex-linked differences in cognitive, personality, and physical characteristics. One frequent observation is that boys have more learning difficulties and are more likely to be aggressive.

Short-term memory (STM; conscious memory, working memory). The minute-to-minute memory system limited to about 7 ± 2 meaningless items. It lasts about 30 seconds and is "post-attentive."

Skewed distribution. A non-normal distribution of test scores, with several scores strung out (skewed) at either the high end or the low end.

Smoothness. Efficient, trouble-free transitions between tasks; the uninterrupted maintenance of *momentum* during a lesson (Kounin). The absence of *flip-flops, dangles,* and *stimulus-bound* interruptions.

SMPY (Study of mathematically precocious youth). Julian C. Stanley's successful mathematics acceleration program. Baltimore area youth, identified by high SAT-M scores, attend fast-paced math classes at Johns Hopkins University.

Social-integration-based education. An educational orientation in which the main goals (outcomes) are social integration and acculturation (e.g., of minority persons) into productive social roles (Mitchell and Spady, 1978).

Social learning theory. A form of learning theory emphasizing learning from social activity. Especially involves observational learning (imitation) and the self-regulation of behavior.

Social reinforcer. Verbal praise, facial gestures such as smiles, nods, or winks, and physical nearness or contact, such as sitting the small student on the teacher's lap or patting the student on the back.

Social-responsibility-based education. An educational orientation in which the goals (outcomes) are a military-like responsibility, loyalty to the system, and good personal conduct; academic achievement plays second fiddle (Mitchell and Spady, 1978).

Sociodrama. Procedure for increasing empathetic understanding of social problems, and for changing attitudes in a proper direction, by having students role play short episodes.

Special education. Education field dealing with handicapped children. The "special ed" teacher processes referrals, diagnoses difficulties, plans programs, prepares reports, teaches "special ed" classes, and confers with parents.

Split-half reliability. The most common form of internal consistency reliability; usually a correlation between even-numbered items and odd-numbered items.

Stages in the creative process. A logical sequence of steps in creative problem solving. The traditional model includes preparation, incubation, illumination, and verification (Wallas, 1926). There are several other stage models.

Standard deviation. A measure of score variability. Very useful in identifying the relative standing of a student.

Standard scores. z scores or T scores. Test scores may be converted to standard scores to identify the relative standings of various students. The z scores are in standard deviation units; e.g., a score which is one standard deviation above the group mean is a z score of $+1.0$. The T distribution has a mean set at 50 and a standard deviation set at 10. Thus a score which is one standard deviation above the group mean is converted to a T score of 60.

Stanine. Distribution of scores divided into nine groups of $\frac{1}{2}$ standard deviation each. A student may score "in the third stanine," etc.

State anxiety. A temporary "state" of anxiety due to temporary circumstances, such as taking a test. See *Trait anxiety.*

State motivation. Motivation as a temporary condition caused by external circumstances, circumstances which the teacher often can control. Contrasts with *Trait motivation.*

Stem. The first part of a multiple-choice question, excluding the alternatives.

Stimulus-bound behavior. The inability of the teacher to resist reacting to irrelevant stimuli *during* a lesson; e.g., "Did we feed the fish today?" or "George, I forgot to ask how your mother is feeling."

Structure of intellect model. Guilford's three-dimensional, 120-celled model of human intelligence based upon five *operations*, four *contents*, and six *products.*

Styles A, B, C. Heil and Washburne's three teacher personality/leadership patterns. The Style A teacher is sentimental, identifying with students; teaching is often unplanned and variable. The Style B teacher is friendly, yet businesslike and responsible. The Style C teacher is anxious, dominating, and unreasonable.

Subjective test. Test whose score may be influenced by the judgment, biases, feelings, etc. of the scorer; usually just essay tests.

Subsumption. Learning. The process of "anchoring" new ideas to ideas already in cognitive structure. The latter may be called "subsumers." "Subsumption theory" is another name for Ausubel's "meaningful verbal reception theory" of learning.

Success-oriented student. One whose history of succeeding inspires confidence and self-esteem. He or she is motivated more by needs to achieve than by needs to avoid failure.

Summative test. Test given at the end of a unit or course used especially for assigning grades; usually norm-referenced, with medium-difficulty items. See *Formative test.*

Superego. Freud's term for the moral part of the personality which struggles with the *Id.* It is a "social conscience" and the source of feelings of guilt.

Superstitious behavior. Responses which are strengthened through accidental reinforcement, or which we incorrectly believe produce reinforcements (Skinner). In fact, there is no cause-effect relationship between the behavior and the reinforcements.

Supply items. Items in which the student recalls and supplies the answer: essay tests (restricted and extended response), short-answer, and completion questions. Contrasts with *Selection items.*

Symbolic. Bruner's third mode of representation, characterized by language and other symbolization. See *Enactive, Iconic.*

Symbolic (token) reinforcers. Refers to the use of poker chips, points, marbles, or Snoopy cards as rewards. These are accumulated and exchanged for backup (or *Tangible*) reinforcers, which the children wanted in the first place.

Synectics methods. Metaphor-based creative thinking strategies devised by William J. J. Gordon. Includes *Direct analogy, Personal analogy,* and *Fantasy analogy* methods.

Tangible reinforcer. The toys, candy, movies, money, hamburgers, or yo-yos used to reinforce cooperation or learning. Sometimes called a "bribe."

Target behavior. Maladaptive behavior to be modified through intervention programs. Might consist of wandering, interrupting, turning in assignments late, etc. See *Goal behavior.*

Task analysis. An analysis of one's definition of mastery, the important task cues, and most importantly the content and ordering of prerequisite subskills. Task analysis is used for formulating objectives and organizing instruction.

Taxonomy of Educational Objectives: Affective Domain. Five hierarchically-organized steps in learning an attitude or value, from the simple reception of affective information to permanent changes in personality and lifetime commitments. The five categories are labeled *Receiving, Responding, Valuing, Organization* and *Characterization by a Value Complex.*

Taxonomy of Educational Objectives: Cognitive Domain. Six progressively more complex levels of learner cognitive activities: *knowledge, comprehension, application, analysis, synthesis,* and *evaluation.* Instructional objectives, classroom activities (e.g., teacher questions), and examinations may be planned around specific levels of the taxonomy. Also known as "Bloom's Taxonomy."

Teacher-centered instruction. About the same as direct instruction. Includes teacher supervision of groups, teacher selection of goals, teacher pacing. The atmosphere is academic but pleasant, not authoritarian.

Telegraphic speech. Clipped speech during the two-word stage of language development. Sentences sound like a telegram; e.g., "Car broke."

Telescoping. Acceleration plan in which three years' work is collapsed into two (or four into three). Content is not missed, as it is when a grade or subject is skipped.

Terman's gifted children. Fifteen hundred gifted students, IQ = 140+, identified in the 1920s. They have been tracked, studied, and written about ever since.

Test-retest reliability. Relationship of test scores to scores on the same test administered at a later time; quantified with a correlation coefficient.

Theory. A set of concepts, principles, and vocabulary used to simplify, explain, and predict. A theory (or a model) also provides a language and a viewpoint and prescriptive guidance. In contemporary psychology and educational psychology, *theory* and *model* may be used interchangeably. See *Model.*

Three-ring model of giftedness. Renzulli's notion that a truly gifted student possesses high creativity, high motivation, and above-average intelligence.

Time sampling. In behavior modification, procedure of recording occurrences of target behavior only during specified time periods; for example, between 10:00 and 11:00 A.M.

Trait anxiety. An enduring personal tendency to be anxious. See *State anxiety.*

Trait motivation. Motivation viewed as a stable, enduring characteristic which differs among individuals. Contrasts with *State motivation.*

Trait theory. The notion that people possess pervasive personality traits which determine their behavior in a consistent fashion across a variety of situations. See *Person-situation theory.*

Transfer. In the present text, the application of school learning to later problems in school or the real world. Transfer may be *positive,* when the initial learning helps later problem solving, or *negative,* when the earlier learning interferes with solving later problems.

Transformational rules. Rules for transforming deep structures (internal meanings, purposes) into surface structures (grammatically correct sentences; Chomsky).

Tutoring. Using students to teach other students who may be the same age, younger, or handicapped. The tutor often benefits both academically and personally from the increased feelings of responsibility, prestige, authority, and competence.

Unconditioned stimulus, Unconditioned response. In classical conditioning, an unconditioned stimulus (e.g., meat) is a stimulus which elicits a response, the unconditioned response (e.g., salivation), without any training.

Validity. The ability of a test to measure what it is intended to measure. See *Content, Construct,* and *Criterion-related validity.*

Values clarification (VC). Procedures for helping students identify and understand their personal values. They *choose* values from alternatives, publicly endorse or *prize* their values, and *act* consistently with the values.

Vicarious learning. Generally, learning by witnessing others receive rewards for correct behavior. A teacher may administer praise to Student A in order to teach Student B the correct behavior; e.g., "I like the way Barbara is sitting up and paying attention" (Got that, Alfred?).

Voucher system. Innovation in which each family is given "vouchers" which may be used to pay private or public school costs. Administrators of public schools worry that the voucher system will put them out of business.

WISC-R (Wechsler Intelligence Scale for Children—Revised). A popular IQ test devised by David Wechsler. Individually administered, it is used with ages 6–16, and produces verbal IQ, performance IQ, and full-scale IQ scores.

"Withitness." Kounin's famous term for the ability of the teacher to let students know that he or she knows what is going on; i.e., having "eyes in the back of your head." It helps reduce deviancy and increases student task involvement.

Written philosophy and rationale. Prepared statement of the reasons for and objectives of a program for gifted and talented students. It should also include an overview of other components, such as selection procedures and programming plans.

Written plan. A detailed description of a program for gifted/talented students, including target students, philosophy and goals, identification procedures, organization and curriculum plans, assignment of personnel, support services, budget, and program evaluation.

REFERENCES

Abt Associates. Education as experimentation: A planned variation model, Volumes III and IV. Cambridge, Mass.: Abt Associates, 1977.

Ackerman, J. M. *Operant conditioning techniques for the classroom.* Glenview, Ill.: Scott Foresman, 1972.

Adelson, J. (ed.). *Handbook of adolescent psychology.* Somerset, N.J.: Wiley, 1979.

Agnew, S. T. Address given to the Farm Bureau. *Psychology Today* **5** (1), 1972, 4.

Aiken, L. R., Jr. Ability and creativity in math. *Review of Educational Research* **43,** 1973, 405–432.

Airasian, P. W. An application of a modified version of John Carroll's model of school learning. Unpublished Masters Thesis, University of Chicago, 1967.

Alexander, L., R. G. Frankeiwicz, and R. E. Williams. Facilitation of learning and retention of oral instruction using advance and post organizers. *Journal of Educational Psychology* **71,** 1979, 701–707.

615

Alexander, T. Synectics: Inventing by the madness method. In G. A. Davis and J. A. Scott (eds.), *Training creative thinking.* Huntington, N.Y.: Krieger, 1978.

Allen, M. S. *Morphological creativity.* Englewood Cliffs, N.J.: Prentice-Hall, 1962.

Allen, V. L. *Children as teachers.* New York: Academic Press, 1976.

Allen V. L., and R. S. Feldman. Tutor attribution and attitude as a function of tutee performance. *Journal of Applied Social Psychology* **4**, 1976, 311–320.

Allport, G. *The nature of prejudice.* Cambridge, Mass.: Addison-Wesley, 1954.

Alschuler, A. S. The effect of classroom structure on achievement motivation and academic performance. *Educational Technology* **9**, 1969, 19–24.

————. *Developing achievement motivation in adolescents.* Englewood Cliffs, N.J.: Educational Technology Publications, 1973.

American Psychiatric Association. *Diagnostic and statistical manual of mental disorders,* second edition. Washington, D.C., 1968.

American Psychological Association. *Standards for educational and psychological tests.* Washington, D.C., 1974.

Ames, C. Children's achievement attributions and self-reinforcement: Effects of self-concept and competitive reward structure. *Journal of Educational Psychology* **70**, 1978, 345–355.

Ames, C., R. Ames, and D. Felker. Effects of competitive reward structure and valence of outcome on children's achievement attributions. *Journal of Educational Psychology* **69**, 1977, 1–8.

Ames, C., and D. W. Felker. An examination of children's attributions and achievement-related evaluations in competitive, cooperative, and individualistic reward structures. *Journal of Educational Psychology* **71**, 1979, 413–420.

Amidon, E. J., and N. A. Flanders. Interaction analysis as a feedback system. In E. J. Amidon and J. B. Hough (eds.), *Interaction analysis: Theory, research and application.* Reading, Mass.: Addison-Wesley, 1967.

Anderson, J. R. *Cognitive psychology and its implications.* San Francisco: W. H. Freeman, 1980.

Anderson, L. M., C. E. Evertson, and J. E. Brophy. An experimental study of effective teaching in first-grade reading groups. *Elementary School Journal* **79**, 1979, 193–223.

Anderson, R. C., and W. B. Biddle. On asking people questions about what they are reading. In G. Bower (ed.), *Psychology of learning and motivation,* Vol. 9. New York: Academic Press, 1975.

Anderson, R. C., R. E. Reynolds, D. L. Schallert, and E. T. Goetz. Frameworks for comprehending discourse. *American Educational Research Journal* **14**, 1977, 367–381.

Andrews, G. R., and R. L. Debus. Persistence and the causal perception of failure: Modifying cognitive attributions. *Journal of Educational Psychology* **70**, 1978, 154–166.

Anonymous. Intelligence: A new *g* from Arthur Jensen. *Report on Education Research* **10**, 1978, 1–3.

Arena, J. I. (ed.). *Building spelling skills in dyslexic children.* San Rafael, Calif.: Academic Therapy Publications, 1968.

—————. (ed.). *Building number skills in dyslexic children.* San Rafael, Calif.: Academic Therapy Publications, 1972.

Arkin, R. M., and G. M. Maruyama. Attribution, effect, and college exam performance. *Journal of Educational Psychology* **71**, 1979, 85–93.

Arlin, M. Teacher transitions can disrupt time flow in classrooms. *American Educational Research Journal* **16**, 1979, 42–56.

Aronson, E., N. Blaney, J. Sikes, C. Stephan, and M. Snapp. Busing and racial tension: The jigsaw route to learning and liking. *Psychology Today* **8** (9), 1975, 43–50.

Arthur, A. Z. Diagnostic testing and the new alternatives. *Psychological Bulletin* **72**, 1969, 183–92.

Atkin, J. M. Behavioral objectives in curriculum design: A cautionary note. *The Science Teacher* **35**, 1968, 27–30.

Atkinson, J. W. The mainsprings of achievement-oriented activity. In G. A. Davis and T. F. Warren (eds.), *Psychology of education: New looks.* Lexington, Mass.: D. C. Heath, 1974, Pp. 220–225.

Atkinson, R. C. Mnemotechnics in second-language learning. *American Psychologist* **30**, 1975, 821–828.

Ausubel, D. P. *The psychology of meaningful verbal learning.* New York: Grune & Stratton, 1963.

—————. Is drill necessary? The mythology of incidental learning. In G. A. Davis and T. F. Warren (eds.), *Psychology of education: New looks.* Lexington, Mass.: D. C. Heath, 1974. Pp. 282–286.

—————. The facilitation of meaningful verbal learning in the classroom. *Educational Psychologist* **12**, 1977, 162–178.

—————. In defense of advance organizers: A reply to the critics. *Review of Educational Research* **48**, 1978, 251–257.

Ausubel, D. P., J. D. Novak, and H. Hanesian. *Educational psychology: A cognitive view.* New York: Holt, Rinehart & Winston, 1978.

Ausubel, D. P., S. H. Schpoont, and L. Cukier. The influence of intention on the learning of school materials. *Journal of Educational Psychology* **48**, 1957, 87–92.

Backman, M. E. Patterns of mental abilities: Ethnic, socioeconomic, and sex differences. *American Educational Research Journal* **9**, 1972, 1–12.

Bandura, A. The role of imitation in personality development. *Journal of Nursery Education* **18**, 1963, 207–215.

_____. *Principles of behavior modification.* New York: Holt, Rinehart & Winston, 1969.

_____. *Social learning theory.* Englewood Cliffs, N.J.: Prentice-Hall, 1977.

_____. The self system in reciprocal determinism. *American Psychologist* **33,** 1978, 344–358.

Barbe, W. B., and J. S. Renzulli (eds.). *Psychology and education of the gifted,* second edition. New York: Irvington, 1975.

Barnes, B. R., and E. V. Clawson. Do advance organizers facilitate learning? Recommendations for further research based on an analysis of 32 studies. *Review of Educational Research* **45,** 1975, 637–659.

Barron, F. *Creative person and creative process.* New York: Holt, Rinehart, & Winston, 1969.

_____. An eye more fantastical. In G. A. Davis and J. A. Scott (eds.), *Training creative thinking.* Huntington, N.Y.: Krieger, 1978.

Bar-Tal, D. Attributional analysis of achievement-related behavior. *Review of Educational Research* **48,** 1978, 259–271.

Bar-Tal, D., A. Raviv, A. Raviv, and Y. Bar-Tal. Consistency of pupils' attributions regarding success and failure. *Journal of Educational Psychology* **74,** 1982, 104–110.

Bates, J. A. Extrinsic reward and intrinsic motivation: A review with implications for the classroom. *Review of Educational Researh* **49,** 1979, 557–576.

Becker, W. C. Introduction. In L. Homme, *How to use contingency contracting in the classroom.* Champaign, Ill.: Research Press, 1970.

Becker, W. C., C. Madsen, C. Arnold, and D. Thomas. The contingent use of teacher praise and attention in reducing classroom behavior problems. *Journal of Special Education* **1,** 1967, 287–307.

Becker, W. C., S. Engelmann, and D. R. Thomas. *Teaching: A course in applied psychology.* Chicago: Science Research Associates, 1971.

Beilin, H. The training and acquisition of logical operations. In M. S. Rothkopf, L. P. Steffe, and S. Taback (eds.), *Piagetian cognitive developmental research and mathematical education.* Washington, D.C.: National Council of Teachers of Mathematics, 1971.

Bellezza, F. S. Mnemonic devices: Classification, characteristics, and criteria. *Review of Educational Research* **51,** 1981, 247–275.

Bem, S. L. The measurement of psychological androgyny. *Journal of Consulting and Clinical Psychology* **42,** 1974, 155–162.

_____. Sex-role adaptability: One consequence of psychological androgyny. *Journal of Personality and Social Psychology* **31,** 1975, 634–643.

Berlyne, D. E. *Conflict, arousal and curiosity.* New York: McGraw-Hill, 1961.

Blake, K. A. *Educating exceptional pupils.* Reading, Mass.: Addison-Wesley, 1981.

Block, J. H. Introduction to mastery learning: Theory and practice. In J. H. Block (ed.), *Mastery learning: Theory and practice.* New York: Holt, Rinehart & Winston, 1971. (a)

————. *Mastery learning: Theory and practice.* New York: Holt, Rinehart & Winston, 1971. (b)

Bloom, B. S. *Stability and change in human characteristics.* New York: Wiley, 1964.

————. Mastery learning. In J. H. Block (ed.), *Mastery learning: Theory and practice.* New York: Holt, Rinehart & Winston, 1971.

————. Recent developments in mastery learning. *Educational Psychologist* **10,** 1973, 53–57.

————. (ed.). *Taxonomy of educational objectives.* New York: McKay, 1974.

————. *Human characteristics and school learning.* New York: McGraw-Hill, 1976.

————. Affective outcomes of school learning. *Phi Delta Kappan* **59,** 1977, 193–198.

Bloom, B. S., M. D. Engelhart, E. J. Furst, W. H. Hill, and D. R. Krathwohl. *Taxonomy of educational objectives, handbook I: Cognitive domain.* New York: Longmans Green, 1956.

Boring, E. G. Intelligence as the tests test it. *New Republic* **35** (June 6), 1923, 35–36.

Bowerman, M. Words and sentences: Uniformity, individual variation, and shifts over time in patterns of acquisition. In F. D. Minitie and L. L. Lloyd (eds.), *Communicative and cognitive abilities—early behavioral assessment.* Baltimore, Md.: University Park Press, 1978.

Bowers, K. Situationism in psychology: An analysis and critique. *Psychological Review* **80,** 1973, 307–336.

Bradley, J. I., and J. N. McClelland. *Basic statistical concepts: A self-instructional text.* Glenview, Ill.: Scott, Foresman, 1963.

Brainerd, C. J. Neo-Piagetian training experiments revisited: Is there any support for the cognitive–developmental stage hypothesis? *Cognition* **2,** 1974, 349–370.

Braun, C. Teacher expectations: Sociopsychological dynamics. *Review of Educational Research* **46,** 1976, 185–213.

Bridger, W. H. Individual differences in behavior and autonomic activity in newborn infants. *American Journal of Public Health* **55,** 1965, 1899.

Brophy, J. E. Research on the self-fulfilling prophecy and teacher expectations. Presented in a symposium entitled "The self-fulfilling prophecy: Its origins and consequences in research and practices." American Educational Research Association, New York, March 1982.

Brophy, J. E., and T. L. Good. Teacher's communication of differential behavioral data. *Journal of Educational Psychology* **61,** 1970, 365–374.

————. *Teacher-student relationships: Causes and consequences.* New York: Holt, 1974.

Brown, G. I., M. Phillips, and S. Shapiro. *Getting it all together: Confluent education.* Bloomington, Ind.: Phi Delta Kappa Educational Foundation, 1976.

Brown, G. I., T. Yeomans, and I. Grizzard (eds.). *The live classroom: Innovations through confluent education and gestalt.* New York: Viking Press, 1975.

Brown, J. L. Effects of logical and scrambled sequences in mathematical materials on learning with programmed instruction materials. *Journal of Educational Psychology* **61**, 1970, 41–45.

Brown, R. *A first language: The early stages.* Cambridge, Mass.: Harvard University Press, 1973.

Brown, R., and M. L. de Bronac-Meade. Reduction of mathematics anxiety: A cognitive behavior modification approach. Paper presented at the American Educational Research Association, New York, March, 1982.

Brown, R., and J. Kulik. Flashbulb memories. In U. Neisser (ed.), *Memory observed: Remembering in natural contexts.* San Francisco: W. H. Freeman, 1982.

Bruininks, V. L. Peer status and personality characteristics of learning disabled and nondisabled students. *Journal of Learning Disabilities* **11**, 1978, 484–489.

Bruner, J. S. On going beyond the information given. In *Contemporary approaches to cognition.* Cambridge, Mass.: Harvard University Press, 1957. Pp. 41–69.

———. *Toward a theory of instruction.* Cambridge, Mass.: Harvard University Press, 1967.

———. *The relevance of education.* New York: Norton, 1971.

Bryan, T. Social relationships and verbal interactions of learning disabled children. *Journal of Learning Disabilities* **2**, 1978, 107–115.

Bryan, T., and J. H. Bryan. *Understanding learning disabilities.* New York: Alfred Knopf, 1975.

Bryant, B. K. Locus of control related to teacher-child interperceptual experiences. *Child Development* **45**, 1974, 157–164.

Budoff, M., and J. Gottlieb. Special class students mainstreamed: A study of an aptitude (learning potential) X treatment interaction. *American Journal of Mental Deficiency* **81**, 1976, 1–11.

Bullock, L., and R. K. Brown. Behavioral dimensions of emotionally disturbed children. *Exceptional Children* **39**, 1972, 740–741.

Bureau for the Education of the Handicapped. *Progress toward a free appropriate public education: A report to Congress on the implementation of Public Law 94-142, The Education for All Handicapped Children Act.* Washington, D.C.: U.S. Department of Health, Education, and Welfare, Office of Education, 1979,

Burns, R. W. *New approaches to behavioral objectives.* Dubuque, Iowa: W. C. Brown, 1977.

Burton, T. A., and A. Hirshoren. Some further thoughts and clarification on the education of severely and profoundly retarded children. *Exceptional Children* **45**, 1979, 618–625.

Butter, E. J. Visual and haptic training and cross-model transfer of reflectivity. *Journal of Educational Psychology* **71**, 1979, 212–219.

Cairns, G. G., Jr. Evaluation of the Youth Tutoring Youth Project, summer 1971. Research and Development Report **5,** No. 9, Atlanta Public Schools, Atlanta, Ga., 1972. (ERIC Document Reproduction Service No. ED 065-455.)

Canfield, J. W., and H. C. Wells. *100 ways to enhance self-concept in the classroom.* Englewood Cliffs, N.J.: Prentice Hall, 1976.

Carlson, R. Personality. In M. R. Rosenzweig and L. W. Porter (eds.), *Annual review of psychology.* Palo Alto, Calif.: Annual Reviews, 1975.

Carroll, J. B. Problems of measurement related to the concept of learning for mastery. In J. H. Block (ed.), *Mastery learning: Theory and practice.* New York: Holt, Rinehart & Winston, 1971.

Carroll, J. B., and S. E. Maxwell. Individual differences in cognitive abilities. In M. R. Rosenzweig and L. W. Porter (eds.), *Annual review of psychology.* Palo Alto, Calif.: Annual Reviews, 1975.

Cattell, R. B. Theory of fluid and crystallized intelligence: A critical experiment. *Journal of Educational Psychology* **54,** 1963, 1–22.

————. *The scientific analysis of personality.* Baltimore, Md.: Penguin Books, 1965.

————. *Abilities: Their structure, growth and action.* Boston: Houghton Mifflin, 1971.

Centra, J. A., and D. A. Potter. School and teacher effects: An interrelational model. *Review of Educational Research* **50,** 1980, 273–291.

Chaiken, A. L., E. Sigler, and V. J. Derlega. Nonverbal mediators of teacher expectancy effects. *Journal of Personality and Social Psychology* **30,** 1974, 144–149.

Chandler, M. Egocentrism and antisocial behavior: The assessment and training of social perspective-taking skills. *Developmental Psychology* **9,** 1973, 1–6.

Chapman, J. W., and F. J. Boersma. Learning disabilities, locus of control, and mother attitudes. *Journal of Educational Psychology* **71,** 1979, 250–258.

Chase, C. I. *Measurement for educational evaluation.* Reading, Mass.: Addison-Wesley, 1974.

Chiland, C. Social adaptation of the child in the latency period. *Canadian Psychiatric Association Journal* **21,** 1976, 192–196.

Chomsky, N. *Aspects of a theory of syntax.* Cambridge, Mass.: M.I.T. Press, 1965.

Chukovsky, K. *From two to five.* Translated by M. Morton. Berkeley: University of California Press, 1968.

Clarizio, H., and G. McCoy. *Behavior disorders in children,* second edition. New York: Crowell, 1976.

Clark, B. *Growing up gifted.* Columbus, Ohio: Charles E. Merrill, 1979.

Clark. C. H. *Brainstorming.* Garden City, N.Y.: Doubleday, 1958.

Cloward, R. I. Studies in tutoring. *Journal of Experimental Education* **36,** 1967, 14–25.

Coffman, W. E. Essay examinations. In R. L. Thorndike (ed.), *Educational measurement.* Washington, D.C.: American Council on Education, 1971.

Colangelo, N., and R. T. Zaffrann (eds.) *New voices in counseling the gifted.* Dubuque, Iowa: Kendall/Hunt, 1979.

Colby, A., and L. Kohlberg. The relationship between logical and moral development. Unpublished manuscript, Center for Moral Education, Graduate School of Education, Harvard University, Cambridge, Mass., 1975.

Coleman, J. S. Equality of educational opportunity. Washington, D.C.: U.S. Department of Health, Education, and Welfare, Office of Education, 1966.

————. Racial segregation in the schools: New research with new policy implications. *Phi Delta Kappan* **57,** 1975, 75–78. (a)

————. Recent trends in school integration. *Educational Researcher* **4** (7), 1975, 3–12. (b)

————. Public and private schools. Invited address to the American Educational Research Association, Los Angeles, April, 1981.

Coles, G. S. The learning-disabilities test battery: Empirical and social issues. *Harvard Educational Review* **48,** 1978, 313–339.

Collins, K. M. A strategy for mastery learning in modern mathematics. Unpublished report, Division of Mathematical Sciences, Purdue University, Lafayette, Indiana, 1970.

Combs, A. W. Humanistic goals of education. In D. A. Read and S. B. Simon (eds.), *Humanistic education sourcebook.* Englewood Cliffs, N.J.: Prentice-Hall, 1975. Pp. 91–100.

Conrad, A. S., and H. E. Jones. A second study of familial resemblance in intelligence. *39th Yearbook, Part II.* Chicago: National Society for the Study of Education, 1940.

Cook, J. M. *Learning and retention by informing students of behavioral objectives and their place in the hierarchical learning sequence,* USOE Final Report, 1969. (ERIC Document Reproduction Service No. ED 036 869).

Cooper, A. M. Pygmalion grows up. *Review of Educational Research* **49,** 1979, 389–410.

Cooper, H., R. Baron, and C. Lowe. The importance of race and social class in the formation of expectancies about academic performance. *Journal of Educational Psychology* **67,** 1975, 312–319.

Corrigan, R. Language development as related to stage 6 object permanence. *Journal of Child Language* **5,** 1978, 173–179.

————. Cognitive correlates of language: Differential criteria yield differential results. *Child Development* **50,** 1979, 617–631.

Covington, M. V., and R. G. Beery. *Self-worth and school learning.* New York: Holt, Rinehart & Winston, 1976.

Covington, M. V., and C. L. Omelich. It's best to be able and virtuous too: Student and teacher evaluative responses to successful effort. *Journal of Educational Psychology* **71,** 1979, 688–700.

Cowan, P. A. *Piaget with feeling.* New York: Holt, Rinehart, & Winston, 1978.

Craik, F. I. M., and M. J. Watkins. The role of rehearsal in short-term memory. *Journal of Verbal Learning and Verbal Behavior* **12,** 1973, 599–607.

Crawford, C. George Washington, Abraham Lincoln, and Arthur Jensen: Are they compatible? *American Psychologist* **34,** 1979, 664–672.

Crawford, R. P. The techniques of creative thinking. In G. A. Davis and J. A. Scott (eds.), *Training creative thinking.* Huntington, N.Y.: Krieger, 1978.

Cronbach, L. J. Comments on James S. Coleman's paper, public and private schools. Presented at the American Educational Research Association, Los Angeles, April, 1981.

Cronbach, L. J., and R. E. Snow. *Aptitude and instructional methods.* New York: Irving Publishers, 1977.

Cruickshank, W., *et al. A teaching method for brain-injured and hyperactive children.* Syracuse. N. Y.: Syracuse University Press, 1961.

Dale, P. S. *Language development,* second edition. New York: Holt, Rinehart & Winston, 1973.

Dalis, G. T. Effect of precise objectives upon student achievement in health education. *Journal of Experimental Education* **39,** 1970, 20–23.

Davis, D. P., O. P. Gray, P. C. Ellwood, and M. Abernathy. Cigarette smoking in pregnancy: Associations with maternal weight gain and fetal growth. *Lancet* **1,** 1976, 385–387.

Davis, G. A. *Psychology of problem solving: Theory and practice.* New York: Basic Books, 1973.

————. In frumious pursuit of the creative person. *Journal of Creative Behavior* **9,** 1975, 75–87.

————. Using personality and biographical information to identify creatively gifted children, adolescents and adults, Presented in a symposium entitled "Psychology of creativity," XXII International Congress of Psychology, Leipzig, Germany, July, 1980.

————. *Creativity is forever.* Cross Plains, Wis.: Badger Press, 1981. (a)

————. Personal creative thinking techniques. *Gifted Child Quarterly* **25,** 1981, 99–101. (b)

————. *The good person book: Affective and humanistic education.* Cross Plains, Wis.: Badger Press, in press, 1983.

Davis, G. A., and G. DiPego. *Imagination express: Saturday subway ride.* Buffalo, N.Y.: DOK Publishers, 1973.

Davis, G. A., and M. O'Sullivan. Taxonomy of creative objectives: The model AUTA. *Journal of Creative Behavior* **14,** 1980, 149–160.

Davis, G. A., J. M. Peterson, and F. H. Farley. Attitudes, motivation, sensation seeking, and belief in ESP as predictors of real creative behavior. *Journal of Creative Behavior* **8,** 1973, 31–39.

Davis, G. A., and S. Rimm. *Group inventory for finding interests. II.* Watertown, Wis.: Educational Assessment Services, 1980.

_____. *Group inventory for finding interests* (GIFFI) *I* and *II:* Instruments for identifying creative potential in the junior and senior high school. *Journal of Creative Behavior*, 1982, in press.

Davis, G. A. and J. A. Scott (eds.). *Training creative thinking*. Huntington, N.Y.: Krieger, 1978.

Davis, J. K., and B. M. Frank. Learning and memory of field independent-dependent individuals. *Journal of Research in Personality* **13**, 1979, 469–479.

Day, H. I., and D. E. Berlyne. Intrinsic motivation. In G. S. Lesser (ed.), *Psychology and educational practice*. Glenview, Ill.: Scott, Foresman, 1971.

Debus, R. L. Effects of brief observation of model behavior on conceptual tempo of impulsive children. *Developmental Psychology* **2**, 1970, 22–32.

DeCecco, J. P. High schools: Decision making in a democracy. In J. P. DeCecco (ed.), *The regeneration of the school*. New York: Holt, Rinehart, and Winston, 1972.

DeCharms, R. Personal causation training in the schools. *Journal of Applied Psychology* **2**, 1972, 95–113.

_____. *Enhancing motivation: Change in the classroom*. New York: Irvington, 1976.

Dennis, W. The effect of cradling practices upon the onset of walking in Hopi children. *Journal of Genetic Psychology* **56**, 1940, 77–86.

DeRose, J. Independent study in high school chemistry. *Journal of Chemical Education* **47**, 1970, 553–560.

Dewey, J. *How we think*. Lexington, Mass.: D. C. Heath, 1933.

Diederich, P. B. *Short-cut statistics for teacher-made tests*. Princeton, N.J.: Educational Testing Service, 1973.

DiStefano, J. J. Interpersonal perceptions of field independent and field dependent teachers and students. Unpublished Doctoral dissertation, Cornell University, 1970.

Dowaliby, F. J., and H. Schumer. Teacher-centered versus student-centered mode of college classroom instruction is related to manifest anxiety. *Journal of Educational Psychology* **64**, 1973, 125–132.

Duchastel, P. Learning objectives and the organization of prose. *Journal of Educational Psychology* **71**, 1979, 100–106.

Duchastel, P., and B. R. Brown. Incidental and relevant learning with instructional objectives. *Journal of Educational Psychology* **66**, 1974, 481–485.

Duchastel, P., and P. F. Merrill. The effects of behavioral objectives on learning: A review of empirical studies. *Review of Educational Research* **43**, 1973, 53–70.

Dunn, L. M. Special education for the mildly retarded: Is much of it justifiable? *Exceptional children* **35**, 1968, 5–22.

Dweck, C. S. The role of expectations and attributions in the alleviation of learned helplessness. *Journal of Personality and Social Psychology* **31**, 1975, 674–685.

Dweck, C. S., and E. S. Bush. Sex differences in learned helplessness: I. Differential debilitation with peer and adult evaluators. *Developmental Psychology* **12,** 1976, 147–156.

Dweck, C. S., and N. D. Repucci. Learned helplessness and reinforcement responsibility in children. *Journal of Personality and Social Psychology* **25,** 1973, 109–116.

Eberle, B., and R. Hall. *Affective education guidebook: Classroom activities in the realm of feelings.* Buffalo: DOK Publishers, 1975.

————. *Affective direction: Planning and teaching for thinking and feeling.* Buffalo, N.Y.: DOK Publishers, 1979.

Egeland, B. Training impulsive children in the use of more efficient scanning techniques. *Child Development* **45,** 1974, 165–171.

Eisner, E. W. Instructional and expressive educational objectives: Their formulation and use in curriculum. *Instructional objectives.* AERA Monograph Series on Curriculum Evaluation: Monograph No. 3, Chicago: Rand-McNally, 1969.

Ekstrom, R. B., J. W. French, H. H. Harmon, and D. Derman. *Hidden figures test—CF-1* (Rev.). Princeton, N.J.: Educational Testing Service, 1975.

Elashoff, J. D., and R. E. Snow. *Pygmalion reconsidered.* Worthington, Ohio: Charles E. Jones, 1971.

Elerian, A. F. Programmed learning: A study in literacy. *Programmed Learning and Educational Technology* **15,** 1978, 69–78.

Elkind, D. *Children and adolescents.* New York: Oxford, 1970.

————. *Child development and education: A Piagetian perspective.* New York: Oxford University Press, 1976.

Ellis, H. C. *Fundamentals of human learning, memory, and cognition,* second edition. Dubuque, Iowa: W. C. Brown, 1978.

Erikson. E. H. *Childhood and society.* New York: Norton, 1963.

————. *Identity: Youth and crisis.* New York: Norton, 1968.

Erlenmeyer-Kimling, L., and L. G. Jarvik. Genetics and intelligence: A review. *Science* **142,** 1963, 1477–1479.

Evans, J. L., R. Glaser and L. E. Homme. A preliminary investigation of variation in the properties of verbal-learning sequences of the "teaching machine" type. In A. A. Lumsdaine and R. Glaser (eds.), *Teaching machines and programmed learning.* Washington, D.C.: National Education Association, 1960.

Evertson, C. M., C. W. Anderson, L. M. Anderson, and J. E. Brophy. Relationships between classroom behaviors and student outcomes in junior high mathematics and English classes. *American Educational Research Journal* **17,** 1980, 43–60.

Evertson, C, M., and J. E. Brophy. High-inference behavioral ratings as correlates of teaching effectiveness. Research and Development Center for Teacher Education, University of Texas, Austin, 1973.

Eysenck, H. J. (ed.). *Behavior therapy and the neuroses.* London: Pergamon Press, 1960.

_____. The effects of psychotherapy. In H. J. Eysenck (ed.), *Handbook of abnormal psychology: An experimental approach.* New York: Basic Books, 1961.

_____. *The IQ argument.* New York: Library Press, 1971.

Eysenck, S. B. G. *Junior E.P.I.* San Diego, Calif.: Educational and Industrial Testing Service, 1965.

Fabun, D. *You and creativity.* New York: Macmillan, 1968.

Farley, F. H. A theory of delinquency. Paper presented at the meeting of the American Psychological Association, Montreal, August, 1973.

_____. Basic process individual differences: A biologically based theory of individualization for cognitive, affective, and creative outcomes. In F. H. Farley and N. J. Gordon (eds.), *Psychology and education: The state of the union.* Berkeley, Calif.: McCutchan, 1981.

Farley, F. H., and T. Sewell. Test of an arousal theory of delinquency. *Criminal Justice and Behavior* **3**, 1976, 315–320.

Featherstone, J. *Schools where children learn.* New York: Liveright Publishing, 1971.

Feffer, M. Developmental analysis of interpersonal behavior. *Psychological Review* **77**, 1970, 197–214.

Feingold, B. D., and M. J. Mahoney. Reinforcement effects on intrinsic interest: Undermining the overjustification hypothesis. *Behavior Therapy* **6**, 1975, 367–377.

Feingold, B. F. *Why your child is hyperactive.* New York: Random House, 1975.

Feingold, B. F., and H. S. Feingold. *The Feingold cookbook for hyperactive children.* New York: Random House, 1979.

Feld, S., D. Ruhland, and M. Gold. Developmental changes in achievement motivation. *Merrill-Palmer Quarterly* **25**, 1979, 43–60.

Feldhusen, J. F., and D. J. Treffinger. *Creative thinking and problem solving in gifted education.* Dubuque, Iowa: Kendell/Hunt, 1980.

Feldman, R. S., and T. Prohaska. The student as Pygmalion: Effect of student expectation on the teacher. *Journal of Educational Psychology* **71**, 1979, 485–493.

Fennema, E. Overview of sex-related differences in mathematics. Paper presented at the American Educational Research Association, New York, March 1982.

Ferrell, J. G. The differential performance of lower class, preschool, Negro children as a function of the sex of S, reinforcement condition, and level of field dependence. Unpublished Doctoral dissertation, University of Southern Mississippi, 1971.

Festinger, L. *A theory of cognitive dissonance.* Evanston, Ill.: Row, Peterson, 1957.

Filby, N. N., and L. S. Cahen. Teaching behavior and academic learning time in the A-B period. Technical Note V-1b, Far West Laboratory for Educational Research and Development, San Francisco, 1977.

Filby, N. N., and R. Marliave. Descriptions of distributions of ALT within and across classes during the A-B period. Technical Note IV-1a, Far West Laboratory for Educational Research and Development, San Francisco, 1977.

Fisher, C. W., N. N. Filby, and R. Marliave. Descriptions and distributions of ALT within and across classes during the B-C period. Technical Note IV-1b, Far West Laboratory for Educational Research and Development, San Francisco, 1977.

Fisher, G. Computer games in the classroom. *The Computing Teacher* **9** (4), 1981, 52–53.

Flanders, N. A. *Analyzing teacher behavior.* Reading, Mass.: Addison-Wesley, 1970.

Flavell, J. H. *The developmental psychology of Jean Piaget.* Princeton, N.J.: Van Nostrand, 1963.

————. *Cognitive development.* Englewood Cliffs, N.J.: Prentice-Hall, 1977.

Flavell, J. H., and H. M. Wellman. Metamemory. In R. Kail and J. Hagen (eds.), *Perspectives on the development of memory and cognition.* Hillsdale, N.J.: L. Earlbaum, 1979.

Fletcher, J. D., and R. C. Atkinson. Evaluation of the Stanford CAI program in initial reading. *Journal of Educational Psychology* **63**, 1972, 597–602.

Forehand, G., and M. Ragosta. *A handbook for integrated schooling.* Washington, D.C.: U.S. Office of Education, 1976.

Forsyth, D. R., and J. H. McMillan. Attributions, affect, and expectations: A test of Weiner's three-dimensional model. *Journal of Educational Psychology* **73**, 1981, 393–403.

Fox, L. H. Programs for the gifted and talented: An overview. In A. H. Passow (ed.), *The gifted and the talented: Their education and development.* Chicago: National Society for the Study of Education, 1979.

Frank, B. M., and J. K. Davis. Effect of field-independent match or mismatch on a communication task. *Journal of Educational Psychology* **74**, 1982, 23–31.

Friend, R. M., and J. M. Neale. Children's perceptions of success and failure: An attributional analysis of the effects of race and social class. *Developmental Psychology* **7**, 1972, 124–128.

Freud, A. Adolescence. *Psychoanalytic Study of the Child* **13**, 1958, 255–276.

Freud, S. *An outline of psychoanalysis.* New York: Norton, 1949.

Frostig, M., and D. Horne. *The Frostig program for the development of visual perception: Teacher's guide.* Chicago: Follett, 1964.

Furst, E. J. Bloom's taxonomy of educational objectives for the cognitive domain: Philosophical and educational issues. *Review of Educational Research* **51**, 1981, 441–453.

Gaeta, J. P. Teacher ratings of students as a function of the match or mismatch in field independence-dependence. *Dissertation Abstracts* **37**, 1977, 7506A.

Gage, N. L. Paradigms for research on teaching. In N. L. Gage (ed.), *Handbook of research on teaching.* Chicago: Rand McNally, 1963.

_____. IQ, heritability, race differences, and educational research. *Phi Delta Kappan* **53**, 1972, 308–312.

Gagne, E., J. W. Moore, W. E. Hauck, and R. V. Hoy. The effect on children's performance of a discrepancy between adult expectancy and feedback statements. *Journal of Experimental Education* **47**, 1979, 320–324.

Gagne, R. M. Problem solving. In A. W. Melton (ed.), *Categories of human learning.* New York: Academic press, 1964.

_____. Curriculum research and promotion of learning. *Perspectives of Curriculum Education.* AERA Monograph Series on Curriculum Evaluation: Monograph No. 1. Chicago: Rand-McNally, 1967.

_____. Learning hierarchies. *Educational Psychologist* **6**, 1968, 1–9.

_____. Domains of learning. *Interchange* **3**, 1972, 1–8.

_____. *Essentials of learning for instruction.* New York: Holt, Rinehart & Winston, 1974.

_____. *Conditions of learning,* third edition. New York: Holt, Rinehart & Winston, 1977.

Gagne, R. M., and L. J. Briggs. *Principles of instructional design.* New York: Holt, Rinehart & Winston, 1974.

Gagne, R. M., and R. T. White. Memory structures in learning. *Review of Educational Research* **48**, 1978, 187–222.

Gall, M. D., B. A. Ward, D. C. Berliner, L. S. Cahen, K. A. Crown, J. D. Elashoff, G. C. Stanton, and P. H. Winne. The effects of teacher use of questioning techniques on student achievement and attitude. Far West Regional Laboratory for Educational Research and Development, San Francisco, 1975.

Gallagher, J. J. Characteristics of gifted children: A research summary. In W. B. Barbe and J. S. Renzulli (eds.), *Psychology and education of the gifted*, second edition. New York: Irvington, 1975. (a)

_____. *Teaching the gifted child*, second edition. Boston: Allyn & Bacon, 1975. (b)

Galton, F. *Hereditary genius.* London: MacMillan, 1869.

Gartner, A., M. Kohler, and F. Reissman. *Children teach children.* New York: Harper & Row, 1971.

Gearhart, B. R., and M. W. Weishahn. *The handicapped child in the regular classroom.* St. Louis, Mo.: C. V. Mosby, 1976.

Gecas, V., J. M. Calonica, and D. L. Thomas. The development of self-concept in the child: Mirror theory vs. model theory. *Journal of Social Psychology* **92,** 1974, 67–76.

Getzels, J. W., and P. W. Jackson. The teacher's personality and characteristics. In N. L. Gage (ed.), *Handbook of research on teaching.* Chicago: Rand McNally, 1963.

Glaser, R. Objectives and evaluation: An individualized system. *Science Education News.* American Association for the Advancement of Science, 1967, 1–3.

Glaser, W. E., and I. G. Sarason. Reinforcing productive classroom behavior: A teacher's guide to behavior modification. Washington, D.C.: U.S. Department of Health, Education, and Welfare/Office of Education, National Center for Educational Communication; U.S. Government Printing Office, 1972.

Glasser, W. *Schools without failure.* New York: Harper & Row, 1969.

─────. "Classroom meetings" from *Schools without failure.* In G. A. Davis and T. F. Warren (eds.), *Psychology of education: New looks.* Lexington, Mass.: D. C. Heath, 1974. Pp. 298–308.

Glucksberg, S., R. Krauss, and E. T. Higgins. The development of referential communication skills. In F. D. Horowitz (ed.), *Review of child development research,* Volume 4. Chicago: University of Chicago Press, 1975.

Glynn, E. L., J. D. Thomas, and S. M. Shee. Behavioral self-control of on-task behavior in an elementary classroom. *Journal of Applied Behavior Analysis* **6,** 1973, 105–113.

Goldbeck, R. A., and V. N. Campbell. The effects of response rate and response difficulty on programmed learning. *Journal of Educational Psychology* **53,** 1962, 110–118.

Goldberg, L. R. The exploitation of the English language for the development of a descriptive personality taxonomy. Paper presented at the American Psychological Association, Montreal, Canada, 1973.

Good, T. L., and J. E. Brophy. *Educational psychology: A realistic approach,* second edition. New York: Holt, Rinehart & Winston, 1977.

─────. *Looking in classrooms,* second edition. New York: Holt, Rinehart & Winston, 1978.

Goodwin, D. L., and T. G. Coates. *Helping students help themselves: You can put behaviorism into action in your classroom.* Englewood Cliffs, N.J.: Prentice-Hall, 1976.

Goodwin, S., and M. Mahoney. Modification of aggression via modeling: An experimental probe. *Journal of Behavior Therapy and Experimental Psychiatry* **6,** 1975, 200–202.

Gordon, A. K. *Games for growth: Educational games in the classroom.* Chicago: Science Research Associates, 1970.

Gordon, W. J. J. *Synectics.* New York: Harper & Row, 1961.

─────. *The metaphorical way of learning and knowing.* Cambridge, Mass.: Synectics, Inc., 1969.

─────. *Making it strange.* Books 1–4. New York: Harper & Row, 1974.

Graham, J., and R. Hess. *Handbook for Project Head Start.* Chicago: University of Chicago Press, 1965.

Greeno, J. G., and R. A. Bjork. Mathematical learning theory and the new "mental forestry." *Annual Review of Psychology* **24,** 1973, 81–116.

Grimes, J. W., and W. Allensmith. Compulsivity, anxiety and school achievement. *Merrill-Palmer Quarterly* **7,** 1961, 247–271.

Gronlund, N. E. *Stating objectives for classroom instruction.* New York: Macmillan, 1972.

————. *Measurement and evaluation in teaching,* third edition. New York: Macmillan, 1976.

————. *Constructing achievement tests,* second edition. Englewood Cliffs, N.J.: Prentice-Hall, 1977.

————. *Stating objectives for classroom instruction,* second edition. New York: Macmillan, 1978.

Guilford, J. P. *The nature of human intelligence.* New York: McGraw-Hill, 1967.

————. *Way beyond the IQ.* Buffalo, N.Y.: Creative Education Foundation, 1977.

————. Some incubated thoughts on incubation. *Journal of Creative Behavior* **12,** 1979, 1–8.

Hakstian, A. R., and R. B. Cattell. *The comprehensive ability battery.* Champaign, Ill.: Institute for Personality and Ability Testing, 1975.

————. Higher-stratum ability structures on a basis of twenty primary abilities. *Journal of Educational Psychology* **70,** 1978, 657–659.

Hallahan, D. P., and J. M. Kauffman. *Introduction to learning disabilities: A psychobehavioral approach.* Englewood Cliffs, N.J.: Prentice-Hall, 1976.

————. *Exceptional children: Introduction to special education.* Englewood Cliffs, N.J.: Prentice-Hall, 1978.

Halverson, C., and J. Victor. Minor physical anomalies and problem behavior in elementary school children. *Child Development* **47,** 1976, 281–285.

Hammill, D. D. Adolescents with specific learning disabilities: Definition, identification, and incidence. In L. Mann, L. Goodman, and J. L. Weiderholt (eds.), *Teaching the learning disabled adolescent.* Boston: Houghton Mifflin, 1978.

Hammill, D. D., and N. R. Bartel (eds.), *Teaching children with learning disabilities and behavior disorders.* Boston: Allyn & Bacon, 1978.

Hanson, J. W. Crisis in the unborn: Fetal alcohol syndrome. Paper presented at the Annual Meeting of the Occupational Medicine Society, Anaheim, California, May, 1979.

Haring, N. G., and B. Bateman. *Teaching the learning disabled child.* Englewood Cliffs, N.J.: Prentice-Hall, 1977.

Hart, F. W. *Teachers and teaching.* New York: Macmillan, 1934.

Hayes, L. A. The use of group contingencies for behavioral control: A review. *Psychological Bulletin* **83,** 1976, 628–648.

Hearn, J. C., and R. H. Moos. Subject matter and classroom climate: A test of Holland's environmental propositions. *American Educational Research Journal* **15,** 1978, 111–124.

Heider, F. *The psychology of interpersonal relations.* New York: Wiley, 1958.

Heil, L. M., and C. Washburne. Brooklyn College research in teacher effectiveness. *Journal of Educational Research* **55,** 1962, 347–351.

Helman, I. B., and S. G. Larson. *Now what do I do?* Buffalo, N.Y.: DOK, 1979.

Herman, T. M. *Creating learning environments: The behavioral approach to education.* Boston: Allyn & Bacon, 1977.

Herrnstein, R. IQ. *Atlantic Monthly,* September 1971, pp. 43–64.

―――――. *IQ in the meritocracy.* Boston: Little Brown, 1973.

Hess, R. D., M. Tenezakis, I. D. Smith, R. L. Brad, J. B. Spellman, H. T. Ingle, and B. G. Oppman. The computer as a socializing agent: Some socioaffective outcomes of CAI. Technical Report No. 13, Stanford Center for Research and Development in Teaching, Stanford, California, 1970.

Hewitt, L., and R. Jenkins. *Fundamental patterns of maladjustment, the dynamics of their origin.* Springfield, Ill.: State of Illinois, 1946.

Hilgard, J. Learning and maturation in preschool children. *Journal of Genetic Psychology* **41,** 1932, 36–56.

Hill, P. W., and B. McGaw. Testing the simplex assumption underlying Bloom's taxonomy. *American Educational Research Journal* **18,** 1981, 92–101.

Hilton, T. L., and G. W. Berglund. Sex differences in mathematics achievement—a longitudinal study. *Journal of Educational Research* **67,** 1974, 231–237.

Hobbs, N. (ed.). *Issues in the classification of children,* Volume 2. San Francisco: Jossey-Bass, 1975.

Hoffman, E. Children's perceptions of their emotionally disturbed peers. *Dissertation Abstracts* **37,** 1976, 952-B.

Hoffman, L. W. Early childhood experiences and women's achievement motives. *Journal of Social Issues* **28** (2), 1972, 129–156.

Holland, J. L. *Making vocational choices: A theory of careers.* Englewood Cliffs, N.J.: Prentice-Hall, 1973.

Homme, L. E. Human motivation and environment. *Kansas Studies in Education* **16,** 1966, 30–39.

Homme, L. E., A. P. Csanyi, M. A. Gonzales, and J. S. Rechs. *How to use contingency contracting in the classroom.* Champaign, Ill.: Research Press, 1979.

Holt, J. *How children fail.* New York: Pittman, 1964.

Hooper, F. H., and N. W. Sheehan. Logical concept attainment during the aging years: Issues in the neo-Piagetian research literature. In W. G. Overton and J. M. Gallagher (eds.), *Knowledge and development,* Volume 1. New York: Plenum, 1977.

Horn, J. L. Human ability systems. In P. B. Baltes (ed.), *Life span development and behavior.* New York: Academic Press, 1978.

―――――. The rise and fall of human abilities. *Journal of Research and Development in Education* **12,** 1979, 59–78.

Horn, J. L., and R. B. Cattell. Refinement and test of the theory of fluid and crystallized intelligence. *Journal of Educational Psychology* **57,** 1966, 253–270.

―――――. Age differences in fluid and crystallized intelligence. *Acta Psychologica* **26,** 1967, 207–229.

Howe, L. W., and M. M. Howe. *Personalizing education: Values clarification and beyond.* New York: Hart, 1975.

Howes, C., and J. Krakow. Effects of inevitable environmental pollutants. Paper presented at the Annual Meeting of the American Psychological Association, San Francisco, August 1977.

Iano, R. P., D. Ayers, H. B. Heller, J. F. McGettigan, and V. S. Walker. Sociometric status of retarded children in an integrative program. *Exceptional Children* **40,** 1974, 267–271.

Jackson, P. W. *The way teaching is.* Washington, D.C.: Association for Supervision and Curriculum Development, 1966. Pp. 7–27.

James, C. D. A cognitive style approach to teacher-pupil interaction and the academic performance of black children. Unpublished master's thesis, Rutgers University, 1973.

Jamison, D., P. Suppes, and S. Wells. The effectiveness of alternative instructional media: A survey. *Review of Educational Research* **44,** 1974, 1–68.

Jensen, A. R. How much can we boost IQ and scholastic achievement? *Harvard Educational Review* **39,** 1969, 1–123.

_____. *Educability and group differences.* New York: Harper & Row, 1973. (a)

_____. Race, intelligence and genetics: The differences are real. *Psychology Today* **6** (12), 1973, 80–86. (b)

_____. *Educational differences.* New York: Barnes & Noble, 1974.

_____. Changing conceptions of intelligence. Paper presented at the American Educational Research Association, New York, March 1982.

Johnson, R., J. Rynders, D. W. Johnson, B. Schmidt, and S. Haider. Interaction between handicapped and nonhandicapped teenagers as a function of situational goal structuring: Implications for mainstreaming. *American Educational Research Journal* **16,** 1979, 161–167.

Johnson, S. B., and B. G. Melamed. The assessment and treatment of children's fears. In B. B. Fahey and A. E. Kazdin (eds.), *Advances in child clinical psychology.* New York: Plenum, 1979. Pp. 108–139.

Jordon, T. J. Self-concepts, motivation, and academic achievement of black adolescents. *Journal of Educational Psychology* **73,** 1981, 509–517.

Jung, J. *The experimenter's dilemma.* New York: Harper & Row, 1971.

Kaestner, E., L. Rosen, and P. Appel. Patterns of drug abuse: Relationships with ethnicity, sensation seeking, and anxiety. *Journal of Consulting and Clinical Psychology* **45,** 1977, 462–468.

Kagan, J. Impulsive and reflective children: Significance of conceptual tempo. In J. D. Krumboltz (ed.), *Learning and the educational process.* Chicago: Rand McNally, 1965.

Kagan, J., L. Pearson, and L. Welch. Conceptual impulsivity and inductive reasoning. *Child Development* **37,** 1966, 583–594.

Kagan, J., B. L. Rosman, D. Day, J. A. Albert, and W. Phillips. Information processing in the child: Significance of analytic and reflective attitudes. *Psychological Monographs* **78** (1, Whole No. 578), 1964.

Kagan, S., L. Zahn, and J. Gealy. Competition and school achievement among Anglo-American and Mexican-American children. *Journal of Educational Psychology* **69**, 1977, 432–441.

Kahl, S. R. Sex-related differences in pre-college science: Findings of the Science Meta-analysis Project. Paper presented at the American Educational Research Association, New York, March 1982.

Kalla, F. Educational technology in the Syrian Arab Republic. *Programmed Learning and Educational Technology* **15**, 1978, 64–68.

Kallman, F. J. *Heredity in health and mental disorder*. New York: Norton, 1953.

Kamii, C. An application of Piaget's theory to the conceptualization of a preschool curriculum. In R. F. Parker (ed.), *The preschool in action: Exploring early childhood programs*. Boston: Allyn & Bacon, 1972.

Kamin, G. *The science and politics of IQ*. New York: Halstead Press, 1975.

Kane, J. H., and R. C. Anderson. Depth of processing and interference effects in the learning and remembering of sentences. *Journal of Educational Psychology* **70**, 1978, 626–635.

Kanfer, F. The many faces of self-control or behavior modification changes its focus. In R. Stuart (ed.), *Behavioral self-management*. New York: Bruner/Mazel, 1977.

Kaplan, S. *Providing programs for the gifted and talented*. Ventura Calif.: Office of the Ventura County Superintendent of Schools, 1974.

Karnes, M. *The Karnes early language activities program*. Champaign, Ill.: Generators of Educational Materials, 1975.

Katz, I. The socialization of academic achievement in minority group children. In D. Levine (ed.), *Nebraska symposium on motivation*, Volume 15. Lincoln: University of Nebraska Press, 1967.

Kauffman, J. M., J. Gottlieb, J. A. Agard, and M. B. Kukic. Project PRIME, mainstreaming toward an explication of the construct. Project No. IM-71-001, U. S. Office of Education, Bureau of Research for the Handicapped, Intramural Research Program, March, 1975.

Kauffman, J. M., and D. P. Hallahan. Learning disability and hyperactivity (with comments on minimal brain dysfunction). In B. B. Fahey & A. E. Kazdin (eds.), *Advances in child clinical psychology*. New York: Plenum, 1979. Pp. 72–105.

Kaye, S., E. Trickett, and D. Quinlan. Alternative methods for environmental assessment: An example. *American Journal of Community Psychology* **4**, 1977, 367–377.

Kelley, H. H. The processes of causal attribution. American Psychologist **28**, 1973, 197–207.

Kennedy, W. A., and H. C. Willcutt. Praise and blame as incentives. *Psychological Bulletin* **62**, 1964, 323–332.

Kerr, M. M., and P. S. Strain. The use of peer social initiation strategies to improve the social skills of withdrawn children. ERIC Document Reproduction Service No. ED 158 551, 1978.

Kersh, M. E. A strategy for mastery learning in fifth-grade arithmetic. Unpublished Doctoral dissertation, University of Chicago, Chicago, 1970.

Kibler, R. J., L. L. Barker, and D. T. Miles. *Behavioral objectives and instruction.* Boston: Allyn & Bacon, 1970.

Kirk, S. A. *Educating exceptional children,* second edition. Boston, Mass.: Houghton Mifflin, 1972.

Kirk, S. A., and W. D. Kirk, *Psycholinguistic learning disabilities: Diagnosis and remediation.* Urbana: University of Illinois Press, 1971.

Kirk, S. A., J. J. McCarthy, and W. D. Kirk. *Illinois test of psycholinguistic abilities,* revised edition. Urbana: University of Illinois Press, 1968.

Kirschenbaum. H. Sensitivity modules. In D. A. Read and S. B. Simon (eds.), *Humanistic education sourcebook.* Englewood Cliffs, N. J.: Prentice-Hall, 1975. Pp. 315–320.

Klausmeier, H. J., J. T. Jeter, M. R. Quilling, D. A. Frayer, and P. S. Allen. *Individually guided motivation.* Madison, Wis.: Wisconsin Research and Development Center for Cognitive Learning, 1975.

Klineberg, O. Negro-white differences in intelligence test performances: A new look at an old problem. *American Psychologist* **18,** 1963, 198–203.

Koberg, D., and I. Bagnall. *The universal traveler.* Los Altos, Calif.: William Kaufman, 1976.

Kohlberg, L. Montessori with the culturally disadvantaged. In R. D. Hess and R. M. Blair (eds.), *Early education.* Chicago: Aldine, 1968.

————. The child as moral philosopher. In G. A. Davis and T. F. Warren (eds.), *Psychology of Education: New Looks.* Lexington, Mass.: D.C. Heath, 1974. Pp. 144–154.

————. Moral stages and moralization: The cognitive developmental approach. In T. Lichona (ed.), *Moral development and behavior.* New York: Holt, Rinehart & Winston, 1976.

Kounin, J. S. *Discipline and group management in classrooms.* New York: Holt, Rinehart & Winston, 1970.

Kounin, J. S., and P. A. Doyle. Degree of continuity of a lesson's signal system and the task involvement of children. *Journal of Educational Psychology* **67,** 1975, 159–164.

Kounin, J. S., and P. V. Gump. Signal systems of lesson settings and the task-related behavior of preschool children. *Journal of Educational Psychology* **66,** 1974, 554–562.

Krathwohl, D., B. S. Bloom, and B. Masia. *Taxonomy of educational objectives. Handbook II: Affective domain.* New York: McKay, 1964.

Krumboltz, J. D. The nature and importance of the required response in programmed instructions. *American Educational Research Journal* **1,** 1964, 203–209.

Kryspin, W. J., and J. T. Feldhusen. *Developing classroom tests.* Minneapolis, Minn.: Burgess Publishing Co., 1974.

Kun, A., and B. Weiner. Necessary versus sufficient causal schemata for success and failure. *Journal of Research in Personality* **7**, 1973, 197–207.

Labouvie-Vief, G., and J. N. Gonda. Cognitive strategy training and intellectual performance in the elderly. *Journal of Gerontology* **31**, 1976, 327–332.

Lahey, B. B., and A. E. Kazdin (eds.). *Advances in child clinical psychology.* New York: Plenum, 1979.

Lancaster, S. L. P. The nature of the relationship between locus of control and academic achievement. Unpublished Doctoral dissertation, University of Virginia, 1974

Lange, P. C. What's the score on programmed instruction? *Today's Education* **61**, 1972, 59.

Lansdown, R., and L. Polak. A study of the psychological effects of facial deformity in children. *Child Care, Health, and Development* **1**, 1975, 85–91.

Lao, R. C. Internal-external control and competent and innovative behavior among Negro college students, *Journal of Personality and Social Psychology* **14**, 1970, 263–270.

Leahy, A. M. Nature-nurture and intelligence. *Genetic Psychology Monographs* **17**, 1935, 235–308.

Lee, J. M., and C. J. Pulvino. *Educating the forgotten half.* Dubuque, Iowa: Kendall/Hunt, 1978.

Lefcourt, H. M. Recent developments in the study of locus of control. In B. A. Maher (ed.), *Progress in experimental personality research.* New York: Academic Press, 1972. Pp. 1–39.

————. *Locus of control: Current trends in research and theory.* Hillsdale, N.J.: Erlbaum, 1976

Lefkowitz, W. Communication grows in a "Magic Circle." *Teacher's Edition: My Weekly Reader,* April 5, 1972. Reprinted in D. A. Read and S. B. Simon (eds.), *Humanistic education sourcebook.* Englewood Cliffs, N.J.: Prentice-Hall, 1975. Pp. 457–459.

Leinhardt, G., A. M. Seewald, and M. Engel. Learning what's taught: Sex differences in instruction. *Journal of Educational Psychology* **71**, 1979, 432–439.

Lenneberg, E. H. *Biological foundations of language.* New York: Wiley, 1967.

Lesh, R. A. The influence of an advanced organizer on two types of instructional units on finite geometry. *Journal for Research in Mathematics Education* **7**, 1976, 82–86.

Levin, J. R. *Learner differences: Diagnosis and prescription.* New York: Holt, Rinehart & Winston, 1977.

Levin, J. R., C. B. McCormick, G. E. Miller, J. K. Berry, and M. Pressley. Mnemonic versus nonmnemonic vocabulary-learning strategies for children. *American Educational Research Journal* **19**, 1982, 121–136.

Levine, F. M., and G. Fasnacht. Token rewards may lead to token learning. *American Psychologist* **29,** 1974, 816–820.

Lewis, B. N., and G. Pask. The theory and practice of adaptive teaching systems. In R. Glaser (ed.), *Teaching machines and programmed learning, II.* Washington, D.C.: National Education Association, 1965. Pp. 213–266.

Lickona, T. (ed.). *Moral development and behavior.* New York: Holt, Rinehart & Winston, 1976.

Lieth, G. O. M. Learning and personality. In W. R. Dunn and C. Holroyd (eds.), *Aspects of educational technology, II.* London: Methuen, 1969.

Lieth, G. O. M., and E. A. Trown. The influence of personality and task conditions on learning and transfer. *Programmed Learning and Educational Technology* **7,** 1970, 180–181.

Lieth, G. O. M., and B. Wisdom. An investigation of the effects of error making and personality on learning. *Programmed Learning and Educational Technology* **7,** 1970, 120–126.

Lindsay, P. H., and D. A. Norman. *Human information processing.* New York: Academic Press, 1977.

Linton, H. B. Relations between mode of perception and the tendency to conform. Unpublished Doctoral dissertation, Yale University, 1952.

Lippitt, R., and M. Lippitt. Cross-age helpers. *National Educational Association Journal* **57** (March), 1968, 24–26.

Lippitt, R., and R. K. White. An experimental study of leadership and group life. In E. E. Maccoby, T. M. Newcomb, and E. E. Hartley (eds.), *Readings in social psychology.* New York: Holt, Rinehart & Winston, 1958. Pp. 496–511.

Lips, H. H., and N. L. Colwill. *The psychology of sex differences.* Englewood Cliffs, N.J.: Prentice-Hall, 1978.

Litow, L., and D. K. Pumroy. A brief review of classroom group-oriented contingencies. *Journal of Applied Behavioral Analysis* **8,** 1975, 341–347.

Lockwood, A. L. The effects of values clarification and moral development curricula on school-age subjects: A critical review of recent research. *Review of Educational Research* **48,** 1978, 325–364.

Lodge, G. A. (ed.). *Growth and development of mammals.* London: Butterworth, 1968.

Long, J. D., and R. L. Williams. The comparative effectiveness of group and individually contingent free time with inner-city junior high school students. *Journal of Applied Behavior Analysis* **6,** 1973, 465–474.

Longstreth, L. E. A comment on "race, IQ, and the middle class" by Trotman: Rampant false conclusions. *Journal of Educational Psychology* **70,** 1978, 469–472.

Looft, W. R., and W. H. Bartz. Animism revived. In G. A. Davis and T. F. Warren (eds.), *Psychology of education: New Looks.* Lexington, Mass.: D.C. Heath, 1974. Pp. 155–169.

Lowenbraun, S., and J. Q. Affleck. The exceptional child and special education. In

S. Lowenbraum and J. Q. Affleck (eds.), *Teaching mildly handicapped children in regular classes.* Columbus, Ohio: Charles E. Merrill, 1976. Pp. 1–13.

Luria, A. A. The mind of a mnemonist. In U. Neisser (ed.), *Memory observed: Remembering in natural contexts.* San Francisco: W. H. Freeman, 1982.

Maccoby, E. E., and C. N. Jacklin. *Psychology of sex differences.* Stanford, Calif.: Stanford University Press, 1974.

MacDonald, F. J. Report on Phase II of the Beginning Teacher Evaluation Study. *Journal of Teacher Education* **27,** 1976, 39–42.

MacKinnon, D. W. Educating for creativity: A modern myth? In G. A. Davis and J. A. Scott (eds.), *Training creative thinking.* Huntington, N.Y.: Krieger, 1978.

MacMillan, D. L. *Behavior modification in the classroom.* New York: Macmillan, 1973.

Madsen, C. H., W. C. Becker, and D. R. Thomas. Rules, praise, and ignoring: Elements of elementary classroom control. *Journal of Applied Behavioral Analysis* **1,** 1968, 139–150.

Mager, R. F. *Preparing instructional objectives.* Palo Alto, Calif.: Fearon, 1962.

―――――. Deriving objectives for the high school curriculum. *National Society Programmed Instructional Journal* **7,** 1968, 7–14.

―――――. *Goal analysis.* Belmont, Calif.: Fearon, 1972.

―――――. *Preparing instructional objectives,* second edition. Belmont, Calif.: Fearon, 1975.

Maker, C. J. *Curriculum development for the gifted.* Rockville, MD: Aspen, 1982.

Malott, R. W. *An introduction to behavior modification.* Kalamazoo, Mich.: Behaviordelia, 1973.

Mannheim, L. A. Healthy children's perceptions of ill children with nonobservable illness. Unpublished M. S. thesis, University of Wisconsin, Madison, Wis., 1980.

Marini, M. M., and E. Greenberger. Sex differences in educational aspirations and expectations. *American Educational Research Journal* **15,** 1978, 67–79.

Marland, S. P., Jr. Education of the gifted and talented, Volume I. Report to the Congress of the United States by the U.S. Commissioner of Education. Washington, D.C.: U.S. Government Printing Office, 1972. P. 2.

Martinson, R. A. *The identification of the gifted and talented.* Ventura, Calif.: Office of the Ventura County Superintendent of Schools, 1974.

Maslow, A. H. *Motivation and personality.* New York: Harper & Row, 1954.

―――――. *Toward a psychology of being,* second edition. Princeton, N.J.: Van Nostrand, 1968.

―――――. *Motivation and personality,* second edition. New York: Harper & Row, 1970.

―――――. *The farther reaches of human nature.* New York: Viking Press, 1971.

Masserman, J. H. *Behavior and neurosis.* Chicago: University of Chicago Press, 1943.

Mayer, R. E. Different problem-solving competencies established in learning computer programming with and without meaningful models. *Journal of Educational Psychology* **67**, 1975, 725–734. (a)

_____. Information processing variables in learning to solve problems. *Review of Educational Research* **45**, 1975, 525–541. (b)

_____. Advance organizers that compensate for the organization of text. *Journal of Educational Psychology* **70**, 1978, 880–886.

McCandless, B. R. Environment and intellectual functioning. In H. A. Stevens and R. Heber (eds.), *Mental retardation: A review of research.* Chicago: University of Chicago Press, 1964.

McCarthy, D. *McCarthy scales of children's abilities.* New York: Psychological Corporation, 1972.

McClelland, D. C. Toward a theory of motive acquisition. *American Psychologist* **20**, 1965, 321–333.

_____. *The achieving society.* New York: Irvington, 1976.

_____. Testing for competence rather than for "intelligence." *American Psychologist* **28**, 1973, 1–14.

McClelland, D. C., and D. G. Winter. *Motivating economic achievement.* New York: The Free Press, 1969.

McFie, J., and J. Robertson. Psychological test results of children with Thalidomide deformities. *Developmental Medicine* **15**, 1973, 719–727.

McNeil, J. D. Concomitants of using behavioral objectives in the assessment of teacher effectiveness. *Journal of Experimental Education* **36**, 1967, 69–74.

_____. The development of language. In P. H. Mussen (ed.), *Carmichael's manual of child psychology,* third edition, Volume 1.

Means, V., J. W. Moore, E. Gagne, W. E. Hauck. The interactive effects of consonant and dissonant teacher expectancy and feedback communication on student performance in a natural setting. *American Educational Research Journal* **16**, 1979, 367–373.

Mehrabian, A. Measures of achieving tendency. *Educational and Psychological Measurement* **29**, 1969, 445–451.

Meichenbaum, D. H. *Cognitive-behavior modification.* New York: Plenum, 1977.

_____. Teaching children self-control. In B. B. Fahey and A. E. Kazdin (eds.), *Advances in child clinical psychology.* New York: Plenum, 1979. Pp. 1–33.

Meichenbaum, D. H., and J. Goodman. Training impulsive children to talk to themselves: A means of developing self control. *Journal of Abnormal Psychology* **77**, 1971, 115–126.

Melton, R. F. Resolution of conflicting claims concerning the effect of behavioral objectives on student learning. *Review of Educational Research* **48**, 1978, 291–302.

Messer, S. Reflection-impulsivity: Stability and school failure. *Journal of Educational Psychology* **61**, 1970, 487–490.

Meyers, C. E., D. L. MacMillan, and R. K. Yoshida. Regular class placement of EMR students, from efficacy to mainstreaming: A review of issues and research. In J. Gottlieb (ed.), *Educating mentally retarded persons in the mainstream.* Baltimore, Md.: University Park Press, 1980.

Michels, T. J., and N. C. Hatcher. Sociodrama in the classroom: A different approach to learning. In D. A. Read and S. B. Simon (eds.), *Humanistic education sourcebook.* Englewood Cliffs, N.J.: Prentice-Hall, 1975.

Miezitis, M. The Montessori method: Some recent research. *American Montessori Society Bulletin* **10**, 1972, 1–28.

Miller, G. A. The magical number seven, plus or minus two: Some limits on our capacity for processing information. *Psychological Review* **63**, 1956, 81–97.

Minskoff, E., D. Wiseman, and J. Minskoff. *The MWM program for developing language abilities.* Ridgefield, N.J.: Educational Performance Associates, 1975.

Mischel, W. Toward a cognitive social learning reconceptualization of personality. *Psychological Review* **80**, 1973, 252–282.

————. On the interface of cognition and personality. *American Psychologist* **34**, 1979, 740–754.

————. Behavioral consistency: Myth or reality? Special debate presented at the American Psychological Association, Montreal, Canada, 1980.

————. *Introduction to personality,* third edition. New York: Holt, Rinehart, & Winston, 1981.

Mitchell, D. E., and W. G. Spady. Organizational contexts for implementing outcome based education. *Educational Researcher* **7** (7), 1978, 9–17.

Moos, R. H. Situational analysis of a therapeutic community milieu. *Journal of Abnormal Psychology* **73**, 1968, 49–61.

————. *Evaluating treatment environments: A social ecological approach.* New York: Wiley, 1974.

————. A typology of junior high and high school classrooms. *American Educational Research Journal* **15**, 1978, 53–66.

Moos, R. H., and B. S. Moos. Classroom social climate and student absences and grades. *Journal of Educational Psychology* **70**, 1978, 263–269.

Morgan, R. F., and T. B. Troy. Learning by teaching: A student-to-student compensatory tutoring program in a rural school system and its relevance to the educational cooperative. *Psychological Record* **20**, 1970, 159–169.

Morris, L. W., M. G. Davis, and C. H. Hutchings. Cognitive and emotional components of anxiety: Literature review and a revised worry-emotionality scale. *Journal of Educational Psychology* **73**, 1981, 541–555.

Moss, H. A. Sex, age and state as determiners of mother-infant interaction. *Merrill-Palmer Quarterly* **13**, 1967, 19–36.

Moursand, D. *Introduction to computers in education for elementary and middle school teachers.* Eugene, Oregon: International Council for Computers in Education, 1980.

Moursand, D. Introduction to microcomputers. Speech presented at the Conference on Microcomputers in Education. Research and Development Center for Individualized Schooling, University of Wisconsin, Madison, July 1981.

Murray, H. *Explorations in personality: A clinical and experimental study of fifty men of college age.* New York: Oxford University Press, 1938.

Muus, R. E. *Theories of adolescence.* New York: Random House, 1975.

Naeye, R. L., W. Blanc, and C. Paul. Effects of maternal nutrition on the human fetus. *Pediatrics* **52,** 1973, 494–503.

Nardine, F. The development of competence. In G. A. Davis and T. F. Warren (eds.), *Psychology of education: New looks.* Lexington, Mass.: D. C. Heath, 1974.

National Advisory Committee on the Handicapped. *The unfinished revolution: Education for the handicapped.* Washington D.C.: U.S. Government Printing Office, 1976.

National Assessment of Educational Progress. *Male-female achievement in eight learning areas: A compilation of selected assessment results.* Denver, Colo.: Education Commission of the States, 1975.

Neisser, U. Memorists. In U. Neisser (ed.), *Memory observed: Remembering in natural contexts.* San Francisco: W. H. Freeman, 1982.

Neisser, U. (ed.). *Memory observed: Remembering in natural contexts.* San Francisco: W. H. Freeman, 1982.

Newburg, N. A. *Affective education in Philadelphia.* Bloomington, Ind.: Phi Delta Kappa Educational Foundation, 1977.

Newhouse, R. C. Reinforcement-responsibility differences in birth order, grade level, and sex of children in grades 4, 5, 6. *Psychological Reports* **34,** 1974, 699–705.

Nichols, J. G. The development of the concepts of effort and ability, perception of academic attainment and the understanding that difficult tasks require more ability. *Child Development* **49,** 1978, 800–814.

———. Development of perception of own attainment and causal attributions for success and failure in reading. *Journal of Educational Psychology* **71,** 1979, 94–99.

Norman, D. A. Memory, knowledge, and the answering of questions. In R. L. Solso (ed.), *Contemporary issues in cognitive psychology.* Washington, D.C.: Winston, 1973.

———. *Memory and attention: An introduction to human information processing,* second edition. New York: Wiley, 1976.

Norman, W. T. Toward an adequate taxonomy of personality attributes: Replicated factor structure in peer nomination personality ratings. *Journal of Abnormal and Social Psychology* **66,** 1963, 574–583.

Novak, D. Children's reactions to emotional disturbance in imaginary peers. *Journal of Counseling and Clinical Psychology* **42,** 1974, 462.

Novak, J. D. *A theory of education.* Ithaca, N.Y.: Cornell University Press, 1977.

Nowicki, S., M. P. Duke, and M. P. D. Crouch. Sex differences in locus of control and performance under competitive and cooperative conditions. *Journal of Educational Psychology* **70**, 1978, 482–486.

Nowicki, S., and B. R. Strickland. A locus of control scale for children. *Journal of Counseling and Clinical Psychology* **40**, 1973, 148–154.

Ornstein, A. C. Techniques and fundamentals for teaching the disadvantaged. In A. C. Ornstein and P. D. Vairo (eds.), *How to teach the disadvantaged.* New York: David McKay, 1969. Pp. 139–152. (a)

————. In defense of slum school teachers. In A. C. Ornstein and P. D. Vairo (eds.), *How to teach the disadvantaged.* New York: David McKay, 1969. Pp. 153–162. (b)

Osborn, A. F. *Applied imagination,* third edition. New York: Scribner's, 1963.

Packer, J., and J. D. Bain. Cognitive style and teacher-student compatibility. *Journal of Educational Psychology* **70**, 1978, 864–871.

Page, S. Social interaction and experimenter effects in the verbal conditioning experiment. *Canadian Journal of Psychology* **25**, 1971, 463–475.

Paivio. A. *Imagery and verbal processes.* New York: Holt, Rinehart & Winston, 1971.

Paivio, A., and A. Desrochers. Mnemonic techniques in second language learning. *Journal of Educational Psychology* **73**, 1981, 780–795.

Palomares, U. H., and T. Rubini. Human development in the classroom. *Personnel and Guidance Journal* **5**, 1973, 653–657. Reprinted in D. A. Read and S. B. Simon (eds.), *Human education sourcebook.* Englewood Cliffs, N.J.: Prentice-Hall, 1975. Pp. 383–387.

Panicucci, C. L., and G. Labouvie-Vief. Effect of training on inductive reasoning behavior. Paper presented at the Annual Meeting of the Gerontological Society, Louisville, Ky.: 1975.

Papert, S. *Mindstorms.* New York: Basic Books, 1981.

Parnes, S. J. Can creativity be increased? In G. A. Davis and J. A. Scott (eds.), *Training creative thinking.* Huntington, N.Y.: Krieger, 1978.

————. *The magic of your mind.* Buffalo, N.Y.: Creative Education Foundation, 1981.

Parnes, S. J., R. B. Noller, and A. M. Biondi. *Guide to creative action.* New York: Scribner's, 1977.

Pavlov, I. *Conditioned reflexes.* Oxford, England: Clarendon Press, 1927.

————. Conditioned reflex theory. In W. S. Sahakian (ed.), *Learning: Systems, models and theories,* second edition. Chicago: Rand McNally, 1976. Pp. 13–30.

Payne, D. A., D. R. Krathwohl, and J. Gordon. The effects of sequence on programmed instruction. *American Educational Research Journal* **4**, 1967, 125–132.

Pediwell, A. The saber-tooth curriculum. New York: McGraw-Hill, 1939. Partially reprinted in G. A. Davis and T. F. Warren (eds.), *Psychology of education: New Looks.* Lexington, Mass.: D.C. Heath, 1974. Pp. 5–13.

Pelligrino, J. W., and R. Glaser. Cognitive correlates and components in the analysis of individual differences. In R. J. Sternberg and D. K. Detterman (eds.), *Human intelligence: Perspectives on its theory and measurement.* Norwood, N.J.: Ablex, 1979.

Perrone, P. A., W. W. Karshner, and R. A. Male. Identification of talented students. In N. Colangelo and R. T. Zaffran (eds.), *New voices in counseling the gifted.* Dubuque, Iowa: Kendall/Hunt, 1979.

Perry, T., and G. Zawolkow. CAI: Choosing hardware and software. *Apple Orchards* **3** (1), 1982, 22–24.

Peterson, P. L., T. C. Janicki, and S. R. Swing. Ability X Treatment interaction effects on children's learning in large-group and small-group approaches. *American Educational Research Journal* **18**, 1981, 453–473.

Peterson, P. L., and H. J. Walberg, (eds.). *Research on teaching: Concepts, findings and implications.* Berkeley, Calif.: McCutchan, 1979.

Piaget, J., and B. Inhelder. *The child's conception of space.* London: Routledge and Kegan Paul, 1956.

Pierce, K. M. Camps for computers. *Time Magazine,* August 3, 1981, 70.

Pine, G. J., and A. V. Boy. *Learner-centered teaching: A humanistic view.* Denver, Colo.: Love Publishing Co., 1977.

Plemons, M. S., S. L. Willis, and P. B. Baltes. Modifiability of fluid intelligence in aging: A short-term longitudinal approach. *Journal of Gerontology* **33**, 1978, 224–331.

Popham, W. J. Objectives and instruction. *Instructional objectives.* American Educational Research Association Monograph Series on Curriculum Evaluation: Monograph No. 3. Chicago: Rand-McNally, 1969.

————. *Criterion-referenced instruction.* Belmont, Calif.: Fearon, 1973.

Popham, W. J., and E. L. Baker. *Systematic instruction.* Englewood Cliffs, N.J.: Prentice-Hall, 1970.

————. *Classroom instructional tactics.* Englewood Cliffs, N.J.: Prentice-Hall, 1973.

Poteet, J. A. *Behavior modification: A practical guide for teachers.* Minneapolis, Minn.: Burgess, 1973.

Premack, D. Reinforcement theory. In D. Levine (ed.), *Nebraska symposium on motivation,* Volume 13. Lincoln: University of Nebraska Press, 1965. Pp. 123–180.

Pressley, M., and J. R. Levin. Developmental constraints associated with children's use of the keyword method of foreign language vocabulary learning. *Journal of Experimental Child Psychology* **26**, 1978, 359–372.

Pressley, M., J. R. Levin, and H. D. Delany. The mnenomic keyword method. *Review of Educational Research* **52**, 1982, 61–91.

Price, R. The taxonomic classification of behavior-environment congruence. *Human Relations* **27**, 1974, 567–585.

Prout, A. T. Behavioral intervention with hyperactive children: A review. *Journal of Learning Disabilities* **10**, 1977, 141–146.

Pulvino, C. J., N. Colangelo, and R. T. Zaffrann. *Laboratory Counseling Programs.* Department of Counseling and Guidance, University of Wisconsin, Madison, 1976.

Purpel, D., and K. Ryan (eds.). *Moral education . . . it comes with the territory.* Berkeley, Calif.: McCutchan, 1976.

Quay, L. C. Academic skills. In N. R. Ellis (ed.), *Handbook of mental deficiency.* New York: McGraw-Hill, 1963.

Raths, J. Teaching without specific objectives. *Educational Leadership* **28**, 1971, 714–720.

Raven, J. C. *Standard progressive matrices.* London: H. K. Lewis, 1958.

Renzulli, J. S. *A guidebook for evaluating programs for the gifted and talented.* Ventura, Calif.: Office of the Ventura County Superintendent of Schools, 1975.

————. *The enrichment triad model: A guide for developing defensible programs for the gifted and talented.* Wethersfield, Conn.: Creative Learning Press, 1977.

————. What makes giftedness? Reexamining a definition. *Phi Delta Kappan,* November 1978, 180–184.

————. Will the gifted child movement be alive and well in 1990? *Gifted Child Quarterly* **24,** 1980, 3–9.

Renzulli, J. S., R. K. Hartman, and C. M. Callahan. Scales for rating the behavioral characteristics of superior students. In W. B. Barbe and J. S. Renzulli (eds.), *Psychology and education of the gifted,* second edition. New York: Irvington, 1975.

Renzulli, J. S., S. M. Reis and L. H. Smith. *The revolving door identification model.* Mansfield Center, Conn.: Creative Learning Press, 1981.

Renzulli, J. S., and L. H. Smith. Developing defensible programs for the gifted and talented. *Journal of Creative Behavior* **12**, 1978, 21–29, 51.

————. Issues and procedures in evaluating programs. In A. H. Passow (ed.), *The gifted and the talented: Their education and development.* Chicago: National Society for the Study of Education, 1979.

Rest, J. New approaches in the assessment of moral judgement. In T. Lickona (ed.), *Moral development and behavior.* New York: Holt, Rinehart & Winston, 1976.

Reynolds, M. C., and J. W. Birch. *Teaching exceptional children in all America's schools.* Reston, VA: Council for Exceptional Children, 1982.

Richardson, S. Some social psychological consequences of handicapping. *Pediatrics* **32**, 291–297.

————. Handicap, appearance, and stigma. *Social Science and Medicine* **5**, 1971, 621–628.

Ridberg, E., R. D. Parke, and E. M. Hetherington. Modification of impulsive and reflective cognitive styles through observation of film-mediated models. *Developmental Psychology* **5**, 1971, 369–377.

Riessman, F. Teachers of the poor: A five-point plan. In A. C. Ornstein and P. D. Vairo (eds.), *How to teach disadvantaged youth.* New York: McKay, 1969. Pp. 402–417.

Rimm, S. *GIFT: Group inventory for finding creative talent*. Watertown, Wis.: Educational Assessment Service, 1976.

Rimm, S., and G. A. Davis. GIFT: An instrument for the identification of creativity. *Journal of Creative Behavior* **10**, 1976, 178–182.

_____. *Group inventory for finding interests. I.* Watertown, Wis.: Educational Assessment Service, 1979.

_____. Five years of international research with GIFT: An instrument for the identification of creativity. *Journal of Creative Behavior* **14**, 1980, 35–46.

Ringness, T. A. *The affective domain in education*. Boston: Little-Brown, 1973.

Rist, R. C. Student social class and teacher expectations: The self-fulfilling prophecy in ghetto education. *Harvard Educational Review* **40**, 1970, 411–451.

Robertson, D. J. Integrate teaching: Children learn from children. In S. L. Sekesta and C. J. Waller (eds.), *The first R: Readings in teaching reading.* Chicago: Scientific Research Association, 1972.

Roddy, J. Integrating normal and severely handicapped children using a peer tutoring approach. Unpublished M.S. thesis, University of Wisconsin, Madison, 1980.

Roediger, H. L., and R. G. Crowder. A serial position effect in recall of United States Presidents. In U. Neisser (ed.), *Memory reconsidered: Remembering in natural contexts.* San Francisco: W. H. Freeman, 1982.

Rogers, C. R. A coordinated research in psychotherapy: A non-objective introduction. *Journal of Consulting Psychology* **13**, 1949, 49–51.

_____. Toward a theory of creativity. In S. J. Parnes and H. F. Harding (eds.), *A source book for creative thinking.* New York: Scribner's, 1962.

_____. *Freedom to learn.* Columbus, Ohio: Charles E. Merrill, 1969.

_____. Regarding learning and its facilitation. In G. A. Davis and T. F. Warren (eds.), *Psychology of education: New looks.* Lexington, Mass.: D. C. Heath, 1974. Pp. 227–235.

Rogers, J. B. An introduction to computers and computing: A high school course outline. *The Computing Teacher* **8** (7), 1981, 30–32.

Root, A. A. What instructors say to the students makes a difference. *Engineering Education* **61**, 1970, 722–725.

Rosenshine, B. *Teaching behaviors and student achievement.* London: National Foundation for Educational Research in England and Wales, 1971.

_____. Content, time and direct instruction. In P. L. Peterson and H. J. Walberg (eds.), *Research on teaching: Concepts, findings and implications.* Berkeley, Calif.: McCutchan, 1979.

Rosenshine, B., and N. E. Furst. Research on teacher performance criteria. In B. O. Smith (ed.), *Research in teacher education: A symposium.* Englewood Cliffs, N.J.: Prentice-Hall, 1971.

_____. The use of direct observation to study teaching. *Second handbook of research on teaching.* Chicago: Rand McNally, 1973.

Rosenthal, R. *On the social psychology of the self-fulfilling prophecy.* New York: MSS Modular Publications, 1974.

_____. *Experimenter effects in behavioral research,* second edition. New York: Irvington, 1976.

Rosenthal, R., and L. Jacobson. *Pygmalion in the classroom: Teacher expectation and pupils' intellectual development.* New York: Holt, Rinehart & Winston, 1968.

Rosman, N. P. Fetal alcohol syndrome. *Neurology Review* (audio cassette), June 1978.

Ross, A. O. The application of behavior principles in therapeutic education. *Journal of Special Education* **1,** 1967, 275–286.

_____. *Learning disability: The unrealized potential.* New York: McGraw-Hill, 1977.

Rothkopf, E. Z., and R. Kaplan. Exploration of the effect of density and specificity of instructional objectives on learning from text. *Journal of Educational Psychology* **63,** 1972, 295–302.

Rotter, J. B. Generalized expectancies for internal versus external control of reinforcements. *Psychological Monographs* **80** (1, Whole No. 609), 1966.

Rotter, J. B., J. E. Chance, and J. E. Phares. *Applications of social learning theory to personality.* New York: Holt, Rinehart & Winston, 1972.

Rubin, R. A., J. Dorle, and S. Sandidge. Self-esteem and school performance. *Psychology in the Schools* **14,** 1977, 503–506.

Ruhland, D., M. Gold, and S. Feld. Role problems and the relationship of achievement to performance. *Journal of Educational Psychology* **70,** 1978, 950–959.

Ryans, D. G. Some correlates of teacher behavior. *Educational and Psychological Measurement* **19,** 1959, 9–10.

Sajwaj, T., M. P. McNees, and J. F. Schnelle. Clinical and community interventions with children: A comparison of treatment strategies. In B. B. Fahey and A. E. Kazdin (eds.), *Advances in child clinical psychology.* New York: Plenum, 1979. Pp. 175–191.

Salvia, J., and J. Yesseldyke. *Assessment in special and remedial education.* Boston: Houghton Mifflin, 1978.

Sanborn, M. P. Career development: Problems of gifted and talented students. In N. Colangelo and R. T. Zaffrann (eds.), *New voices in counseling the gifted.* Dubuque, Iowa: Kendall/Hunt, 1979.

Sanders, N. M. *Classroom questions: What kinds?* New York: Harper & Row, 1966.

Santrock, J. W. *Adolescence: An introduction.* Dubuque, Iowa: W. C. Brown, 1981.

Saracho, O. N. The cognitive styles of teachers and their perceptions of their matched and mismatched children's academic performance. Paper presented at the American Educational Research Association, New York, March, 1982.

Sarason, S. B., F. F. Lighthall, K. S. Davidson, R. R. Waite, and B. K. Ruebush. *Anxiety in elementary school children.* New York: Wiley, 1960.

Sattler, J. M. *Assessment of children's intelligence.* Philadelphia: Saunders, 1974

Sauter, D. L. The development and application of a battery for the exploratory screening for neuropsychological deficits in children exposed to formaldehyde. Unpublished Doctoral thesis, University of Wisconsin, Madison, 1981.

Sayre, S., and D. W. Ball. Piagetian cognitive development and achievement in science. *Journal of Research in Science Teaching* **12**, 1975, 165–174.

Scarr, S. Genetic factors in activity motivation. *Child Development* **37**, 1966, 663–673.

_____. Social introversion and extraversion as a heritable response. *Child Development* **40**, 1969, 823–832.

_____. *Race, social class, and individual differences in IQ: New studies of old issues.* Hillsdale, N.J.: Erlbaum, 1981.

Schaffer, H. R., and P. E. Emerson. The development of social attachments in infancy. *Monographs of the Society for Research in Child Development* **29** (3, Serial No. 94), 1964.

Schaefer, C. E. *Biographical Inventory-Creativity.* San Diego, Calif.: Educational and Industrial Testing Services, 1970.

Scheirer, M. A., and R. E. Kraut. Increasing educational achievement via self concept change. *Review of Educational Research* **49**, 1979, 131–150.

Schumacher, G. M., D. Liebert, and W. Fass. Textural organization, advance organizers and the retention of prose material. *Journal of Reading Behavior* **7**, 1975, 173–180.

Sears, P. S. The Terman generic studies of genius, 1922–1972. In A. H. Passow (ed.), *The gifted and the talented: Their education and development.* Chicago: National Society for the Study of Education, 1979.

Sears, P. S., and A. H. Barbe. Career and life satisfaction among Terman's gifted women. In J. C. Stanley, W. C. George, and C. H. Solano, *The gifted and the creative: Fifty-year perspective.* Baltimore, Md.: Johns Hopkins University Press, 1977.

Sears, R. R. Sources of life satisfactions of the Terman gifted men. *American Psychologist* **32**, 1977, 119–128.

Seddon, G. M. The properties of Bloom's Taxonomy of Educational Objectives for the cognitive domain. *Review of Educational Research* **48**, 1978, 303–323.

Segal, B., and P. F. Merenda. Locus of control, sensation seeking, and drug and alcohol use in college students. *Drug Forum* **4**, 1975, 349–369.

Selman, R. Social-cognitive understanding: A guide to educational and clinical practice. In T. Lickona (ed.), *Moral development and behavior: Theory, research, and social issues.* New York: Holt, Rinehart & Winston, 1976.

_____. The child as a friendship philosopher: A developmental perspective on the meaning of friendship conceptions. Paper presented at the Society for Research in Child Development, Champaign-Urbana, Ill., 1978.

Selman, R., and D. Byrne. A structural-developmental analysis of levels of role-taking in middle childhood. *Child Development* **45**, 1974, 803–806.

Shaffer, H. E., and P. E. Emerson. Patterns of response to physical contact in early human development. *Journal of Child Psychology and Psychiatry* **5,** 1964, 1–13.

Shantz, C. V. The development of social cognition. In E. M. Hetherington (ed.), *Review of Child Development Research,* Volume 5. Chicago: University of Chicago Press, 1976.

Shavelson, R. F., and P. Stern. Research on teachers' pedagogical thoughts, judgments, decisions, and behavior. *Review of Educational Research* **51,** 1981, 455–498.

Shavelson, R. J., J. J. Hubner, and G. C. Stanton. Self-concept: Validation of construct interpretations. *Review of Educational Research* **46,** 1976, 407–441.

Shepard, L. A. Self-acceptance: The evaluative component of the self-concept construct. *Journal of Educational Research* **16,** 1979, 139–160.

Shuey, A. *The testing of Negro intelligence,* second edition. New York: Social Science Press, 1966.

Shulman, L. S. Seeking styles and individual differences in patterns of inquiry. *School Review* **73,** 1965, 258–266.

Shulman, L. S., and E. R. Kieslar (eds.). *Learning by discovery: A critical appraisal.* Chicago: Rand McNally, 1966.

Simon, S., L. Howe, and H. Kirschenbaum. *Value clarification: A handbook of practical strategies for teachers and students.* New York: Hart, 1972.

Simon, S., and S. Massey. Value clarification. *Educational Leadership* **5,** 1973, 738–739.

Skinner, B. F. *The behavior of organisms.* New York: Appleton-Century-Crofts, 1938.

———. *Walden two.* New York: Macmillan, 1948.

———. The science of learning and the art of teaching. *Harvard Educational Review* **24,** 1954, 86–97.

———. A case history in scientific method. In S. Koch (ed.), *Psychology: A study of a science,* Volume 2. New York: McGraw-Hill, 1959. Pp. 359–379.

———. *The technology of teaching.* New York: Appleton-Century-Crofts, 1968.

———. *Beyond freedom and dignity.* New York: Knopf, 1971.

———. *Cumulative record: A selection of papers,* third edition. New York: Appleton-Century-Crofts, 1972.

———. The free and happy student. *Phi Delta Kappan* **55,** 1973, 13–16.

———. Excerpts from "Teaching Machines" and "Why We Need Teaching Machines." In G. A. Davis and T. F. Warren (eds.), *Psychology of education: New looks.* Lexington, Mass.: D. C. Heath, 1974.

Skodak, M., and H. M. Skeels. A final follow-up study of one hundred adopted children. *Journal of Genetic Psychology* **75,** 1949, 85–125.

Slavin, R. E. Effects of biracial learning teams on cross-racial friendships. *Journal of Educational Psychology* **71,** 1979, 381–387.

Slavin, R. E., and N. A. Madden. School practices that improve race relations. *American Educational Research Journal* **16,** 1979, 169–180.

Slobin, D. I. Seven questions about language development. In P. C. Dodwell (ed.), *New horizons in psychology,* No. 2. Baltimore, Md.: Penguin, 1972.

Smiley, M. B. Objectives of educational programs for the educationally retarded and disadvantaged. In P. A. Witty (ed.), *The educationally retarded and disadvantaged. Sixty-sixth Yearbook of the National Society for the Study of Education, Part I.* Chicago: University of Chicago Press, 1967.

Smith, J. A. *Setting conditions for creative teaching in the elementary school.* Boston: Allyn & Bacon, 1966.

Soar, R. S. *Follow-through classroom process measurement and pupil growth: Final report.* Gainesville, Fla.: Institute for Development of Human Resources, College of Education, University of Florida, 1973.

Solano, C. H., and W. C. George. College courses and educational facilitation of the gifted. *Gifted Child Quarterly* **20,** 1976, 274–285.

Solomon, D., and A. J. Kendall. *Individual characteristics and children's performance in varied educational settings.* Rockville, Md.: Montgomery County Public Schools, 1976.

Solso, R. L. *Cognitive psychology.* New York: Harcourt, Brace & World, 1979.

Spearman, C. E. *The abilities of man.* New York: Macmillan, 1927.

Sperling, G. The information available in brief visual presentations. *Psychological Monographs* **74** (Whole No. 11), 1960.

Spielberger, C. D. (ed.). *Anxiety and behavior.* New York: Academic Press, 1966.

Spielberger, C. D., H. F. O'Niel, and D. N. Hanson. Anxiety, drive theory, and computer-assisted instruction. In B. A. Maher (ed.), *Progress in experimental personality research,* Volume 6. New York: Academic Press, 1972.

Spiker, J. M. Assessing the impact of low-level chemicals on development: Behavioral and latent effects. *Federation Proc.* **34,** 1975, 1835–1844.

Spitz, R. A. Hospitalization: An inquiry into the genesis of psychiatric conditions in early childhood. *Psychoanalytic Study of the Child* **1,** 1945, 53–74.

Staats, A. W. *Language, learning, and cognition.* New York: Holt, Rinehart & Winston, 1968.

Stallings, J. A., and D. Kaskowitz. *Follow-through classroom observation evaluation 1972–1973.* Menlo Park, Calif.: Stanford Research Institute, 1974.

Stanley, J. C. The study and facilitation of talent for mathematics. In A. H. Passow (ed.), *The gifted and the talented.* Chicago: National Society for the Study of Education, 1979. (a)

————. The second D: Description of talent (further study of the intellectually talented youths). In N. Colangelo and R. T. Zaffran (eds.), *New voices in counseling the gifted.* Dubuque, Iowa: Kendall/Hunt, 1979. (b)

Stephans, J. *The process of schooling.* New York: Holt, 1967.

Stephans, T. M. *Teaching skills to children with learning and behavior disorders.* Columbus, Ohio: Charles E. Merrill, 1977.

Sternberg, R. J. Factor theories of intelligence are all right most. *Educational Researcher* **9** (8), 1980, 6–13, 18.

————. Intelligence and nonentrenchment. *Journal of Educational Psychology* **73,** 1981, 1–16.

Stinard, T. A., and W. D. Dolphin. Which students benefit from self-paced mastery and why? *Journal of Educational Psychology* **73,** 1981, 754–763.

Stoddard, G. D. *The meaning of intelligence.* New York: Macmillan, 1943.

Strang, L., M. D. Smith, and C. M. Rogers. Social comparison, multiple reference groups, and the self-concepts of academically handicapped students before and after mainstreaming. *Journal of Educational Psychology* **70,** 1978, 487–497.

Strong, S. R. Counseling: An interpersonal influence process. *Journal of Counseling Psychology* **15,** 1968, 215–224.

Suchman, J. R. Inquiry training: Building skills for autonomous discovery. *Merrill-Palmer Quarterly* **7** (3), 1961, 147–171.

Surgeon General's Scientific Advisory Committee on Television and Social Behavior. *Television and growing up: The impact of televised violence.* Washington, D.C.: U.S. Government Printing Office, 1972.

Swanson, B. M., and D. J. Willis. *Understanding exceptional children and youth.* Chicago: Rand McNally, 1979.

Tanner, J. M. Physical growth. In P. H. Mussen (ed.), *Carmichael's manual of child psychology,* Volume 1. New York: Wiley, 1970.

Taylor, C. W. How many types of giftedness can your program tolerate? *Journal of Creative Behavior* **12,** 1978, 39–51.

Terman, L. M. The intelligence quotient of Francis Galton in childhood. *American Journal of Psychology* **28,** 1917, 208–215.

Terman, L. M., and M. A. Merrill. *Revised Stanford-Binet intelligence scales.* Boston: Houghton Mifflin, 1960.

Terman, L. M., and M. H. Oden. *Genetic studies of genius: Mental and physical traits of a thousand gifted children.* Stanford, Calif.: Stanford University Press, 1925.

————. *Genetic studies of genius: The gifted child grows up,* Volume 4. Stanford, Calif.: Stanford University Press, 1947.

————. The Stanford studies of the gifted. In P. Witty (ed.), *The gifted child.* Boston: D. C. Heath, 1951.

————. *Genetic studies of genius: The gifted at mid-life: Thirty-five years' follow-up of the superior child,* Volume 5. Stanford, Calif.: Stanford University Press 1959.

Thompson, G. G., and C. W. Hunnicutt. The effects of praise on the wc achievement of "introverts" and "extroverts." *Journal of Educational Psychol* **35,** 1944, 257–266.

Thorndike, E. L. *Animal intelligence.* New York: Macmillan, 1911.

————. *The psychology of learning: Educational Psychology,* Volume ? York: Columbia University, Teachers College Press, 1913.

Thurstone, L. L. Primary mental abilities. *Psychometric Monographs* **1,** 1ᶜ

Thurstone, L. L., and T. G. Thurstone. *SRA primary mental abilities* Science Research Associates, 1962.

Thurstone, T. G. *Examiner's manual IBM 805 edition, PMA primary mental abilities for grades 6–9.* Chicago: Science Research Associates, 1963.

Tiemann, P. W. Student use of behaviorally-stated objectives to augment conventional and programmed revisions of televised college economics lectures. Paper presented at the meeting of the American Educational Research Association, Chicago, 1968.

Tikunoff, W. J., D. C. Berliner, and R. C. Rist. *An ethnographic study of the forty classrooms of the beginning teacher evaluation study known sample.* Technical Report No. 75-10-5, Far West Laboratory for Research and Development, San Francisco, 1975.

Torrance, E. P. *Torrance tests of creative thinking.* Bensenville, Ill.: Scholastic Testing Service, 1966.

————. *The search for satori and creativity.* Buffalo, N.Y.: Creative Education Foundation, 1979.

Torrance, E. P., and R. E. Myers. *Creative learning and teaching.* New York: Dodd, Mead, 1970.

Torres, S. *A primer on individualized education programs for handicapped children.* Reston, Va.: Council for Exceptional Children, 1977.

Trotman, F. K. Race, IQ, and the middle class. *Journal of Educational Psychology* **69,** 1977, 266–273.

————. Race, IQ, and rampant misrepresentations: A reply. *Journal of Educational Psychology* **70,** 1978, 478–481.

Tulving, E. Episodic and semantic memory. In E. Tulving and W. Donaldson (eds.), *Organization of memory.* New York: Academic Press, 1972.

Turnbull, A. P., and J. C. Brantley. *Mainstreaming: Developing and implementing individualized education programs,* second edition. Columbus, Ohio: Charles E. Merrill, 1982.

Tyler, L. E. *The psychology of human differences,* third edition. New York: Appleton-Century-Crofts, 1965.

Vargas, J. S. *Behavioral psychology for teachers.* New York: Harper & Row, 1977.

Veroff, J. Social comparison and the development of achievement motivation. In C. P. Smith (ed.), *Achievement-related motives in children.* New York: Russell Sage Foundation, 1969.

Veroff, J., L. McClelland, and D. Ruhland. Varieties of achievement motivation. In M. Mednick, S. Tangri, and L. Hoffman (eds.), *Women and achievement: Social and motivational analyses.* New York: Halsted, 1975.

Walker, V. S. The efficacy of the resource room for educating retarded children. *Exceptional Children* **40,** 1974, 288–289.

Wallach, M. A. Tests tell us little about talent. *American Scientist* **64,** 1976, 57–63.

G. *The art of thought.* New York: Harcourt, Brace & World, 1926.

F. How to squelch ideas. In G. A. Davis and T. F. Warren (eds.), *Psychology* *tion: New looks.* Lexington, Mass.: D.C. Heath, 1974.

, C. W. Educational measurements as a key to individualizing instruction promotions. *Journal of Educational Research* **5,** 1922, 195–206.

Watson, J. B. *Behaviorism.* New York: Norton, 1925.

Watson, J. B., and R. Raynor. Conditioned emotional reactions. *Journal of Experimental Psychology* **3,** 1920, 1–14.

Watson, J. D. *The double helix.* New York: New American Library, 1968.

Watts, G. H., and R. C. Anderson. Effects of three types of inserted questions on learning from prose. *Journal of Educational Psychology* **62,** 1971, 387–394.

Wechsler, D. *Wechsler adult intelligence scale.* New York: Psychological Corporation, 1955.

————. *The Wechsler preschool and primary scale of intelligence.* New York: Psychological Corporation, 1967.

————. *Wechsler intelligence scale for children—revised.* New York: Psychological Corporation, 1974.

Weiner, B. *Theories of motivation.* Chicago: Markham, 1972.

————. *Achievement motivation and attribution theory.* Morristown, N.J.: General Learning Press, 1974.

————. An attributional approach for educational psychology. In L. Shulman (ed.), *Review of research in education,* Volume 4. Itasca, Ill.: Peacock, 1976.

————. A theory of motivation for some classroom experiences. *Journal of Educational Psychology* **71,** 1979, 3–25.

————. *Human motivation.* New York: Holt, Rinehart & Winston, 1980.

Welsh, G. S., and F. Barron. *Barron-Welsh art scale.* Palo Alto, Calif.: Consulting Psychologists Press, 1963.

West, C., and T. Anderson. The question of preponderant causation in teacher expectancy research. *Review of Educational Research* **46,** 1976, 185–213.

West, L. M. T., and P. J. Fenshaw. Prior knowledge or advance organizers as effective variables in chemical learning. *Journal of Research in Science Teaching* **13,** 1976, 297–306.

White, J. M., S. R. Yussen, and E. M. Docherty. Performance of Montessori and traditionally schooled children on tasks of seriation, classification, and conservation. *Contemporary Educational Psychology* **1,** 1976, 356–368.

White, R. W. Motivation reconsidered: The concept of competence. *Psychological Review* **66,** 1959, 297–333.

Whitlock, C. Note on reading acquisition: An extension of laboratory principles. *Journal of Experimental Child Development* **3,** 1966, 83–85.

Wiggins, J. S. Circumplex models of interpersonal behavior in personality and social psychology. In L. Wheeler (ed.), *Review of personality and social psychology,* Volume 1. Beverly Hills, Calif.: Sage, 1980. Pp. 395–412.

Willerman, L. Activity level and hyperactivity in twins. *Child Development* **44,** 1973, 288–293.

Williams, F. E. *Classroom ideas for encouraging thinking and feeling.* Buffalo, N.Y.: DOK, 1970.

Willis, S. L., R. Blieszner, and P. B. Baltes. Training research on figural relations and induction abilities in aging: Short-term longitudinal studies. Paper presented at the Annual Meeting of the Gerontological Society, Dallas, Texas, 1978.

Winne, P. H. Experiments relating teachers' use of higher cognitive questions to student achievement. *Review of Educational Research* **49,** 1979, 13–50.

Witkin. H. A., C. A. Moore, D. R. Goodenough, and P. W. Cox. Field-dependent and field-independent cognitive styles and their educational implications. *Review of Educational Research* **47,** 1977, 1–64.

Wittrock, M. C. The cognitive movement in instruction. *Educational Researcher* **8,** 1979, 5–11.

Wolff, P. H. The natural history of crying and other vocalizations in early infancy. In B. M. Foss (ed.), *Determinants of infant behavior,* Volume 4. London: Methuen, 1966.

Wolleat, P. L. Guiding the career development of gifted females. In N. Colangelo and R. T. Zaffrann (eds.), *New voices in counseling the gifted.* Dubuque, Iowa: Kendall/Hunt, 1979.

Wolpe. J. *The practice of behavior therapy.* New York: Pergamon Press, 1969.

Wu, J. J. Cognitive style and task performance—A study of student teachers. *Dissertation Abstracts* **29,** 1968, 176A.

Yando, R. M., and J. Kagan. The effect of teacher tempo on the child. *Child Development* **39,** 1968, 27–34.

Yates, Y. A. *The art of memory.* Chicago: University of Chicago Press, 1966.

Yussen, S. R., and V. M. Levy. Developmental changes in predicting one's own span of short-term memory. *Journal of Experimental Child Psychology* **19,** 1975, 502–508.

Yussen, S. R., and J. W. Santrock. *Child development: An introduction,* second edition. Dubuque, Iowa: W. C. Brown, 1982.

Zelazo, P. R., N. A. Zelazo, and S. Kolb. "Walking" in the newborn. *Science* **176,** 1972, 314–315.

Zeskind, P. S., and C. T. Ramey. Fetal maturation: An experimental study of its consequences on infant development in two caregiving environments. *Child Development* **49,** 1978, 1155–1162.

Zigler, E. The environmental mystique: Training the intellect versus development of the child. *Childhood Education* **46,** 1970, 402–412.

————. Project Head Start: Success or failure? *Learning* **1,** 1973, 43–47.

Zigler E. The effectiveness of Head Start: Another look. *Educational Psychologist* **13,** 1978, 71–77.

Zigler, E., and S. Muenchow. Mainstreaming: The proof is in the implementation. *American Psychologist* **34,** 1979, 993–996.

Zigler, E., and P. K. Trickett. IQ, social competence, and evaluation of early childhood intervention programs. *American Psychologist* **33,** 1978, 789–798.

Zuckerman, M. *Sensation seeking: Beyond the optimal level of arousal.* Hillsdale, N.J.: Lawrence Erlbaum, 1979.

Zuckerman, M., E. A. Kolin, L. Price, and I. Zoob. Development of a sensation-seeking scale. *Journal of Consulting and Clinical Psychology* **28,** 1964, 477–482.

INDEXES

AUTHOR INDEX

653

SUBJECT INDEX